C000008575

Dissertations Upon the Principles and Arrangement of a Harmony of the Gospels. 3 Vols. and Suppl. Dissertations
by Edward Greswell

Copyright © 2019 by HardPress

Address:
HardPress
8345 NW 66TH ST #2561
MIAMI FL 33166-2626
USA
Email: info@hardpress.net

DISSERTATIONS

UPON

THE PRINCIPLES

AND

ARRANGEMENT

OF A

HARMONY OF THE GOSPELS.

BY THE

REV. EDWARD GRESWELL, M. A.

FELLOW OF CORPUS CHRISTI COLLEGE, OXFORD.

———◆———

IN THREE VOLUMES.

———◆———

VOL. II.

———◆———

OXFORD,
AT THE UNIVERSITY PRESS.
MDCCCXXX.

Clar. Press
1. b. 24.

THE CONTENTS

OF

THE SECOND VOLUME.

VOL. II.　　　　　　　b

DISSERTATION II.

DISSERTATION III.

DISSERTATION IV.

DISSERTATION V.

DISSERTATION VI.

DISSERTATION VII.

DISSERTATION VII. APPENDIX.

DISSERTATION VIII. PART I.

DISSERTATION VIII. PART II.

DISSERTATION VIII. PART III.

General prospective survey of our Lord's ministry in Galilee.
  Year the second - - - - 283—319

DISSERTATION VIII. PART IV.

General prospective survey of our Lord's ministry in Galilee. First
  six months of year the third - - 320—345

DISSERTATION IX.

DISSERTATION X.

DISSERTATION XI.

DISSERTATION XVI.

DISSERTATION XVII.

DISSERTATION XVIII.

HARMONY OF THE GOSPELS.

PRELIMINARY DISSERTATIONS.

DISSERTATION I.

On the prophecy of the Seventy weeks, and the second part of the chronology of the Acts of the Apostles.

IT may not, perhaps, be sufficient to have shewn that the first twelve chapters of the Acts, with respect to the times and the periods which they embrace, require to be distributed in a certain manner, unless it can be further demonstrated that the sequel and residue of the history admit of this distribution. For the sake, therefore, of establishing this fact, as well as because the purpose, which I have in view by it, is not altogether foreign to the proper business of a Gospel Harmony, I shall devote the present Dissertation to the remainder of the Acts, from the thirteenth chapter inclusively, to its close; in the course of which I shall necessarily have occasion to consider also the chronology of the Epistles of St. Paul.

The notices of time, or such other indications as might serve to ascertain the chronology of the Acts, are interspersed in the body of the history, and withal of so peculiar a nature, as to render it much easier and much safer, to begin by tracing the course of events from a certain fixed point backwards, than from any certain point forwards. Two such points, each of them within the compass of the time which remains to be investigated, are capable of being determined; and as they may be determined independently of one another, and yet will be found to coincide in a common result, no inconvenience is likely to arise from my beginning with the latest first.

When St. Paul, on the last visit to Jerusalem, recorded in the Acts, was brought before the Jewish Sanhedrim[a], Ananias presided at the Sanhedrim, in quality of the high-priest, and yet St. Paul did not know him to be the high-priest; or rather, he did not know that there was at that time any high-priest.   The true meaning of his reply—οὐκ ᾔδειν, ἀδελφοὶ, ὅτι ἔστιν ἀρχιερεύς—upon which I ground this inference, has been much obscured by the inaccuracy of the authorized version;—I wist not, brethren, that he was the high-priest.   I do not object to the rendering of the historical present, ὅτι ἔστι, by *was*, for that is more agreeable to the genius of our language, as the other is to the idiom of the Greek[b], than the contrary: I object only to the rendering, ὅτι ἔστιν ἀρχιερεὺς, standing absolutely as it does stand, and yet supposed to stand for the name of the high-priest officially, as if it had been expressed, ὅτι ἐστὶν ὁ ἀρχιερεὺς, or as if the whole had stood, οὐκ ᾔδειν, ἀδελφοὶ, τοῦτον ὅτι ἐστὶν ὁ ἀρχιερεύς.

The party who had just reproved St. Paul, speaking under his own impression, had very naturally said: τὸν ἀρχιερέα τοῦ Θεοῦ λοιδορεῖς; and St. Paul, if he had meant to be understood of any particular person as high-priest, would have expressed himself with equal propriety.   There is a case, very much akin to each of these passages, at Acts xix. 2.   St. Paul enquired of the disciples at Ephesus, εἰ πνεῦμα ἅγιον ἐλάβετε πιστεύσαντες; where, as he did not mean the Holy Ghost absolutely, but some one or other of the gifts or the graces of the Holy Ghost, he could not so properly have used the article, as omitted it : Have ye received any Holy Ghost—that is, any gift or χάρισμα of the Holy Ghost—in consequence of your having believed ?   To this the disciples replied, ἀλλ᾿ οὐδὲ, εἰ πνεῦμα ἅγιον ἔστιν, ἠκούσαμεν. No, so far from that, we have not even heard that there

---

[a] Acts xxiii. 1—5.   [b] Vide Acts ix. 26. 38.   xii. 9.   xix. 2.

was any Holy Ghost : we did not know there was any such gift to be received.

On the same principle the reply of St. Paul, οὐκ ᾔδειν, ἀδελ-φοὶ, ὅτι ἔστιν ἀρχιερεὺς, which is so far exactly analogous to this, ought to be rendered in a similar manner ; I did not know, brethren, that there was any high-priest. The correctness of this version, I think, is unimpeachable ; and while that is the case, no words can more plainly declare at what juncture critically the speaker must have come to Jerusalem, or been standing before the council; viz. at a time when there was no regular high-priest, but either some one who was altogether usurping the office, or some one who, at the utmost, was only *pro tempore* acting in his stead. This some one, in either case, was doubtless Ananias; and the history of Ananias is as follows.

Herod of Chalcis, either the year before, or the very year of, his death, that is, either before, or in, the eighth of Claudius[c], removed Joseph the son of Camudus, whom he had appointed to the priesthood a few years before[d], and constituted Ananias the son of Nebedæus in his stead[e]. This was also the year in which Cumanus succeeded to Tiberius Alexander.

After this, some time between the eighth of Claudius, as before, and the end of his twelfth, Ananias was sent to Rome by Quadratus, the governor of Syria[e]; and he was sent upon a charge of high treason. From the time of this mission, consequently, he was no longer high-priest ; but, instead of him, at a point of time coincident with, or at least not later than, the first of Nero, Jonathan, son of Ananus[f], the Annas of the Gospel history, and known in Josephus as Ananus the son of Seth ; which Jonathan was sent to Rome as well as Ananias *[g], and either had been

---

* It is said, indeed, in the Antiquities, xx. vi. 3. that Ananias only, and his son Ananus, who was before captain of the temple, were so sent ; and perhaps this was more probably the case.

[c] Ant. Jud. xx. v. 2.   [d] Ib. i. 3.   [e] Ib. vi. 2.   vii. 1.   B. ii. xli. 5. 6.
[f] Ant. xx. viii. 4. 5.   B. ii. xli. 3.   [g] B. ii. xii. 6.

appointed high-priest at the time of the deposal of Ananias, or was so upon their return in common from Rome[h]: of which return, as they were acquitted of blame by Claudius[i], there can be no doubt in the case of either.

The next high-priest, of whom mention occurs, was Ishmael, a different person from both the former; appointed by Agrippa the younger[k], and before the close of the administration of Felix. Between the first of Nero, then, and the appointment of Ishmael, either there was no regular high-priest at all, or it was Jonathan.

But Jonathan, not long after his appointment, was assassinated at one of the feasts, through the instrumentality of the Sicarii, but by the subornation of Felix[l]. This assassination, therefore, was either in, or after, the first of Nero; yet before the deprival of Felix; and the deprival of Felix was prior to the loss of the influence of his brother Pallas, or, rather, while that influence was still at its height[m]. Now the influence of Pallas with Nero depended altogether on his influence with Agrippina the mother of Nero, and her influence with Nero himself; and as Agrippina was assassinated by Nero, in the month of March, A. U. 812. the fifth year of his reign, so was Pallas himself put to death four years after, A. U. 815. in the eighth or ninth[n]. His influence with Nero, therefore, could not have been at its height later than the fifth of Nero; it had already begun to decline as early as his second, A. U. 808.[o] The deprival of Felix, then, cannot be placed later than the fifth of Nero; nor, consequently, the appointment of Ishmael later than the fourth. It follows, therefore, that between the death of Jonathan, either in, or after, the first of Nero, and the appointment of Ishmael, either in, or before, the fourth, there was no regular high-priest.

The duration of this interregnum may, perhaps, be limited as follows. The appointment of Ishmael is placed in the Antiquities after the sedition between the Jews and

[h] B. ii. xii. 5.   Ant. xx. viii. 5.   [i] Ant. xx. vi. 3.   B. ii. xii. 7.
[k] Ant. xx. viii. 8.   [l] Ant. xx. viii. 5.   B. ii. xiii. 3.   [m] Ant. xx. viii. 9.
[n] Tac. Ann. xiv. 1. 4. 65.   [o] xiii. 14.

the Greeks at Cæsarea ; the sedition at Cæsarea is placed
after the appearance of the Egyptian false prophet ; the
appearance of the Egyptian false prophet is placed after the
assassination of Jonathan ; St. Paul's arrival at Jerusalem
was after that appearance also[p], but two years, if not more,
prior to the removal of Felix[q]; the removal of Felix was
later than all these events, yet not later than the fifth of
Nero.   We may safely conclude, then, that the death of
Jonathan could not have taken place, as not before the first,
so neither after the second, of Nero ; and the appointment
of Ishmael, as not before the second, so neither after the
fourth, of the same reign : and the critical period during
which there might be either no high-priest, or some one
usurping his office, or merely filling it for a time, will lie
between the last half of the second, and the first of the
third, of Nero.   That Ishmael was appointed at the last of
these times I think is implied by a remarkable mistake of
Josephus himself.

Antiquities iii. xv. 3. mention is made of a famine, or
dearth, in Judæa, when Claudius was Emperor, Ishmael
was high-priest, and not long before the Jewish war ; all
which criteria cannot possibly concur together of any famine
in the reign of Claudius whatever, and more especially of
the famine mentioned in the Acts, and considered at large
in the preceding Dissertation.   Ishmael was never high-
priest under Claudius at all ; in the first year of whose
reign Herod Agrippa appointed Simon, called Cantheras[r],
and before the third, Matthias, son of Ananus[s], and Elio-
næus, son of Cantheras[t]: and in the third, or the fourth,
Herod of Chalcis appointed Joseph, son of Camudus[u], and
in the seventh, or the eighth, Ananias the son of Nebedæus,
after whom the succession, until the time of Ishmael, was
perpetuated in Jonathan, the son of Ananus.

The high-priest, then, during the great famine, was Joseph, the son of Camudus ; and though Ishmael had been
so, still what happened at the latest, in the fourth of Claudius,

---

[p] Acts xxi. 37. 38.   [q] Ib. xxiv. 27.   [r] Ant. Jud. xix. vi. 2.   [s] Ib. 4.
[t] Ib. viii. 1.   [u] Ib. xx. 1. 2. 3.

twenty-two, or twenty-three, years before the beginning of the war, could not be said to have happened but a little before it.   The frequency of famines, however, besides the great famine, at this period of contemporary history, is a well-attested fact, and in reality only the completion of our Saviour's prediction to that effect, in the prophecy delivered on mount Olivet.   Suetonius alludes to Assiduas sterilitates, and Tacitus to Frugum egestas, et orta ex eo fames; both towards the end of the reign of Claudius; in which they are followed by Eusebius and by Orosius also[v].   And if Dio does not specify the same things, it is because after A. U. 802. and the marriage of Claudius and Agrippina, he gives no particulars at all, but passes over the rest of his reign in silence.   Yet in the Antiquities, directly after the appointment of Ishmael, in the description of the violences committed by the higher orders of the priests on the inferior, there seems to be clear intimation of some period of dearth[w]. Josephus might mean this, though by a lapse of memory he has assigned it to the time of Claudius, and not of Nero; a lapse of memory which is easily accounted for, if this, like the former, happened in the *third* year of the reigning Emperor, and in the *first* year of the presiding high-priest. And this famine being not quite nine years prior to the war, might well be said to have happened but a little before it.

The power of appointing the high-priest rested at this time with the younger Agrippa, whose dominion, as possessed under Claudius, had been considerably enlarged on the accession of Nero[x].   Towards the end of the reign of Claudius he was certainly absent at Rome[y]; and if the Agrippa, who is mentioned by Tacitus[z], as commanded by Nero to cooperate with Corbulo against the Parthians, and upon the Euphrates, was the same with this Agrippa the younger, it is plain that, whether he was at Rome, or not, in the first of Nero, the execution of that commission kept

[v] Suet. Claud. 18. Tac. Ann. xii. 43. Oros. vii. 6. Euseb. Chron.
[w] xx. viii. 8.   [x] Ant. xx. viii. 4. B. ii. xiii. 2.   [y] xx. vi. 3. B. ii.
xii. 7.   [z] Ann. xiii. 7. 8. 9.

him at a distance from Judæa until the beginning of his second year at least. The expressions of Tacitus, Quæ, in alios consules egressa, conjunxi, demonstrate that Corbulo and his allies were engaged upon it at least till the summer of A. U. 808. If, after this, the high-priest Jonathan, as I consider the most probable state of the case, had been assassinated at the feast of Tabernacles, or, at the latest, at the feast of the Passover next ensuing, and both in the second of Nero, the time when a high-priest was indispensably wanted was the recurrence of the day of Atonement; and, therefore, the time, by which a successor to Jonathan would almost of necessity be appointed, would be against that recurrence, at the beginning of the third of Nero. But the arrival of St. Paul at Jerusalem was certainly at a Pentecost[a]; and if this was the Pentecost between these extremes, it was the Pentecost of the second of Nero, or A. U. 809. To this conclusion every note of time, and every incidental circumstance, disclosed in the history, and any how connected with this arrival, will be found exactly to agree.

I. The Sicarii[b], a race of men who had not started up before the first of Nero, but who continued long after, would now be in existence, and known as a distinct body.

II. The regular high-priest, Jonathan, had been very recently murdered; and no successor as yet appointed in his stead: Ananias, however, who had once been high-priest (and for two or three years) himself, and was probably the vicar of Jonathan, even while he was living, was as likely as any one to be acting for him; and yet could not be known nor recognized as the regular high-priest.

III. The Egyptian impostor, whose appearance is alluded to in the Acts, and which both the Antiquities and the War mention after the death of Jonathan[c], must very lately have been defeated, or at least have appeared in Jerusalem; a conclusion which the suspicion of Lysias, that St. Paul might be this same person, is enough of itself to

[a] Acts xx. 16. xxi. 27. xx. viii. 5. B. ii. xiii. 3. xiii. 5.
[b] Acts xxi. 38. Suidas Σικάριοι. Ant. Jud.
[c] Acts xxi. 38. Ant. Jud. xx. viii. 6. B. ii.

suggest. Josephus also shews that the impostor was not made prisoner, though his followers were attacked and dispersed. All this might have taken place between the passover and the Pentecost of A. U. 809. *

IV. Felix was now the acting procurator, and he had performed such services to the community at large as might give occasion to the complimentary language of Tertullus[d]; for he had, before this, made prisoner Eleazar, a chief captain of the λῃσταί, who had previously infested the country with impunity for twenty years[e]; and he was still em-

---

* As to the means of reconciling the account, which Josephus has given of this impostor, with the above allusion to his history in the Acts, I entirely agree in the solution proposed by Lardner. The interrogation of Lysias related to such of his followers, as he had originally led with him out of Jerusalem, which might be only four thousand ; the account of his defeat in Josephus, to those whom he was bringing back with him thither from the wilderness, when Felix met him and put him to the rout, which might be as many as thirty thousand.

It is manifest from Josephus that he was once, but only once, in Jerusalem, very probably at the feast of the Passover, A. U. 809. and that, before his departure to the wilderness; but that he was returning thither again, by way of mount Olivet, when he was attacked by the Roman governor. The statement of the numbers killed or taken prisoners, in consequence of this attack, relates to a part of his history not mentioned in the Acts ; and however differently it may be represented in the Antiquities compared with the War, concerns the reconciliation of Josephus with himself, not with St. Luke ; yet Dr. Lardner's solution of this difficulty also appears to me perfectly just and natural.

I think, however, that at the time of St. Paul's arrival in Jerusalem, he had not yet returned, nor did so until some time afterwards. The language of Lysias clearly implies that he had been, indeed, in Jerusalem, and led out thence a body of men into the wilderness ; but it also implies that, as yet, no more had been heard, or was known, about him. His defeat, then, by Felix would be properly when St. Paul was at Cæsarea.

[d] Acts xxiv. 3.　　　　[e] Ant. Jud. xx. viii. 5. B. ii. xiii. 2.

ployed daily in capturing, and putting to death, numbers of the same description of persons[f].

V. He had been many years in office, as St. Paul reminds him[g]; which may thus be proved.

Orosius places the appointment of Cumanus in the seventh of Claudius[h]; nor does Josephus, as we have seen in the last Dissertation, militate against this supposition. It is more probable, however, that his appointment is to be placed actually in the summer of his eighth. On this principle the disturbance at the Passover[i], which followed soon after his appointment, may reasonably be supposed to have happened at the Passover in the ninth of Claudius, A. U. 802. Between this and the Passover mentioned in the War[k], shewing that the feast generally only alluded to in the Antiquities was a Passover[l], including the fresh outrage committed on Stephanus, and the insurrectionary warfare with the Samaritans, there could have been only one year's interval; for which conclusion there is this additional reason, that the feast, in going up to which the Galileans were waylaid by the Samaritans, is called ἁπλῶς, ἡ ἑορτή.

The degree of estimation, in which the feast of Tabernacles more particularly was held, justifies us, *a priori*, in supposing the allusion to be to this feast. Τῆς Σκηνοπηγίας ἐνστάσης· ἑορτὴ δ' ἐστὶν αὕτη παρ' ἡμῖν εἰς τὰ μάλιστα τηρουμένη— Ὁ τῆς Σκηνοπηγίας καιρός· ἑορτῆς σφόδρα παρὰ τοῖς Ἑβραίοις ἁγιωτάτης καὶ μεγίστης—Μηνῶν δὲ ὁ ἕβδομος, κατὰ πᾶν ἔτος, ἑορτῶν ἔλαχε τὴν μεγίστην[m]—The usage of Josephus[n], and the similar usage of the Rabbinical writers[o], *a posteriori*, confirm the supposition. On this principle it would be the feast of Tabernacles A. U. 802. or in the ninth of Claudius also, when this event too happened. The next Passover, which was going on when Quadratus paid a visit to Jeru-

[f] B. ii. xiii. 2. [g] Acts xxiv. 10. [h] vii. 6. [i] Ant. Jud. xx.
v. 3. B. ii. xii. 1. [k] ii. xii. 6. [l] xx. vi. 2. [m] Ant. Jud. xv.
iii. 3. viii. iv. 1. Philo De Septen. et Fest. 1183. [n] Ant. xiii. xiii. 5.
B. i. iv. 3. Ant. xiv. xi. 5. 3. 4. B. i. xi. 6. xx. ix. 3. [o] xxii. 2. Compare also Plut. Moralia i. 514. Wyttenbachii. and Ant. Jud. xiii. viii. 2.
Plut. Convival. Quæst. iv. 6. [o] Maim. De Ædificio Templi. i. 16. Annott.
De Sacris Solemn. ii. 4. Annott. De jure jurando. i. Annott.

salem, was consequently the Passover of A. U. 803. the tenth of Claudius.

Now, before he paid this visit, he had already sent the former high-priest Ananias, if not also the newly-appointed high-priest Jonathan, and the procurator Cumanus, all to Rome, to answer for themselves before Claudius in common [p]: they were sent, therefore, between the feast of Tabernacles, A. U. 802. and the Passover, A. U. 803. The result was that not only did the Jews obtain a favourable hearing from the Emperor, but Jonathan, by his personal intercession, is said to have got Felix the appointment to the procuratorship in the room of Cumanus [q]. If so, he would be appointed in the tenth of Claudius, A. U. 803. from which time to A. U. 809. in the second of Nero, he would have been six years in office ; a longer period than had fallen to the lot of any governor since Gratus, or Pilate ; and, perhaps, to be attributed in part to the influence of his brother Pallas (through Agrippina) with Claudius.

VI. Drusilla was now the wife of Felix. Drusilla was one of the daughters of Herod Agrippa and Cyprus, and, consequently, by both her parents a Jewess ; and at the time of her father's death, A. U. 796. she is said to have been six years old, which probably means in her seventh year [r]: in the thirteenth of Claudius, A. U. 806. ten years after, she had been married to Azizus, King of Emesa, who, however, died A. U. 807. or 808. in the first of Nero [s]: and even before his death Drusilla had been persuaded to leave him, and to marry Felix [s]; to whom she continued united until A. U. 832. in the reign of Titus, when both she, and a son whom she had borne him, perished by the eruption of mount Vesuvius [t]. Suetonius, in allusion to this marriage among others, calls Felix, Trium reginarum maritum [u]. It is certain, then, that he and Drusilla were living together in marriage, in the second of Nero, A. U. 809.

---

[p] Ant. xx. vi. 2.   B. ii. xii. 6.   [q] Ant. xx. vi. 3.   B. ii. xii. 7.   Ant. xx. viii. 5.   [r] Ant. xix. ix. 1.   [s] xx. viii. 4.   vii. 1. 2.   [t] Dio. lxvi. 20. 24. 26. 18.   [u] Claud. 28.

VII. St. Paul had not been in Jerusalem for some years before this time[v]. When he last was there, it was, as I shall prove hereafter, A. U. 805. at the Passover in the twelfth of Claudius; from whence to the Pentecost in the second of Nero, there would be four years' and two months' interval: and he came now, as we shall also see, charged with the contributions of the Churches of Asia Minor, and of Achaia, towards the necessities of the Church of Jerusalem; that is, of his nation.

VIII. Felix, who left Paul in confinement behind him, with a view to conciliate the Jews[w], had some reason for wishing to oblige them: the dispute about Cæsarea, in which he had taken so decided a part against the Jewish inhabitants, and in behalf of the Greeks, and when so many lives were lost, must have happened in the fourth year of Nero, and in the last year of his administration[x].

IX. When Paul was tried before Festus, Ishmael had been some time appointed, and was certainly the acting high-priest. And it is observable that this high-priest, whosoever he was, is no longer called the high-priest Ananias, as he had been repeatedly before[y]; but simply the high-priest[z]. Yet Festus speaks still of the high-priests[z], as if there were still more than one of them; and this also would be literally the case; since, though Ishmael might be titular and acting high-priest, Ananias might yet be his vicar, and the next in dignity to him. He is called high-priest by Josephus, even after the appointment of Jesus, the son of Damnæus[a]; and he is still so called, even when Paul's prophecy against him was accomplished, in his being assassinated by the partisans of Manahem, at the outset of the Jewish war[a]. Nor must he be here confounded with the younger Ananus, whose death is also mentioned, but at a later period, and in a different way[b].

I have said nothing hitherto concerning the discrepancy respecting the successive administrations of Cumanus and of

---

[v] Acts xxiv. 17.   [w] xxiv. 27.   [x] Ant. Jud. xx. viii. 7.   B. ii. xiii. 7.
[y] Acts xxiii. 2.   xxiv. 1.   [z] xxv. 2.   xxv. 15.   [a] Ant. xx. ix. 2.
B. ii. xvii. 9.   Acts xxiii. 3.   [b] B. iv. v. 1. 2.   iv. iii. 9. 7.

Felix, which exists between the accounts of Josephus and of Tacitus ; because, however great this discrepancy might be, it must be unquestionable that a Jewish historian ought to be more entitled to credit, in relation to the affairs of Judæa, than a Roman : nor would this be the only instance where Tacitus might be convicted of either a want of correct information, or of a culpable haste and inaccuracy, with reference to this country in particular. But as to Josephus —in this portion of his history he must have written in some degree from personal observation ; for he was thirteen or fourteen years old in the tenth of Claudius, and, if we may believe his own account, so forward in intellectual proficiency, that, even at that age, the doctors of the Law used to consult him on difficult questions[c]. ·

The discrepancy, after all, is not insuperable : Tacitus attests that Quadratus was Præfect of Syria not only before, or in, the eleventh of Claudius, but long after it; and that in the twelfth Felix was governor of Judæa, and had been Pridem impositus[d]. The coins of Quadratus, still extant, begin only from A. U. 808.[e] at which time it is certain he must have been long in office. I should conjecture that he was appointed in the ninth of Claudius, A. U. 802 ; and that he had not long been come into the province when the Jewish and Samaritan deputies, in consequence of the dispute of the two nations, had their audience of him at Tyre. His predecessor, Cassius Longinus, had succeeded to Vibius Marsus after the death of Herod Agrippa, A. U. 796 : and one of his coins proves him to have been in office A. U. 798. at least[f]. Hence he might well be superseded in A. U. 802. Nor is this supposition inconsistent with the testimony of Tacitus[g], who makes Cassius still president of Syria, when Meherdates was sent from Rome to be placed on the throne of Parthia, A. U. 802 : and Cassius the person who conducted him to the banks of the Euphrates. This service would be performed by the summer of that year ;

[c] Vit. 2.   [d] Ann. xii. 45. 54.   xiv. 26.   [e] Eckel. iii. 280.   [f] Ib.
loc. cit.   [g] Ann. xii. 11. 12.

and it would still be possible for Cassius to have been superseded in the ensuing autumn.

Now it is not improbable that, when Cumanus was appointed in the eighth of Claudius, A. U. 801. (the very year before Claudius, a few days after December the 29th, celebrated his marriage with Agrippina[h], whom the influence of Pallas had raised to that dignity above her rivals,) or early in the next year, Felix also might be sent out in some co-ordinate capacity ; and that the high-priest, Jonathan, who is said to have personally solicited his appointment to the procuratorship after Cumanus, first became acquainted with him in Judæa, and not at Rome.

Be this, however, as it may, the two historians are agreed as to the main facts, that the Galileans had gone to war with the Samaritans; that Roman soldiers had been killed; that Quadratus was presiding governor of Syria ; that he had authority to try the Jewish procurator himself; that Felix was, or might have been, present at the trial of Cumanus ; and that all these things might have happened about the ninth of Claudius : while Josephus in particular will shew that the agitation in the province could not have been finally quelled (partly by the punishment of the most turbulent among the Jews, and partly by that of the Roman tribune Celer) before his tenth[i].

Suetonius, by placing the appointment of Felix over Judæa after the adoption of Nero, is so far in favour of Josephus[k]; for it is the practice of this biographer, though he does not relate the whole of any life in historical order, yet to relate such portions of it, as he classes together, in the order in which they followed each other. Nero was adopted by Claudius, according to Tacitus, A. U. 803. *ineunte*[l]; according to Suetonius, in the eleventh year of his age ; which eleventh year was completed December the fifteenth, A. U. 801.[m] This would fix the time of his adoption to A. U. 802. *ineunte*, when he had entered on his twelfth year, at the latest; so that, on this point Tacitus is at va-

---

[h] Tac. Ann. xii. 5. 8. Suet. Claud. 29. [i] Ant. xx. vi. 2. 3. B. ii. xii. 7.
[k] Claud. 27. 28. [l] Ann. xii. 25. [m] Ner. 7. 6. Capitol. Luc. Ver. i.

riance with Suetonius; and yet that Suetonius is more in the right may be proved from Tacitus himself.

At the time of this adoption Nero was committed to the tuition of Seneca[m]; and to this tuition he had been committed fourteen years, in the eighth of Nero[n], that is, between October 13. A. U. 814. and October 13. A. U. 815. This might possibly be the case, if the first year of his tuition was A. U. 801. *exeunte*, or 802. *ineunte ;* but not if it was A. U. 803. Nero, then, must have been adopted in the ninth of Claudius at the latest; and, consequently, Felix, appointed to Judæa after this adoption, might have been appointed in the tenth; but could not have been before it.

The second of the points of time, which I originally proposed to consider, is not less critical than the first; but, after what has been already established, will be found, perhaps, to be even more so.

When St. Paul, upon leaving Athens, was arrived, for the first time, at Corinth, he met there with Aquila and Priscilla, who were recently come from Italy, because Claudius had commanded all Jews to depart from Rome[o]. I have shewn elsewhere[p] that, in almost every instance of a journey from Italy to Asia, Corinth was the regular thoroughfare; and if Aquila was a native of Pontus, it is probable he was returning to Asia; a conjecture, which is so far confirmed by the subsequent course of events, that it appears he left Corinth at the same time with St. Paul, and afterwards settled in Ephesus[q]. Nor had he long been arrived in Corinth when St. Paul also came thither; nor, consequently, had the decree of Claudius, by which the Jews had been expelled from Rome or Italy, been long in force.

Now a great number of Jews, most of them *libertini generis*, or the descendants of such as, having originally been brought to Rome in the capacity of slaves, had recovered their freedom, were living there in the time of Augustus and of Tiberius—and even before that—in the quarter

[m] Ner. 7. 6.   [n] Ann. xiv. 53.   [o] Acts xviii. 1. 2.   [p] Vol. i. Diss. ii. 88.   [q] Acts xviii. 18. 19. 24. 26.

called Trans Tiberim[r]: eight thousand concurred in the petition against Archelaus, sent from the mother country, A. U. 751[s]; four thousand were transported to Sardinia A. U. 772[t]; and at the beginning of the reign of Claudius their numbers were become so considerable, that it was not thought safe, or practicable, to expel them the city, though they were forbidden to assemble together[u]. This being the case, it becomes presumptively an argument that they would not have been expressly driven from Rome at any subsequent period, except for some great and urgent reason; and that they were so expelled some time in the reign of Claudius is attested in general by Suetonius, as well as by St. Luke[v]; though he may have mistaken the cause, or assigned it only in part, when he ascribes it to their constant disturbances, *impulsore Chresto*; for Christianity, as we have seen[w], had certainly reached Rome early in the reign of Claudius; and, even in the time of Lactantius, Chrestus was still a common mistake of pronunciation for Christus[x].

It is a critical coincidence, however, that Suetonius places this expulsion, about the same time with the occasion when an embassy of Parthians and Armenians was present in Rome. This embassy, I have little doubt, is the embassy alluded to by Tacitus[y], A. U. 802. when they came to ask for Meherdates. It is placed also about the same time with the restitution of their liberty to the Rhodians, taken away A. U. 797.[z] which restitution Tacitus places A. U. 806.[a] but Suetonius A. U. 804.[b] in some consulate of Claudius, which must have been his fifth.

Jerome, in his Commentary on Dan. ix.[c] quotes from Apollinarius of Laodicea the following passage: Postea . . ab octavo Claudii Cæsaris anno, contra Judæos Romana arma correpta—. *Ab octavo* means *after the eighth*, and therefore *in the ninth*; just as, in a like expression of Ter-

<hr />

[r] Philo de Legat. 1014.   Suet. Jul. 84.   [s] Ant. Jud. xvii. xi. 1.   B. ii. vi. 1.   [t] Ant. xviii. iii. 5.   Tac. Ann. ii. 85.   Suet. Tib. 36.   Dio. lx. 6.   [u] Dio. loc. cit.   [v] Claud. 25.   [w] Vol. i. Diss. ii. 97.   [x] De Vera Sep. iv. 7.   [y] Ann. xii. 10.   [z] Dio. lx. 24.   [a] Ann. xii. 58.   [b] Nero. 7.   [c] Oper. iii. 1114.

tullian's[d], *a duodecimo,* meant *after the twelfth,* and, consequently, *in the thirteenth.* Now, from whatsoever authority this statement was derived, it is supported by Orosius also[e]; who distinctly places the expulsion of the Jews from Rome in the ninth of Claudius: and what is more, it is entirely in unison with the implicit testimony of Josephus. The disturbance at the passover; the subsequent outrage on Stephanus, the Emperor's freed-man and fiscal procurator; the tumultuary warfare between the Galileans and the Samaritans—all events of the same year, A. U. 802—were the most natural and most likely causes of this act of severity towards the Jews; whose conduct, as regarded at Rome, and until the rupture had been satisfactorily adjusted, partly by the Jewish deputies, and partly by the intercession of the younger Agrippa, would be looked on as a direct rebellion. Tacitus expresses himself strongly to this effect; Arsissetque bello provincia[f]—and Josephus shews that, if actual war was prevented, it was by only the prayers, remonstrances, and entreaties, of the rulers, or chief Jews, themselves; whose efforts and expedients to disarm the infuriated passions of the common people he describes very much to the life[g]. Certain it is, that a breach with the Roman government was never so near at any time before the final revolt as now, and in the last year of Caius; and to these two occasions, in particular, I am persuaded our Saviour alluded in the prophecy upon the mount, when he told the disciples that they should hear of wars and rumours, or tidings, of wars, but should see no actual war: the storm, once and again, should gather over Judæa, on the point of bursting upon it; and once and again, as the event proves, it should be seen to pass away without effect, because the end would not be as yet.

The number of Jews, inhabitants of Rome, was certainly too considerable to be tolerated there, with confidence or safety, if the mother country was in a state of revolt. But the news of what had happened in Judæa, especially of

[d] Vol. i. Diss. xi. 436.   [e] vii. 6.   [f] Ann. xii. 54.   [g] Ant. xx. vi. 1. B. ii. xii. 5.

what had happened after the feast of Tabernacles, (which in A. U. 802. when the Passover was celebrated April 5.[h] must have begun to be celebrated on or about September 30.) would not be received at Rome, under two or three months afterwards; that is, before December, A. U. 802. or January, A. U. 803. at the earliest. The decree of expulsion might follow soon after this; and in two or three weeks time, subsequently, Aquila might arrive in Corinth; where he had certainly been some time, longer or shorter, before St. Paul also came thither. If we place, then, this meeting at Corinth about the spring of A. U. 803. we place it in all probability about the truth.

I have now, I think, ascertained two dates, the earlier of which fixes the time of St. Paul's first visit to the peninsula of Greece; and the later, the time of his last visit to Jerusalem, recorded in the Acts. With a view to the detail of intermediate particulars, I will assume only that he set out on his second general circuit, Acts xv. 36. about the same period in the year as when he set out on his first, viz. May 26. the Pentecost of A. U. 802; or between that, and April 5. the date of the preceding Passover. The subsequent course and direction of his journey along the extent of Asia Minor, from Antioch, through Syria and Cilicia first, by land as far as to Alexandria Troas, and from thence through Macedonia, Thessaly, and Attica, until he came to Corinth, including the time taken up by the residence in particular places, both those, where such residences are not specified, and those, where they are, as at Troas, Philippi, Thessalonica, Berœa, and Athens, do necessarily require that we should allow the space of a year for the transaction of every thing, between Acts xv. 36. and xviii. 1; though this interval is not too little: for it is clear that St. Paul did not make a practice of staying every where; and we may infer from the narrative in the Acts, compared also with the Epistles to Philippi and to Thessalonica[i], that he stayed as long in each of these cities as he had ever stayed any where else;

---

[h] Vol. i. Diss. v.   [i] 1 Thess. i. 6. ii. 9.   2 Thess. iii. 8.   Philipp. iv. 16.

and yet the length of the stay at the latter does not appear to have exceeded three weeks [k].

In the year of our Lord 44. and A. U. 797. in which St. Paul set out on his first circuit, the Passover was celebrated March 31 ; and the day of Pentecost fell on May 21 : and St. Paul's first circuit, we have assumed, began about that time. Between this time, and the Pentecost, May 26. A. U. 802. which we have assumed as the beginning of his second circuit, there was just a five years' interval ; to be filled up, first, by the time occupied on the first circuit before the return to Antioch ; or between Acts xiii. 4. and xiv. 26 : secondly, by the residence at Antioch posterior to the return, but before the beginning of the dispute with the Judaizing teachers ; that is, between Acts xiv. 27. and xv. 1 : thirdly, by the mission to Jerusalem, and the conference there, in consequence of this dispute ; or between Acts xv. 2. and xv. 29 : and fourthly, by the return to Antioch, and continuance of the residence there, posterior to all the former events, but prior to the commencement of the next general circuit ; or between Acts xv. 30. and xv. 35. For one and all of these transactions the period of five years is not too long an interval ; especially, as independent of the duration of the circuit itself, the residence at Antioch both before and after the conference in Jerusalem, it is either affirmed or implied, took up no little time [l].

The details of the five years would be of no importance to our general argument, and so far might be distributed as we pleased. I cannot help conjecturing, however, that the time of the council of Jerusalem, at which the question, whether the Gentile converts to Christianity became subject, in consequence of their conversion, to the Law of Moses, or not, was formally discussed and settled, and which was, therefore, a cardinal period in the progress of the Christian scheme as concerned them, is to be placed A. U. 800. or 801. exactly at seven years' interval from the time of the conversion of Cornelius. This supposition is

[k] Acts xvii. 2.   [l] Acts xiv. 28. xv. 35.

manifestly possible; and it derives some support from the language of St. Peter, Acts xv. 7. ἀφ' ἡμερῶν ἀρχαίων, which is seen from verse 14—lower down—in the speech of St. James, to be equivalent simply to πρῶτον, or at the utmost to ἀπ' ἀρχῆς. The fact alluded to in each instance is clearly the opening of the Gospel to the Gentiles, by the instrumentality of St. Peter in the conversion of Cornelius; and this being spoken of as a somewhat remote event—as what had happened a good while ago, or at first—it is more naturally to be understood of a period of six or seven years, than of merely three or four. But to proceed.

The arrival of St. Paul at Corinth, then, about a year after the commencement of his second journey, would be about the spring of A. U. 808; and, consequently, in the first quarter of the tenth of Claudius, which began that year on January the 24th. The last places which he visited, and, as the course of the history proves, not many weeks before his arrival at Athens, were Philippi, Thessalonica, and Berœa; all which it is to be presumed would be visited A. U. 808: and it is some slight confirmation of the presumption that the language ascribed to the enemies of Paul, first at Philippi, and again at Thessalonica [m], points to a period when Christianity must have pervaded the *world*, which it might be said to have pervaded, when it had once reached Rome; and, also, to the knowledge of some dogma or decree of the existing Emperor, hostile to the Jews, and especially binding on Roman citizens: which might be that very edict of Claudius, which he issued about this time, commanding the Jews to leave Rome and Italy: and, consequently, laying them under a public ban, and forbidding Roman citizens in particular to give them any encouragement.

It is a much more critical circumstance in order to the same conclusion, that the first half of the ninth of Claudius, A. U. 802. when St. Paul set out on this second mission, was, as I shall prove hereafter, the close of a sabbatic year:

---

[m] Acts xvi. 21. xvii. 6. 7.

which was always a year of scarcity among the Jews.   Nor
yet was it the case with the Jews only, that the ninth of
Claudius was a year of dearth ; but according to Eusebius,
in Chronico, it was the case in Greece also.   He speaks of
a famine in Greece, in the ninth of Claudius, A. U. 802;
when the *modius* or *peck* of corn, ($\sigma i \tau o v$,) rose to six drachmæ
or denarii in price, that is, to six times its usual value.
The ordinary price of the modius of bread-corn was one
drachma, or denarius, and not more ; hence it is, that in the
book of Revelations, to express the severity of a dearth, the
chœnix or three half-pints measure of such corn alone,
(that is, so much as would maintain one man for a day,)
is put at a denarius in price ; about eleven times its usual
rate [n].   There are other occasions in the course of contemporary events, as well as before [o], when the price of wheat
rose much higher than usual ; but scarcely any, under ordinary circumstances, when it seems to have been higher
than this.   The use which I make of the knowledge of this
fact is as follows.

It might be collected from 2 Cor. xi. 8, 9. alone, that
St. Paul came to Corinth at a time of dearth, or when he
was likely to have wanted ; nor would he make a merit to
the Corinthians of having taken nothing from them, if there
were not some particular reason why he should.   The same
inference seems to be deducible from 1 Thess. ii. 9. and
2 Thess. iii. 8. also : he *might* have been *grievous* to this
Church, if he had not purposely abstained from being so.
What, then, are we to conclude ? The wants of St. Paul at
Corinth had been supplied by the brethren who came from
Macedonia [p], and the Epistle to the Philippians proves that
they had been supplied from that part of Macedonia [q].   The
time of this supply at Corinth was, consequently, when
Silas and Timothy arrived there from Macedonia [r] ; and
they had brought it with them from thence.

In like manner, the wants of St. Paul at Thessalonica, as
the same Epistle proves [q], had been supplied from Philippi

[n] vi. 6.   [o] Josephus mentions one, Ant. xiv. ii. 2.   [p] 2 Cor. xi. 8. 9.
[q] Phil. iv. 15. 16.   [r] Acts xviii. 5.

also : and though he came to Thessalonica almost on leaving Philippi [s], and though he stayed at Thessalonica perhaps not more than three weeks, yet even there they had ministered *once and again*, that is, on two several occasions, to his necessities.

St. Paul's arrival at Thessalonica would be early in the winter quarter of A. U. 803. when the famine, if there was any such thing in existence, would necessarily have begun to be felt.　His arrival at Corinth was early in the spring quarter of the same year—and the coming of the brethren from Macedonia to him there was certainly not long afterwards.　Yet, in this short time, the Philippians, a single Church, ministered thrice at least to his wants; twice in Thessalonica, and again in Corinth.　All this seems to intimate that there was some pressing occasion for it : something in the state of the times more likely to stimulate the benevolent zeal of his converts in his behalf than usual : which the fact of a period of scarcity, five or six times as severe as commonly, would explain and illustrate at once.

This conclusion is strengthened by the consideration that, for ought which appears to the contrary, from the time of this visit to Greece, to the time of his first imprisonment at Rome, these were the only occasions on which even the most attached and most grateful of his converts, the Philippians themselves, are seen to have rendered any such service to him.　There is no occasion until the time of this imprisonment, when he was likely again to have wanted. Nor can I help conjecturing that the true reason both why this Church in particular was so early and so long among those who supplied his pecuniary wants, and why St. Paul consented to be relieved by them, when he made a point of not accepting relief from others, was the friendship between St. Paul and St. Luke, who, as I have shewn elsewhere, was probably an inhabitant of Philippi.　But to return to the prosecution of our subject.

The course of events from the time of the arrival in Corinth may be ascertained as follows.

[s] xvii. 1.

c 3

St. Paul had been sometime there, before he ceased to preach to the Jews, and began to preach to the Gentile inhabitants of the city [t]; he was there a year and six months longer, even dated from the time of his vision [u], before the insurrection of the Jews in the time of Gallio [v]; and he remained there a good many days still, even after that [w]. It is clear, then, that we cannot compute the whole length of his stay at less than one year, and nine or ten months of another; which, being dated from the spring quarter of A. U. 803. in the tenth of Claudius, will place his departure early in the winter quarter of A. U. 805. in the twelfth.

When he had left Corinth, and was come to Ephesus, he was on his way to keep some feast [x]; concerning which, as it must have been some feast one year and nine or ten months, at least, distant from the spring quarter of A. U. 803. there can be no doubt that it must have been the Passover, A. U. 805. in the twelfth of Claudius, which fell that year on April 3: and by an argument from the Epistle to the Galatians, hereafter, I shall prove demonstratively that it was. Now the length of time necessary for a journey even from Troas to Jerusalem, and even in the summer season, if we make the requisite allowances for such stoppages as would naturally take place by the way, cannot be computed at less than five or six weeks [y], or the interval between Passover and Pentecost: and if so, the length of time necessary for such a journey from Corinth, which is a great deal further—and partly in the winter season, when all travelling took up more time—cannot be computed at less than two months. About one month, then, before the Passover A. U. 805. that is, early in the month of March, St. Paul would be passing through Ephesus, having probably left Corinth early in the February preceding: he would accomplish his purpose by arriving in Jerusalem at the beginning of April: and, as he made no stay there, but simply went up and saluted the Church, he would, con-

[t] xviii. 1—8.   [u] Ib. 8—11.   [v] Ib. 12—17.   [w] Ib. 18.   [x] Ib. 21.
[y] Acts xx. 6. xx. 16.

sequently return to Antioch, between the Passover and the Pentecost of A. U. 805. that is, between April 3. and May 24; about three years from April 5. or May 26. when we supposed that he left it last, A. U. 802.

I have said nothing on the controverted point respecting the vow which is mentioned Acts xviii. 18. because I do not think any certain conclusion can be grounded upon it. The grammatical construction undoubtedly requires that κειράμενος should be referred to Aquila, not to St. Paul, as the proper subject of the vow; and it is equally probable that the vow itself was the ordinary vow of separation, or the Nazirœatus—the minimum for which in respect of time was thirty days, or one month, but the maximum was indefinite [z]. To shave the head, under ordinary circumstances, was to declare the consummation of this vow, and preparatory to offering the sacrifices, which the law required in token of that consummation [a]. But here we have Aquila shaving his head at Cenchreæ; whereas the sacrifices could begin, or be offered, only at Jerusalem.

The doctrine of the Mishna with respect to the Nazirœatus is peculiarly complex, and full of nice distinctions. Among other things it is said that it could not be kept any where but in the land of Israel, Extra terram Israelis [b]; yet we find Aquila keeping it either at Corinth, or at Ephesus: where he was left by St. Paul [c]. It is true, that the due continuance and completion of the vow might be prevented by some accidental pollution; in which case the Nazarite was required to shave his head, and to begin his computation of time afresh. Mere tonsure of the head under such circumstances destroyed the thirty days, but did not oblige to any other ceremonial rite [d]. This might be Aquila's case. But it is not necessary to suppose he had made a vow of separation for a month only; he might have made it for a much longer time—called the Nazirœatus magnus, or a separation of sixty days; which would admirably agree to what we have supposed concerning the distance of time be-

---

[a] B. Jud. ii. xv. 1. Mishn. iv. 346. 11.   [a] Acts xxi. 23. 24. Ant. Jud. xix. vi. 1.   [b] iv. 346. 11.   [c] Acts xviii. 19.   [d] Mishn. iii. 165. 3. 5.

fore the Passover, when Paul left Corinth, viz. as about two months; and also account for Aquila's staying at Ephesus, while St. Paul continued his journey to Jerusalem. He would not go up to Jerusalem until the time of his vow was expired.

If I am right as to the time when St. Paul left Corinth, the attempt of the Jews to prosecute him before Gallio must have been later than the autumn of A. U. 804: whence we may infer that this was in the first year of Gallio's office. It is not necessary for me to trace the history of the province of Achaia, from the time of the partition of the provinces A. U. 727. when Augustus assigned it to the people, to A. U. 768. when it was resumed by the Emperor Tiberius; or A. U. 797. when it was again restored to the people; or A. U. 819. or 820. when it was declared independent by Nero; or A. U. 827. or 828. when, according to the opinion of Eckel [e], its liberty was abolished by Vespasian. Nor is it necessary to prove that, though two only of the twelve popular provinces [f], Asia Proper, and Africa, were strictly proconsular, yet the governors of the remaining ten, who were of prætorian dignity, bore the title of proconsul officially : to this fact a cloud of historical witnesses might be produced, and it is eminently true of the governors of Achaia and of Cyprus, to each of whom St. Luke has applied it [g].

It is certain, from one of the Epistles of Seneca, that his brother Gallio, whom he calls Dominum suum, in consequence of his having served the office either of prætor or of consul, before that Epistle was written, was sometime governor of Achaia [h] : Illud mihi in ore erat domini mei Gallionis; qui cum in Achaia febrem habere cœpisset, protinus navem ascendit, clamitans, non corporis esse sed loci morbum.

If it is reasonable to assume this was in the autumn—and that he was now leaving his government—it might be the autumn of A. U. 805: but not the autumn of A. U. 804. Paul might have been tried before him after the latter, but he

---

[e] vi. 332.   [f] Strab. xvii. 1186.   [g] Eckel. iv. 241.   Acts xiii. 7. 8. 12.
xviii. 12.   [h] Ep. 104.

could not after the former. Moreover, Corinth was the capital of the province, and the proconsul's place of residence —and Gallio was there when St. Paul was brought before him; which also implies that he was brought before him after or in the autumnal quarter of A. U. 804: for we shall see, hereafter, that, from the commencement of the spring quarter, the governors of provinces would not be found stationary in the seat of the proconsular government, but were employed in visiting their province, and administering justice elsewhere. There can be little question that Gallio was serving Achaia as prætor: into possession of which province he might come after three or four years' time—and as his brother Seneca had been made tutor to Nero, A. U. 802. it is nothing unlikely that he might have been admitted to the prætorship, even before that. The number of prætors in the reign of Claudius was annually never less than ten, and sometimes as many as eighteen.

The length of the stay at Antioch is not specified, except in general terms, which would lead to the inference that it was not very considerable ; yet we have shewn elsewhere [i] that it was sufficiently long to allow for the coming thither of Peter also from Jerusalem, and for the arrival of certain persons from James, while both he and St. Paul were still there together. It is probable, therefore, that the latter would not set out on his visit to the churches of Galatia and of Phrygia [k], or upon that circuit of the upper regions, which ended in his finally settling at Ephesus, before the midsummer of this year at least. For this journey, therefore, beginning from Antioch, but embracing the tour of Asia, as far as the Euxine sea, and, possibly, even the Hellespont, we cannot allow much less than eight or nine months. I assume, then, that Paul would not come to Ephesus and settle there, agreeably to his promise, the preceding year [l], before the beginning of the thirteenth of Claudius A. U. 806.

After this arrival, three months were spent before the separation of the disciples, when Paul began to dispute

---

[i] Vol. i. Diss. ii. 89.   [k] Acts xviii. 23. xix. 1.   [l] Ib. xviii. 21.

daily in the *schola* of one Tyrannus; and two years more, posterior to that, before the formation of the design to return, through Macedonia and Achaia, to Jerusalem, preparatory to a journey to Rome: and, even after this, St. Paul himself still remained somewhat longer in Asia—though he had sent Timothy and Erastus into Macedonia —until at last the disturbance excited in Ephesus by Demetrius, whether earlier, or not, than he had always intended, rendered it necessary or expedient that he should leave it [m].

In this account, then, of the residence at Ephesus, there is a positive reckoning of two years and three months, which bring us from the beginning of the thirteenth of Claudius A. U. 806. to the beginning of the spring quarter of A. U. 808. the middle of the first of Nero; and an indefinite reckoning of some time more, the length of which must be otherwise determined. The entire duration of his residence is stated by St. Paul himself, in his farewell address to the elders of the Ephesian Church, when they met him at Miletus, as a τριετία, or period of three years [n]; which, being understood, as it may be, of current years, and not necessarily complete, will determine it as more than two years, but less than three: and I shall shew, hereafter, by a comparison with the Epistles, that the two years and three months, above specified, terminated at, or before, a Passover at least; and that the stay of St. Paul, even after that, extended to, or beyond, the ensuing Pentecost: which would make the whole length of his residence in Ephesus from first to last, a period of two years, and more than six months. This conclusion may be confirmed at present even by what passed in the city, immediately before his departure.

In the speech of the townclerk, the γραμματεὺς, scribe, or recorder, of the city, we meet with the phrase, ἀγόραιοι ἄγονται, καὶ ἀνθύπατοί εἰσιν [o]. The phrase, ἀγοραίους (scilicet ἡμέρας) ἄγειν, is analogous to the Latin, *forum agere*, or

---

[m] Acts xix. 8. 10. 21. 22. 23. 41. xx. 1.   [n] Ib. xx. 31.   [o] Ib. xix. 38.

conventum agere[P], and to our own of *holding a court;* it occurs ῥητῶς in a rescript of Publius Servilius Galba preserved by Josephus, and, what is almost the same, τὰς ἀγοραίους ποιεῖσθαι, is to be met with in Strabo [q]; by the help of which, it seems to be requisite that we should correct ἄγοντι τὸν ἀγόραιον, in Josephus, by ἄγοντι τὴν ἀγόραιον. Now we may infer from Strabo [r], (and the supposition itself is but reasonable,) that the governors of particular provinces, though they had one stated place of residence, which place was the metropolis or principal city of the province, were accustomed to be travelling up and down, during a certain part of the year, and holding these courts, or ἀγοραίους, in other quarters, not in the metropolis. For this purpose, a country was divided into διοικήσεις—which would so far answer to shires or counties—and one court, *forum, conventus,* ἀγόραιοι, was commonly held for the inhabitants of every διοίκησις, at some principal city within the diocese; which would therefore answer to the assize court for the shire or county, in the county town [s]. We may infer also, from Cicero, *locis citatis,* that the times for these annual circuits were from the spring to the summer quarter of the year [t]: that is, from March to May or June: after which period, consequently, it is to be expected the regular governor would not be found in his regular place of residence, but elsewhere.

Ephesus was, certainly, the metropolitan city of the province of Asia [u]; though that province, if Josephus and Philostratus are to be believed, contained five hundred cities; nor was it without reason that it claimed to itself the title of Πρώτη, or Princeps, so frequently, upon its coins [v]. The privilege of the καταπλοῦς, that is, the right of receiving the proconsul, upon his entry into his government, in their city first, was conceded to the Ephesians by law [w]. The ordinary place of the proconsul's residence was, consequently,

[p] Ciceron. Ep. ad Att. v. 21. vi. 2. Suet. Jul. 30. 56. [q] Ant. Jud. xiv. x. 21. Strabo xiii. 901. [r] iii. 229. [s] Plin. H. N. iii. 1. 3. 21. v. 29. 30. [t] Vide also Suet. Jul. 7. Galb. 9. compared with Neron. 40. and 34. [u] Ant. Jud. xiv. x. 11. B. ii. xvi. 4. p. 478. Philost. Vit. Soph. Herod. Att. 3. [v] Eckel. ii. 521. iv. 282. [w] Id. ii. 518.

Ephesus: but, after the month of February, or March, it is probable he would not be found even there. Servilius was holding a court at Tralles, when he issued the edict before quoted; and Julus Antonius was doing the same at Ephesus still, but on the ides of February, when he issued that which on another occasion also is recited by Josephus [x].

Now the language of the townclerk implies neither that any courts of law were then open, nor any proconsul then on the spot; but quite the contrary; his words should be rendered, There are courts held, and there are proconsuls— not, The courts are open, and deputies are present ; which would have required, αἱ ἀγόραιοι ἄγονται, καὶ ὁ ἀνθύπατος πάρεστιν. He asserts, therefore, merely what was commonly the *practice*, but not what was then going on. Nor, if he had meant that the proconsul was on the spot, and not simply that there were such persons as proconsuls, would he have expressed himself in the indefinite manner, ἀνθύπατοί εἰσι—for proconsular Asia, including Ephesus, was never governed by more than one such deputy at a time. And though, as the title of an office, the name of the Γραμματεὺς is recognized upon the coins of Ephesus [y], and, consequently, the office itself is proved not only to have been an actual one, but an office of dignity and authority, something like that of the first civil magistrate among them—still had the supreme Roman governor been in the city at the time, it is not likely that the duty of quelling the disturbance, or dismissing the assembly, which Acts xix. 39. demonstrates to have taken place at an irregular time, and not on one of the stated days of such meetings, would have been left exclusively to him. When all Ephesus was in an uproar, the Roman governor, it might be presumed, would naturally have interfered. The proconsul of Asia, at the time of the accession of Nero, was Junius Silanus; and he had been put to death immediately upon that accession [z] ; nor can it be said with certainty by whom he was succeeded [a]. But this ought to constitute no difficulty, for the province would

ˣ Ant. xvi. vi. 7.   ʸ Eckel. ii. 519.   ᶻ Tac. Ann. xiii. 1.   ᵃ Ib. 33.

not be left long without a governor; and Silanus was made away with in a very short time after October 13. the day of the accession of Nero, A. U. 807.

It is observable also that, in the same speech, the epithet of νεωκόρος is applied to the city of Ephesus[b]; and this title, so expressed, begins to appear on the coins of Ephesus first in the reign of Nero[c]. In the course of time afterwards it came to designate itself δὶς, τρὶς, and even τέτρακις, νεωκόρον. It is apparent, likewise, that the time, when this uproar took place at Ephesus, was some time when the Asiarchs were assembled in that city[d]. This name is descriptive of an office which was annual and elective; and of a body of men returned by a number of cities[e], though, probably, not more than one might be so returned for each; the purpose of whose appointment being purely religious, and especially connected with the annual solemnities in honour of the Ephesian Diana, they would not have been found collected in Ephesus, except at a time when those solemnities were going on[f]. The existence of games called Ephesia, and celebrated at Ephesus in honour of Diana, is a well-attested fact[g]; and concerning the time of the year when they were celebrated, it seems to be certain that it coincided with the spring, or the summer. There is a coin of Ephesus[h] which relates to the games there celebrated, and bears the inscription, ΕΦΕCΙΩΝ. ΝΕΩΚΟΡΩΝ. ΟΛΥΜΠΙΑ. ΟΙΚΟΥΜΕΝΙΚΑ. from which title we may infer that their proper time synchronized with the same part of the year, as the recurrence of the Olympiads; that is, the first full moon after the summer solstice. This full moon, A. D. 55. or A. U. 808. when the moon was eclipsed on July 27. at 5. 30. in the morning, could not fall earlier than June 27. previously: about which time we have shewn, upon other grounds, it is probable St. Paul must still have been in Ephesus. To proceed, then, with the course of our subject.

[b] xix. 35.   [c] Eckel. ii. 519. 520.   iv. 288—306.   [d] xix. 31.
[e] Strabo. xiv. 929.   Philos. De Vit. Soph. Scopelianus. 2.   [f] Eckel. iv.
207—212.   [g] Vide Meursii Græcia Feriata.   [h] Eckel. ii. 521.   Vide
also Philostr. De Vit. Sophist.   Polemo. 4. 9.

After his departure from Asia, there is mention made of
a residence in Macedonia, before the next visit to Greece ;
and after the arrival in Greece, of a three months' residence
there, before the return to Macedonia again ; and after this
return, of the spending the days of unleavened bread at
Philippi, before the departure, finally, to Troas, on the
way to Jerusalem[1]. This Passover spent at Philippi is,
consequently, the Passover next after the departure from
Ephesus, or just one year from the Passover of A. U. 808.
in the first of Nero alluded to above ; and therefore just
three years from the first Passover, since the arrival originally, A. U. 806. It is, consequently, the Passover of
A. U. 809. the middle of the second of Nero. How the
time between this Passover and the departure from Ephesus, A. U. 808. was spent will appear presently from the
Epistles. By the ensuing Pentecost St. Paul was in Jerusalem ; he was, consequently, in Jerusalem at the Pentecost
of A. U. 809 ; and in A. U. 809. at the Pentecost of that
year, the midsummer of the second of Nero, I have already
determined, on other and independent data, that he must
have been there.

All these conclusions I shall further establish, and place
beyond a question, by shewing their agreement with the
internal evidence furnished by the Epistles of St. Paul,
such as I consider to have been written before this visit to
Jerusalem ; which are, in my opinion, the following six,
stated in their order of succession; the First and the Second
to the Thessalonians ; the First and the Second to the Corinthians ; the Epistle to the Romans, or the Epistle to the
Galatians. Each of these I shall consider in its turn.

I. *On the First Epistle to the Thessalonians.*

It must be evident, from those parts of this Epistle,
which mention the preaching of the Gospel in Macedonia
in general, and also at Philippi in particular[k], that it could
not have been written before St. Paul's visit to Philippi[l],
and to other parts of Macedonia, A. U. 802; and from iii. 1.

---

[1] xx. 1. 2. 3. 6.　　　　[k] i. 7. 8.　ii. 2.　　　　[l] Acts xvi. 12.

that it could not have been written before his arrival at
Athens, even after that [m]; and from i. 1. 7. 8. (compared
with 2 Cor. i. 18. 19.) which mentions *Achaia* as well as
Macedonia, that it could not have been written before the
visit to Corinth, A. U. 803. [n] of which it must be superfluous to prove that it was the first, which St. Paul had yet
made to the peninsula of Greece.

Notwithstanding, therefore, the *prima facie* evidence of
1 Thess. iii. 1. compared with Acts xvii. 15. 16. which
proves that St. Paul both came to, and for a time was left
at, Athens, the Epistle could not have been written from
Athens ; and the allusion in it to his being in Athens
would still be true, if he had been there, and had sent Timothy to Thessalonica from thence, though he afterwards
wrote the letter in which he speaks of these things, from
some other place.

Now, when he was first brought to Athens, he was
brought alone; but he sent back a message, by those who
brought him, to Silas (or Sylvanus) and Timothy, whom
he had left at Berœa, that they should come and join him
without delay. We may justly suppose they would comply
with this wish, especially as it is said that he waited for
them accordingly [o]. Yet it is not mentioned that they did;
on the contrary, they are first said to have joined him only
when he was at Corinth [p]. In order to have reconciled
these different intimations together, even in the Acts, we
might have been obliged to suppose that, after rejoining St.
Paul at Athens, according to his desire, either Timothy, or
Sylvanus, or both, must have been sent out by him somewhere again, before his own departure thence, and did not
return to him a second time save at Corinth. This is precisely that state of the case which the first Epistle proves to
have happened; for Timothy had actually rejoined Paul at
Athens, and actually been sent again from thence to Thessalonica, before he himself left it ; and Timothy had rejoined him alone; or, what is equally probable, Sylvanus

[m] xvii. 15. [n] xviii. 1. [o] xvii. 16. [p] xviii. 5.

had rejoined him also, and been sent again to some other quarter, while Timothy was despatched to Thessalonica[q]; (otherwise St. Paul could not have said he had thought proper, or rather consented, to be left at Athens alone;) and Timothy had rejoined him a second time only recently, either at Athens—or, if not there, at some other place, whither St. Paul had proceeded in his absence—after this very errand to Thessalonica, and before the Epistle was written[r]. The same thing is implied of Sylvanus also; for both Paul, and Sylvanus, and Timothy, who are all joined in the salutation at the head of the Epistle[s], must all have been together when it was written.

Now, after Acts xviii. 5. when both of these last are said to have come to him at Corinth, it is manifest they would be together in that place at least; where also it is proved by the Second Epistle to the Corinthians[t] they all continued throughout: and they are there said to have rejoined him from Macedonia generally; as the Epistle itself proves that Timothy in particular rejoined him from Thessalonica, which is the same thing. And if we compare 2 Cor. xi. 9. with Philipp. iv. 15, 16. we shall consider it more than probable that, when Timothy rejoined Paul from Thessalonica, Sylvanus also rejoined him from Philippi; which too would be from Macedonia.

These coincidences place it beyond a question, that the First Epistle to the Thessalonians was written after the arrival of St. Paul at Corinth, and after the return of Timothy and of Sylvanus to him there; and, consequently, from Corinth itself; for there is no proof that St. Paul, during this visit, preached in any other part of Achaia. Moreover, if 1 Thess. iii. 6. 7. be compared with Acts xviii. 5. xviii. 11. we shall conclude that it must have been written at the very beginning of the visit, and not at some later period, when the year and nine or ten months, during which we supposed it to have lasted, were more or less advanced in their progress. Nor is ii. 18. any objection; for the em-

---

phasis laid on the ἐγὼ μὲν Παῦλος clearly implies that he
had wished this once or twice to have rejoined them in
person, and not merely by a messenger ; and coming between ii. 17. which speaks of a separation—πρὸς καιρὸν ὥρας
(that is, a very recent, and as it might be supposed
about to prove, a very brief, separation) and iii. 1. 2. which
speaks of the mission of Timothy, as the substitute of Paul,
it shews that he means some wish which he had formed
since his departure from Thessalonica indeed, but before
his departure from Athens also.

We may venture to pronounce, therefore, with confidence, that the First Epistle to the Thessalonians was written
from Corinth, A. U. 803. soon after St. Paul's arrival, which
we placed about the spring of the year; and the time of the
first determines presumptively the time of the second; which
being written apparently to correct a very important mistake, produced by the first[u], must have been written in a
short time after, and, consequently, in A. U. 803. also. In
fact, iii. 2. of the Second Epistle may probably allude even
to Acts xviii. 6—10. It follows, consequently, that these
two Epistles were the earliest of St. Paul's Epistles in general ; and there are passages in each of them which might
have led of themselves to such a conclusion[v].

II. *On the First Epistle to the Corinthians.*

The First Epistle to the Corinthians was written from
Asia[w], that is, from the province of that name in Asia
Minor ; and it was written from Ephesus within that province[x]. It could not, therefore, have been written before
the commencement of the residence at Ephesus[y], in the
thirteenth of Claudius, A. U. 806.

Again; It could not have been written before Apollos had
visited and preached at Corinth[z], to which place it is evident he proceeded from Ephesus[a]; nor yet before he was

---

[u] 1 Thess. iv. 13—v. 11. 2 Thess. ii. 1—12. [v] 1 Thess. v. 27.
2 Thess. iii. 14. iii. 17. [w] xvi. 19. [x] xv. 32. xvi. 8. [y] Acts
xix. 1. [z] 1 Cor. i. 12. iii. 4. 5. 6. 22. iv. 6. 2 Cor. iii. 1. [a] Acts
xviii. 24. 27.

come back again thence to Ephesus[b]. Now when Paul first
arrived at Ephesus, A. U. 806. he was still at Corinth[c]: if
so, we may take it for granted that the Epistle was not
written immediately after the arrival, nor until some time
in the course of the first year of the residence at least; a
conclusion which is implicitly confirmed by 1 Cor. iv. 11—
13. compared with Acts xx. 31. 34; for St. Paul must have
been some while at Ephesus, for this description of his mode
of employment daily to have been natural and just.

Again; The Epistle was written either at, or just before,
the recurrence of the period of the Passover, and before the
ensuing Pentecost[d]; and it was written after Timothy had
been sent to Corinth, and while he was still absent—but
when St. Paul was waiting for his return at Ephesus,
and for his return in company with others; which implies
that others also had been sent with him[e]. And that after
this Timothy did actually rejoin him, before he wrote any
second Epistle at least, appears from the Second to the Corinthians[f]. If, then, the Epistle had been written before
the point of time specified at Acts xix. 22. which mentions
the fact of a mission of Timothy and of Erastus into Macedonia—this mission, as concerns the former, and perhaps as
concerns the latter too, must have been a second mission,
yet nothing at variance with the Epistle, nor impossible in
the nature of things; and this I believe to have been actually the case.

For, first, at a time posterior to the mission of Timothy,
alluded to in the Epistle, St. Paul had not yet decided upon
going up to Jerusalem, much less upon visiting Rome; but
before the mission specified in the Acts he had already made
up his mind to do both[g].

Secondly, when he wrote the Epistle to the Corinthians,
he had not yet determined, though he might have given some
reason to expect he would determine, on passing through
Macedonia, and so on to Achaia; much less upon making

[b] 1 Cor. xvi. 12.   [c] Acts xix. 1. 2.   [d] 1 Cor. v. 7. 8.   xvi. 8.
[e] iv. 17.   xvi. 12.   xvi. 10. 11.   [f] 2 Cor. i. 1.   [g] 1 Cor. xvi. 3. 4. 6.
Acts xix. 21.

any stay there; but at the time of the mission in the Acts he had decided on doing both[h].

Thirdly, after the mission of Timothy in the Acts, there is no mention of his ever rejoining St. Paul, either at Ephesus, or any where else, before they set out together from Greece to go into Asia[i]; which seems to imply that, after that mission, St. Paul joined Timothy, and not Timothy St. Paul. And this might easily have been the case; for Timothy had been sent into Macedonia, and Paul left Ephesus to go to Macedonia[k], and wrote his Second Epistle to the Corinthians (as we shall see by and by) when Timothy was certainly with him, from thence.

Fourthly, St. Paul's original intention ¦had been to pass through Corinth into Macedonia, and back from Macedonia to Corinth, and thence to set out for Judæa[l]: the plan which he actually adopted was just the reverse of this; passing to Corinth through Macedonia, and back again from Corinth to Macedonia[m].

Fifthly, he had never been at Corinth since his first visit[n]; yet he tells them this was the *third* time he was coming to them[o], that is, the third time he had promised to come to them. Now there is one such promise here, and another in various places of the First Epistle[p], but no instance of a third, unless it had been sent by Timothy at the mission specified in the Acts, or at some other mission, such as we are supposing, prior to, and distinct from, that. And this is much the more probable; for there is no proof in the Acts[q] that Timothy had been sent any where into Achaia; but there is proof in the Epistle, that he had been sent to Corinth; that St. Paul expected he would arrive there; and that he would correct some belief, which had given occasion to the mistaken presumption that St. Paul never intended to visit Corinth again[r]; and that to rectify this mistake, as well as for other purposes, had been one great motive of

---

[h] 1 Cor. xvi. 5.   Acts xix. 21. 22.   [i] Acts xx. 3. 4.   [k] xx. 1.
[l] 2 Cor. i. 16.   [=] Acts xix. 21.   xx. 1. 3.   [m] 2 Cor. i. 15. 23.   ii. 1.
xiii. 2.   [o] 2 Cor. xii. 14.   xiii. 1.   [p] 1 Cor. iv. 19.   xi. 34.   xvi.
2. 3. 5.   [q] xix. 22.   [r] 1 Cor. iv. 17.   xvi. 10.   iv. 18.

his mission itself. And 1 Cor. xvi. 5. the emphasis laid on Μακεδονίαν γὰρ διέρχομαι is another presumptive intimation that he had sent them a message to that effect already ; which message some among them might perhaps affect to disbelieve. Moreover, from 1 Cor. xvi. 10. it appears Timothy had not been sent long before the Epistle itself was written ; and St. Paul considered it possible the Epistle might arrive at Corinth before him.

The drift of all these considerations is to show that the First to the Corinthians was written before the point of time specified at Acts xix. 22 : and consequently before the expiration of the two years' and three months' residence, as mentioned at xix. 10. and xix. 21. at least. If it was written, therefore, about a Passover, it was probably written before its actual arrival ; nor, in fact, could it have been said with propriety, ὥστε ἑορτάζωμεν [s], unless the feast had been still to come.

Now, when he should visit Corinth, the writer considers it probable he might spend a winter there[t] ; which could not be the winter of the year then current, because it would be later than both the Passover, and the Pentecost, of that year[u]. The Epistle, then, was written a year at least before the time when this winter would arrive; and if this winter was the winter which St. Paul actually did spend in Greece, after he left Ephesus, and before the Passover spent at Philippi[v], it was the winter of the second of Nero, A. U. 809. *ineunte ;* and, consequently the Epistle, written one year at least before it, was written in or before the winter of the first, A. U. 808. *ineunte :* and this conclusion may be rendered almost indubitably certain by the following considerations.

The Epistle was written at a time when a collection for the Church of Jerusalem either had been only recently begun, or was still incomplete and going on, at Corinth[w]. The same collection had previously been going on among the churches of Asia, where its origin could not have been

---

[s] 1 Cor. v. 7.   [t] Ib. xvi. 6.   [u] Ib. xvi. 8.   [v] Acts xx. 3. 6.
[w] 1 Cor. xvi. 1.

earlier than the time of St. Paul's last visit to Galatia, which was A. U. 805. This collection had been projected and going forward at Corinth in particular, a year before it was completed in Macedonia [x]; and it was completed, or about to be so, in Macedonia, when St. Paul wrote his Second Epistle to the Corinthians: and it had been projected at least, if not for some time going on, before he wrote his First; for the directions at xvi. 1. are manifestly given in answer to an enquiry of the Corinthians among other things, about which they had written [y], respecting the mode to be adopted in making this collection also: and the collection, we may presume, was in a great measure a proposal of their own, or St. Paul would not write to them in the Second Epistle as he does write [z].

Now, we have seen one instance of a similar collection made at Antioch; to which it was peculiar to have been made in or just after a sabbatic year, and against a period of dearth :. we have seen also that the third of Nero was very probably a year of dearth; and if we turn to the table of sabbatic years—which is given in Diss. vii. App.—it will be seen that the thirty-second in order coincides with the second of Nero, from seed-time in A. U. 808. to the same time in A. U. 809. throughout. It was in this year, at the Pentecost A. U. 809, that the contributions thus made and collected were brought by St. Paul to Jerusalem; and they must have been made and collected, at least before the Passover, when he set out on this journey from Philippi. They had begun to be collected a year before they were completed; and the time of their completion was at hand when St. Paul wrote the Second to the Corinthians; and they had been some little while in progress when he wrote the First. The Second Epistle could certainly not have been written earlier than midsummer A. U. 808. therefore neither could the First later than the Passover of the same year. The truth is, as it appears to me, the collection was projected and begun to be made in Achaia about the au-

[x] 2 Cor. viii. 1—4. viii. 10. ix. 2.   [y] 1 Cor. vii. 1.   [z] 2 Cor. viii. 10—15. ix. 1—5.

tumn of A. U. 807 : and St. Paul was written to, on this subject as well as on others, and returned his answer, in the First Epistle to the Corinthians, early in the winter quarter of A. U. 808.

I have said nothing, in considering the time of this Epistle, on the allusion to the gymnastic exercises of antiquity, which occurs at ix. 24. not because it is not capable of proof that all the most celebrated of these games in former times, the Olympia, the Pythia, the Isthmia, the Nemea, and even others of more recent date, as the Actia, instituted by Augustus, A. U. 724. or 726. were still in being and long after, but because as their number was so great, and their times so various, some of them might fall out every year, and none are referred to in particular. The same remark is applicable to later instances of the same kind, as 1 Tim. iv. 7, 8. and 2 Tim. ii. 5. Allusions of this description, among such a people as the Greeks or the Romans, were always in character, whether suggested by the occasion or not.

III. *On the Second Epistle to the Corinthians.*

The Second Epistle to the Corinthians was not written before St. Paul had determined to go himself to Jerusalem, along with the bearers of the contributions of the churches both of Asia, and of Macedonia and Achaia ; which, however, he had not determined on doing when he wrote the First to the Corinthians [a]. It was not written, therefore, prior to the time when Timothy and Erastus were sent from Ephesus to Macedonia [b] ; nor, consequently, as we may safely presume, to the Pentecost, before which St. Paul did not propose to leave Ephesus [c] ; which we have seen was the Pentecost of A. U. 808. the first of Nero.

Again ; It was not written until St. Paul had both departed from Ephesus ; and passed through Troas ; and come into Macedonia ; as in the history he was made to come directly from Asia ; and was still there [d]. Nor was it written until Titus both had been sent to Corinth from Ephe-

---

[a] 2 Cor. viii. 19.   1 Cor. xvi. 3. 4.   [b] Acts xix. 21. 22.   [c] 1 Cor. xvi. 8.
[d] 2 Cor. i. 8. ii. 12. 13. vii. 5—viii. 1.—ix. 2. Acts xx. 1.

sus, after the First Epistle, and had rejoined St. Paul again in Macedonia, subsequent to his departure from Asia ; and from Macedonia had once more been sent to Corinth [e]. That it was written, then, from Macedonia, after St. Paul left Ephesus, and before he passed into Greece, and consequently sometime between Acts xx. 1. and xx. 3. there can be no question; the only difficulty remaining will concern the time ; or at what period of the interval, so included, it was actually written.

Now that St. Paul spent some months in Macedonia, preaching the gospel there, round about as far even as Illyricum, and exhorting them with many words, before he revisited Greece, appears both from the direct narrative in the Acts, and, as we shall see by and by, indirectly from the Epistle to the Romans. The time when he passed into Greece was about three months, or at the utmost four, before the Passover, March 19.[f] A. U. 809. in the second of Nero : it is possible, therefore, that the Epistle might not have been written before the middle of the autumnal quarter of A. U. 808. or the beginning of the second of Nero: and this appears to me to have been the case.

For it has been proved that it was after the Pentecost of A. U. 808. that St. Paul left Ephesus ; and, consequently, it must have been in the summer quarter that he came into Macedonia : there must have been some interval, and perhaps of considerable length, between the sending of the message, or the formation of the design, alluded to i. 15, 16, 17. (which message we have rendered it probable was sent by Timothy at a time not specified in the Acts,) and the writing of the Epistle ; it must have been written the best part of a year at least since the collection had begun in Achaia, which is, in fact, since the First Epistle had been sent [g] : it must have been written not long before St. Paul expected that he himself should be in Corinth [h] : that is to say, not long before the commencement of the three months' residence there. All these criteria determine its actual time

---

[e] 2 Cor. vii. 6—8—14. viii. 6—16. 17—23.   [f] Vol. i. Diss. v.   [g] 2 Cor. viii. 10. ix. 2.   [h] 2 Cor. ix. 3—5.

to the last quarter of A. U. 808. and the first quarter of the second of Nero : and this conclusion being thus established, I shall point out its accordance with a remarkable note of time, contained in the Epistle itself: the time of the rapture which is stated to have occurred, πρὸ ἐτῶν δεκατεσσάρων [i], referred to the date of the Epistle, or the year then current when it was written.

I shall prove hereafter, in its proper place, by a multitude of examples, that such notes of duration as these are never to be construed either inclusively, or exclusively, of both their extremes, but, if inclusively of the one, exclusively of the other, and conversely : upon which principle, the date of the rapture was the fourteenth year before—exclusive of the date of the Epistle—or the date of the Epistle was the fifteenth year subsequently—inclusive of the date of the rapture—and in either case, if the date of the Epistle was A. U. 808. the date of the rapture was A. U. 794. Now, at Acts xxii. 17—21. St. Paul affirms the fact of an ecstasy, the scene of which he places in the temple at Jerusalem, upon occasion of some visit there, which the context alone must determine to be the first visit after his conversion, when he stayed in Jerusalem only fifteen days [k]. The time of this visit has been proved to coincide with the Passover of the first of Claudius, A. U. 794. exactly fourteen years before the Passover of the first of Nero, A. U. 808. and fifteen before the Passover of his second, A. U. 809.

IV. *On the Epistle to the Romans.*

The Epistle to the Romans was written after the First to the Corinthians, and by parity of consequence, as well as for other reasons, which will shortly appear, after the Second. For Aquila and Priscilla, when this Epistle was written, were at Rome; but when the First to the Corinthians was written they were at Ephesus [l]. The same passage asserts that they had jeoparded their lives for the sake of Paul; which they might be said to have done, after the

[i] 2 Cor. xii. 2.   [k] Gal. i. 18. Acts. ix. 28—30.   [l] Rom. xvi. 3.
1 Cor. xvi. 19.

danger to which they, in common with the rest of St. Paul's companions or fellow-labourers, or, perhaps, they in particular, had been exposed at the time of the uproar in Ephesus[m]; but not, as far as it appears from the history, before that.

Again; It was not written until after the time when St. Paul, having begun from Jerusalem, and by his individual ministry, had made an end of preaching the gospel round about as far as Illyricum[n]. Between the departure from Asia and the arrival in Greece, it has been shewn that there was an interval of five or six months, which must have been spent by St. Paul in Macedonia[o]. Macedonia confined upon Illyricum, and a noble road, branching out from two heads, Apollonia and Dyrrhachium, both upon the Sinus Adriaticus, and close upon the borders of that region, stretched eastward right through the country for an extent of five hundred and thirty-five Roman miles[p], and afforded an easy access to all parts of Macedonia. Its name was the Via Ignatia; and its course is described by Strabo. The expression of St. Paul, μέχρι τοῦ Ἰλλυρικοῦ, does not imply that he had preached in Illyricum itself, but only as far as its borders, or, as we should express ourselves, *up* to it; and this he would necessarily do if, as he is represented in the history, he traversed the whole of Macedonia; for, beginning at its eastern extremity, by which only he could approach it from Asia, he must thus have proceeded to its western, where only it confined on Illyricum. There is no period in the previous history of St. Paul's travels, during which it was possible for the circuit of this country to have been thus made; and in passing thither now, he was merely completing a purpose, which it has been seen that he had formed some time before[q]. The Epistle to the Romans, then, was not written until the circuit of Macedonia was over.

Again; It could not have been written before the three months' residence subsequently in Greece[r] were either com-

[m] Acts xix. 23.   [n] Rom. xv. 19.   [o] Acts xx. 1. 2.   [p] Strabo vii. 467.   [q] Acts xix. 21.   [r] xx. 3.

pleted or drawing to a close; for it was written when not only the mind of St. Paul had been made up about going to Jerusalem, and the collections for the Church of that city, still pending when the Second to the Corinthians was written, had now been completed, but when St. Paul was on the eve of departure; or having no longer room, or occasion for staying, in the parts where he was at the time, was preparing to return to Judæa[s]. I infer, then, that it must have been written at the close of the three months in question; and either from Corinth, where the three months were most probably spent, or at least from Cenchreæ; in which case it was certainly written a little before the Passover of A. U. 809; and this conclusion may be confirmed in various ways as follows.

I. Among the salutations at the end of the Epistle, Erastus the steward, or οἰκονόμος, of the city, saluteth you, is one[t]; and Erastus, it might be conjectured from Acts xix. 22. and it must be almost certain from 2 Tim. iv. 20. was either a native, or an inhabitant, of Corinth, or both. In the same text Gaius, or Caius, is spoken of as the host or entertainer of Paul; and in the First to the Corinthians the name of Gaius is mentioned, as the name of a Corinthian convert, whom St. Paul had baptized in person[u], along with the name of Crispus, (whom the Acts shew to have been really a householder in Corinth[v],) and also along with the name of Stephanus, whom a subsequent passage recognizes as the first-fruits of Achaia[w]. There must have been, consequently, another Gaius, a Corinthian, besides the Gaius, whom the Acts specify by name as a native, or inhabitant, of Derbe[x]. I may observe also, that in the phrase εὐδόκησαν γὰρ Μακεδονία καὶ Ἀχαΐα, and that of Ἐπαίνετον . . . ὅς ἐστιν ἀπαρχὴ τῆς Ἀχαΐας εἰς Χριστὸν[y], this mention of Achaia after Macedonia, or of Achaia, ἁπλῶς, and without Macedonia, is some proof that the writer of the Epistle was himself in Achaia at the time, and known to be so, by those to whom he wrote.

[s] Rom. xv. 23. 25. 26. 31.   [t] Rom. xvi. 23.   [u] 1 Cor. i. 14.   [v] xviii. 8.
[w] 1 Cor. i. 16.   xvi. 15.   [x] xx. 4.   xix. 29.   [y] Rom. xv. 26.   xvi. 5.

II. Among such others, besides Erastus and Gaius, as are also specified by name, and take part in the salutations to the Roman Church along with St. Paul, Timothy and Sopater were actually companions of the writer, when he set out from Greece, upon his journey into Asia[z]. And, in addition to these also, Jason, whose name occurs at Rom. xvi. 21. and whom Acts xvii. 5. 6. 7. prove to have lived in Thessalonica, as well as Aristarchus—whose presence with Paul, and whose relation to that city, are specified at Acts xx. 4—may likewise have been of the number; especially if, while Jason remained at Thessalonica, Aristarchus went on, with St. Paul, to Asia, and finally accompanied him even to Rome, and remained with him there, during his imprisonment, to the last[a].

III. The Epistle was transmitted by Phœbe, a deaconess of the Church of Cenchreæ, and one who had personally ministered to St. Paul; which seems to infer that he had lodged at Cenchreæ in her house[b]. If this inference is right, the exact time and place of the Epistle are both presumptively determined by it. It was written when St. Paul was at Cenchreæ, in the interim between his original purpose of setting out to Syria by sea, and the change of his purpose, in consequence of the conspiracy of the Jews, so as to determine on returning by land; which purpose he executed accordingly, travelling through Macedonia as far as Philippi, and taking ship first on departing from thence. It was written, then, at the point of time specified at Acts xx. 3. when Paul was preparing ἀνάγεσθαι εἰς τὴν Συρίαν; for which purpose it is morally certain he would be in Cenchreæ, not at Corinth. The discovery of the conspiracy of the Jews, who must have intended to execute their scheme against his life as soon as he had put to sea, was made in time to prevent his departure, and would compel him to retrace his steps.

It is entirely in unison with this alleged date of the Epistle that the Romans are told he had longed to see them

---

[a] Rom. xvi. 21.   Acts xx. 4.   [a] Acts xx. 4. · xxvii. 2. Col. iv. 10.
Philem. 24.   [b] Rom. xvi. 1.

for many years back [c]; for he might have conceived this desire when he first became acquainted with Aquila and Priscilla, six years before, A. U. 803: and it is equally so, with the supposition of its place, and the particular juncture of circumstances under which it was written, that he desires the cooperation of their prayers with his own, that he might be delivered or rescued from the malice of the unbelieving Jews[d]; for the conspiracy of theirs against his life might have only just come to light. Nor is it any objection that mention is made, among others, of the household of Narcissus, οἱ ἐκ τῶν Ναρκίσσου[e], though this Narcissus should be considered the same with the celebrated freedman of Claudius, whose death occurred within a month after the accession of Nero, or sometime in November, A. U. 807.[f] They of his household, and ὄντες ἐν Κυρίῳ, and who had been converted to the gospel, might still be described by their relation to Narcissus as before; and ἐκ τῶν Ναρκίσσου no more means of necessity, *those who are now,* than *those who were once,* of the people of Narcissus. There is one more such allusion in verse 10. to persons ἐκ τῶν Ἀριστοβούλου. I cannot help suspecting that this was Aristobulus, the brother of Herod Agrippa, and of Herod of Chalcis; whose death is mentioned by Josephus in conjunction with that of the other two[g] in such a manner, as proves that it could not have been earlier, and probably was somewhat later, than the time of the death of the latter, or A. U. 801. the eighth of Claudius. In this case, he also must have been dead A. U. 809. but perhaps he had not been dead long.

V. *On the Epistle to the Galatians.*

There is no Epistle whose date has been more contested, and more variously represented, than the date of the Epistle to the Galatians; and though I acknowledge the difficulty which exists upon this subject, still the uncertainty about it is not so great, but that two points may be presumptively established; the first with almost demonstrative conviction,

[c] xv. 23. [d] xv. 30. 31. [e] xvi. 11. [f] Tac. Ann. xiii. 1. Seneca's Ἀποκολοκύντωσις. [g] B. ii. xi. 6.

and the second with a high degree of probability: first, that it could not have been written before A. U. 807—and, secondly, that it could not have been written after A. U. 809—the inference from which is that it must have been written A. U. 808. about the same time with the Second Epistle to the Corinthians, and the Epistle to the Romans; but whether between the two, or before, or after, them both, it may not be possible, except conjecturally, to determine.

I. As the Church of Galatia itself was not founded before A. U. 802. the time of the second general circuit of St. Paul [b], it is manifest no Epistle could have been written to any such Church before A. U. 802.

II. The Epistle could not have been written before the time of the visit, to which the Epistle itself alludes, ii. 1; and the time of this visit the very next verse, ii. 2. ascertains in general, as follows. It was the time of some visit to Jerusalem—posterior to either the first or the second of St. Paul's missions to the Gentiles—at least: *I laid before them the Gospel which I am preaching among the Gentiles .... lest haply I should be running, or had been running, in vain*—When they saw that *I am entrusted with the Gospel of the Uncircumcision, just as Peter with the Gospel of the Circumcision*—these expressions admit of no other construction than that St. Paul's commission to the Gentiles had both duly been received, and duly been acted upon, already. The visit to Jerusalem, therefore, when this interview took place, could not possibly be prior to the first of his circuits among the Gentiles, and it must have been posterior even to his second; for it was some visit just fourteen years later than the time of the return from Arabia to Damascus, which followed directly upon his conversion, and was the beginning of his ministry there.

That the time of this return is the date, to which we are to refer the fourteen years specified Gal. ii. 1. follows both from the reason of the thing, that St. Paul naturally refers to the date of his own conversion, and to that of the com-

---

[b] Acts xvi. 6.

mencement of his ministry, as the only proper ἀρχὴ or point
of time, to which the more memorable, or cardinal, incidents
in its progress afterwards ought to be referred; and also
from the analogy of verse 18. of chapter the first. The visit
there specified, at the end of three years, is referred to no
other date. Now the time of the return to Damascus has
been proved to synchronize with about the Passover of the
second of Caius, A. U. 791 : the time of a visit, then, just
fourteen years posterior to that, is the time of some visit
about the period of a Passover, A. U. 805; and this is precisely the time at which, as we have proved already, St.
Paul returned to Jerusalem from his first visit (in A. U.
803.) to the peninsula of Greece : which coincidence, established as it is, upon perfectly independent data, must place
it beyond a question, that the visit upon that occasion, recorded in the Acts, at xviii. 22. and the visit referred to in
Galatians, at ii. 1. were one and the same.

It makes in favour of the same conclusion, that we might
have collected, from the extraordinary earnestness to attend
the approaching feast at Jerusalem, which St. Paul expressed in the Acts[i], that he had special reasons for wishing
to be present at it ; which reasons the Epistle explains at
once, if St. Paul's journey to Jerusalem, ii. 1. was produced
by a revelation, or in obedience to some direct command
from the Spirit. Nor would it be any objection that Barnabas must have accompanied St. Paul to Jerusalem on
this occasion, though after their separation, A. U. 802.[k] we
read no more in the Acts of the former, or of his ever being
in company with the latter. It is clear, from the account
of what passed in Jerusalem, that the object of the attendance of both was something, which intimately concerned
them in their character as the Apostles, κατ' ἐξοχὴν, of the
Gentiles; in which capacity, even after their separation in
the Acts, Barnabas is still acknowledged as the co-partner
of Paul so late as A. U. 807.[l] and is spoken of as still alive,
and, we may justly presume, still engaged in the same cha-

---

[i] xviii. 21.   [k] Acts xv. 36.   [l] 1 Cor. ix. 6.

racter, and in the same occupation, at the close of St. Paul's first, if not also of his second, imprisonment [m]. The same revelation, then, which enjoined the attendance of St. Paul, as one of the great Apostles of the Gentiles, required, we may suppose, the attendance of Barnabas, as the other also; both on the same occasion A. U. 805. The Epistle, then, could not have been written before the time of this attendance accordingly.

III. The Epistle could not have been written before the time of the visit of St. Peter to Antioch [n]; which time, I have proved elsewhere, was in the course of the same year with this visit to Jerusalem also [o]; not longer, perhaps, than the interval between the Passover, and the Pentecost ensuing.

IV. The Epistle could not have been written before St. Paul's second visit to Galatia, Acts xviii. 23: when he proceeded thither from Antioch, in the course of the same year with each of the preceding events, but after them both. The conclusions at which we are already arrived would prove this; but, independent of them, it might have been deduced from the plain import of Gal. iv. 13. alone: Ye know that in weakness of the flesh did I preach the gospel to you, τὸ πρότερον; which means, not simply, at the first, but, the former time, or the time before; and, consequently, distinctly implies that he had been *twice* in Galatia, and neither more nor less than *twice*, before he wrote the Epistle. This use of τὸ πρότερον here is parallel to that of τὸ δεύτερον, and τὸ πάλιν, 2 Cor. xiii. 2: or of τὸ δεύτερον, Jude 5; or of τὰς πρότερον ἡμέρας, Hebrews x. 32; and of many other instances which might be produced; all referring to one or other of two occasions, but only of two, as the subjects of comparison, and each of the same kind. The same reference to a second visit appears, though not with equal clearness, in the literal sense of ἐπιχορηγῶν [p], which may be understood of some *second* supply of the gifts of the Spirit, in addition to a *first*; such as might have been expected

[m] Col. iv. 10. 2 Tim. iv. 11.   [n] Gal. ii. 11.   [o] Vol. i. Diss. ii. 89.
[p] Gal. iii. 5.

upon a second visit of St. Paul. That weakness of the flesh which is alluded to here, as the description of bodily circumstances under which St. Paul first preached in Galatia, is alluded to also in the First Epistle to the Corinthians q, as what had been observable during his residence at Corinth ; and it is a critical coincidence that he came from Galatia, on the first occasion, almost directly to Corinth. If both these allusions are to the same thing, which is denoted by the thorn in the flesh r, the commencement of that infirmity is dated from, or soon after, the rapture, which we have proved to have taken place, A. U. 794 : and it was still in existence, when the Second to the Corinthians was written, A. U. 808 : There is given me a goad for the flesh ; a messenger of Satan, to buffet me ; that I be not elated beyond measure. Had he been speaking of something no longer in being, he would have said, ἵνα με κολαφί- ζοι· ἵνα μὴ ὑπεραιροίμην—There was given me, a goad for the flesh ; a messenger of Satan, that he *should* buffet me, that I *might* not be elated beyond measure.

It follows, then, that the Epistle could not have been written before St. Paul settled at Ephesus, A. U. 806.

But, fifthly, the Epistle could not have been written before the First to the Corinthians, A. U. 807 : nor even before the Second, A. U. 808.

For, first, when the Epistle was written to the Galatians, St. Peter was personally known to them s ; whence we may infer he had already been personally among them : but he was never personally among them before the time of his great Evangelical circuit ; on which circuit I have proved elsewhere t he set out A.U. 805. and in the course of which A. U. 806. or 807. he came to Corinth ; having visited Galatia previously.

Secondly, St. Paul had sometime given instructions to the Church of Galatia, the same in themselves, and manifestly for the same purpose, (the collection going forward in behalf of the Hebrew Church,) which he repeats to the

q ii. 3.   r 2 Cor. xii. 7.   s Gal. i. 18. ii. 7—11.   t Vol. i. Diss. ii. 91.

Church of Corinth [u]. Now no such instructions of any kind are to be found in the Epistle to the Galatians: nor even an allusion, from its beginning to its ending, whence it might be conjectured that such a business as this collection was going on at all. It is reasonable, therefore, to presume that he had either given himself, or sent by some other medium, to the Church of Galatia, the instructions in question *orally*, before he wrote his First to the Corinthians: and that the collection had been made and completed, before he wrote the Epistle to the Galatians : and each of these suppositions is possible ; for he came himself to Ephesus, A. U. 806. directly from a visit to Galatia, and he made this visit to Galatia, directly after his return to Antioch, A. U. 805. At the visit to Jerusalem the same year, before all these things, it had been stipulated that the Gentiles should remember the poor [v], that is, the poor of the Church of Jerusalem, for whom the collection was ultimately intended ; a sabbatic year was about to arrive in A. U. 808 ; and the collection against that year was begun in Achaia, A. U. 807. a year before its arrival ; and, when it was only beginning there, it had been going on some time in Galatia, and by parity of consequence, in the rest of the Asiatic churches. It was begun there, then, before the middle of A. U. 807. at the latest ; and probably it was begun earlier. St. Paul, it is true, was at Ephesus all the year 807 ; and, perhaps, all the year 806. also ; but he might either have left directions with the Church of Galatia, when he visited them himself—in A. U. 805—prospectively against this time— or have communicated with them, when the time arrived, by some other agent. And this appears to me to have been the case.

For when St. Paul was present in Jerusalem, at the Passover, A. U. 805. Titus was with him [w] ; and, therefore, we may suppose, would afterwards accompany him both to Antioch and to Galatia : yet either he did not return with him to Ephesus, A. U. 806—or, if he did, he had been sent somewhither from Ephesus again, before St. Paul wrote the First to the Corinthians, A. U. 807.   For he was not with St. Paul when he wrote that Epistle ; yet, before he wrote the Second, he had come from some quarter to Ephesus, accompanied by another of the brethren, (who is currently believed to have been St. Luke,) and that, a brother charged, (χειροτονηθεὶς,) by common appointment, with the contributions of some Christian societies, distinct from those of Macedonia and Achaia, which must, consequently, have been the Christian societies of Asia ; he had been sent from Ephesus to Corinth ; he had been expected to meet St. Paul (on his way back into Asia) at Troas ; he did not meet him until St. Paul was come into Macedonia ; he had departed again to Corinth from Macedonia, accompanied also by the brother supposed to be St. Luke, out of obedience to a personal wish of St. Paul's, and with a view to expedite and get ready the contributions of Achaia, before he himself, accompanied by the brethren from Macedonia, should arrive at Corinth : and all this before the Second to the Corinthians was written ˣ.

We may conclude, therefore, that Titus and St. Luke were the persons by whose means St. Paul, though himself at Ephesus, had communicated, on the subject of this contribution, with the churches of Asia, and with that of Galatia among the rest ; that this communication was made early in A. U. 807 ; and that the contributions, so raised, were brought to Ephesus, by the same parties, between the Passover and the Pentecost of A. U. 808.   When the Epistle to the Galatians, then, was written, which must have been after A. U. 807. *ineuntem* at least, there is no reason to suppose the least allusion to this subject would be found in it.   And this conclusion is further confirmed by the right version of ii. 10. the only text which could be construed into any such meaning, ὃ καὶ ἐσπούδασα αὐτὸ τοῦτο ποιῆσαι. Had St. Paul been referring, in these words, to any thing about which he was anxious, at the very time when this

---

ˣ 2 Cor. vii. 8. 6. 13—16—viii. 5. 6—16—24. ii. 12. 13. ix. 3—5. xii. 18.

meeting was held at Jerusalem—and much less about which he was anxious still—the merest tyro in the Greek language would have known that he must have written, ὃ καὶ ἐσπούδα-ζον αὐτὸ τοῦτο ποιῆσαι; or else, ὃ καὶ σπουδάζω αὐτὸ τοῦτο ποιῆσαι. As this is not the case, the tense, as it stands, must have either its purely indefinite and historical sense, or it must stand, as it so often stands in Greek, for the preterite ἐσπούδακα : so as to mean ; Which also I endeavoured with the requisite diligence accordingly to do ; *or* which also I have endeavoured with the requisite diligence accordingly to do; or more agreeably to our idiom—The very thing which I also have been diligent to do. Compare Acts xi. 28. 30. xxvi. 10. where similar phrases occur. Each of these meanings will imply that the thing itself, the matter of fact in question, the object of this diligence, which was that the Gentiles should remember the poor of Jerusalem, was already a past fact, and not the object of that diligence any longer ; with this difference between them, that, according to the former, it might have been any length of time past ; according to the latter, it must very recently have been effected.

Thirdly, I observe at Gal. iv. 10. the following allusion ; Ye are observing days, and months, and seasons, and years ; where the mention of years unquestionably denotes sabbatic years—which, the assertion in general must imply, the Galatians either were observing, among other Mosaic rites, at the time when the Epistle was written, or disposed to observe. Now from seed-time A. U. 808. to seed-time A. U. 809. was actually a sabbatic year ; in the course of which year, especially about the time of its feasts, as the Scenopegia, or the Passover, there would also be days in its sabbaths, and months in its new moons, and seasons in the stated times of its legal solemnities, which Galatian or other Christians, who had imbibed the principles of the Judaizing teachers, might think themselves bound to observe. There is a similar allusion at Col. ii. 16. but not with any such distinct assertion of an observance as then going on. If the Epistle was written in the course of a sabbatic year, this allusion might be as true with respect to the Galatians, as natural and just in the writer ; and we have shewn that, though it could not have been written before A. U. 807. yet there is nothing in what has hitherto been said to prevent but that it might have been written in A. U. 808.

For, fourthly, in all the First Epistle to the Corinthians from first to last, I can discover not one distinct allusion to the existence of Judaizing teachers, or to the prevalence of Judaizing principles, in that Church ; whereas, in the Second Epistle, written about a year after the First, they are to be met with in every page [y]. They appear also, sufficiently clearly, in the Epistle to the Romans, written after both the former [z]. I cannot help inferring from this distinction, which is very glaring, and equally remarkable, that these teachers, and their principles, were not yet got into Corinth when the First Epistle was written, but were so when the Second was written. They must have come thither, consequently, in the interval between the Epistles : and, herein, we may observe a critical coincidence between the Epistle to the Galatians, and the Second to the Corinthians. These teachers, we may presume, would arrive in Galatia before they arrived in Corinth ; yet they were only just come among that Church, when the Epistle was written : I marvel that ye are so soon beginning (*of yourselves*) to depart from him who called you in Christ's grace, to another gospel, (which is not another, *or*, as to which, there is not another,)—*of yourselves, I say*, unless there be some who are troubling you, and desiring to pervert the Gospel of Christ [a]—and again, Ye were running well ; who hath hindered you? *or rather*, tripped you up? [b]—and, But he who is troubling you shall bear the condemnation (*of so doing*), whosoever he may be [c]—and again, ὄφελον καὶ ἀποκόψονται οἱ ἀναστατοῦντες ὑμᾶς [d]—and again, O foolish Galatians, who hath bewitched you, not to obey the truth [e]—and again, Are ye so foolish? having begun in spirit, are ye now making an end in flesh ? Have ye suffered so much

---

[y] 2 Cor. ii. 17. v. 12. x. 2. 7. 10. xi. 4. 13—15. 22. 23. [z] Rom. xvi. 17—20. [a] i. 6. [b] v. 7. [c] v. 10. [d] v. 12. [e] iii. 1.

to no purpose ? if, indeed, it be even to no purpose f—all which are clear intimations that these teachers, whether many or one, with the leaven of their principles, were only just come among the Galatians : and St. Paul, as yet, did not know even who they were. Now this is exactly the way in which he speaks of them in the Second Epistle to the Corinthians ; the tenth chapter of that Epistle is a case in point throughout : and at the fourth verse of the eleventh, he applies to some one of these teachers in particular the indefinite description of ὁ ἐρχόμενος; which implies that, though he might be expected to come soon, he was not yet come to Corinth.

Fifthly, the coincidence between the general argument, reasonings, and sentiments, and partially even the expressions, of the Epistle to the Galatians, and of that to the Romans, is a presumptive proof that they were written about the same time, or with a view to the same purposes, arising in part from the same juncture of circumstances, or the same kind of occasion. In order to establish this coincidence we may compare the passages in the margin g. There are other Epistles, as those to the Ephesians and to the Colossians, and those to Titus and the First to Timothy, respectively, of which a similar conformity is perceptible, and which were certainly written together. I cannot, indeed, contend that the coincidence in the present instance is such, as would lead to the inference that one Epistle was

f iii. 3. 4.

g Galatians iii. 6.	with Romans iv. 3.
— 7.	— 12. ix. 6. 7.
— 13.	viii. 1—4.
iv. 5. 6. 7.	viii. 14. 15. 17.
— 4.	— 3.
— 28.	ix. 7.
v. 14.	xiii. 8—10.
— 17.	vii. 13—24.
— 19. 21.	i. 28—31.
vi. 1. 2.	xv. 1. 3.
iii. 6—iv. 1—7. ⎱	⎰ ii. 17—29.
iv. 21—31. ⎬	⎨ iii. 9—
v. 1—6. ⎰	⎱ v. 21.

E 3

written while the other was still fresh in the mind of the writer ; but I think it is such even here as, among other arguments, to prove that both were written within a short time of each other ; in which case the Epistle to the Galatians, as neither so elaborate, nor so regular, nor in all respects so deliberate and premeditated, a composition as that to the Romans, but manifestly written on the spur of the moment, in the first excitement of feeling produced by an unexpected and disagreeable piece of information, that of the defalcation of any of the writer's converts from the sound and sober form of the faith, which they had received from him, we may perhaps conclude was written by St. Paul first.

Lastly, if it is reasonable to suppose that the Judaizing teachers would not leave Judæa, to make converts professedly among the Gentiles, before the last of the Apostles, St. Peter, was himself set out upon his great Evangelical circuit, then if the progress of that circuit did not bring even him to Corinth, before the beginning of A. U. 807. it is not extraordinary that those teachers also should not have arrived there, or even in Galatia, before A. U. 808. Again, Galatians v. 11. is clearly incompatible with an early date, but very much in unison with Acts xx. 3. and Rom. xv. 30. 31. which are synchronous facts and allusions. Again, it is a very ancient tradition, and attested by the subscription of the Epistle itself, that the Epistle to the Galatians was written from Rome ; and though the subscriptions to the Epistles in general are entitled to little consideration, yet, if the Epistle was actually written when St. Paul was on his way to Rome, the tradition may so far have been correct. There is no intimation in any part of the Epistle that he intended to revisit the Galatians in person, but rather the contrary [h]; and, consequently, that at the time when he was writing to them he had no means of addressing them, or of correcting their error, except by letter. This too, I think, would be the case after the point of time specified at Acts xix. 21. and from thenceforward,

[h] Gal. iv. 18. 19. 20.

until he arrived at Jerusalem. It was not, indeed, in the nature of things impossible that he might write the Epistle after this, when he was at Cæsarea ; but the first words of the exordium, Παῦλος .... καὶ οἱ σὺν ἐμοὶ πάντες ἀδελφοὶ, imply that he was somewhere at large, and in the society of his usual companions and fellow-labourers, when he wrote it. He makes use of similar language at Acts xx. 84. speaking of those who had been his companions at Ephesus. Had the Epistle been written while he was any where in confinement, some allusion would have occurred in it to his bonds ; whereas there is nothing of the kind. Nor do I consider the declaration, ἐγὼ γὰρ τὰ στίγματα τοῦ Κυρίου Ἰησοῦ ἐν τῷ σώματί μου βαστάζω[i], to be any exception to the contrary. It is proved by 2 Cor. x. 10. xii. 7. 8. 9. Gal. iv. 18. 14. that this allusion to the *prints* of the Lord Jesus, is an allusion to his thorn in the flesh. The principle of the allusion is illustrated by Philo Judæus[k]. Ἔνιοι δὲ . . . ἵενται πρὸς δουλείαν τῶν χειροκμήτων, γράμμασιν αὐτὴν ὁμολογοῦντες, οὐκ ἐν χαρτιδίοις, ὡς ἐπὶ τῶν ἀνδραπόδων ἔθος, ἀλλ' ἐν τοῖς σώμασι καταστίζοντες αὐτὴν σιδήρῳ πεπυρωμένῳ, πρὸς ἀνεξάλειπτον διαμονήν. This custom was of great antiquity in Egypt ; for Herodotus alludes to it in his own time[l]—ἐς τὸ ἢν καταφυγὼν οἰκέτης ὅτεῳ ἀνθρώπων ἐπιβάληται στίγματα ἱρὰ, ἑαυτὸν διδοὺς τῷ Θεῷ, οὐκ ἔξεστι τούτου ἅψασθαι. And the practice of so branding themselves was expressly forbidden the Jews[m]. St. Paul's thorn in the flesh, whatsoever it was, did as plainly denote whose servant he was—by whose grace, notwithstanding this infirmity, his ministerial labours were crowned with success, and whose strength was made perfect in his weakness—as if the name of the Master whom he served, and whose property he was, had been branded or printed on his body.

The result of these reasonings is to confirm my original proposition, that the Epistle to the Galatians was not written before A. U. 807. nor after A. U. 809. and, therefore, most probably in A. U. 808. but whether before the Second

[i] vi. 17.   [k] De Monarchia. 819.   [l] ii. 113.   [m] Lev. xix. 28.

to the Corinthians, or after the Epistle to the Romans, or between the two, I cannot undertake to determine; nor in fact is it of any importance to do so. The same uncertainty must always exist with regard to the place where it was written, further than simply thus much ; that if it was written in A. U. 808. it was written from some one or other of those quarters, in which St. Paul spent the whole of this year ; that is, the first part he spent in Asia, but the rest, and the chief part, perhaps, in Macedonia, if not in Achaia : and having arrived at this conclusion, I shall resume the course of the subject, which is the continuance of St. Paul's last journey, from Greece to Jerusalem, A. U. 809.

It will appear from the Table of Passovers in Diss. V. of vol. I. that the Passover was celebrated A. U. 809. on March 19. and the Pentecost on May 9. It was by the time of this feast that St. Paul proposed to arrive in Jerusalem [n] ; and that he accomplished this purpose in the interval between leaving Philippi, and being apprehended in the temple, is evident from the presence of the Jews of Asia in Jerusalem, at the time of the latter event [o]. But the same Jews were not present at Cæsarea also, when he was soon after examined by Felix [o]. We may infer, then, that Pentecost was over by this time, and those Jews were returned to their homes. As St. Paul had to travel from Corinth, as far as Philippi, by land, and as he spent at Philippi the Paschal week, which would fall, according to the reckoning above made, between March 19. and March 26. *inclusive*, it is probable that he set out from Corinth about the end of February, and arrived at Philippi about the third week in March. His three months' residence in Greece, then, would terminate about the end of February, A. U. 809. and began, consequently, about the middle or the beginning of December, A. U. 808. which is entirely agreeable to what we had before concluded of the length of his stay in Macedonia.

Between the time of the arrival in Jerusalem, and the

[n] Acts xx. 16. [o] xxi. 27. xxiv. 18.

day of St. Paul's first examination before Felix, there was exactly a twelve days' interval[p]; the accuracy of which calculation may be proved as follows. First, the day of the arrival; secondly, the day of the interview with James; thirdly, the day of St. Paul's entering into the temple with the Nazarites; fourthly, the day when he was seized in the temple, some one of the seven days of purification; fifthly, the day when he was examined before the council; sixthly, the day which preceded the night of his mission to Cæsarea; seventhly, the day of his arrival at Cæsarea; eighthly, the day when he was put on his first audience before Felix[q]. Cæsarea was six hundred stades, or about sixty of our miles [r], distant from Jerusalem, and St. Paul would arrive there the day after he set out; for he reached Antipatris that very night, and Antipatris was more than midway between Cæsarea and Jerusalem [s]. He was put on his first audience on either the fourth or the fifth day after his arrival, and the only point, upon which there can be any uncertainty, is as to which of the seven days' purification of the Nazarites he was apprehended upon in the temple.

The calculation above given will shew that this was either the second or the third of the number. Those twelve days, however, as calculated above, were dated from the day of St. Paul's coming to Jerusalem; but, perhaps, they should be dated from the day *after* this, the day of his entering in to James; which day after, if I am not mistaken, is to be pronounced the day of Pentecost itself. For St. Paul tells Felix, that, in consequence of his long experience of the usages of the Jews, he could easily comprehend it was but twelve days' time, since he had come up to Jerusalem to worship[t]; which yet, with all that experience, Felix could not have comprehended, unless he had previously been aware that the day of Pentecost (which brought Jews from all parts up to worship) had fallen not more than twelve days before.

---

[p] Acts xxiv. 11. [q] xxi. 17. 18. 26. 27. xxii. 30. xxiii. 11. 12. 32. xxiv. 1. [r] Jos. Ant. Jud. xiii. xi. 2. xv. ix. 6. B. i. iii. 5. Vide Arbuthnot on Ancient Weights and Measures. [s] Rel. Pal. ii. 444. [t] xxiv. 11.

On this principle, the day of St. Paul's first audience would be about the twenty-first of May. The day of Pentecost was certainly then past, or the Jewish rulers would not otherwise have come down to Cæsarea from Jerusalem. It is of importance to establish this point; for Paul was again examined by Felix some days after this first occasion, in the company of Drusilla his wife; which would thus fall about the end of May or beginning of June; and it is from this last examination that we are to date the beginning and continuance of his two years' imprisonment at Cæsarea[u]. These two years, therefore, would expire about the end of May or the beginning of June, A. U. 811; and this time of the year in particular, especially while the edict of Claudius, or the rule of Tiberius, before alluded to[v], were in force, was the most likely of all for the arrival of a new governor, and, consequently, the departure of an old. From the middle of April to the beginning of June would be six or seven weeks' interval; the ordinary interval necessary to travel in summer from Judæa to Rome, or from Rome to Judæa. And as Pentecost A. U. 809. fell upon May 9. so A. U. 811. it fell upon May 17. or at the latest upon May 18.

From the time of the arrival of Festus, to the time when he decided upon allowing of the appeal of Paul to Cæsar, there are express notices of more than seventeen days at least[w]; which will bring us to past the middle of June. After this also, there was still some interval before the arrival of Agrippa at Cæsarea; and a still longer interval for the time of his staying there, before his request to hear Paul; and last of all, his audience of Paul accordingly, the day after that request[x]. Even after this audience there was yet some interval or other before Paul, with the other prisoners, was actually delivered to Julius, in order to set out to Italy[y]. On all these accounts it seems impossible to place his final departure for Rome, before the beginning or the middle of August, A. U. 811; which would, conse-

---

[u] xxiv. 24. 27. [v] Vol. i. Diss. vii. 282. [w] xxv. 1. 6—12. 17.
[x] xxv. 13. 14. 23. [y] xxvii. 1.

quently, be towards the close of the fourth of Nero; and this conclusion, I think, may be confirmed as follows.

When they were arrived at Myra in Lycia, they found there a ship of Alexandria, sailing to Italy, in which they embarked[z]. Now this ship was laden with corn[a], the last thing with which they parted; and, consequently, it was corn of that year's harvest. The harvest, in Egypt, was commonly over before the annual rise of the Nile, that is, the summer solstice. Reliqua pars, says Pliny[b] on this subject, non nisi cum falce arva visit, paulo ante kalendas Aprilis. Peragitur autem messis mense Maio. The corn-ships, therefore, with the produce of the year's harvest, would usually set out for Italy in the month of June or July, and arrive in August or September. There is a lively description, in one of Seneca's Epistles[c], of the effect produced by the appearance of the first of these ships, called *tabellariæ*, or packets.

Moreover, when the wind was favourable, the usual route for the Alexandrian corn-ships, bound to Italy, was not in the direction which *this* ship was taking, along the coast of Asia Minor, from east to west, but across the Mediterranean by Malta and Sicily, from south-east to north-west, which is straight in the direction from Alexandria in Egypt to Italy. But this could not be done, unless the Etesian monsoon had ceased to blow, and the southern winds, by which it was commonly succeeded, had set in in its stead. Before that, the ships which left Alexandria in Egypt, bound for Italy, according to the principles of the coasting navigation universally practised by antiquity, were compelled to pursue a very circuitous route, in order to take advantage of the Etesian winds. This seems to have been the case with the ship found at Myra, yet making a voyage, and that with corn, towards Italy.

That the Etesian winds in particular were blowing both when St. Paul left Sidon, and when he came in the direction of Cnidus[d], is manifest from the relative position of

[z] xxvii. 6.   [a] xxvii. 38.   [b] H. N. xviii. 18.   [c] Ep. lxxvii.
[d] xxvii. 3. 4. 5. 7.

Cyprus to the one, and of Myra in Lycia to the other ; but more especially from the fact that, when the ship left Cnidus, instead of pursuing its former course, it sailed under the coast of Crete, in the direction of Salmone, and that because the wind was contrary[l]; for this was to sail directly before the Etesian wind, viz. from north to south. That the northern monsoon, then, was still blowing seems unquestionable ; but that it was about to be succeeded by the southern appears from the change of the wind, when the ship set out again from the Fair Havens in Crete towards Phœnice; for this was with a slight wind from the south[m].

Now the time when the Etesian winds commonly ceased to blow, or continued to blow only very irregularly, is well known to have been about the recurrence of the autumnal equinox, or the middle of the last week in September. It may be presumed, then, that it was not before this time when St. Paul arrived at Crete : and the presumption, I think, is confirmed by the allusion to the νηστεία, or tenth of the Jewish Tisri[n], as past some time, more or less, before they set out for Phœnice.

In the year of the city 811. or A. D. 58. when the fifteenth of Nisan coincided with March 28. the fifteenth of Tisri coincided with September 21. and, consequently, the tenth of Tisri fell on September 16. If we suppose that, before the ship arrived at Lasæa, St. Paul had been about a month on the road, and that the day of the fast occurred either before or soon after they came thither, the time of his departure from Cæsarea would be, as we conjectured, about the middle, or even the beginning, of August. It was the intention of the ship's crew not to have continued their route that year from Crete, but to have passed the winter in the island ; and when they set out from Lasæa to Phœnice, it was only that they might change their present winter quarters, for others which were more convenient. This is a proof that, before they set out, the autumnal equinox, or September 24. was long past; the autumnal equinox

[l] xxvii. 7.   [m] xxvii. 13.   [n] xxvii. 9.

being the time after which the sea was usually considered shut. They had already taken up winter quarters at Lassea, and it was against the prophetical warning of St. Paul that they were about to exchange them for others: he would have had them remain where they were; the pilot and the master of the vessel thought there could be no danger, in removing only to Phœnice.

It seems presumptively certain, then, that they must have set out from Lassæa about the middle of our October, if not later; and as the storm which immediately surprized them lasted fourteen days or more[o], they would finally be wrecked on Malta about the beginning, if not near the middle, of our November. In the fourth month after this shipwreck, (for so I understand the note of time at verse 11. of chap. xxviii. Μετὰ δὲ τρεῖς μῆνας ἀνήχθημεν,) which was consequently some time in February or March, A. U. 812. they resumed their journey; and in something more than a fortnight afterwards, which might possibly be at the middle, or even the end, of March, St. Paul arrived in Rome[p]. His two years' residence there subsequently must be dated from this period: and, beginning with March A. U. 812. it would expire with March A. U. 814.

Upon the arrival of Julius in Rome, he delivered his prisoners to the officer whose duty it was to receive them, and who is called the στρατοπεδάρχης; a very appropriate denomination for the commander-in-chief of the prætorian cohorts, or the Imperial guard; which, since the time of Sejanus in the reign of Tiberius, instead of being distributed in different parts of the city, had been collected together and quartered in a στρατόπεδον, or camp, by themselves[q]. The commander of these forces, from A. U. 804. the eleventh of Claudius, to A. U. 815. the eighth of Nero, was Burrhus[r]; and this is one argument, among others, that the time of St. Paul's first imprisonment at Rome could not have begun later than the eighth of Nero; for, upon the decease of Burrhus, the command was divided be-

[o] xxvii. 27.   [p] xxviii. 12—15.   [q] Tac. Ann. iv. 2.   [r] xii. 42. xiv. 51.

tween two, Fenius Rufus, and Sofonius Tigellinus, as it
had been, even before his appointment, between Lusius
Geta, and Rufius Crispinus.   Had the command been divided at the time of St. Paul's arrival, the extreme accuracy
of St. Luke, I am persuaded, would have induced him to
write τοῖς στρατοπεδάρχαις, not τῷ στρατοπεδάρχῃ.   Nor is it
improbable that the centurion Julius was a centurion of one
of these cohorts; and that the σπεῖρη Σεβαστὴ[a], to which he
belonged, is but a Græcised form of expression for the Latin, Cohors Prætoria.   I do not deny that Augusta, which
would be in Greek Σεβαστὴ, was one of the commonest
names for both legions and cohorts; but if we compare this
description of Julius and *his* cohort with that of Cornelius
and his[b], ἐκ σπείρης τῆς καλουμένης Ἰταλικῆς, it becomes an
argument, that if St. Luke had meant *there* a particular cohort, which bore the name of Σεβαστὴ, as he certainly meant
here a particular cohort, which bore, or once bore, the name
of Ἰταλικὴ, he would have expressed himself accordingly, ἐκ
σπείρης τῆς καλουμένης Σεβαστῆς.

During the whole of St. Paul's imprisonment, the command of these cohorts would still rest with Burrhus; which,
from the personal character of Burrhus himself, may account both for the lenity of his imprisonment previously,
and for his release at last.   The character of his successors,
and especially of Tigellinus, the more influential of the two,
was of a very different kind.   Not but that the character of
Nero himself, before the death of his mother, in his fifth
year, and of Burrhus, in his eighth, was far from being developed in all its atrocity; but as yet stood fair and unsul-
lied; so much so, that it is an observation of later times
upon his reign, as it appeared for some years at first, Dis-
tare cunctos reges Neronis quinquennio; and within this
favourable period it was so ordered by Providence that the
two chief of the Apostles, St. Peter and St. Paul, should,
for the first time, both come to, and depart again from,
Rome.   And here, having arrived at the end of the history

---

[a] Acts xxvii. 1.   [b] x. i.

in the Acts, I might also make an end of the history of St.
Paul, as well as of the present Dissertation.   But there still
remain some of his Epistles, concerning the times of which
I have hitherto said nothing ; and yet the determination of
whose times, when we consider the very different opinions
which are entertained with respect to some of them, may
justly be regarded as necessary even to the confirmation of
our previous conclusions.   For the sake, then, of completing
a subject, the importance of which it is not easy to overrate,
and which would otherwise be manifestly imperfect, I will
take the liberty of dwelling on these points a little longer.

The Epistles which St. Paul wrote from Rome, during
any part of his two years' imprisonment, I believe, were
only the following four, Ephesians, Colossians, Philippians,
and Philemon; the Epistles which he wrote at any time, between the close of that imprisonment and his death, must
consequently have been the remaining four : Hebrews, the
First to Timothy, Titus, and the Second to Timothy. And
all these, I think, were written in the order in which they
are here recited. The proof of these positions may be made
out as follows.

I. Each of the four first of these Epistles contains internal evidence of two facts respecting the situation of the
writer when he wrote them ; first, that he was in confinement ; secondly, that he was in confinement at Rome[u].

II. The remarkable coincidence, both of sentiments and
of language, between the Epistle to the Ephesians and the
Epistle to the Colossians, would be sufficient to demonstrate
that both were written together ; and the identity of the
person, by whom they were sent, is a still more decisive intimation that they must have been sent together[v].

III. If it is reasonable to suppose that Epaphras, who is
mentioned by that name in the Epistle to the Colossians,
and Epaphroditus, who is mentioned by that name in the
Epistle to the Philippians, are one and the same person,

---

[u] Ephes. iii. 1. 13. vi. 19. 20. Col. i. 24. ii. 1. iv. 3. 9. 10. 18. Philem.
9. 10. 13.   Philipp. i. 7. 12. 13. 14. 20. 26. 30. ii. 12. 23. 24. 27.
[v] Ephes. vi. 21. 22. Col. iv. 7. 8.

(which I think cannot well be disputed,) then this Epaphras, or Epaphroditus, was one of the Church of Colossæ, and he had come to Rome before the Epistle to the Colossians was written ; and he was left at Rome when that Epistle was sent [w]. Nor is there any reason to suppose he had yet been taken ill. But before the Epistle to the Philippians was written he had certainly fallen sick, and, on recovering from his sickness, was sent back with the Epistle to Philippi [x]. If so, and if Epaphroditus in the Epistle to the Philippians is the same person with Epaphras in the Epistle to the Colossians, the former Epistle was both written and sent some time or other after the former. Epaphroditus, it is true, came to Rome charged with the contributions of Philippi for the relief of Paul's pecuniary wants [x] ; but he seems to have done this as a voluntary commission [y], which any one, if he was so inclined, might have undertaken ; and he seems to have been on his way through Philippi somewhere else when he undertook it, as even a native or inhabitant of Colossæ might be. Nor is there any expression, respecting Epaphroditus, in the Epistle to the Philippians, which would identify him with that Church, as there is concerning Epaphras, in the Epistle to the Colossians, which proves *him* to have belonged to that [z].

IV. For the same reason, the Epistle to the Philippians was later than the Epistle to Philemon also ; for Onesimus, himself a member of the Church of Colossæ, was sent to Colossæ along with Tychicus, as joint bearer of the Epistle ; and he was sent at the same time with the Epistle to Philemon also ; and the mention of Archippus in both these Epistles alike, with the allusion to the Church in his house, is a proof that all these parties, Onesimus, Philemon, and Archippus, belonged to the Colossian Church alike [a]. These two Epistles, then, Colossians, and Philemon, were certainly written and sent together ; and the name of Timothy is premised to them both ; and the names of Epaphras, Marcus, Aristarchus, Demas, and Lucas, are all subjoined

---

[w] Col. i. 7. iv. 12. 13.   [x] Philipp. ii. 25. 26. 30. iv. 18.   [y] Philipp. ii. 25. 29. 30.   [z] Col. iv. 12.   [a] Col. iv. 9. 17. Philem. 2. 10.

to them both[b]. If so, they were both written before the
Epistle to the Philippians; and the only question remaining
is first, whether they were both written *before*, or both
written *after*, the Epistle to the Ephesians, or both at the
same time with that; and secondly, at what period of the
two years' imprisonment they must each have been written
respectively.

Now there are two or three reasons more particularly,
which may incline us to place the Epistle to the Ephesians
at the head of the rest; first, because the Epistle to the
Colossians resembles an epitome of that, or, in those parts
where they most agree together, is shorter and conciser
than that; secondly, because there is no mention of Epaphras in the Epistle to the Ephesians, as there is in the
Epistle to the Colossians; and thirdly, there is no mention
of Timothy in the Epistle to the Ephesians, as there is in
every other of the Epistles, now written from Rome, besides.
In the Epistles to the Colossians, to Philemon, and to the
Philippians, respectively, his name is combined with St.
Paul's at the outset of the Epistles themselves—it is morally
certain, then, that had he been present, when the Epistle to
the Ephesians was written, his name would have appeared at
the outset of that likewise. And with respect to Epaphras,
it was from him that St. Paul heard of the faith of the Colossians[c]; and this fact appears in the Epistle; and it was
from some quarter or other that he heard of the faith of the
parties addressed in the Epistle to the Ephesians, but not, as
it appears, from Epaphras. I infer, then, that between St.
Paul's writing the Epistle to the Ephesians, and his writing
the Epistles to the Colossians and to Philemon, respectively,
both Epaphras and Timothy came to Rome; and I see no
reason to suppose that they might not have come in conjunction. They seem to have both been at Philippi together, before the mission of Epaphroditus in particular from
thence[d].

It is clear that Timothy did not accompany St. Paul to

[b] Col. i. 1.   Philem. 1.   Col. iv. 10. 12. 14.   Philem. 23. 24.   [c] Col.
i. 2. 7. 8.   [d] Philipp. ii. 19—24.

Rome, but only Aristarchus of Thessalonica, and St. Luke[e]. It is clear also that, when the last of these Epistles, that to the Philippians, was written, Timothy was free and at large; and yet, from the Epistle to the Hebrews[f], it seems equally clear, he must some time have been in confinement at Rome. The Epistle to the Ephesians, then, was written just before Timothy and Epaphroditus arrived from Philippi ; and the Epistles to Colossæ, and to Philemon, just after. Now Philemon is told to provide Paul a lodging [g]—and though this does not imply that he was then at liberty, or expected immediately to return to Asia, yet, I think, it must imply that, humanly speaking, he believed he should soon be set at liberty ; and, consequently, might return in the course of time. The same kind of anticipation is also expressed in the Epistle to the Philippians[h]. It implies, therefore, that his two years' imprisonment was drawing to a close : and if this was actually the case when he addressed these words to Philemon, it follows, as a necessary consequence, that all these Epistles were written within the last twelve months of his imprisonment, or A. U. 813 : the Epistle to the Ephesians, probably, about midsummer, just before the time when Timothy and Epaphroditus might arrive in Italy from Asia; the Epistles to the Colossians, and to Philemon, just after that time ; but all three early enough to be sent to their respective destinations by a common bearer ; and the Epistle to the Philippians last of all, after Epaphroditus had fallen sick and recovered ; which sickness, if we may hazard a conjecture, is a proof that it was written and sent about the autumnal quarter of the year. For it is by no means improbable that this sickness was a fever, due to the peculiar unhealthiness of Rome at the close of the summer quarter. Nor is it any objection, that the Philippians are supposed to have heard of his illness before the Epistle was written[i]: this might easily be the case ; nor is it said, or implied, that any thing had also been since heard from them. They might have had one account from Rome,

---

[e] Acts xxvii. 2.   [f] xiii. 23.   [g] 22.   [h] i. 26. 27. ii. 29.   [i] ii. 26.

sent or carried by some persons who left it *while* Epaphroditus was sick; which account, upon his recovery, was speedily followed by the Epistle; but it is not said that either St. Paul, or he, had had any account in return from them. The anxiety of Epaphroditus was produced by the natural circumstance that he knew they had already heard of his illness—(an illness too to which he had exposed himself, though not a Philippian, for their sake; to supply the lack of their service—that is, in performing what was necessary for the completion and effect of the service which they wished to render to St. Paul)—but could not have heard of his recovery.

It follows, consequently, that St. Paul wrote no Epistles in the first year of his imprisonment; nor, perhaps, was it *a priori* to be expected that he would. The practice of corresponding with the churches, especially with those of their own planting, and where they had preached in person, was not the familiar usage of the Apostles : nor do we find them resorting to it, except upon grave, and even unavoidable, occasions. Now such occasions were not likely to occur in the first year only of St. Paul's imprisonment; particularly if, as I think there is reason to believe, all his letters which he ever wrote to parts beyond the sea, or churches in remote situations, for the convenience and facility of transmission, were written and despatched in the spring or summer quarter of the year.

Before I dismiss the consideration of these four Epistles, I shall still make some observations on the Epistle to the Ephesians in particular. The internal evidence of this Epistle, without any other proof, ought to satisfy every one who is acquainted with the previous history of St. Paul, that it is improperly so called : the language, addressed to the parties for whom it was intended [k], could never be the language in which St. Paul would address the Church of Ephesus above all others; a Church of his own planting, and where three years of his personal ministry, day and

[k] Ephes. i. 13. 14. 15. iii. 1—9—iv. 21.

night, had not long before been spent; to whose elders he had delivered a parting address, in the course of that very journey to Jerusalem, which had ended in his imprisonment at Rome, and who were doubtless well aware of every thing which had befallen him since. The Epistle to the Ephesians, in all these, and other, respects, is absolutely a twin Epistle to the Epistle to the Colossians; and that Epistle, we have the writer's own assurance for knowing, was written to a Church which had never yet seen his face in the flesh [1]. Let the strain of each of these Epistles be carefully contrasted with the strain of the Epistle to the Philippians, written soon after them both, but confessedly to a Church, like that of Ephesus, which St. Paul himself had planted: every thing in the one is in character with that fact; every thing in the other two is out of character as referred to it. There is not a syllable in the Epistle to the Philippians which would not be strictly applicable to the previous, and the existing, relations of the writer and of the parties addressed—or rather, which without that knowledge of the past and the present history of each, supplied by the Acts, would not be almost unintelligible at the present day, instead of appearing, as it does appear, so apposite and natural, so beautiful and pathetic, and yet so unstudied and inartificial. Not so the Epistle nominally addressed to the Ephesians; every thing passes there not as between teachers and converts, bound together by mutual ties of acquaintance, good offices, and endearment, but as between strangers in the flesh, though brethren in Christ; and every thing there, also, is just and natural, on that supposition, but quite the reverse upon the contrary.

If the words, ἐν Ἐφέσῳ, had not appeared in the front of the Epistle, no one would ever have suspected its relation to that Church in particular; and as to the right of the words to stand where they do, I may be satisfied to refer my reader to the editors of the Epistle; it is sufficient for me to observe only that, for an Epistle designed to be catholic,

[1] Col. ii. 1.

whether in a more or in a less extended sense, and, consequently, not meant to be confined to one community of Christians more than another, the words of the exordium, without ἐν Ἐφέσῳ—τοῖς ἁγίοις, τοῖς οὖσι, καὶ πιστοῖς ἐν Χριστῷ Ἰησοῦ, To the saints and faithful in Christ Jesus, who are, are as appropriate as any which could have been chosen. There were persons in the time of Jerome, who understood τοῖς οὖσιν in this sense—and with respect to whose opinion he writes, Alii vero simpliciter, non ad eos *qui sunt*, sed qui Ephesi sancti et fideles sint, scriptum arbitrantur [m]. The grounds of this opinion are ascertained by Basil against Eunomius [n], viz. the absence of ἐν Ἐφέσῳ, and the presence of τοῖς οὖσιν, ἀπλῶς, in ancient copies—which he himself had seen; for it is manifestly absurd to understand his testimony in any other sense—since he declares that it had been so handed down by those before him, and that he had found it so himself in ancient copies: Οὕτω γὰρ καὶ οἱ πρὸ ἡμῶν παραδεδώκασι, καὶ ἡμεῖς ἐν τοῖς παλαιοῖς τῶν ἀντιγράφων εὑρήκαμεν.

Now what had these predecessors of Basil delivered, and what had he found himself in the most ancient copies? What he had found in the most ancient copies was τοῖς ἁγίοις, τοῖς οὖσιν—ἰδιαζόντως, or without ἐν Ἐφέσῳ: and what his predecessors had handed down was the reason of this peculiarity, such as he had just before stated. It is ridiculous to suppose he would mention the testimony of manuscripts at all, except for a various reading; or the testimony of the more ancient manuscripts, as such, except for a various reading which differed from that in the modern. The opponents of our opinion suppose τοῖς οὖσιν ἐν Ἐφέσῳ to have been *always* the reading; and if so, in ancient copies as well as in modern. What, then, could Basil have found in the former, which would not be also in the latter? and, if there was no difference between them, why should he oppose one to the other; or why, in fact, should he appeal to manuscripts at all? It is of little importance, there-

---

[m] Oper. iv. 323.   [n] Lib. ii.

F 3

fore, that the words in question are said to be found in all
the manuscripts of the New Testament now extant; for
there is no manuscript now extant whose age is as great as
that of Basil; and in Basil's time, the more ancient manuscripts were, the more, as it seems, were they free from this
interpolation. Yet they are not, strictly speaking, in the
Vatican.

It is also with singular infelicity, that the authority of
Ignatius has been pressed into the service of the opposite
side; as if he recognized the Epistle to the Ephesians by
that name, and with that designation, in his own time. This
inference is founded on the allusion, in *his* Epistle to the
Ephesians, to St. Paul, followed soon after by the words, ὃς
ἐν πάσῃ ἐπιστολῇ μνημονεύει ὑμῶν ἐν Χριστῷ Ἰησοῦ [o]. I say nothing, here, of the opinion of those who would read μνημο-
νεύω instead of μνημονεύει, and, consequently, refer the words
to Ignatius himself, and not to St. Paul; I contend only
that, the text being taken as it stands, it cannot be rendered
otherwise than, Who in every epistle maketh mention of
you in Christ Jesus: a rendering which will necessarily imply that no one epistle is meant more than another. There
is the same difference in Greek between ἐν πάσῃ ἐπιστολῇ
and ἐν πάσῃ τῇ ἐπιστολῇ, as in Latin between *in omni epistola*, and *in tota epistola;* and the old translator of the
Epistle into Latin, whosoever he was, has shewn that he
understood Greek better than Lardner and others, by rendering the passage accordingly: Qui *in omni epistola* me-
moriam facit vestri in Jesu Christo.

It is an acknowledged principle of Greek construction
that the article is indispensable with a particular and specific reference, as this is supposed to be, to one certain epistle of St. Paul's, among the complex of his epistles in general. This reference here would be equivalent to a quotation; and the article can never be dispensed with before a
quotation. The two passages which Lardner has cited [P], as
instances of what he considers a similar construction, one
from the fifth chapter of Ignatius' Epistle to the Ephesians,

[o] Ignat. Epist. ad Ephes. cap. xii.   [P] Credibility, xvi. chap. 13. 398.

and the other from Ephesians ii. 21. are very unfortunately chosen, since, when they are properly rendered, they both make against himself.

With respect to the first, καὶ πάσης ἐκκλησίας, it would betray a great ignorance of the proper meaning of the word ἐκκλησία, and equal inattention to its primitive use, to restrict it every where to the specific sense of what *we* mean by *the Church*; when it is much oftener to be understood of simply, *an assembly* or *congregation*. Used in the former sense, it might require the article with πᾶσα; used in the latter, it does not. The passage, then, ought to be rendered, If the prayer of one or two be of such force, how much more that of the bishop, and of all an assembly.

With respect to the latter, some editions read πᾶσα ἡ οἰκοδομὴ, as it is; but, admitting that the article, on the authority of the best manuscripts, ought to be rejected, still we may reply, as before, that St. Paul is speaking of no particular building, and, therefore, needed not to employ the article: on the contrary, he is speaking of any such οἰκοδομὴ, ἁπλῶς; and, therefore, was bound to have left it out: for this οἰκοδομὴ is a description of the visible Church; which visible Church is every where founded on one and the same θεμέλιον or base, the Apostles and Prophets, and cemented by one and the same corner stone, Jesus Christ; but consists itself of an infinite number of particular buildings, as many as there are particular Christian societies; any one of the former of which might be called *a building*, or οἰκοδομὴ συναρμολογουμένη ἐν Χριστῷ Ἰησοῦ, just on the same principle that any of the latter might be called *a Church*.

Now it is indisputably clear from Colossians iv. 16. that, at the same time when St. Paul wrote or despatched the Epistle to the Colossians, he wrote and despatched an Epistle to the Church of Laodicea; which Epistle, in point of time, must consequently have synchronized with the Epistle to the Ephesians; and which, it is needless to observe, must either be the same with the Epistle to the Ephesians, or have perished. The reputed existence of such an Epistle is a very ancient tradition of ecclesiastical history; it was admitted by Marcion in *his* canon of Scripture; and it is alluded to by name in the very antique fragment ascribed to the Latin Presbyter Caius [q]; the author of which, whosoever he was, was contemporary with Pius, the tenth Bishop of Rome, and flourished early in the second century. The name of Laodicea occurs five times in the Epistle to the Colossians [r]; and once it is classed with Colossæ and Hierapolis also; both cities of Phrygia, as well as Laodicea, and both contiguous to each other, and to it. It is clearly implied of this city, as well as of Colossæ, and of Hierapolis, that it had never seen Paul's face in the flesh: nor do we know that during the whole of his residence at Ephesus he ever preached in the province of Asia, distinct from Ephesus, or out of Ephesus itself [s].* It is also implied that, to whomsoever he wrote in the Epistle to the Ephesians, he had only just heard of the reception of the gospel, and of its success, among them; and the same thing is true of the Epistle to the Colossians, concerning whose faith and gospel proficiency he had lately received information from their fellow-townsman, or fellow-citizen, Epaphras [t]: and it was the pleasure which these tidings gave him that produced

---

* I consider it no objection to this assertion that Philemon, in the Epistle which bears his name, is told that he owed even himself to St. Paul (19.): though this should imply that he had been converted by St. Paul: and though it should also be conceded that Philemon belonged to Colossæ. It would not follow of necessity that he was converted at Colossæ: it would be equally probable that he might have been converted at Ephesus. My opinion, however, is that he was converted at Rome; after Onesimus, who was his slave, and had accompanied him thither, had run away from him there; and when he was gone back to Colossæ, Onesimus, who might be already acquainted with St. Paul, by some fortunate coincidence was also reclaimed to a sense of his duty by St. Paul; and was sent home again, a convert to the gospel, with this intercessory letter to his master.

[q] Rel. Sacræ. iv. 5. [r] Col. ii. 1. iv. 13. 15. 16. [s] Acts xix. 10—26. xx. 18. 20. 31. 34. [t] Ephes. i. 15—iv. 20. 21. Col. i. 4—9. i. 23. ii. 6—8. iv. 12.

the Epistles to each. All this is very conceivable of an Epistle addressed to Laodicea, but perfectly incredible of an Epistle addressed to the Ephesians.

It is much more reasonable, therefore, to suppose that the present Epistle to the Ephesians is miscalled, than to suppose an Epistle to the Laodicenes, which once did exist, but has since been lost. The mistake, which assigns it to Ephesus, though undoubtedly an ancient one, might have been produced by this fact, that it was sent by Tychicus, whom 2 Tim. iv. 12. appears to describe as an Ephesian; though whether he was so, or not, must always be doubtful; for Acts xx. 4. describes him merely as one of the province of Asia, and by a comparison with xxi. 29. and 2 Tim. iv. 20. would just as much imply that he was a Milesian. It might contribute to the same mistake, that the Second Epistle to Timothy, which was certainly written from Rome, and speaks of Tychicus' being sent from Rome, as it seems, to Ephesus, may have been supposed by many anciently, as well as in modern times, to have been written during St. Paul's first imprisonment; at which time the Epistle to the Ephesians was certainly both written and sent.

It is possible, indeed, that the Epistle might have been sent originally both to Hierapolis and Laodicea in conjunction, and that the name of either in particular was not at first inserted, because it was intended for each; though, as to conjecturing that it was a circular Epistle, designed for a number of churches, if Ephesus was one of that number, and they were not exclusively Hierapolis, Laodicea, and Colossæ, the conjecture can never resolve the difficulty, but leaves it open to as many perplexities as before. I shall conclude, then, with one more remark. Laodicea of Phrygia was one of the cities, which in the first half of the seventh of Nero, A. U. 813. were overthrown by an earthquake [a]; from the effects of which however it recovered of itself. If there is no allusion to any such event in the Epistle, it is because, as we have already had reason to

[a] Tac. Ann. xiv. 27.

conclude, the Epistle must have been written before it happened.

Again, with regard to the Epistle to the Hebrews, which has been ascribed to so many authors—to Barnabas, to Clement, to Luke, to Apollos—it is the most reasonable of all suppositions, and the most in unison with both internal and external testimony, to conclude that it was itself the authentic production of St. Paul, composed, like the Gospel of St. Matthew, as was naturally to be expected, originally in the vernacular language of the Hebrew Church, to which it was addressed, and, like St. Matthew's Gospel also, afterwards translated into Greek: which translation, if we must acquiesce in some one of the various conjectures which have been, or may be, formed concerning its author, I should be more inclined to ascribe to St. Luke, than to any other source. I find nothing in the Epistle, which might be considered to militate against the supposition that it was the work of St. Paul, except this one passage—Πῶς ἡμεῖς ἐκφευξόμεθα, τηλικαύτης ἀμελήσαντες σωτηρίας; ἥτις, ἀρχὴν λαβοῦσα λαλεῖσθαι διὰ τοῦ Κυρίου, ὑπὸ τῶν ἀκουσάντων εἰς ἡμᾶς ἐβεβαιώθη ʳ —in which the writer, whosoever he was, appears to identify himself with the hearers only of the Apostles. But even St. Paul might express himself in this way συγκαταβητικῶς—especially as one who was not by his office, and no where represents himself as, an Apostle of the Circumcision; but, on the other hand, was both by his office, and according to his own uniform representation of himself, the Apostle, κατ' ἐξοχὴν, of the Uncircumcision. In this way too it is that the Apostles themselves may often be found identifying themselves with their converts, and expressing sentiments as applicable to both in common, which, strictly construed, apply only to the parties addressed : and it is still true that St. Paul, though he might receive his commission from our Lord himself, and be made acquainted with Christian facts and doctrines by direct inspiration from above, had yet never heard our Lord, or seen him, while he was conversant in his ministry upon earth. The same consideration of what he himself was by his office, and what they were whom he was about to address, might produce also the absence of his name, and of the usual form of his salutations, from the head of the Epistle; but, as to supposing that he was writing anonymously, and that the Hebrew Christians did not very well know from what source the Epistle emanated, it is both absurd in itself, and directly contradicted also by the Epistle.

The time, and the circumstances, when, and under which, it was written, are a more uncertain, and so far a more important, point, than the question of its author: and yet, with respect to these, we may safely collect first, that it was written from some part or other of Italy, but not, as it appears, from Rome; secondly, when the author himself was at large, but before he had returned to Judæa; thirdly, just after the release of Timothy, who must consequently have been previously in confinement; and while the writer was waiting somewhere or other in Italy, expecting that he would come to him shortly, but not without some degree of uncertainty as to whether he would, or not, before the time when he himself must be departing [w].

Now, if our conjecture, before stated, with respect to the first arrival of Timothy at Rome, was correct, he did not arrive there before the middle of A. U. 813—or the last half of the sixth of Nero; and, when he arrived there, he certainly did not arrive as a prisoner. But if there be any meaning in this allusion of the writer to the Hebrews to the fact of his being released, or set at liberty, it must imply that he had previously been in confinement; it is absolutely impossible that he could otherwise have been released. It follows, then, 'that between the time of the arrival of Timothy at Rome, (soon after which the Epistles to the Colossians, to Philemon, and to the Philippians, were all written, and at the moment of writing which Timothy was at large,) and the time of writing the Epistle to the Hebrews, when he had been just released, he must have been imprisoned,

---

[w] Hebr. xiii. 24. 23. 19. 23.

or someway or other put under restraint at Rome. It is no objection to the fact of such imprisonment that we have no account of it in the Acts; for the history of the Acts had probably expired before it had yet taken place; nor, indeed, is there any mention in the Acts of any thing, which happened at Rome, during St. Paul's two years' sojourn there, excepting the little which transpired at the very beginning of the period. For the same reason, neither can any objection to this fact be taken from Philippians ii. 19—24. and much less from Philemon 22. The actual imprisonment of Timothy, if it ever happened, must have happened after each of these Epistles; and it is manifestly possible that St. Paul, who was still uncertain about the issue of things as it concerned himself [x], might labour under a similar uncertainty respecting the disposal of Timothy. It is by no means certain that, much as might be revealed, upon some subjects, to the Apostles, they yet were aware beforehand of every thing which should happen to themselves, and much less to their friends or followers. That perfect knowledge of his future destiny was the prerogative of our Saviour only. We have St. Paul's assurance to the elders of the Ephesian Church that he was then going up to Jerusalem, not knowing the things which should happen to him there; and, though he adds, Save that the Holy Ghost witnessed in every city that bonds and tribulations awaited him, this does not alter the truth of the assertion; for it is abundantly clear, from a comparison with other passages, that he means, by this witnessing, no revelations made to himself, but communications made to others, in different cities, and through them, to himself [y].

And this, in defect of any other, would still be a sufficient answer to the inference deducible from Acts xx. 25; as though, after such a declaration, St. Paul never could have visited Ephesus again. The inference, however, goes on the supposition that the words are to be rendered; And now, behold, I know that *none* of you, among whom I

---

[x] Philipp. i. 27.   [y] Acts xx. 22. 23. xxi. 4. 11.

went preaching the kingdom of God, will see my face again: whereas, it is my own conviction, both from the order of the terms, and from the emphasis laid on the ὑμεῖς πάντες, that they ought to be rendered; And now, behold, I know that ye will not *all* of you, among whom I went preaching the kingdom of God, see my face again. The fulfilment of this prediction would require no more than that some of the persons, then present, should never see St. Paul again. And this might easily be the case; for between the time of this address, A. U. 809. and the time when St. Paul was first at liberty to come back to Asia in A. U. 816. were eight years complete, or nearly so, at least; and in eight years' time, great changes might take place any where and in any society. In fact it must have been the case; for, first, after St. Paul's departure, grievous wolves would come among the Church of Ephesus, who should not spare the flock; and, secondly, St. Paul is addressing the elders of the Ephesian Church, and them, as it would seem, exclusively. Ephesus, then, and its Church, at this time, were not in want of elders; but, when St. Paul wrote his First to Timothy, which was long after this time, Ephesus and its Church were either still in want of elders, or had but recently been supplied therewith. What, then, had become of the elders whom he was now addressing? Could all have been still alive, or still present in Ephesus? or is it not a natural inference that between the time of this address, and the time of the Epistle to Timothy, the still undisturbed and quiet order of the Ephesian Church had been agitated in some manner or other, and the integrity of its community had suffered in the loss even of some among its governors themselves, which loss could be repaired only by the appointment of fresh?

It is still possible, then, that Timothy, for some reason or other, might be placed in confinement at Rome, after the Epistle to the Philippians itself was written; and if so, in the latter half of A. U. 813. at the earliest; and, therefore, if *his* imprisonment, *a priori*, was likely to last as long as St. Paul's had lasted, his release was not to be expected before the same time in A. U. 815. at the soonest. Let us suppose that this was the case, and, consequently, that the Epistle to the Hebrews, written soon after this release, was written either in the last half of A. U. 815. or in the first of A. U. 816. The probability of both these assumptions may be further confirmed as follows.

It is manifest from Rom. xv. 24—28. that St. Paul had projected a visit to Spain, even before he designed to go to Rome; or rather, that the visit to Rome was something ἐκ παρέργου with respect to this visit to Spain; something which he intended to do by the way, in comparison of that; and over and above, though preparatory to, the execution of his original purpose. And still more evident it is that, for those who would travel either by land or by sea from Asia, or from Greece, to Spain—Italy in general, and even Rome in particular, would lie in the direct line of the course which they must take.

Now if St. Paul had deliberately conceived the design of this visit before he went up to Jerusalem—and if he went up to Jerusalem, though with a particular ignorance, yet under a general assurance that bonds and persecutions awaited him—what reason is there to suppose that the retention of his original design would be prevented by his subsequent imprisonment? Its execution would necessarily be delayed, so long as his imprisonment lasted; but when his imprisonment was over, and he was at liberty to go wheresoever he would, the very proximity of Spain would be an additional motive, for completing his purpose of visiting it. I cannot think St. Paul's intentions of this kind were ever lightly formed, nor, consequently, likely to be easily abandoned: nor, perhaps, would the implicit assumption of some such fact, in the course of his Evangelical ministry, after his confinement at Rome, as a visit to Spain, (for which assumption he himself had furnished such strong grounds of belief *a priori*,) ever have been called into question, if those, who have treated of the history of St. Paul's ministry, had not almost generally fallen into the same mistake of bringing him to Rome too late; and therefore not allowed a sufficient interval of time between the close of his imprisonment, and even the latest possible date of his death, for the transaction of this purpose, and of many others, which must also have intervened. I have obviated this inconvenience by placing the commencement of his imprisonment in the spring of A.U. 812. and, consequently, its termination in the spring of A.U. 814—between which, and even the earliest date of the close of his ministry, which it would be possible to admit, A.U. 818. there would yet be four or five years' interval.

The tradition that he did accordingly visit Spain is the most ancient, and, perhaps, the most authentic, of any such traditions, which ecclesiastical history has perpetuated; for it may be traced up to the time of the presbyter Caius, contemporary with the Roman Bishop Pius, who speaks of Paul's departure from the city to Spain, as a certain and undeniable matter of fact[z]; and even past his time, to the age of Clement, the third Bishop of Rome, and the contemporary of St. Paul himself[a]; for though he does not mention Spain by name, yet if we consider that he was writing from Rome, and that he speaks of the *extreme bounds of the west*, relatively to the geographical position of Rome, it is as certain that, by this description of the limits to which St. Paul's personal labours had extended, he must mean Spain, as if he had expressly named it.

After these two contemporaneous testimonies to the fact in question, I should consider it superfluous to produce any more, depending on the authority of later times. I will observe only that the testimony of the Latin Presbyter supposes Paul to go to Spain *from the city;* and that of Clement supposes him to have evangelized the *whole* of that country: he could not otherwise have preached the gospel to the extreme bounds of the west, which the ancients universally considered to be the Straits of Gibraltar. I think, then, that upon the strength of these two testimonies we are authorized to assume, first, that St. Paul set out to Spain at the close of his imprisonment at Rome; and, secondly,

---

[z] Rel. Sacræ. iv. 4.   [a] Philipp. iv. 3.   Clem. Ep. v.

that he was long enough in Spain to have, more or less, evangelized the whole country.   He would set out, then, soon after the spring of A. U. 814. and he could not, perhaps, have accomplished his purpose, or be likely to leave Spain again, under two years' time at least.   The extent and the populousness of the country, and the very great probability that Christianity had not been previously introduced into it, justify us in asserting this with confidence.

Now that, when he had made an end of the circuit of Spain, he would come back again to Italy, before he could return to Asia, is just as much a matter of course, as that he should have come to Italy at first, before he could travel to Spain.   The time of his return to Italy, if the data on which we ground the conclusion are correct, would be either the latter half of 815. or the first half of 816. and both in the ninth of Nero : and this is the very time when I have already shewn it to be probable St. Paul was writing the Epistle to the Hebrews, and writing it, as the Epistle itself proves, from Italy.   It is some confirmation of each of these conclusions, that the well-known inscription in Gruter [b], the time of which is synchronous with the tenth of Nero, the date of the first general persecution of Christianity, if it be admitted as genuine, proves that the gospel had been introduced into Spain at least by the tenth of Nero; and I think it is some argument of the genuineness of the inscription itself, that, if we are right in the conclusion already established, it must have been introduced there by St. Paul himself, even before the ninth.

The date of the Epistle to the Hebrews will thus be determined to the ninth of Nero ; and that it was the latter half of this ninth, not the former, and, consequently, A. U. 816. not A. U. 815. may further be shewn as follows.

I. The writer was preparing to leave Italy and to return to Asia [c], which we may suppose he would not do except in the spring or summer quarter of the year.

II. That when the Epistle was written, a persecution

<hr/>

[b] ccxxviii. n. 9.   [c] xiii. 19. 23.

was going on against the Church of Judæa, has been made to appear elsewhere[d]; and yet that it was a persecution of no long standing may be collected from xii. 4: Ye have not yet *resisted* unto blood—ἀντιχατέστητε—*more properly*, Ye have not yet been set in opposition unto blood—while striving against the sin of apostasy ; that is, ye have not yet been placed in circumstances under which, while striving against the sin of apostasy, it would be necessary for you to resist unto blood. It appears from x. 34. that the violence of the persecution as yet had been limited to the spoiling or plundering of their goods. But whatsoever it was, that it was the second which they had yet experienced appears also from x. 32. which refers to a former persecution, and yet only one former ; and, therefore, to the persecution in the time of Saul.

Now, as that former persecution was begun by the martyrdom of Stephen, so may it be inferred from xiii. 7. was this second by the martyrdom of those, who are called the ἡγούμενοι of the Church, and who are said to have spoken to them the word of God ; the end of whose conversation among them, that is, the exit, or mode of departing, from the world, which they had finally experienced, they are commanded to remember, in order to imitate their faith—ἀναθεωροῦντες—*literally*, reviewing ; but as a spectacle, which is over and over again brought before the eyes. This description can apply in general to none so justly as to the Apostles of Christ, nor to any of these in particular, (as not only Apostles of Christ, but also the ἡγούμενοι of the Hebrew Church,) as to either James, the one the brother of John, and the other the brother of our Lord ; the former martyred at a time when other of the Apostles were still left with the Hebrew Church, and the latter their first Bishop ; and himself, in the course of time, a martyr also. Both these martyrdoms may be here intended ; but that the latter in particular is alluded to seems to me to follow not only from the reason of the thing, but from the coincidence of the time of the martyrdom itself.

[d] Vol. i. Diss. ii. 132.

We have two accounts of the martyrdom of James, the first Bishop of Jerusalem, and surnamed the Just; one from Hegesippus, an ancient Christian writer, and the other from Josephus^e. The former of these places it at the time of a Passover; and the latter when the younger Ananus was high-priest, and in the first year of the administration of Albinus, but before he was arrived in the province*. The first year of Albinus may be determined as follows.

The history of Jesus the son of Ananus^f demonstrates that Albinus was already procurator and in office, at or after the feast of Tabernacles, πρὸ τεσσάρων ἐτῶν τοῦ πολέμου—and seven years, and five months, before the time when this Jesus himself perished, during the siege of Jerusalem, A. U. 823. The siege was begun at a Passover; and, consequently, at the Passover of A. U. 823: Albinus, therefore, was procurator and in office at or soon after a feast of Tabernacles, seven years, and five months, before this Passover; which could be the feast of Tabernacles A. U. 815. only, the beginning of the ninth of Nero—seven years, and five or six months, before the Passover A. U. 823. when the city was invested by Titus ; and three years, five or six months, or what might be called in current language, four

* I am not ignorant that the words which relate to James, in this account of Josephus—Τὸν ἀδελφὸν Ἰησοῦ, τοῦ λεγομένου Χριστοῦ· Ἰάκωβος ὄνομα αὐτῷ—have been considered an interpolation; but I have seen no argument to this effect, which is not absolutely gratuitous, and resolvable into the ipse dixit of the critic. If all these words are to be given up, the whole section must be pronounced spurious ; for this part and the rest must stand and fall together. The words τοῦ λεγομένου Χριστοῦ may very possibly have been an interpolation, but we have no proof that the remainder, τὸν ἀδελφὸν Ἰησοῦ· Ἰάκωβος ὄνομα αὐτῷ, is justly to be considered so ; nothing, in short, but suspicion and mere possibility—in opposition to the weight of internal and external testimony, from manuscripts, quotations, and recognitions, as far back as we can trace the history of the passage—which is entirely on the other side.

e Euseb. E. H. ii. 23.   Ant. Jud. xx. ix. 1.   f B. Jud. vi. v. 3.

years, before the time in A. U. 819. when the war broke out.

This feast of Tabernacles is undoubtedly the feast alluded to, as next after the arrival of Albinus[g]; which the very circumstance of its not being specified by name would also of itself imply: it is likewise the feast next after the death of James; at the time of which death, or soon after it, Albinus was in Alexandria, and still on his way to the province. As he was travelling through Alexandria, it is clear he had set out from Rome, taking advantage of the Etesian winds; and, consequently, not before the middle of July, when those winds commonly began to blow. Ananus was deposed from the priesthood in consequence of this very act; but he was deposed by Agrippa, not by Albinus; and at a time when Albinus had not arrived further, at the utmost, than Alexandria. By the aid of the Etesian winds, he could not fail to be in Alexandria some time in the month of August. Pliny mentions instances of Prefects who, under similar circumstances, made the passage from the fretum Siculum to Alexandria in seven days, and even in six days; and from Puteoli, in nine [h].

Now Ananus had been three months in possession of the priesthood, before he was deposed; on which principle he must have been deposed in the last half of the eighth of Nero, A. U. 815; and the time of his deposal might have coincided with the month of June or July, in that year. The tradition of Hegesippus, then, that James was put to death at the time of a Passover, may be correct, but it must have been the Passover of A. U. 815—for Ananus might then have been in office; and thus much we may assert with confidence—that he was in office, if not at the Passover, at least at the Pentecost, A. U. 815—the former of which fell out upon April 11. and, consequently, the latter upon June 1. And if St. James was put to death by Ananus, and put to death at some Jewish feast, it must have been at one of these two. Jesus the son of Damnæus was ap-

[g] xx. ix. 3.   [h] H. N. xix. Procem.

pointed by Agrippa in his stead ; and as Ananus must certainly have been deposed, so must a successor to him have been appointed, in the interval between the next feast of Tabernacles, October 6. and the last at least of these feasts.

Though, therefore, the account of Hegesippus contains many other particulars, which appear to me to offend against probability, yet in the main fact he is so well supported by Josephus, that we may, perhaps, implicitly believe him. The death of James, then, and the first year of Albinus, were consecutive upon each other, and both coincident with A. U. 815. the latter half of the eighth of Nero.   The assertion, therefore, of Jerome[i], that St. James suffered in the seventh of Nero, though it is grounded apparently on the alleged authority of Josephus, and also on that of the Ὑποτυπώσεις of Clemens Alexandrinus, is entitled to no credit ; for Josephus certainly does not warrant this inference, nor, if the truth were known, perhaps, did Clement.

Festus, who succeeded to Felix, in the fourth of Nero, died in office[k]; but before his death he had sent the highpriest, Ishmael, and certain others of the chief of the Jews, to Rome[l]; some of whom, including Ishmael, were subsequently detained by Poppæa, whom Josephus calls the wife of Nero.   This may be the mission alluded to in the Life of Josephus[m], ascribed by a lapse of memory to Felix instead of Festus; though it is by no means a necessary supposition.   In consequence of the detention of Ishmael, the priesthood was conferred by Agrippa on Joseph, surnamed Cabi, the son of Simon[n]; and, on the death of Festus, upon Ananus the younger, who held it, as before stated, only three months[o].

It is clearly implied by the account, that Joseph continued in possession of the priesthood a very short time ; and when *he* was appointed, Festus was still alive, Ishmael was in detention at Rome, and Poppæa was then, or, according to the usage of Josephus, might be reputed and called even then, the wife of Nero.   Now she was formally espoused by

[i] Script. Eccles. Catalog. 2.   [k] Ant. Jud. xx. ix. 1.   [l] Ib. viii. 11.
Vit. 3.   [n] Ant. xx. viii. 11.   [o] xx. ix. 1.

Nero, in the eighth year of his reign, A. U. 815. within twelve days after the divorce of Octavia[p]—and not long before the beginning of the month of June—the ninth of which was the time of the death of Nero, as well as of Octavia subsequently to the divorce[q]. But, from the intimacy which had long subsisted between them, she might be called, and would be considered by Josephus, as his wife, from A. U. 811. and thenceforward[r], as early as the fourth or the fifth of Nero.

If, then, we suppose that Ishmael was sent to Rome in the seventh of Nero, *before* A. U. 814. *medium*, and Joseph was appointed high-priest in the eighth, *after* A. U. 814. *medium*, that Festus died, and Ananus was made to succeed Joseph, about the spring of A. U. 815. and that he was again deposed, and Albinus, being sent after midsummer, arrived in the province by or before the feast of Tabernacles, October 6. A. U. 815. at the close of the eighth, or the beginning of the ninth, of Nero, we make no supposition which is not both possible in itself, and entirely consistent with the accounts of Josephus. It is true that Festus, on this principle, must have been three years and six months in office, before his death; but it is also true, that Felix had been eight years in office, before Festus; and Albinus, who must have come into office at midsummer A. U. 815. was not superseded by Gessius Florus before A. U. 817. at the earliest, and possibly not before A. U. 818: for Poppæa, to whom the latter is said to have owed his appointment, did not die before the close of the first six months in A. U. 818; soon after which time Nero put the consul Atticus Vestinus to death, and married Messalina his wife[s]. The war is said to have broken out in the second year current of the administration of Florus; which might still be true of the first part of A. U. 819. when the war broke out, though that administration had begun only in A. U. 818. [t]

[p] Tac. Ann. xiv. 60.   Suet. Neron. 35.   [q] Ann. xiv. 60—64.   Suet.
Neron. 57.   [r] Ann. xiii. 45.   [s] Tac. Ann. xvi. 6. 13.   Suet. Neron.
35. 15. 12.   [t] Ant. Jud. xx. xi. 1.

The propriety, then, of the allusion at Hebrews xiii. 7. though we should understand it of the death of St. James, if the Epistle was written in A. U. 816. a year after the event, must be apparent; and I think this coincidence between the matter of fact, and the allusion to it, should be a strong argument that the Epistle was now written. The reference to the chains of the writer[u] is clearly a reference to some past, and not any present, circumstance of his personal history; which also would be in character in reference to either the imprisonment of St. Paul at Cæsarea, six or seven years before, or to his imprisonment at Rome, three or four. The same conclusion is implied by x. 35. and x. 37; which can be understood of nothing except the approaching visitation of the Jews; for that was also the term of deliverance to their Christian brethren, and in A. U. 816. the visitation, which began about the same time, A. U. 819. was only three years remote: and having arrived at these conclusions, I shall pass to the remainder of St. Paul's Epistles, which are three in number, the two Epistles to Timothy, and the Epistle to Titus.

I. If these Epistles were really written the last of all, they must each have been written between the date of the Epistle to the Hebrews, and the date of the death of St. Paul; concerning which something will be said hereafter.

II. The Second to Timothy was unquestionably the last of the three, and written in the year of Paul's second imprisonment, and, very probably, even of his death; first, because it was written when the writer was again in chains[v], and when he either was, or had been, again in Rome[w]; secondly, because it was written when the writer had a strong and lively presentiment, in his own mind, that the time of his departure was come, that is, that his martyrdom was at hand[*]; under which presentiment, and consoled by the pleasing re-

---

* This appears particularly in his use of the term ἐφέστηκε, verse 6; for that does not denote is at hand——however near——but is come, or actually arrived.

[u] x. 34.   [v] 2 Tim. i. 8. 12. 16.   ii. 9. 10. 11. 12.   [w] 2 Tim. i. 17.

flection that his appointed part had been faithfully and successfully fulfilled, he exults accordingly [x].

III. The resemblance perceptible both in the general design, and in the particular structure, of the Epistle to Titus, and of the First Epistle to Timothy, is a satisfactory proof that they must have been written either together, or within a short time of each other; so that the time and the place of the one would be presumptively the time and the place of the other. Now when St. Paul wrote to Titus, Titus was in Crete[y]; when he wrote to Timothy, Timothy was at Ephesus[z]; and St. Paul had left them in each of these places respectively himself. St. Paul, then, must both have visited Crete, and passed through Ephesus, before he could have written to either. When, however, he left Timothy in person at Ephesus, he was himself on his way to Macedonia[z]; and when he wrote the Epistle to him afterwards, his business in that country was at an end[a]; for he hoped to rejoin him shortly. We may infer, then, that he wrote to Timothy either from Macedonia, or from some other quarter, in its vicinity.

IV. Now, when he wrote the Epistle to Titus, as Titus himself was in Crete, so was St. Paul in the neighbourhood of some Nicopolis[b]; for that he was not at the time *in* this Nicopolis appears from his language, ἐκεῖ γὰρ κέκρικα παραχειμάσαι, not, ἐνταῦθα γὰρ κέκρικα παραχειμάσαι. The winter, too, which he proposed to spend there, must still have been at some distance; for Titus was to come to him while he was wintering there, and Titus was still in Crete; and St. Paul was to send him a message, even after the reception of this Epistle itself, to tell him at what time to come. It is clear, then, that he must have written to him on the present occasion either in the summer season, or at the latest early in the autumnal quarter of some year.

V. There was no Nicopolis in the neighbourhood of Macedonia, at which St. Paul could propose to winter, if he was now any where in that quarter, except the well-known

---

[x] 2 Tim. iv. 6. 8.   [y] Tit. i. 5.   [z] 1 Tim. i. 3.   [a] 1 Tim. iii. 14.
[b] Tit. iii. 12.

city founded by Augustus, to commemorate his victory at
Actium.   Nicopolis, situate on the confines of Thrace, and
of the first division of Macedonia, known by the name of
Nicopolis ad Nessum, Nestum, or Mestum, though otherwise a central city, and very likely to have been selected for
a winter residence by one who was previously in Macedonia,
being founded by Trajan, was, consequently, not yet in
being[c].   The same thing is true of Nicopolis ad Istrum ;
and very probably of Nicopolis ad Hæmum, and ad Ia-
trum. Nor, besides the Actian Nicopolis, was there any city
of note so called, and contemporary with St. Paul, except
Nicopolis in Armenia, founded by Pompey, A. U. 688. and
Nicopolis in Egypt, founded by Augustus, A. U. 724.[d]

Let us suppose that St. Paul means the Nicopolis of
Epirus.   He was not there when he wrote to Titus ; he
might be there when he wrote to Timothy ; and, wheresoever he was, when he wrote to either, it was somewhere not
far from where he was, when he wrote to the other. Before
he wrote to Timothy, he had been in Macedonia, and when
he wrote to Titus, he was in the neighbourhood of Nicopolis ; and each of these things would be the case, if he left
Titus in Crete before he proceeded to Ephesus, and Timothy in Ephesus, before he proceeded to Macedonia ; and
wrote to Titus from Macedonia before he went to Nicopolis, and to Timothy from Nicopolis as soon as he left
Macedonia.

Nor is it any objection that he speaks of rejoining Timothy again in person[e]; for he may intend this to be understood of rejoining him after the winter ; and if he wrote to
him just before, or during, the winter, it could be understood in no other sense. Besides which, he considers it possible he might still be delayed[f], and he writes to him, by
way of precaution, lest this should be the case ; that so Timothy might know how to demean himself in the Church
of God, without St. Paul's presence, as well as with it.   I
conclude, then, that the Epistle to Titus was written from

[c] Cellarii Geogr. ii. xv. 857.   viii. 370.   xv. 859.   [d] Dio. xxxvi. 33.
li. 18.   Strabo. xii. 802. 803.   xvii. 1128.   [e] 1 Tim. iii. 14.   [f] Ib. 15.

Macedonia ; and the First Epistle to Timothy, soon after it, from Nicopolis ; and about the same time, when St. Paul thus wrote to Timothy, though probably before it, it may be conjectured that he sent either Artemas or Tychicus, according to his promise, with his message to Titus in Crete.

VI. If we compare together the places noted in the margins, they must render it unquestionable that no such Epistle as this First to Timothy could have been written before the second of Nero, when the men speaking perverse things had not yet risen up in the Ephesian Church ; nor, consequently, before the seventh, when St. Paul was first released from imprisonment ; nor, if we are right in the date assigned to the Epistle to the Hebrews[h], before A. U. 816. when Timothy himself was in Italy, not in Asia, and only just set at liberty. Nor, as I will venture to say, is there, within the compass of time embraced by the Acts, any instance of a journey of St. Paul's from Asia in general, much less from Ephesus in particular, at which it would be possible, without a contradiction from the history itself, to suppose Timothy might have been left behind, while St. Paul went into Macedonia. There is no instance within that time, upon which Timothy was left any where behind him at all, especially for such a purpose, and in such a capacity, as are implied in the Epistle ; viz. to preside over the house or household of God, and to ordain Bishops, Presbyters, or Deacons. The whole strain of the Epistle in general, and of certain passages more than others in particular[i], is sufficient, on the contrary, to demonstrate that this was the first time, for which he had yet been left in so arduous, and so responsible, a situation, without the benefit of the presence and direction of St. Paul. In other words, it was now only that he had been appointed the Bishop of Ephesus, and, perhaps, of the Asiatic Churches in its vicinity : and it is manifest that, as he had been just appointed to this dignity, when the First Epistle was written, so was he still in possession of it, and still engaged upon it

---

[i] 1 Tim. i. 3—i. 19. 20. v. 15. vi. 3. 10. 21. Acts xx. 30. [h] Heb. xiii. 23. [i] 1 Tim. iii. 15. iv. 12—16.

either at Ephesus in particular, or in Asia generally, when the Second also was written[k].

VII. The winter which St. Paul proposed to spend at Nicopolis[l], before he wrote to Titus, and which we have supposed he was actually spending there, when he wrote to Timothy, if it was some winter posterior to the date of the Epistle to the Hebrews, A. U. 816. when St. Paul was in Italy, could not be the winter of A. U. 816. itself, but at the earliest, of the year 817. the next to that; for it was some winter posterior to the return from Italy—to a visit to Crete—to a visit to Asia—and to a visit to Macedonia— and, perhaps, if Hebrews xiii. 19. and xiii. 23. are to be understood in their natural and obvious sense, before them all, to a visit to Judæa. A winter posterior to all these transactions we can hardly place earlier than two years' time from A. U. 816. *ineunte,* which will bring us to the close of A. U. 817. in the first quarter of the eleventh of Nero. There is no proof in the Acts of the Apostles that St. Paul was ever at Crete, or preaching the gospel there, before his voyage to Rome. We may presume, then, that the visit which he had recently paid it had been his first visit; and Tit. i. 5. which speaks of *his* remaining there, to complete what St. Paul himself had left unfinished, seems to confirm the conjecture. On this principle these two Epistles could not have been written before A. U. 816—and were probably written in A. U. 817—the Epistle to Titus in the summer or autumn; the Epistle to Timothy at the beginning of the winter.

VIII. Besides this visit to the island of Crete, and the subsequent wintering at Nicopolis, the gospel must sometime have been preached in Dalmatia, and Churches founded there also, by St. Paul, before his second imprisonment at Rome[m]. Dalmatia was a province of Illyricum; and Illyricum, as we have seen already, had not been Evangelized, at least by the ministry of St. Paul, before the second of Nero, when he wrote his Epistle to the Romans;

---

[k] 2 Tim. i. 18—ii. 2. 14. 15.   iii. 14.   iv. 12. 13.   [l] Tit. iii. 12.
[m] 2 Tim. iv. 10.

nor, consequently, could have been before the seventh; nor, if St. Paul, as we supposed, went straight from Rome into Spain, before the ninth. Macedonia lay between Illyricum and Epirus; and Nicopolis, where St. Paul proposed to winter, after writing to Titus, and where he was probably wintering when he wrote to Timothy, was equally well situated either for the close of an Evangelical circuit, which had already embraced Illyricum, as well as Macedonia, in the course of that same year, or for the commencement of one, which should embrace it in the next: and this I consider the more probable supposition of the two; that St. Paul had not yet visited Illyricum, when he wrote either to Titus or to Timothy, but that he did visit it, when he left Nicopolis in the course of the year after that.

IX. The general lateness of these two Epistles in particular is implied by many internal evidences, which some may consider minute and superficial, but which appear to me critical and striking. The constitution of the visible Church had now first assumed its settled and definite state, under the government of Bishops, Presbyters, and Deacons, in which it was destined ever after to continue; and to give it which seems to have been the chief employment of the last few years of St. Paul's ministry, and, as we have seen elsewhere [n], very probably of St. Peter's also. The language, sentiments, and manner, of both, are perceptibly different from those of the earlier Epistles; they have much less of the air and character, which would indicate the nascent, and therefore the extraordinary, state of Christianity; and a great deal more of what would apply to its actual condition, at every period of its existence since. These two letters to Timothy and to Titus, respectively, are just what a grave and serious teacher of the gospel, endued with an adequate authority, might have written under similar circumstances, and upon similar topics, with very little modification, even at the present day. They display throughout an experience of the practical effects of Christianity, which

[n] Vol. i. Diss. ii. 131.

could be produced only by time; there is no enthusiasm, no glow, no warmth of colouring, about them; they are serious and earnest, but cool and dispassionate.   They have even a melancholy cast; they contain complaints, which must have been the results of past disappointments, as well as pre-sentiments, the fruit of the foreboding of evil to come. It is clear that the writer considered the present state of things in the Church, as worse than the former, and the future, as likely to be worse than the present: the passions and vices of men had already defeated in practice the natural good effects of the gospel; and they would still more oppose and thwart them hereafter.   Nor is it any objection that, both in the First and in the Second Epistle [o], Timothy is ad-dressed as still a young man; for if he was even twenty, A. U. 802.[p] when Paul first took him with him, instead of what is more probable, not more than fifteen or sixteen, he would be only thirty-six or thirty-seven, and perhaps only thirty-one, or thirty-two, A. U. 819.

The time of the Second Epistle to Timothy, as I have already observed, is the time of St. Paul's second imprison-ment at Rome, and probably also of his death: upon which question I shall now enter.

The truth of the general proposition that both St. Paul and St. Peter suffered martyrdom at Rome, and under the reign of Nero, is so well authenticated, and by a cloud of witnesses, that it would be the height of scepticism to dis-believe it, and an unnecessary waste of trouble to produce the testimonies to it: but as to the more particular, circum-stantial, assertion, that they suffered at Rome in the *same* year, and much more on the *same* day in the *same* year, of Nero, testimony is not uniform to that point—antecedent probability is strongly in opposition to it—we meet with no trace of it in the earliest and most authentic Christian writ-ers, and it begins to appear first, like many other preca-rious assumptions of the same kind, only in the later and the least entitled to credit.   On these accounts, unless very

---

° 1 Tim. iv. 12.   2 Tim. ii. 22.   ᵖ Acts xvi. 1.

unexceptionable testimony could be produced in its favour, we need not hesitate, if the nature of the case requires, to call it into question. The year in which they suffered, whether conjointly or respectively, must certainly be otherwise determined.

I. If it is reasonable to suppose that they would neither of them suffer, before the persecution of Christianity, in the reign of Nero, was first set on foot, and if it is still more certain that they both suffered sometime in the reign of Nero, the extreme limits within which the martyrdom of each must be comprehended will be A. U. 817. in the tenth of Nero, on the one hand, and A. U. 821. in the fourteenth on the other. They could neither of them have suffered before the nineteenth of July in the former year [q], when the city of Rome was set on fire, nor after the ninth of June in the latter, which was the day of the death of Nero. The persecution of the Christians at Rome was certainly begun in consequence of that fire [r], but when once begun, it seems to have been continued independent of it. Suetonius attests the fact of the persecution of Christianity under Nero, as well as Tacitus; but with no allusion to the charge or suspicion of having set fire to the city also—Afflicti suppliciis Christiani, genus hominum superstitionis novæ ac maleficæ [s]—and the same thing is true of the implicit testimony of Juvenal [t],

> Pone Tigellinum—tæda lucebis in illa,
> Qua stantes ardent, qui fixo gutture fumant,
> Et latum media sulcum deducit arena.

And, we have seen, from the language of several of the contemporary Epistles [u], that persecutions against Christianity were going on, more or less generally, in the provinces, before the commencement of this at Rome.

II. It is a very ancient tradition that St. Paul, after his conversion, preached the gospel five and thirty years, until the time of his death [v]. If the date of this conversion was, where we have placed it, A. U. 790. it is impossible that this

[q] Tac. Ann. xv. 41.   [r] Ib. 38—44.   [s] Neron. 16.   [t] Sat. i. 155.
[u] Vol. i. Diss. ii. 132.   [v] Hippolyti Opera. tom. i. Appendix. 31.

fact should have held good of St. Paul ; for five and thirty years from A. U. 790. would place his martyrdom, A. U. 825. some time in the third or the fourth of Vespasian. And if the term of thirty-five years is thus inapplicable to the length of his ministry, how much more the term of thirty-seven !   But, if what is thus asserted of St. Paul be understood of St. Peter, the tradition may possibly be true ; for five and thirty years from A. U. 783. would thus place *his* martyrdom A. U. 818; sometime in the eleventh of Nero.

III. The last half of the twelfth of Nero, A. U. 819. we have proved already, was the beginning of the Jewish war ; that is, it was the beginning of the days of vengeance, or the punishment of the national infidelity and impenitence : and, consequently, implies that the period of their trial previously was arrived and past. Now, with the consummation of this period, it is reasonable to presume that, in the purposes of the divine Providence, the close of the personal ministry both of St. Peter, the great Apostle of the Circumcision, and of St. Paul, the great Apostle of the Uncircumcision, should coincide also ; on which principle, it was not, *a priori*, to be expected that, after the beginning of A. U. 819. either of them should be still alive, or still at liberty to carry on their evangelical labours, as before.

IV. If the ministry of St. Peter expired A. U. 818. and began A. U. 783. it had lasted just five and thirty years between ; if the ministry of St. Paul began, where we have placed it, A. U. 791. and expired likewise, A. U. 819. it had continued just seven years less. Now there was reason, *a priori*, as we have observed elsewhere [w], to expect that this ratio or proportion of time should be found to hold good, between the lengths of their ministries respectively, or of the separate duration of each.

V. The language of testimony is so far in unison with both these conclusions, that of all the dates which are, or which can be, assigned to the year of the martyrdom either of St. Peter, or of St. Paul, the best supported is one or

---

[w] Vol. i. Diss. xiii. 576.

other of these two only, A. U. 818. and A. U. 819[x]; in one or the other of which, therefore, as far as we are bound to be governed by testimony, we must place the death of both, or in the former we must place the death of the one, and in the latter, the death of the other.

VI. There is more authority for placing the death of St. Peter in A. U. 818. and the death of St. Paul in A. U. 819. respectively, than for placing the death of both in either of those years conjointly. Rufinus, in Div. Hieronymum[y]— Petrus Romanæ ecclesiæ per viginti et quatuor annos præfuit —which being dated from the time when he was currently believed in the age of Jerome to have first come to Rome, viz. A. U. 795. places the last year of his bishopric, and by parity of consequence, the year of his death, in the twenty-fourth year current, A. U. 818.

Jerome makes Peter to have suffered, on the same day with Paul, in the thirty-seventh year after the ascension[z]. Referred to A. U. 783. this date of St. Paul's martyrdom, in the thirty-seventh year current, would be A. U. 819.

Hippolytus, περὶ τῶν ιβ΄. ἀποστόλων[a], places the martyrdom of St. Paul five and thirty years after his conversion, which conversion, it is probable, he placed A. U. 784: for it is probable he placed the ascension A. U. 783. This date, as we stated, might be true of the length of the ministry of Peter, but not of the length of the ministry of St. Paul; and, referred to the former, would place its close, as before, A. U. 818.

Orosius asserts that the pestilence at Rome, which began in the last half of A. U. 818.[b] began after the martyrdom of the Apostles Peter and Paul; which might be true of the martyrdom of Peter, if that was A. U. 818. but is contradictory to other, and earlier, testimony, if understood of the martyrdom of Paul. In like manner, Sulpicius Severus places the death of both, just at the time when the Jews

[x] Lardner. Credibility, xvi. chap. xi. Eccles. Catalog. 5. [a] Oper. ut supra. Suet. Neron. 39. [y] Oper. v. 296. [b] Tac. Ann. xvi. 13. Oros. vii. 7. [z] Scriptor.

were breaking out into open revolt[c], viz. A. U. 819. *in-eunte*: which, on the same supposition, would not be true of the time of the death of St. Peter, but might be so of the time of the death of St. Paul.

Epiphanius places the death of St. Peter and of St. Paul both in the twelfth of Nero, but not both at the same time in that year [d] : and this would still be true, if Peter had suffered in the first half of that year, the second half of A. U. 818. and Paul in the second, the first half of A. U. 819.

Lastly, the internal evidence of the Second Epistle to Timothy is most in unison with this supposition, at least as regards St. Paul.

For first, it was certainly written from Rome [e]; and written to Timothy, either as at Ephesus, or as somewhere in Asia [f]. Secondly, it must have been written in the spring quarter of the year; for it desires Timothy would come to him quickly, and that before the winter should arrive [g]. This mention of the winter may be understood even of the autumnal equinox; and it must be understood of some time soon after that, before the close of the autumnal quarter. Now if a letter from Rome was to reach Timothy at Ephesus, in time to produce his arrival at Rome after its receipt, by either of these periods, and especially by the earlier of the two, it could not have been written and sent later than the midsummer previously, at the utmost. If so, St. Paul, when he wrote this last letter to Timothy, must have been at Rome between the spring and the midsummer of some year, which, for argument's sake, I will suppose was A. U. 819.

Now it is clear that he had not long come to Rome; he must very recently have been in Asia: the passages noted in the margin are sufficient to prove this [h]. If so, he wrote the letter in question very soon after his arrival: whence, if he wrote it in the spring quarter of A. U. 819. he arrived

---

[c] Hist. ii. 41. 42.	[d] Oper. i. 107.	[e] 2 Tim. i. 17. iv. 21.
[f] iv. 12. 13. 19. 20. i. 15. 16. 18.	[g] iv. 9. 11. iv. 21.	[h] i. 15—18.
iv. 10—13. 14. 15. 19. 20.

at Rome in the spring quarter of A. U. 819. Moreover, it is also clear from iv. 20—especially as compared with Rom. xvi. 23—that St. Paul, before he came to Rome, had passed through Corinth ; and from various passages, that before he arrived there, he had been in, or was brought from, Asia [i]. It is clear also from iv. 16. 17. that, either in Rome, or somewhere else, he had had one audience at least of Nero, before he wrote the letter ; for Nero only, and deliverance from him, can properly be meant by the *lion*, and the *lion's mouth*, from which he says he had been rescued. The very same metaphor is applied in Josephus [k], by Marsyas the freedman of Herod Agrippa, to Tiberius. The use, too, of the particular tense, ἐρρύσθην, in speaking of this deliverance, implies that it was a recent event ; for ἐρρύσθην is properly, I have been delivered. The whole passage means that he had been saved out of the jaws of a lion ; that is, from a most imminent danger, and where there was apparently no chance of his escaping alive.

Now, it is a critical coincidence that, from the beginning to the midsummer of A. U. 819. Nero would be found at Rome ; but after that time he would not ; because, soon after the departure of Tiridates, who arrived at the beginning of that year, he set out on his visit to Achaia [l] ; and he was still in Achaia, when he despatched Vespasian, after the defeat of Cestius Gallus, in the last quarter of A. U. 819. to Judæa [m]. Nor did he return to Italy before the last year of his reign [n].

If, then, it is reasonable to suppose the first audience of St. Paul was before Nero himself, and at Rome, it was an audience between the spring and the summer of A. U. 819. He seems to have written his Epistle to Timothy soon after the result of this audience ; and, consequently, in the course of the same period ; which agrees with what has been already established. But, before this, it is clear from i. 15. that he must have had some trial or examination in Asia

[i] ii. 15. 18. iv. 13. 20.   [k] Ant. xviii. vi. 10.   [l] Dio. lxiii. 1—8.
Tac. Ann. xvi. 23.   Suet. Neron. 13. 19. 22. 23.   [m] Jos. B. ii. xx. 1
iii. 1. 3. iv. 2.   [n] Suet. Neron. 25. 40.   Dio. lxiii. 19.

also ; with the nature and results of which Timothy himself was acquainted, so that he is only reminded of them.   If this was the case, we may reasonably conjecture it was at his first apprehension, and probably before the proconsular governor; who, in the first half of the twelfth of Nero, A. U. 818. seems to have been either Lucius Antistius Vetes, consul along with Nero A. U. 808. or Barea Soranus[o]. But this is a point of no consequence.

It is much more certainly to be conjectured that, if Paul had been so apprehended and tried in Asia before he was sent to Rome, he had been apprehended and tried at the very beginning of A. U. 819; and it is probable, as in the former instance, that he was subsequently sent to Rome, to be tried in person before the Emperor, because he was a Roman citizen.   His privilege, as that of such a citizen, seems at least to have been respected in the kind of his death, which all authorities are agreed in attesting was decapitation ; whereas that of St. Peter, who was no such citizen, was crucifixion.

The day of the martyrdom, both of St. Paul and of St. Peter, is traditionally reported to have been June 29.[P] and the tradition may have been so far founded in fact, as that the 29th of June might be the day of the martyrdom of one of them, if not of the other : and if St. Paul actually suffered upon any second audience, and soon after his first, it might actually have been the day of his : for his first audience must have been earlier than the month of June at least.

When Nero set out to go to Achaia, he left his freedman Helius at the head of affairs, and intrusted with absolute powers, behind him[q] ; and Helius continued there in the possession of this authority, until a very short time before his return.   The character and cruelty of this man were as atrocious as those of his master ; and every day, during his administration, witnessed some execution or other.   By one of these two, it seems most probable, St. Paul also would be put to death, and soon after writing his Epistle to Timo-

[o] Tac. Ann. xvi. 10. 23.   [P] Chrys. Oper. v. 994.   [q] Dio. lxiii. 12—19.   Suet. Neron. 23.   Tac. Ann. xiii. 1.

thy itself; for there is no reason to suppose he would survive until Timothy, in obedience to his wish, could come to Italy. On *that* principle, though we have rendered it probable that he arrived in the spring, he must have survived until after the autumnal equinox at least.

This circumstance in the situation of the times, when St. Paul suffered, viz. that the Roman empire, or the city of Rome, was then subject to more than one master, seems to be implied in the words of Clemens Romanus, ἐπὶ τῶν ἡγουμένων[r], which have otherwise been much perverted. The expression may be understood of Nero and Helius; and it is only parallel to a similar expression of the historian Dio's, with reference to the very same state of things[s]—οὕτω μὲν δὴ τότε ἡ τῶν Ῥωμαίων ἀρχὴ δύο αὐτοκράτορσιν ἅμα ἐδούλευσε, Νέρωνι καὶ Ἡλίῳ.

As to St. Peter—when he first came to Rome, before his death, and how long he had been there, when that happened—whether he was brought there as a prisoner, or whether he was apprehended in Rome itself—before whom he was tried, and at what time of the year he might be executed—these are points on which we are destitute of all positive information, and can advance only conjectures. The total absence of any allusion to him, in the Epistle to Timothy, seems to me a strong presumptive argument that he was either not alive, or not present at Rome, when that Epistle was written; and this would be the case, if the reasons, which I have assigned, render it probable that he died sometime in A. U. 818. and not in A. U. 819.

As to the time of his death, it is possible that it might happen A. U. 818. about the same time as St. Paul's in the next, A. U. 819. It is a singular circumstance, upon this point, that the Chronographia of Nicephorus[t], in contradistinction to many other more ancient computations of the same thing, makes the length of his sitting at Rome two years' time. If this implies that he came there two years before his death, it would imply that he came there A. U.

---

[r] 2 Ep. i. 5.   [s] lxiii. 12.   [t] Apud Syncell. 411. Par. 1552.

н 2

816. or at the latest, A. U. 817; and this would agree very well with the probable date of his Second Epistle, which might thus have been written from Rome just before, or in the middle of, the persecution against Christianity; and the allusion to his own death, as at hand[u], would in that case be every thing but out of place. There is no way, as it appears to me, of accounting for the assertion of Nicephorus, except this; either that Peter stayed two years at Rome, on his first visit, or came back thither, two years before his death, on his second; in which case he might be said to have sate there two years. The first of these facts has, indeed, been rendered probable elsewhere[v]; but the latter appears more naturally to be what Nicephorus meant. In this case, the date of his martyrdom would be A. U. 818. A. D. 65. as that of St. Paul's would be the ensuing year, A. U. 819. A. D. 66. And having arrived at these conclusions, I shall here make an end of the present Dissertation.

[u] 2 Pet. i. 14. 15.   [v] Vol. i. Diss. ii. 92. 93.

DISSERTATION II.

On the two genealogies.

THE apparent discrepancy of the two genealogies naturally excited discussion even in the earliest ages; and, though there is one method of solution which satisfactorily explains this discrepancy, and that method not more satisfactory, than simple and obvious, yet the adversaries of Christianity, as far back as even the time of Celsus, have always been ready to lay hold on this particular instance of seeming contradiction, as one of the most prominent and most triumphant, which the Gospel history can furnish.

If the genealogies are really distinct, there may, after all, be no contradiction between them; and as this appears to me the true state of the case, I shall mention a few of the considerations, which may contribute to render it *a priori* probable, and be applicable to both in conjunction, before I speak of either in particular.

First, The necessity of some genealogy of our Lord in general must be evident; for if he was the predicted Messias of the Jews, whose birth and descent had been fixed long before to a certain line, the fulfilment of the prophecy in his person could not be made known but by exhibiting his descent accordingly. That their genealogical records were still preserved, among the Jews, after, as well as before, the Babylonish captivity, is too notorious a fact to require proof[a]. The numerous family notices, which occur in the books of Chronicles, Ezra, and Nehemiah[b], *passim,* were doubtless extracted from such records; and so late even as the reign of Domitian, when Josephus composed his own Memoirs[c], he may still be found appealing, in proof of his extraction, to the δημόσιαι δέλτοι, as yet in existence, and yet open to inspection.

---

[a] Jos. Vit. i. Contra Ap. i. 7.   [b] 1 Chron. ix. 1—22. 2 Chron. xxxi. 16—19. Neh. vii. 5.   [c] Ant. Jud. xx. xi. 2.

Again; As our Saviour's parents, whether both really, or both nominally, such—or the one really, the other only reputed so—were necessarily distinct individuals, his descent might be exhibited through either; and, as traced through the one, must necessarily differ from the same descent as traced through the other. Yet the one would be truly an account of his family, as well as the other.

Again; If Joseph was really the father of our Lord, the genealogy of Joseph, according to the flesh, would be the genealogy of our Lord, in the same respect—and it would be superfluous to search for any other. But if Joseph was not really the father of our Lord, that is, if the Christian doctrine of the Incarnation be scriptural and true—a doctrine, which St. Matthew also confirms as plainly as St. Luke—the genealogy of Joseph, according to the flesh, could in nowise be the similar genealogy of Christ. Now the genealogy, which is given by St. Matthew, is obviously the genealogy of Joseph, according to the flesh: the use of the assertion ἐγέννησε, between its several links, from first to last, admits of no other conclusion. If so, it could not be the genealogy of Christ in the natural sense. But it might still be his genealogy in some other sense—as reputed, for instance, the son of Joseph—that is, as naturally the son of the wife of Joseph. It might be, therefore, his genealogy in a civil or political sense. Accordingly, the same Evangelist, who so clearly propounds it as the natural genealogy of Joseph, does by no means propound it as the natural genealogy of Christ; for, when he is arrived at the name of Joseph, instead of continuing, as he had begun, and had proceeded all along until now—Ἰωσὴφ δὲ ἐγέννησε τὸν Ἰησοῦν —he changes his language in a striking manner—Ἰακὼβ δὲ ἐγέννησε τὸν Ἰωσὴφ, ΤΟΝ ΑΝΔΡΑ ΜΑΡΙΑΣ ΕΞ ΗΣ ἐγεννήθη Ἰησοῦς ὁ λεγόμενος Χριστός—It is evident, then, that he intended the previous line to stop short with Joseph—or not to pass on to Christ, except as the son of Mary, whose husband was Joseph. Nor is this all; but, if the words be rightly translated, it is further implied by them, that Joseph did not become the husband of Mary until after the

birth, or at least the conception, of Christ : And Jacob begat Joseph, the husband of Mary, of whom had been born,
or, had been conceived, Jesus who is called Christ.   That
this is a possible meaning of ἐγεννήθη I have no hesitation in
affirming.

Again ; The genealogy of St. Matthew not being the genealogy of Christ, according to the flesh, the general reason,
alluded to already, would require some other to be left on
record, which should be this genealogy according to the
flesh.   But any genealogy, distinct from that of his reputed
father, must be the genealogy of his real mother. St. Luke
has exhibited such a genealogy.   St. Luke's genealogy,
therefore, may be the natural genealogy of Mary, but cannot be the natural genealogy of Joseph.

Again ; If, as it has been asserted, it was not the custom
of the Jews to exhibit the genealogy of females, as such—
that is to say, to deduce a particular line of descent from
a female, as its head—or to trace one back to one—the
truth of which assertion, generally speaking, is incontestable
—the genealogy of Christ, as descended from Mary, would
not be formally exhibited as his genealogy *through* Mary,
but as his genealogy through some one most closely connected with Mary—that is to say, through some one who
stood, or might be considered to stand, in the same relation
to the father of Mary, as Mary herself. Now this could be
none but her husband Joseph, to whom she was already
contracted, before the birth of Christ—and to whom she
was actually united in marriage, at his birth.

It ought to excite no surprise, therefore, that the genealogy of Mary, regarded as the genealogy of our Lord, is
exhibited nominally as the genealogy of Joseph. It follows
only that, as the *natural* genealogy of Joseph, distinct from
Mary's, was exhibited by St. Matthew as the *legal* genealogy of Jesus, so the *natural* genealogy of Jesus, distinct
from Joseph's, is exhibited by St. Luke, as the *legal* genealogy of Joseph. The language of this Evangelist is as
much adapted to the support of this conclusion, as the language of St. Matthew to the support of the former.   For

first, the words ὦν ὡς ἐνομίζετο, premised to the account, by setting forth our Lord merely as the *reputed*, and not as the *actual*, son of Joseph, do clearly imply that the genealogy which follows, apparently *through* Joseph, could not be the natural genealogy of both ; and, if it was real, in respect to either, it could be only imputed, in respect to the other. Secondly, his mode of expressing the relation, between the successive links, seems purposely chosen to describe an acquired as well as a natural relation ; for it is such as to apply to both. This appears most distinctly at the end of all, τοῦ Ἀδὰμ, τοῦ Θεοῦ. It is equally possible, then, at the beginning, τοῦ Ἰωσὴφ, τοῦ Ἠλὶ—and of any intermediate step, as τοῦ Σαλαθιὴλ, τοῦ Νηρί.

Again ; We have but to suppose that Mary, the mother of our Lord, was the daughter of Eli, and the wife of Joseph, and we assign a reason why the descent of our Lord, though in reality *through* Mary, might yet be set forth as apparently *through* Joseph. Tradition seems to have perpetuated thus much—that the names of the Virgin's parents were Joachim (which is but another form for Eliachim, or for Eli) and Anna—which so far agrees with the supposition. And though, if the fact of their marriage be admitted, we may not in strictness be concerned with the further question, how Joseph, the son of Jacob, might come to be contracted to Mary, the daughter of Eli, yet if we may also suppose, what I think is very probable, that Mary was the only child of Eli, and Joseph was the next of kin to her, then the Law of Moses would require their union.

Nor can it be objected to this supposition that the particular provision, by which heiresses were forbidden to match themselves out of their tribe, was no longer in force, or no longer capable of being observed. It could not cease to be in force so long as the Law itself was in being—and as to its observance—while the distinctions of tribes and families continued to be kept up, it was not only practicable, but requisite ; and while there was any kind of property to transmit, whether that was a family landed inheritance, or not, it might still regulate the transmission of that. It is certain that, as both descended from David, Joseph and Mary were of kin; and as both standing at analogous points in the lines of this descent, it is probable they were the next of kin. It is probable also that Mary was an orphan at the time of the annunciation; or that her parents were then dead : and, though she was already espoused to Joseph, it is almost presumptively certain that she was much younger than he. We have seen, elsewhere [d], that the most usual age of marriage for females in Judæa was from fourteen to sixteen; and the canon of Hippolytus, quoted on a former occasion [e], places the annunciation, accordingly, in the fourteenth year of her age. The age of Joseph, at the same period, if Epiphanius is to be credited [f], was not less than eighty—and though we may very well hesitate to believe this assertion in particular, yet there is reason to suppose he was more than arrived at man's estate, and even considerably advanced in years. Joseph was certainly alive when our Lord was twelve years old [g]—but, I think, he was not alive when our Lord was thirty [h] : whereas the Virgin Mary was alive at the crucifixion [i], and, if tradition is to be believed [k], for fifteen years at least afterwards. It would seem, then, that Joseph could not have survived the annunciation more than thirty years, and he might have survived it much less—whereas the Virgin is believed to have survived it at least forty-eight. We may take it for granted, therefore, that he was an old man, and she was still a young woman, at the time of this event; which disparity of age, if it be rightly assumed, must be among the strongest presumptive arguments that they were espoused as the next of kin.

The hypothesis of Julius Africanus, which is the earliest attempt, at reconciling the genealogies, on record, though it professes to be grounded on tradition, and makes Joseph naturally the son of Jacob, and only by adoption the son of Eli, is liable to this great objection, that it supposes Eli to

[d] Vol. i. Diss. viii. App. 306.   [e] Ibid. Diss. xiii.   [f] Vol. i. 1040.
[g] Luke ii. 41—48.   [h] John ii. 12.   [i] Ib. xix. 25—27.   [k] Vol. i. Diss. ii. 120.

have died childless, and Jacob, the father of Joseph, to have married his widow, and raised up seed to Eli in Joseph [l]. In this case the Virgin Mary herself was not the daughter of Eli, and neither genealogy would prove that our Lord was descended from David.

If, then, it be asked why St. Matthew should have given the genealogy of Joseph, as the genealogy of Christ, knowing it to be merely his civil, but not his natural, it may be answered, first, that if the Jewish records did not recognize Mary, though the daughter of Eli, except as the wife of Joseph, her son, who would appear to be his son, must be described accordingly. Secondly, the final end of any genealogical account of Christ being merely to demonstrate his lineal descent from David, if the Virgin Mary was really ἐπίκληρος παρθένος, married to Joseph, as the next of kin, this end would be answered by the line of Joseph, as well as by the line of Mary. The wife of Joseph under such circumstances must have been descended from David, as well as he. Thirdly, what is, perhaps, the true reason, St. Matthew, writing exclusively for the Jews, proposes our Saviour as *their* Messias—and confines his line to David and Abraham accordingly, with a view more particularly to establish his title, as the βασιλεὺς τοῦ Ἰσραὴλ, and, in that capacity, his right to the temporal kingdom of Israel. This temporal kingdom at first was undoubtedly assured to Solomon, and to his posterity according to the flesh [m]; and though this promise may seem to have been revoked in the person of Coniah, Shallum, or Jeconiah, the grandson of Josiah, and even before that in the person of Jehoiakim, the father of Coniah [n], yet a contemporary prophecy, relating to the last king Zedekiah [o], and another prophecy of Jeremiah himself [p], will shew it was never absolutely revoked, but merely for a time suspended. It was taken away from the present possessor, Jehoiakim, Coniah, or Ze-

[l] Euseb. E. H. i. vii.   [m] 2 Sam. vii. 12—16.   [l] Kings i. 13. 30. ix. 5.
[l] Chron. xvii. 11—14. xxii. 7—10. xxviii. 5.   [n] Jer. xxii. 10. 11. 12.
24. 25—27. 29. 30. xxii. 13—19. xxxvi. 30.   [o] Ezek. xxi. 25—27.
[p] xxxiii. 15—end.

dekiah, but only to be reserved until *he* should come whose right it was—and to him it should be restored. This person was doubtless Christ—and his right, as entitled to the crown of Israel, must be as derived from David. For this reason St. Matthew has traced up his descent through the line of Solomon, because the promise of the temporal kingdom was originally assured to David, in the person of Solomon. The right, conveyed by that promise, and transmitted through the descendants of Solomon, was now centred in Joseph—and through Joseph became vested in Christ—a result which would be the same, in whatever sense our Saviour were considered the son, provided he was only the πρωτότοκος, of Joseph. Nor is it any objection that the temporal kingdom has not yet been actually restored to the descendants of David, in the person of Christ. It may be restored hereafter—and that is sufficient for the end in view. But the genealogy of St. Luke, which beginning with Jesus proceeds up to Adam, can have no object except to represent Christ as the promised seed of the woman, in whom all the nations of the earth should be interested alike. It is such a genealogy, therefore, as was to be expected from a Gospel, written expressly for Gentiles, and not for Jews.

I shall now pass to a few observations on each of the genealogies in particular.

First, The descent of the Messias having been gradually restricted, from Abraham downwards, to the line of Isaac, and afterwards of Jacob, became fixed at last to one tribe in the line of Judah, and to one family in the line of David. From the time of David, then, the line of the Messias was necessarily to be deduced through the posterity of David—among whom, if the promise of his birth was ever confined to any in particular, it was so to the children of David and Bathsheba q. The most eminent of this number was unquestionably Solomon. But the promise of the Messias, according to the flesh, is no where restricted to the line of

q 1 Chron. xxii. 7—10. Psalm lxxii. lxxxix. 3. 4. 20—37. cxxxii. 11—end.

Solomon: and, among the children of David and Bathsheba, Nathan is mentioned as well as he [r]. St. Luke's genealogy is derived from Nathan: St. Matthew's from Solomon. If, indeed, the tradition which is mentioned by Africanus [s]—that Matthan, the father of Jacob, and Melchi, the father of Eli, were both at different times married to the same wife, whom he calls *Estha*—were true, then Jacob and Eli, as he supposes, would be brothers: and, if Estha herself was descended from David, Jacob might also be related to Nathan, or Eli might also be related to Solomon: in which case the same things would be true of Joseph the son of Jacob, and of Mary the daughter of Eli. I confess there appears to me some reason for this tradition, partly because it specifies the name of Estha, and partly because it brings the connection between Joseph and Mary still closer than before: for they would thus be the children of brothers by the same mother, but not the same father; and, consequently, cousins of each other.

Again; It is probable that neither genealogy stands exactly as it came from the writer of the Gospel; and, in the mere transcription of names, errors of excess or of defect are things of too common occurrence, and too often exemplified in other instances, to create any surprise here. The number of kings in direct descent from David to Jeconiah, the last king of Judah but one, including them both, is nineteen [t]—in St. Matthew it is but fifteen—and it is evident that, between Joram and Uzzias, in his account, are omitted three names in succession, Ahaziah, Joash, and Amaziah—and between Josias and Jechonias, the intermediate name of Jehoiakim, the father of Jechonias. The certainty of omissions in this first half, between David and Jechonias, may be presumptively proof of omissions in the last half, between Zerubbabel and Joseph.

St. Luke's genealogy contains at present, from Jesus to God, seventy-seven names; and it contained the same number in the time of Jerome [u]. Yet there is authority from

[r] 1 Chron. iii. 5. 2 Sam. xi. 3. [s] Supra loc. cit. [t] 1 Chron. iii. 1—22.
[u] Ep. Crit. Oper. ii. 565.

Africanus [v] to expunge *two*, between Eli and Melchi, viz. Matthat and Levi, (for he writes in this order, τοῦ 'Ιωσὴφ, τοῦ 'Ηλὶ, τοῦ Μελχὶ,) which reduces the number to seventy-five; and *another*, in the second Cainan, which also he does not recognise, between Salah and Arphaxad [w], which reduces it to seventy-four. In the time of Irenæus, however, more ancient than the time of Africanus, the whole number was only seventy-two [x]. We must reduce it, therefore, by two more; which two, I should conjecture, are the second τοῦ Ματθὰτ, τοῦ Λευὶ, in verse 29. coming between τοῦ 'Ιωρεὶμ, and τοῦ Συμεών. With these five omissions the number of degrees is exactly seventy-two: and there is this further reason for the last omission, that without the two names, τοῦ Ματθὰτ, τοῦ Λευὶ, the number of steps from David to Neri in St. Luke, inclusive of both, is exactly nineteen; the number of steps also from David to Jechonias in St. Mat-thew. Now Neri and Jechonias must have been contemporaries; for Salathiel stands in the same relation of son to both: and it is not unlikely that, between each of them and David, the common founder of either line, the number of generations should be equal. The same thing is asserted by Josephus of the number of the high-priests, from the high-priest contemporary with Solomon, who was Zadok, to Jozadak, contemporary with Jechonias [y]. This number was eighteen—which, beginning at Solomon, answers to nineteen, beginning at David.

From the birth of Solomon [z], which the Bible Chronology places B. C. 1033. to the birth of Jechonias [a], eighteen years before his captivity, B. C. 599. are 416 years; which, divided by seventeen, the number of descents between Solomon and Jechonias, is about twenty-four for the average interval between each step. A similar interval is reckoned by Josephus, for the succession of eighteen high-priests, at 466 years [y], which is an average of twenty-five or twenty-six. Most of the kings of Judah had children early. It admits

---

[v] Loc. cit.   [w] Rel. Sacræ. ii. 130.   [x] Contr. Hær. iii. cap. 33. 261.
[y] Ant. Jud. xx. x.   [z] 2 Sam. xii. 24.   [a] 2 Kings xxiv. 8.   2 Chron. xxxvi. 8—10.

of proof that Solomon was only seventeen at the birth of Rehoboam—Joram only eighteen at the birth of Ahaziah —Ahaziah and Joash only twenty-two at the birth of Joash, and of Amaziah, respectively—Jotham only twenty-one at the birth of Ahaz—Ahaz only twelve at the birth of Hezekiah—Amon only sixteen at the birth of Josiah—Josiah only fourteen at the birth of Jehoiakim—and Jehoiakim only eighteen at the birth of Jeconiah.   In the remaining instances the interval is much greater. Jehoshaphat was twenty-eight at the birth of Joram—Amaziah was thirty-eight at the birth of Uzziah—Uzziah was forty-three at the birth of Jotham—Hezekiah was forty-two at the birth of Manasseh—Manasseh was forty-five at the birth of Amon.

St. Matthew asserts that Jechonias begat Salathiel *after*, or *during*, the removal to Babylon. Jechonias was but eighteen years old when he went into captivity [b] ; and though his wives are mentioned as carried into captivity along with him, his sons, or his children, are not [c]—whence we may conclude he had no children then.   Yet, Jer. xxii. 28. a prophecy, which it appears from verse 11. was spoken after he was gone into captivity, an allusion occurs to his seed ; that is, to his seed begotten in captivity. Compare also verse 30.   Accordingly it appears he must have had eight sons [d], the eldest Assir, and the next to him Salathiel.   In the thirty-seventh year of his captivity, that is, B. C. 563. and in the fifty-fifth of his age, Evil-Merodach released him from confinement [e].   But though he might not be too old to have children even after that, Salathiel in particular could not have been of that number ; for in that case Salathiel himself could not have been more than twenty-six, B. C. 536. the last year of the Babylonish captivity—the return from which was conducted by his son Zerubbabel—if Zerubbabel, at least, was his son—which St. Matthew's expression ἐγέννησε, and Ezra iii. 2. Nehem. xii. 1. Haggai i. 1. 12. ii. 1. &c. must place beyond a doubt.

[b] 2 Chron. xxxvi. 9. 10.   2 Kings xxiv. 8—16.   [c] 2 Kings xxiv. 15. Jer. xxix. 2. xxii. 26.   [d] 1 Chron. iii. 17. 18.   [e] 2 Kings xxv. 27.

Both in Josephus also [f], and in the Seventy, Salathiel is but another form for Shealtiel. Salathiel, then, was not born before B. C. 599. nor after B. C. 563 : and B. C. 536. had a son arrived at man's estate, and able to conduct the return of his countrymen. He must have been born, then, soon after B. C. 599.

In one place of his Antiquities Josephus asserts that David reigned and bequeathed the sovereignty to his children, for twenty-one generations [g]; in another, that the kings of the race of David, from the first to the last, were twenty-one in number [h]. Between David and Zedekiah there were certainly twenty-one kings, inclusive of them both; but between David and Zedekiah, even though we reckon in both, there were only nineteen generations. Josephus, therefore, has either spoken inaccurately here, intending *this* assertion as equivalent to the *other*, or, if he is to be literally understood, he included in the number of generations Salathiel and Zerubbabel both—and this would be an important conclusion—for it would prove that he considered them both to be lineally descended (and through Jechonias) from David. Nor would it make much difficulty that he talks of the supremacy, as still surviving with his posterity, in them ; for Zerubbabel, as the chief of the Jews who returned from captivity, did still retain in some sense the dignity, though no longer the title, of their king. But there is no proof in Scripture that any descendant of Zerubbabel succeeded to his father's place, or that the revived supremacy, such as it was, did not strictly expire with him.

As the two lines begin together from David, so they meet together in Salathiel ; whence we may infer that Neri was contemporary with Jechonias. But, if Salathiel was the lineal descendant of Jechonias, he could not be the lineal descendant of Neri. The same supposition, then, is necessary here, as in the case of Joseph and Eli—viz. that Salathiel was the son of Neri in the *civil*, and of Jechonias in the *natural*, sense : and this would be the effect, if he

[f] Ant. Jud. xi. iii. 10.   [g] v. ix. 4.   [h] x. viii. 4.

was married to a daughter of Neri; after which, the two lines, having been previously united in Zerubbabel, would again begin to diverge, through Abiud and Resa, down to Joseph, and to Eli, respectively. This union of the lines in his person was doubtless the effect of the special providence of God. Zerubbabel was the most illustrious of the Jews who returned from captivity; and altogether the fittest, among the posterity of David, to become the founder of the line of the Messias afresh. He was, moreover, himself a type of Christ [i]. Nor were the families of Solomon and Nathan so likely, perhaps, to have been united, at any time, as during the captivity.

The Zerubbabel who is mentioned as the son of Pedaiah, and consequently as a grandson of Jechonias [k], it is reasonable to presume, on many accounts, was a different person from Zerubbabel the son of Salathiel. I. A grandson of Jechonias, by Pedaiah, must have been a younger person than a grandson through Salathiel. II. Among the posterity of this Zerubbabel, neither Abiud nor Resa are mentioned, though many others are. III. The identity of the name would be no objection—for bearing a distinct reference merely to the place of a person's birth, and to the circumstances of his family at the time, it might have been given to others, born during the captivity in Babylon, as well as to one. IV. If there had been only one Zerubbabel, the author of the book of Ezra, who designates him there by his proper relation to Salathiel, and is believed to have compiled the book of Chronicles, would have designated him so here likewise.

Again; If Salathiel was born B. C. 598. or 597. there is this number of years to the time of the birth of Christ—to fill up which period St. Luke's genealogy, (independent of the two names rejected,) from Salathiel to Joseph, who stands in the same relation to Eli as Mary, inclusive of both, exhibits nineteen persons—and from Salathiel to the birth of Christ, nineteen generations—which is an average

---

[i] Hagg. ii. 23. Zech. iii. 8. 9. iv. 6—10. vi. 12. 13.   [k] 1 Chron. iii. 19.

of thirty-one years and one half to each; no very improbable duration; for the age of thirty was as common an age
of marriage for males, as fourteen or fifteen was for females;
of which many instances might be produced.

Μήτε τριηκόντων ἐτέων μάλα πόλλ' ἀπολείπων,
Μήτ' ἐπιθεὶς μάλα πολλά· γάμος δέ τοι ὥριος οὗτος[1].

And as the family of Mary became gradually more and
more reduced in circumstances, early marriages would become so much the less frequent among them.   Within the
same period, dated from the close of the captivity B.C. 536.
down to the time of Alcimus, appointed high-priest by Antiochus Eupator, B. C. 163—162.[m] Josephus reckons up
fifteen high-priests[n], including Jeshua, the son of Jozadak,
who was already arrived at man's estate, when the return
from captivity took place.   Jozadak, the father of Jeshua,
was carried into captivity along with Seraiah his father[o],
eleven years after B. C. 599. that is, in B. C. 588.[p] Jeshua
is not mentioned at this time; but the sons of Jeshua are
mentioned Ezra iii. 9—which from iii. 8. it appears is the
second year after the return, or B. C. 535.   If so, Jeshua
himself was born about B. C. 588—whence to B. C. 163. or
162. are about 426 years; which allows to fourteen generations an average of thirty years and six months each.

To fill up the same period, in the genealogy of St. Matthew, from Salathiel to Joseph, inclusive of both, there are
but twelve names in all—and from the time of the birth of
Salathiel, B. C. 598. to the time of the birth of Joseph,
which, if he was fifty years old at the time of the birth of
Christ, would be about B.C. 54. there would be only eleven
generations, the average of which, to the intervening period
of 544 years, would be as much as fifty years each.   It is
not improbable, therefore, that some names may have fallen
out here—and it is a curious circumstance that, if the four
names which appear to have crept, over and above the proper number, into the corresponding portions of St. Luke's
account, had belonged originally to St. Matthew's, the num-

[1] Hesiod. Opera et Dies. 694.   [m] Ant. Jud. xii. ix. 3. 7.   [n] xx. x.
[o] 1 Chron. vi. 14. 15.   [p] 2 Kings xxv. 18.   [p] 2 Kings xxiv. 18. xxv. 2.

ber of generations from Salathiel to Joseph would have been fifteen ; at an average of about thirty-six years each : which might have squared sufficiently well with St. Luke's.

There are not wanting, however, instances where a few generations are seen to have taken up a great number of years. I could illustrate this circumstance from the Old Testament, compared with Josephus, in several places ; but I shall be satisfied to illustrate it from his account of his own pedigree.

Matthias, surnamed ὁ Κυρτὸς, between whom and Josephus there were just three generations—Josephus, Matthias, Josephus ᑫ—was born in the first year of John Hyrcanus, that is, A. U. 619. or B. C. 135.ʳ From this time to the year of the birth of Josephus, which was the first of Caius, A. U. 790. are 171 years ; which, divided by three, gives an average of fifty-seven years to each. But this interval must be still further enlarged. Between the birth of Josephus, A. U. 790. and the birth of his father Matthias, in the tenth of Archelaus, A. U. 760. there are but thirty years. Between the birth of this Matthias, A. U. 760. and the birth of *his* father, Josephus, in the ninth of Queen Alexandra, A. U. 687. there are seventy-three : and between the birth of this Josephus, in A. U. 687. and the birth of his father, Matthias ὁ Κυρτὸς, A. U. 619. there are sixty-eight. The fact is that men may have children at fifty, sixty, or seventy, as well as at twenty, thirty, or forty —and a given line of descent may be carried on in the one case, as well as in the other. Generations, of about thirty years each, will then only apply, when the calculation is made on the supposition of marriages at a regular time, and of descents in the regular way, from a father to his eldest son. It is not impossible, therefore, that eleven generations only might still have taken up a period of 550 years.

If there have been omissions, at least, in this part of St. Matthew's genealogy, I think they must come after Azor,

ᑫ Vit. I. ʳ Vol. i. Diss. iv. App. ii. 225.

the fourth name from Salathiel on the one hand, and before Matthan, the second name from Joseph, on the other; which materially diminishes the chances of any such omissions at all. Matthan stood second in the time of Africanus[s]—and Azor, I think, was contemporary with Nehemiah; or is the same person who is mentioned by him, among the heads of the people, under the name of Azzur[t], which the Seventy render by 'Aζούρ. Nehemiah was sent to Jerusalem in the twentieth of Artaxerxes[u], B. C. 444. just ninety-two years after the return, B. C. 536; at which time Azor was manifestly arrived at man's estate. Let us suppose that Abiud, the grandfather of Azor, was born soon after the return; which, if Zerubbabel himself was then in the flower of his age, is very likely to have been the case. From his birth to the birth of Zadok, when Azor might be thirty years old, we cannot reckon less than ninety years. It would seem from Nehemiah xii. 47. as if the age, or the government, of Zerubbabel had reached very near to the time of Nehemiah himself, or at least of Ezra, whose mission took place B. C. 458. If Zerubbabel was about thirty B. C. 536. and had lived to be eighty or ninety years old, he would have died not many years before the arrival of the latter.

This conclusion is further supported by the following coincidence also. A son of Joiada, and grandson of Eliashib, was contemporary with Nehemiah, and already of a marriageable age, in the thirty-second year of Artaxerxes[v], that is, B. C. 432. Now Eliashib was the grandson of Jeshua[w], as this son was of Eliashib. The father of Eliashib was Joiakim, and Joiakim (one of the sons, and probably the oldest, of the sons of Jeshua[x]) was not only born, but arrived at man's estate, B. C. 535. the year after the return. This Joiakim succeeded to Jeshua in the priesthood, and Eliashib succeeded to Joiakim. Now in the seventh of Artaxerxes[y], Eliashib was already high-priest; and, consequently, Joiakim was dead. From B. C. 535. to the seventh of Artaxerxes, B. C. 458. there is an interval of seventy-

---

[s] Ut supra.   [t] x. 17.   [u] i. 1.   ii. 1.   [v] Neh. xiii. 28.
[w] Ib. xii. 10. 11.   [x] Ezra iii. 9.   x. 18.   [y] Ezra x. 6.

I 2

seven years; whence, if Joiakim had been thirty at the first of those extremes, he would have been one hundred and seven at the latter. It is probable, then, that he was dead before even the first, and much more the seventh, of Artaxerxes.

His age, therefore, at the return, would be on a par with that of Zerubbabel; and Eliashib, the son of this Joiakim, would correspond, in the line of descent, to Abiud the son of Zerubbabel. It is manifest, therefore, that a grandson of Eliashib would answer to a grandson of Abiud; the latter of whom was Azor, and the former was some son of Joiada, whose name is not mentioned; and both, contemporary with Nehemiah. Moreover, as Azor was now arrived at man's estate, so was this grandson of Eliashib; for the former was among the heads of the people, and the latter was married to a daughter of Sanballat the Horonite.

There is no proof, however, in any part of the book of Nehemiah, which is to be considered his own production, that he was contemporary with any of the descendants of Jeshua beyond this grandson of Eliashib, or the third generation after the return from captivity; which being the case, it is abundantly sufficient to convince us that the Artaxerxes, within whose reign his mission fell, was Artaxerxes Longimanus, the first of that name, and not Artaxerxes Mnemon, the second who bore it. The reign of Artaxerxes Longimanus began B. C. 464; that of Artaxerxes Mnemon B. C. 405. and the twentieth year of the former began B. C. 445; the twentieth year of the latter, B. C. 386. and his thirty-second, B. C. 374. Now Eliashib, born, as we supposed, directly after the return from captivity, was alive not only in the seventh, but as late as the thirty-second, year of this Artaxerxes[z]. This might be the case B. C. 433. the thirty-second of Artaxerxes Longimanus; but is absolutely incredible of B. C. 374. the thirty-second of Artaxerxes Mnemon, as much as sixty years later. Though Eliashib had been born as early as B. C. 535. he would still be only

[z] Ezra x. 6.   Nehem. iii. 1.   xiii. 4—6.

one hundred and two years old, B. C. 433; but B. C. 375. he would be one hundred and sixty: the first of these suppositions is possible; but the latter, if not impossible, is highly incredible.

Moreover, besides Joiada[a], who afterwards succeeded him in the priesthood, he had a son called Johanan, who also was arrived at man's estate—and both before the seventh of Artaxerxes. This is very possible of the seventh of Artaxerxes Longimanus, B. C. 458. seventy-seven years after B. C. 535—and just what we might have expected; for Johanan, though younger than Joiada, might yet be more than thirty when his father was seventy-seven. But there is no mention in Ezra of more than the sons of Eliashib, as neither in Nehemiah of more than his grandsons; had all these parties, however, lived in the time of Artaxerxes Mnemon, it is to be presumed that allusions would have occurred to the sons of his grandchildren also. Between the seventh and the thirty-second of Artaxerxes Mnemon, that is, between B. C. 399. and B. C. 374. Jaddua, the great-grandson of Eliashib, and grandson of Joiada, who was high-priest and an old man, B. C. 332. the year when Alexander besieged Tyre[b], must have been not only born, but of mature age; and yet neither in Ezra nor in Nehemiah is there any mention of him.

I will conclude this subject with one more remark. It is clear from Nehemiah v. 1—6. which belongs to the twentieth of Artaxerxes, that Nehemiah came into Judæa in a period of great dearth and scarcity, which appears to have lasted as long even as his thirty-second[c]. Now it is attested by Strabo, on the authority of Xanthus the Lydian[d], that there was in the time of Artaxerxes Longimanus a very great drought, so that rivers, lakes, and wells, alike were dried up. The period during which Xanthus was writing history is necessarily to be restricted between the first and the twentieth of Artaxerxes[e]; so that any drought of which *he* could make mention must have come within this time.

[a] Neh. xii. 10. 11.   Ezra x. 6.   [b] Ant. Jud. xi. viii. 4—7.   [c] Neh. v. 14.   [d] i. 71.   [e] Vide Clinton's Fasti Hellenici. B. C. 463.

But if some such thing did so take place, it is needless to argue that Judæa would be affected by it, as well as any other part of the Persian empire; still less that if it was so, it would necessarily be subject to a scarcity. The effect of this scarcity seems to have been that, by the twentieth of Artaxerxes, the people had mortgaged their lands and houses, and even their own persons, either to pay the King's tribute, or to maintain themselves and their families, and were very much in debt and distressed. This must have been going on some time to arrive at such an height ; and as there is no allusion to it in Ezra, we may infer that it had begun between the seventh and the twentieth of Artaxerxes, and, perhaps, as near to the latter as to the former ; for, from the measures adopted by Nehemiah, in consequence of the complaints of the people, we may infer that a year of release for property or bondsmen, which was properly every seven years, was either lately past or just at hand. And this, I shall prove elsewhere, would be the case about the twentieth of Artaxerxes.

DISSERTATION III.

Upon the question, who are meant in the Gospels by the 'Αδελφοὶ *of Christ.*

THAT Joseph, before his marriage with the Virgin, had either been married, or had any children, is no where affirmed in the Gospels, nor implicitly to be collected from any intimations which they supply. Upon this point, therefore, it would become us to suspend our judgment, and not to undertake to decide; though, perhaps, the negative—on every account—may be more probable than the affirmative. But that, after his marriage, he continued still childless, or in other words, that the Virgin Mary, as the Romish, and as the modern Greek, Church maintains, after her union with Joseph and the birth of Christ, remained a virgin as much as before, is a tradition which, both as superstitious, and as untenable, may justly be called into question. It is superstitious, because it can serve no good purpose—and it is untenable, because it is repugnant to the scriptural narrative, or to the plain inference deducible from its testimony.

It might be essential to the fulfilment of prophecy that the Messias should be born of a pure and an immaculate virgin—it might be indispensable to the end of the Incarnation itself—but when these purposes had once been answered, it was clearly indifferent whether his mother remained still in her former condition, or not. The estate of matrimony, which God's word had sanctioned from the first, and every where pronounces to be becoming in all, was as open to her as to any one else; and what crime she could commit by entering into it, even after the nativity of Christ, it would be difficult to say. It is probable that her orphan condition, and it is more than probable that the reduced circumstances of her family, would render this not merely a lawful, but even a prudential, expedient. She was con-

r 4

tracted to Joseph before the conception of Christ—she was united to him at the time of his birth—and she continued to live with him, under the name, and in the relation, of his wife, long afterwards.   Even *after* the conception, and *before* the nativity, Joseph was admonished by God to complete the espousals, between himself and Mary, in the usual manner, as if nothing had occurred to prevent it.   It was plainly intended by Providence, then, that they should live together, even after the birth of Christ, in the marriage state ; and if they so lived together, it was equally possible that, even after the birth of Christ, they might have children.   To suppose that they would be commanded to complete their union—and yet not be intended to live in the relation of husband and wife—would be to suppose an effect without a cause ; or a special interposition of Providence, without a special reason to produce it.   It was rather to be expected that, after the conception of Christ, Mary would have remained, as she had remained before it, in her unmarried and single estate.   The denomination of Mary *the Virgin,* except at the time when she was really so, before not merely her marriage with Joseph, but also the conception of Christ, is no where in Scripture ascribed to her.   It is predicted that all generations should call her *blessed*—and the event has fulfilled that prediction—it is not predicted that she could be called *the Virgin*, and this addition to the name of *the blessed* is one of the inventions of men.   But it would not be said, as at Matt. i. 25. even after Joseph had taken her home, that he abstained from the knowledge of his wife, *until* she had been delivered of Christ, if he had abstained from the same knowledge afterwards—nor would our Lord be called, as at Matt. i. 25. and Luke ii. 7. the *firstborn* of Mary, if it were not as certain that she had other children after him, as that she had none before him.   I admit that the name of a *firstborn* may possibly be given even to an *only* child.   But if an only child must be the first, he must also be the last—and had that been the nature of the relation here, both the reason of the thing, and the matter of fact, would have required the Evangelist to say, ἕως οὗ

ἔτεκε τὸν υἱὸν αὐτῆς τὸν μονογενῆ, not τὸν πρωτότοκον—and to
have dropt the other part of the assertion—καὶ οὐκ ἐγίνωσκεν
αὐτήν—altogether.

John ii. 12. Matt. xii. 46. Mark iii. 31. Luke viii. 19.
John vii. 3. 5. 10. Acts i. 14. mention occurs of the *brethren*
—οἱ ἀδελφοὶ—of our Lord ; and Matt. xiii. 55. 56. Mark
vi. 3. of his *brethren* and of his *sisters* both ; and this, at
times, and on occasions, which, it will be seen hereafter,
synchronize with the beginning, with the middle, and with
the very end, of his ministry. The parties alluded to, in all
these instances, were obviously persons, whether male or
female, arrived at maturity ; as, though born of the same
parents, and yet younger than our Saviour, they might still
be, thirty, or thirty-two, years after the birth of Christ.
What kind of relationship would be thus implied, except
the natural one in the ordinary sense of the terms, it would
not be easy to say. The use of the terms ἁπλῶς leads directly to that one conclusion. They could not be the children of any other Mary, distinct from the mother of our
Lord—at least exclusively—because it is always Mary the
mother of our Lord, and not any other Mary, who is mentioned along with them—who was obviously living with
them—and making one of some family with them—which,
it is not probable, she would make with any family but her
own.

It may be said, however, that these might be the children
of Joseph, but by some former, or, at least, some different,
wife ; in which case, they might still be called the ἀδελφοὶ, or
ἀδελφαὶ, of our Lord—and Mary might possibly be living
with them. But the fact of this double marriage of Joseph, as I have observed, is purely a gratuitous assumption
—without countenance from any authentic historical testimony—or even any traditionary, which does not contradict
itself. Nor, except upon one supposition, which would obviously beg the question, viz. that Joseph never could have
had children, either sons or daughters, by Mary, the mother of Jesus, his actual wife, is it more gratuitous, than
unnecessary. If any such other wife of Joseph had once

existed, still, before the commencement of our Saviour's
ministry, that is, before John ii. 12. at least, she must have
been dead ; and, if she was dead before that point of time,
she might have been dead some length of time before it.   It
seems equally clear that Joseph himself was not then alive,
any more than she.   It would follow, therefore, that these
sons and daughters, the fruit of a distinct marriage, were all
older, instead of being all younger, than our Saviour ; and
if the difference of years, between the age of Joseph and
that of the Virgin, was such as has been supposed, much
older too: a conclusion which would involve us in great perplexity.   Nor do I see how it could come to pass that our
Lord should have been so commonly reputed the son of
Joseph and Mary, that is, confounded with their natural
offspring, if he had not brothers or sisters who were naturally their offspring, and justly to be considered such.

Matt. xiii. 55. Mark vi. 3. the names of these ἀδελφοὶ of
our Lord are specified as follows : James and Joses, Simon
and Jude, or Jude and Simon.   John vii. 5.—a point of time
which coincides with the third feast of Tabernacles—his
ἀδελφοὶ, it is said, did not believe in him; and Matt. xii. 46.
Mark iii. 21. iii. 31. Luke viii. 19—all relating to a point
of time one year earlier than the notice in St. John—implicitly confirm St. John.   Yet, Acts i. 14. they must have
become believers *after* the resurrection, and *before* the descent of the Holy Ghost; and 1 Cor. ix. 5. they must have
become, in due time, Evangelists of Christianity itself.   If,
then, they continued unbelievers up to the time of the last
Passover, and yet were converted before the day of Pentecost ensuing, it is probable they were converted by the fact
of the resurrection between.   It would be, consequently, in
their unbelieving state that our Saviour, John xix. 25—27.
committed his mother, in his dying moments, to the care,
not of these his brethren, but of St. John.   And this, I
think, is the best reason why he might pass over them, even
though they had been present;—and (what is much more
probable) had not been absent at the time—to commit his
mother to St. John.   Not but that commentators, both an-

cient and modern, have supposed some relationship between the Virgin and St. John ; which, if the fact of this relationship could be made out, might conspire to produce the same effect.   Be this, however, as it may, still, with respect to the unbelief of our Lord's ἀδελφοὶ, the gospel accounts are not inconsistent with each other.   They will all shew, either directly or by implication, that up to the close of his public ministry his brethren, or some at least who are called by that name, were not believers as yet—but they will none of them imply that they did not become so afterwards.

Now, among those who, even in the lifetime of Christ, were not merely believers, but already Disciples, and already Apostles, of our Lord, Matt. x. 3. Mark iii. 18. Luke vi. 15. Ἰάκωβος Ἀλφαίου is invariably mentioned as one : and if this James was James the first Bishop of Jerusalem, then, Gal. i. 19. and even Joseph. Ant. xx. ix. 1.—this James was undoubtedly known and denominated as the Ἀδελφὸς τοῦ Κυρίου, or τοῦ Χριστοῦ.   There was one, then, even in the lifetime of Christ, known as an ἀδελφὸς, or brother of Christ, who believed in him—and there were others known by the same relation, who did not believe in him. It follows, therefore, either that this one of his brethren was a particular exception from the rest, or that there were a number of persons, all of whom might be called in some sense or other, ἀδελφοὶ, or brethren, of Christ, and yet be distinct from each other ; some of whom believed in him, and others believed not.

Now, according to the Hebrew idiom, the relation of son is extended to every direct remove, however distant, from the fountain head ; and, on the same principle, the relation of brother or sister to every collateral, equally remote.   In proof of this idiom, the very subject under discussion supplies a case in point.   Matt. xxvii. 56. Mark xv. 40. xvi. 1. Luke xxiv. 10.—the Mary, there spoken of, is described as Mary the mother of James—concerning which James, we may take it for granted, he is James the Apostle, the son of Alphæus.   But in the parallel place of John xix. 25. she is described as the ἀδελφὴ or sister of Mary the mother of

Jesus; from both which descriptions we may argue as follows.

If this Mary was really the *sister* of the Virgin, their children would be simply *cousins;* and, consequently, James, the son of this Mary, could not be really the *brother* of Jesus, the son of the other: and therefore ὁ ἀδελφὸς τοῦ Κυρίου, as applied to him, cannot mean the *brother* of the Lord. But if she was not really the *sister*, then, ἡ ἀδελφὴ τῆς μητρὸς αὐτοῦ, as applied to her, does not mean the *sister* of his mother. In either case, then, it will follow that ἀδελφὸς, or ἀδελφὴ, do not strictly denote the relation of a brother or a sister, but at the utmost of a male or a female cousin. The term, therefore, in a given instance, agreeably to the Jewish usage, may imply no more than this. Nor is it possible to escape this conclusion, except by contending that this Mary was really the *sister* of the Virgin, and really the *wife* of Joseph; in which case two uterine sisters must have both borne the name of Mary—both must have been married to Joseph—and living in marriage with him at the same time—which, I think, is directly repugnant to Lev. xviii. 18—and Joseph himself must have borne the other name of Alphæus. All these suppositions are very incredible, and open to the greatest objections. Besides which, Mary is called in the same passage, John xix. 25. ἡ τοῦ Κλωπᾶ, which must be understood with the ellipsis of γυνὴ, agreeably to the Latin idiom—Apicatam Sejani[a]—Agrippina Germanici[b]—Antonia Drusi[c]—Verania Pisonis[d]—in all which there is the same ellipsis of uxor[*]: and Cleopas, if Hegesippus[f] is to be believed, was himself the brother of Joseph. But, Lev. xviii. 16. except in the case provided by the Law, to marry with the wife of a brother, even after

---

[*] So common is this ellipsis, both in Latin and in Greek, that Eckel[e] considers it a great singularity to find the word γυνὴ expressed on some of the coins of Agrippina, the consort of Claudius.

[a] Tac. Ann. iv. 11.   [b] Plin. H. N. vii. 13.   [c] Ib. vii. 19.
[d] Plin. Ep. ii. xx.   [e] vi. 259.   [f] Eus. E. H. iii. xi.

his death[g], was forbidden.   Δύο ἀδελφὰς ἄγεσθαι τὸν αὐτὸν οὐκ
ἐπίτρεπει, οὔτ᾽ ἐν τῷ αὐτῷ, οὔτ᾽ ἐν διαφέρουσι χρόνοις, κἂν τύχῃ τις
ἣν προέγημεν ἀπεωσμένος[h].

It remains, then, that the name of ἀδελφὸς among the
Jews might be applied indifferently to the relation of brother, or to the relation of cousin.   Hence, it may be so applied, Matt. xiii. 55. and Mark vi. 3 ; that is, some of the
persons, there mentioned by name, may be strictly the brethren, and the rest may be merely the cousins, of our Lord.
But how are we to discriminate them asunder ? I observe
that the two first are called James and Joses—the two last
Simon and Jude, or Jude and Simon.   I observe also, and
it appears to me a critical coincidence, that Mary, the ἀδελφὴ
or cousin of the Virgin, who is called, Mark xvi. 1. and
Luke xxiv. 10. Mary the mother of *James*, is called, Matt.
xxvii. 56. and Mark xv. 40. 47. Mary the mother of *James*
and *Joses*.   It is an obvious and natural inference that this
James and this Joses, who are here described as the children of Mary, are the same James and the same Joses, who
were described above, Matt. xiii. 55. Mark vi. 3. as among
the ἀδελφοὶ of our Lord.   I observe also, that Mary is never
called the mother of Simon and Jude—or of Jude and Simon—and, therefore, I cannot assume that these were her
children also.   One of our Saviour's Apostles, besides Judas
Iscariot, was certainly called Jude[i], the same who, Matt.
x. 3. Mark iii. 18. is also called Lebbæus, or Thaddæus ;
and whom Luke vi. 16: Acts i. 13. twice describe by a certain relation to James, which his own Epistle, Jude 1. proves
to be rightly pronounced the relation of brother.   This
Jude, then, as well as James, must have been a son of Alphæus ; but this Jude is never called, like James, a son of
Mary, or consequently a brother, in any sense, of our Lord.
I infer, then, that he was no such son of Mary, though he
might be the son of Alphæus ; and I assign thereby a reason which no commentator, as far as I know, has yet been
able satisfactorily to do, why he should call himself, the

g Jos. Ant. Jud. xvii. xiii. 1.   h Philo Jud. de Legibus Special. 780.
i John xiv. 22.   Luke vi. 16.   Acts i. 13.

brother of James, but not the brother of Christ. Alphæus, whosoever he was, was married to two wives—one, the mother of Jude the Apostle—the other, Mary, the cousin of the Virgin, and mother of James and Joses, and, consequently, ἀδελφοὶ of Christ.

That Alphæus was no uncommon name, among the Jews, may be collected from Mark ii. 14. where Levi is called the son of Alphæus—unless, what is not probable, this Levi also (in other words, St. Matthew the Apostle) was the brother of James and Jude. Hence, if Alphæus is not another name for Cleopas, which also Luke vi. 15. compared with xxiv. 18. shews not to be probable, at the time of our Lord's crucifixion, when, John xix. 25. this Mary is called the wife of Cleopas, Alphæus was dead, and Mary also had been twice married; once to Alphæus, and again to Cleopas. Nor is it unlikely that the marriage at Cana in Galilee, John ii. 1. only three years before xix. 25. was this very marriage of Cleopas and Mary; especially if Mary was the sister or cousin of the Virgin, and Cleopas the brother or cousin of Joseph; for both our Lord and his mother were present at it—which proves it was the marriage of relations —and St. John, who alone mentions this marriage, mentions also alone the consequent relation of Mary to Cleopas.

If now Mary, the mother of James and Joses, was married to Alphæus about the same time when Mary the Virgin was espoused to Joseph, the Apostle James would be about the same age with our Saviour—as we may presume all or most of his Apostles were, at the time when he entered on his ministry. Nor is there any reason to suppose the Apostle Jude would be much older or much younger than James. It will follow, however, that this Jude, the brother of James, the Disciple and Apostle of our Lord, as well as he, is a different person from Jude, who is mentioned along with Simon, as one of the other two ἀδελφοὶ or brethren of Christ. He could not be one of that number, and not a son of Mary, the cousin of the Virgin, and yet a believer in, and an Apostle of, Christ. For the same reason, neither can the other, Simon, be the same with that

Simon, also an Apostle, who is denominated in every catalogue of the Apostles, as Simon the Cananite, or Simon
the Zealot—and both these conclusions, I think, may be
further confirmed as follows.

I. 1 Cor. ix. 5. the ἀδελφοὶ τοῦ Κυρίου are spoken of there,
either among, or distinct from, the λοιποὶ ἀπόστολοι—yet as
Evangelists of Christianity, and as married men. Now,
none of the Apostles, except James, the first Bishop of Jerusalem, is ever spoken of, or described, as a brother of the
Lord: and, concerning this James, the following facts are
almost certain[k], first, that he was not a married man; secondly, that if he had been, he could not have led about a
wife, a sister—he was always stationary at Jerusalem—and
this, we have seen, was eminently true of the time (A. U.
808—A. U. 809.) when the First to the Corinthians was
written, and St. Paul came up to Jerusalem. As St. Paul,
however, in the passage above recited, leads to the inference
that the ἀδελφοὶ τοῦ Κυρίου, one or more, were married men,
so does Eusebius, on the authority of Hegesippus[l], confirm
the inference; shewing that there were persons, πρὸς γένους
κατὰ σάρκα τοῦ Κυρίου, still alive after the destruction of Jerusalem—and descendants of Judas in particular, τοῦ κατὰ
σάρκα λεγομένου αὐτοῦ ἀδελφοῦ—in the reign of Domitian—
and down to the time of Trajan—which descendants he
specifies as his υἱωνοὺς, or grandchildren. The persecution of
the Christians by Domitian Eusebius places in the fifteenth
year of his reign[m]; and Dio Cassius[n] so far confirms Eusebius as to place the death of Flavius Clemens, at that time
consul, on the charge ἀθεότητος, (who is believed to have suffered as a Christian,) in the year of the City 848. or A. D.
95. the last year but one of Domitian. It is manifestly
possible, if Jude was married before A. U. 808. A. D. 55.
that he might have grandchildren arrived at man's estate,
A. D. 95. forty years afterwards.

II. It is affirmed on the authority of the same Hegesippus, in the places of Eusebius above referred to, that the

[k] Eus. E. H. ii. 23. iii. 11. Ib. 19. 20. 32. Vide also Rel. Sacræ.
ii. 120. 121. Africani Epist. ad Aristidem. [m] iii. 18. [n] lxvii. 14.

second Bishop of Jerusalem, appointed upon the death of James, and on the return of the Church, after the Jewish war, was Symeon—which is the same name with Simon—which Symeon suffered by martyrdom in the reign of Trajan, and ἐπὶ ὑπατικοῦ 'Αττικοῦ, that is, before a consular president, Atticus—at one hundred and twenty years old.   It is true that Eusebius calls him, (and so does Hegesippus, if he has been quoted rightly,) the son of Cleopas.   But to this tradition, I think, we are entitled to pay no attention; for Eusebius speaks of Mary also, as the daughter of Cleopas—understanding John xix. 25. ἡ τοῦ Κλωπᾶ, with the ellipsis not of γυνή, but of θυγάτηρ.   There is no proof from Scripture that Cleopas had any children, much less any son who was called Simon.

The time of the martyrdom of Symeon is placed by Eusebius in Chronico, in the tenth of Trajan, A. U. 860. and A. D. 107. in which case Symeon must have been born A. U. 740. or B. C. 14.   But if Cleopas was the brother of Joseph, he would probably be almost as old as Joseph, at the time of the birth of Christ: in which case, though he might have a son fourteen years old A. D. 1. it is not likely he would have married again, A. D. 27. or even that he would then be alive, any more than Joseph.   It is much more probable that Symeon, the second Bishop of Jerusalem, was Simon, the brother of Jude and son of Joseph and Mary, one of the two brethren of our Lord, but falsely reputed the son of Cleopas.   The appointment of Simon, if he also was the brother of our Lord, to be the second Bishop of Jerusalem, was just as natural as the appointment of James, both on that account, and because he was an Apostle, to be the first.

And with respect to the time of his death, I do not see on what grounds Eusebius has referred it to the tenth of Trajan. The language of Hegesippus would imply, that he suffered ἐπὶ Τραϊάνου Καίσαρος, καὶ ἐπὶ ὑπατικοῦ 'Αττικοῦ—that is, before Trajan and Atticus in conjunction—and it is clear that he suffered in Palestine, or somewhere else on the spot. It would follow, then, that he suffered at some time when

Trajan was in the east, for the determination of which time
I might be content to refer implicitly to Eckel[o], who proves
that the Emperor Trajan was once only in the east, and
that upon his Armenian, Parthian, or other, expeditions
in those quarters. The year of his reign when he set out
upon them may be presumptively collected from Dio.

For, first, Licinius Sura was dead before the expedition[p]; and Licinius Sura was not dead before the tenth of
Trajan, in which year he was consul. The same thing appears to be implied of Sosius and Palma also[q]; the latter of
whom, when last mentioned[r], was mentioned as governor of
Syria. This would make the expedition later not only than
the tenth of Trajan, when Sosius was consul, but also than
the twelfth, when Palma was consul.

Secondly, after the commencement of the expedition,
there was one campaign, the same year, in Armenia; another, the next year, in Parthia; a third, after them both,
in Arabia; which third coincided with the nineteenth of
Trajan, A. U. 869.[s] the last but one of his reign. On this
principle, the first year of these wars, and, consequently,
either the year of Trajan's arrival in the east, or the year
after that at the latest, must have been A. U. 867. the
seventeenth of his reign.

It is in unison with this conclusion, that he was wintering at Antioch, after one year's campaign, preparatory to
taking the field again, in the next, when the great earthquake happened there[t]. The time of the earthquake is
ascertained by the death of Pedo, one of the sufferers from
it, and consul ἐπώνυμος at the time, A.U. 868—at the beginning of the eighteenth year of his reign. John Malala
places the earthquake December 13. Ærse Antiochenæ
164[u]; which, if deduced from the epoch of A. U. 705.
would be December 13. A. U. 868—at the end, not at the
beginning, of the eighteenth of the reigning Emperor. At
the same time, according to this historian, Trajan had been
two years in the east; which would place his arrival A. U.

[o] vi. 451—454.   [p] lxviii. 15.   [q] Ib. 16.   [r] Ib. 14.   [s] Ib. 17. 18.
24. 26. 31. 32.   [t] Ib. 24. 25.   [u] Lib. xi. 358.

816. But Malala's authority is not equal to that of Dio; according to whom, if there was one campaign of Trajan's, A. U. 867. another, A. U. 868. a third, A. U. 869. and a fourth, A. U. 870. in the midst of which Trajan was surprised by death, and the campaign in A. U. 868. was posterior to the earthquake, when Pedo was consul, and killed by it, the earthquake could not have happened before the first of January, A. U. 868. at least. And it is possible it might actually happen on the thirteenth of January, A. U. 868. and not on the thirteenth of December, A. U. 867. or 868.

If Symeon, then, was put to death, ἐπὶ Τραϊάνου as well as ἐπὶ 'Αττικοῦ, he could not have been put to death before the eighteenth of Trajan, at the earliest. If Atticus was governor of Syria at the time *, the tenth year of Trajan, at least, seems to be out of the question. For Palma, not Atticus, was certainly president of that province A. U. 858. the eighth of Trajan ᵛ; and the context of Dio ʷ would imply that he was still president in the tenth, at the close of the Dacian war, and later than that, at the time of the death of Sura, which could not well be earlier than the eleventh. Had Symeon, then, suffered in the tenth of Trajan, and before a Roman president of Syria, it would have been ἐπὶ Πάλμου, not ἐπὶ 'Αττικοῦ.

But the testimony of Hegesippus at the same time describes this Atticus, as ὑπατικὸν, one who was of consular dignity, and, therefore, had been consul. The Fasti Consulares exhibit no Atticus as consul before A. U. 896. the sixth of Antoninus Pius : and that was Herodes Atticus, the son of this Atticus, and the contemporary and friend of

---

* It is true that, in Spartian's Life of Hadrian, (Casauboni et Variorum i. 43.) Hadrian is spoken of as legate of Syria, at the time of the death of Trajan : iii. id. August—but this was almost two years after the time when he was wintering at Antioch. Nor does it appear that Hadrian was then in Syria, as the regular governor ; but only as commander of the forces instead of Trajan. Dio, lxviii. 33.

     ᵛ Eckel vi. 418.   ʷ lxviii. 14. 15.

Aulus Gellius [x]. We have the authority, however, of Suidas and of Philostratus, for knowing that Atticus the father was twice consul, and, by virtue of his consular dignity, sometime governor of Asia [y]. The same biographer informs us that he acquired the wealth, which laid the foundation of his future dignity, in the reign of Nerva, and that he was governor of Asia in the reign of Hadrian. His first consulate, then, might fall in the reign of Trajan; but it would fall, probably, late in that reign, rather than early [*]; and if we were to conjecture that he might be consul suffectus in the room of Pedo, A. U. 868. it would not be an extraordinary supposition.

The next year, also, which would be the nineteenth of Trajan, the rebellion of the Jews, in Cyrene, Cyprus, and Egypt, broke out [z]; the connection of which event, as well as of the earthquake, just before, with the persecution in which Symeon suffered, is very probably implied in the account which Eusebius has left of it. For, first, the persecution was not general, but μερικῶς καὶ κατὰ πόλεις, ἐξ ἐπανα-

---

* It appears from the same passage of Philostratus, that Herodes Atticus the younger was a young man (probably not less than twenty) at this time, when his father was governor of the free cities in Asia. Herodes Atticus died at seventy-six years of age, (Vita xv.) and he was not yet dead when the Emperor Marcus Aurelius visited Athens, for the purpose of being initiated in the Eleusinian mysteries. (Vita xii.) This visit, it appears from Philostratus, (Vita Hadriani, iv.) was later, at least, than the consulate of a certain Severus, most probably M. Aurelius Severus, consul A. U. 926: and by Eckel (vii. 63.) it is placed in the consulate of Pollio and Aper, A. U. 929. Vide also Dio, lxxi. 31. Let us suppose Herodes Atticus died at, or about, seventy-six years of age, A. U. 929. He was born, on this principle, A. U. 853. in the third of Trajan: and he would be about twenty, A. U. 873. the fourth of Hadrian. At this time his father was governor of Asia: and ὑπατικός.

---

[x] Noctes Atticæ. i. 2. ix. 2. xviii. 10. xix. 12.   [y] Suidas. Ἡρώδης Ἀττικός. Philostrat. Vit. Sophist. lib. ii. Herodes. 3. lib. i. Polemo. 6. Scopelianus. 6. 7. Nicetes. 4. 2.   [z] Dio. lxviii. 32. Euseb. H. E. iv. 2. Appian. B. C. ii. 90.

κ 2

στάσεως δήμων—the moving cause to which was commonly
some national calamity, as a drought, a famine, or an earthquake; all which the populace were accustomed to lay to
the charge of the ἄθεοι, that is, the Christians.   Secondly,
Symeon was denounced as one of the posterity of David, an
accusation, which the rebellion of the Jews was most likely
to have suggested, and to have rendered dangerous.

The contest does not appear to have lasted more than one
year; and we are told by Dio, *loco citato*, that Lusius, the
commander of the Roman forces, was made governor of
Palestine, in return for his services in the war.   The government of Palestine, then, was probably conferred upon
him in the twentieth of Trajan, A. U. 870: whence, if Symeon was put to death in Palestine, and ἐπὶ 'Αττικοῦ, not ἐπὶ
Λουσίου, he could not have been put to death as not earlier
than the eighteenth of Trajan on the one hand, so neither
later than the twentieth, on the other; the inference from
which is that he was probably put to death in the nineteenth itself.   In this case he was put to death A. U. 869.
A. D. 116; and, therefore, if he was a son of Joseph and
Mary, born after the birth of Christ indeed, but two or
three years before the vulgar era, he might be actually one
hundred and nineteen years old at his death; which, in
round numbers, would easily be called one hundred and
twenty.

III. St. Luke's mention of the name of Simon [a], καὶ Σίμωνα τὸν καλούμενον Ζηλωτὴν, is not exactly to the same effect with that of St. Matthew, Σίμων ὁ Κανανίτης, or that of
St. Mark [a], Σίμωνα τὸν Κανανίτην—that is, there would be no
reason to infer from either of the latter that he was called
Simon the Cananite, as there is, to infer from the former
that he was called Simon the Zealot.   It is commonly believed, indeed, that Simon the Zealot is an equivalent designation to Simon the Cananite.   But this does not appear
to me to be the case.   For in the first place, the Hebrew
root קנא, *zelotypus fuit*, can be no where shewn to have

---

[a] vi. 15.   [a] Matt. x. 4.   Mark iii. 18.

given birth to any such verbal derivative, as קנאן or קנן, from which only Κανανίτης, as equivalent to Ζηλωτὴς, could be transferred into Greek. Secondly, Κανανίτης, or Canan-ite, would be as regularly formed from Κανὰν, or Canan, as Canaanite from Canaan, Horonite from Horon, Canite from Cana, Gaulonite from Gaulon, or the like—all which are nomina *gentilitia*, derived from the names of countries or places, to express the inhabitants or the natives thereof.

Thirdly, There is proof in Strabo that Canan was the name of a certain village, which might be a village of Ju-dæa, and was certainly some village in the east. Speaking of the illustrious men whom Tarsus had produced, he men-tions two philosophers of the name of Athenodorus; one of whom was a contemporary, and preceptor or tutor, of Au-gustus Cæsar; whom he calls the son τοῦ Σάνδωνος, ὃν καὶ Κανανίτην φασὶν ἀπὸ κώμης τινός [b]. This name of Sando, the father of Athenodorus, is evidently not a Greek one—like the name of his son—and Canan, the name of his native village, is still less like the name of a Grecian settlement : not to mention that such Grecian settlements, at least in the east, are commonly known and described as πόλεις, not as κῶμαι. The fact, however, that, either in the neighbour-hood of Tarsus, or in some of the adjacent countries, there was at this time a village, from the name of which Κανανί-της would be regularly derived, and which must, conse-quently, have been called Κανὰν, is placed by this testi-mony beyond a question. I should conjecture that it was either in Phœnicia, or in Judæa, and that Sando, though born there, had afterwards migrated to Tarsus. Simon the Cananite is a designation absolutely identical with Sando the Cananite; and if the latter is taken from the name of this village, the former, it is reasonable to suppose, is taken either from the same, or from another, which bore the same name.

Fourthly, The appellation of Cananite, as equivalent to Zealot, if it was bestowed upon Simon before his ordination

[b] xiv. 961. Dio. lvi. 43.

κ 3

as an Apostle, or relates to any circumstance in his history, prior to that event, would imply that he either was, or had been, a Zealot—which as a term of distinction denotes a follower of Judas of Galilee—the founder of the sect of the Zealots.　Now the followers of Judas of Galilee, and, consequently, the sect which he had just founded, if we may believe the assurance of Gamaliel in the Acts[c], had been extinguished as soon as they appeared ; and, at the time of that deliberation in the Acts, were notoriously dispersed and scattered.　It follows, therefore, that no disciple of our Lord, at the time of his ordination to be an Apostle, whatever might have been his previous history, could still be known and described as *the Zealot*—that is, as a follower of Judas of Galilee.　And if, notwithstanding what he had once been, he was actually no longer such, it would have been not merely an erroneous, but even an unjust and disparaging, manner of describing him, still to represent him as the Zealot.　The name of Zealot was identified from the very first with faction and turbulence—and in the course of time with hypocrisy, violence, and wickedness, exceeding the measure of human.

Besides which, it is reasonable to suppose that all our Lord's Apostles, at the time of their ordination, were in the flower of their age, or neither much younger, nor much older, than himself, who was then in his thirty-second year. The insurrection of Judas of Galilee was produced by the census of Quirinius, A. U. 760. in the eleventh year of our Saviour's age ; and if his followers consisted of men, Simon the Zealot, who could not have been less than thirty, when our Lord was ten years old, would not be less than fifty when our Lord was thirty ; and at the age of fifty, the age when St. Paul or St. Peter were arriving at the close of their Apostolic career itself, he was surely too old to have been ordained one of our Lord's Apostles.

The name of Zealot, then, which is found only in St. Luke, applies to his subsequent history, and to something in his character as an Apostle, which the modesty of St.

Matthew, himself an Apostle, and in consequence of the silence of St. Matthew, which St. Mark also, did not think proper to mention; but which St. Luke might very fitly allude to. The name of Cananite, therefore, may still have been the name of his native place; in which case, his individual distinctness from any brother of our Lord follows as matter of course. Nor is it an unlikely circumstance that, though the son of Galilean parents, he was born by accident at Canan; Canan itself not being any village of Judæa. In this case, all the rest of our Lord's Apostles being Galileans, it might be necessary, for the sake of distinction, to specify the contrary of him.

Hippolytus, περὶ τῶν ιβ΄. ἀποστόλων [d], asserts that Simon the Cananite, whom also he calls the son of Cleopas, was the next Bishop of Jerusalem after James the Just; and that he died at the age of one hundred and twenty. By the Chronicon Paschale[e], his death is placed in the consulate of Syrianus, or Suburanus, and Marcellus, which answers to A. U. 857. or the seventh of Trajan. The same Chronicon makes him a martyr; but Hippolytus, as before quoted, implies that he died a natural death: and there are other circumstances of difference between them, which prove that the Chronicon did not borrow the tradition from Hippolytus: for it calls this Simon the son of James, not of Cleopas; and speaks of the martyrdom of Simon the son of Cleopas, under the next year.

It is manifest, then, that either in these traditions Simon the Cananite, and Simon, the reputed son of Cleopas, with their respective personal history, are strangely confounded together, or it must have been the case, and tradition have some way or other perpetuated it, that they were each of them Bishops of Jerusalem—each after James—and each died at the age of one hundred and twenty—under the reign of Trajan. There is no impossibility in these suppositions, if we assume only that Simon the Cananite first succeeded to James the Just, and then Simon, the reputed

[d] Oper. i. Appendix. 30.   [e] 252.

κ 4

son of Cleopas, to him : and that the former died in the
seventh, the latter suffered martyrdom in the eighteenth or
nineteenth, of Trajan. Simon the Cananite might have been
born A. U. 738. or 739 ; in which case he might be said to
be one hundred and twenty years old, A. U. 857 : and
Simon, the reputed son of Cleopas, A. U. 751. or 752—in
which case he might be called of the same age, A.U. 868. or
869. Nor is it impossible that Simon the Cananite might be a
son of Cleopas; and that this circumstance may have caused
the other Simon to be considered so likewise.   If Cleopas
was the brother of Joseph, and Joseph was past the prime
of life at the time of the birth of our Saviour, Cleopas
might be so too; and therefore it would be nothing incredible that he should then have a son, nor that that son
should be nine or ten years old.   Moreover, Simon the
Cananite might actually have died in the tenth of Trajan,
A. U. 760 : and Simon, the reputed son of Cleopas, not
until his eighteenth or nineteenth ; which would so far account for the confusion respecting that fact also.   In this
case, Simon the Cananite would have been born A. U. 740 :
and been ten years older than our Lord.

These points, then, being presumptively established, I
shall conclude with observing that those, who are called,
Matt. xiii. 56. Mark vi. 3. the sisters of our Lord, may
have been either his sisters, or merely his cousins, as
they were the children of Mary the Virgin, or of Mary the
mother of James.   But I incline to the latter supposition—
because, at the time of this visit to Nazareth, these ἀδελφαὶ
are all said to have been *there*, that is, living there—but no
such thing is implied of the ἀδελφοὶ also—and in fact, they
who are called by this name, Mark iii. 21. and iii. 31. only
a day or two before this visit, are seen to have been in
Capernaum—and if we compare John vii. 3. the scene of
which is Capernaum, were actually settled there, and the
mother of our Lord was living with them.   I consider this,
then, a strong proof of the distinctness of families ; that
those who are called the ἀδελφοὶ of our Lord, with his
mother, were living in Capernaum, at the very time when

those, who are called his ἀδελφαὶ, were living without her at Nazareth. And it is in unison with this distinctness that, John ii. 12. though our Lord, his mother, and his brethren, are all said to have gone down to Capernaum, his sisters are not. Mary the wife of Cleopas, and her husband, might possibly be inhabitants of Nazareth : the latter in particular, if he was a kinsman of Joseph, might even be a native of it. His wife, on the contrary, before her marriage with him, might have been a native, or an inhabitant, of Cana ; and that might be the reason why, though Cleopas lived at Nazareth, their marriage was celebrated there. It was the custom of the Jews to celebrate a marriage among, and with, rather the friends of the female, than those of the male.

DISSERTATION IV.

On the visit of the Magi.

OF the questions connected with this visit, and properly concerning a Harmony—the time of the appearance of the star—and the time of the arrival of the Magi—the latter is to be determined principally by the help of the former: with respect to which, it is possible to establish a maximum—that is, to shew before what time the star could not have appeared—if not a minimum; or the very time when it actually appeared. In order to this, we must reason as follows.

When the Magi were come to Jerusalem, Herod, having privately sent for them, ἠκρίβωσε παρ᾽ αὐτῶν τὸν χρόνον τοῦ φαινομένου ἀστέρος [a]; the answer to which enquiry would ascertain this time, or shew how long before their arrival the star had first been seen. Upon this information he proceeded in limiting the age of the children: it was, κατὰ τὸν χρόνον ὃν ἠκρίβωσε παρὰ τῶν Μάγων [b]. The age of the children, therefore, had a certain relation to what we may call the age of the star; and, if the former could once be determined in either of its extreme limits, the latter would so far be determined also.

St. Matthew has defined this age by ἀπὸ διετοῦς καὶ κατωτέρω [c]. The order was limited to children of two years old and under; that is, it was limited at one extreme, but not at the other; a child above two years old would be exempted from it, a child of two years old, or of any age less than that, would be included in it. Now it was a maxim among the Jews, that the son of a day was the son of a year: Unus dies in anno habetur pro anno integro. The age of puberty is reckoned in a male, at thirteen years and a day, and in a female, at twelve years and a day [d]: a ram, or any other animal, was considered *bimus*, or two years

---

[a] Matt. ii. 7.   [b] Ibid. 16.   [c] ii. 16.   [d] Maim. De Best. Consec. Mutat. Annot. i. 8.

old, which was one year and thirty days old, or thirteen months old in all[e]. On this principle a child of thirteen months old would answer to the limit ἀπὸ διέτους, as well as a child of full two years. And when it is considered that the phrase ἀπὸ διέτους is used here, to fix the *beginning* of a scale of descent, and as understood in its most general, or in its most particular sense, would vary at least to the extent of ten months, it will appear only reasonable to conclude that the first age which, in the popular mode of reckoning, would correspond to the limit prescribed, must have been the age primarily and properly intended. Now this would be the age of thirteen months. Nor is the testimony of Macrobius, while it confirms the material fact, at variance with such a limitation. Cum audisset (Augustus) inter pueros, quos in Syria Herodes, rex Judæorum, intra bimatum jussit interfici, filium quoque ejus occisum, ait, Melius est Herodis porcum esse (τὸν ὖν) quam filium[f] (τὸν υἱόν.) This expression, intra bimatum, is exactly equivalent to St. Matthew's ἀπὸ διέτους καὶ κατωτέρω.

If, then, the order respecting the children was strictly framed in accordance to the information obtained about the age of the star, the utmost limit of the age of the one is the utmost limit of the age of the other; that is, if thirteen months was the utmost limit of the age of the children, the star could not have appeared more than thirteen months before the arrival of the Magi, though it might have appeared less.

The quarter whence the Magi came is not specified, except in general terms, as somewhere in the east. Justin Martyr and Tertullian suppose it to have been Arabia; but more, as it will appear on referring to the passages which contain this opinion[g], to shew the fulfilment of an alleged prophecy, than from any certain knowledge of the fact. From the time of Zoroaster downwards to the age of Christianity itself, the parts beyond the Euphrates—Persia,

---

[e] De rat. Sacrif. i. 14.   [f] Saturn. ii. 4.   [g] Just. Mart. Dial. 304. 5. Tertull. Oper. I. 217. 488.

Bactria, or Parthia—had always been the chief seats of the Magian philosophy.

Τὴν μὲν οὖν ἀληθῆ Μαγικὴν, ὀπτικὴν ἐπιστήμην οὖσαν, ᾗ τὰ φύσεως ἔργα τρανωτέραις φαντασίαις αὐγάζεται, σεμνὴν καὶ περιμάχητον δοκοῦσαν εἶναι, οὐκ ἰδιῶται μόνον, ἀλλὰ καὶ βασιλεῖς, καὶ βασιλέων οἱ μέγιστοι, καὶ μάλισθ' οἱ Περσῶν, διαπονοῦσιν οὕτως, ὥστ' οὐδένα φασὶν ἐπὶ βασιλίαν παραληφθῆναι δύναμιν παρ' αὐτοῖς, εἰ μὴ πρότερον τοῦ Μάγων γένους κεκοινηκὼς τυγχάνοι[h].

That the Magi in the present instance came, accordingly, from those regions, which are as much to the east of Judæa, as Arabia, has been uniformly the tradition of the Church[i]. Theophylact, *in loco*, observes upon the star; Ἀλλὰ καὶ ἀπὸ τοῦ βορείου μέρους, ὅ ἐστι τῆς Περσίδος, εἰς τὸ νότιον ἐκινεῖτο. But, if this was the case, the length of their journey, or the time for which they would be on the road, may presumptively be determined.

I. By Herodotus, a day's journey on foot is computed at 150 stades, and the distance from Sardis to Susa, as exactly a three months' journey[k].

II. Xenophon makes the distance from Ephesus, to Cunaxa in the plain of Babylon, a distance of 535 parasangs, which, on the usual computation of thirty stades to a parasang, and 150 stades, as according to Herodotus, to a day's journey, is a journey of 107 days, or three months, and seventeen days at least[l].

III. The march from Tarsus in Cilicia to Bactria is computed, in Diodorus Siculus, at four months for an army[m].

IV. The Jews, from beyond the Euphrates, in their annual visits to Jerusalem, had δυσβάτους, καὶ ἀτριβεῖς, καὶ ἀνηνύτους, ὁδοὺς περαιοῦσθαι[n].

V. Ἤδη δέ τινες, says Josephus, καὶ τῶν ὑπὲρ Εὐφράτην μηνῶν ὁδὸν τεσσάρων ἐλθόντες[o].

[h] Philo Jud. De Leg. Spec. 792. Vide also, Quod omnis probus liber. 876. Ἐν Πέρσαις μὲν τὸ Μάγων κ. τ. λ. Plin. H. N. xxx. 1. Origen. contra Cels. i. 19. Clem. Alex. Strom. I. 357. [i] Clem. Alex. Strom. i. 359. Irenæus. iii. 213. iii. xviii. 240. Chrys. ii. 37. [k] v. 53. [l] Anab. ii. 2. 6. [m] xiv. 20. [n] Phil. de Legatione. 1023. [o] Aut. Jud. iii. xv. 3.

VI. Tiridates, when he came to Rome, A. U. 819. in the reign of Nero, to receive the investiture of Armenia, had been nine months previously on the road P. Five of these might be taken up in travelling to Italy from Asia Minor q : the preceding four, therefore, had been taken up in arriving in Asia from Parthia.

VII. Nehemiah set out from Susa in the month Nisan ; and in three days' time after his arrival at Jerusalem, he began the rebuilding of the walls, which he had finished in fifty-two days after, by the twenty-fifth of Elul, the sixth month in the sacred year r. Consequently he could not have been less than three months, and, probably was as much as four, in travelling to Jerusalem *.

* I think it of so much importance to establish the positions, respecting the days of the week, and other points, formerly discussed in the tenth Dissertation, and its Appendix, volume i. that whatever opportunity for this purpose the course of the subject may present ought not to be let slip. The allusion to the mission of Nehemiah furnishes me with one among others, of which I shall avail myself accordingly.

The year of the mission of Nehemiah I assume as B. C. 444. In the year after that, B. C. 443. according to Pingré, the moon was eclipsed for the meridian of Jerusalem, April 4. 7. 57. in the evening. Add to this time ten days, twenty-one hours of mean time; and B. C. 444. the moon must have been at the full, April 15. 4. 57. in the evening. Let this date coincide in that year with the fifteenth of the Jewish Nisan.

Between April 15. B. C. 444. *inclusive*, and April 15. A. D. 1. *exclusive*, the interval of time, estimated by tropical days and nights, amounts to 162,167 days, fourteen hours ; or 23,166 weeks, and what may be considered six days of another week.

Now A. D. 1. the tables exhibit April 15. on Friday ; which I should consider to be on Sunday. And this would be the case, if B. C. 444. April 15. had been Monday : for then A. D. 1. April 9. would be Monday, and April 15. Sunday. I assume, then, that B. C. 444. Nisan 15. coincided with Monday.

Nehemiah vi. 15. the wall of Jerusalem was finished in fifty-

P Dio. lxiii. 2. 1.   q Herod. viii. 51.   r Neh. ii. 1. ii. 11. vi. 15.

VIII. Upon the *first* day of the *first* month, says the book of Ezra, began he to go up from Babylon, and on the *first* day of the *fifth* month, came he to Jerusalem[s].

IX. The temple was destroyed at Jerusalem on the seventh day of the fifth month; and Ezekiel heard of its destruction in the land of Chaldea, from one who had escaped, on the fifth day of the tenth month[t].

If the Magi, then, came from this part of the east, they would be four months on the road; and, therefore, if the

two days, on Elul 25. If so, it was begun upon Ab 3: for from Ab 2. *exclusive* to Elul 25. *inclusive*, the interval is just fifty-two.

Now, from Nisan 15. *exclusive* to Ab 2. *inclusive* there would be 105 days, or fifteen weeks; whence if Nisan 15. was a Monday, Ab 3. was a Tuesday; and if the walls were begun on the third of Ab, they were begun on a Tuesday. But, ii. 11. Nehemiah waited, after his arrival, three days, before he began them. This may imply that he arrived on the Friday, and began the work on the Tuesday following; for, then, he would wait only three days, though three days exactly, between. Moreover if the walls were completed in fifty-two days, or seven weeks' and three days' time, the last of the number, Elul 25. would be a Thursday, because the first, Ab 3. was a Tuesday.

On the same principle the first of Tisri, viii. 2. would be a Wednesday; and therefore the twenty-fourth would be a Friday. Now this day was a *fast*,. ix. 1. and as it would seem from x. 31. it was also some day not long .before the sabbath. One of the ordinary fast days among the later Jews is said to have been the *Thursday*; but this fast was manifestly an extraordinary one—and we may collect, perhaps, from ix. 1. 2. 3. that it was very probably a Friday. For, as the reading of the law took up one *fourth* part of the day, and confession took up another, then whether this ceremony began at the first hour of the day, or at the third, it lasted in either case six hours, but no more—and it broke off either at the sixth hour, or at. the ninth. The prayer, and the sealing of the covenant, appear to have followed directly after, and concluded the whole—all, as we may conjecture, just before the arrival of the sabbath.

---

[s] Ezra vii. 9.   [t] 2 Kings xxv. 8.   Ezek. i. 3. xxxiii. 21. 22. xxiv. 21—27. Zechar. viii. 19.

star had appeared thirteen months before they arrived at Jerusalem, it had appeared nine months before they set out. Hence, if they set out at the time of the birth of Christ, the star must have appeared at his incarnation.

They came to Judæa in consequence of the appearance of the star—where is the King of the Jews? for we saw his star, and are come. They came thither, after his birth—where is the King who is born? for we are come to worship him. Now the star must needs have appeared, for the first time at least, either at, or before, or after, the nativity of Christ. If it appeared *at*, or *after*—the age of the Christ, at the time of their arrival, could not have been less than thirteen months; a conclusion which would involve the Gospel Chronology in insuperable difficulties. But if it appeared before the nativity, there is no reason why it might not have appeared at the incarnation. The idea of an early appearance is nothing new, but as old as the time of Chrysostom[u]—and, in fact, seems to have been the traditionary opinion of the Church. Ὁ γὰρ ἀστὴρ, πρὸ τοῦ γεννηθῆναι τὸν Κύριον, ἐφάνη τοῖς Μάγοις. Ἐπεὶ γὰρ ἔμελλον πολὺν ἀναλίσκειν χρόνον κατὰ τὴν ὁδοιπορίαν, διὰ τοῦτο πρὸ πολλοῦ ἐφάνη ὁ ἀστὴρ, ὡς ἂν προσκυνήσωσιν αὐτὸν ἔτι ἐν τοῖς σπαργάνοις ὄντα[v].

I consider it unnecessary to enter on the question what the star itself might be. It was manifestly something preternatural, and yet might be truly a luminous appearance, in the form of a star. But, whatsoever it was, we can scarcely doubt whether the Magi were aware of its meaning; and still less, if it was really a luminous phenomenon, resembling a star, whether they could have divined its meaning for themselves. A star, it is true, in the symbolical language of eastern mythology, and even in the symbolical language of prophecy[w], might be the emblem of a God; these Magi also, though it is clear they could not have been Jews, might yet have been acquainted with the Jewish Scriptures, and parties in the general expectation of the Messias, which at this period had been diffused over the

---

[u] Oper. ii. 45.   [v] Theophyl. Comm. in loc.   [w] Numb. xxiv. 17. Amos v. 26. Isaiah xiv. 12.

East. This, however, must always be an uncertain point; though Origen[x] supposes them possessed of the prophecies of Balaam, and Theophylact goes even further than that: Λέγουσι τούτους τοὺς Μάγους τοῦ Βαλαὰμ ἀπογόνους εἶναι τοῦ μάντεως· εὑρόντας δὲ τὸν ἐκείνου χρησμὸν, τό· ἀνατελεῖ ἄστρον ἐξ Ἰακώβ· νοῆσαι τὸ κατὰ Χριστὸν μυστήριον, καὶ διὰ τοῦτο ἐλθεῖν, θέλοντας ἰδεῖν τὸ τεχθέν. From *their* part in the transaction, it seems much more clear that they acted throughout as instruments. They knew, from some assurance or other, before their arrival, that the Christ had actually been born, but they did not know where: they came to Jerusalem, in the expectation of finding, or of hearing of, him there; but they did not go to Bethlehem, until they were sent. They came, therefore, with a full conviction of the fact of the birth of the Messias in general, but with an entire ignorance, as yet, of all its circumstances. It is most reasonable, then, to conclude, that they were directed throughout by an express command from God: nor is a special revelation more incompatible with the beginning, than with the course, of the same transaction. They were supernaturally assisted in their researches after the Christ, and they were supernaturally admonished what to do when they had found him: it is not less credible that they were supernaturally instructed in the meaning of the star at first. In this case, though it had appeared at the Incarnation, they would not set out until the birth.

But the truth appears to me to be this. The star, which had been seen first at the Incarnation, was seen again at the birth, of Christ; in the former instance to announce the beginning of this great mystery, in the latter to announce its consummation; the one, consequently, thirteen months, the other, four, before the time of their arrival at Jerusalem. No supposition is better adapted to explain the peculiarity of Herod's order, why the age of the children was not to exceed thirteen months, but might be any thing below that. He enquired about the age of the star solely with a view to the age of the Christ; and if the star had appeared once thirteen months, and a second time four months, before the arrival of the Magi, he would not be able to determine which intimated the real age of the Christ; and, therefore, by way of precaution, and little solicitous how many more innocent victims might be sacrificed to his cruel policy, he would naturally so frame his order as to take in children of every age, beginning from thirteen months old, indiscriminately.

Every special dispensation of Providence must have a special purpose in view, and that, an adequate and satisfactory purpose. In this visit and adoration of the Magi, the unanimous concurrence of the Christian world has long since discovered the first distinct intimation of that great mystery or secret, the communication of Gospel privileges to the Gentiles. Regarded in this point of view, the advent of these strangers from the East becomes wonderfully ennobled; they are no longer simple individuals, but the first fruits of the Gentile Church; the manifestation of Christ to them is the manifestation of a Redeemer; the adoration which they pay him is not mere homage, but religious worship. Nor is it less observable, that in all their leading steps, the economy of divine grace with respect to the Gentiles, and the economy of the same grace with respect to the Jews, run parallel together. An angel announces the Incarnation to the Virgin, and a star, whose message is as intelligible as that of an angel, announces it to the Gentiles: a similar angelic vision apprizes the shepherds, and a second appearance of the star apprizes the Magi, of the birth of the Christ: he is presented in the temple, and so far manifested to the Jews first; but he is made known to the Magi, and so far revealed to the Gentiles also, directly after: he is preached to the Jews, for a certain time, by his Apostles, exclusively; at the end of this time he is preached also to the Gentiles; until at last, when every distinction had been levelled, both the Jew and the Gentile are made one, in the unity of a common faith in Christ.

I shall conclude, then, with one more remark. The case of Ezra, in particular, among the other instances cited above, proves it to have been possible that a person, setting out from the parts beyond the Euphrates, on a certain day in the *first* month, might arrive at Jerusalem exactly on the same day in the *fifth* month, of the Jewish year. Hence if the Magi set out on the tenth of Nisan, A. U. 750. they might arrive in Jerusalem on the tenth of Lous, or Ab, the fifth month, afterwards. The tenth of Nisan, in that year, as I have abundantly proved elsewhere[z], coincided with April 6; and, consequently, the tenth of Ab would coincide with August 2. April 6. in that year, was a Sunday, and August 2. was a Saturday. We may consider it probable, that in one week's time after this, consequently about August 9. or 10. the holy family would set out for Egypt; where they would, perhaps, arrive at the place of their abode, August 25. or 26. From this time to March 31. the date of the next Passover, the included term of days is as nearly as possible 215 in all. Vide vol. i. Dissertation x. page 338. 339. note.

[z] Vol. i. Diss. x.

DISSERTATION V.

On the ministry of John the Baptist.

OF the two questions, which naturally belong to the consideration of this subject, first, the question of the entire duration of the ministry of John—and secondly, that of the order or distribution of its parts—the former has been in a great measure anticipated. The entire duration of the ministry of John was necessarily comprehended between the feast of Tabernacles, when we supposed it to have begun, and the day of his imprisonment—both in the thirteenth year of Tiberius Cæsar.

The precise day of the imprisonment of the Baptist may justly be regarded as unknown, and as likely always to be so; yet we have seen sufficient reason to believe that it must have fallen out sometime before the midsummer of A. U. 780. in the last half of Tiberius' thirteenth[a]; and it may be shewn hereafter[b] that, whensoever it fell, it fell on some day between the Passover, John ii. 13. and the feast of Pentecost, next after that; which being the case, even the day itself may not improbably be conjectured.

The ministry of John being entirely preparatory to the ministry of Jesus Christ, the close of the one is either virtually or actually the commencement of the other; and, conversely, the commencement of the one determines either virtually or actually the close of the other. Now the ministry of Jesus Christ had a twofold commencement—once in Judæa, at the Passover, John ii. 13. before the imprisonment of John, and again in Galilee, after it; at the former of which the ministry of John was over virtually, and at the latter, it was over actually. Answerable to this twofold beginning, the ministry of Christ had a twofold conclusion

[a] Vol. i. Diss. viii. Appendix.　　　　[b] Dissert. vii.

L 2

also—one, at the Passover in the sixteenth of Tiberius, when he suffered—and another, on the day of the ascension, before which he was not finally removed into heaven. The interval between these two, which was a period of forty-one days, was similarly employed, according to St. Luke, with the whole course of his ministry preceding ; viz. in shewing himself to the Apostles, and telling them of the things which concerned the kingdom of God[c]: and, consequently, though the personal ministry of Christ, after his death and resurrection, until his reception into heaven, might be strictly confined to his own disciples, and no longer transacted in public, yet, as regards this one particular, the preparation for the future dispensation of the Gospel, which had always been its object before—it must be considered as the same in kind still.

Between the first beginning and the first termination of his ministry, there was an interval of exactly three years—and between the second beginning and the second termination, if they both coincided with ascension-day, there would be the same. Now this duration of the ministry of Christ, from whatever point of time we deduce its commencement, seems to have been a necessary consequence, in order to the fulfilment of prophecy. If, then, it was finally and properly closed on the day of the ascension, in the sixteenth of Tiberius, A. U. 783. we may infer that it finally and properly began at the same time, in his thirteenth, A. U. 780. But it did not finally and properly begin, except after the imprisonment of John. I advance it, therefore, as a probable conjecture, that the day of the imprisonment of John, A. U. 780. was the same day in that year, on which our Saviour ascended into heaven three years after, A. U. 783. This is, in each case, about the forty-first day from the fourteenth of the Jewish Nisan. The entire duration of his ministry must be determined accordingly ; and if we date its commencement from the feast of Tabernacles preceding, it would occupy about seven months in all. On this point, however, something more will be said hereafter.

[c] Acts i. 3.

The second question, or that which concerns the order and distribution of the parts of the ministry of John, supposes the whole to have been directed to more than one purpose—and the separate discharge of its functions in general to have begun at different periods: and as this appears to me to be the truth of the case, I shall enter upon its consideration somewhat at large.

With this view I observe that, if the ministry of John the Baptist was really subservient to distinct offices, both what these were, and in what they differed from each other, is presumptively to be collected from what the accounts of this ministry describe him to have done; and the presumption is so far confirmed by the matter of fact, that, little as each of the Evangelists in particular has recorded of it, that little is substantially the same in all, and furnishes the evidence of more than one effect, and, consequently, of more than one purpose, of his mission; which, whether they could be discharged at the same time, or not, were manifestly distinct in kind.

I. One, and the first, character, upon the public assumption of his ministerial office, in which they represent him, is the character of a κῆρυξ τοῦ εὐαγγελίου; that is, of a herald, or proclaimer, of the tidings of the kingdom, accompanied by the conditions of faith, that is, belief in the tidings, and of repentance, or reform of life, as a consequence of the belief.   In those days cometh John the Baptist, κηρύσσων, proclaiming, in the wilderness of Judæa, and saying, Repent ye ; for the kingdom of heaven is at hand.   Matt. iii. 1. 2.

II. His next character is the character of a baptizer. Then began to go forth unto him Jerusalem, and all the land of Judæa, and all the country round about the Jordan, and were baptized by him in the Jordan, confessing their sins.   Matt. iii. 5. 6.

III. Another, and a third, character is that of a teacher of morals, as well as of a preacher of the kingdom: nor is it any objection that his moral instructions are represented as conveyed not in long or set discourses, but in short and familiar rules of duty, applicable to the parties addressed, and easily retained in mind.   Luke iii. 10—14.

IV. A fourth, and the last, character is that of a harbinger of the Messias, or of one commissioned to bear express testimony to the approaching advent of the Christ. And he proclaimed, (ἐκήρυξε,) saying, There is coming after me He who is mightier than I ; the thong of whose shoes I am not worthy to stoop and unloose.   I, indeed, have baptized you in water, but he shall baptize you in the Holy Ghost.   Mark i. 7. 8.

Besides these characters we meet with no more; and of these, the first and the last alone are really distinct ; the intermediate two are not so much different from, as natural consequences of, the first.   The character of a preacher of repentance could not fail to include the character of a moral teacher also; and the doctrine of the kingdom, as preached by John, being accompanied by the requisition of repentance, grounded upon faith in the approach of this kingdom, baptism was administered as the sign and seal of both.   For the baptism of John was invariably either preceded, or attended, by the confession of sins ; whence, it is manifest, it was designed to attest and confirm the sincerity of the receiver's professing his belief in the prediction of the approaching kingdom, and, in the assurance of that belief, of the truth of his purpose to lead a new life.

The administration of baptism, then, without any regard to the use of this rite among the Jews, in the admission of proselytes, was a necessary part of the office of John—whether as a prophet of the kingdom, or as a teacher of morality—in which might be supposed comprehended the sum and effect of his ministry as both.   The reception of baptism at his hands was the last and most decisive step, to declare the faith of the recipient in both the message and the authority of John.   Hence it is that the final end of his mission, so far as these objects were contemplated by it, might be fitly described as simply and solely *to baptize:* that his ministry, regarded in the complex, might be called *his baptism ;* that his personal denomination, both in the

Gospels, and out of them, was John ὁ Βαπτιστής—John *the baptizer*—that St. Mark and St. Luke have each concisely expressed both his first, and his second, office, in this one description, that John came, preaching or proclaiming the baptism of repentance, unto remission of sins—and that St. Paul, in the synagogue of Pisidian Antioch, employs the same language : John having proclaimed, before the face of his entrance, baptism of repentance to all the people[d].

Now the character, in which the Baptist would first appear, it is presumptively certain, would be his true and his proper character ; a character which, whatever other he might also combine with it afterwards, he could never thenceforward lose, but must have retained to the last. This character was the character of an herald of the kingdom : and the same character, it may be shewn, is the character subsequently assumed by our Saviour. Ἀπὸ τότε, says St. Matthew, that is, from the time of the return into Galilee after the imprisonment of John, and the choice of Capernaum as the place of our Lord's abode, ἤρξατο Ἰησοῦς κηρύσσειν, καὶ λέγειν· Μετανοεῖτε· ἤγγικε γὰρ ἡ βασιλεία τῶν οὐρανῶν[e].

It was in this identical form of words, that he set forth and described just before the office and ministry of John : Repent ye, for the kingdom of heaven is at hand, was his account of the ministry of John ; Repent ye, for the kingdom of heaven is at hand, is his account of the ministry of Christ. It is the same character of the heralds or proclaimers of the gospel-tidings, in which he exhibits both ; it is the same kingdom of heaven, and as still future, or not yet come, which he makes to be announced by both ; it is the same practical inference of the necessity of repentance, and reformation of life, as grounded upon the futurity, and the belief in the futurity, of this kingdom, which he shews to have been inculcated by both. If these words, then, were a correct description of the ministry of John, they must be a correct description of the ministry of Christ; and

---

[d] Acts xiii. 24.　　　　　　　[e] iv. 17.

L 4

if they are a correct description of the ministry of either, the ministry of the other was so far the same.   It is impossible that the kingdom of heaven should mean one thing, as the subject of the preaching of John, and another, as the subject of the preaching of Christ ; or that the part and character of a herald, in relation to it, as supported by John, should not agree with the same part and character, in relation to it, as supported by Christ.   We might as well contend that the doctrine of repentance, and of amendment of life, as grounded upon it by the one, was a different thing from the same doctrine, as grounded upon it by the other.   Nor would it be less absurd to maintain that, if the kingdom of heaven means the same thing, as the subject of the preaching of either, it was future, or not yet revealed, in the time of John, but present, or actually manifested, in the time of Christ ; and not that it was equally future, though shortly to be really disclosed, at the time of the ministry of both.

Now that, in these words, St. Matthew has given us a correct and faithful, however concise a, description of the office and ministry of Christ, is to be inferred not merely from *his* authority, who having been a Disciple, and an Apostle, of Christ, and constantly in attendance upon him, could not be ignorant in what his ministry had consisted, or how he had been employed from the first—but also from the testimony of the other Evangelists, and from certain facts which, as we shall see presently, transpired in the course of his ministry itself.   St. Mark's account of the commencement of the same ministry, i. 14. which I have had occasion to quote elsewhere [d], is substantially to the same effect with St. Matthew's ; but, as fuller and more explicit, is so much the stronger an evidence on the point at issue.   With both, also, we may compare, as not many days later than either, the following text of St. Luke : To the other cities likewise must I preach the gospel of the kingdom of God ; because for this purpose am I sent [e].

[d] Vol. i. Diss. xiii. 526.   [e] iv. 43.

Now any statement of the nature, or the functions, of the ministry of Christ in general, historically premised to the account of it in detail, must, for that very reason, be received as a statement of its nature, and its functions, throughout. For we cannot suppose that it would be otherwise than consistent with itself, from first to last; or that its offices at one time would be essentially different from its offices at another. If, therefore, our Saviour appeared in the proper character of a herald, or an ambassador, of the gospeltidings, at its commencement, he would sustain the same character, and he must be still regarded as such a herald or ambassador, at its middle, and at its close. Nor is this conclusion left to presumption merely. The cardinal points in the course of his ministry, from the time of its commencement, are the several circuits which he made of Galilee: and his employment on any one of these ought, consequently, to be decisive evidence of the object of his ministry from the first. Now his employment upon them all, different as they were in themselves, and distinct as they were in their times, was one and the same; uniformly represented alike, and, on every occasion, reducible to these three heads—of preaching, or proclaiming, the kingdom; of teaching; and of working miracles—in none of which particulars, except the last, is the ministry of Christ, as we have seen, to be distinguished from that of John. The Baptist, indeed, wrought no miracles; and, if we consider for what purpose miracles were to be wrought, viz. as an evidence that he who wrought them, or in whose name they were wrought, was the expected Messias, and, consequently, after, not before, the personal manifestation of the Messias himself, John could not, perhaps, in conformity with his real character, and his proper order of time, have wrought miracles, like Christ, or like the Apostles of Christ. But, in other respects, whether as a preacher of the kingdom, or as a teacher of moral duties, he was absolutely the counterpart, and merely the forerunner, of Christ.

Again; the mission of the Twelve, which took place about the middle of our Saviour's ministry, was the mission

of helpers or coadjutors in the discharge of the functions
of his ministry itself. The reason assigned for the mission
is a clear proof of this : Seeing the multitudes, and pitying
their destitute condition, because they were as sheep, without a shepherd, he said to his Apostles : The harvest to be
gathered, truly, is plentiful ; but the gatherers of the harvest are few. Pray ye, therefore, the owner of the harvest,
to send forth labourers into his harvest [f].

It is plainly implied by these words that the work to be
performed, the business of reaping the spiritual harvest, was
too much for the individual exertions of one person, and,
therefore, required the assistance of more—but the work
itself, whether to many or to few, would still be the same.
How, then, is the object of this errand now described ?
First, in the words of the charge to the Apostles, Go and
proclaim, saying, The kingdom of heaven is at hand [g]—and
in the historical notice of St. Luke, that they were sent to
proclaim the kingdom of God [h]. Secondly, in the declaration of St. Mark, subjoined to the charge, and shewing
how the commission was fulfilled, Having gone forth, they
preached, or proclaimed, that men should repent [i]. Other
purposes there were to which, as the same authority shews,
this mission was also directed, and bringing it down still
nearer to a conformity with the ministry of Christ. For the
Apostles taught as well as he, and the Apostles wrought
miracles as well as he. But this is sufficient to prove that
the business of our Lord's personal ministry at its middle
period was still what it had been at first—and St. Matthew
tells us, that while the Twelve were thus employed in one
direction, by themselves, our Saviour was similarly employed
in another, by himself : or that all, though in different directions, were similarly employed at once [k].

Again ; about a year after this time, and, probably, not
more than two months before the last Passover, the Seventy also were sent out ; in the account of the charge to
whom, preparatory to their departure, as it is recorded by

[f] Matt. ix. 36—38.   [g] Matt. x. 7.   [h] ix. 2.   [i] vi. 12.
[k] Matt. xi. 1.

St. Luke [1], the words, Go and say, The kingdom of God is come nigh unto you, and, Be assured of this, that the kingdom of God is come nigh to you, occur twice with peculiar emphasis. The errand, then, of these Apostles was still the same with the errand of the Twelve, one year before— with the ministry of our Lord, at its commencement—and with the commission of John, from the first : viz. to preach the gospel, strictly so called—to publish the tidings of the approaching kingdom—and to inculcate the great practical duty of repentance, and of amendment of life, necessarily resulting from its expectation. The ministry of our Lord, therefore, at its beginning, at its middle, and at its end, was still the same, and still identified with the Baptist's. In all these instances, the kingdom of heaven, or of God, spoken of as something future, and actually still something future, can mean only the Gospel dispensation—the promulgation of formal Christianity—dated from the day of Pentecost, next after the death and the resurrection of Jesus Christ ; or if it does not mean that, it means absolutely nothing at all, or nothing which we could say it means.

If this, however, be the case, the mission and ministry of John, as far as they were subservient to this future dispensation, were the same in kind with the mission and ministry of our Lord himself, of the Twelve, and of the Seventy, during the lifetime of Christ : they differed in nothing except the order and succession of time : each in his own place, though a distinct place from another's, was still a harbinger in common of the same future kingdom. And this conclusion is irresistibly enforced by the fact, that our Saviour's own part and agency, in this common commission, begin with no delay upon the absolute termination of John's, but not before. No sooner was the Baptist imprisoned, and, consequently, debarred from the discharge of his proper work any longer, than our Lord steps in and supplies his place. Nothing could more clearly intimate the identical nature of their respective missions, the community of end and purpose, to which the personal ministry

[1] x. 9. 11.

of either was to be directed. For Christ, as we have seen, succeeds not merely to the place, but to the very language and proclamation, of John; which was as good as to declare that, though the agent had been changed, the thing done was not altered: the voice of the same proclamation, the dictates of the same awful warning, might still be heard; the mouth of the harbinger, the authority of the teacher only, were distinct. It was John who had pronounced them before—it was the Christ who repeated them now; it was the servant of the Messias who had begun with the command to believe and to repent, at first—it was the Lord of that servant, it was the Messias himself, who was reiterating and enforcing it after him.

I am not aware that, as far as we have yet compared them together, there was any difference between the personal ministry of John, and the personal ministry of Jesus Christ, except this—that John baptized, but Jesus Christ did not baptize. Even during the interval, short as it was, for which our Lord's ministry ran parallel with that of John, though his disciples, as the Evangelist tells us [m], might baptize, Jesus himself, he also tells us, did not: and after the commencement of his own ministry, posterior to the imprisonment of John, until the day of Pentecost, and thenceforward, we read no more of baptism, as administered even by the disciples of Christ. I think we may infer from these facts that it was at no period, in his public career, proper for our Lord himself to baptize; nor for his disciples at any period, except during the interval between the first Passover, and the final return into Galilee, (when John also was still making converts as before,) to do so in the same sense, and to the same effect, with John; that is, with water—as the sign and seal of repentance.

The reason of this difference in two offices, whose separate functions were otherwise so much the same, appears to me to have been in each instance one the reverse of the other, and consequently, very much the same also. John baptized, and with water, because he was not to baptize

[m] John iv. 2.

with the Holy Ghost; Christ did not baptize, nor with water, because he was to baptize with the Holy Ghost. The water-baptism, then, of John, was typical of the Spirit-baptism of Christ, and water, the medium of the baptism of John, was analogous to the Holy Ghost, the medium of the baptism of Christ.   So far, therefore, from introducing a real difference into the office of John, compared with the office of Christ, this distinction brings them nearer to a resemblance than before; making the Baptist so exactly the counterpart of Christ, that even that most important part in the functions of the latter, the mission and effusion of the Holy Ghost, is not without its significant prototype in the functions of the former.   And this may be one reason why the baptism of John, though, as conveyed by the same external medium, but destitute of the same inward grace, it might so far appear the appropriate emblem of Christian baptism in general, should be considered in reality no type, or similitude, of that sacrament, but only of the one baptism, once for all administered, at the day of Pentecost, by Christ himself, upon the first Christian converts, in the communication of the extraordinary graces of the Spirit—and afterwards, as often as those graces were repeated, upon all converts subsequently.

I am led to these considerations partly by the testimony of John himself, who, on a variety of occasions, so distinguishes his own baptism from some baptism of Christ's, as shews him to have had none other baptism in view, but this : I, indeed, have baptized you in water, but he shall baptize you in the Holy Ghost [n] : and, what is still more to the purpose, because it was literally fulfilled at the day of Pentecost, when the Spirit visibly descended in the likeness of tongues of fire : I, indeed, am baptizing you in water— but he shall baptize you in the Holy Ghost, and in fire [o] : partly, by the testimony of our Lord himself, who, as if expressly to remind the Apostles of the typical baptism, which they had heretofore received at the hands of John, tells them on the way to Bethany, before his ascension, John,

* Mark i. 8.   o Matt. iii. 11.   Luke iii. 16.

indeed, baptized in water, but ye shall be baptized in the
Holy Ghost, not many days hence P : a declaration, which
St. Peter afterwards applies to a case in point—the effusion
of the Spirit on Cornelius and his household, even before
they had been baptized with water q : partly, from the testimony of St. Paul, with respect to the twelve Disciples at
Ephesus : John, indeed, baptized with baptism of repentance, telling the people that they should believe upon
him who was coming after him, that is, upon Jesus, the
Christ r.   For this was to imply that John had baptized
with water, as the sign and seal of repentance, but Christ
should baptize with the Spirit, as the sign and seal of ac-
ceptance : and the event gave effect to his words ; for, as
soon as these disciples had been baptized in the name of
the Lord, and Paul had laid his hands upon them, the
Holy Ghost also was poured on them, and they spake with
tongues.   Nor is it improbable, that among the other uses
proposed by the baptism of our Lord himself, to prefigure
this future truth might be one ; for, after the water had
been poured over him by John, the Holy Ghost was poured
on him from above, and not only was poured upon him,
but rested on him, and continued with him.   And if Justin Martyr is to be believed, even a more sensible indication of the same truth was at the same time given. Καὶ τότε,
ἐλθόντος τοῦ Ἰησοῦ ἐπὶ τὸν Ἰορδάνην ποταμὸν, ἔνθα ὁ Ἰωάννης ἐβά-
πτιζε, κατελθόντος τοῦ Ἰησοῦ ἐπὶ τὸ ὕδωρ, καὶ πῦρ ἀνήφθη ἐν τῷ Ἰορ-
δάνῃ, καὶ, κ. τ. λ.s

The same tradition is said to have been contained in the
gospel according to the Ebionites t; between which, however,
and this allusion to it by Justin, there is so much of difference in the circumstances, as to prove that the latter did
not take it from the former.   But, whatever may be thought
of this fact, the baptism of John, which had just preceded,
might be typical of that spiritual unction which followed ;
and both together might concur to intimate that he, who
had received not only the thing signified but the sign, if he

P Acts i. 5.   q xi. 16.   r xix. 4.   s Dialog. 331.   t Epiph.
Oper. i. 137. 138.

baptized at all, would baptize not with water, but with the Spirit ; and, having received so plenteous, and withal so enduring, an unction, that he should baptize with the Spirit. For it was in reference to the plenteousness of that effusion, that John afterwards said to his disciples: The Father giveth not the Spirit by measure [u]——and in reference to the derived communications, bestowed on the church, from the same inexhaustible source, that the Evangelist, at the beginning of his Gospel, declared, Of his fulness have all we received, and grace in return for grace ; that is, grace imparted, in return for grace received [v].

The identity of the ministry of John, and of the ministry of Jesus Christ, in general, may be further confirmed as follows.

I. By the exordium of St. Mark's Gospel, Ἀρχὴ τοῦ εὐαγγελίου Ἰησοῦ Χριστοῦ, υἱοῦ τοῦ Θεοῦ, ὡς γέγραπται ἐν τοῖς προφήταις [w], κ. τ. λ. The beginning of the Gospel of Jesus Christ was, consequently, the beginning of the ministry of John ; and the part, subsequently discharged in the same Gospel by Jesus Christ, was similar to the part, which had been previously discharged in it by John. Nor is it possible to evade this conclusion, except by contending that τὸ εὐαγγέλιον Ἰησοῦ Χριστοῦ means here no more than the tidings of the approach and manifestation of Jesus Christ ; a sense, which, by limiting the gospel entirely to the supposed ministry of John, in this one respect, would lead to the absurd inference that Jesus Christ himself bore no part in the Gospel at all, and would contradict the writer to the Hebrews : Πῶς ἡμεῖς ἐκφευξόμεθα τηλικαύτης ἀμελήσαντες σωτηρίας; ἥτις ἀρχὴν λαβοῦσα λαλεῖσθαι διὰ τοῦ Κυρίου, ὑπὸ τῶν ἀκουσάντων εἰς ἡμᾶς ἐβεβαιώθη [x].

II. By the true drift and meaning of the reply to the question, Ἐν ποίᾳ ἐξουσίᾳ ταῦτα ποιεῖς [y]; the peculiarity of which reply consists in this, that while it appears to decline, it does, in reality, answer, the question. Our Lord, indeed, foreknew that his interrogators would not reply to his own

---

[u] John iii. 34.   [v] i. 16.   [w] i. 1.   [x] ii. 3.
[y] Matt. xxi. 23.   Mark xi. 28.   Luke xx. 2.

question—from heaven; and that they durst not reply to it—from men: he foreknew, therefore, that they would not reply to it at all; and this is the reason why he encounters their question by another. But, suppose them to have answered, what was certainly possible, that the Baptism of John was ἐξ οὐρανοῦ; then, on one implicit admission, viz. that the ministry of our Saviour also was the same in kind with the ministry of John, they would have answered their question for themselves. If John's ministry was from heaven, our Saviour's was so too: and he, who acted by a divine commission, had the clearest right to do those things.

III. By a comparison of Matt. xi. 12. 13. with Luke xvi. 16: the first of which ought to be rendered thus; From the days of John the Baptist, even until now, the kingdom of heaven is suffering violence, and violent ones are seizing on it by force: for all the Prophets, and the Law, taught until John: and the second, delivered on a different and a much later occasion, in like manner, thus; The Law and the Prophets taught until John; since then, the kingdom of heaven is preaching of, and every one is pressing into it. So rendered, and taken in conjunction, the figurative language of each of these passages describes the efforts of men, not yet in possession, but striving with all their might and main to get possession, of some desirable object. It would aptly, for example, personify the exertions of soldiers, who having the reduction, and the spoiling, of some rich, but fortified, place before them, are employing all the arts and expedients of war to take it; are scaling the walls, battering the gates, undermining, and throwing down, every obstacle which keeps them, for a time, from their prize.

It is not, then, implied that the kingdom of heaven was as yet subdued by this holy warfare, or that the violence of these figurative spoilers was actually crowned with success: only that it was on the point of becoming so: and the language of prophecy, which speaks of the future as already present, describes it accordingly even now. But that it does this in conformity to its own idiom merely, appears from the fact that the kingdom of heaven, all the time, εὐαγγελίζεται, is still only preached of, and announced, though every one was pressing into it. The truth is, the very tidings, or news, of its approach were themselves the producing causes of this eagerness to press into it, of this violence exerted to get possession of it : and the publication of those tidings had begun with John. The welcome, the eagerness, the impatience, with which the news had been received, and the approach of the kingdom was already expected, were, consequently, all to be dated from the commencement of the ministry of John : but the same feelings continued to be still kept up (and that the more, the longer the arrival of the kingdom itself seemed to be delayed) since the commencement of the ministry of Christ.

The ministry of John, therefore, was the same in kind with the ministry of Christ, and merely prior in the order of time to that ; which being the case, it follows directly that the ministry of John, compared with the ministry of any prophet who had gone before him, was something novel and *sui generis*. It might be justly said that the Law and the Prophets had all prophesied, or taught, as before, until John appeared ; but that, since then, the kingdom of heaven—a new dispensation, distinct from the Mosaic, though raised up and nourished in the bosom of the Mosaic—had begun, and was continuing, to be preached. The reign of the ancient dispensation, the authority of the former rule of faith, were first superseded by the advent, and the ministry, of John. He might be said to have stood on the middle wall of partition between the Law and the Gospel ; and to have belonged alike to each—consummating the one, and introducing the other. He was neither the last in the order of the Prophets, nor the first in the order of the Apostles ; but something made up of both. As appearing before the Messias, he might be classed with the Prophets of the Law ; and as sustaining the same office with the Messias, he might be classed with the emissaries of the Gospel : and, on all these accounts, while he might still be the same *in genere* with the Prophets, he would be something in particular more than they.

IV. By the right construction and interpretation of that much disputed passage in the Gospel of St. John: Ὁ ὀπίσω μου ἐρχόμενος ἔμπροσθέν μου γέγονεν· ὅτι πρῶτός μου ἦν [z]. The authorized version of this text, upon the whole, is the most correct; though, if we would do entire justice to the force and emphasis of the original terms, we must alter it slightly to the following effect: He, who is coming after me, is become before me; because he was before me. It would be just as absurd to suppose that the first half of this sentence affirms priority of existence, as that the last half affirms priority of rank; for they cannot both be considered to affirm priority of the same thing, without amounting to an identical proposition, or assigning the same thing as a reason for itself. The last clause, ὅτι πρῶτός μου ἦν, ascertains the ground of the assertion, conveyed by the first, ἔμπροσθέν μου γέγονε: whence, if πρῶτός μου ἦν is rightly rendered, He was before me, or affirms priority of existence, ἔμπροσθέν μου γέγονε cannot be rightly rendered, He is before me, or affirm priority of existence also: and if ἔμπροσθέν μου γέγονεν is rightly rendered, He is become before me, or affirms priority of rank—then (though the original Greek might bear it, which, I contend, it never could) πρῶτός μου ἦν cannot be rightly rendered, He was my chief, or affirm priority of rank also.

If, however, the first clause affirms precedence, or priority of rank, the second may very well affirm preexistence, or priority of being; and where the question lay between the comparative personal dignity of the Baptist, and that of Christ, it might still more reasonably assign this very priority of existence, as the sole and sufficient ground for that very priority of rank. The most superficial reader must be sensible that, by the peculiar antithesis of his language, John has it in view expressly to oppose the circumstance of Christ's being advanced before him, to the circumstance, notwith-

[z] i. 15. 27. 30.

standing, of his coming after him ; a use of ὀπίσω, and ἔμπρο-
σθεν, which is the most classical imaginable.

Γνώμης πατρῴας πάντ' ὄπισθεν ἑστάναι.

Soph. Ant. 640.

Καὶ τοὺς ὄπισθεν εἰς τὸ πρόσθεν ἄξομεν.

Ajax. 1249.

. . . . . . Τὰ μακρὰ τῶν σμικρῶν λόγων
'Επίπροσθέν ἐστι, καὶ σαφῆ μᾶλλον κλύειν.

Eur. Orest. 632.

To the effect of this antithesis, and to render the anomaly
more complete, it is evidently necessary that Christ should
be understood to have come after, in the same way, and in
the same sense, in which John himself had gone before ; in
other words, that their personal ministry respectively should
be the same, differing only in the order of succession. For,
generally speaking, it is the first in a common office, and
not the last—it is he who ushers in and begins a business
of any importance, not he, who takes it up and prosecutes
it afterwards—who may be said to have precedence, or to
sustain the more dignified character of the two. But the
successor of the Baptist, even in a common work, was such
as by the superior lustre of his person, and by the superior
authority of his teaching, could not fail to eclipse and to
supersede his predecessor. For he, who was from eternity
—he, who was before the Baptist—and before every other
divinely-commissioned, but merely human, teacher, more
ancient than the Baptist—though he might condescend to
labour in the same vocation with the Baptist, and even in
an order of time posterior to his, yet, by virtue of his essential preexistence, his sublime and mysterious divinity of
nature, could not possibly rank, or long continue to rank,
beneath him, but must be preferred before him. The same
assertion, therefore, of his own subordination to his successor, and the same reason for that subordination, that John
was from the earth, Christ was from heaven—John was
from below, Christ was from above—are not more piously,
than naturally, repeated in that other testimony of the
Baptist's, which holds up the torch to the meaning of this.

M 2

Him it behoveth to encrease, but me it behoveth to decrease: he, who came from above, is above all things: he, who was from the earth, is from the earth, and speaketh from the earth; but he, who came from the heavens, is above all things, and what he hath seen, and hath heard, the same he testifieth[a].

And, hence, we may arrive at a right conception of that peculiar circumstance of distinction, in which the superiority of John to every prophet, who had appeared before him, must be made to consist; a superiority so great, that our Lord himself has said, Among them that were born of women, there hath not arisen a greater than John the Baptist[b]. It was no preeminence of personal sanctity, but a certain preeminence of personal office, which was thus ascribed to *him* in particular. All the prophets before him had been, in some sense, the precursors of the Messias, as well as he; but none of them had been his immediate predecessor, like John : all the prophets before him had a high and a holy office to sustain, the same in one, as in another; none had been admitted to the privilege of sustaining the same office with the Messias, of being the fellow-labourer, and as it were copartner, in his proper work and ministry, of the Lord of the prophets—but John. And in the same sense, in which it might thus be said that John was superior to any prophet before himself, in the same sense might it be said, that the least in the kingdom of God, the least minister of the gospel, among those who should come after him, would be greater than John. For the office and part of one, who merely preceded to announce the approach of this kingdom, and to prepare men's minds for the future preaching of the gospel, could not, in the nature of things, be so dignified and illustrious, as the office and part of one, who should actually begin, or in any way contribute to execute, the predicted dispensation itself.

Nor ought it to be objected to this assertion, that the personal ministry of Christ himself, as being the same with the personal ministry of John, must, on this principle, have

---

[a] John iii. 29—36.   [b] Matt. xi. 11.

been inferior in dignity, or in importance, to the personal ministry of a Christian Evangelist. It is not the disparity of personal characters, but the disparity of personal functions, relatively to a common end, which we are here contrasting together. The personal dignity of Jesus Christ can bear no comparison with that of either Prophet or Apostle; and, as the Lord of the Apostles, as well as of the Prophets, by whom *they* also were commissioned and sent, who inspired *them* with the knowledge of gospel truths, and cooperated with *them* wheresoever they went, the sole and efficient cause of every thing brought to pass by their instrumentality, and even in their proper vocation, was still Jesus Christ. But in every regular and orderly scheme, which has a beginning and an ending—a preparation and a consummation—leading to, yet distinct from, each other—they, who carry into effect, must be considered to do more towards the final result, than they who merely begin. And if the prenunciation of the gospel was to precede, as well as conduct to, its preaching, it is no disparagement of the personal dignity of Christ, who, in his relative place and order of time, could discharge only the former, that his personal office was preliminary, and, therefore, subordinate, to the personal office of his Apostles, who were to be appointed to the latter.

The similarity, indeed, of the personal ministry of our Saviour to that of John, *before* him, and yet its distinctness from that of the Apostles, *after* him, may be a good presumptive argument that there might be something incumbent upon *him*, and to be discharged by *him*, over and above the proper work of *his* ministry; something which could be done neither by John before him, nor by the Apostles after him; something equally necessary to the effect and completion of his own ministry, and to the commencement and discharge of their's; something, consequently, which must be interposed between both; *after* the one, but *before* the other: which something the event alone would prove to have been the death, and the resurrection, of our Lord, with the saving design of each; and next to this,

M 3

which was to happen at the close of his personal career, the collecting, ordaining, and commissioning, of Apostles, during its course—who should publish these saving truths, (and, therefore, commence their ministry, as preachers of formal Christianity,) afterwards.

Lastly—the case of Apollos, who is said to have known only the baptism of John [c]—and still more the case of the Twelve disciples at Ephesus, who had been baptized only into the baptism of John [d]—are sufficient to prove that persons might be disciples, and, consequently, Christians in some sense or other already, who had not been fully instructed in the gospel dispensation as such—or had not received Christian baptism—who were merely believers in the divine legation of John, and had merely received baptism from John, or from some of the disciples of John. Nothing can more clearly imply the subordination of the ministry of John to the same common end with the ministry of Christ; and that common end the dispensation of the gospel, as yet ulterior to both.

These considerations, and others which, if they were necessary, might still be adduced, are sufficient to place it beyond a question that the personal ministry of John is not to be regarded as distinct from the personal ministry of our Saviour, except in the order of succession only: that both were continuous, though separate, parts of the same scheme, or dispensation, in general, which may be called, indifferently, either the Ministration of the Kingdom, or the Ministration of the Messias, as discriminated from the propagation of formal Christianity, or the Ministration of the Apostles. It may be said, however, that prophecy, both ancient and recent, had represented the ministry of John, in a different light, as the ministry of a herald, harbinger, or precursor, specifically in reference to the coming of Christ, and, therefore, distinct from the ministry of Christ. The voice of one, crying in the wilderness, Prepare ye the way of the Lord, make straight his paths [e]—Behold I do send my messenger before thy face, who shall get

[c] Acts xviii. 24. 25.   [d] xix. 1—7.   [e] Is. xl. 3—5.

ready thy way before thee [f]—He shall be mighty before the Lord, and many of the children of Israel shall he turn to the Lord their God. And he himself shall go before him in the spirit and power of Elias, to turn the hearts of the fathers to the children, and the disobedient to the wisdom of righteous: to prepare for the Lord a duly provided people [g]. And thou, child, shalt be called a Prophet of the Highest: for thou shalt go before the face of the Lord to prepare his ways; for the sake of giving knowledge of salvation to his people, by the remission of their sins through the tender mercies of our God; wherewith the dayspring from on high hath visited us, to shine unto those who were sitting in the darkness and shadow of death, whereby to direct our feet safely into the way of peace [h]. To which, we may add the testimony of St. Paul also, as quoted above [i], that John proclaimed, before the entrance of Christ, baptism of repentance unto all the people.

That John was really the predecessor of Christ—that the business of bearing witness to the Messias was part of his commission originally—that the fact of such witness, as delivered by him in more ways, and on more occasions, than one, is actually on record—and, consequently, that even those descriptions, which speak of him as personally the herald of Christ, become strictly applicable to him, and are literally fulfilled in his history—no one can pretend to dispute. There was a man, says the last of the Evangelists, sent from God; his name was John. This man came for a testimony, that he might bear testimony concerning the light, that all might believe through him [k]. I was sent before the Christ—says the Baptist of himself; and, That the Christ might be manifested to Israel, for that purpose came I, baptizing in water [l]. And again; He who sent me to baptize in water, the same said unto me, On whomsoever thou shalt see the Spirit descending, and abiding upon him, this it is who baptizeth in the Holy Ghost [m].

[f] Mal. iii. 1.   [g] Luke i. 15—17.   [h] Ib. 76—79.   [i] Acts xiii. 24.
[k] John i. 6. 7.   [l] Ib. iii. 28. i. 31.   [m] Ib. i. 33.

M 4

The duty, however, of bearing personal testimony to Jesus Christ was so far from being incompatible with the duty of an Evangelist of the kingdom, that, in the case at least of John, the former would necessarily be a consequence of the latter.   For, if John knew that, though not himself the Messias, he was shortly to be succeeded by the Messias, and his own part in their common ministry was sometime to be superseded by his, he could not fail to attest this truth, and to bid the people prepare for the coming of another, after himself, but greater than himself.   And this seems, indeed, to be the exact description of John's personal relation to Christ ; that he had to point him out as his successor in a common office, and, however greater, or more dignified, than himself, yet still as only his successor. In comparison, then, with his proper and primary commission, as a preacher of the kingdom, or ambassador of the gospel-tidings, this duty of bearing personal testimony to Jesus Christ would be a kind of πάρεργον, or secondary purpose ; perfectly compatible with that, yet entirely subordinate to it : and this conclusion may be further supported by the following arguments.

I. If the authority of John, in his original capacity as a Prophet of the kingdom, had not been already acknowledged, his personal testimony to the Messias must, clearly, have failed of its effect : for what weight or sanction could have been given to the character, or the claims, of another, by one, who was still in want of confirmation for his own ?

II. To suppose, for argument's sake, that this business was the great business of his ministry : the testimony of John to Christ before, and after, his baptism must necessarily have been widely different.   Before that baptism, he could bear witness, if to any thing, only to the *future* approach of the Messias ; after it, to his *actual* coming ; before, only to *some* Messias in general ; after, to the *person* of this Messias in particular.   Both these kinds and modes of testimony, it may be said, would be suitable to the office of one, commissioned expressly to bear witness to the Christ ; the former or general, while he was still unknown, the latter or particular, when he had once been ascertained. But the latter, every one must admit, would be much the more effectual of the two, and much the more in unison with the character of a personal witness, and of one who had no other duty to perform, than that of bearing such witness to the Christ.

Is it, then, upon this hypothesis, no difficulty, that out of the four Evangelists, who have all given some account of the ministry of John, *one* only makes mention of his personal testimonies to Christ? Is it no proof, on the other hand, that this duty was subordinate to his duty as a herald of the kingdom, that all four record both his preaching and his baptizing? From the time of the baptism of Christ, when only the person of the Messias became known to John, and from which time forward, but not before it, personal attestations in favour of Christ might be delivered by him, the three first Gospels are totally silent on the subject of the ministry of John: so that had not the last Gospel, though written so long posterior to the first, and expressly to supply their omissions, placed the fact of some such attestations on record, we should have remained for ever in ignorance that John had borne any personal testimony to Christ; that is, that he had ever performed the great, if not the sole, business of his ministry in general. And what are these attestations, recorded by St. John himself? They are three in number, two of them delivered on consecutive days, the third, about a month later; the former confined to the disciples of the Baptist, and the latter, as far as we can judge of it, not purposely, nor primarily, addressed to the rest of the people [t].

III. If we take the Baptist's own account of his original commission [u], as implicitly to be trusted, it will follow that, though given before the commencement of his ministry, it could not be discharged until that ministry was far advanced: and, when so discharged, it would prove to be a commission to bear not a general testimony to the *future* advent, but a particular testimony to the *actual* person, of the

[t] John i. 29. 35. iii. 26—36.   [u] i. 33.

Christ. It was given before the commencement of his ministry; for it was given when he was first sent to baptize; it was a commission to bear witness to the person of the Messias, because it was accompanied by a promise how that person should be recognised. It was, consequently, a commission which neither could, nor was intended to, be executed, until his recognition had taken place—that is, until the baptism, at least, of Christ—when only the promised sign was vouchsafed. But the ministry of John had been going on some considerable time before the baptism of Christ; for this baptism is the last thing which three of the Evangelists record of his ministry at all. The ministry of John, then, had some proper object, distinct from the commission to bear personal testimony to Jesus Christ, which must have been going on before the baptism of our Lord; and, consequently, had been discharged from the first.

There is reason, indeed, to believe that even the first *general* testimony to Christ was much posterior to the commencement of his ministry: at least, if that instance is the instance recorded by St. Luke[v]. And that it is so, may be inferred, I think, from the cause which produced the testimony itself: When the people were in expectation, and all men were reasoning in their own hearts, concerning John, whether he might be the Christ, John answered, saying unto all. The declaration which follows, affirming that he was not the Christ, but only his predecessor, was designed to set them right: whence, it seems hardly to admit of a question, that this must have been the first declaration to any such effect, which had yet taken place. It was very natural that the men of the time should, at first, have considered it possible that John might prove to be the Messias, whom they had all so long been expecting; it was not less natural, or rather it was peremptorily incumbent upon him, that John should disclaim the title, which they would willingly have awarded to him. But he could neither rectify this misconstruction of his real character, until it had begun to prevail, nor yet delay to rectify it, after it had. The

[v] iii. 15—18.

authoritative denial, therefore, with which, in the present instance, he does rectify it, must, on every account, be considered the first of its kind ; and if one such denial, and so expressed, was likely to set the mistake at rest, it would also be the last.   St. Mark's account, then, of a similar declaration [w] will belong to the same occasion as this in St. Luke ; and be only more concise ; while St. Matthew's [x], which is identically the same in terms with St. Luke's, will be this very occasion itself, joined to the account of another passage, and of a corresponding discourse, in the previous history of John.

Now, that the time of this testimony was considerably later than the commencement of his ministry I infer, first, from the reason of the thing ; because the error which produced it, and so widely spread, could not have arisen all at once.   Secondly, because St. Luke has detached this single declaration from the longer discourse in St. Matthew ; obviously as belonging to a later period than the rest.   Thirdly, and chiefly, because it is this testimony of the Baptist's, and as so produced, as well as so directed, to which I believe St. Paul also to have alluded, in the synagogue of Pisidian Antioch [y].

Now, as John was accomplishing his course, he said, Whom do ye suppose me to be? I am not He : but, lo! he is coming after me ; the shoes of whose feet I am not worthy to unloose.

These words of John are manifestly addressed to the people, and as manifestly are intended to rectify some possible mistake, with respect to the truth of his own character. They agree, therefore, so far, in substance, with the same declaration in St. Luke, that both must have belonged to the same occasion in the history of John ; and since the former is said to have taken place, ὡς ἐπλήρου Ἰωάννης τὸν δρόμον, the latter must have done so too ; that is, they must each be supposed to have happened, when the ministry of John was far advanced ; for that could on no principle be said to have transpired when a man was *accomplishing* or *fulfilling* his course, which ensued when it was scarcely begun. The same conclusion results from these premises, as before; that, if even any *general* testimony of John's to the Messias was not delivered, until comparatively late in the duration of his ministry, to deliver such testimony never could have been the principal, much less the sole, or proper, duty of his ministry from the first.

Had this actually been the case, then, it was to be expected that our Lord, or his Apostles, after the formal commencement of *his* ministry, or of *their's*, would often be found appealing to the testimony of John, as to one of the most convincing arguments, (with all at least who admitted the divine legation of John,) which could be urged in his own behalf. But so far is this from being done, that in the three first Gospels, as soon as the Baptist is once removed, by his imprisonment, from the public stage of his ministry, his name and memory are, from thenceforward, as good as obliterated; it is accident, humanly speaking, which causes him to be mentioned again: and as to his testimony, it is not so much as alluded to. That occasion when it might have been supposed, *a priori*, our Lord would have said something expressly on this subject, and when even the necessity of the case might have seemed to require it, was the occasion of his celebrated message: for whatever, as concerned the Baptist himself, might have been the motives to that message, it is indisputable, that *prima facie*, and in the natural construction of the fact by those who were present, to have sent such a message, and to such a person, was in some degree to retract his former declarations in his behalf. Yet, if our Saviour alludes at all to the vacillation of John, it is in figurative language—under the form of an interrogation, dismissed without an answer—or suffered to remain in a dignified silence. Once only, and that in the Gospel of St. John, is it evident that he refers directly to this subject, as such. He who testifieth concerning me is another; and I know that the testimony which he testifieth concerning me is true. Yourselves have sent unto John, and he hath borne witness to the truth. But I receive not my testimony from a man, though I say these things that ye may be saved; he was the lamp which did burn and shine, and ye were willing, for a while, to rejoice in its light. But I have that testimony which is greater than John's; for the works, which the Father hath given me to perform, the very works which I do testify concerning me, that the Father hath sent me[z]. Even in this very passage, then, it is evident that the testimony of John is appealed to solely by way of condescension, or *more humano*—that it is not considered our Lord's proper testimony—that he never supposed the truth of his character to depend upon it—that in comparison of the testimony of the Father, which was manifested in the works, that is, in the miracles, performed by Christ, it was altogether secondary and inferior.

With respect, therefore, to the representations of prophecy quoted above, we may observe, first, that as far as they merely describe the Baptist, under the character of a messenger, or harbinger, commissioned to make known the advent of the Messias, they describe an actual part of his office, which was strictly verified in its functions. Secondly, as far as they proceed, especially the descriptions of the ancient prophets, to delineate the purposes of his mission, under images or terms derived from a well known principle of eastern pomp and state, the preparations usually made for a royal progress, by sending forward persons to form roads and bridges, to level mountains, to fill up valleys, to render the rough places smooth, and the crooked straight,* it is manifest that, though founded in fact themselves, they can apply in figure only to the ministry of John : they pre-

---

* Πέμπουσι δ' αὐτὸν, καὶ σεβίζουσιν μέγα,
Κελευθοποιοὶ παῖδες Ἡφαίστου, χθόνα
Ἀνήμερον τιθέντες ἡμερωμένην.   Æschyl. Eum. 12.

Vide also Diod. Sic. ii. 13. 14. Herod. Polymn. passim. Jos. B. Jud. iii. vi. 2.

[z] v. 32—36.

dict no real change, to be wrought by him, in the face of external nature, but certain moral, or spiritual, changes in the hearts and dispositions, in the principles and practice, of mankind, which should be the effect of his preaching. Now, as descriptive of such moral revolutions as these, in general, they are descriptive of nothing, which might not be understood of the Ministration of the Messias, as such; whose business and whose purpose, from first to last, whether by the instrumentality of John, or by the instrumentality of Christ, it was to bring these revolutions to pass.

They, who should contend that these were changes to be produced by the sole ministry of John, and entirely in subordination to the reception, and the success, of Christ, would be reduced to this dilemma, that either they must suppose the ministry of John to have failed entirely of its effect, or they must acknowledge that our Saviour did that for himself at last, which John, on this principle, must have done for him already before. As moral effects, all such changes must have been produced by moral causes; by the authority and influence of John, preaching the doctrine of repentance, and reinforcing the duties of morality; parts of his office, in which our Lord was so far from differing from him, as not only to continue the same ministry, but even to repeat the very language of his preaching.

I infer, then, that what the Baptist had all along been doing before Christ, and Christ continued still to do after the Baptist, being the same in each case, was done by neither for the sake of the other, but by both for the sake of something else, equally related, and equally ulterior, to the personal agency of each. Not but that, in whatever proportion the general wickedness of the times might have been ameliorated by the preaching of John, the people would be so far the better disposed to attend to, and to profit by, the ministry of Christ; but this is a very different thing, conducing not to the reception of the person, but to the success of the labours, of Christ; nor that, as distinct from, but as the same with, those of John. The efforts of both were directed to one purpose, the preparation of the minds and affections of men for the arrival, in due time, of the Gospel ; and what effect they had each produced would not fully appear, until the Gospel began to be preached. Yet, in whatever degree John might have advanced this work, in the same degree it would be found so much the more forward for the labours of Christ ; and by him be advanced to a still higher degree of perfection. But the ultimate degree of all, the advancement, which should be due to the united efforts of both, could not be fully developed before the close of the ministry of Christ ; nor fully ascertained by the event, until the commencement of the ministry of the Apostles. The seed would be sown, and in part matured, in the time of the Messias and of his predecessor ; the fruit would not appear, nor the harvest be gathered in, before the time of the successors of both. On this subject, however, something more will be said elsewhere.

If such had not been the original design of the ministry of John, would the prophet Isaiah have specified *this*, as the final result of that preparation which he attributes to the spiritual harbinger, that all flesh should see the salvation of God? For what is the salvation of God, but God their Saviour? and what is God their Saviour, but a crucified Saviour? and when was a crucified Saviour revealed, or seen, before the day of Pentecost, when the first Christian sermon was preached? Would the angel Gabriel have said that John should get ready for the Lord, λαὸν κατεσκευασμένον? For what is this duly prepared, or befitting, people, but the members of his future Church, his *peculium* among the Jews, the ἐκλογή, in short, of Israel? Would his father Zacharias have said, that he should go before the face of the Lord to give knowledge of salvation to his people? For when was the knowledge of salvation, that is, the knowledge of a Saviour, communicated in the lifetime of John? or when were the tender mercies of God, fully developed in the remission of sins, before the great forfeit had been paid in the sacrifice for sins, and human redemption was complete? Or when could the dayspring from on high be said to have shone forth, on the darkness of the Gentile world, before the gospel was preached to that world ? Or when were the feet of sinners, whether Jews or Gentiles, safely guided into the way of peace, before Christ, the Way, the Truth, and the Life, the Captain of salvation, and the Prince of peace, had been distinctly proposed in all these capacities, to the Jew first, and afterwards to the Gentile ?

The reasons, which are commonly assigned in explanation of the fact that the personal appearance and ministry of our Saviour were preceded by the ministry of John, though partly founded on a mistaken idea of the proper relation between them, are not less significant, but in many respects more so, when the truth of this relation has been better established. I shall not add, therefore, to the length of the present discussion, by either repeating those reasons, or alleging others in their stead ; but, having said thus much upon the nature, purposes, and discharge, of the ministry of John in general, I shall proceed, in the last place, to adjust the harmony of its parts.

The period of the feast of Tabernacles, A. U. 779. or A. D. 26. has been already assumed as the time when it probably began ; further than which period, in ascertaining this time exactly, it may not be possible to advance. We may conjecture, however, that it would begin after, not before, the tenth of Tisri, and the expiration of the feast itself; after the former, as the day of the great national fast, the recurrence of which would compose the minds of men, of all, at least, who were likely to be duly impressed by it, to a frame of seriousness, reflection, and self-examination, in accordance with the future ministry of John, who was eminently a preacher of repentance, and of amendment of life : after the latter, that so the people might be returned from the feast to their homes ; and the necessity of water, for the purposes of baptism, have been previously provided for, by the recurrence of the autumnal rains. The feast of Tabernacles, A. U. 779. began on September 15. and expired September 22[a] ; and I have advanced a conjecture else-

* Vol. i. Diss. v. 268.

where[b] that the day, when John might enter on his ministry, A. U. 779. was probably October 5. the assumed date of his nativity, when he completed his thirtieth year. Nor is there any thing improbable in this conjecture, but rather quite the reverse. I will observe only that October 5. A. U. 779. when the fifteenth of Tisri coincided with September 15. would coincide with Marchesvan 6. About the second or third week of Marchesvan (in this instance October 12 or 19.) the autumnal rains commonly set in ; the appositeness of which coincidence to the commencement of the ministry of John I need not mention. If it began at this time, it might last, as we shall see hereafter, until the day of his imprisonment, as nearly as possible seven months; but until April 5. the day of the commencement of our Saviour's, at the Passover, John ii. 13. A. U. 780. only exactly six.

The scene of this ministry is laid by St. Matthew, and by St. Mark, at its commencement, in the wilderness of Judæa ; which does not mean an absolute desert, but a plain and champaign country, devoted to pasturage, and, though comparatively remote from the more populous parts, yet not unoccupied by villages. Thus Josephus mentions Βηθαλαγὰν, κώμην οὖσαν ἐν τῇ ἐρήμῳ[c]. It would be absurd, indeed, to suppose that John was sent to preach among solitudes, and not among the haunts of men. The principal scene of his ministry, however, we learn from St. Luke was the Perichorus of Jordan, the proper name of which was the Aulon[d]—described by Josephus[e] as two hundred and thirty stades in length, one hundred and twenty in breadth—intersected by the Jordan—enclosed on either side by mountains—desert and barren, and reaching from the southern extremity of the Lake of Tiberias, to the northern extremity of the Lake Asphaltites. The scene, thus chosen, seems to have been ever after the same—Bethabara, Ænon, or Salem—all contiguous places, or not very remote from each other ; the former in Peræa, or on the eastern side of the

[b] Vol. i. Diss. x. 353.   [c] Ant. Jud. xiii. i. 5.   [d] Hieron. Oper. ii. De Situ et Nominibus.   [e] B. iv. viii. 2.   Ant. xvi. v. 2.

Jordan, the latter in Galilee, or on the west. The locality
of Bethabara continued to be still pointed out by tradition
even in the time of Origen [f]; but whether correctly, or not,
may be doubted. The preponderance of critical reasons
makes rather in favour of *Bethany beyond Jordan*, than of
Bethabara. Such a country was well adapted for the supply of John's peculiar food, ἀκρίδες καὶ μέλι ἄγριον, as the
desert had been previously for the materials of his dress.
Clothes made of hair, in general, are alluded to by Josephus as characteristic of poverty, or a mean state of life [g].

The Perichorus of Jordan, for a great part of its extent,
bordered upon Judæa ; hence, among those who resorted to
the baptism of John, the inhabitants of Jerusalem, and of
Judæa, as well as the people of the neighbourhood, are specified first. It is, however, a circumstance of resemblance
between John's ministry and our Saviour's also, that both
appear to have been almost confined to Galilee, or to the
dominions of Herod Antipas, beyond the jurisdiction of the
Jewish Sanhedrim. The resort to his baptism, in question,
must be placed at no greater a distance of time from his
first appearance, than would be necessary to make the fact
of his appearance, and the nature of his preaching, generally
known : and the manner, in which he received the people,
on what seems to have been the first occasion of a mixed
resort, is recorded by St. Luke [h]. I say a mixed resort, because [i] there were many Sadducees and Pharisees among the
number. The address, as related by St. Luke, is the same
with the address as related by St. Matthew ; and if the parties addressed were, as we suppose, a mixed audience, the
latter might justly describe it as directed to the Pharisees
or Sadducees in particular, the former, to the people in general. St. Luke's τί οὖν ποιήσομεν; shews that these last
considered themselves concerned in it ; while St. Matthew's
γεννήματα ἐχιδνῶν, (an apostrophe contained in St. Luke
also, and twice used hereafter by our Saviour, but in each
instance solely of the Scribes and Pharisees,) as well as the

[f] Comm. in Joh. ii. 131.   [g] B. i. xxiv. 3.   Ant. xvi. vii. 3.   [h] iii. 7—9.
[i] 7—10.

strain of the denunciation in general, obviously levelled against the characteristic hypocrisy, self-righteousness, and carnal trust, of the principal sects, is a much stronger intimation that some of the Pharisees, in particular, must have been present, and singled out ; or that, while all were addressed in common, these were reproved in particular.

The sequel of the same discourse, as found in St. Matthew, I have already observed, was not delivered at the same time with the preceding part ; and yet the Evangelist might attach it to that, both as an actual, though a later, discourse of the Baptist's, as well as that ; and also because, as he proposed to conclude his account of the ministry of John, with the next event, the baptism of Christ, this was the only opportunity, prior to that event, for placing on record so important a fact as that of his personal testimony to Christ. The subject of each discourse is so far akin, as to admit of their being related in conjunction ; and yet so far distinct, that they might have been delivered at different times ; nor will it be denied, on a careful consideration of both together, that there would be a certain abruptness in the transition from the topic of the one, to the topic of the other, which would favour the supposition that they could not originally have been united. In this respect, then, St. Matthew and St. Mark, as we before observed, must be reduced to a harmony with St. Luke, and not St. Luke to one with St. Matthew or St. Mark : and as the commencement of John's testimonies to Christ, whether general or particular, is so far an epoch in his ministry, and as this is the only instance in the three first Gospels of any such testimony at all, it would manifestly be improbable to place it immediately after the beginning of his ministry, or long before the baptism of our Lord himself.

After this account, if we except only the history of the baptism of Jesus Christ, no mention of any circumstance relating to John, but that of his imprisonment, is to be found in the same three Gospels ; and even this fact is alluded to only by the way in St. Matthew and in St. Mark, and, for reasons stated elsewhere, anticipated by three or

four mouths, in St. Luke. From the time of this baptism,
then, the sequel of the ministry of John is to be collected
entirely from the last Gospel; and this will be done hereafter, shewing that the baptism of our Saviour, which, from
the importance of the event itself, and from the nature of
the testimony which John was, thenceforward, enabled to
bear to the Christ, compared with what he had been restricted to before it, was evidently qualified to become a
cardinal point in the course of his ministry, actually was
such; happening about the same time from its commencement, as before its termination. The first public testimony,
after his baptism, borne to our Lord, was probably by the
voice from heaven; and as he was immediately impelled
into the wilderness, the first opportunity, after the same
event, which John could have of bearing witness to him,
would be the opportunity afforded by the deputation and
the question of the Sanhedrim: and his answer to this
question, as far as it conveys any such testimony, is no
longer general and indefinite—speaking of some one, merely
as to come—but particular and definite, so far as to speak
of some one, who was already standing in the midst of them,
and already known to the Baptist, though still unknown
to them. This, then, is that instance of his testimony, to
which, as understood to have been given to himself, though
without any mention of himself, our Saviour referred
above[k].

The obligation to perpetual Nazaritism, from his mother's womb, which might have been daily endangered had
he been brought up amidst the usual society of men[l], seems
to have been the true reason why John was educated, and
lived, in the desert, until the day of his shewing to Israel.
Not but that the existence of eremites, even in his time, might
be no uncommon thing[m]. For the same reason, he would
be excused from attendance at the feasts. Hence, if our
Saviour's life also, until the same period, had been spent in
a similar privacy at Nazareth[n], it would seem impossible to

[k] John v. 33.　　[l] Numb. vi. 2—21.　　[m] Vit. Jos. 2.　　[n] Matt. xiii. 55.
Mark vi. 3.　John vi. 42.　Justin. Martyr. Dial. 333.

doubt that John asserted a matter of fact, when he asserted that he knew not the Christ[o]—even though the assertion be restricted to the person of Christ—before, at least, his baptism: and, if it is implied by St. Matthew's account of what passed between them at the time of his baptism[p], that he must have known him *then*, we have only to suppose that the knowledge in question was communicated to him, on the appearance of Christ—as the knowledge of Saul, and afterwards of David, was communicated to Samuel[q], and the knowledge of the wife of Jeroboam to Ahijah[r]—by a direct inspiration from above—and both facts become consistent. For as to the recognition implied by the descent of the Holy Ghost, and, consequently, not until the baptism was over, however much commentators may have overlooked this truth, nothing is clearer than that this descent was intended to mark out not the person, but the office, of Christ. I, indeed, knew him not, but he who sent me to baptize in water, the same said to me, On whomsoever thou shalt see the Spirit descending, and abiding upon him, this is he who baptizeth with the Holy Ghost. The object of such a recognition, then, was to ascertain our Lord, as him who should baptize in the Holy Ghost, in opposition to John who had merely baptized in water. It had nothing to do with the person of Christ; it opposed the Spirit-baptism of the Messias, to the water-baptism of his predecessor; and it was consistent with the knowledge of the person of this Messias, whether as previously possessed, or as now, for the first time, revealed.

The conduct of the Baptist, therefore, when he would have declined the administration of his own baptism on our Lord, was founded in a genuine humility, and a sincere conviction of the superior dignity of Christ, such as this knowledge of his person would either convey, or imply; and our Lord's answer, by which he impresses on him the necessity of performing his part in that ceremony, rightly

[o] John i. 33. [p] iii. 14. [q] 1 Sam. ix. 16, 17. xvi. 12. [r] 1 Kings xiv. 6.

understood, may instruct us in the final end of his baptism ; with the consideration of which I shall conclude this Dissertation on the ministry of John.

The answer was doubtless emphatic, or specially in reference to the time then present, and to some obligation incumbent, at that time, both on John and on himself in particular. He would not have said, Suffer it to be so *now*, could it have been as well suffered at any other time, before or after it, as at that—nor, For thus it behoveth *us* to fulfil all righteousness—had the same fulfilment, in that one respect, been equally incumbent on others, as on them in particular. I infer, therefore, that the obligation in question was to no moral duty, binding upon moral agents in general, but to some legal requisition, incumbent on these two more especially ; the nature of which we must needs collect from the instance of its observance, which was our Lord's receiving from John, and John's administering on our Lord, one and the same form of baptism ; but each, as part of a further, and a much more important, ceremonial, the consecration of our Lord to his ministerial office, preparatory to his entering upon it.

That the Levitical high-priest was always a type of the Christian, may be taken for granted ; and that John, as the son of Zacharias and of Elizabeth, was competent to have sustained even the character of the Levitical high-priest is not less obvious. That there existed also, under the law, a high-priest, and one only not the high-priest, but, in other respects, superior in dignity, and in the sacredness of his character, to all besides, is proved by various authorities. Κἂν ἄρα τίς που, οὐ λέγω τῶν ἄλλων Ἰουδαίων, ἀλλὰ καὶ τῶν ἱερέων, οὐχὶ τῶν ὑστάτων, ἀλλὰ τῶν, τὴν εὐθὺς μετὰ τὸν πρῶτον, τάξιν εἰληχότων [s]. Constituebatur ... sacerdos, qui dignitate proximus esset a summo sacerdote, sic tanquam in administratione regni est secundus a rege ; is vicarius appellabatur ; idem etiam dicebatur antistes. Is igitur ad dextram summi sacerdotis semper adstabat [t]. And even

---

[s] Philo De Legat. 1035.   [t] Maimon. De Apparatu Templi. iv. 16.

this vicar had two subvicars[u]. Vide also the passages quoted in the margin[v].

In this relation may the Levitical high-priest be considered to have stood to the Christian, in general; and, certainly, John, the representative of the Levitical high-priesthood, the forerunner of the Messias, the paranymph of the spiritual bridegroom, and the greatest prophet among all, who had been born of women, to our Saviour, in particular. Now the consecration of the Levitical high-priest was a necessary ceremony before he could enter on his ministry: much more, then, the consecration of the Christian. But, if our Saviour was not so consecrated upon this occasion of his baptism, it would not be easy to say when he was. I regard his baptism, therefore, as the ceremony of his consecration. And that a priest, as such, could be consecrated only by a priest, and the high-priest himself so properly by none, as by the next in dignity to him, nor, consequently, our Saviour so properly by any, as by John, appears too obvious to require any proof. The true consecration of Jesus Christ might be the effusion of the Holy Ghost; but his previous baptism, as the event proved, was necessary even to that.

We may look upon this baptism, therefore, with all its circumstances and its effects, as constituting his true and his proper consecration; such as was naturally to be expected for the spiritual antitype of the legal prototype. Nor is there any particular, requisite to the integrity of the legal form [w], which may not be seen, *mutatis mutandis*, to have held good in what now took place. The previous ablution of the body of the priest was supplied by the baptism itself, and the agency, which performed that part of the ceremony, was a competent agency; for it was the agency of John. The absence of the sacred chrism[x] was compensated by its antitype, the gifts and graces of the spiritual

---

[u] Ibid. 17.   [v] 2 Sam. viii. 17.   xx. 25.   2 Kings xxv. 18.   Jos. Ant. Jud. viii. i. 4.   x. viii. 2.   xviii. iv. 3.   xviii. i. 1. compared with xvii. xiii. 1. Vit. 38. B. ii. xii. 6.   iv. iii. 9.   [w] Exod. xxix. 1—7.   xl. 12—15.   [x] xxx. 23—33.

unction [y]; and the medium by which these were effused was the medium of the Holy Ghost. The robes of beauty and of holiness, which adorned the person of the priest [z], were the essential innocence, and spotless purity, of the nature of Christ; a much more glorious garb, and much more becoming for the Christian high-priest, than the Aaronical vesture—and always typified by that [a]. More than this I do not know to have been requisite to the inauguration even of the legal high-priest; and, if it answered to all this, the baptism of our Lord, regarded as his inauguration also, would be complete.

[y] Ps. xlv. 7.   [z] Exod. xxviii. 2.   [a] Ps. xlv. 8.

DISSERTATION VI.

On the order of the temptations.

THE order of the temptations is not the same throughout in each of the Evangelists; that is, the second temptation in St. Matthew is the third in St. Luke; and the second in St. Luke is the third in St. Matthew. The order of St. Matthew, too, appears, from the notes of sequence which he employs, to have been the true; nor does the arrangement in St. Luke, who no where affirms his order, militate against this conclusion: and hence it has been inferred that St. Luke does not write after a strict historical method.

But if this inference proceeds on the supposition that the several temptations, distinctly, are still only the particulars of one transaction, it is manifestly illogical; for, notwithstanding any difference in the disposal of the parts, the whole is related in its place—and, if it does not proceed on this supposition, but regards the several temptations as so many detached and independent events, it proceeds upon a false hypothesis, or a mistaken idea of the transaction itself.

I am ready to admit that the order of St. Matthew's narrative, in this instance, may be the real order; yet it would not follow on that account that St. Luke's contains a Trajection. The moral end proposed by the narrative in either, though it must have been partly the same, might have been partly so far distinct also, as to require St. Matthew to observe the actual order of the event, and to excuse St. Luke for making a corresponding change in it.

The temptation, regarded in any point of view, was unquestionably one of the most mysterious transactions in our Saviour's personal history; and, without pretending to unravel the mystery, or to be wise beyond what is written, I am content to profess my belief in the reality of the transaction itself—and in the reality of the parties concerned in it—of that being, who is called the Tempter, the Devil, or Satan, as much as of our Lord himself, whose personal existence no one will think of disputing. For the sake, however, of the present argument, which concerns, in some degree, the first principles of our Harmony, I shall lay, as concisely as possible, before the reader, what I consider to be the most general outline of its nature, and its purposes.

I. Not one of the temptations is to be contemplated by itself, as what it is *in specie,* but as what it is *in genere ;* that is, each of them *familiam ducit,* or is the representative of a class. St. Luke himself has intimated this, when he says at the end of the account, iv. 13. Συντελέσας πάντα πειρασμὸν ὁ Διάβολος, not, πάντα TON πειρασμόν—Every kind of temptation, not, *the* whole temptation.

II. The first temptation, according to the order of St. Matthew, is addressed to a natural appetite ; and, consequently, is a specimen of such temptations as may be addressed to the purely sensual principle : the second is addressed to the ostentatious display of superior worth, goodness, or estimation in the sight of God; that is, to the principle of pride ; and, consequently, it is a specimen of temptations directed against the purely intellectual principle : the third is addressed to the love of honour, wealth, or power ; and, therefore, is a specimen of temptations addressed to a mixed principle ; or a principle partly intellectual and partly moral.

III. The order of the temptations is the order of their strength ; that is, they begin with the weakest, and proceed to the strongest ; for any other order would manifestly have been preposterous—and the end of the whole transaction is to represent our Lord tempted in all points, like unto ourselves, yet without sin ; attacked in each vulnerable part of his human nature, yet superior to every art, and to all the subtlety, of the Devil.

IV. The proximate cause of the first temptation was our Lord's being an hungred at the time ; the proximate cause of the second, we may reasonably conjecture, was the voice from heaven at his baptism : and the proximate cause of the third, it is equally reasonable to conclude, was the expectation of a temporal Messias.

V. The immediate purpose of each temptation is purely tentative : but the object of the two first is to discover whether Christ was the Son of God ; the object of the last is to discover whether he was the true, or a false, Christ. If so, the last temptation in St. Matthew, besides being actually the last in the order of succession, would appear the strongest also in the eyes of a Jew ; because it was directly a temptation that our Saviour should avow himself the Messias, which the Jews expected. For, that to fall down and worship Satan, in the hope of worldly pomp and grandeur, was to renounce the character of the true Christ, and to assume the character of the false, is too obvious to require any proof. If St. Matthew, then, wrote for the Jews, his account of this temptation, besides being more agreeable to the order of the event, would make it appear the strongest also : for the last temptation was one, which the true Christ only could have withstood, and which the false Christs, who came successively after the true, never were able to withstand.

VI. This presumption, however, in favour of the last temptation, is ultimately reducible to the national prejudice in behalf of a temporal Messias ; and, consequently, must have been confined to the Jews. The Gentiles, who partook in no such prejudice, could not, *a priori*, have been prepared (on these grounds at least) so to appreciate its force. To them it would appear in the light of a temptation, simply addressed to the desire of honour, wealth, or power ; and, therefore, of inferior strength to the second. For the history of their own philosophers could furnish instances of persons, whom their natural strength had enabled to surmount the former ; but few, or none, of such as, unassisted by the grace of God, had not fallen victims to the latter. Hence, if St. Luke wrote for the Gentile Christians, as St. Matthew had written for the Jewish, he would as naturally place the second temptation last, as St. Matthew, on the other supposition, had placed the third.

VII. This view of the principle of St. Luke's arrangement is further confirmed by that classification of impure desires, which is given by St. John; and, as it would seem, in reference to this account of our Lord's temptation itself —ʹΗ ἐπιθυμία τῆς σαρκός—καὶ ἡ ἐπιθυμία τῶν ὀφθαλμῶν—καὶ ἡ ἀλαζονεία τοῦ βίου [a]. The desire of the flesh is a description of temptations of the first class; the desire of the eyes, (which are captivated by external pomp and splendour,) of temptations like the second; and the pride of life, or, as it should rather be rendered, the *vain-glory* of life, of temptations like the third; and of each as they stand in St. Luke. This sense of ἀλαζονεία is determined by classical usage. It is specified by Aristotle [b], as the extreme of excess opposed to the mean habit, which he denominates ἀλήθεια; the nature of which being to make its possessor habitually appear what he is, and neither better, nor worse, compared with others, than the truth of his character will warrant, the vice of excess, opposed to it, is that which makes him habitually studious of appearing other than he is, in a sense beyond, and not below, the truth. In a word, it is the habit of arrogance, boastfulness, ostentation—without the foundation of superior excellence, or real desert, of any kind—a description of failing to which the professors of philosophy, anciently, and especially in our Saviour's time, were notoriously liable.

<hr />

[a] 1 Ep. ii. 16.   [b] Ethic. Nic. iv. 7.

DISSERTATION VII.

On the hiatus in the three first Gospels between the time of the baptism of our Saviour, and the commencement of his ministry in Galilee, and on its supplement by the Gospel of St. John.

THE assertion, that the Gospel of St. John is supplementary to the rest, requires it to be proved that, in all those parts, where the former narratives were evidently not continuous, the narrative of St. John comes in critically to connect them, and to fill them up ; and, as this proof is capable of a high degree of precision, I propose to establish it at present in the first, and not the least complete and satisfactory, instance of its kind, with regard to the substance of the sections included between the first and the fourth chapters of St. John.

The former Gospels, after beginning their accounts with the public ministry of John the Baptist, and bringing them down to the time of the baptism of Christ, are altogether silent, if we except the single fact of the fasting and the temptation, upon any intermediate events between the time of the baptism, and the time of that return to Galilee, with which they all concur in representing our Lord's ministry there to have been begun. Unless, then, it could be demonstrated that this return followed immediately on the fasting and temptation, as the fasting and temptation might have followed on the baptism, there will necesearily be some hiatus in the continuity of their accounts ; the measure of which must be the interval between the close of the forty days' fast, and the time of the return into Galilee; an hiatus which will, consequently, be greater or less as this interval is greater or less ; but will be nothing at all solely on the supposition that this interval is so too ; or that the return into Galilee took place, without loss of time, after the forty days' fast. But, that this last supposition is not the case may be proved by the testimony of St. John's Gospel, as follows.

The strictly historical part of this Gospel does not begin, nor proceed, except from the nineteenth verse of chapter the first : the verses before that are all the substance of re-flections, premised by the Evangelist in his own person ; and serving as an introduction or proœm to the whole work, but no portion of its historical matter whatever. It cannot be considered to begin even at the fifteenth verse ; first, be-cause the words, there recited, as the words of some testi-mony of John, are clearly an Anticipation, and clearly re-ferred to, as such ; an Anticipation which the course of the narrative, but only from verse nineteenth, and thenceforwards, goes on to explain and to apply : for this peculiar declaration, ὁ ὀπίσω μου ἐρχόμενος, ἔμπροσθέν μου γέγονε, was first made by John in his answer to the Sanhedrim ; and the first personal application of it to our Lord took place on the following day : secondly, because the reference to the Baptist is plainly to be restricted to this one verse, and what follows, from thence to the eighteenth, is subjoined by the Evangelist himself, in the same spirit, and to the same effect, with the rest of the chapter from the first verse to the fourteenth. The mention of John, then, here is no more historical, than the same mention, in verses six, seven, eight, before ; all which relate, indeed, to him, but evidently in some general and proleptical sense.

Now at the nineteenth verse of chapter the first, we have the account of a fact which could not have been prior, at the earliest, to the baptism of Jesus ; nor, consequently, to the beginning of the forty days' fast ; but must have been sometime, either more or less, posterior to both. And we may go further than this ; the fact in question, we may contend, was not only by some time, either more or less, posterior to the baptism, and to the beginning of the forty days' fast, but cannot, on any principle, be placed earlier than on the very last day of the forty days' fast itself. For, on the day after this fact, John, says the Evangelist[a], saw

* i. 29.

Jesus walking towards him; and, from the testimony which he immediately bears to him, it is clear that Jesus had been already baptized; for he had seen the Holy Ghost descending and abiding upon him. This appearance, then, of Jesus to John was necessarily posterior to the baptism; and if it could not be shewn to have happened between the baptism, and the temptation, it must have been posterior also to the temptation.

Now the testimony of each of the Evangelists, who record the temptation, is express to the point that Jesus was led, or impelled, by the Spirit, without any perceptible delay, from the scene of his baptism, to the scene of his fasting and temptation; and the testimony of St. John, who alone records this appearance, is not less express to the point that in two days after it[b], Jesus was proposing to return into Galilee, and in five days after it[b], was actually in Cana of Galilee. It would be the height of extravagance to suppose that all this could have happened between the time of the baptism, and the beginning of the forty days' fast; which being the case, the appearance of Jesus to John, and, consequently, the deputation from the Sanhedrim, to interrogate John, which had its conference with him the day before, both of them later than the baptism, were both of them later than the fast—or, could not have happened, at the earliest, the former before the day after, and the latter before the very day of, Jesus' return from the wilderness, when the forty days' fast was over.

After the account of this fast, and of one return into Galilee, subsequent to it, there is an account of a Passover, attended by Jesus at Jerusalem[c]; and, after this Passover, of a residence, longer or shorter, in the land of Judæa[c]: and after this residence, of another return into Galilee; prior to none of which events, except, perhaps, the last, and that only after our Lord was departed from Samaria, is it capable of proof that John had yet been cast into prison. It is evident, then, upon the whole, that between John i.

---

[b] i. 29. 35. 44. ii. 1.　　　　　　　　[c] ii. 13. iii. 22.

19. and iv. 1. that is, between the proper historical commencement of his Gospel, and the beginning of the account of this journey, through Samaria, into Galilee, we have a narrative of matters intermediate to the two extremes, of the baptism, fasting, and temptation, (where the former Evangelists left off their accounts,) on the one hand, and of the imprisonment of the Baptist, followed by the return of Jesus into Galilee, (at which they resume them,) on the other. It follows, therefore, that whatever be the length of time included between these two points in the Gospel of St. John, for that length of time, whether greater or less, there is an interruption of the continuity of the other Gospels; which interruption this portion of St. John's does manifestly contribute to supply. The question, then, which we have still to consider, is, how far it contributes to supply it; or whether the historical matter furnished by St. John is an exact measure of the historical matter omitted by the rest; and the affirmative of this question will be sufficiently proved if it can be shewn that St. John has begun, where they had broken off, and has left off, where they had begun again; and has given a connected detail of particulars between. To examine, therefore, each of these points in their order; and first the two extremes.

The second journey into Galilee, recorded by St. John, is either the same, or not the same, with that return, recorded by the other Evangelists, which they make to precede the beginning of our Lord's ministry there. If it is the same, one part of our assertion is established; for, from that time forward, St. John suspends, and they continue, the course of the subsequent history, down to the arrival of the second Passover. If it is not the same, then this second journey *into* Galilee must have been followed by a second journey *out* of it; and this second journey *out* of it, by a third journey *into* it, at least; the two former, both prior to the imprisonment of John, but posterior to Jesus' residence in Judæa previously specified; (of none of which things is there the least hint in the Gospel history;) and the last only, coincident with that return into Galilee, pos-

terior to the imprisonment of John, which was the beginning of our Lord's ministry there.   The improbability of
this hypothesis is too great to require its refutation ; and,
though it were true, yet, instead of diminishing, it would
only enlarge, the hiatus in the former accounts; nor do I
know of any harmonist who maintains it.   The second journey of St. John, then, into Galilee, may be implicitly considered the last journey, at least into Galilee, from any
other quarter, before the formal commencement of our Saviour's ministry there ; in which case, the coincidence between his Gospel, and the Gospels of the other three, at
one of the extreme points in particular, becomes indisputable : and this coincidence at one, and the second, extreme, when once made out, may justly be urged, as a presumptive argument for the same kind of coincidence at the
other, and the first.

It has been already shewn that the earliest historical fact,
recorded by St. John, is one of the most memorable, and,
yet, probably one of the latest, events, in the ministry of
the Baptist—his solemn reply to the solemn interrogation
from the Jewish Sanhedrim.   It has been shewn also, that
the time of this event could not have preceded the forty
days' fasting, and the temptation ; though it might have
coincided with the expiration of the latter.   It may be said,
however, that, provided it followed sometime, it might have
followed *any* time, after them ; and, consequently, that it
cannot be concluded with certainty, how far the account of
this event in St. John joins on directly to the account of
the fast, and of the temptation, in the rest : which I am
ready to admit.   But it may be rendered presumptively
certain that there could have been no great interval between
them ; and it has been shewn that there might have been
none ; the one might have happened on the very day when
the other was over.

Jesus came to Bethabara, or wherever else it was that
John was baptizing, πέραν τοῦ Ἰορδάνου, on purpose to be
baptized ; and as soon as that was done, he was led away,
at once, to the wilderness, to undergo his fasting, succeeded

by his temptation.   Whatever be supposed the locality of
this wilderness, the appointed scene of each of these events,
it must have been some wilderness, to arrive at which would
carry him either to the east, or to the south, of Bethabara—
and, consequently, away from Galilee, not towards it.   The
Talmudic writers acknowledge no more than two deserts as
such—one of which would be the scene of the fasting and
the temptation—the desert of Judah, which lay to the
south, and the desert of Sihon and Og, which lay to the
east, of Galilee[d].   There was no desert to the north, except,
perhaps, the great desert of Syria—to which it would be
absurd to suppose our Saviour was carried.

Hence, in order to return from this wilderness, even upon
his way to Galilee, he would have to come back to Bethabara, or in that direction in general, by which he had before
proceeded from it.   The other Evangelists, having brought
him from Galilee to Bethabara, before the baptism and
temptation, either leave him still in Bethabara after them,
or, at least, do not make him return all at once into Galilee:
for, according to them, even after the baptism and temptation, when John was still at large, there must have been
some time during which Jesus was absent from Galilee, or
they would not suppose him to return thither first after John's
imprisonment only.   The narrative of St. John, in particular, as it certainly takes up their's, posterior to the baptism
and temptation in general, so manifestly finds our Saviour
either still at Bethabara, or but recently returned unto it.
If, then, he had quitted this neighbourhood, before the
point of time where *their* accounts expired, he must yet
have come thither again, at, or before, the point of time
where *St. John's* account begins.   The probability, indeed,
is that he was only just returned, when the testimony recorded John i. 29. was delivered by John; and that this
was the first opportunity, since the baptism of Jesus, which
he had had for delivering any such testimony at all.   On
the second day, after this time, Jesus himself was preparing

---

[a] Rel. Pal. i. 376. vide also 1 Macc. v. 24. Ant. Jud. xii. viii. 3.

to return into Galilee; and in three days after, he was actually in Cana of Galilee; and as he had come from Nazareth, the place of his previous residence, in order to be baptized, so, if he would arrive at Cana, he must pass through, or by, Nazareth again, upon his return. Nor did he come to Bethabara, as the course of events subsequently proves, to commence his ministry, but to be baptized, and, perhaps, to undergo the spiritual trial and probation, consequent upon his baptism, as a preparation for it. These ends being accomplished, he would naturally return into Galilee; and continue there, until the time should arrive, when it would be necessary for him to appear in Judæa, where first he designed to commence his ministry. The very purpose of a two days' residence at Bethabara, as it was, might be the express desire of affording John the necessary opportunity of reinforcing his former *general*, by a renewed *particular*, testimony to himself—such as is afterwards referred to John iii. 26. by the followers of the Baptist; and, perhaps, for the sake of some of the chief of his future disciples, the foundation of whose faith in Jesus seems now to have been laid.

We may consider it, therefore, sufficiently probable that the point where St. John's Gospel begins is, on the whole, directly contiguous to the point where the other Gospels break off; and, consequently, that the coincidence between them, at the first of the extremes, is as critical and complete as that at the second: in which case, the remaining question, or what concerns the intermediate detail of particulars, admits of so easy a decision, that we may be satisfied with referring to the bare inspection of the narrative; and proceed to the consideration of another—much more difficult, as well as more important—the question, what is the precise interval of time, comprehended by these details, from the one of the above extremes to the other.

The notes of time, interspersed in the body of the narrative, for the period in question, being collected together, and stated in their order, will stand as follows.

I. The intervening Passover, John ii. 13. being regarded

as a fixed point, up to which we must trace the series of particulars before, and from which we are to deduce them afterwards—first, from the time of the conference with the Sanhedrim, to the time when our Lord was preparing to return into Galilee, was one day.

II. From the time when he was preparing to return into Galilee, to the beginning of the wedding feast at Cana, were three days.

III. From the beginning of this feast, according to the usage of the Jews [c], to its conclusion, there might be as many as seven days, but there could not be more.

IV. After the feast at Cana, the time taken up by the residence of our Lord in Capernaum, which St. John states at *not many days*, we may estimate at seven successive days.

These calculations being laid together, the whole interval between the time of the conference with the Sanhedrim, and the time of the departure from Capernaum, to attend the Passover, John ii. 13. will amount to eighteen days. From Capernaum to Jerusalem would be a journey of not more, at the utmost, than three days' time [f]—and we may assume that our Lord would arrive in Jerusalem, neither after the fourteenth of Nisan, the day of the Passover itself, nor, probably, before the tenth, the day when the Paschal Lamb was appointed originally to be taken up, and the day on which we have conjectured that he himself had been born, and the day when, as it will be shewn hereafter, he presented himself in the temple of God, before the fourteenth of Nisan in the last year of his ministry, as the true Paschal Lamb—then ready to be offered up. The entire interval, then, between the time of the conference with the Sanhedrim, and the arrival in Jerusalem, by the tenth of Nisan, before the first Passover, may be computed at twenty-one days—and that, probably, rather above than under the truth. To this we must add the forty days' fast —subsequent to the baptism, and before the temptation—

[c] Gen. xxix. 27. Judg. xiv. 12. Tobit. xi. 19.   [f] Jos. Vit. 52. Rel. Pal. i. 331.

the time taken up by the temptation itself—and the time taken up in travelling first from Bethabara to the scene of the temptation, and, secondly, from the same scene to Bethabara back again—and we shall obtain the whole measure of time between the baptism, and the arrival in Jerusalem, John ii. 13. On none of these points can there be much uncertainty. The temptation must have been transacted in less than one day after the close of the fast, if not on the last day of the fast itself : and though the scene of the fast had been the great wilderness to the south of Judæa, as I should be disposed to believe it was, even this would not be more than one or two days' journey from Bethabara. Beersheba, on the verge of this desert, was only nineteen miles distant from Hebron [g] : Tekoah, only six miles from Bethlehem, stood upon its borders also ; Ultra, says Jerome [h], nullus est viculus, ne agrestes quidem casæ, et furnorum similes, quas Afri appellant mapalia. Tanta est eremi vastitas, quæ usque ad mare Rubrum, Persarumque, et Æthiopum, atque Indorum, terminos, dilatatur. Maimonides confirms Jerome, by making the distance of the wilderness, into which it was usual to carry the escape goat on the day of expiation, only twelve miles from Jerusalem [i]. Peræa, in which Bethabara was situate, was still nearer to this wilderness. Strabo [k] reckons it only three or four days' journey, from Jericho, to Petra in Arabia deserta. And this is confirmed by Diodorus Siculus, xix. 95. who mentions an instance of a march performed in three days and nights, from Idumæa—much further than Jericho—to Petra ; a distance of 1200 stades, or 150 Roman miles : at the rate of 25 such miles to the *day*. The same passage informs us that Petra was situated in the wilderness—two days' journey distant from the inhabited country : in which case, from the banks of the Jordan, to that desert, could be merely one day's journey. Jerome [l] also makes it only a three days' journey from Gerara (which he places contiguous to Beer-

[g] Euseb. et Hieron. Oper. ii. De Situ et Nominibus. [h] Oper. iii. 1370. Præfatio in Amos. [i] De Sol. die. Exp. iii. 7. Annot. [k] xvi. 1107. [l] Oper. ii. 525. 526.

sheba, and, consequently, on the verge of Arabia deserta,) to Jerusalem. I am persuaded, therefore, that one day's journey would suffice to bring our Saviour to the scene of his fasting and temptation, if that was the wilderness of Arabia Petræa—and one day's journey might bring him back from it again—and that a period of forty-one days might account for the transaction of every thing between.

The whole interval, then, between the baptism of Jesus Christ, and the arrival in Jerusalem at the first Passover, may be very probably computed at sixty-four or sixty-five days, or something more than two months in all; a computation critically in unison with the testimony of St. Luke to the age of our Lord at his baptism, on the supposition that he was born about the Passover; which testimony we concluded to mean that he was less than three, but more than two, months within the full age of thirty[m]: and it is manifest that a more liberal allowance of time, should any parts of the period in question be considered to require it, which would still make the whole less than ninety, though greater than sixty, days in all, might square with the same testimony likewise. The Chronicon Paschale supposes it a period of seventy-six days[n]; and that may be about the truth.

II. The calculations belonging to the next half of the detail, deduced from the Passover downwards, will stand as follows.

I. The time of the stay in Jerusalem, which cannot be stated at longer than the duration of the Paschal feast[o], may be computed from the tenth of Nisan to the twenty-second.

II. The time of some residence in Judæa, posterior to the departure from Jerusalem[p]; neither the place, nor the duration, of which are specified. With regard to the one, then, we may conjecture with certainty only that it was some quarter of Judæa bordering on Samaria, and in the vicinity of water; the former, because our Lord is seen to have tra-

---

velled thence direct to Sychar, the latter, because converts were made and baptized there by his disciples: and with regard to the other, it must be determined on independent grounds, and, for the present, will be left indefinite.

III. After the expiration of this residence, when Jesus set out for Galilee[q], there is the length of his journey to Sychar, and the time of his continuance there; the former of which I estimate at one day's journey, and part of a second at the utmost—and the latter is determined by the Evangelist himself as of two days' length, the first of which might be the day of the arrival itself. It is well known that Sychar lay upon the high road between Jerusalem and Galilee; and its distance from the former is computed, in the Jerusalem Itinerary, at forty Roman miles. But our Saviour was not at Jerusalem before he set out for Sychar; and he might be somewhere in Judæa much nearer to it than Jerusalem itself. Sebaste, according to Josephus[r], (though his statement must probably be understood with some latitude, and perhaps was meant of the frontiers of Judæa, not of Jerusalem,) was only one day's journey from Jerusalem; and Sychar was seven or eight miles nearer to it than Sebaste. I assume, then, that our Saviour had made one day's journey complete, and possibly travelled seven or eight miles on a second, before he arrived at Sychar. On the third day after this arrival he would continue his journey into Galilee; a single day's journey, or at the utmost two, would suffice to bring him there; and this second return would be complete.

We observe, therefore, that no part of the period between the tenth of Nisan, and the time of this arrival in Galilee, admits of doubt or uncertainty, except the intermediate portion which was passed in Judæa. It is herein, consequently, that a difference of opinion between harmonists begins to appear; and it is upon the length of this interval in particular, that the true measure of the hiatus in the former accounts, as supplied by the last, will mainly depend. This hiatus, as far as the time of the preceding

q John iv. 1. 2.   r Ant. Jud. xv. viii. 5.

Passover, was sufficiently determinate; and could not have exceeded two months and one half in all: but from the time of this Passover downwards, to the time of the return into Galilee, it is left to conjecture only, for no other reason than the indefiniteness of the interval, supposed to have been transacted in Judæa. Nor is the length of this period of slight importance in itself; for the duration of the ministry of the Baptist is greatly affected by it: and still less so with respect to the merits of different schemes, whose opinions upon this particular question, instead of squaring together, as they necessarily would square, if they were all agreeable to the truth, may vary by many months, either in excess, or in defect, in respect to both each other and the reality. Yet, notwithstanding this uncertainty, I think it may be shewn that our Saviour's stay in Judæa was neither more, nor less, than a month; or, in other words, that he set out, on his return into Galilee, within forty days after the tenth of Nisan.

It is clear from the testimony of St. John, that the ministry of the Baptist went on, as before, for some time after the ministry of our Lord was begun; that is, while the disciples of Jesus, wheresoever he was in Judæa, were baptizing there, John, also, was still baptizing in Ænon, near Salem; or that they were baptizing in conjunction, and converts were resorting to each. This united ministry continued some time; but the reputation of Jesus must have been daily increasing above the reputation of John, and the popularity, if I may so call it, of the baptism administered by his disciples, must have been daily becoming superior to that of John's; as the intermediate event, John iii. 25. 26. alone would be sufficient to prove.

The eyes of the Pharisees, then, which had been hitherto fixed, with no friendly intention, upon John, began naturally to be turned towards Jesus; the knowledge of which fact, and the implied desire of retiring from their observation, are assigned as the reasons[a], which determined him to remove out of Judæa, (where he was necessarily subject to their inspec-

       [a] John iv. 1—3.

tion, if not to their jurisdiction,) into Galilee, where he would be comparatively safe from both. All this time the ministry of John was still going on, and, though with diminished celebrity, it had not yet ceased. The very procem of the fourth chapter, rightly translated, demonstrates this; When, therefore, the Lord knew that the Pharisees have heard that Jesus is making and baptizing more disciples than John, he left Judæa, and went away again unto Galilee. To justify such a mode of speaking, both must have been making disciples, and baptizing, at the same time; but Jesus in greater numbers than John. If so, when our Lord set out on this return, John was not yet cast into prison; but, according to the other Evangelists, by the time that he arrived in Galilee, on this very return, he was. Now, in the course of the journey, even after leaving Judæa, and before he arrived in Galilee, besides the time taken up in travelling thither, he spent two days at Sychar. If, then, when he first set out from Judæa, John was still at large, he was not imprisoned before Jesus came into Samaria; and if, when he was returned into Galilee, John was no longer at liberty, he must have been imprisoned before he arrived there. He must have been imprisoned, consequently, while Jesus was still in Samaria; and if this was actually the case, then, however near they may approach to an inconsistency, St. John and the other Evangelists will be critically in unison with both each other and the matter of fact.

It has been already assumed[t] that ascension-day, or the forty-first day from the fourteenth of Nisan, *exclusive*, having been the precise termination of our Saviour's personal ministry at the latest of its extremes, A. U. 788. in the sixteenth of Tiberius, the same day was, very probably, its precise beginning at its other extreme, A. U. 780. in the thirteenth of the same reign; and the ministry of our Saviour in person, from the time of the imprisonment of John, having taken up and perpetuated *his* ministry, not only in the order of succession, but also in the kind and character

[t] Diss. v. supra.

of its functions, it became a highly plausible conjecture that the precise beginning of our Lord's ministry was the precise termination of John's—or, in other words, that the day of the imprisonment of John, which must have been some determinate day in particular, was the very day, A. U. 780. in the thirteenth of Tiberius Cæsar, on which our Lord ascended into heaven, A. U. 783. in the sixteenth. It has been shewn also[u] that, whensoever he was imprisoned, it is most likely he was imprisoned some time in the spring. Now, by a reference to the table of Jewish feasts in Dissertation v. of vol. i. the day of Pentecost, A. U. 783. will be seen to have fallen on May 26—and, consequently, ascension-day, ten days before that, fell on May 16. If we are right, then, in the conjecture upon which we are proceeding, May 16. the date of the ascension into heaven, A. U. 783. was also the date of the imprisonment of John, A. U. 780. It was the date also of our Lord's arrival in Galilee, and, consequently, of his departure from Sychar. The day of his arrival in Sychar, therefore, was either May 14. or May 13—the former, if the day of his arrival was included in the days of his residence there; the latter, if it was exclusive of them. Now the same table of feasts will shew that the Passover was celebrated A. U. 780. on April 9—and the Paschal feast would expire upon April 16. which coincided with Nisan 21. In this case, if we suppose our Lord to have left Jerusalem upon April 17. or 18. and to have arrived at Sychar on May 13. or 14. the length of the previous residence in Judæa, to the time when he set out for Galilee, might be twenty-six or twenty-seven days, very little less than one month; and in support of this conclusion we may argue further as follows.

I. It is not inconsistent with the fullest import of the terms, in which the Evangelist speaks of its duration, καὶ ἐκεῖ διέτριβε[v]. The same expression occurs[w] to describe another similar residence in Judæa, of which it is capable of proof that it could not have lasted even so long as a month.

---

[u] Vol. i. Diss. viii. Appendix. 315. [v] iii. 22. [w] xi. 54.

II. It is adequate to account for the intervening particulars on record ; the commencement, continuance, and
progress, of the work of baptizing by our Lord's disciples—
the increasing celebrity of his reputation—the comparative
decrease of John's—the jealousy, produced by this cause in
the disciples of the latter—the attention to the conduct, or
the pretensions, of Jesus, beginning to be excited in the
Sanhedrim—the expediency, on prudential considerations,
of withdrawing himself from their personal cognizance, and
the commencement, accordingly, of his journey into Galilee.
And yet it may not be more than sufficient for this purpose, or no more than we may well suppose would be requisite to bring all these things to pass.

III. That a little before this departure John was baptizing in Ænon, near Salem [x], and no longer at Bethabara,
because there was *much water there*, after what has been
elsewhere observed already [y], and what will be shewn more
fully hereafter, may justly be considered a proof that the
rainy season had been some time over, and water was beginning to be scarce; which would necessarily be the case
a little before the feast of Pentecost, or nearer to midsummer than to the vernal equinox ; but not at the opposite
quarter of the year.   According to Eusebius and Jerome [z],
Ænon and Salem were both about eight Roman miles distant from Scythopolis, the ancient Bethshan, which Josephus [a] places at one hundred and twenty stades from Tiberias, the southern extremity of the Lake of Galilee.   Whether they were on the Galilean or the Peræan side of the
Jordan, is decided in favour of the former by John iii. 23.
26. where Ænon is opposed to πέραν τοῦ Ἰορδάνου.

IV. If St. John's computation of hours, throughout his
Gospel, is, as there is good reason to conclude [b], the same
neither with the Jewish, nor with the Roman, which were
in fact alike, but with the modern—the sixth hour, when
our Lord arrived at Gerizim [c], was either six in the morn-

[x] iii. 23.   [y] Vol. i. Diss. ix.   [z] Oper. ii. De Situ et Nominibus.
[a] Vit. 65. p. 97.   [b] Vide Townson's Discourses on the Gospels. Discourse
viii. part i. and ii.   [c] iv. 6.

ing, or six in the evening; at both which times after the
autumnal equinox, and near midwinter, it would necessarily
have been dark; but at each of which times, after the vernal equinox, and near to midsummer, it would still be open
day.   The very distance of the frontiers of Judæa from
Sychar confirms this conclusion in the present instance; for
we cannot calculate this distance, from any part of Judæa, at
less than twenty-seven or twenty-eight miles[d]—and from the
neighbourhood of Jerusalem, or of Jericho, it would be half
as many more.   If our Lord had travelled this distance in
one day, he could not have arrived before six at night; and
if he had travelled twenty miles of it on one day, he would
accomplish the other seven or eight, before six in the morning of the next.

That he arrived at the usual period of some meal appears
from iv. 8. and that both πρωΐ, the first hour of the day,
and ὀψία, the last but one, were such stated periods among
the Jews, is also a well known fact.   In the summer season,
too, the morning or evening, and not the middle of the day,
is notoriously the most convenient time for travelling, in
the east, and the most commonly selected for that purpose;
and yet, in the same season, the heat of the sun even at
that time, and especially in the morning, would be such before six o'clock, that one who had travelled for an hour or
two after sunrise, might well be weary, as Jesus is said to
have been[e].

It favours the presumption, respecting the time of his
arrival at Gerizim, that shortly afterwards a Samaritan
woman was found coming thither to fetch water: for the
customs of the east have always been invariable, both in
assigning this kind of menial service to the women in particular, and in fixing on morning or evening for sending
them upon it[f].   That there were wells, likewise, of great
antiquity, and of very elaborate construction, still to be met
with in Judæa, is attested by Origen, contra Celsum [g]. Ὅτι

[d] Rel. Pal. ii. 416. 423. iii. 1007.   [e] iv. 6.   [f] Gen. xxiv. 11. 1 Sam.
ix. 11. Mark xiv. 13. Luke xxii. 10.   [g] iv. 193. Vide also Euseb. et
Hieron. Oper. ii. De Situ et Nominibus. Φρέαρ ἔσκον.

δὶ καὶ φρέατα ἐν γῇ Φιλιστιαίων κατεσκεύασται ὑπὸ τῶν δικαίων, ὡς ἐν τῇ Γενέσει ἀναγέγραπται, δῆλον ἐκ τῶν δεικνυμένων ἐν τῇ Ἀσκαλῶνι θαυμαστῶν φρεάτων, καὶ ἱστορίας ἀξίων, διὰ τὸ ξένον καὶ παρηλλαγμένον τῆς κατασκευῆς, ὡς πρὸς τὰ λοιπὰ φρέατα.

That the woman came out of the neighbouring city is so obviously implied in the account, as to make it super-fluous even to remind the reader of this fact, had not Bretschneider, in his paradoxical work on the genuineness of St. John's Gospel, thought proper, from iv. 7. ἔρχεται γυνὴ ἐκ τῆς Σαμαρείας, to suppose it was meant that she came from the city of Samaria—two hours' journey at least from Mount Gerizim—and to draw an inference, from the absurdity of such a supposition, disparaging to the accuracy of the Evangelist[h]. By so doing he has betrayed, in the first place, a want of discernment, or a want of candour, in not perceiving, or not acknowledging, that γυνὴ ἐκ τῆς Σαμαρείας, in this passage, is plainly equivalent to ἡ γυνὴ ἡ Σαμαρεῖτις, in another[i]; and both describe merely a native of Samaria, in opposition to one of Judæa, or of Galilee: secondly, an inattention to contemporary history; that there was now no city of Samaria, but, since the ancient Samaria had been rebuilt by Herod, that its modern name was Se-baste[k]. Nor is it of any use to oppose to this assertion the tes-timony of Acts viii. 5. which speaks of πόλιν τῆς Σαμαρείας: had that meant the city of Samaria, the Greek idiom would have required εἰς πόλιν, or εἰς τὴν πόλιν, Σαμάρειαν: as at Acts xi. 5. ἐν πόλει Ἰόππῃ. We know not, consequently, what city of Samaria is intended here: but, if it was the city of which Simon Magus himself was a native, then, ac-cording to Justin Martyr[l], it was a city called Gitton. Thirdly, a total disregard to the context[m]; which shews clearly that the city from which this woman came, and the city to which she returned, and the city near which our Saviour had originally arrived, and where he subsequently stayed two days, were all one and the same, Shechem, Sy-chem, Sicima, or Sychar; for it is called by each of these

---

[h] iii. 17. 98.   [i] iv. 9.   [k] Jos. Ant. Jud. xiii. x. 2. xv. viii. 5. B. i. ii. 7.   [l] Apol. i. 38.   [m] iv. 5. 8. 28. 30. 39.

names indifferently; situated formerly within the tribe of Ephraim[n]; and, after a Roman colony had been planted either on its site, or within one Roman mile of its site[o], better known by the name of Flavia Neapolis, and the birthplace of Justin, the Philosopher and Martyr, himself[p]. Its proximity to Mount Gerizim is attested by Josephus— Σίχιμα…κειμένην πρὸς τῷ Γαριζεὶν ὄρει—Τὸ ὄρος τὸ Γαριζεῖν ὑπέρκειται δὲ τῆς Σιχίμων πόλεως[q].

The rate of travelling anciently for a day's journey on foot, which, in Arbuthnot's Tables of ancient Coins, Weights, and Measures, is estimated at thirty-three English miles, is probably beyond the truth; since, one day with another, we cannot suppose it to have much exceeded the standard of five or six and twenty even Roman miles. It is repeatedly asserted by Josephus, that the ordinary length of the journey from Galilee to Jerusalem, even by the shortest route, viz. through Samaria, was an interval of three days' time; though it is certainly possible that it might be accomplished in two. The calculation of Reland[r] will shew that from Jerusalem, through Bethel, or Bethar, and by Sychem, or Neapolis, the usual, and at the same time the most direct, route to the lake of Tiberias in Galilee, was a distance of seventy-three Roman miles; which is an average of twenty-four Roman miles to a day.

This ordinary or average rate of travelling for pedestrians is well illustrated by a case in point, the distance between Cæsarea and Joppa, and the length of time taken up in travelling over that. This distance, by the help of the Itinerarium Hierosolymitanum, and that of Antoninus, conjointly, is calculated by Reland[s] at forty-one Roman miles: for though that is properly the distance between Cæsarea and Lydda, or Diospolis, yet Lydda and Joppa, referred to Cæsarea, in point of distance, were on a par.

Now, if we compare together Acts x. 30. 3. 33. 8. 9. 23. 24. it will appear that the messengers of Cornelius were

[n] Josh. xxiv. 32.   [o] Itinerar. Hieros. Ap. Rel. Pal. ii. 416.   [p] Apol. i. 1.
[q] Ant. Jud. xi. viii. 6. v. vii. 2. Vide also iv. viii. 44. v. 1. 19.   [r] Pal. ii.
416. 423.   [s] Ibid. ii. 445.

despatched from Cæsarea the day after his vision of the angel—they arrived in Joppa, the day after they set out, about the sixth hour of the day—Peter set out with them back on the following morning—and they all arrived in Cæsarea about the ninth hour of the ensuing day—on the *fourth* day from the day of the vision *exclusive*.   It thus appears that the distance between Cæsarea and Joppa, or forty-one Roman miles, was as nearly as possible one ordinary day's journey and a half, and yet at the rate of twenty-six or twenty-seven miles to a day.

The distance of Bethel, or Bethar, on the confines of Samaria and Judæa, was twenty-eight Roman miles from Sychar[t]; a distance which might, therefore, be accomplished, without any great or unusual exertion, in one day's time. Hence, if we may only assume that the place of our Saviour's residence in Judæa, before this departure, through Samaria, into Galilee, was Bethel or its vicinity, it becomes a probable inference that he had travelled from thence to Sychar in one day; and, consequently, arrived in the evening.   Now Bethel was contiguous to Ephraim; and it is rendered probable that our Lord was residing at Bethel, or near it, on this occasion, because we have St. John's assurance that he was residing at Ephraim[u], and, consequently, near it, on the only similar occasion, hereafter, which is specified in the course of his history.   This, then, is the conclusion in which we may finally acquiesce; viz. that Jesus arrived at Sychar after travelling one whole day; and, therefore, if he arrived at the sixth hour, he arrived at six in the evening.   The day of his arrival, it has been shewn already, was probably May 13; the dates of his two days' residence would be, consequently, May 14. and 15; and the day of his departure into Galilee would be May 16: upon which coincidences, as I shall have occasion to revert to them again hereafter, I shall make no further remark at present, except this: that, according to my own calculation of the days of the week, May 13. was a Thursday, and May 16. was a Sunday.

[t] Pal. ii. 416. 423. iii. 637.   [u] xi. 54.

V. When our Lord was actually arrived in Galilee, the Galileans, it is said[v], received him gladly—having seen all things which he did in Jerusalem at the feast—for they also went to the feast. This feast, twice referred to, it is impossible to doubt, is the feast, spoken of first ii. 13. and again ii. 23. that is the feast of the Passover in the thirteenth of Tiberius Cæsar; and the miracles performed at that feast are the miracles referred to, expressly at ii. 23. and implicitly at iii. 2. We may conclude, then, that our Lord had never been in Galilee, since the time of the attendance of the Galileans at this feast, and the time of the performance of those miracles, which they had seen, and still remembered to have seen, performed at this feast, until now, when he came among them directly from Samaria. It follows, therefore, that he must have come among them in the interval between that feast and the next, that is, between the Passover and the Pentecost, both in this year; and not between the Passover, and any other feast, later than that.

For, if the favourable reception, now given to him by the people of Galilee, was solely on the strength of the miracles which they knew and remembered him to have performed, when they and he had met in conjunction at the Passover, the inference appears to me irresistible that he, and the people of Galilee, had never met again, or, at least, had met no where, either in Jerusalem, or out of it, where miracles had been performed, or by the people of Galilee in particular had been seen to be performed, from that time to this. This might be both possible and probable, if our Lord had performed miracles before the eyes of the Galileans, at one feast, and come among them in person, before the next, and spent the intermediate time, apart from Galilee, where he performed either no miracles, or none which were known to, or observed by, them; but it would not be so on any other supposition, either that Jesus and the people of Galilee had met again in Jerusalem, at other feasts, since the Passover, and yet no miracles, which might be known and remembered as well as those at the Passover,

[v] John iv. 45.

had been then performed; or that, though other feasts had since transpired, Jesus and the people of Galilee had met at Jerusalem only at the feast of the Passover, before them all.   Each of these hypotheses would carry with it its own refutation.   During the short interval of a single month, between the close of the Paschal week, and the return into Galilee, when our Saviour was somewhere in Judæa, it would be nothing incredible that the Galileans should have seen, or even heard, nothing of him, and yet, that, when he actually appeared among them, they should still have retained a strong and lively recollection of his miracles, at the Passover, not long before : but it would be utterly inconceivable either that our Lord himself should have passed upwards of the eight first months of his ministry, in comparative inactivity—or that if he, and the people of Galilee, had ever met in Jerusalem again, the proofs of his character, or his mission, exhibited eight months before, should be the only grounds of conviction, to account for the chearfulness of his reception among them, long after.

VI. Οὐχ ὑμεῖς λέγετε· ὅτι ἔτι τετράμηνόν ἐστι, καὶ ὁ θερισμὸς ἔρχεται; ἰδοὺ, λέγω ὑμῖν, ἐπάρατε τοὺς ὀφθαλμοὺς ὑμῶν, καὶ θεάσασθε τὰς χώρας, ὅτι λευκαί εἰσι πρὸς θερισμὸν ἤδη. John iv. 35. The natural inference from such an address as this is that the speaker is calling the attention of his hearers to some sensible fact ; and though, beneath this sensible illustration, a spiritual meaning may be couched, this would make no difference ; for every sign is something *per se* as well as in its signification—and even where the external medium is most analogous to the inward verity, or the sign as such is the best qualified for its proper signification, this nature of its own must remain the same as before.   Whatever end, then, our Lord might have in view by the contemplation of a sensible image, he would still be referring to such an image—to the observation of an actual fact—to the state of the country around him—the ripeness of the corn, and, therefore, the approach of the harvest season.   To lift up the eyes, in the first place, and to survey the fields, in the next, are manifestly literal acts—which it would be absurd to understand in any but the literal sense ; yet they are designed for one effect, which is the sensible impression in question ; and, therefore, this sensible impression also was intended to be a literal impression.

A figurative import, as put upon this result, however incongruous to the simplicity of the acts which precede it, can still make it signify only one thing ; viz. that the fields were crowded with those, among whom the spiritual harvest of our Saviour's ministry either had begun, or was about to begin ; which crowding, at least, must have been a matter of fact : and if so, the crowds, which were thronging the fields at the time, must have been the crowds of Samaritans, flocking from Sychar—for our Lord was now on Gerizim, and near no place but that—and these inhabitants of Sychar must have been the proper subjects of our Saviour's ministry, as either already begun, or about to begin hereafter : in which case, I would put it to the judgment of my reader, whether the resort from Sychar, produced merely by the report of a single woman, even had it now taken place, and our Lord and his disciples had not still been alone on the mountain, could have been so considerable as to fill the country ; and still more, whether Samaritans as such in general, or they in particular, could on any principle be supposed to be meant by the proper subjects of our Saviour's ministry, either present, or to come ; of that ministry—which had yet been begun only in Judæa, and was still to be prosecuted, or resumed afresh, only in Galilee—and ever after to be continued among the inhabitants of these two regions, the lost sheep of the house of Israel.

There is no proof that our Saviour was ever in Samaria at all, except on this occasion, at the very beginning, and on another, at the very end, of his ministry, and, then, also as only travelling through, not preaching in, that country : but there is proof that on two occasions [w]—once, actually, and a second time, virtually—he forbade those, whom he sent out to assist in the discharge of his own commission,

---

[w] Matt. x. 5.   Luke x. 1.

and, consequently, among the same persons, and on the same work, with himself, either to enter into a city of Samaritans, or to go away into the direction of the Gentiles; which was to place Samaritans and Gentiles on a par. It is not, indeed, to be denied, that the work of our Saviour's ministry, or rather those among whom, and for whom, this work was to be performed, are figuratively called the harvest; and the metaphor, when so applied, is perfectly just and beautiful. But it is never so applied except ἁπλῶς; never in such strange and incongruous terms as the fields *being white* for the harvest; between which, and the idea of a concourse or resort of people, however great, there is no possible affinity whatever. The fields being ripe, or the fields being full, for the harvest might have answered in some measure to this idea; but the fields being white for the harvest can answer to nothing but the sensible fact of the forwardness of the corn, when its original green, or brown, is actually changed to a light yellow, resembling white.

What, then, shall we say to the first part of the declaration? The allusion is to a proverb—and its connection with what follows must be thus explained. When the seed is first sown, is it not a common saying, there are yet four months, and the harvest, or reaping time, will come? Lift up your eyes, survey the country round about, and be convinced, by the whiteness of the fields, that the four months are drawing to a close, and the season of the reaping is at hand. The end, which is proposed by the reference to this natural phenomenon, may also be explained as follows. This ripeness of the visible and the natural harvest, now that the period requisite to the maturity of the seed is accomplished, may be an earnest to you of the ripeness of that, as yet unseen, and spiritual, harvest, to bring which to maturity will be the object of *my* personal labours; but to reap which will be the object of *your's*; a ripeness, consequently, which will then be complete when *my* ministry is over, and *your's* is about to begin.

Our Lord is speaking prophetically, and in the usual style

of the language of prophecy, he is speaking of what was still future, as if it were already past. For he proceeds: Ἐγὼ ἀπέστειλα ὑμᾶς θερίζειν ὃ οὐχ ὑμεῖς κεκοπιάκατε· ἄλλοι κεκοπιάκασι, καὶ ὑμεῖς εἰς τὸν κόπον αὐτῶν εἰσεληλύθατε ˣ——where, if any one should take these words to relate to a *past* mission of the disciples, he would be bound to· shew when, and where, and for what purpose, that mission had taken place. But, if they do not relate to a *past*, they must relate to a *future*, mission; and the way to render them will be this. I *shall* send you to reap that which you *shall* not have laboured for; others *shall* have laboured for it, and you *shall* enter into the effect of their labour. Two, as yet future, occasions, in the course of our Saviour's lifetime, there were, when the disciples were sent out; once, upon the mission of the Twelve, and again, upon that of the Seventy; neither of which, however, can here be meant; because the state of the case supposes not one set of agents or workmen, assisting another, and all preparing for a common result, but one set of agents or workmen, succeeding to another, and stepping in by themselves to a certain·result; whereas both the Twelve, and the Seventy, were sent out, as we have seen ʸ, in the former of these capacities, not the latter, and as fellow-labourers, with both our Saviour and the Baptist, in the work which they each had to perform.

There would, however, be a third such mission—but after his death—the mission of the Apostles in their proper character of the emissaries of Christianity, completing the purpose of the ministry of our Lord in his lifetime, by the commencement, the continuance, and the consummation, of that scheme of formal Christianity, the establishment of the kingdom of heaven upon earth, to announce which, and to prepare for its reception in its proper time, was the object both of his ministry and of the Baptist's. This mission is here intended; and, as referred to this, every thing becomes easy and natural. The effect of our Saviour's personal ministry, and that of the Baptist's, would be to have sown the seed, and to have raised to maturity the crop—but not

---

ˣ iv. 38.   ʸ Vol. ii. Diss. v.

to have begun the reaping, or gathered in the fruit—that should be reserved for the ministry of the Apostles.   And, therefore, he proceeds ; And he, that shall reap, shall earn his wages, and shall gather together fruit against everlasting life; that both he who is sowing, and he who is reaping, (or he who is to sow, and he who is to reap) may rejoice in common.   For herein, that is, by this dispensation of one ministry succeeding, and giving effect to, another, the saying shall truly consist, that he who is sowing is one, and he who is reaping is another : the ordinary sense of which proverb was merely to express the uncertain event of human schemes, by which it so often happens that the same hand does not both sow and reap ; one party has had the anxiety and toil of the acquisition, another steps in to the enjoyment.   How natural and pertinent, at the outset of our Saviour's ministry, such reflections as these would be, is too obvious to require any proof.

There were two seasons of harvest among the Jews ; the season of barley-harvest, the first-fruits of which were to be consecrated at the Passover, and the season of wheatharvest, of which the same thing was true at the Pentecost[z].   Of wheat-harvest, in particular, Jerome, in Amos iv. 7. writes thus : Prohibui a vobis imbrem, cum adhuc superessent tres menses usque ad messem : quæ appellatur pluvia serotina, et agris Palæstinæ, arvisque, sitientibus vel maxime necessaria est ; ut ne, quando herba turgeret in messem, et triticum parturiret, nimia siccitate aresceret. Significat autem vernum tempus extremi mensis Aprilis ; a quo, usque ad messem frumenti, tres menses supersunt[a]. Between each of these seasons, and the corresponding seedtime, there was literally an interval of four months : Consider now, from this day and upward, from the four and twentieth day of the ninth month. . . . Is the seed yet in the barn? . . . from this day will I bless you[b]. On which Jerome —Igitur decimus est mensis, eo tempore quo semina latitant in terra, nec futura fæcunditas conjectari potest[c].   Casleu,

[z] Philo de Decalog. 766. De Victimis. 837. De Septen. et Fest. 1192.
[a] Oper. iii. 1400. 1401.   [b] Haggai ii. 18. 19.   [c] Oper. iii. 1702.

then, which in a rectified year would answer nearly to our December, was one seed-time, four months before Nisan, or the time of barley-harvest ; and, according to Maimonides [d], the wheat, designed for the bread, Ad altaris ferta, et libamina, was sown seventy days before the Passover, so as to be ripe at the Pentecost, or fifty days after it; that is, the harvest was just one hundred and twenty days, or literally four solar months, later than the sowing-time. Diodorus Siculus asserts the same thing of Egypt—Τὸ σπέρμα βάλλοντας, μετὰ τέτταρας ἢ πέντε μῆνας ἀπαντᾶν ἐπὶ τὸν θερισμόν [c].——Nor, as we have seen from Pliny, was wheat-harvest in that country ever later than the month of May. At the time of the Exodus from Egypt, when the vernal equinox coincided with April 5. the flax and the barley, it is said [f], were both destroyed by the hail, because both were at that time in the ear ; but the wheat and the rye were not destroyed, because they were neither of them arrived at maturity. The plague of hail must have been some time in the month of March, and very probably in its former half.

But that no literal seed-time could have been meant is well argued by Origen, in his Commentary upon the place, ii. 230. If the time, says he, when Jesus spake these words, was four months before the harvest, it was evident that it was winter. One harvest, at least, begins to take place in Judæa about the time of the month, called among the Hebrews Nisan, when they are celebrating the Passover ; so that they sometimes make their unleavened bread of new grain. But let us suppose that the harvest is not about that month, but about the next to that, the month which is called among them Jar ; even in this case, a four months' time before that month is the depth of winter. When, then, we shall have shewn that, when he spake these words, it was about the season of harvest, either then at its maturity, or drawing, perhaps, to a close, we shall have demonstrated what we propose.

Of the appearance of things in the winter, Jerome in Za-

---

[d] De Reb. Alt. interd. vii. 4.   [e] i. 36.   [f] Exod. ix. 31. 32.

chariam gives this description ᵍ—Octavus apud Hebræos mensis, qui apud illos Maresvan .... apud nos November, dicitur, hyemis exordium est, in quo, æstatis calore consumpto, omnis terra virore nudatur, et mortalium corpora contrahuntur.

Even on the testimony of this passage, therefore, which has been the chief reason why some Harmonists (among whom Archbishop Newcome is one) have thought it necessary to place the journey through Samaria in the month of December, we may consider it almost demonstratively certain, that it coincided with the acme of wheat-harvest, or was but a little before it ; which coincidence would be the case, if it occurred, where we suppose it to have occurred, about a fortnight before Pentecost. For I have supposed these words to have been spoken on May 13. and the feast of Pentecost was coincident with May 30.

There is yet another argument in favour of the same conclusion, taken from the order and succession of Sabbatic years at this time, which, though not less strong than any thing yet mentioned, I have reserved for an Appendix to this Dissertation, by itself : and this point being thus presumptively established, it remains only that we should state the order of facts during the rest of St. John's account, before it breaks off—and so make an end of the subject for the present.

After our Saviour's arrival in Galilee, he is brought again to Canaʰ : but, before this, we meet with the observation ⁱ, For Jesus himself bore witness that a prophet hath no honour in his own country ; where, by his own country, Nazareth, the reputed place of his birth, and the actual place of his bringing up, may very well be meant. Now, if we consult the maps of Judæa, it will be seen that one, who was travelling from Samaria to Cana, would pass by Nazareth : and there is an account, in St. Luke ᵏ, of a visit to Nazareth, at which the truth of the assertion that a prophet has little honour in his own country was verified by the event. It may be imagined, then, that this visit to Naza-

ᵍ Oper. iii. 1707.   ʰ iv. 46.   ⁱ Ib. 44.   ᵏ iv. 16.

P 4

reth, in St. Luke, preceded the visit to Cana, in St. John; and that the observation in question was expressly premised in reference to it : but this conclusion would be premature.

For, first, the first miracle, after the return into Galilee, was wrought on this visit to Cana[1]; and, secondly, before Jesus came to Nazareth, one miracle, or more, had been performed at Capernaum[m]. Now the miracle performed in Cana came to pass in Capernaum ; for it was performed by our Lord *at* Cana on a sick person *in* Capernaum ; and if the visit to Nazareth was only sufficiently later than the visit to Cana, for the news of the miracle to have been spread from Capernaum to Nazareth, before our Lord came thither, this might be the miracle referred to. Now Nazareth was nearer to Capernaum, than Cana to Tiberias—and yet, according to Josephus[n], a man might ride from Tiberias to Cana, in a single night.

The use of the plural, ὅσα ἠκούσαμεν γενόμενα, though in reference even to a single miracle, is so natural in relation to events made known by hearsay, and so familiar to the idiom of the Greek tongue, besides being exactly parallel to Mark v. 19. 20. and Luke viii. 39. as to constitute no objection.

The visit to Cana, then, preceded the visit to Nazareth, and supplies a link in the chain of the account, which would otherwise be perceptibly missed : for, however true in itself it might be, that miracles had been performed in Capernaum—neither the truth of the fact, nor the propriety of the allusion to it, would have appeared from St. Luke, independent of the light reflected upon them by St. John. And such being the benefit of the coincidence between the two accounts, it is unreasonable to question whether what possesses so happy an effect, in clearing up the obscurity of a former Evangelist, was so intended, or not, by a later. The declaration, therefore, at verse forty-four, relates to nothing which Jesus can be supposed to have said, but to something

[1] John iv. 54.   [m] Luke iv. 23.   [n] Vit. 16. 17.

which he was about to suffer : he had not yet testified, but he was shortly to testify, in his own person, that a prophet hath no honour in his own country; and when he did testify it, it was by the example of the reception, which he experienced, on the part either of his townsmen of Nazareth, in particular, or of his countrymen of Galilee, in general, with both of whom his ministry, though formally begun among them first, yet ultimately failed alike. It is not improbable, that this very visit to Nazareth was with a view to have begun his ministry there; and the previous visit to Cana, with the second miracle which then took place, recalling, perhaps, the remembrance of the first also, might have been designed, among other uses, to prepare for this result. But on this subject something more will be said elsewhere [o].

[o] **Diss. viii. part ii.**

DISSERTATION VII.

APPENDIX.

Coincidence of a Sabbatic year with the beginning of our Saviour's ministry.

IT is a well-authenticated fact, that the Sabbatic year was as strictly observed among the Jews, after the return from captivity, as it had ever been before it—and, perhaps, more so[a]—Καὶ τὸ ἕβδομον ἔτος ἀνείσφορον εἶναι—Χωρὶς τοῦ ἑβδόμου ἔτους, ὃν Σαββατικὸν ἐνιαυτὸν προσαγορεύουσιν· ἐπειδὴ ἐν αὐτῷ μήτε ἀπὸ τῶν δένδρων καρπὸν λαμβάνουσι, μήτε σπείρουσι[b]—Vide also the sequel of the same section. If this, then, was the case, and the journey through Samaria, considered in the last Dissertation, had coincided with any part of a year of rest, it must be morally improbable that an allusion should, at that time, have been made either to the usual period of sowing the seed, or to the ripeness of the corn, and the proximity of the harvest. Nor would it constitute any difficulty that our Lord was in Samaria, and not in Judæa; for the Samaritans, as we may collect from the following passage in Josephus, observed the Sabbatic year, as well, and at the same times, as the Jews: Ἀξιούντων ἀφιέναι τὸν φόρον αὐτοῖς τοῦ ἑβδοματικοῦ ἔτους· οὐδὲ γὰρ αὐτοὺς σπείρειν ἐν αὐτῷ[c].

A year of rest began with seed-time in one year, and continued until seed-time in the next : and its observance consisted in leaving the lands uncultivated, the gardens and the vineyards untouched[d]. There was, consequently, neither

---

[a] Maimon. De anno Jubilæi. passim.   [b] Jos. Ant. Jud. xi. viii. 5.
xiv. x. 6.   [c] Ant. Jud. xi. viii. 6.   [d] Exod. xxiii. 10. 11. Lev. xxv.
2—7.

harvest, nor ingathering, during it, except of such productions of the soil as might have sprung up of themselves ; and that, too, not as the property of the owners of the soil, but as open to all, or as especially the right of the poor and the stranger.

Now there is clear proof, in contemporary history, of four different Sabbatic years—and at great intervals of time from each other—any one of which being assumed as actually such, a table may be constructed of others, either before, or after, it—as may be requisite. The first of these years bears date from the seed-time of the 150th year of the Æra Seleucidarum—the first year of the Maccabean Dynasty, as such—that is, B. C. 163[e] : the second, from the seed-time in the first year of John Hyrcanus, dated from the death of his father—that is, the seed-time, B. C. 135[f] : the third, from the seed-time of the year when Jerusalem was taken by Herod and Sosius—that is, as we have seen elsewhere, B. C. 37[g] : the fourth, from the seed-time of the year, before the destruction of the city, and of the temple, of Jerusalem, by Titus—that is, A. D. 69 [h].

Besides these, there are three more, which, if not expressly declared to be such, have yet been proved, on grounds of strong presumption, to have been so[i].

The truth of the fact, in each of these instances, will be made apparent by the following Table, which extends from 150. Æræ Seleucidarum, to A. D. 70. the year of the destruction of Jerusalem—and, proceeding merely on the assumption that the first of the number was a Sabbatic year, renders it demonstratively certain that the rest were all so likewise. Each of these coincidences, to which any argument is attached, is denoted by an asterisk.

e 1 Macc. vi. 26—49—54. Jos. Ant. Jud. xii. ix. 3. 5.   f Ibid. xiii.
viii. 1. B. i. ii. 4. Vide also vol. i. Diss. iv. Appendix ii.   g Ant. Jud.
xiv. xvi. 4. xv. 1. 2. vol. ii. Diss. iv. Appendix i.   h Maim. De anno Jub.
i. 4. Mishna, and the Sedar Olam.   i Vol. i. Diss. iv. Appendix i. 199.
Diss. xiii. 565. vol. ii. Diss. i. 37. 51.

Table of Sabbatic years, from B. C. 163. or 150. Ær. Sel. to A. D. 70 : every such year extending from the first of Tisri in one year, to the first of Tisri in the next.

Sabbatic years.			Urbis Conditæ.				B. C.	
*I.	-	-	*591	to	592	- -	*163 to	162
II.	-	-	598		599	- -	156	155
III.	-	-	605		606	- -	149	148
IV.	-	-	612		613	- -	142	141
*V.	-	-	*619		620	- -	*135	134
VI.	-	-	626		627	- -	128	127
VII.	-	-	633		634	- -	121	120
VIII.	-	-	640		641	- -	114	113
IX.	-	-	647		648	- -	107	106
X.	-	-	654		655	- -	100	99
XI.	-	-	661		662	- -	93	92
XII.	-	-	668		669	- -	86	85
XIII.	-	-	675		676	- -	79	78
XIV.	-	-	682		683	- -	72	71
XV.	-	-	689		690	- -	65	64
XVI.	-	-	696		697	- -	58	57
XVII.	-	-	703		704	- -	51	50
XVIII.	-	-	710		711	- -	44	43
XIX.	-	-	*717		718	- -	*37	36
XX.	-	-	724		725	- -	30	29
*XXI.	-	-	*731		732	- -	*23	22
XXII.	-	-	738		739	- -	16	15
XXIII.	-	-	745		746	- -	9	8
XXIV.	-	-	752		753	- -	2	1

Sabbatic years.			Urbis Conditæ.				A. D.	
XXV.	-	-	759		760	- -	6	7
XXVI.	-	-	766		767	- -	13	14
XXVII.	-	-	773		774	- -	20	21
*XXVIII.	-	-	*780		781	- -	*27	28
XXIX.	-	-	787		788	- -	34	35
*XXX.	-	-	*794		795	- -	*41	42
XXXI.	-	-	801		802	- -	48	49
*XXXII.	-	-	*808		809	- -	*55	56
XXXIII.	-	-	815		816	- -	62	63
XXXIV.	-	-	822		823	- -	69	70

Of the above years that, with which I am chiefly concerned at present, is the twenty-eighth in order, from A. U. 780. or A. D. 27. to A. U. 781. or A. U. 28.   It is in this year, but in the first half of this year, A. U. 780. or A. D. 27. and, consequently, before the periodical return of the Sabbatic year, which would not begin until the September following, that I suppose the journey through Samaria to have taken place.   There would be the regular harvest in this year, and an allusion to the approaching season of reaping, or to the fulness of the fields around, might now not only be possible, but, if there was still any vestige remaining of that particular Providence, which at a former period of the Jewish history had been pledged to bless the sixth year in a triple proportion to any other [k]—peculiarly apposite and striking.

On any other hypothesis, which should place this journey in the month of December the same year, as there could be no regular seed-time, or process of sowing, then arrived, or going on—so neither could there be any allusion to them—much less any literal allusion, such as would necessarily imply that they were then arrived, or then going on.   I look upon this coincidence, which, even according to my own arrangement, treads as closely on the verge of an inconsistency, as without falling into it was possible, to be one which could have been produced by the matter of fact alone.

It is not, however, to be disguised from the knowledge of the reader, that the calculation of Sabbatic years, according to the received principles of the modern Jewish reckoning, (principles, which have been sanctioned by the authority of many learned chronologers,) would differ from the above, so far as in each instance to antedate the year in question, by placing it in the year before.   Yet, notwithstanding this, there can be little hesitation what mode of computation, in a case of this kind, ought to be followed, instead of what—whether the computation of the Jewish Rabbins, or that of the book

[k] Lev. xxv. 20—22.

of Maccabees, and of Josephus. The author of that book, and the Jewish historian, each of them contemporaries with all, or with part, at least, of the events which they record, could not have been ignorant what years were observed in their own time, and among their countrymen, as Sabbatic years ; nor by what rule their recurrrence was determined. Much more inconceivable is it that four distinct, and very distant, years, such as those produced above, every one of which, as referred to its place in contemporary history, or the succession of synchronous events, admits of being determined on purely independent grounds, (which have nothing to do with the assumption that it was, or was not, a Sabbatic year,) should all be asserted to have been such, and all be found, on comparison, to be such, if they had not each been actually such. No such coincidence between them could be the effect of chance ; and yet the assertion, though individually, and independently, made of each, is implicitly true of all ; for if any one of them was a Sabbatic year, the rest must have been so likewise.

With respect, indeed, to the last, or the year before the destruction of Jerusalem, the assurance, *a priori*, might be said to have rested on tradition merely ; but this year was in all respects so memorable, and so characterized in the annals of Jewish history, by its momentous and melancholy interest, above all others before or after it, that what tradition had perpetuated of this year, even *a priori*, it might be supposed, would be implicitly to be trusted ; and tradition had certainly handed down this fact, that the temple was destroyed, and Jerusalem was taken, by Titus, In exitu anni Sabbatici—when a Sabbatic year was drawing to its close. There is nothing in Josephus, which can be shewn to militate against it, and there are some things, which may virtually be considered to confirm it ; for I do not say that he has any where expressly asserted it.

He speaks in one passage of the harvest of a certain year, and such of its productions as were ripe, which the context shews was just after the Passover of A. U. 821. the beginning of the third year of the war, and the year of the death of Nero[1]; and in another, directly after, with a fresh allusion to its productions, he speaks of the land as ἐνεργὸς at the time[m]; which is clearly a description of no Sabbatic year. In another passage he alludes to magazines of corn, which had been sometime laid up in Jerusalem, and were destroyed by the contending parties, in their rage against each other, a little before Titus invested the city[n]. Now Titus laid siege to the city at the Passover, A. U. 823 : these magazines, then, could have consisted in no part of the stores from the harvest A. U. 823. but they might have been formed in part out of those of the harvest in the year before, the harvest of A. U. 822. He speaks in another[o] of the besieged, in Jerusalem, creeping out of the city by night, in search of grass and wild herbs, to allay their hunger—and such like extremities—which, by implying the absence of all but the spontaneous productions of the ground, would so far describe a Sabbatic year.

But the most decisive indication of this fact appears to me to be furnished at v. xii. 4. where it is said, that the Roman army was supplied, during the siege, in whatever abundance, with corn not grown, nor procured, on the spot, but imported from Syria and the neighbouring provinces. Since the midsummer of A. U. 822. when Vespasian had been declared Emperor, and even from that of A. U. 821. when Nero had been deposed, the progress of the war had been altogether suspended, and Judæa in great measure evacuated by the Roman armies—until Titus renewed hostilities, by laying siege to the city, in the spring of A. U. 823. Hence, if from the autumn of A. U. 822. to the summer of A. U. 823. had not been a Sabbatic year, it is morally certain that the country would have been, more or less, cultivated as usual; and the Romans, who came before Jerusalem at the Passover, but did not take it before the following September, would have surprised each description of harvest, both the barley-harvest, and the wheat-harvest, still on the ground. In this case, they must have been converted, at

[1] B. iv. vii. 2. ix. 2.   [m] iv. ix. 7.   [n] v. i. 4. xiii. 7.
[o] v. x. 3. xiii. 7. vi. iii. 3.

least in part, to the supplies of the besiegers; and Josephus could scarcely have failed to give some hint, which would have led to this discovery.

The question which concerns the succession of Sabbatic years, at this period of Jewish history, has nothing to do with the further question of the years of jubilee; for since the return from captivity, though the former were still observed, the latter, according to Maimonides[p], were not. At what time, even after this return, that observance itself began is a very uncertain point; there is no distinct evidence of it, either in the book of Ezra, or in that of Nehemiah, or in the writings of the contemporary prophets, Haggai, Zechariah, or Malachi: and it would be premature to conclude from Neh. viii. 1. 2. that, because the reading of the Law then took place, viz. on the first day of the seventh month, this was necessarily a year of release. What year of the mission of Nehemiah even this might be, whether the same year with that of the building of the wall, which would be its first year, or some other later than that, (for he was twelve years in Judæa altogether,) would be uncertain; but whatever year it was, the reading of the Law, as part of the ceremonial of the year of release, was fixed to the feast of Tabernacles, that is, to the fifteenth of the month Tisri at the earliest[q]; whereas this reading took place on the first: which proves that, however natural and appropriate such an act might have been, at any time, in itself, yet as referred to that specific direction, it was out of course. Such a ceremony, however, on the first of Tisri would coincide with the feast of Trumpets, Lev. xxiii. 24. Numb. xxix. 1: which was probably the true reason why it then took place; for the feast of Trumpets was a sabbath.

There is no strictly authenticated instance of a Sabbatic year, after the return from captivity, before B. C. 163. or the first year of Judas Maccabæus as such; from which, if we calculate backwards, and we suppose the Jews to have returned from captivity in the first of Cyrus, B. C. 536. the

[p] De Ann. Jub. i. 3.

[q] Deut. xxxi. 10. 11.

second year after that return *exclusive*, or B. C. 534. ought to have been such a year; for 534—163=371. a number divisible by seven without a remainder. According to the Jewish reckoning, the year before this, or B. C. 535. would have been so; and this being only one year after the return, almost before the new colony could have settled themselves in the country, and certainly before they could yet have entered on the full enjoyment of its increase—the very supposition is enough to convict it of an absurdity. In the third year after their restoration, the Jews might, perhaps, have kept a year of rest; but none so early as the second.

I do not think, however, that any such observance was yet begun, or at least had been duly kept up, from after the return, until the period of that covenant solemnly entered into in the time of Nehemiah by both princes and people; one article of which was, that they would leave the year of rest, as well as observe the other ritual ordinances of the Law[r]. The precise date of this covenant also may be an uncertainty; but we may conclude, from its very nature, it would much more probably be made, while a Sabbatic year was still a year or two distant, than when it was either arrived, or on the point of arriving. If it was made in the first year of Nehemiah's mission, (which on every account appears most probable—see vi. 15. ii. 1. 11. viii. 2. 13. 14. 18. ix. 1. 38. x. 31.) it was made in B. C. 444. one year before a Sabbatic year; which, calculated backwards, from B. C. 163. as before, would first fall out in B. C. 443.

The decision of this whole question, indeed, would be easy, if the results established in preceding Dissertations of the present work might be implicitly taken for granted. For I have shewn in the Appendix to Dissertation x. of vol. i.[s] that the cycle of Sabbatic years, as such, began B. C. 1520. or B. C. 1513. indifferently, either in the year of the Eisodus itself, or in the year next after the division of lands, B. C. 1514; and I have proved the accuracy of this computation by its agreement with a case in point, the date of a

---

[r] Neh. ix. 38. x. 1—31. [s] Page 390.

Sabbatic year, B. C. 709. after the deliverance of Jerusalem from the invasion of Sennacherib, in the reign of Hezekiah. Let us consider B. C. 1507—B. C. 1506. the first Sabbatic year as such. On this principle B. C. 534—B. C. 533. would be the hundred and fortieth as such; for $1507-534 = 973 = 7 \times 139$. In like manner B. C. 443—442. would be the hundred and fifty-third; for $1507-443 = 1064 = 7 \times 152$.

There is an intimation in the book of Jeremiah[t], from which it may be collected that, according to the Bible chronology, the ninth year of Zedekiah, B. C. 590—589. coincided either wholly or in part with a year of release[u]. The covenant, to which that passage alludes, was entered into first at a time when the Chaldean army was before Jerusalem; and broken again upon their temporary departure to oppose the Egyptians[v]. After this the siege of the city was resumed on the tenth of Tebeth, the tenth month in the Jewish year, and the ninth of the reign of Zedekiah[w]; and prosecuted from that time forward, without any second interruption, until the ninth day of the fourth month, in the eleventh of the reigning King. I think there can be little question concerning this fact; and, therefore, that the previous siege, which was raised for a time by the approach of the Egyptians, made no part of this eighteen months' interval, dated from the tenth of Tebeth, in the ninth of Zedekiah—but was a prior incident belonging to the earlier part of the same year; either the summer, or, at least, the autumn. Nor is it to be supposed, had this not been the case, that the Chaldean army would first have laid siege to Jerusalem in the tenth month, (or in other words, the depth of a Jewish winter,) unless that siege had been merely the *resumption* of what had been begun before, and not the *commencement* of what had never been attempted as yet. Nor is it likely that the expedition from Egypt, which was manifestly intended for the relief of Jerusalem, would have been made except in the summer time, at the usual season of mi-

[t] xxxiv. 8—22. .   [u] Exod. xxi. 2.   Deut. xv. 12.   [v] Jer. xxxiv. 21.
xxxvii. 5—11.   [w] 2 Kings xxv. 1.   Jer. xxxix. 1.   Ezek. xxiv. 1. 2.

litary operations in general ; nor, consequently, that the report of its approach, which was manifestly received just after the siege had been begun, could have been received except in the summer.

If so, the siege, which was broken up for a time by the rumoured approach of the Egyptian army, was altogether a different transaction from the siege, which was begun in the tenth month afterwards. Yet there is no reason why both should not be supposed to have made part of the transactions of the same year: the one, about its middle, as the other much nearer to its end.

On this principle, the first siege also would be laid in the ninth of Zedekiah, and, according to the Bible chronology, sometime in B. C. 590. about its middle. At this particular juncture, a year of release was either arrived, or at hand ; which, if the latter was the case, might extend from B. C. 590—B. C. 589. If B. C. 709—B. C. 708. was actually a Sabbatic year, then B. C. 590—B. C. 589. must have been, or ought to have been, one also: for $709-590=119=7\times17$: whence if B. C. 709—B. C. 708. was the first of the series, B. C. 590—589. was the eighteenth.

In Pingré's Tables of Eclipses, I find an eclipse of the moon B. C. 590. on March 12. at 8. 45. in the morning, for the meridian of Paris ; or 10. 57 in the morning, for the meridian of Jerusalem. The next mean full moon to this would fall April 10—at 11. 41. in the evening: in which case the 15th of Nisan would coincide with April 11. and, therefore, the 15th of Tisri with October 5. From the 15th of Tisri *exclusive*, to the 10th of Tebeth *inclusive*, the interval is eighty-three days. And from the 5th of October *exclusive*, to the 27th of December *inclusive*, it is the same. In this case, the tenth of the Jewish Tebeth coincided with the twenty-seventh of the Julian December ; and the siege of Jerusalem, which began on the former, began also on the latter. If it began, therefore, B. C. 590. it began B. C. 590. *exeunte ;* and if it lasted, from the time of its beginning to the time of its close, eighteen months in all, and if the last month of the siege expired on the tenth of the fourth month of the Jewish year, B. C. 588—the sixth month expired on the tenth of the fourth month of the same year, B. C. 589—and, consequently, the first began on the tenth of the tenth, B. C. 590.

Now it has been shewn [x], at least with presumptive certainty, that B. C. 588. when the 14th of Nisan coincided with April 17—April 17. was a Sunday. On the same principle, December 27. B. C. 588. was a Tuesday—and, therefore, December 27. B. C. 590. was a Saturday. The siege of Jerusalem, then, was begun on the Jewish sabbath; and it has been shewn [x] that it ended on the same. For the ninth of the fourth month, (when Zedekiah attempted to escape by night from the city,) if the premises on which I founded this conclusion were correct, has been demonstrated to have been a sabbath. B. C. 588. if Nisan 14. coincided with April 17. and April 17. with Sunday—Thamuz 9. coincided with July 9—and July 9. with Saturday [*].

* It is possible, indeed, that the tenth of Tebeth, B. C. 590. might have coincided with December 28: in which case, while the siege would expire on the Saturday as before, it would begin on the Sunday—a circumstance of agreement, which would bring the analogy between the first siege, under Nebuchadnezzar, and the last, under Titus, to a degree of correspondence truly remarkable.

[x] Vol. i. Diss. x. 359. note.

DISSERTATION VIII.

PART I.

General prospective survey of the ministry of our Lord in Judæa.

THE entire history of our Lord's public ministry is divisible into that part of it, which was discharged in Judæa, and that part of it, which was confined to Galilee: and these parts were not only distinct in themselves, beginning at different times, and proceeding subsequently at different times, independent of each other, but are recorded in distinct and independent Gospels. The ministry in Judæa began before the ministry in Galilee; and the history of the ministry in Judæa is confined almost totally to St. John —the history of the ministry in Galilee, almost as exclusively, to the other three Evangelists. A general and prospective survey of our Saviour's public ministry must regard it in each of its parts—and as that part which relates to Judæa was both prior to, and ever after, distinct from, that which relates to Galilee, it will properly begin with, and make an end of, the former, before it passes on to the latter.

The times and occasions of the ministry in Judæa are likewise twofold; the times and occasions when our Saviour was visiting Jerusalem, and the times and occasions when he was residing elsewhere in Judæa. The first instance on record of any attendance at Jerusalem is the attendance at the Passover, John ii. 13; which has been fully considered already [a] : and the first instance of any residence in Judæa, apart from Jerusalem, is that which begins to be recorded, John iii. 22. and is supposed to continue, or go on still, to the time of the return into Galilee, iv. 1. 2. 3; which also has been discussed in the preceding Dissertation. Of any instances of attendance at Jerusalem, posterior to the first, I shall speak by and by ; but of any similar residence in Judæa, out of Jerusalem, the only other instance,

[a] Vol. ii. Diss. vii. supra.

distinct from the first, is that which is specified at John xi.
52—for Ephraim, though it might border upon Samaria,
was, notwithstanding, a city of Judæa. The length of this
residence, as well as the period in the course of our Lord's
ministry to which it belongs, will require to be considered
hereafter, and must, therefore, for the present be dismissed.

Besides these two instances, however, there is none other
on record, either in St. John's Gospel, or out of it, during
which there is any reason to suppose our Saviour was residing in Judæa : for as to Bethabara, which is mentioned at
John x. 40. as the scene of a temporary residence also, it is
proved, by a comparison with other passages [b], to have
been probably in Peræa ; and we may take it for granted
was either in Peræa, or, at least, in Galilee. Now each of
these occasions stands entirely independent of the rest of
the course of our Lord's ministry—the former, as very
early in his first year—and the latter, as very late in his
third—and they are the only occasions, on which, as we
shall better perceive hereafter, from the course of that ministry in general, there could have been an opportunity for
the occurrence of any such residence in Judæa ; and, consequently, *a priori*, any reason to suspect it. I take it for
granted, then, that, excepting these two occasions in particular, our Lord was never resident in Judæa, either for a
longer, or for a shorter time, in the course of his ministry
altogether.

With regard, in the next place, to the times and occasions of the attendances at Jerusalem, these were, in every
instance, the times and occasions of an attendance at some
of the feasts : and there are *five* such instances actually on
record ; two, of attendances at a Passover [c]—one, of an
attendance at a feast of Tabernacles [d]—one, of an attendance at a feast of Dedication [e]—and one, which is left indefinite [f]—but, besides these, there are no more. The occasion
of each of these visits is so far exactly determined ; and as

[b] i. 28. iii. 23. 25. 26.　[c] ii. 13. xii. 1.　[d] vii. 2—10.　[e] x. 22. 23.
[f] v. 1.

to what period, in the course of our Lord's ministry generally, they are also each to be referred to, will appear, in due time, hereafter. The only question, which seems to require our consideration at present, is this—whether the *five* instances, thus recorded, embrace *all* the instances of our Saviour's attendance in Jerusalem, at any of the feasts? or, whether there is reason to suppose he might ever have been up to Jerusalem, in the course of his ministry, at times and on occasions, distinct from these, and not recorded by St. John? The affirmative, upon the former question, and the negative, upon the latter, appear to me to be the truth.

For, first, the Gospel of St. John is supplementary to the rest not only in general, and even where they may all relate to transactions in Galilee, or elsewhere out of Judæa, but especially so, with respect to the transactions in Judæa. It was in this department of their common history, that the preceding accounts were principally, or rather totally, defective; since, with the exception of the history of passion-week, that is, of seven or eight days before the close of our Lord's public ministry, it is a notorious fact that they no where speak of any visit to Jerusalem; they no where, except by implication, prove him to have been in Judæa at all. The reverse of this is true of St. John; the whole scene of whose accounts, with the same exception of a very little transacted in Galilee, or on the other side the Lake of Tiberias, is placed in Judæa. The entire history of our Lord's ministry in this country must thus be collected solely from St. John: it is reasonable, therefore, to presume that he has furnished the data necessary for that purpose; and if so, that the instances of attendance at Jerusalem, which he has specified as such, are actually all which occurred. These visits of our Lord to that city were cardinal points in the discharge of the ministry in Judæa; the incidents which then transpired were always of a peculiar kind, and eminently deserving of record. They prove not merely the fact of our Lord's compliance with the legal requisitions, which enjoined such attendance, at stated times, on all the male Israelites, but what was still more to be ex-

Q 4

pected from him, his anxiety to convince the Jews, strictly so called—his brethren according to the flesh—of the truth of his character by both his discourses, and his miracles, on the spot.   Add to which, that at periods of time, distinct from these, when St. John's Gospel demonstrates him to have been present in Jerusalem, there are intimations in it also, that he was either engaged elsewhere, or purposely absenting himself from Judæa; and that, from a comparison of the other accounts with St. John's, it is almost certainly to be inferred that he must have been engaged elsewhere—he could not possibly have been in Judæa—all which is presumptively in favour of the general conclusion that, except on those occasions when St. John records the fact of his presence in Jerusalem, our Saviour was never there.

Secondly, the same conclusion will be still further confirmed, if it can be shewn that our Lord was under no absolute necessity of attending upon *all* the legal solemnities; for, then, we shall be free to suppose that, for prudential reasons, or any other adequate consideration, he might sometimes have omitted to attend them.   And this assumption will be proved to a demonstration, if there was any integral period in the duration of his ministry collectively, for which there must have been *many* instances of the recurrence of stated legal solemnities, and yet there is *no* instance of our Lord's attendance at Jerusalem upon any: in proof of which assertion we may reason as follows.

The last instance of his attendance at Jerusalem, before the close of his ministry in public, is the attendance at the Passover, John xii. 1. the fact of which, also, it is needless to observe, is attested by the other Evangelists, as well as by St. John.   The attendance immediately before that is the attendance at the Encænia [g] ; and that this was the Encænia, belonging to the same year with the Passover after it, if it requires any proof, may be shewn as follows.

The departure from Jerusalem at this feast was premature, and occasioned by the renewed attempt on our

[g] x. 22.

Lord's life [h]——he retired at that time to Bethabara [i]——and at Bethabara, he received the message of the sisters of Lazarus [k]——two days after that message he returned to Judæa [l]——and this return could not have been long after the recent attempt on his life [m]. The raising of Lazarus, then, followed soon after the Encænia——and this raising itself was the cause of a speedy departure from Jerusalem again [n]——the retreat to Ephraim, therefore, was also soon after the Encænia. From Ephraim, as I shall shew elsewhere, our Lord returned into Galilee, to begin that very circuit, the last event of which was the arrival at Bethany, six days before the Passover.

There can be no question, therefore, that the Encænia, John x. 22. is the Encænia directly preceding the Passover, xii. 1. It is as little to be doubted that the same Encænia is the feast of that name, immediately subsequent to the feast of Tabernacles, vii. 2. or that the attendance at the feast of Tabernacles, vii. 10. was an attendance directly prior, in the order of time, to the attendance at the Encænia, x. 22. The very conversation which is recorded, x. 22 ——39. as the whole of the particulars which transpired at this attendance, possessing so clear and so decided a reference to the first half of the same chapter [o], (which belongs, as I shall shew more fully in its proper place, to the attendance at the feast of Tabernacles,) must be sufficient to prove this. The feast of Tabernacles in question, as well as the Encænia, and the Passover, before considered, are consequently all to be comprehended within the last six months of our Saviour's ministry; and, beginning with the first of these, we possess clear proof that he attended them all in their order. Let us observe, however, what is the case with any feasts anterior to these; or with any attendance, on some earlier occasion than any part of the last six months in question.

I. The remonstrance of our Lord's brethren, at the time of this very feast [P], is plainly to be ascribed to the fact, that

[h] Ib. 39.   [i] Ib. 40.   [k] xi. 3.   [l] Ib. 6. 7.   [m] Ib. 8. 16.   [n] Ib. 54.
[o] 1—21.   [P] John vii. 2—9.

they knew him to have been absent from Judæa—and from Jerusalem in particular—for some time past; much longer than can be supposed intended by the ordinary interval between any two of the feasts, even those which were most remote from each other. The fact too, that, when our Lord did go up to this feast, he went up to it, not at its commencement, but at its middle—not openly, but ὡς ἐν κρυπτῷ —is sufficient proof that he had special reasons for avoiding publicity even on this occasion ; and, therefore, a presumptive argument that, for similar reasons, he might have totally omitted to attend on other occasions before it.

II. The uncertainty of the Jews, especially of the Jews of Jerusalem q, before the actual appearance of Jesus, as to whether he would attend the feast, or not, is most naturally accounted for, by supposing them aware that he had not been seen at any of the feasts for some time past. Nor is it any objection that a similar uncertainty is again expressed on a much later occasion r, when it could not but be known that he had attended at the two feasts before : there might still be the same uncertainty about his attendance at *this* feast in particular, if experience had proved that it was not his custom to attend *every* feast in general ; nor could it be unknown also that, on each of those occasions before, his life had been several times attempted ; and that there was actually an edict of the Sanhedrim against him, leading in its consequences to the same result, which was ready to be enforced on this.

III. Among the other circumstances which transpired at this feast, our Saviour is represented s as alluding to some past, but some well known, event—and that, clearly, a miracle performed by himself—as the cause of all the hostility which had begun, and still continued, to be entertained against him. Now, with regard to this miracle—the matter of fact itself—the consequences ascribed to the fact—the parties addressed—the drift of the reasoning employed upon it—the circumstances before and after this point of time in

q John vii. 11—13.   r xi. 56.   s vii. 21—23.

the narrative—demonstrate it to be some individual, and specific, miracle—wrought upon the spot—wrought in the cure of an infirm person—wrought upon some sabbath day —and followed by a resolution, on the part of the Jews, grounded upon this fact as such, to take away·the life of him who had performed it : all which criteria meet together in the history of the miracle recorded at John v. 1—16. as performed at the pool of Bethesda—performed on the man who had been thirty-eight years in his infirmity—performed on a sabbath, and succeeded by a specific determination, on the part of the rulers of the Jews, for this supposed contempt of the sabbath, to effect the destruction of Jesus.

To this miracle, then, our Saviour was now referring ; which being the case, if the miracle was performed at the time of the feast, v. 1. and is referred to, for the first time, here, at the feast of Tabernacles, vii. 2. the conclusion appears to me irresistible : this was the first time, since the performance, when there was an opportunity of referring to it ; our Lord, and the people of Jerusalem, had never met again, from that period, until this, when they met at the feast of Tabernacles. The context confirms the conclusion ; for as it specifies no attendance at Jerusalem since the time of the feast, v. 1. so it can be understood to refer to none else *now*, or at vii. 2. The reason of the thing alone is sufficient to convince us that, to a past transaction like this, and for the purpose of justifying himself on such a score as this, our Lord would revert with the *first* opportunity, which might occur, *after* the transaction itself ; but not that he would often do this, or be perpetually recurring to it : and, consequently, that it would be equally absurd to suppose either that he might frequently have been up to Jerusalem, and never alluded to it until now, or that, as often as he had been up to Jerusalem before, so often he had alluded to it already. The discourse, which followed and is related from v. 17. to the end of the chapter, was not so much a justification of that one particular act which had preceded, as a general exposition of the proofs of our Sa-

viour's divine legation—a general defence of his character—
and a general expostulation with the unbelief of the Jews:
and that specific resolution of putting him to death, produced by this particular act, though it might ultimately be
resolvable into it, yet was not formed, or systematically
acted on, as a rule and principle of the conduct of his enemies thenceforward, until after his departure from Jerusalem. The very manner in which the Evangelist records the
formation of the resolution—Καὶ διὰ τοῦτο, ἐδίωκον τὸν Ἰησοῦν
οἱ Ἰουδαῖοι, καὶ ἐζήτουν αὐτὸν ἀποκτεῖναι, ὅτι ταῦτα ἐποίει ἐν σαββάτῳ.——And therefore it was, that the Jews began to per-
secute Jesus, and to seek to kill him, because he did such
things on a sabbath day—implies as much.

The use we may make of the reference in question is,
consequently, this; that our Lord had never been present
in Jerusalem, attending upon any feast, between the time
of the feast, John v. 1. and the time of the feast of Tabernacles, vii. 2; a conclusion demonstratively certain of the
feast of the Passover, vi. 4. which is one of the number;
and that upon independent grounds also: first, from the
testimony of the other Evangelists—each of whom records
the first miracle of feeding, as well as St. John, and all of
whom shew how our Lord was employed before and after
it—secondly, from the declaration of St. John himself, vii. 1.
that, After these things (meaning the discourse in the synagogue of Capernaum, only a day or two later than the miracle, and, consequently, also before the Passover) Jesus
walked in Galilee; for he would not walk in Judæa, because the Jews were seeking to kill him.

Now, between the Passover, John vi. 4. and the feast of
Tabernacles, vii. 2. there would be an interval of six months
at least, during which our Lord could not have been in Jerusalem; and if the feast, referred to at v. 1. was a Passover
also, between that and the Passover, vi. 4. there would be
an interval of at least twelve months more: so that for
eighteen months at least, between the feast, John v. 1. and
the feast of Tabernacles, vii. 2. (during which there would
be *five* different legal solemnities, viz. the Pentecost, Taber-

nacles, and Encænia, of the first *twelve* months, and the
Passover, and Pentecost, of the last *six*,) our Lord could
not once have been up to Jerusalem.   It will be said, however, that this conclusion depends on the assumption that
the feast mentioned, John v. 1. is a feast of the Passover—
and not any other feast ; the truth of which assumption
may be rendered presumptively certain as follows.

I.   The absence of the Greek article in speaking of this
feast, unless its presence would infallibly have denoted the
Passover, proves nothing at all ; but leaves the question as
open as before.   The truth is that, as the Jewish calendar
contained at least three feasts, all of equal antiquity, and of
equal authority, the article could not stand κατ' ἐξοχὴν before one, any more than before the rest, unless that one had
come, in the lapse of time, to be placed, for some reason or
other, at the head of the rest ; a circumstance of distinction
which, as I have shewn elsewhere[t], from Josephus and from
other authorities, (and which St. John's expression, directly
after—ἦν δὲ ἐγγὺς ἡ ἑορτὴ τῶν Ἰουδαίων, ἡ Σκηνοπηγία—contributes critically to confirm,) might have held good of the
feast of Tabernacles, but could not of the feast of the
Passover.

II.   If the feast, John v. 1. was not the next Passover to
ii. 13. the Passover, vi. 4. must have been so ; and the feast,
v. 1. must have been some feast between the two ; and, consequently, some feast in the first year of our Saviour's
ministry ; *after* the Passover, belonging to that year, but
before the Passover, at the beginning of the next : that is, it
must have been either the Pentecost, or the feast of Tabernacles, or the Encænia, within the first twelve months of
his ministry.   It could not have been the Pentecost ; for, as
I have shewn in the last Dissertation, our Lord's return
into Galilee out of Judæa, was just before the arrival of
this feast.   Nor could it have been the Encænia ; for the
Encænia fell out in the depth of winter, at which time no
such assemblage of sick and infirm persons, as was supposed
at the time of this feast, could have been found about the

pool of Bethesda. Nor could it have been the feast of Tabernacles; because at that feast of Tabernacles, and in the first year of his ministry, our Lord was engaged upon the circuit of Galilee : and it is a general argument why it could have been no feast in the first year of our Lord's ministry whatever, that, as I have in part observed already, the strain of the reflections, from v. 17. to the end, which were then delivered, would be incompatible with such a supposition. The ministry of our Saviour, and, consequently, the trial of the Jews, must have been going on at least for one year, before the futurity of his rejection—and the consequent fact of their infidelity—could be so far certain, as to admit of their being argued with, as we find them argued with on this occasion.

III. There is, in each of the three former Evangelists[v], an account of a miracle performed on the sabbath day, and in the presence of our Lord's enemies, and followed by a specific design, on their part, to put its author to death: there is also, in each of these Gospels, immediately before this account, an instance of another supposed breach of the sabbath, which, though it is not said to have been followed by the same resolution, is yet seen to have been followed by the same kind of offence, and at the commission of the same kind of crime, which afterwards produced that. It is manifest, then, that, at this particular juncture, the Scribes and Pharisees had not merely made up their minds to reject our Lord, but also to reject him on this score—his systematic breach and contempt, as they construed this part of his conduct, of one of their most sacred laws, the obligation of the Sabbatic rest—and, with this feeling, they were not only watching his actions, and putting the most sinister interpretation upon them, but prepared, with the first favourable opportunity, to go even to the length of effecting his death. Their present conduct is the more remarkable, because the very first miracle which any of these Evangelists relate—the miracle performed on the demoniac in the

---

[v] Matt. xii. 9—14. Mark iii. 1—6. Luke vi. 6—11.

synagogue at Capernaum [v]—and another, the same day, in
the cure of Peter's wife's mother—were both wrought upon
the sabbath ; the former, publicly ; and the latter, not in
secret ; yet were both performed without any such effect.
It took some time, then, either to convince our Lord's enemies of his non-observance, in this respect, of their tradi-
tional law, or to confirm them in their unbelief—so as to
except against this circumstance in his demeanour particularly.   This instance, therefore, may be justly considered
not merely the first instance of any such exception, to be
found in the three first Gospels, but also the first which
could be found there ; the first, which it came within their
plan to have recorded, until they notice the present.   It is
an instance, consequently, perfectly distinct from John v.
1—16. not simply as taking place on a different scene of
things—somewhere in Galilee, and, certainly, not in Jerusalem—but also as taking place at a different juncture of
time ; and, therefore, since that in St. John was the first instance of its kind, this in the other Evangelists was later
than that : in which case, how aptly, and yet how critically,
the former comes in to prepare for, and illustrate the latter,
is too obvious to require any proof.

Now, in St. Luke's account of the transaction immediately prior to this, which was the walking through the corn-
fields on the sabbath day[w], a term is employed to denote
the sabbath in question, which, it will be shewn hereafter,
was intended to denote the *first regular* sabbath after the
sixteenth of the Jewish Nisan, and, consequently, either in,
or directly after, the Paschal week.   Either in, or directly
after this week, then, our Saviour was travelling *on* a sabbath ; and he performed the ensuing miracle, as I shall also
shew with a degree of probability amounting almost to a
certainty, in the neighbourhood of the Lake of Galilee—
and, perhaps, at Capernaum—on the next sabbath, or the
next but one ; which miracle was followed on that account
by the design against his life.

What, then, is a more obvious conclusion than that, at

<hr/>

[v] Mark i. 21—28. Luke iv. 31—37.   [w] vi. 1—5.

the former of these times, he had been up to Jerusalem;
and, at the latter, was got back to Capernaum? If so, we
have evidence at Luke vi. 1. of an attendance at a Passover,
which the course of events from that time forward in the
same Evangelist, (as well as in St. Matthew and in St.
Mark,) compared with St. John, proves to have been at
least one year before the Passover, John vi. 4. when the
miracle of feeding took place.   No reasonable person, then,
will hesitate to conclude, that the attendance at Jerusalem,
John v. 1. which must have been prior to the Passover,
vi. 4. as well as to the miracle, Luke vi. 6—11. must have
been the attendance at this Passover itself : the account of
which, if we admit the fact, St. Luke and his predecessors
had manifestly omitted, and the circumstances of which,
notwithstanding this omission, were yet necessary to explain both Luke vi. 1—5. and vi. 6—11. which they all
three do record.   These are coincidences which in my
opinion do as plainly and as strongly determine the time
and occasion of the visit to Jerusalem, at John v. 1. to have
been the time and occasion of the attendance at the second
Passover, as if the statement of both had been *totidem ver-
bis* prefixed to the account *.

    * Among the arguments intended to prove that the feast, inde-
finitely mentioned John v. 1. could not be a Passover, none,
perhaps, is more confidently put forward, and none is in reality
more weak and inconclusive, than the following—that the events,
which are recorded in the fifth chapter of St. John, are not sufficient to have occupied a year, and another Passover is mentioned
directly after at vi. 4. It would have been strange, indeed, if they
had been intended to occupy a year—since it must be self-evident
that very possibly they did not occupy a single day.   But this
argument proceeds upon the supposition that St. John's Gospel is
entire and complete in itself; and that it neither has, nor was intended to have, any supplemental relation to the rest : a supposition, which is purely precarious, and not more precarious than
contrary to the matter of fact.   The truth of the supplemental
relation of this one Gospel in particular is among the few positions, which happily do not admit of a question—and while this

We may conclude, then, with as much certainty as the nature of the case admits of, that for the whole of *eighteen* months, before the last feast of Tabernacles, our Lord had never been present at Jerusalem; and with regard to any attendance there, between the commencement of that period, and the time of the Passover, John ii. 13. the conclusion, thus established, demonstrates of itself that he was under no necessity of attending; and, therefore, might not have attended. Prudential reasons chiefly seem to have produced his absence after the Passover, John v. 1. and from that time forward; but any adequate motive, such as the commencement and prosecution of his ministry exclusively in Galilee, might have produced the same absence before. The feast of Pentecost, in the first year of his ministry, is certainly out of the question; and enough has been said to render it probable that both the feast of Tabernacles, and the Encænia, in the same year, must be excepted likewise. I shall therefore make an end of this review of the ministry in Judæa, with one or two observations more, by way of corollary.

I. We have confirmed the presumption, otherwise established as it was, of the regular order, and the supplementary relation, of St. John's Gospel; for we have shewn

is the case, it is not to be considered whether St. John's Gospel, *per se*, between v. 1. and vi. 4. supplies matter sufficient to have occupied a year, but whether St. Matthew's, St. Mark's, and St. Luke's, in that portion of their Gospels respectively, the true place of which is between these extremes in St. John's, can presumptively be shewn to have done so. And upon this point there is so little room for doubt, that the affirmative may be confidently asserted. The interval in question between John v. 1. and John vi. 4. is in fact our Lord's second year—and with respect to *that* year, as it was the fullest of incident itself, so its incidents have been the most minutely related, of any. From its beginning, by the attendance at this Passover, to its ending, by the miracle of the five thousand, there is no part of it which was unemployed—nor the mode of whose employment it is not possible clearly to ascertain.

that, as he proposed to fill up the omissions of the other Evangelists in general, so he has actually filled them up, where they most stood in need of supplements; viz. in the history of the ministry in Judæa, in particular.

II. We have discovered, in the several gospel histories laid together, satisfactory proofs of *four* distinct Passovers, which must have been consecutive at least; the Passover, John ii. 13—the Passover, John v. 1—the Passover, John vi. 4—and the Passover, John xii. 1: and, if they were consecutive in a direct order, (as no one, who believes them to be distinct, can reasonably think of disputing,) they make up a period of three years in all. Our Lord's ministry began at the first, and ended at the last: it continued, therefore, three years between.

III. It is a remarkable fact, that after so long and systematic an absence from Jerusalem, as eighteen months before the feast of Tabernacles, John vii. 2. our Lord attended every feast, for the next six months, in its order. These attendances come in, it is true, to supply an entire, or at least a partial, blank, for the same length of time, in the other Gospels. But, what is also remarkable, these six months are the *last* six months of his ministry—beginning at the feast of Tabernacles, and expiring at the feast of the Passover: which being the case, the reason of the fact must be sought for in the moral of the parable of the barren fig-tree [x]; and will thence be found to have been due to some necessity, more especially incumbent on our Saviour for the concluding period of his ministry, to be diligent both *in* Judæa, and *out* of Judæa, with a view either finally to convince the Jews, and bring about the national penitence and conversion, or, at least, to leave them, without excuse, to the ultimate consequences of an invincible unbelief.

IV. As *three* out of the *five* feasts, which he actually attended, were feasts of the Passover, this circumstance proves how much more important in his estimation was his attendance at the Passover, than at any other feast; and,

[x] Luke xiii. 6—9.

consequently, how much closer a connection there was between the facts of his history, and the purpose for which he came into the world, and the Passover, than any other feast.

V. It is also remarkable that, whereas the name of every other feast in the Jewish year, occurs in the Gospels, and the attendance of our Lord, once at least in the course of his ministry, at every other feast, is specified in the Gospels, the feast of Pentecost is not even mentioned, much less said to have been attended in person by him. I consider this a proof, in the first place, that his ministry out of Judæa began, as I have supposed, at the time of this feast, and was every year renewed, with increased activity, at the time of this feast ; and, secondly, that the peculiar events, which in all probability occurred—one in each year—about the period of this feast—the call of the Apostles as disciples first—their ordination as Apostles afterwards—and our Lord's Transfiguration—bore a concealed reference to something beyond themselves, and to the facts of the future Christian history. For, I have shewn elsewhere[y], that the time of the feast of Pentecost, from the first effusion of the Holy Ghost, to the mission of St. Paul among the Gentiles, was the great and cardinal point, through a period of fourteen years, in every step towards the more full and complete promulgation of the Gospel.

[y] Vol. i. Diss. xiii. vol. ii. Diss. i.

R 2

DISSERTATION VIII.

PART II.

General prospective survey of the ministry of our Lord in Galilee.

THE history of the ministry of our Lord out of Judæa is almost entirely the history of his ministry in Galilee; and for this we are as much indebted to the three first Evangelists, as for the history of the ministry in Judæa to the fourth.

The formal commencement of this ministry is placed by them all [a] with the return into Galilee, posterior to the imprisonment of the Baptist; the coincidence of which with the return, mentioned in the fourth chapter of St. John [b], has been demonstrated at large elsewhere [c]. The time of the return, it has also been shewn, was very probably not earlier, though it might have been somewhat later, than the fourteenth day before the feast of Pentecost, A. U. 780. May 16: to which day we considered it necessary, for the reasons there alleged, to assign the imprisonment of the Baptist. If the ministry in Galilee, then, was begun after this return, it would be begun about the period of the feast of Pentecost, in general; and the exact time of its commencement, in particular, is specified by St. Matthew: Ἀπὸ τότε ἤρξατο ὁ Ἰησοῦς κηρύσσειν [d]—where the note of time, ἀπὸ τότε, is to be referred to verse thirteenth before; which speaks of our Lord's taking up his abode at Capernaum. It was so long, consequently, after the actual return into Galilee, as might suffice to bring him to Capernaum, in order to take up his residence there; but no longer.

Now the first transaction, posterior to this return, as we saw from St. John, was the performance of the miracle in Cana, upon an inhabitant of Capernaum: the next, as it

---

[a] Matt. iv. 12. Mark i. 14. Luke iv. 14.   [b] John iv. 1. 3. 43.   [c] Vol. ii. Diss. vii.   [d] iv. 17.

appeared from St. Luke, was the visit to Nazareth; and the last only, as it appears also from the same Gospel [c], was the coming to Capernaum, preparatory to settling there. That these events were consecutive upon each other, and in the above order, there can be little question; and the description, attached to the name of Capernaum, as a city of Galilee, (a description which occurs here, for the first time and for the last, in St. Luke,) is sufficient to prove that the period of this visit to Capernaum, in that Evangelist, is the same with that of the similar visit, in St. Matthew [f]; in other words, that Matt. iv. 13. and Luke iv. 31. are coincident in point of time. It would not follow, however, that the leaving of Nazareth, which is also mentioned in the former, as previous to the settling in Capernaum, has any connection either directly or virtually with the close of the incident in the latter [g]: the words imply no more than that whereas, before this return into Galilee, Nazareth had been our Saviour's home, so after it, and from this time forward, Capernaum became so in its stead.

The notice, therefore, which is found in St. Luke [h] prior even to the visit to Nazareth, is partly the account of an effect, which had been already produced, and partly proleptical, in reference to what was thenceforward about to take place. The fame of Jesus had actually been diffused through Galilee, even before this return, by the miracles which he was known to have performed at the preceding Passover [i]; and it would be still more generally disseminated by the miracle at Cana also: the news of which is seen to have reached Nazareth before he arrived there. The visit to Nazareth, and the discourse which ensued in the synagogue of that place, considered as a case in point, demonstrate both the truth of the assertion that our Lord began now to teach—and to teach in their synagogues—and also the reality of the effect, ascribed to his teaching, that he was glorified of all; for all, who heard him in the synagogue at Nazareth, are said [k] to have borne witness unto

[c] iv. 31.   [f] iv. 13.   [g] iv. 16—30.   [h] iv. 14. 15.   [i] John iv. 46.
[k] iv. 22.

him, and to have marvelled at the words of grace, which were proceeding out of his mouth. The declaration, then, is to be understood proleptically—of what thenceforward began to take place—not historically, or of what had already taken place. A visit, indeed, to Nazareth, and an instance of teaching, confined to the synagogue of that place, could by no means have come under the denomination of the commencement of his ministry, on a large and comprehensive scale. Nor, though St. Luke mentions here the fact of some teaching, does he mention on the same occasion the fact of any preaching also; nor, indeed, before the time when he shews our Lord to be actually engaged on the circuit of Galilee [1].

As to St. Mark [m], this declaration also is not inconsistent with the statement of St. Matthew [n]; for it may be understood simply of the final end—always proposed by this return—which was certainly such a formal publication of the gospel of the kingdom, as is here asserted; or, since *he* says nothing, like St. Matthew, of the choice of Capernaum, in preference to Nazareth, yet by the incident, which he proceeds to record [o], shews that our Lord was then either there already, or near it, there is no reason why Mark i. 14. 15. should not be considered to harmonize exactly with Matthew iv. 17 : and each of them should not relate to the same point of time.

Before, therefore, we can properly enter on the survey of our Lord's ministry henceforward, there are two things which will deserve some notice, because they were preliminary, or at least prior, even to its commencement; first, the propriety of the choice of Capernaum, as the place of his stated abode; and, secondly, the propriety of the time, the period of the feast of Pentecost, at which we suppose his ministry to have begun.

First, the necessity of some fixed place of abode for our Saviour must be obvious. He could not always be in motion, or engaged upon his circuits; there must have been periods, throughout the whole duration of his ministry, of

[1] iv. 43. 44.   [m] i. 14. 15.   [n] iv. 13—17.   [o] i. 16.

greater or of less extent, for which, upon various accounts, he would be stationary; and if he was stationary on some definite spot, the great business of his ministry would much better be promoted, than otherwise. The resort of the multitudes from all parts, for the sake of his miracles, or of his instructions, even when he was not himself professedly employed in dispensing both to them at their own homes, could not be more encouraged, or more facilitated, than by their knowing that, though not present among them in person, he might still be found in one place. It is as little to be questioned both from this passage of St. Matthew, compared with another [p], and with the parallel accounts of St. Mark and of St. Luke [q], and from the allusion, twice repeated [r], to some peculiar honour and distinction, as conferred upon Capernaum, above every other city of Galilee, (which is best explained by considering *this* the place of our Saviour's residence, as the *rest* were of his temporary visits,) that Capernaum was selected for the purpose. Nor was there any other city which we should consider *a priori* more likely to have been so chosen, except Nazareth, the place of his infancy and his education, and probably the birthplace also of most of his relations.

It is some confirmation of this presumption, that the first instance of his beginning to teach publicly occurred in the synagogue of Nazareth: an opportunity for believing in him was thereby given to his countrymen; and given to them before any others; which preference it is reasonable we should attribute to the natural and the amiable motive of a regard for the spiritual welfare of his fellow-townsmen in particular. What might have been the result of the experiment, had it succeeded according to our Lord's benevolent desire, it may not be possible to say; but the failure of this first trial, and the similar disappointment of a second, made at a later period in his ministry, demonstrate that the disposition of the people of Nazareth was rooted in unbelief; and it is equally certain, from the reproach of the

[p] ix. 1.   [q] Mark v. 21. Luke viii. 40.   [r] Matt. xi. 23. 24.
Luke x. 15.

Nazarene, so early and so permanently fixed upon our Lord himself, that the disposition of the rest of the Jews also was as little in favour of Nazareth. The renunciation of his former place of abode, as the first step towards the discharge of his public ministry, might, consequently, be just as necessary in condescension to the prejudices of the people at large, as a natural effect of that rude and violent treatment of himself.

Among the causes, then, which produced the choice of Capernaum, these may be reckoned as of some weight. Another might be that there was one family there, the family of the nobleman, whose son had been recently restored to health, already prepared to receive and to acknowledge our Lord. Nor is it an improbable conjecture that this nobleman was Chuzas, the steward or fiscal procurator of the Tetrarch of Galilee; whose wife Johanna is mentioned among those who ministered to our Lord's wants upon his circuits of Galilee [s]; and again among those who visited his tomb on the morning of the resurrection [t]. A third reason, as specified by St. Matthew [u], was the accomplishment of prophecy [v]; which, having predicted that the land of Zebulun and of Napthali, by the way of the sea, (that is the sea of Galilee, concerning which Jerome, *in locum* [w], observes, Mare autem hic appellat lacum Genesareth...in cujus littore Capharnaum, et Tiberias, et Bethsaida, et Chorozaim, sitæ sunt,) should be the principal scene of the Messiah's ministry, and the principal partakers in its benefits, required him to make choice of some place of residence, critically situated on the confines of both. Such would Capernaum be; for it lay at the north-eastern extremity of the lake. And, according to Josephus,—Ζαβουλωνῖται δὲ τὴν μέχρι Γεννησαρί-τιδος ... ἔλαχον—Τὰ δὲ πρὸς τὰς ἀνατολὰς τετραμμένα ... καὶ τῆς Γαλιλαίας τὰ καθύπερθεν, Νεφθαλῖται παρέλαβον [x].

A fourth reason, and specified also by St. Matthew, was its proximity to the lake; and the consequent facility which

[s] Luke viii. 3.   [t] xxiv. 10.   [u] Matt. iv. 14—16.   [v] Is. ix. 1. 2.
[w] Oper. iii. 83.   [x] Ant. v. i. 22.

it afforded of avoiding the importunity, or the pressure, of the multitude, when they became inconveniently great, by teaching them from the sea, and not on the land ; but, especially, for conveying himself speedily away, when the excitement produced by his miracles would have led the people to some rash act—or, when the malice and scrutiny of his personal enemies, the Scribes and Pharisees, were more pertinacious than usual—tempting him with insidious questions, watching his actions with a sinister intent, or, in consequence of some recent miracle, inflamed against him with more violence than ever ; and rendering it only prudent to retire for a while from their immediate vicinity, or their observation.   It may be said, indeed, that any city, on the shore of the lake, might have answered these purposes as well as Capernaum.   But it is to be remembered, that Capernaum was also the native place, or at least the residence, of the four chief of the Apostles, Peter and Andrew, James and John, and, perhaps, of more among them ; as of Matthew, and possibly of Philip ; whose convenience might, perhaps, be consulted, in fixing on this, and not on any other, place. Besides, if any one will inspect the maps of Palestine, he will see that it lay as nearly as possible in the centre of the four great divisions of that country, Peræa, Decapolis, Trachonitis, on the east, and the north—the two Galilees, and Samaria, on the west—and Judæa Proper, on the south: and, consequently, was equally favourable for the resort of the people to our Lord, from all those parts alike.   It was as conveniently situated also, for the beginning and the conclusion of general progresses, or circuits, of Galilee, as any, which could have been selected ; and its distance from Tiberias, one of the seats of the Tetrarchal government, which was as great as possible, the one lying at the upper, and the other at the lower, extremity of the same lake, might be some motive for choosing it, in preference to any other city on the lake.

Besides, as Galilee was among the most populous regions of Palestine, so was the land of Gennesaret, the capital of which may be considered as Capernaum, among the most fertile, and most populous, parts of Galilee; as Josephus bears witness in the following passage.

A region, of the same name, extends along the lake of Gennesar, the natural beauty of which is admirable. For such is the fertility of the soil, it rejects no kind of plant; and they, who cultivate it, have left no sort unplanted there; and such is the temperature of the climate, it suits the most different wants of nature. In addition to palm-trees, which thrive best by heat, and figs and olives, in their vicinity, which require a milder air, nut-trees, the hardiest of plants, flourish there in the utmost abundance. It might be said that nature had been purposely ambitious of forcing herself to collect upon one spot discordant principles; and that the seasons, with a salutary conflict, each, as it were, challenged exclusively the possession of the country: for not merely does it so unaccountably nourish the different productions of as many different periods of the year, but it also preserves what it nourishes. The noblest of the kind, such as grapes and figs, it supplies for ten months without ceasing: and fruits of every other description, growing old on the trees round about, are supplied for the whole year. For, besides the temperature of the air, it is watered by a very fertilizing spring, which the natives call Capharnaum ... In length, the region extends along the lake, which is called by the same name, as far as thirty stades, and in breadth, as far as twenty[y].

To these reasons, others, if they were necessary, might be added; but, as these may suffice, I shall over and above observe only, that the selection of Capernaum, as a fixed place of residence, is no proof that our Lord possessed any house of his own therein; nor, consequently, of any inconsistency with that moving and pathetic declaration, twice repeated[z], The foxes have holes, and the birds of the air have nests; but the Son of man hath not where to lay down his head. The first instance of his using any house in Capernaum was in the use of the house of Simon and

[y] B. iii. x. 8.   [z] Matt. viii. 20. Luke ix. 58.

Andrew[a]: there is proof, after this, of his being entertained in the house of Levi, or Matthew, also[b]: but there is no proof of his ever living in a house of his own, or in what may not justly be considered as only the house of some friend, or some disciple.   The visit to Capernaum, in St. John[c], was clearly a passing visit; and, though after a certain time, his mother and his brethren are both spoken of as resident in Capernaum[d], yet even they either had no house of their own, or none in which our Lord was living along with them.   That he was regarded, however, legally as an inhabitant of Capernaum, is indisputably proved by the incident relating to the tribute money[e].

Secondly; if our Saviour's ministry began about the feast of Pentecost, the proceedings in the Synagogue at Nazareth could not have been much prior to the same time. But the passage, recited from Isaiah[f], may be said to militate against this conclusion; for that passage is part of the Haphtoroth, or portion of Scripture, appointed for the daily service of a much later period of the year, viz. after the feast of Tabernacles itself.   Admitting, however, that the passage was part of some such section, still we might contend that this objection was taken from the order of the Jewish lessons, as they *now* stand; which order could never be demonstratively shewn to be the order in which they *always* stood; or the order in which they stood in our Saviour's time.   The ground of such an objection, therefore, would be much too precarious to overturn every other argument which, from a variety of considerations both might be, and has been, urged to a contrary effect.   There is no authentic instance supplied by the New Testament, distinct from this, of a passage recited from either the Law or the Prophets, which might have been compared with it, and with the arrangement of the Jewish lessons at present: if, however, that part of Scripture, which the Eunuch was reading to himself, when Philip was commanded to join

[a] Matt. viii. 14. Mark i. 29. Luke iv. 38.   [b] Mark ii. 15. Luke v. 29.
[c] ii. 12.   [d] Matt. xii. 46. Mark iii. 21.   [e] Matt. xvii. 24.   [f] Is. lxi. 1. 2.

him[g], was part of the lesson for the day, that passage was taken from the fifty-third of Isaiah, and the time, when he was reading it, was soon after the feast of Pentecost[h]. The sixty-first of Isaiah, therefore, could not well have been in course *before* the feast of Pentecost, if the fifty-third was so *after* it; and if either of them had been in course then, neither could well have been in course at the feast of Tabernacles, more than four months later.

This leads me to observe, that the proceedings at Nazareth, on the occasion in question, at least with respect to our Saviour's conduct, though produced and justified by the special reasons of the case, were yet entirely out of course. He was preparing shortly to commence his ministry; and he prepares so to commence it by citing an illustrious prophecy—applicable solely to himself—but as the Messias of Israel, and as the Saviour also of mankind. There is no one particular, in that enumeration of the various offices to which he declared himself anointed—that is, ordained and commissioned—which must not be understood in a spiritual sense; there is none which, without an absurdity, could be literally received and construed. And they are spiritual purposes, and spiritual benefits, which, though they might be notified or proclaimed in the lifetime of Christ, could be verified only after his death. The reference also to the Spirit of God, as the efficient cause of the unction, by which the Christ had become consecrated to one and all of these functions, is more apposite, *a priori*, to the supposition of the feast of Pentecost, than of any other period; for that was a time which the previous history of the Jews, in the Dispensation of the Law, and the future history of Christianity, in the Dispensation of the Gospel, shew to have been especially, and, κατ' ἐξοχὴν, appropriated to the agency of the Spirit. The exordium of the prophecy ought to be rendered thus: The Spirit of the Lord is upon me for the purpose whereunto he hath anointed me. He hath sent me to preach the Gospel to the poor: and the rest.

[g] Acts viii. 32.   [h] Vol. i. Diss. xiii. 549.

It is said, indeed, that, when he stood up to read, the book of Isaiah was put into his hands; but, unless it could be shewn that every separate book of the Old Testament was contained in a separate roll, and not the whole, or many parts of the whole, in one, which is the case with the most ancient manuscripts, both Hebrew and Greek, still, this circumstance would prove nothing on the point at issue: the offering of the book of Isaiah would imply no more than the offering him the volume of the Scriptures in general, or the volume of the prophets in particular.   Be this, however, as it may, the volume, it is certain, was put into his hands closed, or rolled up; for he had to unfold it for himself; and, it is manifest, that he unfolded, or opened, it expressly to find out the passage in question.   Whether, then, the preliminary act of delivering him the book of Isaiah was regular, or irregular, his finding out, and reciting aloud, the first part of the sixty-first chapter was clearly his own doing, and, obviously, to be accounted for by the appositeness of the passage recited to the time and occasion of a formal commencement of his ministry.   It is evident, also, that as he rolled up the book, and gave it back again to the minister, after he had read this verse, and no more, he always intended to read only this verse, and no more; but it would be absurd to suppose only this verse, and no more, the proper lesson for the day; the different sections, as they now stand, being generally of much greater length than our own divisions into chapters, which are intended for the same purpose: in which case, it may well be questioned whether he was reading any part of the lesson for the day at all.

Nor can it be said that, perhaps, he was doing no more than what, on such occasions, might usually have been done: viz. first reciting a verse, and, then, proceeding to expound it; for it would be false to say that any exposition, even of this verse, is actually subjoined; and, it must be evident, from his closing the book, and returning it to the servant, to be restored to its place, that, when he has recited this one verse, he has done with the passage; he means to recite no more. The circumstance mentioned immediately after, that, when he had done each of these things and was sat down, but before he had yet added a word, the eyes of all in the synagogue were steadily fixed upon him, is an intimation that what he had just been doing was something novel and unexpected ; the nature of such an exordium raised the anticipation of more of the like kind to follow it, and sharpened the attention of the observers accordingly. When, therefore, they heard him proceeding to apply the scripture directly to himself, though they wondered at the gracious words which issued from his mouth, yet, the reflection immediately occurring, who it was that spoke them, the scandal, produced by this reflection, was too strong even for the natural impression, which had preceded, from the words themselves, and from the manner of him who delivered them.

To proceed : though the ministry of our Saviour, so far as concerned the assumption of his character as the Messias, and his beginning to act in that character, had certainly commenced in Judæa, and so early as the last Passover, still he had never yet done that which is meant by Preaching, or Proclaiming, the Gospel of the kingdom ; and calling on all men, by repentance and amendment of life, to prepare for its manifestation : because John, who had been hitherto the proper instrument in the discharge of this commission, before this return into Galilee, had not yet been cast into prison. The beginning, continuance, and final completion, of such a ministry, on his part, from this time forward—the mission of the Twelve, and of the Seventy— each in their proper order of time, and both agreeing, in their final end and purpose respectively, with the description of the ministry of our Lord, at this very period, and of that of the Baptist, long before—demonstrate, as we have argued at length elsewhere, an unity of design and of functions in the common ministry of all. The kingdom of heaven, in each of these instances, as the subject of one and the same proclamation, is necessarily one and the same also; and being what the Baptist, and the Messias—what the

Twelve, and the Seventy—each in their proper order, concurred to announce in common, and to announce as future, it can be understood of nothing which was to come to pass in the lifetime of Christ ; it can be understood of nothing, therefore, but of the future Dispensation of the Gospel. The actual promulgation of the Christian religion, that is, the first open establishment of the kingdom of heaven, took place on the day of Pentecost—from which the actual Dispensation of the Gospel begins to be dated.   With reason, then, might the first intimation of its futurity, the first public and authoritative declaration of the tidings of this kingdom, which proceeded from the mouth of our Lord himself, have coincided with the same period also.   Besides, the great business of our Lord, as a moral teacher, while he continued among mankind, was to revive, reinforce, and enlarge, the moral part of the ancient Law: the first sermon delivered from the mountain would alone be sufficient to prove this.   Hence, as the Law was originally given and instituted at this period of the year, and the feast of Pentecost itself was appointed in commemoration of that event, we have here an additional proof of the propriety with which the revival and republication of the Law, as made by the teaching of our Saviour, might coincide with the same period.   Nothing could tend more directly, in the estimation of all observing and reflecting persons, to point him out as the original and independent Lawgiver—promised by Moses, like unto himself—or as the great Prophet and Teacher, who should come into the world, than such a coincidence.

These preliminary considerations having been thus disposed of, we may observe, that from the time of the formal commencement of our Saviour's ministry in Galilee, it admits of no other distribution than into the times and occasions when he was resident at Capernaum ; the times and occasions when he was making the circuits of Galilee ; and the times and occasions when, though doing neither of these things, he was yet, for special reasons, travelling in Galilee, or elsewhere.   His circuits themselves, though all under-

taken for a common purpose, are still to be distinguished
into such as were *general,* or extended to the whole of the
country; and such as were *partial,* or extended only to
some portion of it. Subject to these limitations this ministry will now be considered ; not so as every where to de-
scend into particulars, but to be satisfied with the outline of
things ; and more especially with a view to determine, as
accurately as either the general reasons of probability, or the
special reasons of the case, may allow, the times and the
places, belonging to each separate transaction, through the
several years of its duration : in order to which, we may
premise that the earliest intimation of the commencement of
the first year, though really upwards of five weeks later
than its actual date, which occurs in the three first Gospels,
is the return into Galilee, after the imprisonment of John:
the earliest intimation of the beginning of the second is the
walking through the corn-fields on the sabbath ; and the
earliest intimation of the arrival of the third is the question
concerning eating with unwashen hands : all of them notices
not merely of such integral periods in themselves, as the
several years of the ministry of Christ, but, what is equally
remarkable, supplied, and each in the same relative order,
by all the three first Evangelists ; or only in the last instance of all, and that for a reason which is easily to be assigned, omitted by St. Luke in particular. Some of the
topics, which would thus have come within the present
scheme, will be found to have been already anticipated ; in
which case, we must be allowed to refer to the results of
former enquiries : and some will require to be discussed by
themselves hereafter ; in which case we must reserve their
proper consideration for another opportunity.

If, then, our Lord, as we have conjectured [k], came into
Galilee not before, not yet, possibly, much later than, the
thirty-sixth day from the sixteenth of Nisan, he came thither
about fourteen days before the feast of Pentecost ; and the
first things done, after the return, as we have also seen,

[k] Vol. ii. Diss. vii.

were the visits to Cana, to Nazareth, and to Capernaum, respectively; all which might have followed upon the return, and upon each other, within fourteen days' time. The visit to Nazareth was prior to a sabbath; and the visit to Capernaum was prior to a sabbath also: but still there is no reason why these sabbaths might not have been successive, or the teaching in the one place only a week, or at the utmost a fortnight, prior to the teaching in the other: for our Saviour might have gone down directly from Nazareth to Capernaum, (the distance between which was not more than one day's journey,) as soon as the expiration of the sabbath would permit of it; and, after what had happened in Nazareth, it is not likely he would make any longer stay there; while St. Luke, from his manner of relating the two facts in conjunction, may be considered to imply that he left Nazareth, and went to Capernaum, even without delay.

The question, therefore, which we have still to propose here, is, whether the visit to Nazareth, followed by the teaching there, and the visit to Capernaum, followed by the teaching there also, supposing them to have been only one or two weeks asunder, were both prior, or both posterior, or the one prior, and the other posterior, to the day of Pentecost? I consider it probable myself that the day of Pentecost fell between the two, and, consequently, that the visit to Nazareth might be prior to this day, but the visit to Capernaum, or the teaching there, was posterior to it: and that this was a possible event, may be shewn as follows.

The day of Pentecost, as being the fiftieth in order from the sixteenth of Nisan, reckoned as the first—or the first day of the eighth week, as that was of the first, between the Passover and Pentecost—would necessarily fall on the same day of the week in every year as that: and A.U. 780. A. D. 27. in the first year of our Saviour's ministry, the sixteenth of Nisan coincided with April 11. and both with the first day of the week [1]. The same thing, therefore, must

---

[1] Vol. i. Diss. v. and x.

have held good of the day of the ensuing Pentecost, May 30. Now, it might have been, even *a priori*, conjectured that one of the days, which were spent by our Saviour at Sychar[m], was very probably spent there because it coincided with a sabbath : and if he came there on the evening of the thirteenth of May, and departed thence again, on the morning of the sixteenth, this was actually the case; for May 13. A. U. 780. was Thursday, and May 16. was Sunday.

Upon this supposition, Jesus would proceed to Cana at the beginning of the week ; and we may suppose would arrive there also at the beginning of the same. The miracle on the sick person in Capernaum might be performed soon after his arrival : and it is some confirmation of this conclusion, that the miracle, which was so performed in Cana, could not have been performed either *on* the sabbath, or on the day *before* the sabbath, at least ; for the nobleman would neither have invited our Lord to come down to Capernaum upon the sabbath, nor have travelled back thither himself on that day.

It might, therefore, have been performed on the third or the fourth day of the week, and yet the fact of the performance be already known in Nazareth, or in any place no more remote from Capernaum than Nazareth, before the sixth or the seventh. In this case, the sabbath, which was passed in Nazareth, might be the sabbath next but one before the day of Pentecost, May 22 ; and that it was some sabbath either two or three days at least *before*, or two or three days at least after, that *day*, though we had no other data to reason from, might safely be concluded from the fact that the inhabitants of Nazareth, the male part of them especially, were still in the place[n]; that is, they were either not yet gone up to the feast, or already returned from it—to each of which things, besides the one day taken up by the observance of the feast, two or three days' journey would be absolutely necessary.

[m] John iv. 40. [n] Exod. xxiii. 14—17. xxiv. 23. Deut. xvi. 16.
Jos. B. Jud. ii. xix. 1.

At the same time, after this visit, when the people of
Nazareth might be preparing to set out to Jerusalem, our
Lord might depart to Capernaum : for, though we cannot
suppose that he also, like the rest of the people of Galilee,
would return to Judæa, (which he had so recently left,) for
the sake of attending the feast in common with them, yet
neither can we suppose that, after what had just befallen
him, he would stay much longer in Nazareth.   The day of
Pentecost, then, May 80. would be spent by him in Galilee,
and probably in Capernaum : the next sabbath day, after
the day of Pentecost, June 5. would be the sabbath on
which his ministry in that place was first formally begun ; and the first Sunday after the same date, June 6.
would be ascertained by the narrative itself as the very
day, on which he set out upon the first circuit of Galilee.

One week, at least, of his history, it is true, would continue, even on this supposition, unaccounted for ; but it
would be a week transacted in Capernaum, where the inactive periods of his ministry in general, by which I mean
the intervals between his journeyings abroad, appear in
other instances so to have been transacted ; and, if the
day of Pentecost fell sometime within it, or at its very commencement, it would be a week of inaction not altogether
unnecessary.   For, though our Lord himself might not
have gone up to Jerusalem, to the approaching feast, the
rest of the nation would go ; by whose going and returning
to their homes, which would be requisite before he could
enter on his ministry among them, six or seven days would
be taken up[o].

This point, then, being presumptively established, the
first event, posterior to the choice of Capernaum, and distinctly on record, is the call of the four disciples, Simon
and Andrew, James and John; the particulars of which
are given by St. Matthew and by St. Mark[p], but, for rea-

* [o] Macc. x. 34.   Jos. Ant. Jud. xiii. ii. 3.   [p] Matt. iv. 18—22.
Mark i. 16—20.

s 2

sons which will appear elsewhere, are omitted by St. Luke;
who yet, by shewing at a subsequent point of time[q], that
Simon, and others with Simon, his acquaintances, were already attached to, and already disciples of, our Lord, recognizes implicitly the fact of their previous call.   The
scene of this transaction being laid by each of the Evangelists in the neighbourhood of the lake of Tiberias, and the
call being followed by the entering of all the parties together
into Capernaum, we cannot doubt that the transaction took
place in the vicinity of Capernaum, and not on some other
quarter of the lake.   Capernaum was the residence, and,
probably, the native place, of Simon and Andrew, two out
of the four ; and the residence of James and John, the
other two, also; each of whom was a partner with the rest
in the same occupation of fishermen.   Now the call is related by St. Matthew, after he had said that Jesus came to
Capernaum, and settled there; which may be thought to
imply that he had been sometime, longer or shorter, at Capernaum before it : nor would this be at variance with St.
Mark[r], unless the entering into Capernaum, there spoken
of, after the call, were also affirmed to be the first instance
of the kind, since our Saviour came thither.   It is a more
critical assertion that they are said, immediately after, to
have gone into the synagogue on the sabbath ; for this
would imply that the call could not long have preceded the
sabbath ; and St. Luke, by making the beginning to teach,
in this same synagogue, the very next thing apparently to
the coming down to Capernaum, leads to the same inference[s].

Laying all these intimations together, we may conjecture
that Jesus had been at Capernaum about a week before he
began to teach, and that he called the four disciples the day
before that event itself : a conjecture perfectly in unison
with the conclusions already established, and in fact borne
out by them.   The instance of teaching, which followed, we
may justly conclude was the first instance of the kind which

[q] iv. 38.   [r] i. 21.   [s] iv. 31.

had yet occurred, if for no other reason, at least for this—that, in both St. Mark and St. Luke, the specific observation upon the characteristic of his manner of teaching, that it was with authority, is found subjoined to it here, once for all : the nature of which argument I shall have occasion to explain more at large elsewhere.

The call of these disciples *now* is a proof that they had never been called as yet ; the readiness, with which they obey the call even now is a proof that they must have been prepared to receive it before: and such a preparation would imply both a previous acquaintance with our Saviour, and a previous disposition to believe in him ; the fact, and the reasons of which, though they do not appear in the account of the three first Evangelists, are yet satisfactorily ascertained by St. John[t].

For it is seen, from this narrative, that all these four persons were either disciples of John the Baptist, or at least believers in his divine legation, before they could have acquired either of these relations to Jesus Christ. Two of them, (Andrew, and as there is every reason to suppose, the Evangelist St. John,) are specified by name as such ; and as the other two were brothers of these respectively, and all four connected by a common acquaintance with each other, and a partnership of trade, it is reasonable that we should conclude the same thing also of them. Simon, one of them, was present at Bethabara, as well as Andrew and John, attending on the Baptist ; and though James might not have been there exactly at this time, he might still have been a disciple of the Baptist ; or his name in particular may be suppressed by the Evangelist, on the same principle for which he suppresses his own ; because it was the name of a brother. Besides these four, Philip and Nathanael also must have been believers in John.

Now the act of the Baptist, by which he pointed out Jesus, as he was walking, to Andrew and John, under the emblem of the Lamb of God[u], who should take away, or rather should carry, the sin of the world, (for on this point

[t] i. 35. to the end.   [u] i. 36.

s 3

St. Chrysostom observes, οὐκ εἶπεν ἔλυσεν, ἀλλ᾽ ἔλαβε καὶ ἐβάστασεν· ὃ περὶ ἁμαρτιῶν μᾶλλον εἰρῆσθαί μοι δοκεῖ τῷ προφήτῃ συμφώνως Ἰωάννῃ τῷ λέγοντι· Ἴδε ὁ ἀμνὸς τοῦ Θεοῦ, ὁ αἴρων τὴν ἁμαρτίαν τοῦ κόσμου[v],) was certainly designed to point him out to them as the Messias; and so, it is clear, they understood it[w]; but, that it was also designed to intimate that they must thenceforward cease to be his disciples, and become the disciples of Jesus, does not so clearly appear. They followed him, indeed, in consequence of what John had said; but it was more out of curiosity than from any other motive; for, on his turning, and asking, What seek ye? it appears from their answer, that they wished merely to learn where he dwelt. He invited them to come and see; and they abode with him for the rest of that day; the mention of which circumstance, as such, distinctly implies that they continued with him at that time no longer than for that day; and the mention, at verse forty-fourth, of the day after proves equally that what happened, and is related, between[x], happened that same day.

Now, neither as they became acquainted with Jesus at first, nor in the course of what subsequently passed between them, is any thing seen to have transpired, which can be construed into a call, *from* our Lord, *to* them. The peculiar manner in which he apostrophizes Simon in particular —Thou art Simon, the son of Jonas; thou shalt be called Cephas—seems, on the contrary, expressly intended as if to bar that construction: for, if these words conveyed a call of Simon, they conveyed also the name of Peter; but the name of Peter was neither given, nor assumed, until a year at least from this time, when Simon was ordained an Apostle. Simon, therefore, did not receive any call now. Hence, though these four disciples, or three of them, at least, might from this time forward have become believers in our Lord, as in the Messias, yet, that they would attach themselves to him does by no means follow; or if they did so, it would be of their own accord.

---

[v] Oper. ii. 190.　　　[w] John i. 42.　　　[x] i. 40—43.

It is true, that on the following day Jesus addressed to Philip the words which, elsewhere, are used to convey a call, ἀκολούθει μοι[y]; but Philip was not one of the four; and, if he had been, it would have made no difference: for, the context plainly demonstrates that this was no call to become a disciple, but merely an invitation to return with the speaker into Galilee.   Nor is it probable, that, whatever predisposition to believe in our Lord might have been raised in John's disciples by their Master's testimony, he himself would formally call any in general, before he had formally commenced his ministry in any sense—either in Judæa, or in Galilee—of which things he had yet done neither: nor that, when he had commenced his ministry, he would formally call any in particular, prior to the four principal disciples, Simon and Andrew, James and John.   I much question whether he himself in person ever called any to become disciples, except these four, and St. Matthew; though he must, in person, have ordained all the Twelve to be Apostles.   But these four, in particular, if he did not actually call until so long after, it must be evident he never could have called so long before.

Yet our Lord, it will be said, was attended by disciples from this time forward, in his journeyings to and fro, before both the Passover, John ii. 13. and the return into Galilee, iv. 2. 43.   There is no proof, however, that these were disciples who had been called by him, or who had not attached themselves to him of their own accord, as some of them, doubtless, must have done to John also before him.   Besides, the word μαθητής is used in St. John, indiscriminately, for a simple believer in Jesus, as much as for one of his professed followers[z]: so that the mere term itself would prove nothing on the point at issue; and yet I should be entirely disposed to allow that among those who are mentioned by this name, on the several occasions between John ii. 2. and v. 1. some may be included who afterwards became regular disciples, and even Apostles; provided they had yet received no call

[y] John i. 44.   [z] iv. 1. vi. 66. vii. 3. viii. 31. ix. 27. 28. xviii. 19. xix. 38.

s 4

from our Lord in person, and were still held in attendance
upon him solely by their own choice, and their own act.   In
this case, there might be occasions when they would not be
about him, but engaged, on their own business, elsewhere :
and, certain it is, that until he himself had formally entered
on his own ministry, and they had, as formally, been called
to attend upon him, they could not consider themselves, in
any sense, bound to give up their ordinary occupations entirely, nor to be constantly in his society : they did not, as
we shall see hereafter, consider themselves bound to do this,
even after they had both received such a call, and made a
circuit of Galilee, along with him ; much less at any time
before that.

St. Peter, in a passage[a] which has been recited elsewhere[b], defined the qualifications of the future Apostle, who
was to succeed to the place of Judas, as the qualifications of
one who should have companied with them, since the time
for which the Lord Jesus, having begun from the baptism
of John, to the day of his reception into heaven, went in,
and went out, among them ; where, by the baptism of John,
I shewed was meant the ministry of John, and, by beginning
from that baptism, beginning from the close of that ministry, and entering upon his own.   The passage, then, virtually affirms that neither St. Peter, nor any of the rest,
who were Apostles at that very time, had received their call,
or begun to company regularly with Jesus, themselves, before the same period ; whereby it is critically in unison with
the testimony of the three first Gospels.

It is not improbable, that if Simon, Andrew, and John,
were originally disciples of the Baptist, before they became
acquainted with Jesus, they might continue so afterwards,
until the time of their Master's imprisonment ; and that it
is from personal knowledge, or as one of the parties who
had witnessed this last and most memorable of the testimonies of John to our Lord—in which too there is a clear
reference to what had passed before[c]—that St. John records

---

[a] Acts i. 21. 22.   [b] Vol. i. Diss. viii. 295.   [c] i. 28—37.

the conversation, which stands in the third chapter of his Gospel, from verse the twenty-sixth to the end.   After the imprisonment of the Baptist, these, among others of his followers, might have returned to their former homes, and to their usual occupations ; in which case, when our Lord came from Nazareth to Capernaum, he might find them all there, a little before, or a little after, the feast of Pentecost.

Or, though this conjecture should not be admitted, still it must be acknowledged that they had attached themselves to him of their own accord, and, therefore, might leave him again for a time.   Some disciples of our Lord certainly accompanied him as far as Sychar[d]; it does not appear that any accompanied him thence[e]; it is probable that he went alone to Cana[f], and it seems indisputable that he must have gone alone to Nazareth, and afterwards to Capernaum[g].   To suppose those disciples had been with him at the former place, whom he called immediately after at the latter, would be absurd in the extreme.   It is possible, then, that, while our Saviour himself remained at Sychar[h], the disciples, who all accompanied him thither, but who could have no inducement to remain, but every inducement not to remain, in a town of Samaria, continued their journey the same day, or the next, into Galilee; which, if they arrived at Mount Gerizim at six o'clock in the evening, and in the middle of summer, was very easy to have been done.   It makes in favour of this supposition, that if they arrived at Gerizim on the evening of May 13. they arrived on the evening of a *Thursday*—and as Sychar, according to Reland[i], was only twenty-one Roman miles distant even from Scythopolis, it would be manifestly possible for them to arrive in Galilee, long before the recurrence of the sabbath.

The feast of Pentecost was not like either of the other two great solemnities, a seven days' or an eight days' feast, but, as its name implies, a one day's feast.   Three days were all that were necessary to travel from Capernaum to Jerusalem, or back again—and in the summer season, when

[d] John iv. 8.   [e] iv. 43.   [f] iv. 46.   [g] Luke iv. 16. 31.
[h] John iv. 40.   [i] Palæstina ii. 423.

travelling might be equally convenient in the night, even less. Hence, though the four disciples in question, like the rest of the male, and grown up, Israelites, might have been in Jerusalem on the Sunday, and detained there all that day, yet by setting out the next morning, or even, at the expiration of the sabbath of Pentecost[k], that same evening, they would be returned to Capernaum, and might be found pursuing their occupation as fishermen, on the lake, at any time on either Thursday or the Friday following. Though Pentecost was observed as a Sabbath, of which both the Law and Josephus supply proofs, οὐχ ἔστιν δὲ ἡμῖν οὔτε ἐν τοῖς Σάββασιν, οὔτε ἐν τῇ ἑορτῇ (scil. τῇ Πεντηκοστῇ.) ὁδεύειν[l], yet the distance from Jerusalem to Capernaum was not more than sixty miles; which the common people of Galilee, who could not afford to be absent from home, and especially in the middle of summer, when the corn harvest was at its maturity, longer than they could help, by travelling thirty miles a day, might accomplish, if necessary, in two days; and by travelling five and twenty, would accomplish with ease in three. On this point, then, there can be no difficulty: and I shall conclude this digression, the length of which must be excused by the interest, and by the importance, of its subject, with one more observation merely, viz. on the delicacy of our Lord, in not having expressly called any of the disciples of the Baptist, so long as their Master was still upon the stage of his public ministry himself—and yet the apposite and well-timed coincidence of their being called by him now, when John, by his imprisonment, had been finally removed from view.

The teaching in the synagogue at Capernaum was followed by a miracle at the same time, and in the same place; both these facts being the first instances of their kind in the course of our Saviour's ministry, which are specified by any Gospel but the last. The history of the miracle[m], in the two Evangelists who record it, is remarkably similar—down

---

[k] Lev. xxiii. 21.   Numb. xxviii. 26.   [l] Ant. Jud. xiii. viii. 4.
[m] Mark i. 23—28.   Luke iv. 33—37.

to the very letter of their accounts—and would be alone sufficient to prove that St. Mark did not write *from*, though he might have written *after*, St. Matthew, who omits the miracle altogether; while St. Luke wrote *distinctly* from, though he must have seen, St. Mark.   The next event, viz. the cure of St. Peter's wife's mother, which St. Mark and St. Luke do both relate in its proper order[n], and St. Matthew out of it[o], belongs to the same day, directly consequent upon the former.   The place of this miracle, then, was Simon's house in Capernaum; the time of it, the Sabbath-day—after the service of the synagogue was over—and, as we may collect from the critical circumstance of her arising and ministering unto, that is, waiting upon, them, about the usual period of some one meal in the day; which, if it was the noonday's repast, would be, upon the Sabbath, the sixth hour, or twelve of the clock with us, one hour later than on the week-days[p].   The next event, which was the performance of sundry miracles of healing and dispossession, on such as needed them[q], is shewn, by the mention of sunset, to have belonged to a time later than the expiration of the Sabbath; that is, about the end of the twelfth hour on the same day.

The next morning, and, consequently, the morning of the first day of the week, (which, if it was the first Sunday after Pentecost, would be June 6.) having passed the night in the house of Peter, Jesus retired early to a solitary place, for the sake of private prayer[r].   The object of this prayer, it is reasonable to presume, was preparation for the circuit of Galilee, about to begin; the place, it is equally probable, was the same mountain in the vicinity of Capernaum, to which he is seen to have resorted, for a like purpose, hereafter; and from which he delivered his two sermons.   Here, at day-break, he was rejoined by the disciples, and by the multitude, who had followed him thither from Capernaum. With this time, then, that is, from the morning of the first

[n] Mark i. 29—31.   Luke iv. 38. 39.   [o] Matt. viii. 14. 15.   [p] Jos. Vit. 54.   [q] Matt. viii. 16. 17.   Mark i. 32—34.   Luke iv. 40. 41.   [r] Mark i. 35—39.   Luke iv. 42—44.

day of the week, answering to Sunday with us, and, probably, within seven days since the recurrence of the feast of Pentecost, consequently on June 6. we must date the commencement of a circuit of Galilee; which evidently set out from Capernaum, and, though it was confined to Galilee, yet was evidently general in that country, and on all these accounts the first of its kind, and as complete as any. The intention of making such a progress, in his departure from Capernaum itself, is implied by the answer to Simon, and the people, when they would have detained him, or prevailed upon him to return to that city; Let us go to the neighbouring κωμοπόλεις—(κώμας καὶ πόλεις) towns or cities —that I may preach there also; for, for this purpose am I come forth [q]; that is, from Capernaum, which he had just left. This is the circuit described by St. Matthew also [r]: St. Luke says, it was discharged in the synagogues of Galilee; St. Mark, in the synagogues throughout all Galilee; and St. Matthew, that it went round all Galilee; and each of them, that it consisted in teaching, and preaching—or proclaiming—and performing miracles: from the unity of which descriptions, and from the identity of place and of time assigned to it by the narrative in each instance, it is impossible to doubt whether it is one and the same in all these Evangelists, or not.

The expediency of undertaking such a progress, as soon after the public commencement of the ministry in Galilee as possible, must be undeniable: the question which we have to consider is chiefly its probable duration; a question of so much the more importance in the present instance, because prospectively useful even for instances of the like kind again; since, whatever length of time might have been occupied by one such circuit, the same, it may be supposed, would be taken up by another. There are, accordingly, two measures by which this duration must be presumptively determined; one, the absolute periphery of the country, or the number of miles which a general circuit of Galilee would embrace; the other, the absolute number of its towns and

[q] Mark i. 38.   [r] iv. 23—25.

villages, or the number of places which such a circuit might be expected to visit.   To the application of the former criterion, it would be necessary to know how many miles our Saviour would travel each day ; to that of the latter, what stay he would make in each place—both which may be very uncertain points.   Yet this last criterion appears to me on every account the more appropriate, and certainly the more feasible, of the two ; for every circuit, whether in Galilee or elsewhere, undertaken in the course of our Lord's ministry, having been undertaken for the benefit of the inhabitants, is surely not to be estimated merely by the number of miles which he would travel in a day—even though this number could be determined ; but by the number of places which he would visit, and the length of the stay which he would make in each—both which may much more presumptively be conjectured.   Nor is it to be supposed that he would merely perambulate Galilee in a circle, and, consequently, pass through such towns and villages only as lay on the line of his route : the expression, περιῆγεν ὅλην τὴν Γαλιλαίαν, in reference to this circuit, must be understood and interpreted, conformably with others, περιῆγεν ὁ Ἰησοῦς τὰς πόλεις πάσας καὶ τὰς κώμας [s]—and, διώδευε κατὰ πόλιν καὶ κώμην [t], in reference to circuits subsequently undertaken. What he did on one general progress, unless there were special reasons, or special intimations, to the contrary, (which, however, would be true of no circuit but the last,) he may justly be considered to have done upon another, and he would, perhaps, be more likely to do on the very first of all, than on any other which came after it.   I do not, therefore, think it necessary to enter upon any examination of the geography of Galilee, with a view, at least, to the present question ; for it would lead to no satisfactory result : those who desire a description of either this part of Palestine, or any other of the scenes of our Saviour's ministry, may consult Josephus [u], or the Palestine of Reland, who has collected almost every thing which could have been adduced on this subject.

* Matt. ix. 35.   t Luke viii. 1.   u Vit. 37. B. iii. iii.

But as to the number of towns and villages—διακόσιαι
καὶ τέσσαρες, asserts Josephus [v], κατὰ τὴν Γαλιλαίαν εἰσὶ πόλεις
καὶ κῶμαι—not one of which contained fewer than fifteen
thousand souls [w]; and many of them, especially the cities,
we may justly presume, would contain a vast number more.
Though, however, we should assume the average population
of every town or city as only 15,000—and though we
should understand the specified number of such towns and
villages as intended of both the Galilees, yet even on these
suppositions, the population of Galilee would amount to
3,060,000 souls in all: which, I think it may be rendered
exceedingly probable, was half the population of Judæa in
general.

The whole longitude of Palestine from Dan to Beersheba, that is, from Beersheba to Cæsarea Philippi, is estimated by Reland [x] at 156 Roman miles; of which 52
miles, or one third, at least, must be assigned to the length
of Galilee, Upper and Lower, in particular. And as the
latitude or breadth of the country (that is, of the habitable
part of the country, west of the Jordan) was sufficiently
uniform, if the population of every part had been on an
equal scale, the population of the whole in general would
have been three times the population of a third part in particular. On this principle the whole population of Palestine, west of the Jordan, must have been estimated at
9,180,000 souls: a calculation, which may, perhaps, justly
be considered as beyond the truth. The great populousness of Judæa is indeed a circumstance often insisted on
by profane writers [y]; and Strabo tells us the small district
of Jamnia and her suburbs only could bring into the field
an army of 40,000 men : which implies a general population of at least 160,000. There can be no question, in
short, that in proportion to its comparative size the province of Judæa was probably the most populous in the
empire. But however numerous its population might be,
we cannot suppose it was more so than that of Egypt; yet

[v] Vit. 45.   [w] B. iii. iii. 2.   [x] ii. 423.   [y] Diod. Sic. xl. Eclog.
Tac. Hist. v. 5.   Strabo. xi. 1079.

even the population of Egypt, A. U. 819. thirty-nine years after A. U. 780. is estimated only at 7,500,000. exclusive of Alexandria [z]. Nor is it to be supposed that Judæa, west of the Jordan, in particular, was more populous in the time of our Saviour, than all Judæa, generally, in the reign of David. Yet from the result of the census in the reign of David, which (exclusive of the tribes of Levi and Benjamin only) gave a gross military population of from 1,300,000 to 1,600,000 [a]. if this be considered a fourth part of the whole, the whole cannot be estimated at more than from six to seven millions in all.

Agrippa tells the Jews of Jerusalem, in the passage from Josephus' History of the War, before referred to, that Egypt paid more to the Roman government, by way of tribute, in one month, than they—by which I understand him to mean the Jews of Jerusalem and Judæa as such—paid to it in a year. It seems to me a reasonable inference that, if the tribute of Judæa Proper was a twelfth part of that of Egypt, the population of Judæa Proper was a twelfth part of that of Egypt; especially as it may be collected from the context, the particular description of tribute, upon which the comparison turns, is the poll-tax as such, or the tribute levied *per capita*. Whatever was the amount of this tax, whether one drachm or denarius (which seems to be the most natural inference from the circumstances of the question relating to the tribute money) or two, yet if it was only uniform, and the same in Judæa as in Egypt, for the reign of Augustus, or of Tiberius, or of any other Roman Emperor, down to the twelfth of Nero—the number of persons who paid it in Egypt is stated, from the public returns, as 7,500,000 : exclusive of the population of Alexandria : which, on the same principle of computation, it may, perhaps, be collected from Diodorus Siculus [b], must be stated at 300,000. more. The whole will thus amount to 7,800,000 : a twelfth part of which would be 650,000 : representing the population of Judæa Proper, as in the twelfth of Nero, on the same scale as the other sum the population of Egypt, at the same period.   The very statement of this result seems to require we should understand it of the male and adult part of that population merely; and this, being reckoned at a third part of the gross, gives us about 2,000,000 as the sum total of the gross—which, it would be admitted, *a priori*, might be very probably about the truth.

At the Passover, A. U. 819. from the number of victims computed to have been sacrificed, and on an average of ten men only to every victim, Josephus reckons the numbers who attended at 2,700,000 [c]—all of whom must be understood as adults, and very probably males, exclusively.   If these consisted altogether of the natives of Palestine, the amount of *their* number, in particular, would make the population of the country in general, 8 or 9,000,000.   But it is unquestionable that, among those who attended at the Passovers, besides the inhabitants of Palestine itself, vast numbers of the Jews of the Dispersion must also be included.   Let us suppose that these constituted one third of the whole—that portion of the native population, who attended at this Passover, would be about 2,000,000.   And as the average, on which the computation is founded, is confessedly the lowest possible—and instead of *ten* persons to every victim ought rather to have been fifteen, the mean between ten, as the least, and twenty, as the greatest, comprehended in the same paschal company—their numbers cannot well be stated at less.   On this principle, also, the whole population of Palestine must be stated at about 6,000,000.

I know not what argument is to be founded upon the assertion in the same passage of the War, quoted above, that the whole population of Jerusalem, at the time of its siege and destruction, as made up of those who survived, and of those who perished, was 1,197,000; but I think it does not militate against the former conclusion.   The ordi-

[c] B. vi. ix. 3.

nary population of Jerusalem may be rated at about 200,000 : all above this number, in the present instance, which we will call a million of souls, were made up of strangers. Now among these strangers—it is probable that during the war there would be no Jews of the Dispersion : for, independent of the risk which they themselves must have run in coming at such a time, it is clear that the Roman government, out of whose dominions, or through whose dominions, they must all have passed, to arrive in Judæa, would not, if possible, have permitted it. In the fifth year of the war, too, after Galilee had been reduced and laid waste, and nothing but Jerusalem, and Judæa Proper itself, still remained to oppose the Romans, it is not likely that any strangers would resort to Jerusalem at the intervening Passover, except the native Jews as such—or from its vicinity more immediately. The numbers, then, who appear to have been assembled at the last Passover, can be no just criterion of the numbers who attended the Passover in general ; nor, perhaps, of the population of any part of the country but Judæa Proper. And if we suppose that half its entire population was collected in the metropolis on this occasion, as that appears to have been little short of a million, the entire population could not be much less than two millions.

The population of Jerusalem may, perhaps, be estimated from the proportion of the size of Jerusalem to that of Alexandria in Egypt. The entire circumference of Jerusalem was 33 stades [d]; that of Alexandria, 110 or 120 [e]. It is probable, however, that these last numbers are both exaggerated ; for Alexandria did not cover more ground than Rome ; yet even the circumference of Rome, A. U. 827. or 828. when Pliny was writing, did not exceed 13 Roman miles, or 104 stades. (H. N. iii. 5.) Quintus Curtius states its circumference at 80 stades ; which is much more in proportion to that of Rome. Perhaps we may assume it at 90.

[d] Jos. B. v. iv. 3 xii. 2. Vide also Contra Apion. i. 22. 1 188. Strabo xvi. 1083. [e] Stephanus De Urbibus. Plin. H. N. v. 10. Jos. B. ii. xvi. 4. Strab. xvii. 1126.

In this case the size of Jerusalem was rather more than one third of the size of Alexandria.   In wealth, grandeur, and number of inhabitants, Alexandria acknowledged no rival but Rome. Its population consisted partly of Greeks and partly of Jews ; whose respective amount must have been very nearly balanced, or they could not so long, and so bitterly, have disputed with each other the exclusive mastery of the city.   Accordingly, of the five quarters, called after the first five letters of the Greek alphabet, into which it was divided, two were occupied chiefly by the Jews [f] ; whence we may infer that their numbers constituted very nearly two fifths of the whole, or two fifths of the free, population at least. In the time of Diodorus Siculus this free population is computed at 300,000.[g] If the Jews were two fifths of this, their numbers would amount to 120,000 : and it would agree to this conclusion, that, at the beginning of the Jewish war, they lost at once as many as 50,000—which the context would imply to be almost one half of their whole number [h]. Yet this calculation of Diodorus is probably rather under, than above, the truth : it may not take in more of the free population than adults of either sex—and if we add to these the non-adults belonging to the same, (probably one third of the whole,) and, to both, the slave population, which in great cities was at least equal to the free, the gross amount of its population cannot be stated at less than 6 or 700,000.   The population of Jerusalem was probably not more than one third, yet greater than one fourth, of that of Alexandria ; and, therefore, may be stated on the same scale as that, at about 200,000.[*]

[*] The population of Seleucia upon the Tigris is stated by Pliny, H. N. vi. 26. at 600,000 : and Seleucia was not a greater city than Alexandria—Strabo. xvi. 1066.   Moreover, as the Jews of Alexandria lost 50,000 of their numbers at once, so did the Jews of Seleucia (and not much before the same time) an equal amount of their's—Ant. Jud. xviii. vi. 8. 9.

In the time of Hecatæus the Abderite, whose age was about Olymp. 117. B. C. 312. Jerusalem was supposed to contain

[f] Philo in Flaccum. 973.   [g] xvii. 52.   [h] B. Jud. ii. xviii. 7. 8.

There is an assertion in Dio [i], that the Emperor Hadrian, in his war with the Jews, destroyed to the ground 985 κώμας 120,000 inhabitants—Jos. Contra Apion. i. 22. 1188. This statement is, perhaps, not to be implicitly depended on ; for the same account of Hecatæus, in other respects, besides a mixture of truth, contains much which is false : as for instance, the alleged extent of the walls of Jerusalem—fifty stades—instead of not more than thirty-three. There can be no question, at least, that in the lapse of above three centuries the population of the city would be greatly encreased : so that if it was even sixty or seventy thousand merely in the time of Hecatæus, it might be 200,000 in the time of our Saviour. The same writer estimates the number of priests as such, in his time, at 1500 : and though this should be understood of one only of the four φυλαὶ, into which they were divided, yet, Jos. Contra Apion. ii. 7. 1245. each of these φυλαὶ contained 5000, at least, apiece. If the priests had multiplied in a threefold, or a fourfold, proportion, the rest of the population may be supposed to have done the same.

Nothing, it is true, can be more uncertain, and more liable to lead to contradictory conclusions, than calculations respecting the magnitude of ancient cities, or the populousness of ancient nations. For example, the inhabitants of Rome itself have been estimated by some learned men, as the result of such calculations, at 13 or 14,000,000. Yet in the time of Augustus, according to the Ancyran monument, and the rate of the Congiaria which he distributed among them at different times, the *plebs urbana* never exceeded 320,000 : only 20,000 more than Diodorus' statement of the population of Alexandria. If we were to multiply this by three, it would give a gross amount of no more than 960,000. Nor do I think the population of Rome, in the time of Augustus, can justly be estimated at more than a million of souls. The population of Carthage, at the time of the third Punic war, is estimated by Strabo (xvii. 1176.) at 700,000 souls : and the periphery of its walls, at 360 stades. If this statement be correct, the periphery of Carthage amounted to 45 Roman miles ; or nearly quadruple the extent of Pliny's statement of the walls of Rome. It is probable, however, that there is here some error in the text of Strabo. One *part* of the walls, viz. that part which

[i] lxix. 14.

T 2

ὀνομαστοτάτας : an assertion which, after what has been said, can hardly be received as true. For if Galilee, a third part of Judæa, and the most populous of all, contained only 204 κῶμαι, or πόλεις, indifferently, is it to be supposed the other two parts contained 781 ? If the assertion had been that the Romans destroyed 685 such *vici*, or κῶμαι, (than which there was scarcely any thing else in Judæa,) it might have squared very well with Josephus ; for, then, allowing 204 to Galilee, we might have assigned 480 to the rest of the country. The assertion must certainly imply that Hadrian laid waste the whole country; but, unless upon one supposition, that the villages or towns *out* of Galilee, though so much more numerous, were proportionably less populous, than those *within* it, it cannot be received, as it stands, without being at variance with Josephus. If Dio is right as to the number of towns in Palestine generally, Josephus must have underrated the number in Galilee in particular ; or, if he has not done that, he must have overstated their population. It is not likely, however, that the Jewish historian should have been mistaken on either of these points : and it is much more probable either that Dio has exaggerated the actual number of villages destroyed, or that his text has been corrupted to 985 instead of 685: which might possibly have been the case : for χ the numeral note for 600. imperfectly

extended across the isthmus or neck of land, the only direction where the city was accessible except by sea, is stated in the text, as it stands, at 60 stades ; but Appian, De Rebus Punicis, viii. 119. makes it only 25. If we reduce the whole statement of Strabo on the same scale, the periphery of Carthage must be reckoned at about one half of 360 ; that is, about 180 stades. Nor would this be much at variance with the statement of the epitomiser of Livy (lib. li.) which puts it at 23 Roman miles, or 184 stades. But even this is considerably greater than the alleged extent of Rome, 13 miles, or 104 stades. If 700,000, then, is a just estimation of the population of Carthage, A. U. 608. with a circumference of 180 or 190 stades, can more than a million be a correct account of that of Rome, in the time of Augustus or Pliny, with a periphery of 80 or 90 stades less ?

or rudely formed, admits of being confounded with ℶ the numeral note for 900.

To revert, however, from this digression. If Galilee contained, within its limited extent, 204 towns, and more than three millions of souls, the half of the population of Judæa, we need no other answer, than the statement of this fact, to a question which may probably have often occurred to reflecting minds—why the ministry of our Lord, for by far the greater part of its duration, was exclusively confined to that country? There might be many and sufficient reasons why it should not have been permanently discharged in Judæa as such ; and if any part must be fixed upon, distinct from that, what could be fitter than Galilee? What scene could be more favourable for the spiritual harvest, on which he was preparing to enter? or what tract of country in the Roman empire, at the same juncture of time, could be shewn to have been, in proportion to its extent, so thickly peopled as this? Where, in short, could our Lord's ministry have both been fixed, and been discharged, so as to be fixed and discharged among his brethren, according to the flesh, as such—so as to dispense its benefits on the widest possible scale—with more propriety than here?—where, perhaps, half the population of the country, in general, was ready assembled, within a third of the territory, in particular.

Now I will not assume, though the language employed by the Evangelists would almost justify us in assuming, that, in the course of the same progress, however general, our Lord would visit each of these towns and villages in its turn ; I will assume that he would visit only one half of the number ; and, what is no extravagant supposition, that he would pass, upon an average, one day in each. I will assume also that, for every week of the continuance of the progress, he would necessarily be stationary somewhere during the four and twenty hours of the Sabbatic rest. Even upon this calculation, which every one will allow to be moderate and reasonable, the duration of a circuit would never be less than three months, and, probably, never less than four. This, then, we may assume, in every instance of what is perceived to have been a general circuit, not other-wise limited, as the nearest approximation to the exact measure of its continuance: and, consequently, the circuits, which began about the feast of Pentecost, would be over about the feast of Tabernacles; of which fact we shall find, if I am not mistaken, incidental notices supplied, on more than one occasion, by the gospel-narrative itself. And it is a general argument in favour of its truth, first, that, on this principle, a circuit would commonly begin after wheat-harvest was over, and terminate when seed-time was ready to begin; the effect of which would be that the people every where would be enabled to attend upon our Saviour, with the least inconvenience to themselves: and, secondly, that it would coincide with the period of the year, when travelling could best be performed only in the morning and the evening of the day, and resting throughout it, so ob-viously necessary for the purpose of teaching, would not be more necessary for that purpose, than expedient in itself.

The course of the present circuit, we may conjecture from St. Matthew[k], was, upon the whole, as follows—first, along the western side of the Jordan, northward; which would disseminate the fame of Jesus in Decapolis: secondly, along the confines of the Tetrarchy of Philip, westward; which would make him known throughout Syria: thirdly, by the coasts of Tyre and Sidon, southward: and, lastly, along the verge of Samaria, and the western region of the lake of Galilee—the nearest points to Judæa Proper, and to Peræa—until it returned to Capernaum. In the course of the progress, if he visited Bethsaida, he might be joined by Philip[l]; if he visited Cana, by Nathanael[m]; and if there was such a village as Iscara[n], by Judas Iscariot also. All our Lord's disciples were natives of Galilee, and, therefore, first became disciples in Galilee. No incident, however, is expressly recorded as having transpired on the circuit itself; a circumstance by no means more peculiar to this first, than

[k] iv. 24. 25.   [l] John. i. 45.   [m] xxi. 2.   [n] Chrys. Oper. ii. 219.
Theophyl. Comm. in Matt. 51. 160.

to any other, of the number, except the last; for these periods in our Lord's ministry, though in themselves integral portions of its whole duration, and as full of action and employment as any, are invariably the least related in detail of all.   The first sermon from the Mount[o], delivered, as I apprehend, at the close of the circuit, is so far an exception to this assertion.   If it was delivered on what tradition has pointed out as the mountain of the beatitudes, it was delivered near to Capernaum; and, therefore, either at the very beginning, or at the end, of the circuit; the latter of which is much the more probable supposition: the former would be inconsistent with both the cause alleged for the sermon[p], and what happened at the outset of the circuit[q].   Whether this is the same sermon with the sermon on record elsewhere[r], or distinct from that, is a question which must be considered hereafter by itself.

The next event, and posterior to this circuit of Galilee, because an event which took place on the lake of Capernaum, and, consequently, supposed our Lord to have been returned to Capernaum, is the miraculous draught of fishes[s]; a very different transaction, as I shall prove elsewhere, from the call of the four disciples in St. Matthew, or in St. Mark[t]. The time of this event, then, could not be earlier than the first feast of Tabernacles, when the circuit would expire; and it might be later. The first feast of Tabernacles in the course of our Saviour's ministry began October 4. and expired October 11.[u]

The cure of the leper, which is next recorded[v], we may conclude, for the following reasons, did not take place in Capernaum, nor, consequently, while Jesus was still resident there even after his return. First, Luke v. 12. is much too indefinite to be understood of so well known a city as Capernaum, especially after the mention of the lake[w], just before: secondly, the miracle took place some-

---

[o] Matt. v—viii. 1.   [p] v. 1.   [q] Mark i. 35—39. Luke iv. 42—44.
[r] Luke vi. 20—end.   [s] Luke v. 1—11.   [t] Matt. iv. 18—22. Mark
i. 16—20.   [u] Vol. i. Diss. v.   [v] Matt. viii. 2—4. Mark i. 40—45.
Luke v. 12—16.   [w] v. 1.

where near the desert[x], and, therefore, we may presume, not in the land of Gennesaret : thirdly, the entering into Capernaum, Mark ii. 1. is opposed to the entering into Capernaum, i. 21. before, as a second instance of the kind to a first ; which implies either that our Lord had never entered Capernaum again, as yet, since his departure thence at i. 35. or that if he had, he had left it again before the return, ii. 1 : fourthly, lepers were forbidden by the Jewish law to enter into the towns or the villages ; they were condemned to live apart from society, and to wear their clothes rent, as a mark of their situation[y]. If this was the case, even St. Luke's expression, As he was in one of the cities, must not be too strictly understood ; nor further than to denote that, when this leper, probably having seen him from afar[z], fell down before him, he was in the neighbourhood of some one city.

We possess, then, in this fact, an intimation that, posterior even to the first circuit of Galilee, Jesus was engaged somewhere distinct from Capernaum, which otherwise we should not have discovered ; and the discovery is so far valuable, that it helps to account for an integral period of time, between the close of this first circuit, and the arrival of the next Passover—an interval of nearly six months ; for which, however, only two or three circumstances are left on record. Part of this time might be spent in Capernaum, after the return—part, and perhaps the greatest portion, in the studied seclusion and privacy which followed the miracle, and were intended to avoid the effects of its notoriety itself. For he did not return to Capernaum, except δι' ἡμερῶν[a]—which may mean a considerable time ; and when he did return, it was not far from the close of the first year of his ministry.

And hence we may infer that this cure of the leper was the first specific miracle of the kind, which had yet been performed ; and that this is the true reason why each of the three Evangelists concurs to relate this one, but no other of

[x] Luke v. 16. Mark i. 45. [y] Lev. xiii. 45. 46. 2 Kings vii. 3. Jos. Contra Apion. i. 31. [z] Vide Luke xvii. 12. [a] Mark ii. 1.

the same description again.   Such miracles as these, considered in a symbolical point of view, were peculiarly characteristic of a Messias, who should make atonement for sin ;
as the plague of leprosy itself was of the spiritual or moral
taint of sin ; and it is evident, from the account of our Saviour's miracles, both the general and the specific, as hitherto given, that, like those which he empowered the
Twelve, and also the Seventy, to perform in his own lifetime, limiting their power to these, they had yet consisted only in the cure of diseases, strictly so called—νόσοι
καὶ μαλάκιαι—and in the ejection of unclean spirits ; that is,
in the simplest kind of miracles in general.   The great notoriety produced by this miracle, and, consequently, the necessity of withdrawing himself for a time, which it imposed
on our Lord, make in favour of the same conclusion.   It is
added, however, by St. Luke, that the multitude found him
out, even in the deserts, that is, in the less populous parts
of the country; (for, wherever he was, and however desirous
of concealment, still he could never be absolutely hid[b];)
and that they still resorted to him, to hear him, and to be
healed from their infirmities ; so that this retirement, long
as it might continue, was not idly or unprofitably spent.
Yet Jesus himself, though pursued by the people, kept
purposely Withdrawing into the deserts, and praying.

The next event, the cure of the paralytic[c], is clearly to
be placed in Capernaum, and in some private house, (probably Peter's,) our Lord's usual abode there.   Nor could
it have been long after the return ; for the bringing in of
the paralytic was produced, according to St. Mark, by the
news of this return; and hence the presence of Scribes from
all the surrounding villages, (κῶμαι,) which St. Luke alludes
to, is very probably to be explained.   They might have
come with our Saviour to Capernaum, as part of the resort
mentioned before ; for Josephus also adverts to the κῶμων
γραμματεῖς by name[d], as a sort of village schoolmasters, or

[b] Mark vii. 24.   [c] Matt. ix. 2—8.   Mark ii. 1—12.   Luke v. 17—26.
[d] Ant. Jud. xvi. vii. 3.   B. i. xxiv. 3.

as a class of inferior municipal magistrates; who might consequently be met with every where.

With regard to the call of Levi[e], which certainly took place the same day, the only question would be, whether it took place on the way to, or on the way from, the lake; a question, which St. Matthew, and St. Luke, may leave in doubt, but St. Mark decides in favour of the latter; shewing that Jesus, before he called Levi, had made an end of teaching. We may infer, therefore, that the cure of the paralytic happened early in the day, and the call of Levi comparatively late; for our Lord commonly resorted to the lake, for the purpose of teaching, in the morning[f]—whence, if the entertainment, on record in St. Mark and in St. Luke[g], was given by Levi the same day, and in consequence of his call, it would be a supper; and this, as we shall see hereafter, would be the strongest argument that each of these occasions must have been distinct from Matthew ix. 10—15. On this question, however, I shall enter elsewhere, by itself. With the facts, hitherto considered, the Gospel accounts of the first year of our Saviour's ministry are brought to a close.

---

[e] Matt. ix. 9. Mark ii. 13. 14. Luke v. 27. 28.
Matt. xiii. 1. compared with Mark iv. 35. iii. 20.
Luke v. 29. to the end.

[f] Luke v. 1. 5.
[g] Mark ii. 15—22.

DISSERTATION VIII.

PART III.

General prospective survey of our Lord's ministry in Galilee.

THE first intimation of the second year, which we possess, is the history of the walking through the corn-fields [a]; concerning which, I have shewn elsewhere [b] that the disposition, thus manifested, of our Lord's enemies to take exceptions against his conduct, or, what was the same thing, the conduct of his disciples, for supposed infractions of the sabbath, is a new feature in the gospel narrative; which, however frequently it may recur hereafter, cannot be traced farther back than the time of the transactions in Jerusalem, John v. 1—16. I argued from this coincidence that the feast there specified was the feast of the Passover, next in order after the same feast, John ii. 13. and before the same, John vi. 4. This Passover, therefore, and the incidents which ensue so soon upon it, discriminate the close of that one and the first year of our Lord's ministry, which might be called the *acceptable year* of the Lord; during which the rulers of the Jews either had not yet made up their minds to reject him, or not begun to conspire against his life; but from which time they did both: and this conclusion we may proceed to confirm a little more fully as follows.

The walking through the corn-fields in question is placed by St. Matthew and by St. Mark simply upon the sabbath; but by St. Luke on a sabbath which he calls the Σάββατον δευτερόπρωτον: a designation which ranks among the ἅπαξ λεγόμενα of the New Testament, and, like another of the same class, τὸν ἐπιούσιον [c][*], has created no small diffi-

---

[*]The meaning of this term, to which an allusion has thus occurred, may be explained as follows.   The

[a] Matt. xii. 1—8. Mark ii. 23—28. Luke vi. 1—5.   [b] Diss. viii. Part i.   [c] Matt. vi. 11. Luke xi. 3.

culty how to explain it. Knowing the great exactness of this Evangelist, I am persuaded it was not without design

The use of ἡ ἐπιοῦσα is just as common as the use of ἡ αὔριον—with the ellipsis in each instance of ἡμέρα—for *to-morrow*, or *the morrow*, in opposition to σήμερον, *to-day*, or *this day*. Vide Acts vii. 26. xvi. 11. xx. 15. xxi. 18. xxiii. 11.

From the former of these, considered as a substantive, the adjective ἐπιούσιος in the kindred signification of *of*, or *belonging to, the morrow*, would be regularly derived. The words of the petition, then, are equivalent to these—τὸν ἄρτον ἡμῶν, τὸν τῆς ἐπιούσης, δὸς ἡμῖν σήμερον, Give us this day our bread of the morrow : and the bread of the morrow is a genuine Hebraism for the bread which is wanted to day. The bread of to-day is in one sense the bread of the morrow ; for it is the bread which must sustain us until the morrow. It is the bread, ὁ εἰς τὴν ἐπιοῦσαν—the bread which is wanted *against* the morrow. The change which St. Luke has made in the terms of St. Matthew, places this relation in a still clearer light : Τὸν ἄρτον ἡμῶν τὸν ἐπιούσιον δίδου ἡμῖν τὸ καθ' ἡμέραν, xi. 3. Give us every day our bread of the morrow ; or, more literally, Give us, for the day, our bread of the morrow.

While I am upon this subject of the ἅπαξ λεγόμενα which occur in the gospels, I will take the liberty of adding one more, peculiar also to St. Luke ; yet not so much from the peculiarity of the word, as from the peculiarity of the sense in which it is used. This is in the use of ἀνάστασιν, ii. 34—the difficulty of understanding which text, so long as this word was considered to possess there its common signification of resurrection, has often been painfully felt by myself, and, probably, by others also. But the word ἀνάστασις possesses another sense, in which it is equivalent to ἀναστάτωσις, *overthrow* or *subversion ;* of which these are specimens from the best Greek classics.

Φράζων ἅλωσιν, 'Ιλίου τ' ἀνάστασιν.

Æsch. Agam. 572.

. . . . Οὐδ' ἐμάνθανον
Τρέφων δι' ἆτα, κἀπαναστάσεις θρόνων.

Soph. Ant. 532.

Μητρακτόνους τ' ἀγῶνας, οὓς οἱ 'μοὶ γάμοι
Θήσουσιν, οἴκων τ' 'Ατρέως ἀνάστασιν.

Eur. Troad. 367.

that he added a specific description to a note of time, which
his predecessors had left indefinite ; and, knowing his great

> . . . . Εἰς δ' ἀνάστασιν
> Δόμων περαίνει πολλάκις τὰ τοιάδε.
>
> Eur. Dictys. Fragm.
>
> . . . . ˙Ἱπ-
> πιοχάρμας τε κλόνους,
> πολέων τ' ἀναστάσεις.
>
> Æschyl. Persæ. 109.

A multitude of others might be produced from Philo, Josephus,
and the contemporary writers. Equally common are ἀναστατήρ,
ἀναστάτης, ἀνάστατος, and ἀναστατόω, in their analogous sense. The
latter occurs thrice in the New Testament itself. Acts xvii. 6.
xxi. 38. Gal. v. 12.

In this sense of overthrow, subversion, or prostration, must
Luke ii. 34. εἰς πτῶσιν καὶ ἀνάστασιν, be understood : I. Because
the whole prophecy is ominous, and melancholy ; predicting evil,
and no good, both to the infant Christ—and to his mother the
Virgin—and to the many in Israel ; to which it would manifestly
be repugnant, were ἀνάστασις to retain its more usual meaning.

II. Because the same many in Israel are described as the subjects of both the πτῶσις and the ἀνάστασις in question ; that is, if
the former means falling, and the latter rising again, the same
many, who are the subjects of the falling, are the subjects also of
the rising again : and these terms being manifestly ἀντίστοιχα, the
one implies the undoing of the effect of the other. Hence, in
whatever sense the many were to fall, in the contrary sense they
would be to rise again. If their falling, then, predicts their unbelief, their rising again must predict their belief ; that is, the
prophecy would imply that the same many in Israel should both
reject and believe in Christ—that Christ should be set to produce
both the belief and the unbelief of the same persons—in which
case, it would both involve a contradiction in terms, and be contrary to the matter of fact. Christ was certainly rejected by the
many in Israel, and so far might be set to occasion their falling ;
but the same many persisted in the rejection, and so far never
rose again from their fall.

III. Because πτῶσις is not absolutely tautologous with ἀνάστασις : the one declares the antecedent—the other the consequent—

precision in the use of terms also, I am persuaded that, peculiar as this denomination may be, if a better, or one more expressive for his purpose in selecting it, could have been found, he would not have employed this.

The word is compounded of two elements, δεύτερος and πρῶτος, each of them alike significant; and, rendered according to the genius of the Greek language in its compound phraseology, it denotes, *first after the second;* and not, *second after the first; primo-secundus,* not, *secundo-primus.* This being the case, its very construction holds out the torch to its meaning, and confirms the conjecture of Scaliger, to whom the merit of the discovery is due: the Σάββατον δευτερόπρωτον, here spoken of, must be some sabbath, considered as first, reckoned after something second, not as second, reckoned after something first.

By the original appointment of the Law[d], the computa-

or the one, the cause—and the other, the effect. Persons must fall, before they can lie prostrate; and πτῶσις is falling—ἀνάστασις is prostration. In like manner, a person must often stumble, even before he can fall; and as Symeon implies here that the many must fall, before they should be prostrate, so does St. Paul, Rom. xi. 11. that they must stumble, before they should fall.

And this leads me to observe, lastly, that the whole prediction is nothing more than a prediction of the rejection of the Jews, because of their rejection of Christ—whom it sets forth as an obstacle, placed in their way, that so they might stumble over it, fall, and be prostrate. It agrees, therefore, with Rom. x. 32. where St. Paul is reasoning on the same dispensation. They, *that is,* the Jews, have stumbled at the stone of stumbling; and both are but the repetition of a more ancient description for the same causes and the same effects; Behold, I do set in Sion a stone of stumbling, and a rock of offence. This stone of stumbling, and rock of offence, was Christ—and the scandal of the cross—concerning which Symeon might consequently well say. Behold this child is set for the falling and subversion of many in Israel. Compare also 1 Pet. ii. 7. 8. which confirms this interpretation.

[d] Lev. xxiii. 10. 11. 15. 16. Deut. xvi. 9.

tion of weeks preliminary to the day of Pentecost, which every one knows to have been seven in number, was required to begin and to proceed from a certain day in the feast of unleavened bread, (which is called the morrow after the sabbath,) as the first of its extremes inclusive; which morrow after the sabbath the Sadducees understood to mean the morrow after the *ordinary* sabbath, and the Pharisees, the morrow after the *extraordinary;* which always fell, by appointment, on the first day of the feast.   The computation of the Sadducees, consequently, began always with the first day of the week; and, therefore, Pentecost, according to them, necessarily fell every year on the first day of the week: the computation of the Pharisees began with the sixteenth of Nisan, which could not be the first day of the week, unless the fifteenth before it had been the seventh. These modes of reckoning would naturally sometimes coincide, and Josephus has specified a case in point when they did so[c]—ἐνέστη ἡ Πεντηκοστὴ ἑορτὴ μετὰ τὸ Σάββατον.* And,

* The particular year, in which this coincidence happened, has been the subject of great controversy, and difference of opinion, among the learned; nor, perhaps, can it ever be exactly determined.   The circumstance, to which Josephus alludes, happened some time in the reign of Antiochus, surnamed Euergetes, and Sidetes; whom Eckel, Doct. Numm. Vett. iii. 235. calls Antiochus the *seventh:* and the most general opinion has been that it happened the year before the assumed year of his death, in battle against the Parthians, B. C. 130. Period. Julian. 4584.   But Eckel has shewn, from his extant coins, that he was alive so late as B. C. 127. Period. Julian. 4587.   On this subject, therefore, historical testimony, and the evidence of coins, are decidedly committed together; unless indeed the authority of the second book of Maccabees, which speaks of the death of a king Antiochus, Ærae Seleucidarum 188. and consequently B. C. 125. or 124. in the temple of Nanea in Persia, (i. 10—16.) be by any admitted, as corroborative of the testimony of the latter.

From the detail of events in the eighth chapter of this thirteenth book of the Antiquities, I should clearly infer that, whe-

* Ant. xiii. viii. 4.

whichever of them might be the right one, it is truly remarkable that, in the year when our Saviour suffered, if the
Friday on which he suffered was the fourteenth of Nisan,

ther right or wrong in itself, Josephus meant to place the time of
this expedition, upon which Hyrcanus accompanied Antiochus,
and in the course of which he halted two days, upon the borders
of the river Lycus, in the year next after his invasion of Judæa,
and siege of Jerusalem. That invasion was made in the *first* year
of Hyrcanus, but early in the spring—and, consequently, B. C.
134 : and the siege of Jerusalem, begun about the time of the
spring rains in that year, continued until the feast of Tabernacles;
soon after which, Antiochus received the submissions of Hyrcanus, and made peace with him. It agrees with this statement
that the invasion of Judæa is placed in the fourth of Antiochus,
dated from the death of Tryphon ; and the death of Tryphon
(Eckel iii. 234.) was A. U. 616. or B. C. 138. The fourth year
from that date might synchronize with B. C. 134.

Now the year after this pacification with Antiochus, B. C. 133.
being understood, as I think the account of Josephus obviously
supposes it to be understood, of the year when Hyrcanus accompanied Antiochus in his Parthian expedition—B. C. 133. Period.
Julian. 4581. is to be understood as the year when the day of Pentecost fell on the first day of the week. It may be proved, by a
reference to Pingré's Tables of Eclipses, that there was a mean
full moon for that year, and the meridian of Jerusalem, on March
28. Hence, if March 28. coincided with Nisan 15. March 29.
coincided with Nisan 16.

Between March 29. B. C. 133. *inclusive*, and the same day,
A. D. 1. *exclusive*, the interval, expressed by tropical days and
nights, is 48,577 such days and nights, with five hours, thirty
minutes, twenty-one seconds, over : or, this fraction of time being
disregarded, 6939 weeks, four days, exactly. A. D. 1. according
to the Tables, March 29. was a Tuesday, or, as I should consider
it, a Thursday ; and March 25. was a Sunday. Now March 29.
B. C. 133. would fall on the same day of the week as March 25.
A. D. 1. If so, March 29. and, therefore, Nisan 16. B. C. 133.
was a Sunday ; or the day of Pentecost, which was always the
same day of the week as the 16th of Nisan, actually fell out after
the sabbath.

the Sunday, on which he rose again from the dead, must have been the sixteenth ; and it was indifferent from what point the calculation of time, until Pentecost, the appointed period of the diffusion of the Holy Ghost, might otherwise have begun.   In that year the fifteenth of Nisan and the seventh day of the week coincided.

That the computation of the Pharisees, however, was either the more correct in itself, or, at least, the computation in vogue throughout the period of the Gospel history, appears from the authorities in the margin[f]; all of which shew that the day of Pentecost was understood to fall on the fiftieth day, inclusive of each extreme, from the day of presenting the wave-sheaf ; and that day to fall on the day after the fifteenth of Nisan, or the first day of the feast of unleavened bread ; and, consequently, always on the sixteenth of Nisan, the second day of that feast.   It is this second day of the ἄζυμα, the day of the consecration of the δραγμὴ, or the first-fruits of the new barley, which, by an apparently felicitous, and an equally reasonable, conjecture, Scaliger concluded to be meant by the first of the elements in the compound denomination, δευτερόπρωτον.   It was necessary to reckon seven weeks, or rather as the original Hebrew expresses it, seven *sabbaths of days*, in succession, from the second day of the Azyma, as their common ἀρχὴ, down to the fiftieth after it inclusive.   What, then, would seem more natural, than that these weeks, or these sabbaths of days, should have been, or might have been, denominated respectively according to their order of succession, as referred to this common beginning? the first seven days, collectively, the first sabbath after the second, (σάββατον δευτερόπρωτον,) the next seven days, the second sabbath after the second, (σάββατον δευτεροδεύτερον,) and so on, to the seventh sabbath after the second, or the σάββατον δευτερέβδομον.

Notwithstanding, however, the great apparent probability of this conjecture, it is liable to an objection which, perhaps,

<hr />

[f] Philo, De Decal. 766. De Sept. et Fest. 1191. 1192.   Jos. Ant. iii. x. 5. 6. Maim. De Sacrif. Jug. vii. 1. &c.

will be considered to possess some weight.   The Jews were commanded to number weeks as such, from the ἀρχὴ in question, not *sabbaths ;* whence, if they made use of any such denominations, to express the order and succession of the parts of the computation, as these, they would be denominations for the order and succession of weeks, not of sabbaths.   But, whatever be the origin or import of the denomination in St. Luke, it is a denomination for a sabbath as such, and not for a week.   It is a denomination also for the ordinary sabbath as such—it cannot be understood even of some day, which, though a sabbath, was merely an extraordinary one.   The parallel places of the other two Evangelists, who specify this sabbath ἁπλῶς, and the allusion to *another* sabbath as such, Luke vi. 6. in opposition to vi. 1. which, at least, must have been the ordinary sabbath, appear to me demonstrative of this.

If so, however, it would seem to follow that, though σάββατον δευτερόπρωτον might express the first sabbath, or week of days, after the sixteenth of Nisan, the σάββατον δευτεροδεύτερον the second, and so on—and though this use of the phrase might actually be proved to have been current among the Jews—yet it would not be strictly a case in point. The σάββατον δευτερόπρωτον of St. Luke is not meant of a week, which was δευτερόπρωτον in any sense of the term, but of a sabbath, or seventh day, in particular which was so. It will follow also, that though the cognate denomination δευτεροδεύτερον might be applied to the second week of days, referred to the same beginning, with just as much reason as that of δευτερόπρωτον to the first, it is not equally obvious whether a similar denomination could have been applied to a sabbath as such; whether, in short, another sabbath could have been called δευτεροδεύτερον, because one had been called δευτερόπρωτον.   There might be special reasons for calling a certain sabbath δευτερόπρωτον, which would not make it necessary to call another δευτεροδεύτερον, δευτερότριτον, or the like.

The literal version of St. Luke's words—Ἐγένετο ἐν σαββάτῳ δευτεροπρώτῳ—would be this: It came to pass on a sabbath which was *second-first* : upon which, as it seems to me, two constructions only can be put.   It was some sabbath, which must be considered as both *second* and *first*, without reference to any thing else ; or it was some sabbath, which must be considered *first* in reference to something *second*.   Now, how a sabbath, of any kind, could be considered ἁπλῶς a second, as well as a first, it would be difficult to say ; but a sabbath as such, which fell upon the seventeenth of Nisan, might be described as first in reference to something second. If it followed the sixteenth of Nisan, it might be called δευτερόπρωτον ; for the sixteenth of Nisan, referred to the feast of Ἄζυμα, was something δεύτερον, and the seventeenth of Nisan, referred to the sixteenth, was πρῶτον.   A sabbath, then, which fell upon the seventeenth of Nisan, referred to the *second* day of the feast of Ἄζυμα, might be said to be δευτερόπρωτον : and, if St. Luke had any special reason for discriminating this sabbath in particular, he might give it such a name accordingly.   Now we may perhaps conceive some such reason in the nature of the material action, supposed to have been performed on this day ; which was the eating of the corn by the disciples as they went along.   Had it not been some day after the sixteenth of Nisan in general, the disciples would not have been eating corn at all ; had it not been a sabbath-day which fell after the sixteenth of Nisan, they would not have been eating corn on the sabbath-day in particular.

It is a singular confirmation of this conclusion, that A. U. 781. A. D. 28. the ordinary sabbath-day actually fell on the seventeenth of Nisan.   The Passover was celebrated that year on March 29. and March 29. was Wednesday. If so, the seventeenth of Nisan coincided with April 1. and April 1. was Saturday.   This, then, appears to me the true import of the phrase in question.   It was meant to denote one particular day—a sabbath which fell on the seventeenth of Nisan as such ; and, therefore, on the day immediately after the sixteenth.   And it was meant to denote that day on account of the incident which transpired on that day. Had not our Saviour's disciples been eating corn on the sabbath, the Pharisees could not have taken exceptions at their conduct ; had not that sabbath fallen *after* the sixteenth of Nisan in general, they could not have been eating corn upon it at all : that it fell on the day after that sixteenth in particular might be due to the circumstances of the case. But if this was the case, and it was necessary to describe the relation of the day to the sixteenth in particular, this circumstance of its falling might give rise to the denomination in question.

Nor would it be any objection that the miracle, related John v. 1—16. which I have supposed to have been performed at this Passover, was yet performed on the sabbath. That miracle might have been performed on the fifteenth of Nisan, and even on the twenty-first, and yet would have been performed on the sabbath. It is my opinion, however, that it was performed on the *tenth :* which, when Nisan 14. coincided with March 29. must have coincided with March 25. And when March 29. was Wednesday, March 25. was Saturday.

Those who are curious to see the explanations of the same term, proposed by the ancient commentators, may consult Epiphanius, or Chrysostom[g]. Suidas also has preserved one of the number, which approaches so near to the interpretation of Scaliger, that it might almost have suggested it[h]. Σάββατον δὲ δευτερόπρωτον, ἐπειδὴ δεύτερον μὲν ἦν τοῦ Πάσχα· πρῶτον δὲ τῶν Ἀζύμων. However much these opinions may differ from each other, yet they all concur in placing the time of this sabbath about a Passover. The material fact itself proves thus much, if no more : the disciples could not have plucked ripe corn, if ripe corn had not been to be found ; but ripe corn could not have been found except at barley-harvest, or at wheat-harvest ; that is, at the Passover, or at Pentecost. Respecting the ripeness of the corn, that is, barley, at the first of these periods, Josephus furnishes a case in point[i]. Nor would any one,

---

[g] Epiph. Oper. i. 158. 159. Chrys. Oper. ii. 262.   [h] Σάββατον.
[i] Ant. Jud. xiv. ii. 2. B. iv. vii. 2.

at either of them, have presumed to eat of this corn, unless it had been previously consecrated to their use by the usual offering of the first-fruits[k]; for, says Josephus, καὶ τότε λοιπὸν δημοσίᾳ ἔξεστι πᾶσι καὶ ἰδίᾳ θερίζειν[l], but not before. The feast of Pentecost I consider to be quite out of the question: it must, therefore, have been the Passover.

Nor is it any objection that ripe corn is mentioned here, and yet we have endeavoured to prove elsewhere[m] that this time would be the middle of a year of rest. The corn in question was such as, even in a year of this kind, might have been produced of itself; for something invariably sprang up from the relics of the last year's harvest; which was eminently, too, the right of the public, or of any one but the owners of the soil in particular[n]. And this would be the best reason (if any reason, beyond the general permission applicable to such cases, already conceded by the Law[o], is considered to be necessary) which could be assigned for the disciples of our Lord eating freely of it, as they went along.

Moreover, by what is called, in the Rabbinical writers[p], the seventh of the constitutions of Joshua, or, in other words, by what had been from time immemorial the custom of the land, it will appear that, except during a Sabbatic year as such, when every field necessarily lay fallow, travelling through corn fields for convenience sake never would have been allowed, until after reaping-time, and up to seed-time; much less through standing corn, or fields as yet uncut. Maimonides observes[q], Non constituebatur annus intercalaris anno Sabbatico; cum enim illæ, quæ e terris incultis sponte sua nascerentur, fruges publici juris essent, si annus augeretur solido mense, non liceret reperire unde Deo libaretur ille qui præscribitur a lege manipulus, atque panes illi duo: which, if correct, proves all we have been contending for, both that there were spontaneous produc-

[k] Lev. xxiii. 14. Josh. v. 11.　　[l] Ant. Jud. iii. x. 5.　　[m] Vol. ii. Diss. vii. Appendix.　　[n] Exod. xxiii. 10. 11. Lev. xxv. 5. 6.　　[o] Deut. xxiii. 24. 25. Jos. Ant. Jud. iv. viii. 21.　　[p] Maim. De Primitiis Animantium. iii. 6. Annott. Rel. Pal. i. 261.　　[q] De rat. Interc. iv. 15.

tions of the soil, even in a Sabbatic year—that these were the public property—that these, whether of barley or of wheat, required still to be consecrated, in such a year, as well as in any other, before they could be touched.

If, then, our Saviour was now at Jerusalem, attending on the Paschal feast, and not yet preparing to return into Galilee—and if he was merely walking a sabbath-day's journey during the Paschal week—still by the next sabbath-day he might be again in Galilee.   The Paschal feast would expire on the twenty-first of Nisan, which, if the seventeenth coincided with Saturday, would fall on the Wednesday : nor would it be impossible that in two days' time afterwards Jesus might be returned to Galilee. The next event[r], therefore, which also happened on a sabbath, might have happened on the following sabbath, and certainly on the next but one ; and this conjecture is further confirmed by the consideration of the place where it happened.   For Mark iii. 1. compared with i. 21. and the use of the article, in the mention of this synagogue ἀπλῶς, by all the Evangelists, (which use shews it to be the synagogue most commonly frequented by our Lord of any, or the single synagogue of some place which had no other synagogue but that,) and especially the reference to the lake, so directly after[s], to which he is supposed to have retired from wheresoever he was, prove, almost to a demonstration, that this place could have been only Capernaum, and the synagogue of Capernaum.   At the time of the miracle now performed, he must, consequently, have been got back to Capernaum ; though he might only just have been so.   I shall pause, therefore, here, to make a few observations.

In the account of the miracle which ensued, the supplementary character of the two last Evangelists, in relation to the first, is strikingly illustrated.   St. Mark supplies matter not to be found in St. Matthew, and St. Luke not only does the same, but, if I am not much mistaken, something else : which may be thus explained.

---

[r] Matt. xii. 9—14. Mark iii. 1—6. Luke vi. 6—11.   [s] Mark iii. 7.

It appears from St. Matthew that the observers of our Lord, whom St. Luke shews to have been some of the Scribes and Pharisees, suspecting his intention of healing the man, anticipated him by a question—Is it lawful to heal on the sabbath-day? to which, however, he made no answer at the time, except by ordering the man to stand forth. When the man had so done, then, according to St. Luke, he addressed them in the following words—I will ask you a certain thing—in which, and in those which follow, there is a reference, first, to the question which they had just put to him—and, secondly, to the *animus* with which they had put it: and their purpose, as implied by this *animus* in respect of himself, is made the ground of the vindication of his own, with respect to the man—both being understood in reference to the sabbath-day. He himself was designing to do good, they to do evil—he to preserve a life, they to destroy one—both, upon the sabbath-day. The passage, then, ought to be rendered in conformity to a well known ellipsis in Greek construction, of which numerous examples may be produced from these Evangelists themselves[t]: I will ask you a certain thing. Is it more lawful to do good on the sabbath-day, or to do evil? Is it more lawful to save a life, or to destroy one?

The answer to this question was the answer to their own; and this question is addressed to the consciences of the parties. They made him no reply: there ensued, consequently, a pause—during which he might look round upon them in anger, mixed with concern for the obduracy of their hearts, according to St. Mark ; and then subjoin the words, which close the account in St. Matthew, and have nothing to answer to them in St. Mark or in St. Luke ; or he might do the reverse : for either arrangement may hold good. Yet in this answer, according to St. Matthew, there is a critical coincidence with the preceding account by St. Mark or by St. Luke, which justifies our position of it. The question of his adversaries had been, Is it lawful to heal

[t] Luke xv. 7. xviii. 14. Matt. xviii. 8. 9. Mark ix. 43. 45. 47.

U 4

(θεραπεύειν) on the sabbath-day? our Lord's reply is, It is lawful to do well (καλῶς ποιεῖν) on the sabbath-day. Whence this change in terms? because his own expressions, ἀγαθο-ποιῆσαι, and κακοποιῆσαι, which are tantamount to καλῶς ποι-εῖν, and κακῶς ποιεῖν, had been only just pronounced, and were still uppermost in his memory. To return, then, from this digression.

The effect of the miracle, as we have had occasion to observe elsewhere [u], was a specific design of the Pharisees, in which the Herodians also joined, against our Saviour's life. The mention of this party, if they were, as their name implies, either the followers, or the partizans, of Herod the Tetrarch, seems to intimate that he was now in the dominions of Herod, and, consequently, it was necessary, or politic, that the Pharisees, in order to give effect to their own designs, should interest in their behalf a sect who were peculiarly his creatures. For the opinions, however, of the ancients concerning this sect, we may refer to the authorities in the margin [v].

In consequence of this conspiracy, which, notwithstanding its secresy, was known, by his preternatural discernment of the thoughts, to our Saviour, St. Matthew, exemplifying the fulfilment of prophecy [w] in the meek and inoffensive demeanour of the Christ, relates that he withdrew from thence, followed by the multitudes, and healing them all: St. Mark is more explicit, and shews that he retired in the direction of the lake, and that the place of his abode, during his absence, was the vicinity of the lake [x].

To this absence, then, I think we may assign the duration of a partial circuit, now begun, but confined to the neighbourhood of the lake, which yet might occupy the time until the arrival of the next feast of Pentecost, May 19. a period, at the utmost, of only five weeks, or a month. For, first, the cause of his departure from Capernaum was such as to warrant the expectation that he would be some time away; and St. Matthew's application of the prophecy

[u] Diss. viii. Part i. Comm. in Marc. 204.   [v] Epiph. Oper. i. 45. Cbrys. ii. 442. Theophyl. [w] Isaiah xlii. 1—4.   [x] iii. 7—12.

in question to it implies the same thing : secondly, the multitudes by which he was attended, and at the close of the circuit, as they are represented by St. Mark, consisting of such numbers, and from such distant regions, could not have been assembled about him, all at once : thirdly, the injunction that a small vessel (πλοιάριον) should constantly be in waiting upon him, προσκαρτερῇ αὐτῷ, specified by the same Evangelist also, appears a decisive intimation that he was all the while in the vicinity of the lake of Galilee. The vessel itself was one of that description, which Josephus shews to have been abundantly numerous on the lake of Tiberias, so much so that, on one occasion, he himself speedily collected together as many as two hundred and thirty [y]—each of which required at least four persons to man it, and was capable of carrying sixteen, or more, with ease—so that our Saviour, and his usual train, when that became his Twelve Apostles, might be about their ordinary complement. The purpose for which this vessel was retained proves that it was not wanted at all times, but only occasionally ; that is, when the importunity of the people, bringing their sick friends, or infirm persons of any kind, to press upon him became too great—or when he might be desirous, as we find him at other times desirous, to address them from the sea, and not from the land.

This circuit, then, would extend along the land of Genesaret [z], described above, towards the southern extremity of the lake. The lake itself, Josephus has described as follows [a].

The lake is called Gennesar after the neighbouring region; and though it is forty stades in breadth, and one hundred and forty in length, still it is both sweet, and very fit for drinking. . . . . It is clear also, terminating on every side upon a sandy beach . . . and there are species of fish in it, which both in taste and in appearance excel such as are to be found elsewhere. The Jordan divides it in sunder .... Beginning its course .... this river passes through

---

[y] B. ii. xxi. 8. Vide also Mark iv. 36. John vi. 23.   [z] Mark vi. 53.
[a] B. iii. x. 7.

the marshes and quagmires of the lake Semechonitis; after which, having travelled through another hundred and twenty stades, it cuts the lake of Gennesar right through, just after passing by the city Julias; and then, traversing a considerable tract of country which is desert, it discharges itself into the lake Asphaltites.

Ergo ubi prima convallium fuit occasio, in lacum se funditur, (Jordanes,) quem plures Genesaram vocant, xvi. mille passuum longitudinis, vi. mille latitudinis [b]. The lake Asphaltites was three hundred stades distant from Jerusalem, or from the frontiers of Judæa [c]; and the Aulon, which is the name of the desert region, through which the Jordan flowed, between this lake and the lake of Tiberias, was two hundred and thirty stades in length.

In the course of the circuit, Magdala, which certainly lay on the western, or on the south-western, side of the lake, might be visited; and, among those, out of whom demons are said to have been cast, Mary of Magdala, mentioned for the first time not long after [d], might be one. There is no proof, however, nor any reason to suppose, it ever crossed the lake, or passed, as yet, either into Decapolis, or into Persea.

The last event which took place upon it, just before our Lord returned to Capernaum, and, probably, when the feast of Pentecost was at hand, was the ordination of the Twelve Apostles [e], where St. Luke rejoins St. Mark, though St. Matthew for reasons assigned elsewhere [f], omits this fact altogether. The circumstances of the ordination, the sermon which followed upon it [g], its distinctness from the former in St. Matthew [h], will be considered by themselves hereafter. The προσευχὴ τοῦ Θεοῦ, alluded to [i], may be understood either of earnest and fervent prayer, or of some place of prayer, or Proseucha, itself. Josephus calls the Proseucha of Tiberias μέγιστον οἴκημα [k], and Epiphanius de-

---

[b] Plin. H. N. v. 15.   [c] Ant. Jud. ix. i. 2. xv. vi. 2.   [d] Luke viii. 1. 2.
[e] Mark iii. 13—19. αὐτόν. Luke vi. 12—16.   [f] Vol. i. Diss. iii.   [g] Luke
vii. 17. to the end.   [h] v. i.—viii. i.   [i] Luke vi. 12.   [k] Vit. 54.

scribes one, in his own time, near Sychar, as follows[1]. There is also at Sicima in what is now called Neapolis, about two miles distant, without the city in the plain ground, a house of prayer, or an oratory; in shape resembling a theatre—so much in the open air and in a free space does it stand—built by the Samaritans, in their imitation of all the customs of the Jews.

The ordination took place as soon as it was day; the sermon, consecutively delivered, must have been over soon after; and then Jesus returned to Capernaum[m]; where, either when he was still on the way to his usual place of abode in that city, or soon after his arrival there, and, certainly, in the course of the same day, he was met by the petition of the centurion[n]. On the following day, probably early in the morning, he set out to Nain; concerning which place Jerome observes[o], Naim . . . usque hodie in secundo milliario Thabor montis ostenditur, contra meridiem, juxta Ændor.

The time of the year when Jesus set out on this journey was about the period of the feast of Pentecost, May 19. The distance of Nain from Capernaum was not more, at the utmost, than might be accomplished in an ordinary day's journey, of twenty-five or twenty-six Roman miles[p]; and, as he is said to have gone thither expressly, it is most probable he went thither in one day. On this principle he would arrive in the evening—and the evening being the usual time of burial among the Jews, it would be the less surprizing that, as he approached to the gates of the city, he should have fallen in with the funeral procession of the widow's son[q]. In towns surrounded by walls, observes Maimonides[r], Nullus humatur homo mortuus, nisi septem optimates jubeant, vel civitas omnis. Now, according to Josephus[s], the following was one of the humane laws of Moses: Πᾶσι τοῖς παριοῦσι, θαπτομένου τινὸς, καὶ συνελθεῖν καὶ

---

[1] Oper. i. 1068.　[m] Luke vii. 1.　[n] Luke vii. 2—10. Matt. viii. 5—13.　[o] Oper. ii. 470. De Situ et Nominibus.　[p] Rel. Palæst. ii. 497. iii. 904.　[q] Luke vii. 11—17.　[r] De Ædificio Templi. vii. 13.　[s] Contra Apion. ii. 26.

συναποδύρασθαι ἐποίησε νόμιμον. Independent, then, of the natural impulse of pity, which is so beautifully and so movingly illustrated by our Lord's conduct on this occasion, we should need no other explanation of it than the existence of such an acknowledged rule ; nor could we assign a better reason for the performance of the miracle which ensued. To restore the only child of this distressed and widowed mother to life was the fittest consolation, which such an one as our Lord could bestow upon her.

The rumour of the miracle, which was obviously the first of its kind, being disseminated through the surrounding regions, produced, among its other effects, the celebrated message of John[t]. Concerning the place where this message would be received by our Saviour, there seems to be little doubt it would still be Nain ; but, with regard to the quarter, whence John might have sent it, there can never be the same presumptive certainty. It was sent by him, it is true, from prison ; and Josephus, as we have seen elsewhere[u], makes him to have been both originally imprisoned, and ultimately put to death, in Herod's castle of Machærus ; the distance of which from Nain was, probably, a three days' journey. The news of the miracle, however, was carried to John by some of his own disciples, who, being, as we may conjecture, Galileans, and having access to him in prison, might make him acquainted with it, even at that distance, in a few days after its performance. Nor if the report of the miracle could be diffused throughout all Judæa[v], could it fail to pass into Peræa also. We have only to suppose that Jesus remained long enough in Nain, even after the miracle, both for the news of that event to have reached John, and for the arrival of his own message in consequence of it. But this, it is obvious, might not have been more than a week.

The answer of our Lord to the messengers of the Baptist was returned on the same day when they arrived ; and either directly after it, or the next day, he was invited by

[t] Luke vii. 18—35.   Matt. xi. 2—30.   [u] Vol. i. Diss. viii. Appendix.
[v] Luke vii. 17.

a certain Pharisee, named Simon, to eat bread in his house[w]. The nature of this meal is not specified; but, if it was the noonday's, and the day itself not a sabbath, its time would be about the fifth hour of the day. During the entertainment, a woman in *the city*[x], (so she is described,) who had been, and—in allusion to her former mode of life—who was still, a sinner, came and anointed the feet of Jesus as he lay at meat. This allusion to the city, of which, it is implied, she was either a native, or an inhabitant, can be understood of no city but that which had been twice mentioned before, viz. Nain[y]. It proves, consequently, that our Lord was still in Nain; it proves, also, that this penitent sinner could not have been Mary Magdalene, who was either a native, or an inhabitant, of a very different place, Magdala. Nor can the reference, which follows next, ἐν τῷ καθεξῆς[z], with the ellipsis of χρόνῳ, be understood of any thing but the whole course of proceedings since the first day of the arrival at Nain[a]; not merely since the day of this one among the subsequent incidents, the unction in the house of the Pharisee.

It seems to be implied, therefore, that our Lord made some stay at Nain; and, to judge from the sequel, his object in going thither was to commence a circuit of Galilee; for which purpose, it was conveniently situated—lying almost in the centre of the country. That such a circuit is represented as beginning from the city, where the last event had taken place, and as continued thenceforward by travelling up and down—such is the meaning of the term διώδευε —through cities and towns in order, accompanied by the Twelve, and by certain women, whose names are mentioned, not only because they attended our Lord, but also because they ministered, of their substance, to his wants; and that the business of this circuit was the same as before, to preach, or publish, the tidings of the kingdom, is placed beyond a question by Luke viii. 1—3. It is clear, also, that it did not cease until it was terminated at Capernaum; for the

[w] Luke vii. 36. to the end.   [x] Ib. 37.   [y] Ib. 11. 12.   [z] viii. 1.
[a] vii. 11.

next event[b], the delivery of the parable of the sower, was certainly posterior to the return to Capernaum, and yet produced, according to the same testimony, in part by the resort of the multitude from every city ; such as might have been the effect of the circuit itself.

The fact of this circuit, it is true, rests upon the single authority of St. Luke. St. Mark, after the ordination of the Twelve, which certainly took place *out* of Capernaum, adds, καὶ ἔρχονται εἰς οἶκον[c]—which would still be true, though, since the ordination, Jesus and the Twelve had both visited, and left, Capernaum, and been any where else ; provided that they had returned thither again, before what begins to be next related.   There would be, on this principle, an interruption in the continuity, but no impeachment of the entire truth and correctness, of St. Mark's narrative.   Indeed, the very particular which it mentions next —καὶ συνέρχεται πάλιν ὄχλος—contains an intimation that, since iii. 7—12. (when our Lord was described as surrounded by immense multitudes, and from every part, as it was) he must have been somewhere else ; during which interval he had ceased to be attended by those multitudes, and, being now come back to Capernaum, was beginning to be surrounded by new.

The omission, by St. Mark, of the intermediate circuit, is, in reality, (as we have observed elsewhere[d],) the natural consequence of its omission by St. Matthew also ; for which omission likewise some reasons were there alleged : while its omission by both might be the very motive to produce its express mention by St. Luke.   A similar omission, as we shall see hereafter, produces a similar supplement on another occasion, of even greater extent than this.   Nor will any one pretend to deny that, if the course of events from Mark ii. 23. to iii. 19. be carefully compared with the similar course of events from Mark iii. 19. to vi. 56. which brings the account to the close of our Saviour's second year, there must have been an hiatus of at least four months in duration ; which hiatus could not have come any where be-

[b] Luke viii. 4—8.   [c] iii. 19.   [d] Vol. i. Diss. i. and iii.

fore or after Mark iii. 19. but might have critically fallen out there—if we suppose the intermediate circuit in question—between ὃς καὶ παρέδωκεν αὐτὸν, and καὶ ἔρχονται εἰς οἶκον.

I assume, then, that the close of this circuit is indicated here, by the return of our Lord, with his disciples, to Capernaum there alluded to: and from this point of time, as the sequel demonstrates, must be dated also the course of proceedings at Matt. xii. 22. The reference, however, in the τότε, at the beginning of this verse, cannot be understood of what went before; it must be understood solely of what comes after; for he shewed, xii. 15. that our Lord had left Capernaum—and he shews, xii. 46. that he was there again—and, yet, no mention of his return is interposed. The notice of time, then, in question, is to be construed according to the idiom of this Evangelist in other like instances; as an admonition to the reader, to attend to what is about to be related—and to the course of events thenceforward—but nothing more.

We possess, therefore, at Luke viii. 1—3. an evident proof of another circuit of Galilee; which set out from Capernaum, before it began at Nain; and, after visiting city and village in order, terminated again at Capernaum: on all which accounts it must be pronounced a general circuit, and, as only one other such has yet been ascertained before it, a *general* circuit the second of its kind. The time taken up by it, on the same principle as before, would be three or four months at least; and if it began about the feast of Pentecost in our Lord's second year, (which was May 19.) it would be over about the feast of Tabernacles, (which began September 23.): and this conclusion may be further confirmed as follows.

I. The parable of the sower, delivered soon after—though probably not before the close of the feast, and, consequently, the first week in our October, at the earliest—may well be supposed to contain a reference to the labours of the field at the time; not only because the season, if it was what we describe it, would obviously permit this, but especially, be-

cause the past year, dated from seed-time to seed-time, had
actually been a Sabbatic year. When this was over, the
labours of agriculture would be renewed, at their accustomed
period, even with more activity than ever. If so, it is a
natural presumption that the parable was delivered at seed-
time, and, therefore, after (but probably not long after) the
feast of Tabernacles at least.

II. The storm on the lake of Galilee, which happened
in the evening of the same day, has been conjectured to intimate that the autumnal equinox was either arrived or past;
both which would be the case after the expiration of the
feast of Tabernacles, October 1. A similar phenomenon
occurs at the time of the ensuing Passover, and, consequently, about as much later than the vernal; and these
two instances are sufficient to prove that the weather, on
the sea of Tiberias, at other times so settled and regular,
could have become disturbed or tempestuous only at the
cardinal points of the year.

III. The most decisive argument in proof of this fact
appears to me to be supplied by Mark iii. 22. in the mention of the Scribes, who are said to have come down from
Jerusalem. Theophylact observes[e], Εἰ δὲ πᾶσαι αἱ χῶραι
εἶχον Γραμματεῖς καὶ Φαρισαίους, ἀλλὰ οἱ ἐντιμιώτεροι ἐν Ἱερου-
σαλὴμ ἦσαν· διὸ καὶ οὗτοι ἐφθόνουν μάλιστα. It is very true, as
St. Luke proves[f], that Scribes, and probably Pharisees,
were to be found in every part of the country, as well as
in Jerusalem; but the presence of Scribes from Jerusalem,
who had come down on purpose upon this occasion, is intended of something more than usual. After a certain time,
which I believe was John v. 1. the time of the second Passover, whenever this circumstance is expressly mentioned,
there is reason to conclude that it implies a feast to have
recently transpired, and a feast which had passed without
being attended by our Saviour. After such times, therefore, more especially, these men appear to have been sent
down from Jerusalem expressly, to inquire after Jesus—to

[e] Comm. in Matt. 85.   [f] v. 17.

discover where he was—and to watch and report upon his conduct. The second feast of Tabernacles was one of the solemnities which, as it has been shewn already, he could not personally have attended; accordingly, Scribes and Pharisees from Jerusalem are perceived, immediately afterwards, to be in his company. The third Passover is another feast, of which it is still more certain that he did not keep it in person; and, directly after that also, the presence of the same description of persons, and from the same quarter, tempting him with insidious questions, is found to be specified. It strengthens the argument, that they are seen, in each instance, to be attending upon him in Capernaum, our Lord's stated place of residence in general—and, as it would seem, during the intervals of the feasts, which he had not gone up to in person, more particularly. If the same intimations do not recur, at any such periods, *after* the third Passover, it is because our Lord either attended the feasts himself, or was travelling before and after them, or purposely kept aloof from Capernaum.

With the return to Capernaum on this occasion, the three Evangelical accounts coincide, and for a time go on, together. Yet the length of the stay there, as far as it is related in detail, I think it is possible to demonstrate, could not have exceeded two full days; the cause of so short a residence having been, in all probability, the first instance of the blasphemy against the Spirit, on one of those days, and its repetition, or something very like its repetition, by the same persons (those, in each instance, who had previously come down to watch our Lord) on the next. With a view to this demonstration, it will be necessary to harmonize briefly the several accounts in somewhat of a particular detail; by doing which, I shall shew that Jesus visited Gadara, for the first time in the course of his ministry, on the first of these days, but did not return to Capernaum until the next.

I. The second general circuit of Galilee being concluded, our Saviour and his disciples return to Capernaum, and there ἔρχονται εἰς οἶκον.

r Mark iii. 19.

II. Besides the multitudes who would naturally accompany him wheresoever he went, this return to Capernaum, and the news of his being resident there, might collect more. But, between the return and the resort of the multitude (συνέρχεται πάλιν ὄχλος[h]) we have supposed that the feast of Tabernacles possibly intervened. The people who had hitherto attended on our Saviour, and, perhaps, his disciples themselves, (though that is by no means certain,) all, in .short, but himself, it may be presumed, would go up to this feast ; and the resort next specified would be strictly a *new* resort. To all these the ministerial attentions of our Lord were indefatigable—so much so, that neither he, nor his disciples, had time even to eat.

III. His relations, therefore, who[i] also were living in Capernaum, consisting of his mother, and his brethren—Joseph, in all probability, having been long since dead—apprised of these circumstances, and afraid, as we may suppose, for his health, go forth for the purpose mentioned Mark iii. 21. and at a time, which the preceding verse may very well imply was the time of some repast, probably the morning's.

IV. Before their arrival, the demoniac, blind and dumb, is brought to our Lord, and healed[k] ; after which the blasphemy, on the part of the Pharisees—the discourse in answer to it—the demand of a sign from heaven—the refusal of that demand—the sequel of the refutation of the blasphemy—as recorded by St. Matthew and St. Mark, either wholly, or in part, are all consecutively delivered[l].

V. At the end of the whole, our Lord's relations now arrived ; and, finding the entrance of the house beset, sent a message to him within[m]. By refusing to attend to that message, the object of which was to interrupt the functions of his ministry, our Lord not only reproved his relations for their improper, though, perhaps, well-meant, interference with his duties, but, also, by the pointed contrast between his disciples and them, intimated to the multitude that, in

[h] Mark iii. 20.   [i] John ii. 12. vii. 3.   [k] Matt. xii. 22. 23.
[l] xii. 24—45. iii. 22—30.   [m] Matt. xii. 46—50. Mark iii. 31—35.

disregarding the claims of private duty, he was obeying the claims of public; he was only sacrificing an inferior to a superior obligation.

VI. After this, and, probably, not much later than the third hour of the day, the time which is known, in classical writers, by the ἀγορᾶς πληθώρα, he leaves the house where he was, and repairs to the lake[n]; where he delivers a series of parables, for the first time in the course of his ministry, himself, with his disciples, on shipboard, and the people standing on the land[o].

VII. Having made an end of these parables, but probably explained none of them as yet, not even to his own disciples, (concerning which more will be said, in its proper place, hereafter,) he returns to the house which he had lately quitted, and secludes himself there, with his disciples, for the rest of that day[p]. The multitude, however, still continued without, in the same numbers as before. The time of the return was probably the time of the usual noonday's meal, or not much after it; and while our Lord and his disciples were still alone within, he explains, at their request, all or most of the preceding parables, and adds a few more in private.

VIII. During this explanation, perhaps when that of the sower was just completed, his relations make a second attempt to see him, the effect of their former failure; and, being again disappointed of admission, they transmit a second message to him, like the former; which is answered substantially, but not verbally, as before[q].

IX. After sunset[r], in the evening of the same day, he leaves the house (where he must, consequently, have remained secluded ever since his return from the lake) a second time; and, finding the multitudes still numerous about it, as the best expedient for dismissing them, he gives commandment to cross the lake[s].

X. On the way to the lake accordingly, the incidents re-

[n] Matt. xiii. 1. [o] xiii. 2—35. Mark iv. 1—34. Luke viii. 4—18.
[p] Matt. xiii. 36—52. Mark iv. 34. [q] Luke viii. 19—21. [r] Mark iv. 35. [s] Matt viii. 18. 23. Mark iv. 35. 36. Luke viii. 22.

corded Matt. viii. 19—22. must be supposed to have happened. Arrived at the lake he embarks, and sets sail; and,
by the help of what follows, it may be shewn that he neither returned the same night to Capernaum, nor landed at
Gergesa until the morning; and, consequently, that he
must have spent the night on the lake.

I. His motive, in going to the other side at all, was to
oblige the multitude to disperse, or, at least, to relieve himself from their importunity: and this effect was more likely
to ensue if they thought he was gone away for the night,
than if they expected to see him shortly come back.

II. The breadth of the lake, according to Josephus, was
forty stades; and, according to Pliny, six Roman miles.
It was after sunset, or in the evening, when they set out;
and a storm was encountered by the way. If they were
going in the direction of Gadara, that was not over against
Capernaum, but considerably lower down to the south-
east [t]: and, even if they were proceeding to Gergesa, still
the passage could not take up less than an hour, and the
storm, which intervened, would doubtless add to its
length.

III. After the autumnal equinox, it would be dark
within an hour from sunset, and much more within two or
three.

IV. When Jesus returned to Capernaum, the multitude
were found collected on the shore of the lake, and anxiously
waiting to receive him [u]. This might naturally have been
the case on the following morning; but it could scarcely
have happened the same night. Their anxiety, too, for the
return of our Lord might be produced by the fact of the
storm the preceding evening—they could not as yet know
whether Jesus and his disciples had survived that storm,
and they would be impatient to see them again on that
account.

V. Before, and during, the storm, all the Evangelists
agree, our Lord was asleep. No solution of this fact is so

[t] Jos. Vit. 9. 10. 65. p. 97.   [u] Mark v. 21. Luke viii. 40.

probable as that he was composed to rest for the night. The reluctance of the disciples to awaken him, until the danger was become imminent and pressing—the answer returned just before to the scribe [v], beautiful and pathetic as it is—are pertinent, also, and significant, if Jesus was gone to sleep for the night—or was preparing to pass the night, in the open air, upon the sea.

VI. When he landed at the opposite side, the demoniac is said to have seen him a *great way* off [w]. If so, it must have been broad daylight at the time; or the landing could not have taken place until the following morning.

VII. This demoniac, it is also said, was by *night* and by *day* [x] among the tombs. If he met our Lord in the morning, just as he was landing from the ship, this circumstance would both explain the reason, and confirm the truth, of the assertion.

VIII. There was, near the place, a large herd of swine, feeding in their usual pasture, at the time; which herd, it is much more probable, had been brought there that morning, than kept out there all night, or not yet driven home. If it was not customary to keep them out all night, they would be driven home by sunset at almost any period of the year; and, after the feast of Tabernacles, whatever might be usual at other times, no description of cattle, and much less swine, would have been found in the fields all night.

IX. The people of the city, as well as of the neighbouring country, were all up, and stirring, at the time; or they could not have been so instantly alarmed by the report of the keepers of the swine, and so instantly brought out in a body, to see what had happened, and to request our Lord to depart from their coasts.

X. If he returned (as after this request he is said to have returned) immediately [y], and yet that same night, then he must have been entertained, at a most unusual hour for a supper, that same night—he must have been

[v] Matt. viii. 20.   [w] Mark v. 6.   [x] v. 5.   [y] Matt. ix. 1. 10.

applied to by Jairus[z], and have raised his daughter, at a still later hour, that same night—he must, consequently, have set out to his house either in the dark, or by torchlight—the miracle of the issue of blood, performed by the way[a], must have been performed under corresponding circumstances—and yet nothing can be clearer than that every thing relating to it must have been transacted in the open day[b].

We may consider it, therefore, almost demonstratively certain, that Jesus neither came back from Gadara the same evening, nor, in all probability, landed there until the next morning. Whatever occurred on the other side occurred, consequently, in the morning; and, perhaps, so early in the morning, as to allow of his returning to Capernaum in time for the usual morning's repast; or not much later than it[c]. His finding the people, on the shore, ready prepared for his reception, and his being at meat in the house of some disciple, when the application of Jairus was made to him, would both, on this supposition, be naturally accounted for. The command too, to give the daughter of Jairus, as soon as she had been restored to life, something to eat[d], might be intended as much to denote what was usual, and in course, at the time, and, therefore, to attest the completeness of the effect in the recovery of health or strength, as for physical reasons of any kind, known to our Saviour, though concealed from us.

The next events to this, the cure of the two blind men, and the dispossession of the dumb demoniac[e], and the repetition of the blasphemy, committed the day before, by some of the same persons in general, who had committed it then, were consecutive upon the last miracle, and, like every thing else since the return from Gadara, were included in the compass of one and the same morning—which is the second morning since the point of time indicated at Mark iii. 19. or Matt. xii. 22. In consequence of the last event,

---

[z] Matt. ix. 18.   [a] Ib. 20—22.   [b] Mark v. 30—33.   [c] Matt. ix. 1. Mark v. 21. Luke viii. 40.   [d] Mark v. 43. Luke viii. 55.   [e] Matt. ix. 27—31. Ib. 32—34.

in particular, it would seem that Jesus determined again to leave Capernaum, and the vicinity of the Pharisees; which he does, first of all, by a visit to Nazareth [f]; intending, as we may collect from the sequel, to commence, in the next place, another general circuit from thence, as he had lately commenced one from Nain.

This visit, the second instance of its kind, is placed by St. Mark after the raising of Jairus' daughter; and by St. Matthew after the dispossession which followed on the same day. By both, consequently, it is placed in a similar order, and at the same point of time, or nearly so. Nazareth, like Nain, was not more than a day's journey distant from Capernaum; so that, had the preceding events happened all in the morning, it might have been possible to arrive there in the course of the same day; and, certainly, sometime in the next. How long this was before the sabbath on which Jesus entered into the synagogue, and taught, we cannot exactly determine. As, however, he would neither set out to Gadara, nor return from it, on a sabbath, the visit to Nazareth, the day after he returned to Capernaum, or the third day since he had gone to Gadara, could not have been more than half a week, and probably was less than that, before the recurrence of a sabbath. The mention of this visit is omitted by St. Luke, because he had already particularized the former.

That it was the prelude to a circuit, undertaken immediately after it, appears, first, from Mark vi. 6; which affirms that Jesus began to go about the villages around, teaching: and, secondly, still more clearly from Matt. ix. 85; which shews that he began to go round all the cities and all the villages, teaching, and preaching, and performing miracles, as on every similar occasion before: a description, applicable to nothing but the fact of a general circuit, and that also the *third* of its kind since the commencement of our Lord's public ministry, and the second which had transpired in the course of the present year. Its relative posi-

[f] Matt. xiii. 53—58.   Mark vi. 1—6.

tion in the narrative of St. Matthew is clearly equivalent to the place which it similarly occupies in St. Mark; and on this point there can be no difficulty. St. Luke may have omitted it, partly because he had specified another, so recently, before it; partly because St. Matthew and St. Mark had both recorded this, as they had both passed over that. Yet he also, as well as they, relates the fact of the mission of the Twelve; a fact, which arose out of the circuit itself—as Matt. ix. 36—x. 1. is sufficient to prove.

The immediate motive to a second progress over all Galilee, so soon after the former, I cannot help ascribing to the recent transactions in Capernaum. The rooted malignity, twice consecutively displayed, of the Pharisees, in imputing our Lord's miracles to Beelzebub, seems to have determined him to remove at once from their vicinity; in which case, he could not, perhaps, be otherwise employed, at this period of his ministry, than upon a general circuit. That, between the close of the last such progress, and the expiration of the present year, there was room and opportunity for another like this, no one will deny; and, did we not suppose something of that kind to have now intervened, that we could not fill up the hiatus in the continuity of events, or account satisfactorily for the disposal of the residue of the year, is equally indisputable. Its duration, I assume, as in former instances, to have been about three or four months; whence, if it began in October it might be over in February; and, whatever time it occupied in particular, yet along with the mission and ministry of the Twelve, which arose out of it, that it must have taken up on the whole about six months will appear more clearly from the sequel.

Towards the middle, if not the beginning, of this circuit, for reasons which have been stated in the first volume [g], I think it most probable that, after an imprisonment of about eighteen months in duration, John the Baptist was put to death. The account of this death is related by St. Matthew and St. Mark [h], though in the way of an historical di-

---

[g] Diss. viii. Appendix.   [h] Matt. xiv. 1—12.   Mark vi. 14—29.

gression; whereas St. Luke[i], though he makes Herod say, John have I beheaded; but who is this? and, therefore, plainly supposes the fact of his death, yet enters into no explanation of the allusion. For this omission it would not be easy to account, except by admitting that he must have considered his readers already too well aware of the fact, to render any such explanation necessary; and, consequently, that he also considered them to be previously acquainted with the Gospels of St. Matthew, or of St. Mark, which only could have made them aware of it. If so, he must have written after one, or both, of them—and had seen either that one, or both, of them.

This circuit, like every other but the last, we may presume would terminate at Capernaum; where, like every other also, it had originally begun: and, therefore, that the mission of the Twelve, which took place at, or towards, its close, took place from Capernaum. It is certain that, after their mission, they rejoined our Lord at Capernaum; and it is not probable they would be sent from one quarter, and be expected to rejoin him at another. The reference to some city[k], in the course of the charge, where both Christ and they were present at the time, can be understood of no city with so much propriety as of this. No city was so likely to have been the place where our Lord would stop to commission, and despatch, his Apostles upon a circuit by themselves, as Capernaum, their common residence and his. It strengthens the argument, that there is every reason to conclude the Seventy also were sent, upon a similar mission, from the same place. Besides, the Twelve, if they were ever called as disciples, were almost all called there, and, when they were ordained as Apostles, were certainly all ordained there; with which it was but consistent that they should proceed on their first Apostolic errand from thence. The reference also in μετέβη ἐκεῖθεν[l], compared with the different passages elsewhere, in which we meet with a similar reference to specify some exact place, yet in-

---

[i] Luke ix. 7—9.   [k] Matt. x. 23.   [l] Matt. xi. 1.

dependent of any thing before or after [m], it will be concluded can be properly understood only of so well known a
place as Capernaum.

The length of the time, for which the Apostles would be
absent, must be determined by the interval between the
probable close of our Saviour's circuit just before, and the
precise period of their return.   This period was certainly
just before a Passover, which fell out in the middle of April;
and we have assumed that they were probably despatched
three or four months after a feast of Tabernacles, which expired on the first of October.   They might therefore be
sent upon their ministry in February, and return to our
Lord in March; the duration of their absence being one
half, or one third, of the length of our Lord's circuits in general.   And, indeed, if three or four months was the ordinary duration of one of these, as performed by our Lord
singly, one month or two months must have been sufficient
for the discharge of their's, begun, and going on while it
lasted, in six different companies, and in six different directions, at once.   The mission of the Seventy, in the ensuing
year, is a case in point; and that mission, it is probable, did
not occupy even so much.

We have no account of the proceedings of the Apostles,
subsequent to their departure, except that they did—what
our Saviour had always done—*preach*, and *teach*, and work
miracles of a certain description; and that, wherever they
went, they were sustained by the attendant providence of
their Master [n].   From the notice, however, which occurs at
Matt. xi. 1. it may be safely collected that, while they were
absent on the work of their commission, our Lord himself,
also, was not inactive; but similarly engaged, in the cities
and the synagogues, apart from them.   We possess, therefore, in this intimation, an evidence of the manner in which
his time, likewise, was occupied, between the close of the
last circuit, and the arrival of the next Passover; viz. in
a kind of circuit, similar to what he had undertaken, at

[m] Matt. xv. 21.   Mark vii. 24. x. 1.   [n] Mark vi. 12. 13.   Luke ix.
6. xxii. 35.

other times, before, but necessarily on a more limited scale, and completed within a much shorter time. Of such partial circuits this will, consequently, be the second instance, which has yet occurred ; and both this, and the first, will be events of the same year. It was over, however, before that of the Apostles ; for they found Jesus at Capernaum, on their arrival ; and were taken by him, with little or no delay, as the motive assigned for the act is sufficient to prove, to the other side of the lake, to a place which St. Luke shews was the desert of the city of Bethsaida [o].

On the position of this city something will be said elsewhere ; at present, I assume that it was in Decapolis : and, consequently, this will be the first occasion, upon which there is any proof that our Lord had yet visited the dominions of Philip, and the second, upon which he appears to have crossed the lake. The history of the transactions on the other side, and from that time forward to the return [p], is one, and the first, of the only two instances in general, when the four Gospels all coincide, and go along, in the narration of facts, with each other. The harmony—as resulting from their united accounts—is as follows.

I. The season of the year in general is ascertained by John vi. 4. which states that the Passover was at hand ; and the circumstance, which also he specifies, that there was much grass in the place, is a proof that the spring was far advanced. The Passover fell this year, which answers to A. U. 782. and A. D. 29. as late as it possibly could, viz. upon April 16 : and the year had, consequently, been intercalated. If we fix the time of the present transaction about the close of the Jewish month Veadar, or the beginning of the Jewish month Nisan, the end of our March, or the beginning of our April, we may, perhaps, not be far from the truth [q].

II. It is distinctly affirmed by St. Mark [r], that the multitude saw our Lord and his disciples setting out ; and, con-

---

[o] Mark vi. 30—32. Luke ix. 10. Matt. xiv. 13. John vi. 1.   [p] Matt. xiv. 13—36. Mark vi. 32—56. Luke ix. 10—17. John vi. 1—21.   [q] Vide vol. i. Diss. x. 349.   [r] vi. 33.

cluding, as we may suppose, whither they must be going, that they ran before in great numbers, to be ready to meet them on the opposite side. As Capernaum, and also Bethsaida, were contiguous to the northern extremity of the lake, and not very far from each other [a], with the Jordan only between them, the breadth of which at this part of its course could be nothing considerable, (for according to the ocular testimony of Maundrell, at the ford in the neighbourhood of Jericho, much beyond this part, it was but sixty feet across,) though this might require a great effort of speed, yet it was not impossible to be effected. Hence if both parties had set out from Capernaum at the same time, early in the morning, they might both meet at the other side of the lake again, before it was noon : or by the middle of the day.

III. Consistently with this supposition, when Jesus arrived, ἐξελθών—which can be understood, perhaps, of nothing but his landing from the ship—both St. Matthew and St. Mark affirm that he beheld the multitudes ; that is, he found many of them on the spot ; and by this unexpected spectacle—implying the extraordinary exertion which they had made to keep pace with the ship, and, consequently, their great zeal and eagerness to be about him, and to hear him—was so touched as to be moved with an impulse of compassion ; and his original purpose of conveying himself from them, or of consulting his personal ease and convenience, was changed into the contrary one of ministering to their spiritual wants. St. John, who says [t] that he went up into the mountain, and sat down with his disciples, before he speaks of his seeing the multitudes, is not inconsistent with St. Mark or St. Matthew, but merely supplies some particulars omitted by them. For, in the first place, the attitude, in which he describes our Saviour, is the attitude of one who had either made an end of teaching, (which is, perhaps, the more probable supposition,) or was preparing to teach : in which case, John vi. 5. will take up and continue Mark vi. 34. as well as Matt. xiv. 14. or Luke ix. 11.

[a] Jos. Vita. 72.   [t] vi. 3.

Secondly, as to the resort of the people, which our Lord, on lifting up his eyes, is said to have beheld [u], there is no reason whatever why this resort should not be understood either of the multitude, already collected, as following him up into the mountain, or of the accession of numbers, which, in addition to those already on the spot, would be momentarily arriving from other parts.

IV. Though Jesus had left Capernaum that very morning, yet the business of teaching the people, and performing miracles on such as needed it, might evidently be over by the ninth hour of the day : the period of ὀψία πρωΐα—in opposition to sunset, the period of ὀψία δείλη. At this time the day might strictly be said to have begun to decline, and Luke ix. 12. would be critically in unison with Matt. xiv. 15. Mark vi. 35 : the usual supper-hour, too, or at least the season of the evening's repast, among the Jews, would not be far off.

V. The multitude, then, having been miraculously fed— a business, which, if we consider their numbers, might easily occupy the time from the ninth hour to sunset, at least—Jesus dismisses his disciples at a period of the day which John vi. 16. might describe accordingly ; with a charge to return to Bethsaida in Galilee ; the site of which was in the region of Gennesaret, between Capernaum, and the southern extremity of the lake. The time of their departure, then, would not be earlier than the second ὀψία, or δείλη ὀψία—as not merely St. John, but St. Matthew and St. Mark [v] also, clearly imply that it was. Meanwhile our Lord himself withdrew to the mountain ; and either persuaded the assembled people to retire, or would be speedily concealed from their observation by the shades of night.

VI. When the disciples in the vessel had got about thirty stades [w], or three miles, on their course, about two thirds of the distance across the lake, (the slowness of their progress in so many hours being critically accounted for by the opposition of the wind, the direction of which must have been

● John vi. 5.   ● Matt. xiv. 23.   Mark vi. 47.   ● John vi. 19.

south-west, a natural circumstance at this time of the year, when the prevailing wind was always the southern,) Jesus appeared to them about the fourth watch of the night— Peter descended to meet him on the sea—and he was afterwards received into the ship. The fourth watch would begin at the ninth hour of the night, or our three in the morning: and as our Lord was visible at a distance, before he came near enough to be recognized—but at first only indistinctly—perhaps the time of his appearance was just the dawn of day, or between four and five in the morning. For, as to the supposition that he might have been visible by moonlight—in the first place, the weather being rough and boisterous, the moon would have been obscured by clouds. In the second, if the time of the month was what I have supposed, about a fortnight before the Passover, the end of Veadar, or the beginning of Nisan, there could have been no moon at all; and the very turbulence of the weather argues this, rather than the contrary.

VII. As the disciples, when they were originally dismissed, had been sent away to Bethsaida [x], not to Capernaum—and, as, on taking Jesus into the ship, they were miraculously transported at once to the quarter where they wished to go [y], they would land, before sunrise in the morning, not at Capernaum, but somewhere in the district of Gennesaret, more to the south, as St. Mark and St. Matthew [z] do both imply. St. John's expression—ἤρχοντο πέραν —εἰς Καπερναούμ [a]—it is clear, even from the sequel of his own account, means no more than that they were proceeding to the other side in the direction of Capernaum—or that Capernaum was ultimately the quarter where they wished to arrive—both which facts were literally true. For, though they might land at Bethsaida first, yet, from the spot where they did land, our Lord finally proceeded to Capernaum.

VIII. Having landed, then, after day-break, he would find the people of the country on the alert—by these he might soon be recognized—and, upon the recognition, and

---

[x] Mark vi. 45.   [y] John vi. 21.   [z] Matt. xiv. 34. Mark vi. 53.
[a] John vi. 17.

during his subsequent progress through the highly populous region of Gennesaret, back to Capernaum, (a progress
which could scarcely fail to pass through cities, and villages,
as well as the open country, by the way,) those things
might ensue which are described accordingly[b]. Nor would
it follow from this supposition, that the time taken up by
the progress, before it arrived at Capernaum, needed to be
more than one day. The note of time, then, in St. John's
Gospel, τῇ ἐπαύριον[c], admits just as well of being understood
of the day before the meeting in the synagogue at Capernaum, as of the day after the miracle of the feeding at
Bethsaida. The day of this meeting, it has been seen elsewhere[d], was probably the sabbath-day, and such a sabbath-
day as coincided with the seventh of April: for the Thursday before was probably the day of the feeding, and both
coincided with the fifth of April—our assumed date for the
true day of the nativity of Christ. With the discourse,
mysterious, figurative, and interesting, as it is, which ensued
in the synagogue on this meeting, the particulars of our
Lord's second year are obviously to be brought to a close.
And now, at the termination of this discourse, the first distinct allusion, anywhere on record, to the future treachery
of Judas, is found to occur[e]; and so exactly a year before
its completion, that it is found to be now predicted on
Saturday the seventh of April, as it will be found hereafter
to be consummated on Friday the fifth of April.

[b] Matt. xiv. 35. 36. Mark vi. 54—56.   [c] vi. 22.   [d] Vol. i.
Diss. x. 350. 351.   [e] John vi. 70. 71.

DISSERTATION VIII.

PART IV.

General prospective survey of our Lord's ministry in Galilee.

As the history of the preceding transactions shewed the Passover not to have been far distant, so the account of the question, which follows next in order[a], shews it to be arrived, and past; for the mention of Scribes and Pharisees, Mark vii. 1. from Jerusalem, as such, is in my opinion an implicit testimony both that the feast was over, and that it had not been attended by our Lord in person. We cannot suppose, therefore, that the ensuing circumstances transpired earlier than some few days after the twenty-first of the Jewish Nisan, which answered in the third year of our Saviour's ministry to April 23. though they might transpire in a short time after it. That the place where they happened was Capernaum, at which also the account of St. John, when it closed, obviously left our Lord, seems scarcely to admit of a question : and these points being all presumptively certain, I shall observe, upon this Passover, that it was the only feast of its kind, which Jesus did not personally attend in Jerusalem. I have already shewn, indeed, that he was under no absolute necessity of attending all the feasts in their order; of which we cannot have a better proof than the fact that, out of the four great solemnities which recurred in each of the years of his ministry, by far the chief part were not attended by him. I have shewn also that, of those which he did attend, he attended none so regularly as the Passover; and of the four Passovers in the course of his ministry he attended every one but this : and, in addition to the prudential reason which might have occasioned his absence from this, there was, perhaps, another—in the peculiarity of the time, when the Passover itself fell out. If the Passover was celebrated this year on the six-

[a] Matt. xv. 1—20. Mark vii. 1—23.

teenth of April, the year was intercalated, and the Passover fell as late as it possibly could. The fourteenth of Nisan coincided, in this year, with the Julian April 16. and the tenth of Nisan with the Julian April 12. neither of which days had any connection with our assumed date of the nativity, the Julian April 5. This was not the case with the other years of his ministry, especially the first and the last ; the times, on which those two days then fell out, are remarkable for this connection. It was not equally the case even with the Passover in his second year, when the fourteenth of Nisan coincided with March 29. and the tenth with March 25—for the 25th of March, though not the day of our Saviour's birth, was yet the date of the vernal equinox ; and the tenth of Nisan would coincide with that. But to return from this digression.

As to the method of reconciling the accounts of St. Matthew and St. Mark, which certainly stand in some need of adjustment, it will be the subject of a Dissertation hereafter : and I shall observe at present only that, no where in his Gospel does the latter in particular write so plainly like an original and independent authority, not as the mere copyist of the former ; and that the probable reason, why St. Luke omits all mention of the transaction in question here, is because something very similar to it occurred, and is related by him to have occurred, hereafter.

The question now put, and its answer, were followed by our Saviour's departure from Capernaum [c] into the parts of Tyre and Sidon ; consequently beyond the precincts of either Galilee ; and more immediately in the vicinity of the Tetrarchy of Philip. This quarter though he might often have approached in the course of his circuits heretofore, there is no proof that he had ever yet visited, or resided in, personally ; and, consequently, he could be known there, perhaps, only by report. His motive in visiting it even now, we learn directly from St. Mark [d], was concealment ; though, such was his reputation, and such the attention

[b] xi. 37. to the end.   [c] Matt. xv. 21.   Mark vii. 24.   [d] vii. 24.

paid to all his movements, that, as the same testimony acknowledges, he could not be hid. The final end of this concealment itself was, in my judgment, to escape the observation of his pertinacious enemies, the Scribes and Pharisees; and I consider such a visit, to such a quarter, an argument that he must have left Capernaum soon after the last transaction, the effect of which, as St. Matthew informed us [e], was not to diminish, but to widen, the breach between them, and to aggravate their ill-will towards himself. He might choose the parts of Tyre and Sidon, not merely on account of their remoteness from Judæa, though that was some days' journey in extent [f], but because it was a Gentile country, into which they would scruple to follow him; or at least because of their proximity to the dominions of Philip, the only one among the sons of Herod who seems to have been a good and just prince [g]; and more likely to afford shelter and protection, within his government, to an innocent party, persecuted by the most powerful and unprincipled of the Jewish sects, than the Tetrarch of Galilee.

I should not consider it improbable that, like Elijah in the days of Ahab, our Lord might bend his steps, on this occasion, in the direction of Zarephath, or Sarepta; for that was midway between Tyre and Sidon [h], and, according to Jerome, situated on the high road. One thing is clear; viz. that the miracle, performed on the daughter of the Syro-Phœnician woman, must have been performed almost as soon as he arrived, and directly after he had entered some house [i]; which circumstance enables us to harmonize the two accounts of it accordingly.

The comparison of the Evangelists renders it self-evident that St. Matthew, from verse 22. to 24. *inclusive*, begins with relating what took place in public; and from verse 25. to the end, proceeds to what took place in private; whereas St. Mark, from first to last, confines himself to the latter only. The woman first made her application to our Lord

---

[e] xv. 12.   [f] Jos. Cont. Apion. ii. 9.   [g] Ant. Jud. xviii. iv. 6.
[h] Ant. Jud. viii. xiii. 2.   Hieron. Oper. ii. De Situ et Nominibus.   [i] Matt. xv. 22—28.   Mark vii. 25—30.

in public, and before he had entered into any house; for this is what is meant by her crying *unto him*, in verse 22. and her crying *after them*, in verse 23. For, even subsequent to this, she is said, at verse 25. to have come and worshipped him ; which denotes that she fell down at his feet. This part of the transaction begins to be intimated by St. Mark, at verse 25. when Jesus was already in private ; and, consequently, it is from this point of time that the two narratives coincide, and go along together.   The harmony, which may thence be established, will be exhibited in its proper place hereafter.

The notoriety of this miracle, which had been conceded solely to the importunity of maternal tenderness, and to the more than usual display of the constancy and strength of faith, could not but interfere with our Lord's desire of privacy, and seems, in fact, to have been the motive which determined him to leave the same parts again, before he had yet made any stay in them.   When he did this, both St. Matthew and St. Mark attest that he came to the sea of Galilee in general[k], and the latter, that he came thither through the coasts of Decapolis in particular.   It is evident, therefore, that he must have travelled first from the confines of Tyre and Sidon eastward, aloof from Galilee as before, until he crossed the Jordan in some part of its course between its springs and the northern extremity of the lake of Tiberias; and afterwards southward, through the dominions of Philip all the time, in which Decapolis also would be included.   And this, likewise, was a part which, though he might frequently have approached before, he had never yet visited, or resided in, personally.   Nor does it appear that he was visiting it even now for the purpose of preaching in it, but for the sake of retirement.   All this time he was confining himself to a distant quarter, where he would either be personally unknown, or at least very imperfectly known, except by fame; and intentionally keeping away from the regions which had been hitherto the scene of his ministry. And though, wherever he went, he might naturally be fol-

[k] Matt. xv. 29.   Mark vii. 31.

lowed about by the people of the country in general, yet it would not be by those of that country, in particular, before whom, and among whom, the two last years of that ministry had been almost exclusively transacted.

The part of Decapolis, to which he came, being some part which bordered on the lake, we may conclude from Matt. xv. 29. (as alluding to some well-known mountain, such only as could be properly designated by the use of the article) as well as from the course of subsequent events, that he came to the same desert of Bethsaida, and to the same individual mountain within that desert, where he had, not long before, fed the five thousand. How long after that miracle he would thus revisit its vicinity, it may not be possible to say ; except that, if the account of his motions hitherto has been continuous, we may reasonably conjecture it was at no great distance of time.

Upon this mountain, and in this region, did Jesus remain, attended by the multitudes which had either accompanied him thither, or resorted to him since his arrival, or both, at least three days[1]; which he employed in teaching the people, and in performing miracles; a vast number whereof is specified summarily[m], but one only (which might have taken place on the first day of the three) in detail ; a miracle performed upon a deaf and dumb person[n], the account of which is due, perhaps, more to the peculiar circumstances of the cure, and to the singular solemnity of our Lord's manner in working it, than to the novelty, or remarkableness, of the miracle itself.

On the third day, as it may be clearly collected from the testimony of each Evangelist, and, probably, about the same hour of the day as before, or, at least, at the usual time of some meal in the day, the second instance of miraculous feeding took place[o]. It took place, consequently, on the same locality as the former, and at no great distance of time after it ; and, in the material fact, it was altogether so

---

[1] Matt. xv. 32.   Mark viii. 2.   [m] Matt. xv. 30. 31.   [n] Mark vii.
32. to the end.   [o] Matt. xv. 32—38.   Mark viii. 1—9.

similar to that, that St. Luke, who had recorded the one, might very well omit the other.*

* It is observable that, in the account of this miracle, both the Evangelists agree in calling the baskets, by which the fragments were measured, σπυρίδας—and, in the account of the former miracle, they all agreed in calling those, by which the fragments at that time also were measured, κοφίνους. We may presume, then, that so regular a distinction between these two things, was not unintended : and the same conclusion is implied in the terms of our Lord's joint reference to both the miracles, Matt. xvi. 10. 11. Mark viii. 19. 20. so soon after the second.   What, however, was the real difference between these two kinds of baskets, it would be hard to say.   That the Jews were accustomed to carry *cophini* about with them, we may safely collect from Juvenal,

> Nunc sacri fontis nemus, et delubra, locantur
> Judæis, quorum cophinus, fœnumque, supellex.
>
> III. 13.

And again,

> Cum dedit ille locum, cophino fœnoque relicto
> Arcanam Judæa tremens mendicat in aurem.
>
> VI. 541.

It may be inferred from both these passages, that the use of the cophinus was chiefly to serve its owner as a *couch*, and of the hay, which seems to have gone along with it, as *bed* or *bedding*. May we infer from this, that both the κόφινοι and σπυρίδες were wanted by those, who attended our Saviour, to provide them with the means of sleeping so long as they remained ἐν ἐρήμῳ, and in his company.   That the σπυρίς, at least, was large enough to contain a man, may be collected from Acts ix. 25. in the account of St. Paul's escape from Damascus.   But why were the people in the former instance all provided with κόφινοι, and in the second, all provided with σπυρίδες ?   I should conjecture, because in the former instance the miracle was wrought about the feast of the Passover, and in the latter about the feast of Pentecost.   Critics, at least, are agreed in deriving the name of the σπυρίς from πυρὸς triticum ; and Hesychius explains it accordingly, τὸ τῶν πυρῶν ἄγγος.   It is needless to observe, that Pentecost was the season of *wheat*-harvest, as the Passover was of the *barley*-harvest : and

It is manifest that, previously to the miracle, Jesus intended to have dismissed the multitude, and his supplying them with food beforehand was only a benevolent precaution, that so they might be able to travel to their respective homes. Yet its effect, as in the former instance, would doubtless be also to accelerate his own departure, lest, as St. John expressed himself then, they should come, after the experience of two such miracles, (the latter of which could not fail to recall to their minds the former likewise,) and make him by force their king. The mention of the ship[p], in which he accordingly embarked, and the consequent fact of his departure by sea, in which both the Evangelists are agreed, though both also suppose that he came to Bethsaida, originally, by land, is critically to be explained by the proximity of Bethsaida to Capernaum, on the one hand, and by the three days' previous stay, on the other. It is nothing incredible that the ship had either been brought to him, or expressly been sent for, from Capernaum, on one of those days. The article prefixed to the mention of it, $\dot{\alpha}\pi\lambda\tilde{\omega}\varsigma$—as $\tau\dot{o}$ $\pi\lambda o\tilde{\imath}o\nu$—shews that it was some ship which was regularly employed on such occasions—and since the point of time specified Mark iii. 9. (where the circumstance was first expressly alluded to) might be considered to be always attending on his motions in the vicinity of the lake. Nor is it improbable that the ship which is designated in the places annexed[q], and called indifferently sometimes $\pi\lambda o\tilde{\imath}o\nu$, sometimes $\pi\lambda o\iota\acute{\alpha}\rho\iota o\nu$, in all these instances might be one and the same, and the property of Simon Peter.

hence, if there was any difference between the $\kappa\acute{o}\phi\iota\nu o\varsigma$ and the $\sigma\pi\upsilon\rho\acute{\iota}\varsigma$ as such, or any appropriation of one of them to one season of the year, and of the other to another, the former might be wanted about the Passover, and the latter about Pentecost. Now the miracle in the first instance, it has been shewn elsewhere, took place not long before the Passover; and the miracle, in the second, might have taken place almost as little before the Pentecost.

[p] Matt. xv. 39. Mark viii. 10.   [q] Luke v. 3. Mark iii. 9. iv. 1.
Matt. xv. 39. Mark viii. 10. John xxi. 3. 8.

St. Matthew says that, upon leaving this quarter, Jesus came into the confines of Magdala—St. Mark, that he came into the parts of Dalmanutha. It follows, therefore, that Magdala and Dalmanutha were either different denominations for the same region, or separate denominations for distinct, but contiguous, regions. And as our Lord before was at Bethsaida, on the eastern side of the lake, and, we shall see hereafter, in order to arrive at Magdala, would have to cross εἰς τὸ πέραν, we may infer that each of these regions, whether in themselves the same, or adjacent, were yet situate on the western side of the lake.

If this, however, was the case, they would be somewhere in the vicinity of Capernaum ; and probably not more than half a day's journey distant from it ; for the sea of Tiberias, even on Pliny's calculation, was but sixteen Roman miles long ; and upon that of Josephus was not quite so much. The Pharisees, therefore, whom the first transaction, in the course of this present year, had left at Capernaum, might soon hear of Jesus' arrival so immediately in their neighbourhood, and, consequently, might go forth on purpose (as the assertion of St. Matthew, xvi. 1. and of St. Mark viii. 11. are most naturally understood to imply) from Capernaum to Magdala or Dalmanutha—to find him out, and to question with him, there, as they had recently done in Capernaum.

The demand of a sign [r], which now ensued, is the second instance of the kind in the three first Gospels, at least upon record ; and it is a proof of the *animus* with which they, who preferred it, were actuated on this occasion, as well as upon the former. The arrival of our Lord in these parts was, consequently, not much posterior to his last departure from Capernaum : and as each of the Evangelists tells us that, when he had answered the demand of the Pharisees, he immediately left them, and sailed away again, it is evident he made no stay here ; and it becomes a presumptive inference that the true cause of so speedy a departure was,

[r] Matt. xvi. 1—4. Mark viii. 11. 12.

as before, the desire to remove himself from the vicinity or
the observation of so troublesome and malicious a sect:
whose hostility against himself was now as confirmed and
inveterate in the principle, as their ingenuity and contriv-
ance were active and indefatigable in the effect. I shall
pause, therefore, for the sake of a few observations upon
the transaction itself.

In the history of this also, the account of St. Mark would
not easily be reconcileable to the account of St. Matthew, if
both were supposed to be coincident, and to go along with
each other, throughout. But if the former is supplementary
to the latter, and, as far as they differ, (which is in the account of our Lord's reply,) begins where that ends, there is
an admirable congruity between them. Now the answer,
which St. Matthew ascribes to him, is altogether such as he
might have returned, (and we may take it for granted, he
did return,) on the spot. The conduct and the language,
ascribed to him, on the other hand, by St. Mark, are altogether the conduct and the language of one, reflecting
upon what had occurred; and making some observations
respecting it to others, and not to the parties before addressed. For, in the first place, he sighed, and sighed
deeply, before he uttered any thing—as one might have
done who was revolving in his mind this new proof of the
obduracy of the people—and, secondly, he expressed himself thus, Why does this generation σημεῖον ἐπιζητεῖ; where
there may be an emphasis in ἐπιζητεῖ, so as to signify *fla-
gitat;* What makes this generation so repeatedly ask for a
sign? for this was not the first instance of the kind. Lastly,
Verily I say unto you, or, as it is much stronger in the
original—εἰ δοθήσεται τῇ γενεᾷ ταύτῃ σημεῖον—is the Hebrew idiom for conveying the most solemn asseverations,
and tantamount to an oath. Yet he had told the enquirers, just before, that the sign of the prophet Jonas should
be given them; so that some sign was to be given. This
last declaration in particular could, therefore, not have
been coincident with any part of Matthew xvi. 4. It was
not likely to have been addressed to the enquirers at all; nor

does it appear, from St. Mark's account, that though accosted by them our Lord said any thing whatever to them. But it might have been spoken to his own disciples; that is, it might have passed in private—at the end of the former conference—and when the parties concerned in that had been dismissed.   In this case, all is consistent with St. Matthew, and in the highest degree natural and probable in itself.   But to proceed.

It is implied by each of the Evangelists [s] that, when Jesus departed, he went away εἰς τὸ πέραν; and they each of them record by the way [t] the discourse, between our Lord and his disciples, respecting the figurative caution to beware of the *leaven* of the three principal sects—a caution which, from the accidental circumstance of their having forgotten to lay in, before their departure, any supply of bread, (implying that, in their journeyings to and fro, they were accustomed to carry with them their own provision, and also that their departure from Magdala had been precipitate and sudden,) and because they were aware that the mutual animosity of the Jewish sects made them avoid, as much as possible, all dealings, even of buying and selling, with those of an opposite αἵρεσις, or party, the Apostles interpreted literally.   The question, then, as to the site of Magdala and Dalmanutha, depends on the construction of the terms εἰς τὸ πέραν; thát is, the direction in which they were sailing.

Now St. Mark makes them land at Bethsaida [u], and relates the performance of a miracle on a blind man there [v]. There was certainly a Bethsaida in Galilee [w], which Jerome also alludes to as situated on the Lake of Tiberias. If Jesus was sailing towards this Bethsaida, he was sailing from east to west, and Magdala and Dalmanutha lay on the Persæan side of the Lake.   But there was also a Bethsaida in Decapolis [x]—which Josephus mentions by name [y]: Κώμην . . Βηθ-

---

[s] Matt. xvi. 5.   Mark viii. 13.   [t] Matt. xvi. 5—12.   Mark viii. 14—21.
[u] viii. 22.   [v] Ib. 22—26.   [w] John i. 45. xii. 21.   Mark vi. 45.
Matt. xi. 21.   Luke x. 13.   [x] Luke ix. 10.   [y] Ant. xviii. ii. 1.
B. ii. ix. 1.   Vita. 72.

σαῖδὰν, πρὸς λίμνῃ δὲ τῇ Γεννησαρίτιδι—and places a furlong distant from the banks of the Jordan. This village, or κώμη, the Tetrarch Philip, some time in his reign before the present period, enlarged from the rank of a village to that of a city, and called Julias, in honour of the daughter of Augustus. If our Lord was sailing towards this Bethsaida, he was sailing from west to east; and Magdala and Dalmanutha were situated accordingly. And this I apprehend to have been the case; because, directly after, he is said to have gone forth at once into the towns of Cæsarea Philippi [z], that is, into the dominions of Philip. It is reasonable to suppose he was on the verge of those dominions previously: which he would be at Bethsaida in Decapolis. Besides which, Bethsaida of Galilee was too near to Capernaum to have suited his purpose of concealment. Nor is it any objection that St. Mark calls it a village; for so it might still be, if Philip had begun to enlarge it only after the accession of Tiberius: and as to its new name of Julias, this would never supersede with the common people its original Hebrew name of Bethsaida. Lastly, Mary ἡ Μαγδαληνὴ, that is, Mary of Magdala, was doubtless a Galilean; and, therefore, her native place was situated in Galilee. Had it been on the eastern side of the lake, she would have been a native of Peræa.

The miracle, performed at Bethsaida, is one of the most singular, and, in a certain point of view, one of the most instructive, on record. It is one of the most singular, because it was performed at twice; and yet was not imperfectly performed on either occasion; it was perfect in each instance with regard to the effect so far produced, but the ultimate effect was more complete than the primary. It is the most instructive, because it contributes to illustrate, and even demonstrably supplies the evidence of, a natural and necessary effect of some of the most remarkable of our Saviour's miracles, which, notwithstanding, though as real as any, and, perhaps, the most wonderful of all, is the most recondite, and the least likely to appear externally.

[z] Matt. xvi. 13.   Mark viii. 27.

The possession of a natural faculty of any kind, and the power of using that faculty according to its natural purposes, are very different things, especially in the case of those who, having been born destitute of the former, should be suddenly endued therewith. Every physiologist is aware that, under such circumstances, the free use of the faculty would be by no means an immediate and necessary consequence. The possession of the faculty, and even the power, as such, of using the faculty, might both be communicated at once; but if no more were communicated at the same time, the complete, natural use of the faculty could be acquired only by degrees, requiring space and time; and the party, restored to the possession, if left to himself, would be as helpless and destitute for some while longer, as if he had continued in his original state.

In every instance of our Saviour's miracles, and, indeed, of the miracles of the Apostles generally, this free and immediate use of the faculty communicated is perceived to have been as much an effect of the miracle, as the simple capacity of the use. The miracle, therefore, in all such cases, must have been attended by a double effect—the communication of a certain power or faculty, not before possessed, or not before capable of being exerted—and the ability to exert it freely on the spot. Whatsoever, then, would be previously indispensable to such an exertion must have been communicated also; in other words, the subject of the miracle, with regard to the use and enjoyment of a certain sense or faculty, must have been placed at once in the same state as if he had never wanted it, or had never been unable to exert it.

On this principle, one who had been born dumb, and was afterwards thus endued with the faculty of speech, if he was enabled at once to converse, besides the power of utterance, must have had the knowledge of articulate sounds—in other words, the gift of a language, as such—bestowed over and above upon him: the communication of the faculty of hearing must have been accompanied by the communication of all the ideas, of which the sense of hearing is the medium : the gift of the faculty of sight by the gift also of all, which are essential to the use and effect of sight : and so in every other case likewise.

These auxiliary or concomitant effects of such miracles may justly be considered not the least extraordinary or admirable of any; and the use of the miracle, now performed at Bethsaida, it appears to me is this, that, with regard to the evidence of such effects, it is a case in point, and what seems to have held good in the secret process of this miracle, we may reasonably conclude, would be equally true, under the same circumstances, of every other. The faculty of sight, and the power of using that faculty, were both communicated in this instance, and both communicated at twice, and as far as the one was communicated so far it was immediately attended by the other. As the faculty was communicated gradually, so the power was developed gradually —but the use of the faculty still kept pace with the power of using it. The ideas of vision clearly went along with the exercise of the powers of vision, and if the ideas were not all at once distinct, it was because the faculty was not all at once complete, or the power of its use all at once developed. But the man could comprehend what he saw, and could discriminate between what he saw, as far as he could see them, even from the first : the use, then, of the faculty of sight was still in proportion to the extent of the possession, or the degree of the power of its use; and, considered in reference to that, it was as adequately exercised at first, when objects were seen confusedly, as at last, when every thing was perceived distinctly.

But to return from this digression. While Jesus was yet on the way to Cæsarea Philippi and its vicinity, according to St. Mark[a], and while he was praying by the way, apart, with his disciples, according to St. Luke[b], the memorable confession of Peter, and, directly after it, the first instance —and, by St. Matthew and St. Mark, critically specified as such—of any particular prediction concerning the rejection,

[a] viii. 27.　　　　　　　　　　[b] ix. 18.

the death, and the resurrection, of the Christ (which, consequently, begin to be thus foretold about a year before the event) must have taken place[c]. This prediction, like every other instance of its kind subsequently, as well as the rebuke of Peter[d] which arose out of it, and the original question, which produced the confession, must have been delivered, apart from the multitude, in the presence of the Twelve alone. But the doctrine of self-denial, and of the duty of taking up the cross, which followed upon the offence, and the rebuke of the offence, of Peter, because it concerned all, was delivered in the audience of all[e]. Our Lord is said to have expressly called the people to him, before he proceeded to discourse upon that.

The next event on record is the Transfiguration[f], which seems to have been, at least in their primary sense, the fulfilment of the concluding words in the above discourse, as they are reported by each of the Evangelists. And so Theophylact understood it : Οὐδὲν ἕτερον ἡ μεταμόρφωσις ἦν, ἀλλ' ἢ τῆς δευτέρας παρουσίας προμήνευμα[g]. The distance of this transaction from the last is differently represented—by St. Matthew and St. Mark, at six days afterwards—by St. Luke, at about eight. The expression of the latter, however, ὡσεὶ ἡμέραι ὀκτὼ, is so guarded, that it must be evident he did not intend to affirm the fact of eight entire days, but either of seven whole days, and part of an eighth, or of six whole days, and parts of two more days. And as to the expression of St. Matthew and St. Mark, μεθ' ἡμέρας ἕξ—I shall shew hereafter that this may, and perhaps must, be understood of six whole days, and a part of a seventh ; in which case there will be no difference between the two statements, except of one day, and this may be explained as follows.

Luke ix. 37. our Lord and the three Apostles are said to have come down from the mountain, τῇ ἑξῆς ἡμέρᾳ—which seems to me to imply very plainly that the Transfiguration

---

[c] Matt. xvi. 13—21. Mark viii. 27—31. Luke ix. 18—22.   [d] Matt. xvi. 22. 23. Mark viii. 32. 33.   [e] Matt. xvi. 24. to the end. Mark viii. 34 —ix. 1. Luke ix. 23—27.   [f] Matt. xvii. 1—9. Mark ix. 2—8. Luke ix. 28—36.   [g] Comm. in Luc. 234.

had taken place the night before.   And this conclusion is
further confirmed by the circumstances before and during
the event itself—that Jesus went up into the mountain, for
the purpose of private prayer ; in order to which he is not
seen to have retired apart at other times, except in the
night, or early in the morning—that the Apostles were
sleeping at the commencement of the Transfiguration, and
were awakened on purpose to behold it—that the whole
transaction, awful and mysterious as it was, would be rendered still more solemn and impressive, if it had happened
amidst the darkness and stillness of the night.

On all these accounts, I think, we may infer that our Saviour took the three Apostles up into the mountain either
at the close of the preceding day, or, what is equally probable, sometime in the ensuing night—that the Transfiguration occurred soon after, and, therefore, in the night as
such—that when this was over they did not come down
until the following day.   Now in this case, from the day of
the confession of Peter, reckoned as the first, to the day before the Transfiguration, reckoned as the last, the interval
might be exactly *seven* days and six nights—but from the
same time to either the night of the Transfiguration, considered as part of the same Jewish νυχθήμερον, or to the morning of the day when it was over as such, the interval might
be *eight* days and seven nights, or what St. Luke would
call ὡσεὶ ἡμέραι ὀκτώ.   If St. Matthew and St. Mark go by
the former rule, and St. Luke goes by the latter, it is manifest that their statements may both be correct, and will be
consistent the one with the other.   It is a probable conjecture, though I have not the means of rendering it demonstrably certain, that both the prediction of the Transfiguration, and the Transfiguration, took place on the same day
of the week, either the Jewish sabbath as such, or the
Christian Sunday as such.   If either of these was the case,
then both modes of speaking concerning the distance of
time between them would be strictly true.   Let me assume
that Christ was transfigured this year at the same distance
of time from the day of Pentecost, at which he ascended

into heaven the next.   The day of Pentecost this year fell upon June 6. and the day analogous to ascension-day before that was May 27.   A. D. 29. May 27. according to the Tables was Friday, but, according to my computation, was Sunday.   Moreover, the day of Pentecost itself the next year fell upon May 26. and May 26. on the first day of the week.

The scene of the Transfiguration is described by the Evangelists simply as a high mountain—the other particular, κατ᾽ ἰδίαν, which might be understood to belong to the same description, being rather to be understood of the taking the Apostles apart.   Yet I can discover no good reason for questioning the ancient ecclesiastical tradition, which supposes it to have been Mount Tabor—called by Josephus, τὸ Ἰταβύριον ὄρος[h], situated in Lower Galilee, between the great plain of Galilee, and Scythopolis, the ancient Bethshan—on what was formerly the confines of the tribes of Issachar, and Napthali—accessible only on its northern side, rising to an altitude of thirty stades, and consisting, at its summit, of a level and grassy surface, the circumference of which was almost four Roman miles.   Jerome also describes it as[i] Mira rotunditate sublimis, distans a Diocæsarea (the Sepphoris of Josephus) decem millibus, contra orientalem plagam.   Nor is it any great objection that Jesus was previously in the vicinity of Cæsarea Philippi; for a week's interval would be more than sufficient in order to travel thence to Mount Tabor.   And that the Transfiguration happened somewhere in Galilee may be presumptively conjectured from the mention of Galilee, Matt. xvii. 22. Mark ix. 30—so soon afterwards.   Nor is it improbable that either this mountain, or the mountain of Beatitudes, near to Capernaum, was the very mountain on which our Lord was manifested in Galilee[k], after his resurrection; especially if, according to Adamnanus[l], its distance from the lake of Gennesaret is to be computed at merely three miles.

[h] Ant. v. v. 3. xiv. vi. 3. B. iv. i. 8. Vita. 37.   [i] Oper. ii. De Situ et Nominibus.   [k] Matt. xxviii. 16.   [l] Rel. Palæstina. i. 333.

With regard, however, to the further question of the time, the history of our Saviour's motions hitherto has been so continuous, and the proof that, since he quitted Capernaum [m], he stayed little or no time in any particular place, is so clear and decisive, that I am persuaded whatsoever has been recorded, from that time to this, might all be comprehended in the few first weeks after the third Passover. The Transfiguration, both in itself, as regarded the material fact, and in its secret meaning, as regarded what was probably its moral end and purpose, must be considered on every account one of the most memorable transactions in our Saviour's life; which not only have the three first Evangelists recorded, accordingly, with proportionate distinctness, and and the fourth [n], if I mistake not, in no obscure terms alluded to [*], but to arrive at which, as it appears to me, was the specific object of this part of their accounts from the first. The minuteness with which they relate the particulars of the intermediate events, from the beginning of the year, down to the time of this single transaction, compared with the brevity of their narratives for many months afterwards, is implicitly an argument that they were desirous to arrive regularly at this: but, having done so, had nothing of equal interest or importance to dwell upon, for some time after. I place it, therefore, between the third feast of the Passover, and the third feast of Pentecost; concerning both which we have the clearest proof that our Lord attended neither of them in Jerusalem. The circumstances of the narrative, directly afterwards, shew that the feast of Pentecost was either still to come, or already past; the former of which suppositions is just as probable as the latter. It might have happened, therefore, ten days before it, on the day which we have conjectured, May 27.

The first event of the ensuing day was the conversation,

---

[*] Ποῦ δὲ ἐθεάσαντο τὴν δόξαν; Ἴσως μέν τινες ὑπολήψονται ὅτι ἐν τῷ ὄρει τῷ Θαβώρ. Theophyl. in Johann. 568. Οἷς ἔδειξε τὴν δόξαν ἐν τῷ Θαβώρ. Id. in Matt. 164.

[m] Matt. xv. 21. Mark vii. 24.   [n] John i. 14.

between our Lord and the three Apostles, as they came down from the mountain, respecting the traditionary doctrine that Elijah should personally reappear before the advent of the expected Christ°——a topic evidently suggested by the presence of Elijah along with Moses, in the recent colloquy which they had witnessed. The next, and directly after, was the cure of the demoniac ᴾ, which the rest of the Apostles, that is, the NINE who had not been with our Lord on the mountain, were unable to effect——though this might be the only instance of any such failure, since the original communication of miraculous power, adequate to effects like these——and a failure even in this instance perhaps to be ascribed to the absence either of our Lord himself, or of their companions——and the diffidence, or want of faith, which might thence have been occasioned in the rest *.

* Or, what is equally possible, it is simply to be ascribed to the nature of the cure itself, and to the peculiar obstinacy of the spirit with whom these Apostles had to contend. For there is no reason why evil spirits, though they durst not but yield obedience to the commands of Christ himself, might not refuse submission, especially in his absence, to the commands of men, though empowered and assisted by him. I say this is at least a conceivable case; for it is just as possible that wicked spirits, under certain circumstances, should refuse obedience to the will of God, as that wicked men should. It excited the surprize of the Seventy, that *even the spirits were subject to them;* though they acted by an undoubted divine commission, in their ejection—— and the reluctance with which the demon, in the present instance, submitted even to the commands of our Lord himself, by evacuating the body of which he had taken possession, appears from the violence of his effects on the subject, just before the dispossession, and at the time of it. It is needless to observe that this miracle, and that upon the demoniacs at Gadara, are the most singular and striking of their kind; and it is probable they were both left on record expressly to shew that the fiercest or most refractory of evil spirits were alike subject to the control, and,

° Matt. xvii. 10—13. Mark ix. 9—13. Luke ix. 37. ᴾ Matt. xvii. 14—18. Mark ix. 14—27. Luke ix. 37—42.

The allusion to the mountain[q], as close at hand, and also the critical circumstance, that the multitude, when they saw our Lord, were amazed and astonished[r], and running up to him began to salute him—a very lively description of the effect produced by his appearance, and implying either that it was sudden and instantaneous, or that there was something, in his person and aspect, more than usually divine and resplendent, (the still visible emanation of that heavenly glory and transcendent majesty with which they had lately been illuminated,) or both—are proofs of direct continuity in the order of all these events. After the miracle, as we may collect from Matt. xvii. 19—21. compared with Mark ix. 28. 29. he must have retired to some private house, where the nine Apostles, apart from the people, enquired of him why they had been unable to perform the miracle, having, probably, performed many like it before. The answer shews that there was something peculiar in this case, such as Origen[s] observes to have happened, under the same circumstances, in his own time also: Δυσίατόν ἐστι τὸ νόσημα τοῦτο, ὡς καὶ τοὺς ἔχοντας χάριν θεραπεύειν δαιμονῶντας ὅτε μὲν ἀπαυδᾶν πρὸς τοῦτο, ὅτε δὲ, μετὰ νηστειῶν καὶ προσευχῶν, καὶ πλειόνων καμάτων, ἐπιτυγχάνειν. The criterion, therefore, of such obstinate cases of possession was the exhibition of those symptoms externally, which might be produced naturally by epilepsy, but, in these instances, were due to demoniacal agency. In answer, then, to this enquiry, the similitude of the grain of mustard seed, for the efficacy of the miracle-working faith, though for the first time, might very pertinently be found on record.

however little inclined to acknowledge any other superiors, alike implicitly submissive to the will, of Christ. Our Lord's final address to this spirit, as reported by St. Mark, is such as we never find ascribed to him elsewhere—and might have been purposely intended to mark the contrast between himself and his disciples. Τὸ πνεῦμα τὸ ἄλαλον καὶ κωφὸν, ἘΓΩ σοι ἐπιτάσσω· Ἔξελθε ἐξ αὐτοῦ, καὶ μηκέτι εἰσέλθῃς εἰς αὐτόν.

---

q Matt. xvii. 20.   r Mark ix. 15.   s Comm. i. 312.

Posterior to these transactions we meet with no more particular details—yet, I think, there is enough to imply a continued residence in Galilee, before the return to Capernaum preparatory to the next feast of Tabernacles ; first, because, John vii. 1. it is said, After these things (that is, the events in the synagogue at Capernaum) Jesus walked in Galilee ; for he would not walk in Judæa. St. John, then, was aware that a considerable portion of our Saviour's time, during the first six months of this year, had been passed in Galilee, and, consequently, was so from this time forward to the feast of Tabernacles : for, hitherto, there is no proof that he had *walked* (that is, lived and resided) in that country at all ; unless his visiting the regions of Tyre and Sidon—his journeying to and fro in the dominions of Philip—his crossing or recrossing the lake, without landing, or continuing any length of time, upon the Galilean coast—are to be considered such.

Secondly, because, Matt. xvii. 22. for some time at least *after* the preceding events, but *before* the return to Capernaum, xvii. 24. they were *conversant*, that is, living and residing, in Galilee—and, Mark ix. 30. when they departed from the vicinity of Tabor, it was to *journey along* through Galilee. The same passage shews that, all this time, Jesus was still desirous of privacy—οὐκ ἤθελεν ἵνα τις γνῷ—and, as it is implied in each of the accounts, the only memorable particular, which transpired throughout it, (and that, apparently, at the *beginning*, rather than the *end*, of the progress,) was the repetition[t] of the same particular prediction, concerning his death and resurrection, which had been once delivered before. If, then, the detail is resumed, it is so only with the account of the last part of the journey—the account of the return to Capernaum[u]—the particulars of all which, down to Matt. xviii. 35. Mark ix. 50. and Luke ix. 46—50. I shall have occasion to consider elsewhere. Nor shall I observe, for the present, on any part of it, except what relates to the demand of the tri-

* Matt. xvii. 22. 23. Mark ix. 31. 32. Luke x. 43—45.   * Matt. xvii. 24. Mark ix. 33.

bute—or the incident recorded Matt. xvii. 24. to the end; for this incident also, rightly estimated, will be found to support the same conclusion, that our Lord had been absent from Capernaum, ever since the last Passover, and returned to it a little before the next feast of Tabernacles.

That Judæa, from A. U. 691. B. C. 63. and thenceforward down to A. U. 819. A. D. 66. became and continued tributary to the Roman government seems to be clearly implied by the passages quoted in the margin [v]: and that this tribute was paid in the shape of a poll-tax is not incredible. That it was not, however, the tribute intended in the present instance appears from the drift of the reasoning addressed to Peter. Our Lord argues that the acknowledged exemption of the children, or the near relations, of kings, from all such tributes or services as they impose upon strangers, would be a just ground of exception—in his own particular instance—from the demand in question. This argument supposes, then, that he himself stood in the relation of son to him, for the benefit of whose service the tax was understood to be levied—a supposition, which would manifestly be true, if the tax was levied for the service of the temple, and our Saviour himself stood in the relation of Son to the God of Israel. And, as proceeding upon the assumption of such a relation, we may observe by the way, the reasoning itself is a strong and convincing testimony to the proper sonship, and, in the capacity of son, to the proper relationship, of Jesus Christ—which those, who deny this relation, will not easily evade or impugn.

There can be little doubt, therefore, that the tribute in question was the tribute required from every male Israelite, above the age of twenty—once in the year—and to be paid into the corban, or treasury of God, for the current expenses of the Temple-service [w]. The original appointment of this tribute is thus recorded by Josephus: Τὸ πλῆθος

[v] Ant. Jud. xiv. iv. 4. 5. Ib. vii. 1. B. i. vii. 6. Ib. viii. 8. Ant. xiv. xi. 2. B. i. xi. 2. Tac. Ann. ii. 42. Matt. xxii. 15—22. Philo De Legatione. 1020. 1021. Ant. Jud. xviii. vi. 3. B. ii. xvi. 4. 482.   [w] Exod. xxx. 13—16. 2 Chron. xxiv. 9. Nehem. x. 32.

ἀθροίσας πάλιν εἰσφορὰν αὐτὸ προσέταξεν εἰσφέρειν, σίκλου τὸ ἥμισυ καθ' ἕκαστον· ὁ δὲ σίκλος, νόμισμα Ἑβραίων ὤν, Ἀττικὰς δέχεται δραχμὰς τέσσαρας [x]. Hieronymus—in Ezechielem [y]: Siclus—id est stater—habet drachmas quatuor.

The continuance of the same tribute ever after—its re-cognition by the Jews of the Dispersion as well as of the mother-country—the peculiar denomination of τὸ δίδραχμον, or τὰ δίδραχμα, by which it was known—its collection into banks or exchequers in every city—especially among Gen-tile communities—in order to be taken up at proper times, and by proper persons, to Jerusalem—are facts abundantly confirmed by Philo, Josephus, and others [z]. Τὸ δίδραχμον τῷ Θεῷ καταβάλλειν—ὃ ἑκάστοις πάτριον. The same tax, so paid before to the sacred treasury, the Jews were com-manded by Vespasian to contribute to the rebuilding of the Capitol at Rome—and the imposition continued to the time of Pliny, where he speaks of the balsam-tree : Servit nunc hæc, et tributa pendit, cum sua gente [a].

It is asserted, indeed, by the Rabbinical writers, that the tax for the temple was ordinarily due, and ordinarily to be collected, at the Passover [b]; but it would be much more probable, *a priori*, that it would be really due, and really required to be paid, at a time to which the payment of every other legal tribute, whether in money, or in kind, appears to have been appropriated—that of the feast of Taber-nacles. In this case the collectors of it at Capernaum, by demanding it now, would be making provision for an ap-proaching feast of that description—and, therefore, the re-turn of our Lord to Capernaum, after which they immediately demanded it, could not have been long before the same time.

I do not know that the authority of the Rabbins is of much weight with regard to any of the customs in our Sa-

---

[x] Ant. iii. viii. 2.   [y] Oper. iii. 722.   [z] Ant. Jud. xviii. iii. 5. ix. 1. Vide also xiv. vii. 2. x. 8. xvi. ii. 3—5. vi. 2—7. B. v. v. 1. vi. vi. 2. Philo De Legatione. 1014. 23—33. 35. 36. Philo Quis Rer. Div. Hæres. 506. De Monarchia. ii. 822. Ciceron. Orat. Pro Flacco. 28.   [a] Jos. B. Jud. vii. vi. 6. Dio. lxvi. 7. Plin. H. N. xii. 25.   [b] Mishna. ii. 176. 1. &c.

viour's day—but, even upon their own shewing, the tribute of the half-shekel might be, and was in fact, paid, at each of the three great feasts [c]. Ter in anno curant de conclavi; in spatio semestri (fifteen days) ante Pascha—in spatio semestri ante Pentecosten—et in spatio semestri ante Scenopegiam [d]: upon which the Commentary of Maimonides is to the following effect : Tempore festi Paschatis publicabatur adducendam oblationem primam de loco propinquiori ; et illi, qui remotiores erant, adducerent tempore festi Pentecostis ; et illi, qui remotissimi erant, adducerent tempore festi Tabernaculorum. So also Bartenoras. It is plain too from 197 §. 5. that all this tax was never received the year when it might become due ; and some of the thirteen chests, into which it was appointed to be received, were expressly reserved for arrears, under the name of *sicli veteres.*

The course of events, from this period forward, is to be collected from John vii. 2. and will be found to be regularly carried onwards by him as far as xi. 54 : where, in like manner, it will be perceived to be again taken up by Luke ix. 51 : by whom, also, it will be carried forward to xviii. 15 ; where his account will again be finally rejoined by Matt. xix. 13. and Mark x. 13. and, after an interval of almost six months, all will proceed in conjunction (St. John likewise from xi. 55. in its proper place) to the close of the Gospel history. The proof of these positions would evidently be necessary to the completion of our present undertaking; but, as it would anticipate what will come more conveniently hereafter, I cannot now enter upon it. I shall conclude, therefore, this review of our Saviour's ministry, so far as it has yet proceeded, with a general summary of its results.

We have brought down the history of the ministry in Galilee, through a period of nearly two years and six months—to the arrival of the third feast of Tabernacles; and the whole of this period we have seen to be so fully

[c] Exod. xxiii. 15. 17. xxxiv. 23. Deut. xvi. 16. 17.　　　[d] Mishna. ii. 184. 3.

taken up, that we may conclude we possess, in its history, a continuous outline, if not a particular detail, of the course and succession of events. During the first year there was no proof of any chasm in this continuity, except for the interval between the first feast of Tabernacles, and the second feast of the Passover; which, yet, we had apparently good reason to believe was filled up either by a studied privacy, such as the occasion required, or by a stationary abode in Capernaum. During the second year there was no proof of any interruption whatever; it was full of action and employment throughout. The same observation holds good of the first two months of the third : and the remaining four, belonging to the first half of this year, were passed, as before, either in an intentional seclusion, or in a residence, of greater or less continuance, at Capernaum.

In this period upon the whole we have discovered clear evidences of *three general,* and at least *two partial,* circuits —the two last of the *general,* and each of the *partial,* within the compass of the same year, and the first of the general during the first six months of the year before it. All these were begun originally from Capernaum, and all were terminated finally at Capernaum, and all were confined to the precincts of Galilee. The ministry of our Lord, during the whole of this period, was so strictly limited to Galilee, that, excepting the single occasions when he visited Jerusalem, we have no proof that he was ever out of it: we have no proof that he once crossed the lake before the middle of his second year—nor that he visited Decapolis, Tyre, or Sidon, or journeyed in the dominions of Philip, as such, before the beginning of his third : nor even then expressly and formally for his usual purposes of teaching or preaching, but rather for the sake of privacy and concealment. In like manner we have no proof, at least from the three first Gospels, that he was ever in Peræa, until he is described as passing thither in the course of his last journey to Jerusalem—nor that he was ever in Samaria except on the two occasions, John iv. 4—early in his first year—and Luke ix. 52. late in his third : and as to the occasions when he was resident in Judæa, or visiting Jerusalem, they have been considered already by themselves.

During the first half of the third year in particular, though it is presumptively certain that, almost the whole of the time, he was constantly journeying from place to place, yet it is also certain that he was not journeying upon a circuit, or, strictly speaking, with a view to the usual functions of his ministry at all : so that we have no proof as yet of any fourth circuit within this period, similar to those which had preceded in the two former years. Different as our Lord's conduct, for thus much of the present year, may, consequently, seem in comparison of his conduct heretofore, it is not more so than in comparison with his conduct for the remainder of this year itself : a circumstance which proves indisputably that he had motives for desiring the concealment of his person, and suspending the course of his ministry, affecting this portion of its duration, but none before or after it.

These motives, it is probable, were twofold ; partly to escape from the excitement of the multitude on what had been hitherto the exclusive theatre of his personal agency— lest the accumulated effect of so many wonderful works, combined with their own ardent, but unfounded, hopes and expectations, now grown more enthusiastic than ever, should lead them to some rash act, such as openly casting off the Roman yoke, and declaring Jesus their King— partly to avoid the society of his enemies, the Scribes and Pharisees, who had long been resolved upon his death, and waited only for a favourable opportunity of effecting it. Hence it was that, for a considerable interval of time, he continued to travel in parts where he was comparatively a stranger—and possibly might not be recognized—whither also the Pharisees were not likely to follow him, or, if they did, where they would have less influence than in Galilee or in Judæa. The effect of a protracted absence might be to abate the ardour, and to diminish the expectations, of the common people, on the one hand, and to dispense with the necessity of preserving his life, from the malice and machinations of his enemies, by supernatural means, on the other. It was the least of two evils to abstain, for a time, from coming in contact with his adversaries, and exasperating their hostility to its utmost pitch, until the purposes of the divine Providence were ripe for execution, rather than to suffer those purposes to be prematurely accelerated, or to frustrate the ebullitions of sudden violence by actual recourse to miracle.   With the last six months, however, of the present year—that is, from the time when this review of his ministry previously has been brought to a close—the period was either arrived, or at hand, during which the course of external events, considered as the instrumental or secondary means, by which the same Providence designed to work in the gradual consummation of its own effects, was to be so controlled and accelerated as to terminate naturally in his death.   With the arrival of this period, then, the season of temporary precaution or concealment was past, and our Lord had no longer any measures to keep with his enemies : and it will be seen accordingly that he again appears in public, even among those whom he had hitherto seemed most to avoid, with more openness, regularity, and boldness, than he had ever assumed before.

DISSERTATION IX.

Comparison of the call of the four Disciples, (Matt. iv. 18
—22. Mark i. 16—20.) *and of the miraculous draught
of fishes*, (Luke v. 1—11.)

THE differences observable between the account of the
miraculous draught of fishes, in St. Luke, and the account
of the call of the four disciples, Andrew and Peter, James
and John, in St. Matthew, or in St. Mark, are the following; which I shall be satisfied with simply laying before
the reader—and, after that, shall leave him to decide upon
them for himself, whether the occasions, to which these accounts respectively relate, can possibly be both the same.

I. According to St. Mark, Jesus, before the call, was
walking by the shore of the sea—according to St. Luke, he
was *standing* by the lake of Gennesaret: according to the
former he was alone, or, at least, doing nothing at the time
—according to the latter there was a multitude about him,
which he himself was preparing to teach.

II. According to St. Mark, he never quitted the land—
according to St. Luke, he went on board a ship: according
to the former he continued to walk on along the shore—according to the latter, he actually put out to sea.

III. According to St. Mark, both the ships were first
seen *upon* the sea—according to St. Luke, drawn up on the
shore : according to the former, they were seen one after
the other, and in different situations, on the sea—according
to the latter, both together, and in the same situation, on
the land.

IV. According to St. Mark, Andrew and Simon were
seen first in their ship, and then James and John, in their's
—according to St. Luke, neither were seen in either—the
fishermen had left both the ships: according to St. Mark,
Andrew and Simon were seen *letting down* their net, James
and John, *preparing* to let down their's—according to St.

Luke, they were all seen washing their nets on the shore. In the one case they were all beginning to fish—in the other they had all done fishing.

V. According to St. Mark, Simon and Andrew, as the first seen, were the first called; and, as seen by themselves, were called by themselves; and then James and John—according to St. Luke, if seen at all, or called at all, they were all seen together, and all called together.

VI. According to St. Mark, the call in each case was made *from* the land—according to St. Luke, in the *midst* of the sea: according to the former, Simon and Andrew (and very probably James and John also) were called in these terms[a]—Δεῦτε ὀπίσω μου, καὶ ποιήσω ὑμᾶς γενέσθαι ἁλιεῖς ἀνθρώπων—according to the latter, if any were called, they were called in these[b]—Μὴ φοβοῦ· ἀπὸ τοῦ νῦν ἀνθρώπους ἔσῃ ζωγρῶν: according to St. Mark, they were called at twice, two of them distinctly from the other—according to St. Luke, if any were called, all were called at once, and all in the person of one.

VII. According to St. Mark, in obeying the call, Simon and Andrew forsook only their nets—James and John only their ship—according to St. Luke, they all forsook every thing—their nets—their ships—and the booty which they had taken. Nor could these representations, however different, have been otherwise. It is plain, according to St. Mark, that the disciples could have nothing more as yet to forsake, than their ships or their fishing tackle; for they were only beginning to fish, and had not made any cast. But according to St. Luke, they had just enclosed a prodigious draught.

VIII. According to St. Mark, the effect ensued in obedience to an invitation—the disciples forsook what they did forsake, because Jesus had bade them follow him—according to St. Luke, it was a voluntary act—they forsook what they did forsake, of their own accord.

I am well aware that, among these various inconsistencies,

[a] i. 17.   [b] v. 10.

there are some which the tortuous ingenuity of criticism, aided by an unscrupulous facility of supposition in the addition of circumstances not expressed, and, therefore, gratuitous, might perhaps twist, or smooth down to an agreement : but there are more which no dexterity of accommodation, nor laxity of interpretation, would be able to render otherwise than, *recta fronte,* at variance with each other : and taken all together they constitute a chain of facts which, as so many evidences of distinctness, or as what logicians would call *circumstantiæ individuantes,* must be indissoluble. Yet, in addition to these, we may add the following considerations also.

I. It is morally certain from St. Matthew and St. Mark[c], that the parties to whom they allude were just beginning to fish—and from St. Luke[d], that they had just done fishing. Moreover, the time of the transaction in St. Luke was evidently the morning[e]; and, consequently, the previous fishing had been going on in the night. It had begun, therefore, the evening before. And that evening would naturally be the time, when fishermen on the lake would ordinarily begin to fish, may be concluded not only from the reason of the thing (that they would commonly begin then, when the inhabitants of the deep are known, by experience, to be most active, and most on the alert, and, therefore, the most likely to be caught) but also from an instance in point, which is seen to have been begun in the evening—and like this to have lasted until the morning[f]. The time of the call, then, in St. Matthew or St. Mark, we may take it for granted was the evening; and the time of the miracle in St. Luke was unquestionably the morning. At this season of the year, which I have supposed to be after the feast of Pentecost, A. U. 780. that is, after May 30. the Jewish evening, which began at sunset, would begin about 8. P. M : and the Jewish morning, which began at sunrise, would begin at 4. A. M : and those, who had commenced their labours on the sea, at the first of those periods,

[c] Mark i. 16. 19.   Matt. iv. 18. 21.   [d] Luke v. 2.   [e] Ib. 5.
[f] John xxi. 1—4.

being unsuccessful, might very naturally continue them until the latter. It was a familiar practice with the people of the East to take their morning's repast at πρωΐ, or sunrise, throughout the year; and among other modes of making it, anciently as well as still, one was to repair to the water side, and breakfast on the newly-taken fish. The instance referred to from St. John is an illustration of this fact.

II. It came to pass, says St. Luke⁵, as he was standing by the side of the lake of Gennesaret, that he saw two ships, drawn up on the shore; and, having entered into one of them, *which was Simon's*, he prayed him to put back a little from the land. Now this mention of the name of Simon is clearly in allusion to iv. 38. before, and supposes him already known to the reader from that. But even the mention of his name *there* would be much too abrupt and indefinite, was there not, throughout the Gospel of St. Luke, a tacit reference to the Gospels of St. Matthew or of St. Mark. From either of those Gospels it might certainly be known who Simon was, prior even to the allusion at Luke iv. 38. and, consequently, his name might there be mentioned, as a well-known name, even without any previous allusion, or additional description, might be mentioned. It is implied, therefore, in this account that, before the transaction to which it relates, our Saviour and Simon were previously acquainted, and understood by its readers to be so.

III. The call in St. Luke was preceded by an act of teaching, which was, consequently, either the first of its kind, which had yet taken place, or not the first. If it was the first—then our Saviour had not yet begun his ministry in public; and if he had not yet begun his ministry in public, though he might now have called certain persons to be his disciples, he could not now have been surrounded by a multitude. If it was not the first, he must already have begun his ministry—and he might, consequently, have been surrounded by a multitude. But, from Acts i. 21. 22. a passage which we have had occasion to produce elsewhere[h], it must be certain that he had previously called the disciples.

IV. The anxiety of the people, on this occasion, to press upon him, is a parallel instance to Mark iii. 9. 10. iv. 1. and to other instances, which might be produced, both in the cause—their desire to hear him, or to come close to him—and in the effect—that it made it necessary he should retire on board a ship, and address them from the sea. On all these other occasions it may be observed in common, that they are decidedly later than the commencement of his ministry in general ; and, if the present instance happened after the first circuit of Galilee, it will be so far in unison with the rest. Nor, indeed, could it be otherwise, especially at the very outset of his ministry. To have attracted crowds in such numbers—to have produced this importunate eagerness to get about our Lord—or to hear him—so as to make it necessary he should retire beyond their reach, his reputation must have been spread far and wide—he must have become generally known as a prophet or teacher, or as a performer of wonderful works. Now this never could have been the case, before the intervention of one public progress over Galilee, at least.

Besides, it is utterly incredible that, when preparing to begin his ministry by teaching the word of God, he should have made choice of the lake of Capernaum, and the locality of a fisherman's boat, instead of the city, and the synagogue, itself. His preaching and teaching—even upon the first circuit—were confined to the synagogues of Galilee, as such—nor is there any proof that he taught in the open air, except towards the close of all, when he delivered the sermon from the mount. The truth, indeed, is, that he called the disciples in question, before he began to teach, that is, to enter on the work of his ministry, any where—and when he began to teach, or to enter on the work of his ministry, as such, it was in that place—the synagogue of Capernaum—and on that day—the day of the sabbath—which from his piety, and, with very few exceptions, from

[h] Vol. I. Diss. VIII. 295.

his uniform practice ever after, it might naturally be expected it would be. And as he first began to teach *there* and *then*, so the first miracle, in confirmation of his teaching, was wrought there and then.

V. The mere perusal of the narrative from v. 1—4. is sufficient to satisfy an unprejudiced reader that the instance of teaching, now recorded, was in the ordinary discharge of our Lord's ministerial functions. He was teaching as a matter of course—he was preparing to do nothing, which he had never yet done before, when the people were resorting to him—he had often taught *them*, and they had as often been taught by *him*, before they were addressed on this occasion.

VI. The manner of our Saviour's teaching was distinguished by a peculiar property, which the Evangelists designate as the teaching of one ἐν ἐξουσίᾳ: as the manner which would be assumed by one, who had a right to command, and a right to be obeyed—who was entitled to an implicit deference to his *own* word and will—who was authorized both to teach men their duty, and to expect their performance of what he taught. Now this manner was so novel and striking, that each of the Gospel historians, except St John, has distinctly noticed it—but, what is not less remarkable, has noticed it *once* for all : having specified it in a single instance they never recur to it again. That single instance, however, is also the *first* instance—the occasion, on which they do notice it, is the *first* occasion which it came within the scope of their accounts to record : and both these things, *a priori*, were very naturally to be expected. A constant identical property of our Saviour's teaching might justly be specified once for all—but, if it were to be specified once for all, that single occasion would most naturally and most fitly be the first. Now the instance of teaching on the lake is accompanied by no such characteristic remark—whence we may infer it could not have been the first—but the instance, recorded before that, in the synagogue of Capernaum, it is absolutely certain, is [i] : whence it would be a

---

[i] Luke iv. 32.

similar inference that this instance was the first. If so, the
teaching in the synagogue preceded, in point of time, the
teaching on the lake—the one is clearly the first on record
in St. Luke—and might be the first ἁπλῶς—the other is
not. But the call of the disciples preceded even that teaching in the synagogue. Much more, then, did the same call
precede this teaching on the lake.

VII. St. Peter addresses our Saviour by the title of ἐπι-
στάτης [k]—the use of which term is one of the idioms of St.
Luke. In his Gospel it occurs six times; but in no other
Gospel besides; and it occurs always as personally directed
to our Saviour—and, in every instance but the last, as addressed to him by the Apostles in the sense of Ῥαββὶ, or
Διδάσκαλος—the ordinary title which disciples, among the
Jews, every where gave to their masters. The use of the
term, then, is peculiar to the relation of master and of disciple—so that, on this principle, Peter would be a disciple
already, at the very time when he is supposed to have received his call. And, according to my distribution of the
preceding events, this was truly the case—for he had been
called four or five months before : but, on any supposition,
which should make his original call accompany the miraculous draught, there must be so far a manifest absurdity.

Nor is this all : for the same text proves that Peter was
acquainted with the *power* of our Saviour, and, however
unsuccessful they had been until then, yet, if they let down
the net at his command, that they could not fail to enclose
a draught. It is clearly implied, therefore, that he knew
our Saviour to be capable of performing miracles, and, consequently, that he had seen him perform miracles before.
On our principles this, also, would necessarily be the case—
for, besides the miracles which he must have witnessed in
Capernaum [l], (one of them wrought upon his own wife's
mother,) *before* the commencement of the circuit, he must
have had ocular testimony of a vast number more, performed upon the circuit itself [m]. But, upon any other sup-

[k] v. 5.   [l] Luke iv. 33—41.   [m] Matt. iv. 23.

position, how could the same thing have been the case? If the disciples had never yet received a call, could they yet have seen a miracle? Would not the miracle, which now ensued, and which had not yet been performed, have been the very first miracle on record any where, except in St. John? Ever after *this* miracle they might well have had an entire confidence in the supernatural power of Jesus; but how could they have had it before?

It is true, as we perceive from the result, that St. Peter appears surprized even at his own success. But this does not prove that he expected *no* miracle—but only that he did not expect *such* a miracle: the success which he experienced exceeded his most sanguine hopes. Hence his first, and his most natural, impression is that of awe; as in the presence of a superior Being. The admiration of the effect is lost in the contemplation of the cause—and he falls down at the feet of Jesus, as a sinful man would prostrate himself before his all-pure and almighty Creator.

VIII. If the miraculous draught was really a part of the transaction of the call, there is no reason to be conceived or assigned for its omission. A miracle like this—the first instance of any miracle in the three original Gospels—a miracle expressly wrought for the conviction of the four first and chief of the Apostles—was surely, on every account, deserving of a distinct notice. Besides, without the history of the miracle, the history of the call would have been not only incomplete, but unintelligible. The call, upon this principle, must have arisen out of the miracle, and the miracle must have introduced the call—the call must have applied the miracle, and the miracle have justified the call. Neither, then, would have been perfect without the other—nor could the end proposed by the history of the one have been attained except in conjunction with the history of the other.

IX. The foundation of the whole mistake, with respect to the presumed Trajection in St. Luke, is the assumption that the account of the miraculous draught is an account of the call of the four parties who witnessed it—an assumption altogether precarious. For, that the words addressed to Peter convey no call, must be self-evident—and, that none is implied in the material fact itself, appears from this consideration—that the very same kind of miracle—on the very same sea of Galilee—and in behalf of most, if not of all, of the very same persons—was again performed after the resurrection [n]. If, therefore, it implied a call *now*, it must have implied a call *then;* that is, the Apostles could not have been called until after the resurrection.

The truth is this. The miracle was a symbolical act, and contained a latent prophecy: the import of the symbol being the future success of these same parties, as Apostles, who had had such success, as fishermen. It illustrated, therefore, in respect to their future character and employment, certain truths—all adumbrated by something correspondent at present—the weakness of the instrumental agency—the efficiency of the accompanying power—each made distinctly visible in the grandeur, and, consequently, the disparity, of the result. They had been, as fishermen, the instruments of Christ in letting down the net and enclosing the fish; and they should be, as Apostles, his instruments also in propagating the Gospel, and catching mankind. In the former capacity, as left to themselves, they had been able to do nothing—as assisted by him, they had made a prodigious capture: as the emissaries of the Gospel, unaccompanied by Christ, they would be able to effect still less—as endowed and assisted by him, they should evangelize the world. It was faith in the divine cooperation which had led to their success now; it would be faith in the same cooperation which should lead to their still more splendid success hereafter.

It may be said, however, that a symbolical miracle, containing such a moral end as this, might very fitly have preceded or accompanied an original call. But this original call, as we shall see elsewhere, was not a call to become Apostles, but merely to become disciples; and those, who had been called in the latter capacity, were yet not ordained

[n] John xxi. 1—4.

in the former, until at least a year afterwards. A transaction, therefore, like the present, which, as concerned disciples, was not so much a call, as the ratification of a call, and as concerned Apostles, was not so much an ordination, as an intimation of an ordination, comes in most significantly and most appositely, where St. Luke has placed it, *after* the one, and *before* the other.

The true light, then, in which we ought to regard it, is that of something which bears an equal relation to the situation of the four parties, both as still disciples, and as sometime to become Apostles. It is not a call for the first time addressed to them, but the confirmation of a call already received : it is not an appointment to the office of an Apostle, but an implicit indication of such an appointment ere long. The language of our Lord, in St. Luke, we saw was not to be reconciled to his language, in St. Matthew : the latter did strictly convey a call, the former no such thing. Yet each declaration, under the circumstances of its own account, is so natural and proper, that in the estimation of any candid judge this alone would be enough to vouch for the reality of either, and yet its distinctness from the other. When Jesus saw Peter and Andrew, in St. Matthew or St. Mark, they were only beginning to fish, and had yet enclosed nothing ; he calls them, therefore, as he could call them, solely in allusion to their occupation—Come after me, and I will make you fishers of men. When he speaks to Peter, in St. Luke, he had just made a wonderful draught; he addresses him, therefore, in allusion to his recent success—Henceforth, thou shalt be catching men.

There would still be so much affinity between the final end of the present transaction, and the ultimate design of the original call, that St. Luke, who proposed to relate the one, might very well be induced to omit the other—especially as two of the Evangelists had recorded that, but both had passed over this. We may now perceive also the distinct force and meaning of that additional circumstance, in his account, that the four disciples, having brought their ships to land, *forsook all*, and followed Jesus. This was

A a 2

not said before—and the reason is that their call was either not fully complete, or not fully comprehended, until now. It is not surprising that, though called as disciples by our Lord himself—yet, as mere disciples, placed only on a footing of equality with many others, who had attached themselves to him of their own accord—they should not all at once have considered it necessary—especially in the first year of our Saviour's ministry—and during the times when they were stationary at Capernaum—to give up their usual occupations, or to bid adieu to every concern but the business of attending on him.   This was what multitudes never did, who yet were his disciples during the whole course of his ministry; and this was what the Apostles, had they always continued in the simple estate of disciples, nowise distinguished from the rest, never could have been expected to do.   Henceforth, however, they devoted themselves wholly to Jesus—they began to be convinced that their original call had some greater, and more exclusive, end in view—and to act upon that conviction.   Now, then, it might first be said, Lo! we have forsaken all things, and followed thee; what, therefore, shall be our's?   And, among the other moral uses of the present narrative, this may reasonably be considered one—to do that justice to the faith and the self-denial of Christian Apostles, which their own modesty had not allowed them to do for themselves—by shewing under what peculiar circumstances of temptation to the contrary—viz. after a rich and valuable capture—they were induced to give up every thing, for the sake of attaching themselves to Jesus.

I think, then, it must now be admitted that, beyond these moral uses, (the proper exemplification of which was still future,) the history of the miraculous draught has nothing in common with the history of the call of Simon and Andrew, James and John : and if so, that there is no proof of a Trajection in this part of St. Luke.   Nor is this conclusion of slight importance.   The disproof of a transposition in the present instance ought to facilitate the eviction of the same conclusion in other instances ; for there is not, perhaps, a single instance of a supposed irregularity which has been more confidently assumed than this; with what reason I leave the reader to judge. But if this is no such thing—others, also, however confidently they may have been assumed, which yet, *a priori*, are not more presumptively so than this, may turn out upon examination to be quite the reverse.

DISSERTATION X.

On the call of Levi, and the entertainment which followed the call: or Mark ii. 13—22. Luke v. 27—39. *compared with* Matt. ix. 9—17.

THE call of Matthew the Publican, who is designated by the name of Levi also, must be assigned to the first year, and to the last six months of the first year, of our Saviour's ministry; and, even as so assigned, took place probably nearer to the end, than to the beginning, of that time. It would not, however, follow from this fact that he was not yet a disciple, by which I understand a simple believer in Christ—much less that he was not yet even acquainted with our Lord—but merely that he had not received any personal call—he had not given up his usual occupations, whatsoever they were, to attach himself to Christ.

The readiness with which he obeys the call is in fact a proof that he was predisposed for its reception, and, consequently, was a disciple of our Lord already in the same sense, and to the same effect, as many others, both before and after the present time, who yet never experienced a personal invitation from our Lord himself. The calls of any among the Apostles, as ascribed to our Saviour, and left on record, were not calls to become disciples in the strictest sense of that term—such as could have been applicable to none except to persons before unacquainted with himself—but a personal compliment to the parties in question, such as might be paid, for special reasons, even to those who were believers previously. Nor is Matt. viii. 22. or Luke ix. 59. any difficulty; unless it could be shewn that these were calls addressed to persons not yet disciples, or even not yet ordained Apostles—all of whom had certainly been appointed to their office, long before the time of either of these incidents, and especially of the last. On this account, more particularly, I am persuaded that every instance of a personal call, as addressed to those who were first disciples, and afterwards became Apostles, has been carefully placed on record—and, consequently, that such instances are five in number, four of the disciples called at the beginning of the year, and this of St. Matthew at its end. In all these cases it is the effect, which ensued upon the call, not the mere call itself, that we are bound chiefly to attend to. St. Matthew had not yet renounced his secular occupation—he was sitting at the Publican's booth, or the receipt of custom, when he was accosted by Christ: he rose up, in obedience to the invitation—and, from that time forward, forsook every thing to follow him.

The call of Matthew, considered as the same person with Levi, is related by each of the three first Evangelists—though by St. Matthew it is related out of its place. In each of them, also, there follows, upon the account of the call, an account of an entertainment, which St. Mark and St. Luke distinctly ascribe to Levi, and in direct connection with his previous call; but which St. Matthew does not less clearly refer to the time of the return from Gadara, and just before the application of Jairus, followed by the raising of his daughter. As both this application, and the subsequent miracle, are related in their proper place by St. Mark and by St. Luke also, and that at a part of their narrative which comes much later than the present—it follows that, if this entertainment is the same in each of these instances, they must have admitted an Anticipation by giving an account of it here. But, as I cannot acquiesce in this conclusion, it becomes incumbent upon me to shew that the occasions themselves were, in all probability, distinct.

I. It is clearly implied in St. Mark and St. Luke[a], that the entertainment which they record was given in the house of Levi: but it is by no means certain that the entertainment, recorded by St. Matthew, took place in the same. Matthew ix. 10. which is all the allusion to the house in question, supplied by his account, alludes to the house where our Saviour was accustomed to reside in Capernaum:

[a] Luke v. 29. Mark ii. 15.

A a 4

it is manifestly the same house, which is implied or mentioned in many other passages[b], after a similar manner—the house of his ordinary residence as such. The very use of the article, in speaking of it so repeatedly ἁπλῶς, demonstrates the same conclusion; for the article would not be thus used except of some well known and definite house; nor could any house be such except the stated place of his abode. Now, unless this house had been Levi's or Matthew's from the first, the entertainment, Matt. ix. 10. given in this house, could not have been given in the house of Levi. But, if it was not given in the house of Levi, it could not be the same with the entertainment of Levi, which was certainly given in the house of Levi. And that this house was not the house of Levi from the first may be collected from Mark ii. 1. and Matt. ix. 2. 9. which shew that our Lord was in the habit of using or frequenting this house before even the call of Levi himself. The truth is that, if it was the house of any disciple, it was that of Simon or Andrew, not of Levi or Matthew[c].

II. The entertainment given by Levi, as recorded by St. Mark and St. Luke, not only followed after his call, but, it is plainly intended to be understood, was meant as an acknowledgment of his call. But the entertainment in St. Matthew was at least six months later than the call; and even subsequently to the call, the mere call to become a disciple had been succeeded by a much greater dignity—the ordination to the rank of an Apostle. What would be more natural than that a mark of respect or gratitude, designed in acknowledgment of the call, should have ensued immediately upon the call—what more unnatural, and more improbable, than that the call should have taken place six months before, and the entertainment, which commemorated it, should have taken place six months after? Nothing but the most special reasons could have produced this anomaly, or accounted for the unnatural interval, under such circumstances, between the cause and its natural effect: and the

---

[b] Mark ii. 1. iii. 19. 31. Matt. ix. 2. 28. xii. 46. xiii. 1. 36. xvii. 25.
[c] Matt. viii. 14. Mark i. 29. Luke iv. 38.

existence of any such reasons would be the strongest of arguments for keeping the two things as distinct in the account, as they were in themselves—for relating the call in one place, and the entertainment, which arose out of the call, in another.

III. It would be in vain to deny the truth of the assumption, on which this reasoning is founded, that the entertainment of Levi was intimately connected with the call of Levi; and, therefore, that the time and occasion of the former were, necessarily, the time and occasion of the latter. The accounts of both the Evangelists place this assumption beyond a question. But, even though the entertainment had been entirely independent of the call, still this would have been no inducement purposely to antedate the account of the former, in order to join it to the account of the latter—but quite the contrary—for it would have been to establish a connection between them which really did not exist, nor ever was supposed to exist. Nor can it be said that the Evangelists have agreed to blend both the accounts in one, with a view to preserve unbroken the history of the same person : because both the incidents had some reference to Levi. The truth is that the history of the entertainment has nothing at all to do with the history of Levi as such. It is given purely and solely on its own account, and from its connection with the history of our Lord.

The entertainment was rendered memorable by two circumstances which transpired at it—the exception, for the first time taken, against the condescension of Christ in eating with publicans and sinners—and the question, for the first time put, concerning a breach of the law of tradition, apparently sanctioned by his example, which breach related to fastings. Both these exceptions were such, as in the nature of things could have transpired only at some feast, or when our Saviour, in some house or other, was sitting at meat : but at what feast it might be, or in what house he might be sitting at meat, would be perfectly indifferent, and purely accidental.

The course of events, however, from this time forward

(which is the close of our Lord's first year) before the return
from Gadara (which coincided with the middle of his second)
will furnish a case in point to shew that such exceptions,
and on such grounds, had already begun to be taken against
our Saviour, and to be matter of public notoriety : which
case, if the account given of the feast of Levi is regular
where it stands, even the Gospel of St. Luke will prove to
be critically apposite and just—but on no other principle
whatever.   In the history of his reflections, as they ensued
upon the message of John, and the departure of his messengers, ἰδοὺ ἄνθρωπος φάγος καὶ οἰνοπότης[d], can be understood of
nothing but the supposed contempt of the law of fastings—
and, τελωνῶν φίλος καὶ ἁμαρτωλῶν, of nothing but his alleged
promiscuous intercourse with persons of that description.
Each of these, if Luke v. 30. and 33. had really preceded,
would be explained at once—but if not, would be little better than unintelligible.

IV. The entertainment, which was given by Levi, is called
δοχὴ μεγάλη[e]—a description which can scarcely imply less
than the principal meal of the day.   Now this meal, universally among the ancients, and at this period of ancient
history more especially, was the last meal in the day, that
is, the meal of supper.   If so, the feast given by Levi was
a supper ; and, consequently, the feast intended at Matt.
ix. 10. it it was the same with that, was a supper also.
The application, then, of Jairus made *at* this feast was
made *at* a supper—his daughter, therefore, was raised—the
issue of blood was staunched—the blind men were restored
to sight—the demoniac was dispossessed—all in the night-
time as such—which is a tissue of absurdities from first to
last.

Besides this, I have shewn elsewhere[f] that the return from
Gadara, Matt. ix. 1. just before the feast, took place early
in the morning—and certainly not at night—the feast in
St. Matthew, then, might be the usual morning's meal, but
neither the noonday's meal, nor, much less, a supper.
But if it was the morning's meal, it could not be the feast

[d] vii. 34.   [e] Luke v. 29.   [f] Vol. ii. Diss. viii. 305—310.

of Levi—for that feast was a *great feast*—but the morning's repast was the simplest and lightest of all in the day,
and, therefore, not a great feast.   Besides which, the idea
of a great feast conceived, prepared for, and executed, between the short interval of landing on the beach at Capernaum, and receiving the application of Jairus, as the feast of
Levi, in this case, must have been, is little better than the
idea of an impossibility.   That there was no great interval
between the return from Gadara, and the arrival of Jairus,
may be concluded from this consideration only—that two
of the Evangelists, St. Mark and St. Luke, connect these
facts so closely together that they have been thought even
to contradict St. Matthew—as though Jairus had met our
Saviour upon the shore of the lake, and he had not time
actually to go to his house.   Nor can it be said that Levi
was, perhaps, aware of the intended return from Gadara,
and made his preparations, accordingly, before the departure thither.   If Levi was Matthew, Matthew, also, must
have gone to Gadara—and, as I have shewn elsewhere,
both the visit to Gadara, and the return from thence, were
equally unexpected events ; which no one but our Saviour
himself could have foreseen, or been prepared for, at the
time.

V. Upon a certain occasion[e], where the context fixes the
import of the declaration to the sacrifice of temporal possessions, Simon Peter in his own name—and in the name of
the rest of the Apostles—says to our Lord, Lo ! we have
forsaken, *or* renounced, all things—and followed thee.   The
answer of Jesus, recognizing the fact of the sacrifice, and
promising a corresponding reward, establishes the truth of
the declaration.   From the time, then, when the Apostles
became stated followers of our Saviour, they must have
given up all that they had, or might have—they must have
bound themselves to a voluntary poverty—they must have
bidden adieu to their worldly possessions, and worldly occupations, by which they had hitherto supported themselves, and by which they might, otherwise, have supported

[e] Matt. xix. 27.

themselves still, on purpose to attend on Christ. Now it is surely inconsistent with this fact, and at variance also with the plain meaning of the Evangelist's assertion—Luke v. 28—that Matthew, who had forsaken ἅπαντα, in obedience to the call of Jesus, and thenceforward devoted himself to his Master's service, should yet, six months or more afterwards, have retained the means of giving him a *great* entertainment. *One* such entertainment, immediately *after* his call, and in gratitude *for* his call, it is very possible he might have given; but many such entertainments, and however long afterwards, if he had once forsaken all things, he never could have given—nor ever have been expected to give.

VI. The motive, in fact, of Levi's feast, if it was really such as we suppose, is so natural and becoming as almost of itself to establish the point in dispute—in which case the modesty of St. Matthew, who was Levi himself, might induce him to suppress the account of the feast, and, consequently, of what transpired at it, where both were too intimately connected with his own personal history. At another opportunity, however, if the same things happened again, and no longer possessed this relation to himself, he would still be free to mention them. But with St. Mark and St. Luke the state of the case would be just the reverse: they could have no such inducement to suppress the account of the feast, and of its incidents, at their first occurrence—yet, having recorded them in their proper place before, they might justly be excused if they omitted to record them again. There is no good reason, but this, to be assigned why *two* independent authorities should each have agreed to give an arbitrary position to a matter of fact, which would have come equally well in its own place—much less why, in so doing, they should set themselves, apparently, in opposition to a third and a prior authority, whose order was perfectly correct. A later Evangelist might rectify the transpositions of an earlier; but it is absurd to suppose he would knowingly disturb his regular accounts. St. Mark and St. Luke are regular in their order every where else—why, then, should it be presumed that they were intentionally irregular here? Every body must see that, by omitting the account of the sitting at meat *after* the return from Gadara, but *before* the application of Jairus, they have exposed themselves, *primâ facie*, to the suspicion of an inconsistency with St. Matthew. It is not to be imagined that they would have incurred this risk for any reason, but one so natural as this—viz. that the intermediate particulars, however instructive, necessary, or curious, had all been actually anticipated already. For it is a rule with them both—and especially with St. Luke—to record nothing of the same kind twice.

VII. If the circumstances of the two accounts be compared together, it will appear that neither the questions, which are seen to have been put, nor the answers, supposed to have been returned, on each occasion, were identical: and, therefore, that the occasions themselves may still have been distinct.

I. St. Matthew's account of the circumstances of the first question is this; It came to pass, as he was sitting at meat in the house, that many publicans and sinners *came* and sate down, along with Jesus and his disciples—St. Luke's is this; And Levi made a great entertainment for him in his own house; and there was a great multitude of publicans, and of others, who were sitting at meat along with them. The former of these notices describes an *ordinary*— the second, an *extraordinary*—occasion of the kind in question. The parties, who were guests along with Jesus and with his disciples, on the one, came of their own accord; on the other, came because they had been invited. And this might well be. Into our Lord's *usual* place of abode even publicans and sinners might reasonably be encouraged to enter; into a strange house they would have access only by permission of the owner. Their presence in the former instance was doubtless due to the desire of hearing Jesus; but their presence in the latter was much more probably the effect of their acquaintance with Levi, who himself was one of their body.

II. At Matt. ix. 14. the disciples of John were present, and put the question, there recorded, *themselves*—at Mark ii. 18. Luke v. 30. 33. it does not appear that the disciples of John were even present ; but it plainly appears that, whether present or not, they did not put the question themselves ; it was put by others concerning them. And this is a circumstance of distinction which can never be got over, and ought to be decisive of the question.

III. With regard to both the questions and the answers in each instance, St. Mark and St. Luke, who undoubtedly relate the same occurrence, agree more exactly with each other, than either of them with St. Matthew. But if they had each been relating the same things, this was not, *a priori*, to be expected—all should have agreed alike, or all should have differed alike.

For example—in the answer to the first question, the first part of ix. 13. which occurs in St. Matthew's account, does not occur in their's. Nor is it any objection that the same text is cited Matt. xii. 7. but wanting in the parallel places of Mark ii. 27. 28. and Luke vi. 4. 5 : for this second instance of its omission would not be a case in point. This text would be the only omission in the present instance— whereas there are other omissions also in the second : it would have been purposely excepted, and by itself, in the one—only in common with more matter, in the other.

Should it be further objected that Luke v. 30. is not so close to Mark ii. 16, as Mark ii. 16. is to Matt. ix. 11. (the former as addressed to the disciples about *themselves*—both the latter as addressed to the disciples about *their Master*) the answer is, both questions were put ; why the disciples were eating—and why Christ was eating—with publicans and sinners. As it is, they amount to the same thing ; for a reproach that the disciples of Jesus did so and so is a reproach that their Master did the same—nor could the particular charge in the present instance be preferred against them, without including also him. They were all alike eating in the company of such persons, and it would be indifferent of whom the question might be asked.

Again, in reporting the answer to the second enquiry at Matt. ix. 15. our Lord is described to have used the remarkable term πενθεῖν, instead of νηστεύειν, as at Mark ii. 19. and Luke v. 34. These words were not synonymous, neither in themselves—nor in the estimation of the parties who asked the question : to *fast* was not necessarily to *mourn*, especially as a mere formality, as a stated part of the ceremonial of religion, but nothing more. In the use, therefore, of such a term, with respect to his own disciples, our Lord had an occasion in view, not yet indeed arrived, but sometime to arrive, of more than mere formal fasting—an occasion of real grief and mourning, expressing themselves in the outward significant acts of fasting and prayer—an occasion which Theophylact (in locum) describes most correctly as follows : Ἔσται οὖν καιρός, φησιν, ὅτε ἐμοῦ παθόντος, καὶ ἀναληφθέντος, νηστεύσουσιν ἐν λιμῷ καὶ δίψῃ, διωκόμενοι [h]. This prophetical allusion to the future sufferings of the Apostles, we may justly contend, was too remarkable to have been purposely suppressed, yet too obscure to have been purposely introduced. If our Lord, in St. Mark or in St. Luke, had made use of the word πενθεῖν, they would have retained it ; if, in St. Matthew, he had made use of νηστεύειν, he would not have changed it.

St. Luke's account of this answer, in general, differs on the whole from St. Mark's, only as a supplementary might differ from a partial—of which Luke v. 36. compared with Mark ii. 21. affords a luminous proof. I have little doubt that, as resulting from the harmony of both together, our Lord's words ought to stand exactly as follows : Καὶ οὐδεὶς ἐπίβλημα ῥάκους ἀγνάφου ἐπιρράπτει ἐπὶ ἱματίῳ παλαιῷ· εἰ δὲ μὴ, αἴρει τὸ πλήρωμα αὐτοῦ, τὸ καινὸν, τοῦ παλαιοῦ, καὶ χεῖρον σχίσμα γίνεται [i]. Εἰ δὲ μήγε, καὶ τὸ καινὸν σχίζει, καὶ τῷ παλαιῷ οὐ συμφωνεῖ ἐπίβλημα τὸ ἀπὸ τοῦ καινοῦ [k]. The correctness of this arrangement is proved by the reason of the thing. The two arguments tend to the same *reductio ad absurdum ;* but they are perfectly distinct from each other, and, notwith-

[h] Commentar. 48.   [i] Mark ii. 21.   [k] Luke vi. 36.

standing a like state of the case, suppose two very different consequences. The first goes on the assumption that an old garment cannot *sustain* a piece of new cloth—whence, that, which is designed to fill up a rent, only enlarges it, and makes it worse than before : the second, on the assumption that an old garment will not *match* with a piece of new cloth—whence, both the new is cut to provide a patch for the old, and the patch of new cloth, being put upon the old, will not suit to, nor assort with, the old.

Lastly—as to the objection from the antecedent improbability that two distinct occasions, requiring a defence in terms so much alike, should yet have arisen in the course of our Saviour's ministry, however great this improbability might be, it must still succumb to the evidence of the fact. But the improbability itself is not so great. No part of his public conduct was more uniformly on principle—nor, consequently, more uniformly obnoxious to the cavils of those who were disposed to find fault with it, than this unreserved intercourse with publicans and sinners. The passage quoted from Luke vii. 34. proves it to have soon become a standing reproach against him ; and there are two other instances, Luke vii. 36—50. xv. 1—10. both later in their occurrence than the present instance, upon which similar exceptions, and the defence against them, are found on record. As to the renewal of the question concerning fasting, if those who put it in the first instance were *not* the disciples of John, and those who put it in the second were *so*, the occasions must have been distinct. Such a question, at that time, was very possible from them—for John was not as yet put to death. But he had been long suffering imprisonment ; and this may be one reason why our Lord, in answer to *their* question, made use of the word πενθεῖν— which he had not used in his answer to the former. *They* might have cause to fast and to mourn even *then*—his own disciples would have cause to do so only some time to come.

DISSERTATION XI.

On the ordination of the Twelve—and the Sermons from the Mount.

THE concurrent testimony of St. Mark and St. Luke establishes the fact that, until the present period of our Saviour's ministry—which is the first quarter of its second year—not only had not the Twelve been yet ordained to their office, but even the name of Apostle was not yet in being. Hitherto, then, they had been merely disciples—distinguished, perhaps, by nothing above the rest of the disciples in common, except that all, or some, of them might have been personally called by our Saviour—as the rest of the disciples had not. But from this time forward they were expressly discriminated from the rest, and formèd into a body, or society, of their own.

Of the ordination itself St. Matthew has given no account—though, as far as the commencement of that circuit in the neighbourhood of the lake, of which the ordination appears to have been the conclusion, his narrative goes along with St. Mark's—and his silence is naturally to be explained by the consideration that he was himself one of the Twelve, and that it might not become the modesty of a Christian Apostle to record his own appointment, by the choice of Christ himself, to so high and so illustrious an office.

In a part of his Gospel, however, which follows not long after this time ª, he speaks of the Twelve, as of a body already in existence, and known by that name as such; whence, it is clear, he recognises implicitly the fact of their previous ordination. On the same occasion he introduces also the catalogue of their names, which agrees, upon the whole, with the lists of St. Mark and St. Luke; and the isolated, yet natural, manner, in which he brings in this ca-

ª x. 1.

VOL. II.

B b

talogue [b], is a strong internal evidence that he kept it back, in its proper place, only from a motive of genuine Christian humility. The same conclusion follows from the way in which even here he speaks of himself : for he puts his own name after that of Thomas ; though, according to the order of St. Mark and of St. Luke [c], it should have taken precedence of it ; and he adds to his name the designation of ὁ τελώνης—a designation, in the opinion at least of his countrymen, expressive only of reproach—and which the other two, with a becoming regard to the memory of a Christian Apostle, accordingly omit.

As this event was the last, the most solemn, and the most important, which transpired in the course of the preceding circuit, the Gospel of St. Luke, which had accompanied St. Mark's as far as the beginning of the circuit, but not further, rejoins it again at this point. If, then, the proof of a position like this, which seems to be so clearly made out by the direct testimony of two Evangelists, and by the indirect testimony of a third, viz. that the appointment and ordination of the Twelve as Apostles were some time posterior to their call as disciples, required any more confirmation, there are two distinct considerations, which must place it beyond a question. First, the regular occurrence, from this time forward, but never before it, of the phrase Οἱ δώδεκα, to express the Apostles, in opposition to the rest of the disciples; a phrase to be met with in St. Matthew eight times, in St. Mark ten times, and in St. Luke eight times. Besides this, there are instances also of the phrase Οἱ δέκα, to express the rest of the Twelve in contradistinction to two— and of the phrase Οἱ ἕνδεκα, to express them all but one —which, consequently, amount to the same thing. This uniformity of designation, which yet begins to appear only now, and hereafter, must be a demonstrative argument that, until now, and hereafter, there was no such distinction, among our Lord's disciples, in being, as that of some one body in particular, opposed to the rest in general. The

[b] x. 2—4.   [c] iii. 18. vi. 15.

very name of Apostle had not yet been bestowed upon any —the only person who had borne it hitherto was our Lord himself—the Shiloh or Apostle of the Father—and, if we look at the precise point of time at which, as it is, the Twelve were chosen, and at the use which is made of their services directly afterwards, it may be concluded that the imposition of this name on them now referred as much to something immediate, as to something remote—to their part and character of Gospel-missionaries in our Saviour's lifetime, as well as after his death. St. Mark in particular declares this to have been the direct cause, and the primary purpose, or final end, of their appointment[d] : Ἵνα ὦσι μετ' αὐτοῦ, καὶ ἵνα ἀποστέλλῃ αὐτοὺς κηρύσσειν, καὶ ἔχειν ἐξουσίαν θεραπεύειν τὰς νόσους, καὶ ἐκβάλλειν τὰ δαιμόνια.

Secondly, the regular occurrence, from this time forward, but not before it, of the name of Peter. St. Mark and St. Luke[e] both shew that, when our Lord appointed Simon Barjonas an Apostle, he gave him also, agreeably to a well-known custom of the East, and to many similar instances which might be produced from the Old Testament, a *new* name, in allusion to his office itself—the name of Cephas, or Peter : and it is a curious circumstance, displaying in an eminent degree the extreme accuracy of both these Evangelists, their strict attention to propriety, as well as to the truth and fidelity of history, in the least things, not less than in the greatest, that, speaking of him before this period, they invariably call him Simon ; speaking of him after it, they invariably call him Peter. His name of Simon, up to this time, occurs in St. Mark five times ; but his name of Peter after it occurs eighteen times ; in St. Luke, up to the same period, the former name occurs eight times ; after it, the latter occurs eighteen times.

There is one exception, indeed, to the rule in St. Luke— at v. 8—at least if the text be genuine. But, even there, the name of Peter is merely added to that of Simon ; and, after all, it is most probable that this addition itself was

---

[d] iii. 14. 15.   [e] iii. 16. vi. 14.

originally a marginal annotation, which some time or other crept into the text. As to St. Matthew, who did not intend to record, in its proper place, the appointment of the Twelve themselves, nor, consequently, the change of the name of any one of them, he introduces St. Peter[f] by a reference to both his names, from the first—and, except in the catalogue of the Apostles as such—to intimate that he really received the name of Peter first when he was first consecrated an Apostle—he speaks of him ever after, by no name but that of Peter.

St. John's allusion to this name at i. 43. of his Gospel, I have shewn elsewhere[g], was entirely prospective. Our Lord's address to Peter at that time contained a *prophecy,* which was designed to have both a *literal,* and a *typical,* fulfilment—a *literal,* when the name of Peter was actually substituted for the name of Simon—and a *typical,* when, by the instrumentality, or personal agency, of Peter in particular, the foundation of the Christian church was laid among the Jews first, and afterwards among the Gentiles. Nor can the meaning of this address, before the time of the change, be better illustrated than by a comparison with another, which occurred after it. In St. John it is, Thou *art* Simon; Thou *shalt be called* Peter—in St. Matthew it is, Blessed art thou, Simon . . . Thou *art* Peter[h].

As to the imposition, at the same time, of a name on the two sons of Zebedee, viz. Boanerges, it is not a case in point; for being imposed alike on each, it could not be borne, as a *personal* denomination, by either. We may argue, therefore, as follows. Simon was not yet an Apostle, when he had not yet received the name of Peter: but he had not yet received the name of Peter until now—which is the first quarter of our Lord's second year; he was not yet an Apostle, therefore, until now. He had been a disciple, however, for at least a year. And what was true of Peter, we may take it for granted, was true, *a fortiori,* of the rest. All the Twelve, then, had been some time dis-

---

[f] iv. 18.　　　[g] Vol. ii. Diss. viii. 262.　　　[h] Matt. xvi. 17. 18.

ciples before they became Apostles. We do not, it is true, possess an express account of the call of any but these five, Peter and Andrew, James and John, and Matthew—and it is not improbable, as I have observed already elsewhere[i], that our Lord himself actually called none but these five. For, unless it could be supposed he would himself call every one, who became his disciple, there is no difficulty in conceiving that some, who were subsequently appointed Apostles, might, nevertheless, originally have voluntarily become disciples, as well as that a vast number of others must, of their own accord, have become disciples, who yet never were appointed Apostles. Yet St. Peter's description of the qualifications, necessary to constitute a successor in the Apostleship to the vacant place of Judas, referred to under a former head[k], it is self-evident would be most properly applicable to those who had become, and continued to be, disciples, from the first.

How long after their original call, the ordination of these five, and of the rest, may have taken place, it is not possible absolutely to determine; but the period to which I have assigned it (assuming only that the consecration of the four chief of the Apostles, at least, fell out about the same time in this year, as their original call in the year before) agrees as well to the course of events, before and after the ordination, as any; and it derives this further support from the final end of the appointment itself, that it supposes the ordination of the Twelve—which must have taken place at some determinate time or other—to have taken place at that time in general, when the divine Providence, in the maturity of its own counsels, designed they should enter upon their Apostolical office itself—the time of the feast of Pentecost.

From this period that Peter assumes a kind of pre-eminence among the Twelve, as the Twelve assume among the disciples, and, next to Peter, Andrew, James, and John, is supported by too many facts to be disputed. We may in-

---

[i] Dissertation x. supra.   [k] Vol. i. Diss. viii. 295.

fer, then, that the order in which the Apostles were called to our Lord, and consecrated—an order, which must have been determined by his own discretion—was deliberately intended, and was accordingly understood, to determine the order of precedence among them. Jesus called to him, from among the disciples, such as he would—and those whom he called, he made his Apostles. As by calling them all in general, out of the disciples in general, and by appointing them to a separate office and relation, he made them all so far distinct from the disciples as such—so by calling them one by one, in particular, and consecrating them one by one in particular, and, consequently, some of them before the rest, he seems to have conferred on some of them an honorary rank and precedence, above the rest— for in the community of name and office, and of personal relation to himself, it is manifest there was no difference between them—they were, and they must have been, all equal. One thing is certain ; in each of the catalogues the name of Peter stands first—and the name of Iscariot stands last ; the one, confessedly chief, the other, confessedly the least deserving, among the whole body. The intermediate names are somewhat differently arranged in the different lists ; but there is no variation between them which does not admit of being explained.

If we take the order of St. Matthew's catalogue, x. 2—4. and compare with it St. Mark's, iii. 16—19. and St. Luke's, vi. 14—16. or Acts i. 13. they will stand, in juxta-position, as follows:

Matt.		Mark.		Luke.		Acts.
1 Simon		1 ———		1 ———		1 Peter
2 Andrew		4 ———		2 ———		4 ———
3 James		2 ———		3 ———		2 ———
4 John		3 ———		4 ———		3 ———
5 Philip		5 ———		5 ———		5 ———
6 Bartholomew		6 ———		6 ———		7 ———
7 Thomas		8 ———		8 ———		6 ———
8 Matthew		7 ———		7 ———		8 ———
9 James Ἀλφαίου		9 ———		9 ———		9 ———

Matt.	Mark.	Luke.	Acts.
10 Lebbæus, or Thaddæus	10 Lebbæus	11 Judas Ἰακώβου	11 Judas Ἰακώβου
11 Simon ὁ Κανανίτης	11 ———	10 Simon ὁ Ζηλωτής	10 Simon ὁ Ζηλωτής
12 Judas ὁ Ἰσκαριώτης	12 ———	12 ———	12 Matthias.

We perceive, then, that in St. Mark's catalogue Andrew is put after James and John; in St. Matthew's and in St. Luke's (as contained in the Gospel) he is put before them. But the order of St. Luke in the Acts agrees with this of St. Mark—whence we may infer that the order of the Apostles originally, (that is, in our Saviour's lifetime,) according to which Andrew might take precedence of James and John, was altered after the ascension, and when they were all to enter on their own ministry; and that St. Mark has given the order of the names, not as it was at first, but as it was ultimately designed to be, and as it afterwards became. Or, what is equally probable—since none of the Evangelists *affirm* their order, if we except the two extreme names of all, it was indifferent in what order the intermediate names might be recited. The four Apostles, who were either the first called as disciples, or, with the exception of Matthew, the only persons who were so called among the Apostles, stand, in every instance, at the head of the list—and the subsequent history of the church both in the Acts and in the Epistles, proves that these in particular, either all, or three of them, Peter, James, and John, were eminently pillars of the church.

Some stress has been laid on the circumstance that two of the Evangelists, St. Matthew and St. Luke, record the names in couplets—as if Jesus had called the disciples to him two and two together; or, at least, that he sent them out afterwards—when they were sent two and two together—in the couplets in question. This conjecture is not improbable: for Peter and Andrew, James and John, it is exceedingly likely would be so ordained, and so despatched upon *their* commission in particular, whether any of the rest were so, or no. But St. Mark observes no such method; and St. Luke observes it only in part; whence we may conclude that the circumstance in question was accidental, or not, at least, intentionally specified, with a view to any such construction.

The wisdom or expediency of suffering the Twelve to become at first, and for some time after to continue, merely disciples—in order to the trial of their faith in, and attachment to, Christ, if not to their personal conviction—before they were elevated to the rank of Apostles, must be obvious. Our Lord's knowledge of the human heart is, *a priori,* a sufficient voucher that, in making choice of these, he was choosing those, who, in point of every moral requisite, were the fittest to be selected for a new and peculiar relation to himself, and for the instruments by which, in the course of time, he designed to work in the propagation of his Gospel. As to natural or acquired abilities, without the divine assistance, the greatest must have been as inadequate to the end in view, as the least. Their subsequent history confirms the presumption. The only exception would seem to be in the original admission, and the ultimate apostasy, of Judas. But this was unquestionably necessary, and therefore, as naturally intended, for the fulfilment of prophecy. If it was requisite that Jesus should be at last betrayed by one of his own Apostles, it was also requisite that one of his own Apostles should have been, from the first, capable of becoming a traitor.

In the number of the Twelve, there is an evident reference to the number of the Tribes; and one Apostle seems to have been chosen for every Tribe, because, as the event demonstrated, both in the original publication of Christianity, and ever after, they were in a peculiar manner the Apostles of the Circumcision, and sent, like their Master, to the lost sheep of the house of Israel. An extra, and, consequently, a thirteenth, Apostle, and though from among the Jews, yet from among the Jews of the Dispersion, was appointed in the fulness of time, and in the person of Saul, for the sake of the mission to the Gentiles. This adaptation of the number of the Apostles to the number of the Tribes is peculiarly exemplified in those words of our Saviour[l]; Verily I say unto you that, when the Son of Man, in the regeneration, shall sit upon his throne of glory, ye also, who have followed me, shall sit upon twelve thrones, judging the twelve tribes of Israel. The number twelve, then, seems to have been something, from the first, absolutely essential to the integrity of their body, and so understood accordingly. Hence, even before the day of Pentecost—or rather, *against* that day itself—the reparation of the defect in that number, produced by the apostasy of Judas, when Matthias was appointed in his stead[m], was yet but a necessary precaution.

The selection, nomination, and ordination, of the Apostles being expressly attributed to our Lord himself, whatever honour, or privilege, present or to come, was thereby conferred on the Twelve, it was an honour, and a privilege, in obtaining which they themselves were totally uninstrumental. The object proposed by their appointment St. Mark defines as twofold—that they might always be with Christ, and that he might send them to preach in his name —whence it must be as clear that they had not hitherto always been with him, as that they had not hitherto been sent to preach in his name. It is clear also that this definition is intended of the immediate, or proximate, end of the appointment—not of the future, and the more remote. But even the mission in question did not take place until sometime after the appointment—and it is manifest that the gift of miraculous power, alluded to here, was no gift bestowed at present, but merely designed to be bestowed, when the mission also, for the discharge of which it would be necessary, should be ready to commence. In the circumstance, however, of such a mission, and in the communication of thus much of miraculous power, subordinate to it, the Seventy were afterwards put upon a par with the Twelve. The true dignity, therefore, the real authority, or the exclusive prerogatives, of the apostolical office and character do not

[l] Matt. xix. 28.   [m] Acts i. 15—26.

fully appear until the day of Pentecost. Their peculiar privilege, during the remainder of our Saviour's ministry, consisted in this one respect, that, henceforward, they were always with him, and about him—as even *they* had not always been heretofore—and as the rest of the disciples never were.

If we consider the momentous consequences which, though still in futurity, hung upon this appointment of the Twelve —and, though still in futurity, yet, to the omniscience of Christ, were even then as good as present—we shall confess that, next to the great business of suffering for mankind, this was, and would be regarded by our Lord himself as, the most important act of his lifetime upon earth. Nor does he enter on it without a corresponding degree of preparation—nor proceed in it without an equal gravity and solemnity. The night before he spends on the mountain apart, in earnest prayer[n]—as soon as it is day, he calls to him the whole of his disciples[o]—out of this number he selects twelve by name, whom he invests with a new, and a peculiar, designation, expressive of the same relation to himself, in which he had appeared and acted with reference to the Father. For Jesus Christ was the Shiloh, or Apostle, of the Father—and the Twelve were the Shilohs, or Apostles, of Jesus Christ. To this relation and this title, it is probable that he consecrated them—either one by one, or two by two—with prayer and the imposition of hands: for by prayer, and the imposition of hands, do the Apostles, now consecrated to their office (and, we may presume, in imitation of what had been done unto themselves) consecrate others to any Christian function hereafter; and as Jesus was parted from them at last, while in the act of lifting up his hands over them, and of blessing them[p], so, with the same affectionate solemnity may he be supposed to have ordained them at first. After this, he delivers a sermon, which is a repetition of part of the former on the mount: Matt. v— viii. l. But, as this brings us to the controverted ques-

[n] Luke vi. 12.   [o] Luke vi. 13. Mark iii. 13. 14.   [p] Luke xxiv. 50. 51.

tion itself, whether these sermons are actually the same or distinct, it is now time that we should enter particularly upon it.

We may take it for granted that these two discourses, related, as they are, by two distinct Evangelists, and in two distinct places of the Gospel-history, are either, so far as they go together, totally the same, or totally different: for, as to their being partly the one, and partly the other, (though such an opinion may have been entertained,) it appears to me too absurd a supposition seriously to be refuted. Now, if they are each distinct from the other, then both may be given in their proper time and place. But, if they are to be pronounced the same, the question of a transposition will concern the order of St. Matthew, and not the order of St. Luke. No commentator or harmonist can reasonably suppose that the latter records *his* sermon out of its place, however many may have thought that St. Matthew has not recorded *his* in its own. By the proof, therefore, of the distinctness of the discourses—if that can be made out—it must still be understood that we are establishing the accuracy of St. Matthew, and not of St. Luke.

I. With a view to this conclusion, and as a kind of presumption in its favour, the order of St. Matthew, we may observe, is regular as far as v. 1. The first transposition which occurs, independent of the sermon itself, occurs at viii. 14.ᵃ

II. Those, who contend that he has antedated the sermon in question, are obliged to detach the introductory remark, at v. 1—as premised to the sermon—from the historical circumstances at iv. 24. 25. the close of the preceding chapter: by doing which, for the sake of a harsh and distorted hypothesis, they offer violence to the most simple and natural explanation of the course of events, imaginable. *That* conclusion represents our Lord as followed, or surrounded, by prodigious multitudes—*this* introduction, that seeing the multitudes, observing their numbers, and desiring

ᵃ Vol. i. Diss. iii. 153. 154.

to teach them, he went up into a mountain accordingly.
Who, on perusing these statements, could hesitate to infer
whether the discourse, which follows, was produced by the
circumstances, which preceded, or no?

III. I have shewn long since that, before this discourse
on the mountain, Jesus had both begun, and been making,
his first general circuit of Galilee. I have ventured, also,
to define the *course* of this circuit [r]—shewing in what manner, even from the very route, which it appears to have
taken, it would make him known in the regions, specified by St. Matthew as furnishing the attendance in question. At the close, also, of the circuit about the lake, and
at the time of the ordination of the Twelve, he was certainly accompanied by multitudes[s]; but it was not exactly
by multitudes from the same quarters as before. For among
these multitudes people from Idumæa are mentioned by St.
Mark—but among *those*, none such are mentioned by St.
Matthew; and it must be self-evident that a circuit towards
the south of Galilee, and along that side of the Jordan, was
much more likely to make our Lord known in Idumæa, and
to attract people after him from thence, than a circuit towards the north, and along the other.

IV. The circuits, which our Lord ever undertook, all
began from, and, if we except only the last, all ended at,
Capernaum. After making, then, for any length of time
soever previously, the progress of Galilee, he would still be
returning to Capernaum at last. It is reasonable to presume that the concourse of his followers would become
greater, the longer his journeying had continued, and would
be greatest when he was nearest to his journey's end. But
when do we find him attended by a more than usual resort
of people, especially in the early periods of his ministry,
and not, at the same time, described as desirous of teaching them? The discourse in St. Matthew, whensoever and
wheresoever it was delivered, was delivered on a certain
hill—and some hill, even St. Luke shews, there was in the

---

[r] Vol. ii. Diss. viii. 278.   [s] Mark iii. 7. 8. Luke vi. 17.

vicinity of Capernaum. It might have been delivered, then, at the close of the first circuit of Galilee, and from this very hill.

V. The discourse unquestionably contains an illustrious instance of our Lord's teaching—and it is not the less remarkable that, however illustrious, it is a single and a solitary instance of any thing of the kind, to be met with in the same Gospel. Numerous are the occasions, even after this, when it is affirmed that our Saviour taught—but on no occasion, except this, is it recorded what he taught. There is but one exception (the instance of the teaching in parables) which could be produced to the contrary; and that is an exception which would rather confirm, than invalidate, the assertion. On other occasions, the account of our Lord's discourses, even as recorded by St. Matthew, cannot, upon any principle, be said to be accounts of his teaching as such —or of such moral and practical discourses as this upon the mount. Compare with this the Apostolical commission— the denunciation of woes—and the prophecy on Mount Olivet[t]—which are the longest and fullest in the narration of all but this; and it will be acknowledged that they are *sui generis*, in contradistinction to this. I infer, then, that it did not come within the design of St. Matthew's Gospel, to specify the particulars of our Lord's public teaching more than once, that is, more than once *for all*—in which case it is morally absurd to suppose he would select any but the first opportunity for the purpose; and equally so, that this first opportunity should not have occurred before the second year of our Saviour's ministry.

VI. The occurrence of the remark on the manner of our Lord's teaching—which is at the end of the whole[u]—makes in favour of the same conclusion : for this is a remark, which in each Gospel occurs only once for all, but in each after the first instance of teaching, which they record. Our Lord's teaching was begun in the synagogue at Capernaum, and, when he was engaged on this present circuit, he still taught

[t] Matt. x. xxiii. xxiv. xxv.　　　　　[u] Matt. vii. 28. 29.

we are told in the synagogues of Galilee. If so, he still taught before within a limited sphere, and a corresponding audience—but now he teaches in the open air, and an innumerable congregation. It is by no means certain whether this was not the very first instance of any such teaching, which had yet occurred—and, if that was the case, it would be, on all accounts, one of the most memorable incidents of its kind, and one of the most deserving to be placed on record.

VII. The brevity of the historical, compared with the fulness of the discursive, matter in St. Matthew is a clear proof that he was more anxious to relate our Lord's conversations than his actions : and, in this preference, he has shewn only a due regard to the more useful, and so far the more important, part of his narrative. The miracles of our Saviour were designed for unbelievers; his sermons for believers : the latter might be wanted, and continue to be profitable, when the former had produced their effect ; for miracles could convince only their sensible witnesses—discourses might instruct and edify at all times ; the benefit of the former, then, would be partial and temporary—but the benefit of the latter, universal and perpetual. Now the compendious manner, in which he despatches the detail of events, from the beginning of the ministry of Christ, to the circuit of Galilee—and from that circuit, to the sermon on the mount—contrasted with the copious and minute account, which he has given of the sermon in particular, must be an internal evidence that the history of the sermon is what he chiefly had in view. He expedites every thing else, in order to arrive the sooner at this : but he arrives the sooner at this, not by antedating this, but by postponing other things : and when he is arrived at it, he dwells and dilates upon it, with an enlarged and comprehensive particularity, singularly opposed to the brief outline, the succinct and cursory notice, of every thing which precedes it.

VIII. The historical circumstances, which preceded or followed the two sermons, are of such a kind as to be decisive of their distinctness. Let us compare them together.

St. Matthew's sermon took place during, if not at the close of, a general circuit of Galilee—St. Luke's, during, if not at the close of, a partial circuit round the lake: St. Matthew's, before such an audience, as might have been collected by such a circuit—St. Luke's, before such an audience, as was more probably to have been collected by the other: St. Matthew's was produced by the presence and contemplation of the multitudes—St. Luke's, by the presence and contemplation of the newly-ordained Apostles: the moving cause in the former instance was a simple regard to the spiritual necessities of the people at *any* time—the moving cause in the latter was a specific regard to the event of the recent ordination: St. Matthew, who suppresses the fact of the previous ordination, could have no inducement to record the subsequent sermon—but St. Luke, who relates the former, for that reason only might naturally subjoin the latter: the disciples might be primarily addressed by both —but the multitudes, as well as the disciples, were addressed by the one—the disciples alone, and not the multitude, by the other.

St. Matthew's discourse was delivered on the mountain— St. Luke's was delivered on the plain: Jesus went up to the mountain, before the one—he came down from the mountain, before the other: he was on the plain, then, before St. Luke's—and he was on the mountain, before St. Matthew's. The use of the article, in speaking of this mountain, is natural and correct. There was, certainly, a hill in the vicinity of Capernaum, where two such discourses might have been pronounced; and this being both a single hill in itself, and the scene of a double, memorable, event, the use of the article, in alluding to it, would be not merely justifiable, but necessary. On the same principle, other mountains, which had been the localities of remarkable transactions—as the mountain where our Saviour twice fed the people—the mountain on which he was transfigured— the mountain on which he appeared after the resurrection —are similarly alluded to as τὸ ὄρος—the well-known, memorable, scene of such and such an event.

The attempt to reconcile these different statements by supposing that Jesus came down from the mountain, to the plain ground, at first, on purpose to heal the people, or perform his miracles, and afterwards retired up to the hill again, on purpose to teach them, or to deliver his sermon, like many other expedients invented to explain away similar differences, is altogether a gratuitous assumption, without a shadow of countenance from the text; and besides, it makes our Saviour do that at last, which, it is clear, he had no intention of doing at first—viz. retire from the people, as if he wished to avoid them, whom he had come down from the hill on purpose to get near to. In St. Matthew's account, he continues all the while on the mountain; and, when he has done speaking, he descends, followed by the people, to the plain—in St. Luke's, he continues where he was; on the level ground; and, when the sermon is over, it is from thence that he goes to Capernaum. In St. Matthew, he assumes the attitude of sitting before he begins to speak—which was as good as to intimate that he was about to begin to teach—in St. Luke, he delivers his discourse standing—with his disciples and the people around him. Both attitudes are equally natural under the previous circumstances of the case—standing, on a level situation—sitting, upon a rising ground. In St. Matthew, he takes his seat *first*, and the disciples draw near to him *afterwards*—in St. Luke, he has them about him from the first: in the latter, it would seem as if the disciples and the people stood upon higher ground; for Jesus, when he began to address them, *lifted up* his eyes to them—in the former, they must have stood upon lower.

IX. The circumstances, which followed upon the sermon in either account, have been considered elsewhere [v], and their differences pointed out. All these conclusions, however, will be still further confirmed by the comparison of the two discourses themselves.

The sermon in St. Matthew contains one hundred and

---

[v] Vol. i. Diss. iii. 151—153.

seven verses—the sermon in St. Luke, thirty. There is, consequently, an excess on the one hand, and a defect on the other, of seventy-seven verses—or more than two thirds of the whole. It would be difficult, however, to assign a reason why one Evangelist should have recited so much, and the other so little, of the same discourse—or why a part should have been omitted or recorded, and not the whole. Nor can it be replied that St. Luke has comprised, in thirty verses, the substance of one hundred and seven— or that *his* sermon is the epitome of St. Matthew's—for, on this principle, the outline in both the discourses ought to have been the same; the particulars only must have differed. But the state of the case is quite the reverse: the topics in St. Matthew are many, and various, and distinct —the topics in St. Luke are few, and simple, and closely connected. The discourse, in the latter, touches only here and there on the former—but, wherever it does so, instead of exhibiting the compressed and meagre features of an epitome, it dwells and dilates upon the subject under discussion with a richness, an emphasis, and an amplification, both of sentiments and of language, superior to the fulness of the supposed original; and preventing the discourse, with such a peculiarity of structure, from being confounded with even the idea of a *selection* out of St. Matthew's—much less with an *abstract* of it. For the same redundancy stands in the way of the former hypothesis, as much as of the latter.

It is a rule of St. Luke's—proving both the perfect knowledge of his subject which he possessed, and the consummate skill with which the course of his narrative was shaped from the first—to relate nothing twice in his own Gospel; however much may occur *once* there, which, taken in conjunction with St. Matthew or St. Mark, his own Gospel might shew to have been related *twice*. Such things happened more than once; and his rule of proceeding with respect to them is as follows—if they had been related, in the first instance of their occurrence, by his predecessors, he reserves his own account of them for their second—if they would have come twice over in his own account, he either relates them *once* for all at first, or, if he omits any part of them then, he supplies the omission by relating it again at some other opportunity. On this principle, the rest of the discourse in St. Matthew, over and above his own, if both the discourses were one and the same, ought to be found somewhere else in his Gospel. But this is not the case. Twenty or thirty verses of it may, perhaps, occur—but more than forty, or almost one half of the whole, would still remain totally unaccounted for.

The apparent identity of the exordiums and the conclusions of the two sermons, respectively, is said to have mainly determined the judgment of Grotius in considering them the same. Let us see, however, how far the nature of these exordiums in particular ought to have led to such an inference.

Both the discourses begin with beatitudes, consecutively delivered—of which St. Matthew's exhibits nine, and St. Luke's four. Now nine cannot possibly be the same with four—and, if it can be shewn that St. Luke records only four beatitudes, because only four were actually pronounced, it will follow that the occasion, upon which he records these four, must have been totally different from that, upon which St. Matthew records the nine.

Now, besides recording certain beatitudes, St. Luke has recorded also certain woes—but St. Matthew no such thing; and as woes in general are the reverse of beatitudes in general, so these woes in particular are the reverse of those beatitudes in particular. The structure of St. Luke's exordium is singular, and a genuine specimen of Hebrew parallelism: he recounts four beatitudes, and he recounts four woes; he recounts the beatitudes first, and the woes next; the order of the beatitudes is the counterpart of the order of the woes, and the particular subject of each beatitude is the ἀντίστοιχον of the opposite woe. I argue, then, that the number and order of the woes, which follow, are decisive as to the number and order of the beatitudes, which precede : each of them is a check upon the other, and a limitation of the other. There could have been only four beatitudes—

because there are but four woes : there could be only four woes, because there were only four beatitudes.

Besides this, is it no symptom of disparity, that the beatitudes in St. Matthew—as far as the ninth—are all indirect, or couched in the form of general *gnomæ*—St. Luke's are all direct, and immediately addressed to the disciples? This circumstance alone is sufficient to decide the question ; for the very change of manner in the ninth beatitude is a proof that the discourse in St. Matthew had begun, and until then had proceeded, differently. Were this also a proper place to explain either of the sermons particularly, it might be shewn, on the ground of the woe specifically opposed to each beatitude, that the terms πτωχοὶ, πεινῶντες, κλαίοντες, in the three first beatitudes of St. Luke, must be literally understood—of the really poor, the really hungry, the really mournful and disconsolate, in this life—whereas, it is equally clear that the same terms in St. Matthew are to be figuratively understood; of the poor in spirit—of the hungry and thirsty after righteousness—of the sorrow produced by repentance and the sense of sin. These objections would remain, though the beatitudes, and the other particulars of each exordium, so far as they agree together, had all been related alike. It happens, however, that, neither with their order, nor with their enunciation, is this the case; St. Luke's fourth beatitude is St. Matthew's ninth—and, what is still more extraordinary—his second and his third are just the reverse in St. Matthew—that is, what answers to his second comes after what answers to his third—and, as to the language and expressions, they are different in every instance throughout.

A comparison of the conclusions, and of the intermediate parts, would only confirm the same result. But, as it would require the examination of verse by verse, and not merely of paragraph by paragraph, and as the effect would be still the same—the eviction of discrepancies upon discrepancies, affecting not simply omissions, or what would be wanting in one, though supplied by the other, but the arrangement and expression of what they would be found to relate in common—I may be excused from entering at large upon it.

The sermon in St. Luke exhibits all the evidences of an original, and of an uniform, composition. Its topics are determinate, consistent, and natural—mutually connected together—and applicable to the case of the newly-ordained Apostles, as enforcing duties either eminently Christian in themselves, or, in their primary relation, peculiarly incumbent upon them. But there is no such leading idea, no such exclusive reference, predominant in St. Matthew's— one purpose of which (though only to a certain extent, and for a limited portion of the whole) is to reinforce parts of the decalogue—and, therefore, to characterize the teacher more as that original, and independent, Lawgiver, promised by Moses [w], and expected by the Jews, than as the Master and Instructor of the Apostles. The tone and manner of the first sermon—the general sentiment—the spirit and character—of the former—may, indeed, be discovered in the second : both the discourses were manifestly the offspring of the same mind, and there is a family likeness between them. But, as even in the children of the same parents, or members of the same family in common, the individuating characters of each are not so indistinct or imperceptible as to allow of our confounding them together. I have judged it best, therefore, to disturb the position of neither—but to leave each where it stands upon record. It is an additional reason for coming to this determination, that though the business of teaching the people as such must have been our Saviour's regular employment, if any thing was so, yet, in all the Gospels put together these two are the only occasions upon which we have the least account in detail of what he taught—and to confound these two together, or to suppose the occasions identical, would, manifestly, be little desirable.

[w] Deut. xviii. 15—19.

DISSERTATION XII.

On the beginning to teach in Parables, and on the time and place of their interpretation.

UPON the particular exposition of the parables, which were now delivered, it would manifestly be improper to enter in the present work ; nor shall I notice the subject of the Gospel narrative, in this portion of the whole, further than as concerns the business of a harmony—the consideration of a certain historical difficulty—with respect to which there exists some degree of perplexity, and which, to say the least of that degree of perplexity, no harmony ought to pass over (as most of those with which I am acquainted have, nevertheless, passed over) unexplained.

With regard to the time, or the manner, of this beginning to teach in parables, as well as to the order of succession, in which these first of the number were pronounced, there is little or no difficulty. On each of these points the testimony of the several Evangelists, is either obviously consistent, or easily to be reconciled together. Thus much, however, is distinctly implied by the express words of St. Matthew and St. Mark—and not called in question merely by the silence of St. Luke—that our Lord began to teach in parables, for the first time, upon this occasion; and, consequently, that he had never delivered a parable before : a conclusion, which the course and succession of the Gospel-history hitherto must of itself confirm. There is no parable, nor any vestige of a parable, like those which were now pronounced, and those which are seen to have been pronounced hereafter, to be met with in it. The word, παραβολὴ, it is true, may occur—but, wherever this is the case, it stands for a very different thing from what we consider to be meant by a parable: as, if I thought it necessary, I could very plainly demonstrate.

It is agreed, also, that when our Lord began thus to

c c 3

teach in parables, it was upon the shore of the lake of Capernaum—to which he had repaired on purpose—and sitting on board a small vessel, at some distance, indeed, from
the land, but not so far as to be out of the hearing of the
people. This, we have often seen, was his familiar practice,
when in the vicinity of the lake; or when he would avoid
the pressure of the multitude. And hence, perhaps, it is
that, speaking of the ship in question, both the Evangelists
make use of the article—meaning probably the very ship,
which had been appointed ª to attend upon him, and to be
ready for such services as these, when he was last in the
neighbourhood of the lake.

The difficulty, to which I allude, concerns the time and
manner of delivering those interpretations of two of the
present parables—the seed, and the tares—which Jesus is
perceived to have vouchsafed at the request of his disciples.
It must be evident from Matt. xiii. 36. that the interpretation of the latter could neither have been asked, nor have
been conceded, before the dismissal of the multitude, and
the return of our Lord to Capernaum. This interpretation,
therefore, as well as the request which produced it, must
have been posterior to the day's teaching in public; or
strictly a part of what afterwards took place in private.
But the interpretation of the former parable St. Matthew
himself interposes, before he recounts the second—and the
other two Evangelists—whether they record any more parables than the first, or not—yet subjoin the explanation of
the first, before they proceed to the next. This interpretation, too, was produced by a request of the disciples—yet
the fact of such a request does not appear from St. Matthew
—it is supplied by St. Mark and St. Luke alone.

The question, then, which we have to consider, amounts
substantially to this—whether the request, which produced
the exposition of the parable of the sower, was preferred
and answered on the spot—or, like that which produced
the interpretation of the parable of the tares, was preferred
and answered, after our Lord had returned into private.

ª Mark iii. 9.

And here, as we have frequently had occasion to observe, the testimony of the less explicit, the less circumstantial, the less positive, among the Evangelists, it is just and reasonable, should be estimated altogether in conformity to the testimony of the more so.

Now, at the close of St. Mark's account of this day's teaching, we meet with the following observation [b], which does not occur in either of the other two : And in many such parables spake he the word unto them ; so as they were able to hear him: but, without a parable, spake he not unto them : in private, however, he expounded every thing to his own disciples. This statement must be understood to affirm that, for that day, and while he was still in public, Jesus spoke in nothing but parables—taking care only that what he himself pronounced aloud, from the ship and the sea, might be heard by the people on the shore : but that, when the day's teaching was over, and the people had been dismissed, he explained to his disciples what he had been teaching.

There is nothing, it is true, said about the disciples requesting this explanation—but neither is any thing said to the contrary : and, with regard to the *fact* of any explanation, the mention of this further circumstance was clearly unimportant. There was one parable, also, the last on record, which he did certainly interpret of his own accord ; and, upon the authority of this assurance of St. Mark's, whether the interpretations of more were requested, or not, we should be bound to believe they were given. The great point of distinction, which the Evangelist would impress upon us, is the marked difference of our Saviour's conduct, in respect to the same thing, the understanding of his parables, towards the people in general, and his disciples in particular. He explained to the one what he had disguised from the other—that is, he conceded a special favour and indulgence to the one, but denied them to the other. Now the parables had been pronounced, at first, in the hearing of the disciples, as well as of the multitude ; and they had

[b] iv. 33-34.

c c 4

been as unintelligible, at first, to the former, as to the latter. He could not, then, explain them even to the disciples, except in private—for as to rendering κατ' ἰδίαν, *aside,* or *apart,* in any sense distinct from *in private*—or supposing that every parable was explained on the spot to the disciples, after and as it had been just pronounced to the people, such a construction would be little better than absurd. According, therefore, to St. Mark, no interpretation of any of the parables could have been delivered, except in private; and out of the three such explanations, which are on record, two, it is obvious, were delivered in private.

But again; before he subjoins the interpretation of the parable of the sower, he premises the following words, in allusion to the circumstances under which it was granted : c"Οτε δὲ ἐγένετο καταμόνας, ἠρώτησαν αὐτὸν οἱ περὶ αὐτὸν, σὺν τοῖς δώδεκα, τὴν παραβολήν. The received translation renders the first part of this sentence, And when he was alone ; its full meaning, however, is, But when he was *become* alone—when he was *got* by himself. Now, what could be understood by these words, except his returning into private? Before, he was in the company of the multitude ; and, therefore, not by himself: or, if it should be objected that he was in the ship, and the people on the shore, I would ask, if that is what was meant by his being alone, how would it be possible to have become more alone? Besides, if the rest of the disciples, along with the Twelve, put this request, and put it in public, they must have put the request, along with the Twelve, and put it in public, on board the ship ; and, therefore, have all been with Jesus, as well as the Twelve, in the ship. But, though this might have been the case with the Twelve, it is not probable it would be the case with more. The vessels, which navigated the lake of Tiberias, were certainly capable of holding more than a complement of twelve persons. But, if we consider for what purpose our Lord had taken up his position on the ship—viz. not to interfere with the business of his teaching, but to avoid the proximity of the crowd—it is not likely that he would

c iv. 10.

admit thither more than his constant attendants, which were merely the Twelve.

The same conclusion is further confirmed by the first words of our Lord's answer to the request itself [d] : To you it is conceded to know the μυστήριον—*that is*, the secret, of the kingdom of God—ἐκείνοις δὲ, τοῖς ἔξω—they are all conveyed in parables. Here, as the disciples are clearly denoted by the *you*, so the multitudes, opposed to them, are as clearly to be understood by the ἐκείνοις, τοῖς ἔξω. Now these words, also, would be inadequately rendered, To those without. The mere use of ἐκείνοις δὲ, that is, But unto them —would have been enough to distinguish the people in general, from the disciples in particular : the addition of τοῖς ἔξω, which defines and limits even the demonstrative pronoun, opposes them so much the more. The words, then, should be understood to mean, But unto them, those, I say, who are without : it is as if Jesus had begun by saying Unto you, τοῖς ἔσω, such and such privileges are conceded— but to those other, τοῖς ἔξω, just the reverse.

It is clearly, therefore, implied that, at the time when this conversation was passing, Jesus and the disciples, οἱ περὶ αὐτὸν, were somewhere *within*, and the rest of the people were somewhere *without*. If so, our Lord and his disciples, were in private. For in what sense could the multitude be called οἱ ἔξω, and our Lord's immediate attendants be opposed to them as οἱ ἔσω, if both were alike in the open air, and still in public? Is it a sufficient account of the distinction that the one were in the ship, and the others were not? or, while all were in common in public, could there possibly be room for such a division between any one part, and the rest, as that of οἱ ἔξω, and οἱ ἔσω? No such distinction occurs in St. Matthew, or in St. Luke : the former of whom has simply ἐκείνοις, and the latter, τοῖς λοιποῖς.

It must be some confirmation of the same conclusion, that our Lord's disciples, from their habitual respect to their master, would surely not have presumed to interrupt him, while engaged in the delivery of a series of parables, and as

[d] Mark iv. 11.

they might perceive, of nothing else.   Still less would they
do this to gratify their own curiosity.   It is possible, that
under such circumstances they might ask him *why* he was
teaching in parables ; that is, in a manner so different from
usual—so contrary to the plainness and simplicity, which
had characterized his doctrine hitherto.   The surprize and
novelty of the thing itself might lead to thus much—especially if a pause in the continuity of his discourse might
have supplied the opportunity—but they would not account
for more.

Besides, if our Lord explained any of his parables in
public, as he first delivered them, this would have endangered the very end of teaching in parables at all.   For, if
the explanation, as well as the parable which it explained,
was delivered in public, what was there to prevent the
people, who had heard the parable, from hearing also the
explanation ? It is some argument, too, that the interpretation is said to have been begun by οὐκ οἴδατε τὴν παραβολὴν
ταύτην ; καὶ πῶς πάσας τὰς παραβολὰς γνώσεσθε [c]; We cannot
suppose that the reference here is intended of any parables,
but those which were actually now delivered—five of which
are placed on record—as more than five, perhaps, were
spoken.   If the words, then, are to be rendered thus, Have
ye not understood this parable ? how then will ye understand them all ? they will imply that all had been delivered
already, and all had been understood, or not understood,
already—but that this being the simplest, and easiest, and,
consequently, the most likely to have been comprehended,
of any, if this had been mistaken, it would be much more
difficult to make them comprehend the rest.

What, then, shall we say to St. Matthew's testimony, who
has certainly interposed this interpretation between the parable to which it refers, and the parable of the tares, which
follows next ; and, as it would seem, in answer to a question from the disciples ?

I. He does not say the disciples put any request, as soon
as Jesus had done speaking the parable—he uses his ordi-

[c] Mark iv. 13.

nary form of expression—implying that, except when our
Lord's followers, even the Apostles, had occasion to prefer
some enquiry, or otherwise to come to him, but of their own
accord, they were accustomed to keep at a certain distance
from him [f]; *The disciples came to him, and said :* an assertion which would be equally true of what might have been
done afterwards, as much as then.

II. The question, which he shews they actually put, is
not, as in the other two Evangelists, the question, *what
might this parable be ?* but the question, *why art thou
speaking to them,* that is, to the people, *in parables ?* a
question, not only very different from the other, but, under
the circumstances of the case, much more likely to have
been put. If our Saviour, hitherto, had never taught in
parables—so that a parable, until now, was an unheard-of
thing—if, now, he began, and continued, to teach in nothing
else—more especially, if the kind of parables, which he first
employed, was the allegorical—a kind, in its own nature designed for mystery and concealment—nothing could be
more reasonable than that the disciples should have been
surprized and perplexed, by this sudden change in the
manner of his public address—nor than that, under the influence of these feelings, as soon as a pause occurred—which
was manifestly the case at xiii. 9—they should have enquired into the causes of the change.

It is not likely, however, that both the questions on record should have been put in conjunction ; or, though they
had been, still it would be morally certain St. Matthew's
would be first put, and first answered. It is certain, also,
that St. Matthew mentions only one of them, St. Mark
and St. Luke mention only the other : but, if both were
put at once, no good reason can be assigned for the omission in either case. If, however, two different questions
were really put, and really answered, each at a different
time and place, then such an omission would be conceivable.

It is certain, likewise, that the answer to St. Matthew's

[f] xiii. 10.

question, as recorded by him[g], however obliquely it may be
given, is yet a proper answer to the previous enquiry—because the very words of the enquiry are repeated in verse
13. and the rest, before and after this verse, is so connected
with it, as to be necessarily the substance of one and the
same reply. It is evident, also, that the answer to St.
Mark's question[h] is all a proper answer to that one and the
same enquiry, which is again alluded to at verse 13. Notwithstanding, too, the apparent substantive resemblance of
verses 11—13. in St. Mark (agreeing almost *verbatim* with
verse 10. in the parallel passage of St. Luke) to some parts
of St. Matthew's account, still there is so much real difference between them, that we should not know on what
principle to regard them as the identical account of an
identical discourse at the same time and place.

To specify no more than one single instance : it is surely
a proof of great disparity that, in quoting the words of
Isaiah, St. Matthew describes our Lord to have said, Ὅτι
βλέποντες οὐ βλέπουσι, and St. Mark, Ἵνα βλέποντες...μὴ ἴδωσι.
The former is the natural mode of assigning the *producing
cause,* the latter, the *final end,* of the effect in question.
According to the one, he is made to reply, and very appositely to the question which precedes—For this reason am
I speaking to them in parables, because that, seeing, they
do not see—and according to the other, though no longer
with any express reference to such a question, yet equally
appositely under the circumstances of the case—To those,
who are without, they are all made known in parables ; to
the intent that, seeing, they may not see.

The harmony, then, of the several accounts will stand as
follows.

I. Matthew xiii. 10—17. is regular—containing the answer actually returned to the question actually put, at the
close of the *first* parable, why art thou speaking in parables?

II. Mark iv. 10—25. and Luke viii. 9—18. assign the
similar reply to the similar enquiry, what might that parable

[g] 11—17.   [h] iv. 10—25.

be? but after the day's teaching in public was over. In both, parts of what had been already related by St. Matthew, and in answer to the former question—concerning the singular privilege, conceded to the disciples, in being favoured by the disclosure of truths, purposely concealed from the rest—are found to be repeated; but so naturally, and so pertinently to the occasion, that their recurrence can be considered no objection. Nor is this account in St. Mark a proper Anticipation; because he specifies, at the outset, the true time to which it belongs; and shews, thereby, that he had nothing in view by it, except to connect the interpretation as closely as possible with what it interprets —for the mutual advantage of both.

III. Matthew xiii. 18—23. is, consequently, a proper Anticipation, being given without any such intimation; yet it is an Anticipation, which may be vindicated on the same principle—the principle of subjoining the explanation directly to the parable explained. The intermediate question might have been truly put and answered, as it is represented to have been; and if so, it would furnish an opportunity for continuing the discourse of our Lord—once begun upon this subject—to another, not much unlike it. He might have this further inducement also, that the substance of the answer to the first question was again premised, though very briefly, to the interpretation accorded to the second.

IV. Our Lord's teaching being afterwards resumed, in the parable of the tares, might be uninterruptedly continued, through the rest of the parables on record, and perhaps more, until he returned to his private abode in Capernaum —where, consequently, as it is shewn by St. Matthew himself, the enquiry about the parable of the tares, which led to its explanation, must first have been put. To conclude then.

The number of parables, related as now delivered, whether in public or in private, is eight: seven of which are found in St. Matthew, three in St. Mark, and one in St. Luke. Of St. Matthew's seven, four are peculiar to his Gospel; and of St. Mark's three, the second is peculiar to his; St. Luke's one, as well as its interpretation, is recorded by them all : it is in fact the parable of the sower.

Of these omissions, St. Matthew's may, perhaps, be accounted for by supposing that many more such parables, as this one which is wanting to complete the eight, might have been now delivered; and, consequently, that omissions of more or of fewer, among the whole number, might be expected in all the accounts.   On this subject I cannot enter at large at present; or else it might be shewn that these minor parables are related, rather as specimens of the class to which they belong, and as instances of the many figurative modes of describing some historical circumstance or other, in the future Christian dispensation, upon which this day's teaching, continued as it was through no little time, was probably occupied, than as a complete enumeration of all which had been actually spoken.

St. Mark's omissions are obviously in unison with his characteristic conciseness in the account of our Lord's discourses as such—a conciseness the true reason of which has perhaps been alleged elsewhere[i].

With regard to St. Luke, two out of the seven, which he omits, come over again in another part of the Gospel-history, and are recorded by him there[k]: three others, which were delivered in private, he might naturally omit, because, as neither the beginning, nor the ending, of this day's teaching are specified by him in particular, he neither brings our Lord out of a certain house, to commence his discourse on the lake, nor takes him back thither, when it was over. Besides which, it is a general reason for *his* omissions, and also for St. Mark's, that the parables omitted being all of them prophecies, and prophecies which, at the time when they composed their Gospels, had long been more or less fulfilled, to have recorded them as they were first delivered, would have been to record the prediction after its fulfilment by the event.   The same objection does not apply to their account in St. Matthew; whose Gospel, we have shewn, was

---

i Vol. i. Diss. ii. 122.   k xiii. 18—21.

written early in the history of the progress of Christianity, and before it had been preached among the Gentiles[1].

But, indeed, the general conciseness of St. Luke, in the account of this whole transaction, must satisfy an impartial reader that it was designed; and, in all probability, was due to his knowledge of the minute and adequate relation, which the same things had experienced from his predecessors; especially from St. Matthew. Hence, had not the one parable, which he does record, been the first of its kind, and expressly interpreted by our Lord himself—so as to constitute an era in his ministry—a remarkable change in his manner of teaching—and, above all, a specimen of both the method of instruction by parables, and the mode of understanding and interpreting them—I consider it not unlikely that he would have passed over even this.

As to the verbal agreement between the several accounts, it is greater between St. Matthew's and St. Mark's, than between either and St. Luke's—a distinction, which holds good also in other instances; and, for the reasons alluded to before, was, *a priori*, to be expected. In the account, however, of the parables, as such, verbal coincidences are, perhaps, not to be expected on the same grounds, as in the relation of our Lord's other discourses. For every such parable consists of a history, the basis of which is an action; and hence, though it may be related as something originally conceived and pronounced by our Saviour, it would no more require to be related in the same form of words throughout, than the common facts of his personal history—which are all given, under different forms of narration, as the same history of what he did, or suffered.

[1] Vol. i. Diss. ii. 121.

DISSERTATION XIII.

On the question concerning eating with unwashen hands,
Matthew xv. 1—20. Mark vii. 1—23.

IN order to compare these accounts, the most convenient
distribution of the narrative is into what took place with
the Pharisees, and with the multitude, in public[a], and what
with the disciples in private[b]. The difficulty of reconciling
them is much greater as concerns the former, than as concerns the latter: and with regard to each there is proof of
one omission, at least, in St. Matthew, supplied by St.
Mark—first, the immediate cause of the question of the
Pharisees[c]—and, secondly, the renewal of the conversation
in private, after the decision in public, when Jesus and
the disciples were come into some house[d]—neither of which
things are specified, though they may be implied, in St.
Matthew.

Independent, also, of this distinction, the account of St.
Mark is in other respects the fuller and more particular of
the two. Not to mention the substance of vii. 3. 4—containing so minute an historical explanation of the customs
of the Jews—which he premises to the ensuing narrative,
there is nothing in St. Matthew, correspondent to vii. 8. 9,
and, perhaps, to vii. 12. 13—in St. Mark; vii. 16. also, is
peculiar to the latter. It is true, that xv. 12. 13. 14. may
be found only in St. Matthew: but this is an integral part
of the account, which might be detached from the rest and
omitted, without prejudice either to what goes before, or to
what follows after, it. This omission, therefore, in St. Mark
is not like the omissions in St. Matthew, which were partly
the omissions of facts, necessary in the way of explanation,
and partly the concise representation of what was more fully
expressed by the speaker. Had St. Mark, indeed, in what

[a] Matt. xv. 1—11. Mark vii. 1—16.   [b] Matt. xv. 12—20. Mark vii. 17—23.   [c] Mark vii. 2.   [d] Mark vii. 17.

he records along with St. Matthew, been found to abbreviate some things, while he enlarged upon others—instead of being more circumstantial throughout—the argument from the comparative particularity or conciseness of either would have been neutral.

With regard to this single omission, which I am persuaded was intentionally made, it is sufficiently accounted for by considering to what it relates. The part in question is a prophetical denunciation, levelled against the Pharisees; whose *persons,* and not whose *doctrines,* are denoted by the figurative language, which it employs. They had taken offence at the recent decision[e]; and the disciples, who report this fact to their Master, apprehended some evil consequences from it. The declaration subjoined is intended to reassure them; and predicts that, in due time, both they and their followers should come to nothing. Let *them alone,* that is, *leave them to themselves,* and they will run blindly to their own destruction. They were no plantation of the Father's planting—and, therefore, should at last be rooted out. All this is certainly prophecy; but prophecy with a limited application; and, like the longer and more particular denunciations, which occur hereafter[f], personally regards only the Scribes and the Pharisees of that generation, and should be fulfilled only in their personal history. If, however, St. Mark wrote for Gentiles—or at least for persons unacquainted with Jewish sects, and Jewish usages, (of which the very notice, premised above, is a sufficient proof,) it does not appear what particular interest in the fate of a sect or party, among the Jews, they were likely to take: nor, consequently, why such denunciations, having been already recorded in full by St. Matthew, might not be purposely omitted by St. Mark. Such seems to have been the principle, on which he acted, every where else: for neither in his account of the ministry of John—nor in his account of the ministry of Christ—do any of the penal denunciations, with a special and a limited reference, which stand so prominently in St. Matthew, occur in St. Mark. His omission of all the personal matter, in reply to the charge of dispossession by the agency of Beelzebub, and his similar omission of the whole of Matthew xxiii. are cases in point.

This evidence, then, of the greater circumstantiality of St. Mark in the present instance must go some way in reconciling his account to St. Matthew's; but it will not, as in other instances, be all which is necessary for that effect. The existing differences are such as do not admit of being adjusted, simply upon this principle; for they involve a question not so much of omission and supplement, as of order and statement. The first part of our Lord's reply, in St. Mark, is the last, in St. Matthew; and the last, in St. Matthew, is the first, in St. Mark; that is, Mark vii. 6—8. answers to Matt. xv. 7—9—and Matt. xv. 3—6. answers to Mark vii. 9—13—with respect to which, I shall, notwithstanding, endeavour to shew, first, that St. Matthew's order may have been, and I believe was, the true; yet, secondly, that St. Mark's may not be at variance with it.

St. Matthew's order, we may presume, is the true, first, because the reply of our Lord, as recorded by him, is recorded continuously, and as *one* reply, without interruption from first to last.

Secondly, because the terms of the first sentence of this reply are so clearly accommodated to the terms of the demand just before ᵍ, that no one can doubt whether the former was immediately retorted upon the latter, or not. Why do thy disciples transgress the tradition of the elders? Why do ye also transgress the commandment of God? There cannot be a more perfect specimen of antithesis: one expostulation is opposed to another—one set of persons are contrasted with another—an instance of the breach of one law is met by an instance of the breach of another.

From the conduct of Jesus at last, it is evident that he never intended to answer the question of the Pharisees to

<hr />

ᵍ xv. 3. 2.

them : he meant to reserve his decision for the people. He knew that they had some sinister purpose in preferring the demand; or, at least, that to enter upon the question, on its own grounds, before *them*—to explain to *them* how utterly insignificant in the sight of God were all forms of merely external purity, unaccompanied by the purity of the heart, would necessarily fail of its effect. His answer, therefore, is entirely an *argumentum ad homines. He* does as good as promise to explain unto *them*, why his own disciples transgressed the tradition of the elders, if *they* would first explain to *him*, why their disciples, in obedience to that tradition, transgressed the commandment of God.

Thirdly, because, though the hypocrisy of the interrogators could not but be known to our Lord, and could not but be justly the subject of *his* reproaches, from the first, yet, for the sake of those about him, it might still be necessary openly to expose that hypocrisy, before he reproached them with it: in which case, it was more likely he would begin as St. Matthew represents him to have begun, than as St. Mark.

The instance of hypocrisy, with which he accordingly reproaches them, consisted in this case, as in other cases of the like kind, in straining off a gnat, and swallowing a camel—in resenting a small offence, and deliberately sanctioning a greater. There is no comparison, in point of force and obligation, between the laws of God, and the laws of men; yet even on their own admission the laws of tradition, being every where spoken of as the traditions of the *elders*, or of *those of old time*, were not the laws of God, but the laws of men. To the existence of this law of tradition Josephus bears distinct testimony [h]—and he attributes it also to the Pharisees, whose origin he first mentions [i] as contemporary with Jonathan, the successor of Judas Maccabæus. It is true that the pretended zeal for the law of tradition was grounded, or affected to be grounded, on a zeal for the authority of God—the laws of tradition, as it was main-

---

[h] Ant. Jud. xiii. x. 6. [i] Ib. v. 9.

tained by the Rabbins, being originally derived from the will or commands of God. But the traditionary word of God—to admit for argument's sake the existence of any such word—could possess at the utmost only an equal, and, certainly, not a superior, authority in comparison of the written : and, if in a given instance the doctrines or precepts of the one were diametrically repugnant to the doctrines or precepts of the other, they could not both have been derived from the same authority, or both still retain the same authority—one of them must needs be false, or must needs succumb to the other. The same legislator can never deliberately contradict himself—nor, while a certain injunction still remains in force, exact at one time what he had directly proscribed at another. Much less is it possible for two contrary requisitions both to have proceeded from God ; or, if in a given instance there should be any conflict between two rules of duty, each of them professing to emanate from him, that both could have been derived from the same divine source, or both be entitled, as such, to the same consideration, and obedience.

Now whatever authority was ascribed to the oral or traditionary word of God, it was not denied that his written word continued the same ; the law of tradition might pretend to explain the law of Moses, but it did not pretend to abrogate it, or to say it was no longer of effect. The written word of God, then, being always professedly acknowledged as the genuine, authentic, record of the will and commands of God, yet the traditionary word being also considered the same, it follows that, on this principle, there were two genuine, authentic, records of the will of God, and two authoritative rules of duty, the law of Moses, and the tradition of the elders. If these, therefore, were each of them what they professed to be, they must agree together ; but, if there was any thing in the one flatly contradictory to something in the other, one of them must be a false pretender to its title—which one might be the law of tradition, but, even on the admission of the Pharisees, could not be the law of Moses.

The ordinances of bodily ablutions, and the other precepts of external purity, in an alleged breach whereof the offence of the disciples consisted, being no where prescribed in the written word of God, rested exclusively on the authority of tradition—and the laws of tradition being all similarly founded, any instance of a direct contradiction between them, and the written word of God, would be sufficient to discredit the whole system, and to justify the inference that what would lead to such consequences as these could never be the dictate of eternal truth and justice, instinctively recognized by the consciences of mankind, but a gross and palpable delusion, either founded in fraud and cunning, or the fruit of error and infatuation. Many such examples of traditionary rules of duty, at variance with the plainest maxims of moral and religious truth, there might have been produced—but that, which our Lord insists upon, in the present instance, as among the most criminal of all, and among the most flatly repugnant to both the written word of God, and the natural sense of right and wrong, is the perversion of the vow of Corban, as sanctioned by the law of tradition.

The existence of the vow of Corban in his own time is recognized by Josephus : Καὶ οἱ Κορβᾶν αὐτοὺς ὀνομάσαντες τῷ Θεῷ· δῶρον δὲ τοῦτο σημαίνει κατὰ Ἑλλήνων γλῶτταν [k]. Δηλοῖ δὲ . . δῶρον Θεοῦ [l]. By this vow both property and persons might become devoted to God ; and what had been once thus appropriated never after could be put to any other use [m]. One of the earliest instances of such a Corban was, in my opinion, the devotion of the daughter of Jephthah to perpetual virginity [n]—which I am persuaded was of no other description : the next was the consecration of Samuel, whom Hannah, his mother, solemnly dedicated to the Lord even before his conception [o]; and whom Eli, in allusion to this dedication, calls by a beautiful metaphor the loan which was lent to the Lord [p]—interceding with God

[k] Ant. Jud. iv. iv. 4. [l] Contra Apion. i. 22. [m] Lev. xxvii. 28.
Deut. xxiii. 21—23. [n] Judges xi. 30. 31. 37—39. 40. [o] 1 Sam. i. 11.
[p] Ib. ii. 20.

that for the sake of this loan, and as it were in acknowledgment for the use of this loan, he would bless his parents with a numerous family besides.

But, in order to the natural effect of the vow of Corban, it must have been *bona fide* made; and when made, it was to be *bona fide* fulfilled. It could never stand good as the result of ignorance, or inadvertency; much less as a subterfuge from other duties. The law of tradition, however, had perverted it to all these abuses; affixing so superstitious a value to the mere pronunciation of the terms δῶρον ἔστω—that, of whatsoever they might have been said, it became thenceforward restricted from its proper use and purpose, yet not necessarily appropriated to the service of God. Hence, if a son, whether in the heat of passion, or coolly and deliberately, had only said to his parents—δῶρον ἔστω, ὃ ἐὰν ἐξ ἐμοῦ ὠφεληθῇς—may every thing of mine, which might be useful to thee, be δῶρον—though, from such a mode of vowing, nothing became consecrated to God, yet every thing was tied up from his parents—he had debarred himself from doing good to them again—he would be as much guilty of impiety, if he turned his means or opportunities, ever after, to their benefit, as if his goods and possessions, his soul and his body, having all been inalienably appropriated to God, had subsequently been put to any other use: yet, strange to say, for any purpose but that one, he was just as much his own master, he was as free to do what he pleased with his own, as before. Thus was a rash and inadvertent, or even designing and malicious, expression rendered perpetually binding on the conscience—the name of religion, and the honour of God, were prostituted as a cloke for unnatural wickedness—and even the road to repentance was effectually blocked up; for, as our Lord continues [q], a son after that, though he might wish it, would not be permitted to honour his parents—he would be kept to his word, against his own inclinations—he would be held as amenable to spiritual or temporal censures, for services rendered to them, as if he had applied a *bona fide* Corban

[q] Matt. xv. 5.

to any profane use. Such monstrous hypocrisy, or such palpable self-delusion, as are implied in this doctrine, are scarcely to be credited of any set of persons who did not find their interest in it—or if the general wickedness of the times did not render it, as a means of evading the simplest and plainest duties, only too palatable to the world at large. Yet this explanation of the doctrine is capable of being confirmed by the testimony of the Rabbins themselves; and I shall produce the necessary proofs of it by and by.

In the mean while this breach of the fifth commandment, as authorized by the law of tradition, has a case in point, in the breach of the third also—which is just as strongly insisted on, Matthew xxiii. 16—22. All these distinctions tended alike to refine away the sanctity of oaths; and, consequently, to sap the foundations not merely of a religious veneration for the name and the attributes of God, but of mutual faith and trust among men—for which there can no longer be any safeguard, when oaths, the most deliberate and solemn of the modes of conviction, are no more of any effect. Amidst all such distinctions between *one* oath, which was good, and *another*, which was nothing, we may trace a common feature of resemblance, which proves, more than any thing, the impurity of their origin; and that they were the contrivances of fraud and cunning—invented for the purpose of deceiving. That mode of swearing, which was *a priori* the most natural and probable, is in each instance pronounced good for nothing—and that, which was the most unnatural, and the least likely to occur, is in every instance alone made binding. But, which of these distinctions would be most serviceable for the sake of deception, nobody can question.

For the proof of the explanation referred to, the reader may consult the authorities in the margin [r]. This one passage from Maimonides would be sufficient to establish it: Si quis . . . ita dixisset, sit—mihi Corban ista massa panis . . . atque idem exinde massam illam panis comedisset, hic

---

[r] Pococke. Not. Miscell. ad Portam Mosis cap. ix. Maim. De Jurejur. Dithmari. vi. 15. Annott.

sane prævaricatione obstringeretur ; quamvis eadem massa panis reliquis hominum licita fuisset [s]. Vide, however, the other cases which he supposes in the same passage. Hence, that maxim of the Talmud, Votum (scilicet, Corban) etiam in legem cadit—juramentum, non item—Corban might excuse from the obligation of written precepts—an oath, could not : and it must have been some such practical knowledge of the perversion of this kind of vow which, according to the testimony of Theophrastus, induced the Tyrians, neighbours of the Jews, to forbid it expressly by law among themselves [t].

St. Chrysostom's account of it approaches very nearly to the above. They taught, says he [u], the young men, under a cloke of piety, to despise their parents . . . . If any parent said to his son, Give me this sheep which thou hast—or this calf—or any other such thing—they used to say, This is Corban for God—with which thou wishest to be obliged by me—and thou canst not receive it. And so it was that a double evil was committed : for neither did they bring it to God, and yet, as if they intended to bring it, they deprived their parents of it—both mocking their parents under pretence of God, and God, under pretence of their parents.

The account of Origen is not equally correct ; and yet he confesses he should never have discovered it, such as it is, if he had not been taught it by a native Jew [v].

It sometimes happened, says he, that the lenders of money, meeting with unreasonable borrowers, who were able, but not willing, to repay them the loan, dedicated what was due to them to the account of the poor, for whom contributions used to be cast into the treasury, according to his ability, by each of those who were willing to communicate unto them. They said, therefore, sometimes to the borrowers, according to their own language, It is Corban, that is, a gift, what thou owest to me ; for I have dedicated it to the account of the worship due to God, viz. unto the poor. Upon that, the borrower as indebted no longer to

---

[s] De Sacrorum Abusu. iv. 9.   [t] Jos. Contra Apion. i. 22.   [u] Oper. ii. 325.
[v] Comm. i. 245.

men but to God, and to the worship due to him, was as it were compelled, even though against his inclination, to repay the loan......

What then the lender used to do to the borrower some of the children sometimes did to their parents ; and said to them, whatsoever thou mightest be benefited in by me, father or mother, this know that thou receivest from the Corban ; upon the footing of the poor who are dedicated to God. Upon that, the parents when they heard that it was Corban, dedicated to God, which they were giving to them, were no longer willing to receive it from their children, though they might be altogether in want of necessaries. The elders, therefore, delivered such a tradition to the laity —that, whosoever should say to his father, or his mother, that what is given to any of them is Corban, and a gift, the same was no longer a debtor to his father or mother, in giving the things which are wanted for the necessaries of life.

To return, then, from this digression. It may now be considered evident that St. Mark, beginning his account of our Saviour's reply, vii. 6. begins with the latter part of it first ; and, therefore, that what follows from vii. 9. to 13. either was repeated in the course of the reply, or is given by way of recapitulation. And this I believe to have been the case ; as the following comparison of his account with St. Matthew's, beginning from the point where they first agree, perhaps will shew.

I. To set aside the historical matter, Mark vii. 3. 4. the question of the Pharisees, vii. 5. may still be correctly recorded, as well as at Matthew xv. 2. If the Pharisees came to our Lord in a body, then, unless they spoke by one man, both forms of the question might be put—or, what is equally probable, as the substance of both questions is the same, meaning that the interrogators came to our Lord, on such and such an occasion, to put such and such a demand; that this fact is represented in the shape of a direct interrogation may be due to the principle of the ancient historical simplicity; according to which every thing is stated directly which more refined history expresses indirectly.

II. The latter part of our Lord's reply, Matt. xv. 7—9. admits of being harmonized with Mark vii. 6—8. thus :

Matt.	Mark.
Ὑποκριταὶ	... ...
καλῶς προεφήτευσε περὶ ὑμῶν	καλῶς προεφήτευσεν Ἡσαίας
Ἡσαίας	περὶ ὑμῶν
... ...	τῶν ὑποκριτῶν,
λέγων·	ὡς γέγραπται·
Ἐγγίζει μοι ὁ λαὸς οὗτος	Οὗτος ὁ λαὸς
τῷ στόματι αὐτῶν,	... ...
καὶ τοῖς χείλεσί με τιμᾷ·	τοῖς χείλεσί με τιμᾷ,
ἡ δὲ καρδία αὐτῶν	ἡ δὲ καρδία αὐτῶν
πόρρω ἀπέχει ἀπ' ἐμοῦ.	πόρρω ἀπέχει ἀπ' ἐμοῦ.
Μάτην δὲ σέβονταί με,	Μάτην δὲ σέβονταί με,
διδάσκοντες διδασκαλίας ἐντάλ-	διδάσκοντες διδασκαλίας ἐντάλ-
ματα ἀνθρώπων.	ματα ἀνθρώπων.

The account will then be concluded by Mark vii. 8: for the allusion to the washings of cups and quarts is critically in reference to what was premised at vii. 3. 4; and on that ground alone might justly be considered a part of what was actually said.   It is more necessary to remark that, with vii. 8. the Evangelist suspends the thread of the discourse; and when he resumes it at vii. 9. it is with the historical premonition, καὶ ἔλεγεν αὐτοῖς : which might as well be rendered, He said, moreover, unto them, as, And he said to them ; the first, a mode of speaking proper for a recapitulation, and the second, one proper for a continuation.

We may suppose, then, that by the pause at vii. 8. the Evangelist designed to imply that Jesus made an end of speaking *there ;* and what follows from vii. 9. was intended to explain vii. 8. The command of God was not renounced or broken, by holding the tradition of men, in the washing of cups and quarts—which were mere formalities, and so far purely indifferent—but in the much more serious instance of the perversion of the vow of Corban, and in such instances as resembled that.   This was what our Saviour meant; and what St. Mark knew him to mean; and what, therefore, by citing the first part of the reply (which, otherwise, he might not have referred to at all) he considered it necessary to explain. This part of St. Mark, then, viz. vii. 9—13. must be harmonized with Matthew xv. 3—6. and the way to harmonize them is as follows :

	Matthew.	Mark.
I.	xv. 3.	... ...
II.	... ...	vii. 9.

which will ensue upon it with equal emphasis and propriety; for it is in the nature of irony to dwell on a subject, and to repeat the same thing in other words. Why do ye, also, transgress the commandment of God, for the sake of your tradition? With reason do ye annul the commandment of God, that ye may observe your tradition.

III.	xv. 4. 5.	vii. 10. 11.

Between these there is no other difference, except that the former says, ὁ γὰρ Θεὸς ἐνετείλατο, and the latter, Μωσῆς γὰρ εἶπε. Both, however, point to the same commandment, and the same commandment of God—and the reason why St. Mark ascribes it in part to Moses, and St. Matthew ascribes it to God, is that the passage, which follows, is made up of two quotations, one from the decalogue, actually the words of God, the other from Exodus xxi. 17. Lev. xx. 9. one of the precepts of Moses, as such.

IV.	xv. 6.	vii. 12. 13.

Καὶ ἠκυρώσατε τὴν ἐντολὴν τοῦ Θεοῦ διὰ τὴν παράδοσιν ὑμῶν.

Καὶ οὐκέτι ἀφίετε αὐτὸν οὐδὲν ποιῆσαι τῷ πατρὶ αὐτοῦ ἢ τῇ μητρὶ αὐτοῦ· ἀκυροῦντες τὸν λόγον τοῦ Θεοῦ τῇ παραδόσει ὑμῶν, ἧ παρεδώκατε. Καὶ παρόμοια τοιαῦτα πολλὰ ποιεῖτε.

For as to the words Καὶ οὐ μὴ τιμήσῃ τὸν πατέρα αὐτοῦ, ἢ τὴν μητέρα αὐτοῦ, Matt. xv. 5. they are no part of our Saviour's observations, as such, but of the same traditionary quotation, which began at ὑμεῖς δὲ λέγετε—just before.   Ye say that, whosoever shall say to his father, or to his mother, Be it δῶρον, whatever might be useful to thee of mine, he shall by no means honour his own father, or his own mother. The structure of the original proves this: the redundant καὶ, which has given so much trouble to the critics, is a clear mark of a quotation; being neither more nor less than the Hebrew *vau* redundant.   It will follow, on this principle, that in St. Mark's account, between vii. 12. and vii. 11. after ὠφεληθῇς, there is an ἀποσιώπησις—which must be filled up from St. Matthew's.   And, indeed, the direct form of verse 12. compared with the indirect of verse 11. cannot be otherwise explained.   Ye say, if a man does so and so—and ye no longer suffer him: which is an anacoluthon.   The assertion, corresponding to the assumption, would, thus, evidently be wanting—and we must have understood it, though it were not expressed: If a man does so and so, *he shall not do so and so*—and ye no longer suffer him.

With regard to the rest of the narrative, or Matt. xv. 10—20. Mark vii. 14—23. there is little or no difficulty. The brief, idiomatic, and sententious, form of Matt. xv. 10. 11. in the address to the multitude, may be considered a proof that these were our Saviour's very words ; which St. Mark, for the sake of avoiding the ambiguity of the expressions *coming out of the mouth*, or, *going into the mouth*, has changed for what they were intended to denote, *coming out of a man*, or, *going into a man—coming out of the heart*, or, *going into the heart*.   It is possible, however, that our Lord might have first pronounced Matt. xv. 11. and then added Mark vii. 15. 16; connecting them by a γάρ.   Οὐδὲν γάρ ἐστιν ἔξωθεν...ἀκουέτω.

The remainder of the conversation, that is, with the disciples in private, is most easily to be adjusted together.   I will observe only that ἀκμὴν, Matt. xv. 16. is simply equivalent to οὕτω, Mark vii. 18: after which they proceed, as the Harmony will shew in its proper place, almost in common, to the end. I shall conclude, therefore, with the following general remarks.

First, as I observed on a former occasion, St. Mark, who throughout this account supplies so much more original matter, did not write as the mere abbreviator of St. Matthew. Secondly, premising it all obviously for the benefit of Gentile readers, he must have written after the Gospel had begun to be preached, and probably had been some time preached, to the Gentiles. Thirdly, speaking of the sect of the Pharisees, and of such and such customs, as still in being, he wrote before the destruction of Jerusalem. Fourthly, St. Luke, who records elsewhere[w] an incident very similar to that which gave occasion to this whole discourse, and, though writing professedly for a Gentile, premises no similar explanation, may justly be supposed to carry St. Mark's Gospel—which does supply this explanation—along with his own; and, therefore, to have written *after* St. Mark; as St. Mark, for a like reason, must have written *after* St. Matthew.

[w] xi. 38.

DISSERTATION XIV.

On the first instance of the dispute among the disciples concerning precedence.

As I have considered it necessary to detach Mark ix. 33—end, and Luke ix. 46—50. (which, as far as it extends, is obviously the same with that) from Matt. xviii. 1—9. and much more from the remainder of this chapter, the grounds of the separation require to be distinctly stated.

For this purpose, the course of events needs not to be traced further back than to the time of the return to Capernaum, which is seen to have now taken place. While our Lord, accompanied by the Twelve, was still on his way to that city, but before they were actually arrived at it, we learn, from the express testimony of St. Mark, and the implicit testimony of St. Luke, that a dispute occurred among them on the subject of preeminence—which, though known to Jesus at the time, he did not, however, think proper to reprove at the time.

Again; when they were now come to the city, but not yet arrived at the house, to which they were going, in the city, we learn, from the account of St. Matthew[a], that the collectors of the didrachma applied to Peter—apart from Jesus, if not from the rest of the Twelve—with the enquiry, Doth not, or, will not, your Master pay the didrachma? This application to Peter, in particular, might be the effect of accident; or, what is more probable, and seems to be implied in the question itself, it was made to him in the name of the other Apostles, as all being the regular attendants of Jesus—and, perhaps, to him, as holding a certain rank or precedence among that body. This circumstance, also, though known to our Lord, at the time when it happened, as well as the former, was not noticed by him at the time, any more than the other.

[a] xvii. 24.

When, however, they were all come into private, before Peter had informed him of this application, and, consequently, before any other business could have been transacted, he shewed him, in the manner recorded Matt. xvii. 25—end, that he was already aware of it—and by Peter's own admission, who had so recently acknowledged him as the Son of God[b], ought to have been considered by him exempt from a tribute, imposed for the service of God. That he might not, however, give unnecessary offence, he sends him to the lake, to angle for a fish—in whose mouth he should find a stater—and with this he instructs him to pay the tax in Jesus' behalf, and in his own.

This coupling of Peter with Jesus, in the proposed payment, seems to have been a necessary consequence of the piece of money being a stater—and no especial compliment to that disciple himself—for the value of the stater amounting to two didrachma, or an entire shekel, it was just equivalent to the requisite tribute from two persons. And that the coin, provided for the purpose, was a stater might be due, in like manner, to the circumstance that there was no single coin in circulation, exactly equal to two drachmæ, or the half shekel of the sanctuary. Hence, had any other Apostle, and not Peter, been sent upon this errand, no doubt he would have been commissioned to pay the tax for himself and for Jesus in conjunction, as well as Peter.

I have made this observation merely because some commentators have thought that, by the working of a special miracle in his behalf, as well as of Jesus, a kind of distinction having been conferred upon Peter, it might have produced the dispute, which afterwards occurred among the disciples. Now, it should be remembered that Capernaum, whence Peter was despatched, was at some distance from the lake—that he has to go to the lake, and to return thence—and to find out the collectors of the tribute, and to discharge his commission to them—before he can come back to the house. There was room, then, for much to have transpired in this house, during his absence, at which he could not possibly have been present—at least throughout it—and something of this kind seems actually to have taken place.

For all the particulars, connected with the history of the tribute money, are related by St. Matthew only; whose account is such as clearly to imply that nothing else could have preceded in the house, after their arrival in it, before this event. Yet St. Mark expressly, and St. Luke by implication, do each of them shew that, as soon as Jesus, with the disciples, was come into the house, he enquired about the subject of the dispute by the way. This enquiry, then, could not have preceded the departure of Peter; but took place either during his absence, or after his return.

Now the disciples, according to the same authority, though questioned by our Lord himself, made no answer to the enquiry as so put; because, as we are also informed, the subject of the dispute had been which was the greatest; that is, because, for some reason or other, they did not venture to acknowledge the subject of the dispute. But, according to St. Matthew, xviii. 1. either then, or some time after, they came to Jesus of their own accord, to prefer the very same question. And if *this* fact should appear inconsistent with *that*, xviii. 21—a little further on—may assist us to explain the inconsistency.

Peter is there mentioned as present, and as a hearer of the discourse which had just been pronounced; a discourse, which it is needless to observe arose solely and directly out of the question, xviii. 1. itself. If so, Peter must have been present, when that question was put; and, consequently, he had executed his commission, and returned to the house, before that question was put. When the disciples, therefore, were interrogated by our Lord himself, and made him no answer, (which must have been almost as soon as they were got into the house,) Peter would be away—when they came to him, with the same question, of their own accord, he must have been returned. The two occasions, therefore, and whatever else arose in consequence of each, would be entirely distinct: when Jesus put *his* question, Peter was absent—when the disciples put *their* question, Peter was present. What is recorded between the two must, consequently, have transpired *after* his departure, and *before* his return: and this is that part of St. Mark and St. Luke respectively, which I mentioned above.

In defence of the same conclusion we may further reason as follows.

If the disciples proposed to Jesus, of their own accord, the very question which they had not specified at his request, it is clear that they must have had some reason for their silence, distinct from the mere subject of their dispute. The absence of Peter, when Jesus made his enquiry, might possibly be that reason; and his return, combined with other considerations, about to be mentioned, might have led to the putting of their question. It is a singular fact, that up to this period of the Gospel-history there are no instances on record of any dispute among the followers of our Lord, upon this subject of their comparative personal superiority—but after the present period there are. It is not less singular that this first instance of such a dispute followed, at no great distance of time, upon the Transfiguration. At the Transfiguration three only of the Apostles, Peter, and James, and John, were permitted to be present; and these had been strictly commanded to conceal the fact not merely from the knowledge of the world at large, but even from their fellow-disciples, until the Son of Man should be risen from the dead: a prohibition which, St. Luke informs us, they were accordingly careful to observe.

Now the Transfiguration was altogether so mysterious and remarkable a scene—it exhibited our Saviour in so novel, and so unexpected, a character—it invested him with a personal glory and majesty, so different from his former habitual humiliation—that the privilege of being present at such a transaction must have appeared to the three disciples a very high distinction, conferred exclusively on themselves; and which the very injunction of secrecy, consequent upon it, could not fail to enhance in their estimation. To have been eyewitnesses of an event—and even to have taken some part in it themselves—which they were not permitted so much as to mention to others, could not be regarded in any other light.

If, then, on the ordinary principles of human conduct, it was antecedently probable that the singular favour, extended to these three, in being alone admitted to such a personal and sensible manifestation of the glory of Christ, as had never been before, nor was ever after, vouchsafed, should have raised in their minds some idea of their own superiority either in personal rank and preeminence, or in the degree of their Master's comparative estimation of his disciples, then, that so soon after this event, but never before it, the followers of our Lord should be found disputing upon this very subject, seems strongly to corroborate the presumption of the cause, to which this dispute should be referred.

It is certain that, at this time, even the most intimate of our Saviour's followers were not exempt from the common mistake of their age, and their nation—that the kingdom of the Messiah, which they all expected shortly to appear, would be a temporal kingdom. Nor was it unlikely that, under the influence of such a mistake, their very simplicity of purpose, their devoted attachment to Christ himself, should have been mixed up with somewhat of selfish and worldly considerations. They could not believe that their Master was to become a great and victorious monarch, possessed of honours, wealth, and power, at his disposal, and not also believe that *they*, his chosen attendants, his most immediate and confidential followers, who had sacrificed their all to attach themselves to him, should sometime be signally distinguished and rewarded. Nor was it unnatural that, with such expectations in common, and all being actuated by the same ambition, they should have regarded each other as rivals and competitors, the success of one of whom would be prejudicial to the interests of another— that they should have been mutually envious or jealous— each setting himself above another—proud of imaginary distinctions—presuming on whatever might flatter this desire of personal superiority, and regarding with an evil eye any marks or expressions of real, or supposed, partiality, conceded to some, but denied to the rest. It would have been much more extraordinary had nothing of this kind ever happened—or ever been recorded to have happened —among them, than that in one or two instances, as is the case, there should be actual proof of its existence.

The Twelve Apostles, in particular, who had been selected by our Lord himself from the body of the disciples in general, and, by his act also, had been in common invested with privileges, withholden from the rest, could not fail to be persuaded that they stood, or were destined to stand, ever after their ordination, on peculiar ground. And if there was, as there seems to have been, from the first a kind of order or gradation in the dignity of the Apostles themselves, by which four of them more especially, Peter and Andrew, James and John, were advanced to the head of the rest, these four might be disposed, from the first, to think more highly of themselves, than they ought to have thought. Certain it is that, in the course of their common attendance upon Christ, many circumstances subsequently transpired which, by drawing a kind of distinction between these and the rest, would have a tendency to unite them together, and to discriminate them from the rest. Besides which, each two of them were brothers; and so would naturally hold together; and our Lord's demeanour towards them, upon numerous occasions, was such as to designate one of them, Peter, for the acknowledged head, and in some sense the representative, of the whole body—and another, John, as the personal and intimate friend of himself. Between these two in particular, there seems to have been always a good understanding, and a degree of intimacy of which there is no proof in the case of any two among the rest—an intimacy which (if it is not even to be traced back to the time, when both they and their brethren were connected by the ties of a common partnership, before any had yet become followers of Christ) our Lord's employing them, distinct from the rest, on more occasions than one, upon confidential commissions, tended either to produce, or to cement ; and of which their subsequent history in the Acts supplies fresh proofs.

As, therefore, the disputes among the Twelve, on the subject of preeminence, begin to be dated from the time of the Transfiguration, but not before it, it is not an improbable conjecture that they were produced by that event itself—in disposing the three Apostles, who had witnessed it, to believe that their Master's kingdom, such as they all expected, was now at hand ; and, consequently, that personal honours and advancements, of some kind or other, might safely be anticipated by them all.   In this expectation, each would be eager for the highest rank ; and measuring the extent of their future, by the degree of their present, distinctions, each would be anxious to appear and to be acknowledged the greatest.   In all these instances, the point in dispute among them, whensoever it is stated, seems to have been as much the question who was, even then—as, who should be, hereafter, the greatest.   Compare in particular Luke xxii. 24. which is a case in point.   The four disciples, who, as we have seen, had private, antecedent, reasons for holding together, might begin to take too much upon them, in comparison of the rest.   The natural ardour of the disposition of Peter is proved by his whole history—and that the sons of Zebedee, besides being persons of some rank and property originally, were by no means deficient in ambition, or the desire of individual aggrandizement, appears from their memorable petition, preferred some months after the present time.

In every dispute, then, upon this subject Peter, and the sons of Zebedee, we may presume would take an active, and probably even a leading, part.   When, therefore, the disciples were questioned about their dispute, if Peter was absent, as it would appear he must have been, they might not, or they could not, know what to reply.   Nor would it be any objection to the supposition of *his* absence in particular that the Evangelist, proceeding to recount the discourse which our Lord delivered, of his own accord, in consequence of their silence, tells us he called to him previously, τοὺς δώδεκα [c]. Ever after the appointment of the Apostles, and so long as their number consisted of Twelve, the phrase οἱ δώδεκα is a denomination equivalent to οἱ ἀπόστολοι; and as ordinarily employed means no more than that. After the fall of Judas, and before the substitution of Matthias, they are called on the same principle οἱ ἕνδεκα. It is not except in a special case, where a part of the whole body were expressly to be opposed to the rest, that the phrase οἱ δέκα occurs—as for instance, to discriminate the rest of the Twelve from the sons of Zebedee. Now no such discrimination could possibly have been here intended by St. Mark; for he makes no mention of the departure of Peter; and, therefore, in speaking of the Twelve, could not have used a term, which would have implied that he, or any other of them, was absent. There is a similar instance of the use of terms Luke xxiv. 33. 1 Cor. xv. 5. compared with John xx. 24. Besides, the discourse which follows, whensoever it might have been pronounced, was doubtless designed not for a part of them, but for all; and whether heard at the time by all, or not, would doubtless be repeated to all.

Yet the act, which by both St. Mark and St. Luke is distinctly attributed to John, I cannot help thinking is a proof, even in them, that Peter was absent. The material fact itself, the dispossession of spirits in the name of Jesus, by one who followed not with them, would be rendered sufficiently probable by Matt. xii. 27. or Luke xi. 19. which shew the practice of exorcism to have been common, among the Jews, in our Saviour's time; and it is actually confirmed by a case in point, the case of the sons of Sceva [d]. Josephus has given an account of one Eleazar, a famous exorcist, in the time of Vespasian [e]; and described also a certain plant, which was to be found only at Machærus [f], of great repute in such exorcisms. He confirms, too, the fact in his own time, or at least the popular belief in his own

---

[c] Mark ix. 35.   [d] Acts xix. 13. 14.   [e] Ant. Jud. viii. ii. 5.
[f] B. vii. vi. 3.

time in the fact, of the reality of demoniacal possession—
and designates demons themselves as the spirits of wicked
men. Et propter hoc, observes Irenæus[g], Judæi usque
nunc hac ipsa adfatione dæmonas effugant; quando omnia
timeant invocationem ejus, qui fecit ea. Compare also
Justin Martyr, Dial. 321. and Origen, contra Celsum, iv.
183. 184. which prove that the custom continued with the
Jews long after the Gospel period.

Now this interruption (for it must be regarded as one)
taking place in the midst of our Lord's discourse, and almost as soon as he had begun to speak, is evidently made
in the name of the body; and concerned a question relating
to the rights and privileges, real or imaginary, of the body.
That John, therefore, was the spokesman in this instance,
and not Peter, which is contrary to every other case in
point, is some ground for the presumption that Peter was
not present at the time.

It is not a less probable account of the origin of their
own question, so soon after, that Peter might then have returned, and been informed of what had passed in his absence. St. Matthew is express[h] that the question was put
the very same day, upon which the incident occurred with
respect to the tribute-money, and not long after the mission
of Peter himself. The phrase, ἐν ἐκείνῃ τῇ ὥρᾳ, ἐν ἐκείνῃ τῇ
ἡμέρᾳ, is among the number of *his* idioms—as the phrase,
ἐν αὐτῇ τῇ ὥρᾳ, ἐν αὐτῇ τῇ ἡμέρᾳ, is among those of St. Luke.
He is equally express that it was put by the disciples of
their own accord. It is evident from more than one instance of the fact in the Gospel-history, that, neither when
travelling from place to place, nor when stationary in the
same house, did the disciples approach indiscriminately to
the person of their Master. Hence, upon one occasion, as
they were going to Jerusalem for the last time, we find it
accordingly specified that, ἦν προάγων αὐτοὺς ὁ Ἰησοῦς, καὶ
ἐθαμβοῦντο, καὶ ἀκολουθοῦντες ἐφοβοῦντο[i]. Nor can we doubt
that to this custom of the Master's always walking before,

or at the head of, the disciples [k], is to be traced the origin of that usual mode of designating the act of becoming a believer in, or a disciple of, Christ, by *following after* him—and even of that highly mystical, though apposite and beautiful, description of the relation between the Messias and his true church, which takes up so much of the tenth chapter of St. John's Gospel; and in one of the most striking and characteristic of its circumstances, that of the Shepherd's walking to and fro, at the head of his flock, and of the sheep's being taught to follow him, is derived from an actual fact in pastoral life among the Jews. The phrase, προσῆλθον οἱ μαθηταί, is consequently to be literally understood—as implying that they came to Jesus formally, and for the express resolution of their own doubt.

Besides this, however, the very terms, in which the question is couched, are an internal, and almost a convincing, evidence that something had passed before, omitted, indeed, by St. Matthew, but obviously such in possibility as would thus have been supplied by St. Mark. Classical readers need not to be reminded of the difference between these two propositions, τίς μείζων ἐστὶν, and, τίς ῎ΑΡΑ μείζων ἐστὶν—ἐν τῇ βασιλείᾳ τῶν οὐρανῶν; nor English readers of the plain distinction between saying Who is greatest, *and* Who, *then*, is greatest, in the kingdom of heaven? Both would imply the same doubt, and both would solicit its resolution—but the latter would also imply that something must have preceded, known to both the speakers, and the party addressed, such as might have suggested the question; which the other would not. The particle ἄρα, in its proper inferential sense, is never useless, or without signification, either in the Gospels, or out of them [l]; and the received translation, having omitted it here altogether, is chargeable with an inaccuracy. If the disciples, having been previously questioned, on a certain point, by our Lord, without returning an answer, had subsequently resolved, of their own accord, to ask him about it—or if, without having

[k] Vide also 2 Kings ii. 3. [l] Matt. vii. 20. xii. 28. xvii. 26. xix. 25. 27. xxiv. 45. Mark iv. 41. xi. 13. Luke i. 66. viii. 25. xii. 42. xxii. 23.

been questioned concerning the point in dispute, yet knowing that he was aware of it, they had agreed to refer it to him—this is the very form of words, with which they would be likely to approach him : Tell us, what *then* is the case—which *then* is the greatest in the kingdom of heaven ? It is certain, however, from St. Mark's account, that no such reference as this could have voluntarily proceeded from the disciples, prior to any question of our Lord's : if it was made, then, at all—as it is equally clear from St. Matthew it must sometime have been made—it must have been made after our Lord's question had been put ; and, consequently, after what he did and said, when *his* question, though put, had met with no answer from *them*.   And this point being once established, whatever account we may give of the origin of the subsequent question (which I think is sufficiently explained by supposing the return of Peter in the mean time, and his being made acquainted with what had passed in his absence) the entire distinctness of this part of St. Mark and of St. Luke, from any part of the eighteenth chapter of St. Matthew, follows as matter of course.

A critical comparison of the narratives themselves will go far to substantiate the same conclusion.

For, not to insist on minute, and merely verbal, discrepancies—of which many might be pointed out—it must be evident that the discourse in St. Mark, beginning εἴ τις θέλει [m], and ending with εἰρηνεύετε ἐν ἀλλήλοις [n], (excepting only the interruption from 38—40. alluded to above,) is an integral discourse, not only delivered at the same time, but relating to a kindred topic, the common moral—the winding up—of which are contained in the ἔχετε ἐν ἑαυτοῖς ἅλας, καὶ εἰρηνεύετε ἐν ἀλλήλοις, with which it concludes.   No one, however, will say this of the discourse in St. Matthew, beginning xviii. 3. and extending to xviii. 35. The subjects of this discourse cannot be considered by me at present ; or I think it might be shewn that, besides the topic of giving offence, which predominates almost exclusively in St. Mark's,

[m] ix. 35.   [n] Ib. 50.

many others are combined with it, which, however gradually they may be deduced from that, are yet very different from it. If St. Mark was recounting what passed on the same occasion, it is a natural question, why was so much less related by him, than by St. Matthew? especially as that principle, which accounts for so many omissions, under similar circumstances, in St. Luke, is not applicable here to him ; viz. that he passed over some things at present, because he knew they would come again elsewhere. No part of what he would thus have omitted here is discoverable any where in his Gospel afterwards. Or though we should confine ourselves strictly to the topic of giving offence in both, there would still be the substance of 10—14. in St. Matthew, relating unquestionably to that topic, or most intimately connected with it, which yet would be wanting in St. Mark.

The omission of the parenthetic matter in St. Mark, 38—40. referring to the interruption which proceeded from John, is another presumptive proof that St. Matthew's narrative belongs to a distinct time and occasion, from St. Mark's. Whatever, in the course of the Gospel-history, might have tended to the credit of the Apostles, St. Matthew, himself an Apostle, may be found with a genuine Christian humility almost invariably to omit—and St. Mark and St. Luke, who were not Apostles, especially the latter, almost as regularly to notice. But, with respect to what might have tended to their discredit, the reverse is generally the case—and such was the nature of the interruption in question, whether in reference to the fact itself, as proceeding from a jealous impatience that the Apostolic privileges should be usurped by any who were not Apostles, or in reference to the oblique censure, passed upon the act by our Lord.

The omission also in St. Mark of what might have answered to verse 7. in St. Matthew is not unimportant; if, as it may be shewn, this verse assigns the very ground, or principle, of that strict personal duty, with regard to personal causes of offence, on which the discourse begins to insist from ix. 43. downwards. Nor is it without its use to observe how contrary to the characteristic fulness of St. Matthew, in his account of our Lord's discourses, it would be, to suppose that *he* has blended together in verse 8. the two first of those scandals, of each of which St. Mark has made a distinct proposition—much more, that he should have omitted entirely the conclusion subjoined to each verse in St. Mark, ὅπου ὁ σκώληξ αὐτῶν οὐ τελευτᾷ, καὶ τὸ πῦρ οὐ σβέννυται—a quotation from Isaiah [o], which, in addition to its natural force and simplicity of meaning, our Saviour, by thrice repeating, had stamped with peculiar emphasis and solemnity.

On the supposition that our Lord, in St. Matthew, is merely repeating what he had lately said in St. Mark, all these circumstances of difference are easily explained. With a general agreement of both the sentiments and the language, such as could not fail to ensue while each was still fresh in the mind of the speaker, there must still be some particular discrepancies—unless he was purposely studious of novelty or refinement—and those points, which had been the most laboured before, it is natural should be the most summarily referred to now ; and what had been insisted on with the greatest emphasis then, on that very account would bear to be the least prominently brought forward afterwards.

I shall conclude, therefore, by observing barely that it is no objection to this supposition of a second discourse, and on the same topic of self-abasement, or Christian humility, that it implies the parties addressed to have been little benefited by the first. Had there been no second instance of any such dispute among the disciples, as this, the disposition, which produced the first, we might conclude must have been eradicated by the rebuke, which had been given to the first. But as it is, there are many more instances— all of them later in their occurrence than the present time. Our Lord's repeated injunctions in favour of humility would not have been necessary, if his first had wrought their full effect. It is remarkable, however, that at the very moment when he was lecturing his Apostles on meekness, forbear-

[o] lxvi. 24.

ance, and self-abasement—in the midst of a discourse levelled distinctly against pride, ambition, selfishness—John
addresses him, not more in his own behalf, than in the
name of the rest, and in a manner, which seems to expect
approbation, not to be afraid of censure—complaining of
some stranger who had usurped the privileges, belonging as
they thought to them alone. This circumstance must prove
very clearly that neither the influence of authority, the most
acknowledged—nor the meaning of language, the most
simple and positive—nor the sense of duty, the most unquestionable—nor the fervour of attachment, the most sincere—nor the strength of faith, the most undoubting—nor
the possession of miraculous power, however preternatural
—could as yet effectually renovate and transform the Apostles, or eradicate from them that principle of self-love,
which is the root and spring of every malicious, and worldly,
feeling. This was reserved for the powerful energy of
Christian charity, which is the offspring of Christian holiness, and both in its cause, and in its effect, is the gift of
divine grace only. We may observe, however, that the
prohibition of these disputes is more strong and emphatic,
in the later, than in the earlier, cases of their occurrence—
which, also, was naturally to be expected.

DISSERTATION XV.

On the supplementary relation of John vii—xi. 54. *to the three first Gospels.*

THAT they, who are called in the Gospels the 'Αδελφοὶ of Christ, were living, at this period of the Gospel-history, in Capernaum, as well as he, may very probably be collected from what was related elsewhere [a]. It is true that, at the visit to Nazareth, soon after that occurrence, some of his relations are spoken of, under the same denomination, as still resident there [b]: but these, it should be distinctly observed, are only his *sisters*—the names of his brethren, indeed, are also alluded to, as the names of persons well known in Nazareth ; but they are not alluded to as living, or as present, in Nazareth at the time. There is no proof that the sisters of our Lord, whatever we may understand by that name, were living at Capernaum ; and, for ought which appears to the contrary, they might all be married, or all be settled, in Nazareth.

The Gospel of St. John, then, which, after the close of chapter vi. and the general statement contained in vii. 1. resumes the thread of the account with the conversation between our Lord and these his brethren, vii. 3—9. and at a time when the feast of Tabernacles was just at hand [c], resumes it either with the return of Jesus to Capernaum, Matt. xvii. 24. Mark ix. 33. Luke ix. 46—or with his residence there, subsequent to the return, and before the arrival of the feast. The same conclusion is deducible from the use of the terms μετάβηθι ἐντεῦθεν—which being stated, and intended to be received, ἁπλῶς can be understood, as in other cases of the like kind, only of Capernaum : not to say that our Lord's brethren, who as yet did not believe in him themselves, nor, consequently, attend upon him, as his dis-

---

[a] Matt. xii. 46. Mark iii. 21. 31. Luke viii. 19.   [b] Matt. xiii. 55. 56. Mark vi. 3.   [c] John vii. 2.

ciples, wheresoever he went, were so likely to meet him in
no place, as in this—the common residence of them all.

This being the state of the case, it is my object in the
present Dissertation to complete in part what was left unfinished, at the close of the eighth—by shewing that, as St.
John resumes the Gospel-history where the former Evangelists had, for a time, suspended it, and, consequently, in
this instance, as well as in others, has written with a view to
supply the omissions of his predecessors, so he continues it
down to the time where they had resumed it again; and,
therefore, has so supplied those omissions, that what he has
added of his own is an exact measure of what was deficient
in them. The antecedent probability of such a supplement
was no where greater, than here; for no where in the
former Gospels was there a larger omission, or more room
for supplementary matter, than here; the chasm, in the
continuity of their accounts, amounting in all of them to
four months, and in two of them to almost six.

First, then; that Judæa and Jerusalem are what the brethren of our Lord mean when they talk of the *world*, and
of his shewing himself unto the *world*, must be too evident
to require any proof; or if it did, the proof would be supplied by the answer of our Lord; which shews that he understood their words of a specific admonition to go up to the
approaching feast. The ultimate cause of the admonition,
we have seen elsewhere [d], was the fact of his continued absence from Jerusalem, for the last eighteen months—a fact,
which could not be unknown to his brethren, and, if they
themselves were ignorant of its motive, might naturally excite their surprize. The time of the conversation in question, then, we may conclude, would be about the usual time
of setting out from Galilee to attend the feast of Tabernacles; that is, three days at least before the tenth of Tisri,
the day of the fast, and of the atonement; to attend upon
which was as much a matter of obligation, as to be present
for the whole of the feast which ensued [e].

[d] Vol. ii. Diss. viii. 233. 234.   [e] Lev. xvi. 29—end. xxiii. 27—32.
Numb. xxix. 7—11.

The reply of our Lord[f] does not—as it has been falsely represented—assert that he should not go up to the feast at *all*, but merely that he should not go up *yet*; and he assigns a sufficient reason for delaying his attendance, in the danger to which *he* would be exposed by going up too openly, or too soon. He suffered his brethren, therefore, and, perhaps, even his Apostles, to set out at the usual time before him; and when all had been some while gone, he set out, and arrived, himself οὐ φανερῶς, ἀλλ᾽ ὡς ἐν κρυπτῷ[g]. Neither, then, his departure, nor his arrival, would be known except to those whom he might have apprized in confidence of his intentions—that is, as we may presume, only the Twelve.

The feast of Tabernacles began on the fifteenth of Tisri, and lasted from thence, for eight days in all, to the twenty-second inclusively[h]. Yet, Deut. xvi. 13—15. Lev. xxiii. 40—42. Neh. viii. 18. Ezek. xlv. 25. the feast as such is specified as a feast of *seven* days only, and the dwelling in booths, peculiar to it, is similarly also restricted. We must consider, therefore, the feast as such to have extended only from the fifteenth to the twenty-first of the month, inclusively; and the Jews, as we shall see by and by, always understood it accordingly. The middle day between these extremes would, consequently, be the eighteenth—and, ἤδη ...τῆς ἑορτῆς μεσούσης[i], our Lord first appeared in the temple: a description, however, which is not so determinate as critically to denote the middle day exactly, but also either the day before that, the seventeenth, or the day after it, the nineteenth; though, perhaps, one of those days it must denote.

We may suppose, then, our Lord would set out from Capernaum about the fourteenth of Tisri, and arrive in Jerusalem about the sixteenth. In the mean while, there would be abundance of time, since the tenth of the same month, or even earlier, as well as, apparently, some cause, for those reasonings, discourses, and conjectures, of the

[f] John vii. 8.   [g] vii. 10.   [h] Lev. xxiii. 34. 39. Numb. xxix.
12—35.   2 Chron. vii. 8—10.   [i] vii. 14.

people, concerning either the character of Christ, or the probability of his attendance, which are summarily related, John vii. 11—13.

Secondly, from this time forward there is no evidence to be discovered of more than, perhaps, *three* distinct days in the course of proceedings—two of them consecutive, the last day of the feast, the twenty-first of Tisri, and the day after that, or the twenty-second. The third, I shall endeavour to prove, was probably the nineteenth.

For first, to judge from the practice of our Saviour, at other times, when he resorted to the temple for the purpose of teaching, as at vii. 14. he resorted thither about the usual period of the morning service—that is, before πρωΐ—and passed the remainder of the day in the temple. The course of proceedings from vii. 14. will consequently begin about this period of the day—and what follows, as far as vii. 29. is so connected with vii. 14. and the rest, that all must have belonged to the same occasion. The same thing is true of vii. 30. as specifying a fact, the natural consequence of vii. 29; that our Lord's enemies would have seized upon him on the spot, but that his hour was not yet come.

With regard, however, to vii. 31. this connection is not so apparent. In conjunction with vii. 32. it merely accounts for the fact why the Pharisees sent officers to apprehend Jesus: a measure which, being produced by the observations of the multitude, vii. 31. could not have preceded—however soon it might have followed on—those observations. And these in particular might be the effect of that day's teaching, vii. 14. or the effect of any day's teaching, posterior to it—and it would still be equally true that they were made, as reported at vii. 31. They might, then, have been made on some other day of our Lord's appearing in public, and not on the first day of all—and it is some confirmation of the conjecture, that they contain a reference to miracles as performed, and still a performing, before the eyes of the observers. Now there is no proof that miracles were performed on the day of the appearance in public first, vii. 14. It is a much stronger argument to the same effect that, if vii. 31. does not belong to a different occasion from vii. 14—30. the mission of the officers, which is specified as the next event, vii. 32. and as produced by vii. 31. could not have taken place until long after the cause which produced it.

We may take it for granted that these officers would not be sent on one day, and return to those who sent them on the next—but be sent upon their mission, and return to report its success—on the same day in either case. Their mission is related at vii. 32—their return and report are related at vii. 45—and, between, a note of time is interposed at vii. 37. which shews that both their mission, and their return, if they took place on the same day, took place on the last and great day of the feast. This day, I shall shew by and by, was Tisri 21. But the last day of the feast cannot surely be considered the day of our Lord's appearance—for no day about the *middle* can possibly be confounded with the last day, or the *end*, of the feast. Unless, then, it could be shewn that the allusion at vii. 37—40. is an Anticipation of the order of time—or, unless it could be shewn that the officers of the Pharisees were sent on one day, and returned upon another, it will follow either that they were not sent on the same day, when the observations of the people were made—or those observations were not made on the middle day of the feast. If so, between vii. 14. the time of the first appearance in public, and vii. 32. the time of the mission of the officers, there is proof of the omission of one day at least; which, if the time implied vii. 14. was Tisri 19. vii. 32. compared with 37. will shew to have been Tisri 20: for the time implied vii. 37. was Tisri 21.

According to Josephus[k], every magistrate, whatever was his rank, had two ὑπηρέται, Levites—which implies that the magistrates themselves were priests. On this principle the Sanhedrim would have at least 144. Now these officers, vii. 32. must be considered distinct from the parties specified vii. 44. just as the parties specified vii. 30. on the same

[k] Ant. Jud. iv. viii. 14.

principle are not to be confounded with the officers, vii. 32. In each of these places, and elsewhere also, as oft as there is occasion for it, such persons are described indefinitely, as some of the Jews in general; but the officers both vii. 32. and 45. and 46. are specified by name, and described by their relation, as such. We may reasonably conclude, therefore, that the Pharisees in question—the superiors and employers of these men, to whom they stand in the relation of ὑπηρέται, or servants—are the members of the Sanhedrim, properly so called: and this conclusion is confirmed both by the mention of the Ἀρχιερεῖς, or heads of the courses, vii. 45. along with the Pharisees, and by the designation of Nicodemus, vii. 48. and vii. 50. as one of them. Nicodemus, as well as Joseph of Arimathea, was a ruler of the Jews, and a member of the Supreme Council[1].

The mission of the officers, then, was a common act of the Sanhedrim. If so, they were assembled before it—and it is evident they were assembled after it: their place of assembly also, as I shall shew elsewhere, was the vicinity of the women's court. They continued assembled, therefore, all the time that the officers were away. We cannot doubt, then, that both their mission and their return happened the same day; and the report, it is manifest, whensoever it happened, happened late in the day: for after a short consultation among themselves, in consequence of the report, the council broke up, and every man went to his own home[m]—Jesus, also, returned from the temple to the Mount of Olives[n]: and that all this was for the night appears from the mention of his return in the morning[o]. Unless, therefore, it should be supposed that, after despatching their officers, the Sanhedrim would sit a whole day, without either hearing from them, or desiring to know the success of their errand, even these officers could not have been sent until late in the day.

The proceedings of this day, then, as far as they are recorded, cannot include the proceedings of an entire day.

---

[1] John iii. 1. Luke xxiii. 50.   [m] vii. 50—53.   [n] viii. 1.   [o] viii. 2.

The first fact is the mission of the officers—the last is the separation of the council for the night, posterior to their return: between these there could have been, at the utmost, no very great interval of time. The partial account of this one day, however, which we suppose to have been the last of the feast, is presumptively an argument for the equally partial account, or even the entire omission, of the proceedings on any day before this. It was the fact of the mission of the officers, for such a purpose, and the supernatural restraint whereby it was frustrated, which seems to have given birth to the account of this day's proceedings at all. The Sanhedrim never before, nor after, took so bold and decisive a step, as this; nor, consequently, ever before or after, was the immunity of our Lord's person so seriously endangered as now. Yet the attempt of his enemies was defeated without any violence—without any concealment of his person—and by a coercion, however extraordinary or not to be expected, of a purely moral kind. This instance of the disappointment of one of the most deliberate designs upon his safety is unique in the Gospel-history—and more memorable, on every account, than even those occasions when, to preserve himself from sudden violence, he had recourse to miracle on the spot.

That the particulars of this day, notwithstanding, as far as they are related, are consecutively related, is sufficiently apparent from the narrative itself. The mission of the officers was the first thing, and their return and report were the last. Between these, vii. 33. 34. not only are distinctly addressed to them, and shew our Lord to have been acquainted with the purpose of their mission, but must have been addressed to them immediately on their arrival—and might be the very cause to excite that involuntary dread and reverence, by which they were subsequently overruled.

Soon after, the libation of water, which is justly supposed to be alluded to, as a passing ceremony, vii. 37—39. would begin to be celebrated—at least, if the time of the mission was late in the day—and, agreeably to our Saviour's invariable principle of drawing instruction from the occasion, it would furnish a striking opportunity for the prophetical declaration, which he pronounced accordingly. The ceremony consisted in fetching water from the fountain of Shiloh—carrying it in procession round the altar of burnt-offerings, accompanied by the recitation of Isaiah xii. 8—With joy shall ye draw water, out of the wells of salvation—and finally pouring out a libation thereof on the sacrifice upon the altar. The primary intention of all these ceremonies was both to commemorate the miraculous supply of water in the wilderness—and to typify the anticipated blessing of heaven, in the recurrence of the autumnal rains, against the arrival of seed-time. But the appositeness of the ceremony to the future facts of the Christian history—which is the application our Lord makes of it—is too plain and perceptible not to have been remarked by almost every commentator. Isaiah viii. 6. too, the waters of Shiloh are figuratively employed as a description of the Messias himself.

Now so far as concerned the simple libation of the water —the ceremony, according to the Rabbins, took place every day during the continuance of the feast; which they also call, and consider, a seven days' feast only[p]. On the seventh day, however, that is upon the *last* day of the feast, (vide the note of the translator of Maimonides, §. 8.) not only was this part of the ceremony performed as usual, but, besides that, and distinguishing this day, κατ' ἐξοχὴν, not merely as the *last*, but also as the *great*, day of the feast, there was a procession of the Priests and the Levites, carrying in their hands branches of the palm, and the citron; and singing the great Hillel to instrumental music; which procession encompassed the altar of burnt-offering, preparatory to the water-libation, seven times. The whole ceremony is particularly described, from the Rabbinical writers, by Dithmar in his note upon Maimonides, De jurejurando, i. 7. The women's court—our Lord's usual place of abode[q]

---

[p] Mishna ii. 276. 9. Maimon. De Sacrific. Jug. x. 6.   [q] John viii. 20.

—was the quarter where the people assembled to witness it; and though the same ceremony was performed both morning and evening, still it is a critical circumstance that the evening's libation is described as much the more joyous and solemn of the two; and if our Lord alluded to either, it must have been the evening's libation, to which he did allude: the time of the allusion admits of no other conclusion. The impression produced on the people, vii. 40. 41. by this application of the ceremony to himself, aided, perhaps, by the traditionary reference to the Messias, which even the Rabbins made of it, would be a very natural circumstance; and leaves it scarcely open to a question, whether it was not to this incident more especially, that the emissaries of the Pharisees alluded, in their own justification, vii. 46. shortly after.

We may come, then, to this conclusion, that John vii. 14. belongs to the nineteenth of Tisri, as somewhere about the middle of the feast—between which, and vii. 31. a whole day, the twentieth of the month, will be omitted. From vii. 31. the account will proceed, as we shall see hereafter, to the twenty-first, and the twenty-second, of Tisri in order. The twenty-first of Tisri will be the day, on which the Pharisees sought to apprehend Jesus—and they might choose to defer their attempt until this day, which was the last of the feast, for prudential reasons—lest the people should have been excited to any commotion on the one hand, and lest the opportunity of effecting their purpose should be lost on the other. The former might have been the consequence, upon any earlier day in the feast; and Jesus himself might be gone from Jerusalem, after the last. For the twenty-second of Tisri was necessarily a sabbath—upon which no such violence could have been attempted even by them.

On the twentieth of Tisri, the day after vii. 14. our Lord might not have visited the temple, perhaps because (vii. 30.) a specific design had been formed, the day before, against his life—or if he did visit it, nothing more memorable than usual occurred, while he was there. And this is no improbable supposition; for even the events of the last day of the feast, though the most specified in detail of any, are yet specified only in part, and for the sake of such circumstances, however beautiful or interesting in themselves, as yet transpired only upon that part : and the same thing is true of the account of the next day's proceedings also—to which we must now pass.

The note of time, viii. 2. renders it certain that the history of another day begins to be there recorded; and viii. 1. that it begins to be recorded in direct continuation of the preceding. As that day, then, was the twenty-first, this must have been the twenty-second, of Tisri; and the twenty-second of Tisri, whensoever it fell, was by appointment an extraordinary sabbath. Ἀνίενται ἀπὸ παντὸς ἔργου κατὰ τὴν ὀγδόην ἡμέραν [r]. It was, also, as the Rabbinical writers denominate it, the *clausula,* or closing day, of the feast ; that is, a kind of supernumerary to the rest, and in some sense a restauration of the solemnity afresh [s]. The same note of time, ὄρθρου δὲ πάλιν, fixes the period of the return on this day to the period of πρωΐ, or even an earlier period still— such also as appears on other occasions to have been our Saviour's rule in this respect [t].

The event, therefore, which is next related, viii. 3—11. not only is consecutively related, but, from the nature of the fact itself, was such as must have happened early. The adulteress was brought before Jesus, as recently surprized, and in the very act—κατελήφθη, ἐπ᾽ αὐτοφώρῳ, μοιχευομένη— She hath been detected, in the very act, committing adultery. If, then, she had been just detected, and in the act, the act had just been committed; and if she was detected in the act, and brought as soon as detected, she must have been brought early in the morning. Such an act was not likely to have been surprized in the day-time.

It is of the more importance to mark this conclusion, because at viii. 12. when the preceding transaction was now over, and our Lord had resumed his teaching, there is an evident and striking allusion, either to the rising of the sun,

[r] Ant. Jud. iii. x. 4.   [s] Num. xxix. 35—38.   Maimon. De Sacrific. Jug. x. 5.   [t] Matt. xxi. 18.   Mark xi. 20.   Luke xxi. 38.

which would take place at the proper hour of πρωΐ, or to
the trimming of the sacred lamps, which synchronized with
the time of morning sacrifice—or perhaps to both—for the
time of both would be the same, and as nearly coincident as
possible. This allusion is established not merely by the
consideration of the circumstances of time and place, and
the well-known principle of our Saviour's usage, but by the
exception of the Pharisees, against the declaration itself[t]:
for this exception implies that there was something in the
declaration, more solemn and more emphatic than usual.

The series of conversations, now begun, will consequently
proceed from the hour of πρωΐ—and down to viii. 59. the
time of our Lord's departure from the temple, produced by
the attempt to stone him, it is so connected by its proper
notes of sequence and coherency, that it must have proceeded consecutively. I can discover no point in the whole
detail, where it is possible to imagine a pause, except perhaps viii. 20; because the subject of discourse, though afterwards continuing the same, or passing gradually from one
associated topic to another, is yet there perceptibly changed
from what it was before. But though such a pause had
taken place here, there is no reason to suppose it would be
a pause of any long continuance, or that the sequel of the
discourse to viii. 59. did not take place consecutively, and
on the same spot with viii. 12—19.

This appears, first, from viii. 40. νῦν δὲ ζητεῖτέ με ἀποκτεῖναι, which implies a reference to viii. 20. where such a purpose is plainly recognized—and, secondly, from viii. 59.
ἐκρύβη, καὶ ἐξῆλθεν ἐκ τοῦ ἱεροῦ, διελθὼν διὰ μέσου αὐτῶν. He
first became invisible, then passed through the midst of
them, and so went out of the temple. For he was previously surrounded by the people in the treasury—and the
treasury lay in the women's court—and the women's court
was the second of the courts of the temple. The woman
taken in adultery must have been brought to him there;
for, we may presume, she could be brought to him in none
but her own court. Our Lord, therefore, had continued in

[t] viii. 13.

one place, since viii. 2. to the time of viii. 59. The period of this final departure, it may consequently be justly supposed, would not be much later than the beginning of morning service; that is, it would be about the second or third hour of the day. It followed immediately on viii. 58. when the Jews first took up stones; and it was produced by the necessity of a hasty retreat.

Now the narrative goes on to say, He went out of the temple, and so passed upon his way—and as he was passing he saw a man, blind from his birth [u]; the natural inference from which words is that the observation of this blind man, and the miracle which ensued upon it, both followed directly upon the departure from the temple—and therefore both happened the same day. It is highly inconsistent to suppose that the Evangelist means Jesus went out of the temple, and so passed on, *one* day, and observed, and healed, the blind man, *another*—not that he did both the same day, and as he was passing on the same occasion. Now Acts iii. 2. supplies a case in point to prove that such, as from bodily infirmities of any kind were obliged to depend upon charity, resorted to the gates or the avenues of the temple—and resorted thither at the times of prayer in particular. This man was evidently an object of the former description [v], and known for such—who was accustomed to resort and to sit somewhere, begging—and the time, when Jesus left the temple, was, as we have supposed, about the middle of morning prayer. It is highly probable, then, that the blind man had been brought, that very morning, to some one of the approaches to the temple, since our Lord first went in; and was accordingly discovered there by him, upon his again coming out.

This discovery was followed by his cure—and that cure was wrought upon a sabbath day [w]. But there is no reason to suppose this means the ordinary sabbath—the absence of the article would rather imply it was *a* sabbath, not *the* sabbath. The 22d of Tisri would always be a sabbath, on

[u] viii. 59. ix. 1.   [v] ix. 8.   [w] ix. 14.

f f 4

whatever day of the week it might fall; but it could not be the sabbath unless it fell on the seventh : and though this might sometimes happen, yet it was not the case in the present instance.   For A. U. 782. A. D. 29. when Nisan 15. fell upon April 17. and April 17. on Tuesday, Tisri 15. would fall on October 11. and October 11. according to the Tables, on Tuesday—but according to my own mode of reckoning the days of the week, on Thursday.   Upon this principle the tenth of Tisri would answer to October 6. and October 6. to Saturday—the nineteenth would answer to October 15. and October 15. to Monday—the twenty-second would answer to October 18. and October 18. to Thursday.   We began the detail of the course of events, as we assumed, with Tisri 19. and we have conducted it down, as we assume also, to Tisri 22; that is, from Monday October 15. to Thursday October 18. in the last year of our Saviour's ministry.   And that the 15th or 22d of Tisri this year did actually fall on the Thursday is proved by the fact that the 15th of Nisan the next year (which was the year of our Saviour's passion) actually fell on the Saturday. The next year was not intercalated—therefore, from the 15th of Tisri *exclusive* to the 15th of Nisan *inclusive* the number of days was 177: or 25 weeks, and two days over. Hence if the 15th of Tisri had fallen on Thursday, the 15th of Nisan would fall on Saturday : and *vice versâ*, if the 15th of Nisan fell on Saturday, the 15th of Tisri must have fallen on Thursday.   Now the 15th of Nisan did fall on Saturday : therefore the 15th of Tisri must have fallen on Thursday *.

Meanwhile it is no difficulty, even on the supposition of a sabbath, that the woman, taken in adultery, had been brought to our Lord the same morning—nor that the Jews

---

* The 15th of Nisan A. U. 783. A. D. 30. coincided with April 6: and from October 11. *exclusive* to April 6. *inclusive* the interval is 177.   Hence if October 11. was Thursday, April 6. would be Saturday; and if April 6. was Saturday, October 11. must have been Thursday.

had attempted to stone him. The object in bringing the woman was insidious ; and might be twofold, according to the event. If our Saviour had condemned the woman, he might be said both to have usurped a civil jurisdiction, and to have sanctioned a breach of the sabbath ; and if he had refused to condemn her, he might be said to have countenanced the crime of adultery. And as to the attempt at stoning—it was the effect of a zeal, as they conceived, for God, and to resent the crime of blasphemy—a crime, which the law required to be punished at any time, and in any place, on the spot [x] : Περὶ μὲν γὰρ γονέων ἀδικίας, ἢ τῆς εἰς τὸν Θεὸν ἀσεβείας, κἂν μέλλῃ τις, εὐθέως ἀπόλλυται [y].

With respect to the sequel of the chapter, and especially from ix. 13. and forward, the scrutiny, produced by the miracle, as arising out of the notice attracted by the miracle, it is reasonable to conclude, would follow not long after it, and, consequently, in the course of the same day. The miracle was performed so early in the morning, that there was abundance of time for this purpose : nor does it constitute any difficulty, that the miracle was wrought on a sabbath. If it was wrought thus early on the sabbath, and yet was not enquired into, in the course of the sabbath, either it attracted no notice, as soon as it was performed, (which would be palpably at variance with the fact,) or though it might have attracted notice on the sabbath, no body thought of enquiring into it on the sabbath. But such an enquiry would have been no breach of the sabbath —for it was not a formal act, instituted by order of the Sanhedrim, nor directed to any judicial, or legal, purpose, but the natural result of circumstances, and intended merely to ascertain the truth of the miracle. The man was conducted by those, who had known him before, to the Jewish authorities, of their own accord. A question, concerning the breach of the sabbath, did certainly arise out of it ; but that would be rather an argument that the investigation took place on the sabbath—the 22d of Tisri—a day of holy

[x] Lev. xxiv. 15. 16.   [y] Jos. Contra Apion. ii. 30.

convocation—at which time, the Sanhedrim would necessarily be assembled together, as the account, at ix. 13. and 24. evidently supposes them to have been, in their usual place in the temple. From the temple, also, the ejection alluded to, ix. 34. 35. amounting to a formal act of excommunication, may most naturally be supposed intended.

To the time of this excommunication, every thing from ix. 13. the beginning of the account, was manifestly regular and uninterrupted: the sequel of the transaction from ix. 35. to the end, which describes our Lord's interview with the man, who had never yet seen him in person, may, consequently, be justly considered to have happened the same day—especially as Jesus, when he heard of the man's ejection, seems purposely, and of his own accord, to have found him out. This honour he might shew him, because he knew the sincerity and firmness of his faith, and what declaration of it he would make, on being openly called upon to do so ; or rather, because he was the first, and as yet the only, example of any believer, who had suffered shame and reproach, and suffered them willingly, for his name's sake.

Now if the sequel of the ninth chapter belongs to this day, the first part of the tenth, 1—21. delivered consecutively upon that, must also belong to the same ; and, therefore, be part of the proceedings still at the feast of Tabernacles. It has been supposed, however, a part of the proceedings at the next visit to Jerusalem, when our Lord attended the Encænia ; and, consequently, it becomes necessary to discuss the question of its proper relation a little more at large.

I. The tenth chapter commences abruptly—with no allusion to the time, the place, or the occasion, when, where, and in consequence of which, the ensuing discourse was delivered. This might be natural enough, if it was actually delivered, with little or no delay, after the close of the preceding chapter ; but on no principle would it be so, if it was not delivered until at least two months later.

II. This abruptness is not more inconsistent with the reason of the thing, than with the practice of St. John—

than who, no Evangelist is more careful to note the circumstances of all the transactions which he records in detail;
and to whose accuracy, in this respect, the present instance
would constitute a singular exception, if the tenth chapter,
for part of its extent at least, standing, as it does stand, isolated and independent of all connection, is not to be considered merely the continuation of the dialogues, which had
been so long going on.

III. The omission of the necessary notices of time, or of
place, at the beginning of the chapter, cannot be said to be
supplied by what occurs at verse 22. in its course—shewing
that our Lord was then in Jerusalem—walking in the porch
of Solomon—and attending the feast of Dedication.   It is
obviously a begging of the question to say this notice is *re-
flexive*, not *prospective*—intended for what had just preceded, and not for what was about to follow—which is its
natural use and purposé.   Besides, if that were the case,
the principal verb, ἐγίνετο, must possess the force of either
the imperfect, *was taking place*, or the pluperfect, *had
taken place*—instead of its simple, historical, and natural,
sense, *did take place*.   This notice may be a very proper
introduction to the rest of the chapter, such as the reason of
the thing, and the usage of St. John, might have authorized
us to expect; but it cannot serve as such for the first part :
and its very position between the two, after the one, but before the other, ought on every principle of consistency to be
a proof that it is to be understood, and was always designed
to be understood, of the latter, and not of the former.

IV.   When the discourse in question, x. 19. was over, we
find it subjoined, σχίσμα οὖν πάλιν ἐγίνετο—the reference in
which is either to ix. 16. or to vii. 43—each of which is a
similar instance—before ; and more probably to the latter,
than to the former ; because the parties in this instance, as
well as in that, are the Jews at large, and not, as in the
other case, the Pharisees in particular.   Both these instances occurred at the feast of Tabernacles—so, then, may
we presume, did the third.

V. That our Lord's hearers at the Encænia should still

have been the same, either wholly or in part, with his hearers at the Scenopegia, two months before—more especially, if they were in each case the Jews of Jerusalem, as such—can excite no surprize. Nor is it more extraordinary, in reference even to these, that what had happened at the feast of Tabernacles should be remembered at the feast of Dedication. The intermediate interval was much too short to obliterate from the memories of men, heated by the daily conflict of feeling and opinion, and sharpened to vigilance and attention, by the strongest incentives which can banish indifference, all traces of the remarkable incidents, which that age of wonder was daily bringing forth. The cure of the blind man, performed at the feast of Tabernacles, must have been still distinctly remembered at the feast of Dedication[z]—and if, for a period of two months' time, our Lord's miracles could be carried in mind, why might not his discourses also?

VI. The question, x. 24. which was now put to our Saviour, implies a state of mind wavering between doubt and conviction; it shews an expectation of *some* Messias, and a secret belief, mixed up with considerable uncertainty, that Jesus was he. This uncertainty the enquirers would evidently charge upon our Lord himself—ἕως πότε τὴν ψυχὴν ἡμῶν αἴρεις; that is, how long dost thou raise our expectations, and yet keep us in suspense? how long dost thou alternately gratify, and alternately disappoint, our hopes? They complain, therefore, of some difficulty in comprehending the true character of Christ; that he gave them reason, at one time, to think so and so of it, and, directly after, just the reverse—and whatever this difficulty might be, producing the ambiguity and suspense of judgment in question, the very request, which they proceed to subjoin, is a proof that, in its cause, it must be ascribed to the *words*, and not to the *actions*, of the party addressed.

If thou art the Christ, tell us so, παρρησίᾳ. Παρρησία in its proper sense is freedom of speech—and in its secondary, openness or simplicity of speech. Hence it is opposed to

[z] x. 21.

παροιμία, or παραβολὴ, as speaking without disguise, and without reserve, is opposed to speaking in figure, or with a partial concealment of the truth. The request of the Jews, therefore, amounts to this—that if Jesus were the Christ—the Christ which they expected—he would use no mystery, nor evasion—he should tell them so at once. I say the Christ which they expected—for about none else can they be supposed to enquire; and this distinction is not unimportant. To be the true Christ, and to be the Christ which the Jews expected, were very different things; and however plainly our Lord might have declared himself the Christ, in the former capacity, the enquirers would still judge of his meaning, from their own notions concerning the Christ, in the latter; between which, and the truth of the fact as regarded the former, there would be the utmost discrepancy. Admitting the Jews to be sincere in their complaint of the obscurity, which still hung over the decision of this great national question, whether Jesus of Nazareth was the Christ, we may justly suppose this obscurity due to the conflict of new and unexpected truths, with old and inveterate prejudices.

The actions of our Lord could not be mistaken—his language might; the former seemed regularly to designate him as the expected Messias—the latter as invariably to shake the conclusion. His miracles were, at all times, plain and intelligible tokens of his divine power, and attributes; his professions, or discourses, concerning himself, his offices, and his relations, were purposely veiled in obscurity—were never delivered except under the cloud of allegories and figures. To penetrate into the meaning of these descriptions, until they had been cleared up by the event, and further illustrated by the enlightening influx of the Spirit, explaining all, and teaching how to apply them all, was manifestly impossible even for our Lord's disciples—much more for a prejudiced, a bigotted, and an incredulous, Jew. These topics, in the lifetime of our Saviour, and whensoever, in his public addresses to the people, or his more confidential communications with his followers, he touches upon them, were truly secret and mysterious truths—the ἀπόρρητα and μυστήρια of the Gospel.

A very remarkable, and as concerns the Jews at large the first, instance, on record, of the allegorical method of instruction in the personal character, relations, and functions, of a spiritual Messias, pursued to any length, took place, as we have seen, at the beginning of this year—when the recent miracle of the loaves and fishes furnished our Saviour with the associated, but mystical, emblem, applied to himself, of the living bread, which came down from heaven. The harshness and obscurity of this metaphor shocked the prejudices, and led to the desertion, of many who, until then, had kept company with Jesus; what, then, must have been its effect upon the unbelieving multitude ! So necessary it is, if we would estimate rightly the perplexity, which would attend the original delivery and reception of those beautiful pictures, which to our apprehensions delineate so forcibly, and so correctly, the true nature and functions of a spiritual Messias, that we should place ourselves in the situation of the men of the time. With every allowance for the good disposition and the docility of the hearers, there would still be ample room for the operation of an implicit faith—for the surrendry of their own judgments—and for the sacrifice of their personal notions of truth, or of fitness, out of pure deference to the authority of the speaker.

In the recent conversations at the feast of Tabernacles, repeated instances must have occurred, when the same figurative style of speaking would be employed. In one— which is actually on record—our Lord describes himself as τὸ ὕδωρ τὸ ζῶν—in another—as τὸ φῶς τοῦ κόσμου—both, descriptions arising out of remarkable coincidences of time, and circumstances—both, publicly delivered—and both, followed by a strong impression upon the audience. But the last, the longest, the most memorable, case in point must have been the allegory of the true shepherd, and his sheep —if that also was now delivered. The impression made by this description of the Messias would be the liveliest, and the difficulty of comprehending the description, under which it would leave the hearers, could not have been the least. It was not, like the former two, a mere comparison or illustration—extending only to a single point of resemblance—but an allegory of just dimensions, and considerable length—embracing a variety of particulars, all of which had their foundation in the facts of a real, but their interpretation in the facts of a future, history. The symbolical picture was laid before the spectators in all the simplicity, and consequently in all the obscurity, of the most circumstantial detail—and the Jews, as we are told by the Evangelist[a], understood not what it meant. As with the contemplation of objects placed in too bright a light, the very simplicity of the external features rendered the substantial and latent truths so much the more difficult to be discovered. The images in their obvious acceptation were familiar enough—the counterpart, intended beneath them, was the most profound and mystical which can be conceived.

After the delivery of the allegory, and after a pause, expressly, as it would seem, interposed to discover its effect upon the hearers, our Lord proceeded to apply the description to himself[b]—which would leave no doubt that it related to Jesus Christ, and to Jesus Christ in the character of the Messiah. But what light did this application reflect on the previous obscurity of the picture? Though the image of the shepherd and his flock might be sufficiently clear in itself—and as metaphorically employed for the relation between a king and his subjects, or even between God and his people, might be no uncommon figure in their own Scriptures, yet its application to denote the relation between the Christian Messias and his Church must as yet have been unexampled, and unintelligible. Besides, there was additional matter, mixed up with the application itself, which would serve only to perplex it the more. Our Lord, x. 7. affirmed himself to be the θύρα τῶν προβάτων, as well as the ποιμὴν ὁ καλός—*through* whom the sheep must gain admission into the fold, as well as *under* whom they must be fed,

[a] x. 6.   [b] x. 7.

maintained, and protected, there.   This was to use a metaphor almost as harsh, and fully as incomprehensible, as that of the bread which came down from heaven. He spake also of a wolf, from whose ravages the flock should be in danger—and he more than insinuated that it would be necessary for himself, the keeper and guardian of the flock, to die in opposition to this enemy—yet, strange to tell! the death of the shepherd should be the salvation of the sheep. He spake too of other flocks, distinct from his flock among the Jews, yet sometime to be united to it—and he affirmed it to be a part of his office, and an illustrious feature in his character as the true shepherd, that he should abolish all distinctions, and gather together innumerable flocks, into one fold, and under one shepherd.

Much more than this he said likewise, and equally hard to be understood—which I cannot enter upon at present. If the Jews, then, had merely not comprehended his words before, now they charge him with raving, and being mad: He hath a demon, and is mad—why listen ye to him[c]? And even they, who thought otherwise, judged so not from superior penetration, but from greater humility of disposition— and because the miracles of our Saviour held out the torch for his words, and made them receive what he said, whether intelligible to themselves or not, as the words of truth and soberness, and as the oracles of divine wisdom, neither deceiving, nor deceived.

It is incontestable that the Jews expected a Messiah, who should deliver their country from a foreign yoke—be a triumphant conqueror—and a mighty potentate: and the event proves that they were determined to receive none else. The personal demeanor of our Lord had given them little encouragement to hope he would ever declare himself such; had he but done this, however indirectly, the nation would have become believers to a man. The negative influence of long and systematic opposition to the national wish, combined with the positive effect of the national degeneracy in religion and in morality, was the true and sole

[c] x. 19. 20.

cause, humanly speaking, of his final rejection by both rulers and people. But had all, who eventually became disbelievers, yet ceased to hope that Jesus might still be the Messias? The proceedings, when he entered Jerusalem, only four days before his crucifixion, will not allow us to assert this. However slow and reluctant to make such an avowal of his character he might himself appear—his actions spoke a language not to be misunderstood; and clearly demonstrated that, were he inclined to assume it, no one was better qualified to realize the glorious and enthusiastic picture of the ideal deliverer—so dear to the national wish. If, notwithstanding the experience of the past, they still clung to the same delusive hope, it would be a motive for watching every word, and every act, of our Lord only the more intensely; and when, in lieu of plain assurances, according with their desires, and easily reconciled to their preconceived expectations, they continued to hear declarations, in their obvious sense flatly repugnant to their belief, and in their secret meaning far beyond their comprehension, great in proportion would be their disappointment.

The present remonstrance, x. 24. it appears to me was produced by some such cause as this—by a long-suppressed feeling of impatience at finding their hopes and their wishes so often excited and encouraged, and again dejected and discouraged. There is no necessity, then, for the violent and improbable hypothesis that St. John has arbitrarily joined together the account of the proceedings at the feast of Dedication, with the account of the proceedings at the feast of Tabernacles—yet has given no notice to that effect. The last discourse, recorded to have happened at this feast, as it must be clearly referred to x. 26—30. in the renewal of the conversations at the next, so would be quite sufficient to account for the connection between them, though each of them should have taken place, as they are related, asunder.

The transactions, then, which belong to the feast of Tabernacles as such, must be considered to be still continued down to x. 21; after which, it is probable, Jesus would

leave Jerusalem, and according to his usage return to
Capernaum.   The two months' interval, between this feast
and the next, we cannot suppose to have been spent in
Judæa—especially as there is no intimation to that effect
in St. John—but we may suppose it to have been spent in
Galilee; because Matt. xix. 1. and Mark x. 1. compared
with the circumstances of the history before and after
them, may safely lead to the inference that all, or by far
the greatest part, of the time between the third feast of
Tabernacles, and the ensuing Passover, before the point of
time when our Lord passed into Judæa out of Peræa, must
have been spent in Galilee: in which case, St. John would
naturally be silent about it.   But if this interval was spent
in Galilee, we may take it for granted it would be spent at
Capernaum.   Our Lord's circuits, for the present, were all
over, and the winter-season was at hand: no place would
be so likely to be made the scene of a temporary, but stationary, residence, as the usual place of his abode; and had
he not been known to have remained there, for some time
after the last return which they mention, St. Matthew and
St. Mark would not have described his final departure
thence so soon, apparently, after that return—though in
reality six months later.

The feast of Dedication, John x. 22. is evidently the feast
next in order to the feast of Tabernacles, vii. 2: and it is
another presumptive proof that, either our Lord had been
absent, all the intermediate time, from Jerusalem, or nothing had since occurred upon the spot, similar to what
had taken place before, that we meet upon this occasion
also with the mention of a renewed attempt to stone him[d].
The πάλιν in this allusion can be referred to viii. 59. an incident at the feast of Tabernacles, only.   We may conclude, therefore, that since the time of the feast of Tabernacles our Saviour and the Jews of Jerusalem had not met
again, until they met in Solomon's porch; or if they had,
that nothing had again occurred, like what had occurred
before.   The former of these suppositions is confirmed by

[d] x. 31.

the silence of St. John—and the latter is negatived by the experience of the past; for had they ever met again as before, something, it may justly be presumed, would have arisen to make the adversaries of Jesus desirous of stoning him as before.

The proceedings at this feast, beginning with x. 22. cannot embrace more than a single day; and being prematurely terminated by the attempt upon the life of Christ, these proceedings themselves are probably the whole of what then transpired; at least in public. After the day of that attempt Jesus appeared no more openly—and until that day he does not seem to have visited the temple: the conversation in the porch of Solomon, which took place upon that day, took place on the first opportunity furnished by his appearance in public.

The feast of Dedication began on the 25th of the Jewish Casleu, and lasted for eight days in all. The 25th of Casleu is the 69th day *inclusive*, from the 15th of Tisri *exclusive*; and consequently in the third year of our Saviour's ministry, when Tisri 15. fell upon October 11. Casleu 25. fell upon December 19. The first of the eight days, then, coincided with December 19. and the last with December 26: a statement, sufficient by itself to prove that the feast of Dedication this year fell out in the midst of a Jewish winter [c]—which yet would not be always the case. But this year the Passover had fallen as late as it could fall, and, therefore, so had every other feast: if the Passover had fallen as early as it could fall, the feast of Dedication would have fallen out a month earlier—which would not have been so much in the winter. Moreover, when Tisri 15. (as we have proved was the case) fell upon Thursday, Casleu 25. must have fallen on Wednesday: the first day of the feast, then, was a Wednesday; and, consequently, so was the last. The particular day, on which the conversation in Solomon's porch transpired, must be uncertain—but if we may conjecture that Jesus repaired to the temple in this instance about the same time as in the former, viz.

[c] John x. 22.

μεσούσης ἤδη τῆς ἑορτῆς—it might have taken place on the last day of Casleu, Sunday December 23. or the first day of Tebeth, Monday December 24. If our Lord retired from Jerusalem soon after the attempt on his life, he would consequently retire thence before the end of the month of December.

The quarter to which he retired is simply described as the region beyond Jordan [f]—the reference in the πάλιν being to vi. 1. previously ; where a similar visit to the country on the other side the lake, and consequently beyond the Jordan, had been already recorded. That this place was Bethabara, where John, at one period of his ministry was certainly baptizing [g], and which also was situate beyond the Jordan, would not be a necessary consequence. The reference in τὸ πρῶτον, x. 40. does not specify Bethabara as such—or relate to the incident recorded i. 28. which happened there ; but merely to the order of time between the ministry of John, and the ministry of Christ ; for the former was prior, and yet only preparatory, to the latter : though it may still be true that the scene of John's ministry might be changed in the course of its continuance from the eastern side of the Jordan, where it had begun, for the western, into which it subsequently passed [h].

It is not, indeed, improbable that Bethabara might be a general name for the Aulon, or Perichorus of Jordan, on its eastern side—or for some part of it, nearer to the southern extremity of the lake of Tiberias, than to the northern extremity of the lake Asphaltites ; and, consequently, to the ford in the vicinity of Jericho. The denomination itself means *house*, or *place*, of passage—and might obviously be given to any of the fords of the Jordan : and there was one such ford, opposite to Scythopolis, and, therefore, not far from Tiberias [i], besides the ford near Jericho. The most ancient manuscripts, however, in the time of Origen, instead of Bethabara beyond Jordan, read Bethany beyond Jordan [k]—and the exception which he takes against this

[f] x. 40.   [g] John i. 28. iii. 26.   [h] i. 28. iii. 23. 26.   [i] Relandi Palæst. i. 279.   [k] Commentar. ii. 130.

reading, and his consequent correction of the text for Beth-abara, are neither of them founded upon just critical grounds, but on mere presumption of what ought to be. Among the thousand towns and villages which were com-prized in all Palestine, it would be nothing extraordinary that many should have borne the same names; which in our Saviour's, or St. John's, time might still be in exist-ence, and still known as distinct, but, by the time of Ori-gen, after the numerous desolations which the country had suffered, might have become totally extinct : and even their names have perished with them.   Moreover, if the text of St. John had originally exhibited Bethabara, and Bethany, as Origen himself contends, was a name so completely un-known on the other side the Jordan, who would have thought of corrupting it for Bethany? But his own ex-ample proves how natural and obvious it would be, under such a presumption of the truth, to change Bethany into Bethabara*.

On this point, however, it is not necessary for me to dwell; I make these observations merely to shew that, by retiring into this quarter in particular, our Lord would be nearer to Galilee, than to Judæa—though strictly in neither at the time—and if he was less than one day's journey re-moved from Capernaum, he would be more than two days' journey distant from Jerusalem.   This quarter, however, was one, which he had probably never visited, since the commencement of his ministry—at least so as to reside within it—and, yet as it had been the principal, if not the exclusive, scene of the labours of John, it was but natural that its inhabitants should still remember both his preach-ing in general, and his testimonies to Jesus in particular : which accounts for the belief of many upon our Lord[1].

The length of the residence, in these parts, is not speci-fied; but I have shewn elsewhere[m], that it was speedily

---

* Bethany is the reading adopted by Griesbach; for whose reasons the reader is referred to his edition of the Gospels.

[1] x. 41. 42.   [m] Vol. ii. Diss. viii. 232. 233.

followed by the return to Jerusalem, preparatory to the raising of Lazarus: the time taken up by which return, and by the performance of the miracle, it is possible satisfactorily to determine.

Lazarus began to be sick, while our Lord was still in this neighbourhood—and, whatever we may conjecture concerning the nature of his sickness, (which its rapid consummation seems to designate as a species of fever,) his death had not yet taken place, when the news of his illness was brought to Jesus [n]—for he speaks of him as still sick, but not yet dead, when he says, This sickness is not unto death. When our Lord, however, set out to return, it is certain that he was then dead [o]. Now he set out upon the return, the day but one after he received the message [p]. The death of the sick man, then, took place either on the day when the message was received, or the day after it.

When Jesus arrived at Bethany, he had been either four days dead, or four days in the tomb, or both [q]; for it was the custom of the Jews to commit the bodies of the dead to the grave as soon as possible—so that the burial of Lazarus on the day of his death itself, especially if he had died of a fever, would be nothing extraordinary. The distance of the quarter where our Lord would receive the first intimation of his sickness, I have shewn, was probably more than two, but less than three, days' journey from Jerusalem. Hence if he had received the message of the sisters on *one* day—Lazarus had died and been buried on the *next*— and Jesus himself set out on the *third*—he would arrive at Bethany in the course of the *fifth*; when, as it is asserted in the narrative [r], the dead man would actually have been three days, and part of a fourth day, in the grave.

This being the case, it seems superfluous to prove that our Lord must have arrived within seven days of the death at least. But, according to Josephus [s], the time of mourning lasted for that number of days; during which it was customary to receive and entertain, οὐκ ἄνευ ἀνάγκης, the re-

[n] xi. 3—5.   [o] Ib. 7—14.   [p] Ib. 6.   [q] Ib. 39.   [r] Ib. 17. 39.
[s] B. Jud. ii. i. 1.

lations or the friends of the dead; and in consequence of this necessity, many, whose means were not adequate to the expense, ofttimes were reduced to poverty. Now this mourning for Lazarus, and this resort of his friends to the house of the sisters, were still going on at the time of our Lord's arrival [t]. His arrival, then, took place within *seven* days after the death.

The miracle ensued so soon after the arrival, that Jesus did not even enter the village [u], but, until he had performed it, continued without—going only in the mean while to the tomb; the situation of which, according to the usage of the Jews, except in the cases specified elsewhere, would necessarily be somewhere apart [v].

It appears, then, that the death of Lazarus would ensue, in the natural course of things, the day after our Lord heard of his sickness—and he himself was too far from Jerusalem to have travelled thither in one day, or even in two days. He could not, therefore, have returned to restore him to health on the spot—and as to working a miracle in this instance, as he had sometimes done before, by an act of volition, or by mere word of mouth, it is manifest that the sisters did not expect this from him [w]; and, had he even done so, neither would the splendour of the miracle have been so great, nor its evidence have been so decisive—for the distance of the author from the subject, that is, between the cause and the effect, of the cure, must have had a tendency to obscure its truth. The miracle might have been equally real, but its reality would not have been so apparent. This, therefore, was most probably the reason why, after hearing of the illness of Lazarus, he yet remained two days where he was.

The news of the miracle was taken, soon after its performance, by some of those who had witnessed it, and communicated to the Pharisees [x]: and the effect of this communication was the resolution, concluded and from that day forward acted upon, of putting our Lord to death [y]. The

[t] John xi. 19. 31.   [u] Ib. 30.   [v] Vol. ii. Diss. viii. 299.   [w] xi. 21. 32.   [x] Ib. 46.   [y] Ib. 47—53.

formation of such a purpose, which it is implied by xi. 54. was known to Jesus, induced him again to depart from Bethany—and no longer to remain publicly in Judæa.

The quarter to which he retired was Ephraim—a city which Epiphanius, as well as St. John, places on the borders of the desert country ᶻ—Συνοδεύσαντός μοι ἐν τῇ ἐρήμῳ τῆς Βαιθὴλ, καὶ Ἐφραΐμ, ἐπὶ τὴν ὀρεινὴν ἀνερχομένῳ ἀπὸ τῆς Ἱεριχοῦς: and which Jerome describes as Villa prægrandis, Ephræa nomine, contra septentrionem, in vicesimo ab Ælia milliario ᵃ.

At Ephraim the Gospel of St. John leaves our Saviour for the present ; and brings him back to Bethany only six days before the next Passover ᵇ.   The question which we have now to consider is whether any of the three former Gospels had found him at Ephraim ; and, having taken up the course of things after the retreat thither, had brought him from thence to Capernaum, before the last circuit itself.   This Gospel I believe to have been St. Luke's : and on the proof of this position I shall enter in the next Dissertation.

ᵃ Adv. Hæres. i. 133. Vide also Joshua xvi. 1.   ᵃ De Situ et Nominibus.
ᵇ xii. 1.

DISSERTATION XVI.

On the supplementary relation of Luke ix. 51—xviii. 14. *to the two first Gospels.*

IT is generally agreed that, so far as ix. 50. the Gospel of St. Luke accompanies the Gospels of St. Matthew, and of St. Mark ; but from ix. 51—xviii. 14. it goes along, apparently, by itself. On the supposition, then, of the regularity of his Gospel throughout, the intermediate matter, between these extremes, would be peculiar to St. Luke, and, as the mere statement of the extremes themselves is sufficient to prove, it would be no small portion of the whole.

The point of time, at which St. Luke ceases to accompany St. Matthew, and St. Mark, is the return to Capernaum, prior to the last feast of Tabernacles ; and the point of time, at which he rejoins them, is with the close of the last journey up to Jerusalem, when our Lord either had already passed, or was just on the eve of passing, out of Persæa, into Judæa [a]. On the same supposition, therefore, of St. Luke's regularity, as before, it follows that the whole intermediate matter, peculiar to his Gospel, belongs to the interval of time between that return to Capernaum, and that passage from Persæa into Judæa—an interval, which, as we have had reason to conclude already, could not comprize less than the last *six* months of our Saviour's ministry, and possibly might comprize even more.

Throughout the whole of these details, which we suppose to be thus comprehended, there are numerous historical notices, some express—others implicit—which demonstrate that our Lord, all the time, was travelling and teaching—and travelling and teaching upon his way to Jerusalem. There are evidences, therefore, that a journey to Je-

[a] Matt. xix. 1. 13. Mark x. 1. 13. Luke xviii. 15.

rusalem, all this time, was still going on—and going on with
the utmost publicity ; a journey, expressly undertaken in
order to arrive at Jerusalem—and, wheresoever it might
have begun, and whatsoever course it might take meanwhile, yet known, and understood, to be tending to that
one point, and ultimately to be concluded by arriving there
at last.   There are, consequently, evidences of a circuit as
such ; and, if it is a circuit belonging to one and the same
occasion, of a circuit begun, and conducted, on a very general scale—the *fourth* of the kind, which the Gospel-history
has yet supplied.

All these indications are of manifest importance, in fixing
the period to which the whole of Luke ix. 51—xviii. 14.
inclusively is to be referred.   During the last six months of
our Saviour's ministry, there were three feasts—all which
he attended personally in their order—the third feast of
Tabernacles, the third feast of Dedication, and the fourth
Passover : between which feasts, and these intimations of
the direction, or the circumstances, of his motions, preparatory to arriving at Jerusalem, there is this kind and degree of congruity, that they may all most easily, most obviously, and most naturally, be understood of a journey,
preparatory to the last Passover, but they can none of them,
with any propriety, be understood of a journey preparatory
to either of the other two feasts, which most immediately
preceded it.

For there is none of these indications, which does not
prove that, while our Lord was thus travelling up to Jerusalem, he was travelling in the most open manner—and attended by crowds of followers, wheresoever he went.   But
it is certain from John vii. 10. that he went up to the third
feast of Tabernacles in a manner the most opposite to this—
and until he appeared in the temple, about the middle of the
feast, that he had been seen, much less had been publicly
accompanied from Galilee, by nobody.   If the same thing
is not expressly asserted of the feast of Dedication ensuing,
it is yet very plainly implied.   The incident in Solomon's
porch, x. 22. which transpired at that feast, we had reason

to conclude, in the preceding Dissertation, was produced by the sudden discovery of the presence of Jesus, as he was walking in that porch : and the same prudential motive, which had required the concealment of his purpose of attending at the feast of Tabernacles, would much more require the same secrecy at the feast of Dedication ; for if his life had been in danger before the former feast, it was much more so at the latter. These indications, then, of the motions of our Lord, of their direction, their final end, or their circumstances, preparatory to some visit to Jerusalem, cannot be referred to the visit at the feast of Dedication : and we have seen that neither can they be referred to the visit at the feast of Tabernacles ; it remains, therefore, that they must be referred to the visit at the feast of the Passover : a conclusion, which may further be confirmed as follows.

I. The last journey to Jerusalem, and the attendance at the last Passover, are the only journey to Jerusalem, and the only attendance at any feast, which the three first Gospels have placed on record. Yet St. John's Gospel proves that our Lord must have been up to Jerusalem five several times besides. Now all these indications in St. Luke may clearly be referred to that one journey—and it is a strong presumptive argument of the necessity of this reference, that no visit to Jerusalem, as such, is specified by him, but the last; nor, consequently, could any journey, preparatory to such a visit, be specified by him, but the last. It is a similar argument, that xviii. 15. in St. Luke, a point of time, which, as well as the rest, belongs to this journey, coincides with Matt. xix. 13. and Mark x. 13—both, points of time which indisputably belong to the last journey to Jerusalem, as such, and to a period of the journey, when it was not far from Jerusalem itself.

II. From all these indications in St. Luke it is distinctly to be collected, that Jesus was still travelling *to* Jerusalem —nor before xviii. 15. or rather, xix. 29. is there any proof that he was already arrived there. All these indications, therefore, may alike belong to the visit at the last Passover,

and to the journey preparatory to that visit, if this journey
had been going on from ix. 51—xviii. 15. or xix. 29 : but
not, upon any other principle.   Much less, then, can they
be referred to different visits—one at the feast of Tabernacles—another at the feast of Dedication—and to the different journeys respectively preparatory to each.   For, in
each of these instances, the Evangelist is still giving an account of the events, which happened *by the way*—he says
nothing as yet of what happened at the journey's end.   But
as the journey was begun for the sake of arriving at Jerusalem, the account of the journey could never have been
complete without an account of the journey's end—events
by the way would never be related except as preliminary to
the relation of events which ensued upon the arrival at Jerusalem.   These are decided objections to the supposition
of journeys before either the feast of Tabernacles, or the
feast of Dedication ; and they are just as decidedly arguments in favour of a journey before the last Passover : for
both the arrival at Jerusalem, and the events which ensued
upon that arrival, as well as the journey which conducted
unto it, will all be as clearly specified upon this principle,
as they will be omitted to be specified on the other.

III. If some of these indications belong to a journey
before the feast of Tabernacles—others, to a journey before
the feast of Dedication—and others, to a journey before the
feast of the Passover— then, between some of the number,
and the rest, our Lord must have been up to Jerusalem,
and come back again—and be returning thither a second,
or a third, time afresh ; yet no notice is interposed to that
effect : he is still represented throughout as travelling in one
direction, and, for ought which we can discover to the contrary, as travelling on the same occasion.   All this would
be consistent and natural, if this occasion was the occasion
of the last journey to Jerusalem ; for, then, it is impossible
that any other representation could have been given.   But
not so—if the occasions themselves were distinct—and many
weeks, not to say months, asunder.   This would be to introduce inextricable confusion and perplexity.   For with

such a strange amalgamation of accounts, who could undertake to separate them—and to say thus much of the whole belongs to such a time, and thus much to such another?

IV. The regularity of St. Luke's Gospel, up to ix. 51. has been, I think, so fully established, that we may justly assume the fact of its regularity for the remainder also—and the assumption will be confirmed, upon its own grounds of proof, hereafter. This being the case, there can be no question that Luke ix. 50. coincides with a point of time which answers to the middle of the *third* year of our Saviour's ministry—that is, Luke i—ix. 50. inclusive brings down the series of the Gospel-history to within six months of its close. The sequel, therefore, or Luke ix. 51—to the end, must all be comprized within these six months, or a very little more—and as ix. 51. in particular synchronizes with a point of time nearer to, or further off, either of the extremes in question, it will take up the whole, or merely some part, of it in general.

Now, such is the notice premised to this division[b]—Ἐγίνετο δὲ ἐν τῷ συμπληροῦσθαι τὰς ἡμέρας τῆς ἀναλήψεως αὐτοῦ, καὶ αὐτὸς τὸ πρόσωπον αὐτοῦ ἐστήριξε τοῦ πορεύεσθαι εἰς Ἱερουσαλήμ— that it could not have been premised to any thing but the occasion of our Lord's last journey to Jerusalem. The words should be rendered thus—Now it came to pass, as the time for his being taken up was beginning to be fulfilled, that he himself also steadfastly settled his countenance, to go to Jerusalem. It would be a waste of argument, to prove that the time of his being taken up—αἱ ἡμέραι τῆς ἀναλήψεως αὐτοῦ—can bear no other construction than that of the period appointed for his reception into heaven. There are analogous phrases in ἡμέρας ἀναδείξεως—the time when the Baptist should be manifested—in καιροὶ ἀναψύξεως —the seasons when refreshment should come—καιρὸς τῆς ἐμῆς ἀναλύσεως—the time for St. Paul's being released—and the like[c]. That this period was a definite period appears clearly from John xiii. 1. xvi. 28. xvii. 1. 11—and from

---

[b] ix. 51.   [c] Luke i. 80.   Acts iii. 19.   2 Tim. iv. 6.

many other passages of Scripture which might be quoted.
That it coincided with the period of the ascension is equally
evident, both from the necessity of the case, and from the
very expression employed to designate it. 'Aνάληψις the act
of taking up, or being taken up, is regularly derived from
the verb ἀναλαμβάνω—and this verb, or some synonymous
one—such as ἀναβαίνω, ἀναφέρομαι, ἐπαίρομαι—are the verbs
invariably employed, in speaking of our Lord's ascent into
heaven[d].

The period of the ascension, as we have seen elsewhere,
was also the final close of his ministry—for until then, and
even after the resurrection, he had still been in some sense
present with his disciples on earth, appearing unto them, at
intervals, for the space of forty days, and λέγων τὰ περὶ τῆς
βασιλείας τοῦ Θεοῦ[c]—but, after the ascension, he was no
longer present, in any sense, as before. The period of the
ascension, then, or in other words, the close of our Lord's
personal ministry, is very clearly here pointed out; and the
whole of the notice both in the language, and in the sentiment, is much the same with what St. Luke had specified
not long before, as the topic of the colloquy on the mount,
when Moses and Elias appeared in glory, and spake to our
Lord of his ἔξοδος, or departure, which he was about to bring
to pass in Jerusalem[f]. The same conclusion follows from
the peculiarity of the phrase τὸ πρόσωπον αὐτοῦ ἐστήριξε—
which describes the feelings or resolution of one, who is em-
barking on a business of more than usual seriousness, or
more than usual danger—such as was the last journey to
Jerusalem in particular, the most solemn and momentous
event in our Saviour's history, and not to be consummated
except by his death and passion, with all their ignominious
and all their afflicting circumstances—every one whereof
was well known beforehand to himself. Besides which—
but whether by an intentional, or an unintentional, coincidence, I do not say—they are the very terms, or nearly so,

[d] Mark xvi. 19. Acts i. 2. 11. 22. 1 Tim. iii. 16. John xx. 17. Acts ii.
34. Rom. x. 6. Eph. iv. 8. 9. Luke xxiv. 51. Acts i. 9.   [e] Vol. ii.
Diss. v. 148. Acts i. 3.   [f] Luke ix. 31. Compare 2 Pet. i. 15.

in which the prophet Isaiah makes the Messiah allude to his approaching sufferings, and express his determination to bear them all[5]: Therefore have I set my face like a flint, and I know that I shall not be ashamed.

There can be little question, then, that at Luke ix. 51. the approach of the last Passover, and the occasion of the last visit to Jerusalem, begin to be distinctly pointed out ; and, consequently, that both the third feast of Tabernacles, and the third feast of Dedication, were already passed: that is, that two months at least, out of the six which we have assigned to this period in general, had now elapsed. If so, the course of events, from this time forward to the close of our Saviour's ministry, cannot embrace more than four months, and may embrace even less.

Now it is said that he prepared to execute his intention of proceeding to Jerusalem, by sending messengers in the first place to a certain village of Samaria : whence it must be evident he had to pass through Samaria. Samaria extended across the western division of Palestine, between Judæa and Galilee—and if a person, travelling towards Jerusalem, had to pass through Samaria, one of the two following suppositions must necessarily be the case—either he was in Galilee, and passing from thence directly to Judæa— or he was in Judæa, and passing from thence directly into Galilee—intending in each case that his journey should terminate at Jerusalem in the end. That the latter supposition was actually true of our Saviour's case, at the time, may be shewn, by the help of St. Luke's narrative itself, as follows.

The mission of the Seventy[h] took place in the course of the journey now undertaken, and after the passage through Samaria. The mission of the Seventy, then, took place either in Galilee, or in Judæa. But the mission of the Seventy was preparatory to a circuit of our Lord himself— they were appointed, and sent before his face into every city, and every place, whither he himself was about to come. If the mission, then, took place in Galilee, the circuit, which followed it, began in Galilee; but if the former took place in Judæa, the latter also began in Judæa. Now no circuit of our Lord's ever began in Judæa—nor, unless Judæa, and not Galilee, had been, like Galilee, the proper scene of his ministry from the first, could any of his circuits as such have begun in Judæa. Every circuit, whether general or partial, which had yet been undertaken, we have seen, had all been undertaken in Galilee, and all been confined to Galilee. The notion of a circuit begun in Judæa, to arrive at Jerusalem, unless the circuit had been confined to Judæa, and much more the idea of a passing on purpose from Galilee, through Samaria, preparatory to such a circuit in Judæa, is preposterous. Even after the mission and return of the Seventy, when our Lord had begun his progress in their track, it is certain that, for a part of the time at least, he was still within the dominions of the Tetrarch of Galilee; and as to the circuit's being undertaken in Judæa, and much more its being confined to that country, at a time when it must be apparent the progress was got into Judæa, there is no proof of its doing more than travel, with the necessary diligence and despatch, along the high road from the passage of the Jordan to Jerusalem. The mission of the Seventy, then, took place in Galilee, and the passage through Samaria, before their mission, was, consequently, a passage from somewhere in Judæa, to somewhere in Galilee. If so, our Saviour was previously in Judæa.

Now the last notices in the former Evangelists, St. Matthew and St. Mark [1], clearly represented him to be in Galilee: but this was a little before the feast of Tabernacles, and, consequently, two months at least before Luke ix. 51: within which time, it is manifestly possible he might both have left Galilee, and returned thither again, prior to Matt. xix. 1. or to Mark x. i. The Gospel of St. John, to a certain extent, confirms this possibility by the matter of the fact; for, after shewing that our Lord was thrice at Jerusa-

---

[1] Matt. xviii. 35. Mark ix. 50.

lem within that time, it brought him, as we saw, to Ephraim —and there for the present it left him.

The utility of this Gospel, and its critical adaptation to the rest, must, consequently, now begin to be strikingly exemplified : for, if our Lord, according to the authority of St. Matthew and of St. Mark, in the course of the last circuit, passed directly into Judæa out of Peræa, and directly into Peræa out of Galilee, he must have returned from Ephraim sometime after St. John left him there, and come again into Galilee sometime before St. Matthew and St. Mark take him thence. If he had not again left Ephraim —which was in Judæa—he could not have come into Judæa, out of Peræa ; and if he had not returned into Galilee, he could not have passed into Peræa, out of Galilee. Now Ephraim lay, indeed, in Judæa—but close upon the verge of Samaria ; and one who was desirous to return into Galilee thence it is .morally certain would pass by the readiest route, and, consequently, through the country between. It is such a return in the present instance—a return from Ephraim, through Samaria—which I suppose to be the return into Galilee, recorded by St. Luke, preparatory to the mission of the Seventy ; a supposition so simple, consistent, and probable, that its mere statement is enough to vouch for its correctness; and, while it is perfectly in unison with the accounts of each Gospel in particular, it perpetuates, connects, and fills ʼup, most completely and most satisfactorily, the united accounts of all.

It may be objected, however, and it is the only material objection, that the motive assigned to the rejection of Jesus by the Samaritans[k], because his face is said to have been going to Jerusalem—his face was as though he was going to Jerusalem—is at variance with our supposition ; and would lead to the inference that the course of the journey lay actually in the direction of Jerusalem. And had the Evangelist been speaking of the *direction* of the journey, and not of the purpose of him who had undertaken it, this inference might have been just. But from the word πρόσω-

[k] ix. 53.

πον in this instance, distinctly in allusion to the same term as used before[1], it is manifest this is not the case.   Jesus *settled* his *face*, it was then said, to go unto Jerusalem— the Samaritans saw his *face*, it is now said, that it was going to Jerusalem ; that it was as of one going to Jerusalem. In all these cases, the meaning of the term is the same; and as it signifies in the first only a fixed purpose and de- termination, it can signify no more in the two last.

It is sufficient to explain the words, and, on the principle of the old religious and national animosity between the Jews and the Samaritans, to account also for the conduct of the latter, that, when Jesus departed from Ephraim, to pass through their country, it was known, or on probable grounds it was collected, that he was repairing to Galilee, intending to commence a public tour to Jerusalem, from thence.   Even upon this occasion, he set out with more state and solemnity than he had ever observed before—for he sent forward mes- sengers to prepare for his reception.   These messengers must have been acquainted with his intention, and were probably some two of the Apostles—perhaps James and John—who resented the affront of their Master so much more warmly than the rest.   The Samaritans might learn the fact of the same intentions, either from these emissaries, or from the direction and appearance of his outward progress itself ; nor is it surprizing that some of them should have been little disposed to respect a Jewish prophet—though that prophet might be our Saviour himself—if he was personally un- known to them, nor had ever resided, much less preached, in their country, except for the two days which, at the out- set of his ministry, he had spent at Sychar.

This description of things, however, is not less reconcile- able to the idea that the course of the journey, in this pas- sage through Samaria, was not, at the time, in the actual direction of Jerusalem, but merely designed to terminate there at last—than another, which occurs sometime after[m]; It came to pass, as he was going to Jerusalem, that he went through the midst of *Samaria* and *Galilee.*   There is

[1] ix. 51.   [m] xvii. 11.

no authority for changing the order of these terms, or putting *Galilee* before *Samaria*—in which case, whatever occasion was taking our Lord to Jerusalem, St. Luke must
be understood to affirm that he went through Samaria *first*,
and through Galilee *last*—in other words, that, for one part
of his journey, the direction in which he was proceeding
was as much *away* from Jerusalem, as in the rest it might,
or it must, have been *towards* it. Nor is it a parallel case,
as I shall shew hereafter, to quote Luke xix. 29. though
our Lord came to Bethany before he came to Bethphage—
and Bethphage was nearer to Jerusalem than Bethany.
Directly after this notice in St. Luke, xviii. 15. compared
with Matt. xix. 13. Mark x. 13. proves that he was either
in Judæa, or on the point of passing into it. The truth is,
all these occasional notices from ix. 51—xvii. 11. belong to
the course and continuance of one and the same journey,
begun from Ephraim, and terminated at Jerusalem; but
visiting in the interim Galilee, and Peræa, also; the particulars of which even St. Luke does not relate in detail, but
only here and there—with such admonitions interspersed,
as may serve to keep the reader in mind what Jesus was
doing, where he had been, or where he was, and what end
he had in view by the journey all the time.

As the feast of Dedication expired upon the third day of
the tenth sacred month—and, as we have seen, there could
have been no great interval between the departure from
Jerusalem, subsequent to the attendance at that feast, and
the departure from Bethany, subsequent to the raising of
Lazarus, all, which we should now be concerned with, would
be the length of the stay at Ephraim. St. John's expression, κἀκεῖ διέτριβε [n], taken in any latitude we may please,
cannot necessarily apply to more than one month's residence. In this case, our Lord would leave Ephraim, to
return into Galilee, two months at least before the recurrence of the Passover—that is, about the end of January—
and there would still be sufficient time both for the mission
and the return of the Seventy, and for his own subsequent

[n] xi. 54.

H h 2

circuit, made as proposed in their route.   It can scarcely be doubted that, having despatched the Seventy, from some certain place, he must have waited there until their return——but, as soon as they rejoined him, have set out directly afterwards.   And hence, with nothing interposed after the account of their mission, except the account of their return, we find him immediately after on his way himself.

Now, though the place itself is not distinctly specified, yet enough has been said to prove that it must have been somewhere in Galilee ; and if it was any where in Galilee, it is so likely to have been no where as Capernaum.   This circuit was the last, and so far if not the longest, yet the most important circuit ; and as every former circuit had originally set out from Capernaum, it is reasonable to suppose this in particular would do so.   Capernaum was our Lord's place of abode——and if he had to await the return of the Seventy any where, he would most naturally wait for it in his usual home.   His ministry in Galilee had been begun by a circuit, which set out from thence——and it was only consistent that it should be closed also by a circuit, beginning from the same.   The Twelve, as we have shewn was highly probable, were sent from Capernaum ; and the same thing, *a priori*, was just as likely to be the case with the Seventy.   Besides which, our Lord is expressly said to have set out *thence*[o], before he passed from Galilee, into Peræa, and from Peræa, into Judæa.   And though no positive conclusion may be deducible from Luke x. 15. a part of the charge to the Seventy, preparatory to their departure, yet, if these words were delivered in Capernaum, and on the spot, it must be acknowledged they would lose nothing in point of force and propriety, but be wonderfully enhanced as to both.

If, however, our Lord really began his last circuit in Galilee, the probability that he would begin it from Capernaum is so great, that no one, who admits the former, will think of disputing the latter : and the former, in addition

* Mark x. 1.

to what has been already said, allows of being directly and demonstratively proved, as follows.

I. On the morning of the crucifixion, the rulers of the Jews denounced our Saviour to Pilate in these words[P]; But they insisted, saying, He stirreth up the people, teaching throughout all Judæa, having *begun* from *Galilee, ἕως ὧδε*— in which there is evidently an accusation, grounded on the alleged tendency of his ministry either for its whole course and duration in general, or for some portion of its course and duration in particular. It implies, therefore, either that the whole tenor of our Lord's public ministry, from first to last, had been to *stir up* the people, or that some part of it at least had been to that effect: and that this latter construction, not the former, is what they mean, appears from the language employed in *ἕως ὧδε*—describing not the continuance and discharge of a ministry, but the progress and direction of a circuit. The adverb *ὧδε*, throughout the New Testament, in which it occurs fifty, or sixty, times, is never once used except of place—the phrase *ἕως ὧδε*, then, can have no meaning in this instance, but that of *unto here—as far as this place.*

Two extreme limits are, consequently, pointed out—one, Galilee—the other, Jerusalem—the former as that where the alleged conduct of our Saviour first began, the latter as that where it had ended; the former, therefore, denoting the place of the commencement of a circuit, the latter, the place of its termination—the period and the course of which in the mean time, as they would have Pilate to believe, had been directed to this one purpose, of going about, and stirring up the people. As it is certain, then, that our Lord's last journey ended at one of these extremes, Jerusalem, so, upon the same authority, it must be supposed that it began at the other, in Galilee: it must have been known to his accusers, when they advanced this charge against him, that on some recent occasion he had set out from Galilee, and had travelled gradually from place to place, teaching the people wheresoever he came, until at last he arrived

P Luke xxiii. 5.

H h 3

in Jerusalem; it must have been known also that he had done this with so little secrecy or reserve—he had attracted so much notice—he had raised, and been attended by, such numerous crowds—he had entered Jerusalem itself with so much publicity and state—that he might be said to have stirred up the people—to have agitated the public mind—and to have sown the seeds of tumult or disaffection, wherever he had appeared.

The outward characteristics of our Lord's last progress were, unquestionably, such as to admit of a sinister construction : for, knowing that this last journey was to terminate in his own death and passion—a death and a passion, which were to be transacted in the most conspicuous manner—he had as designedly courted publicity and observation, upon this occasion, as he had ever studied concealment, before; and from the time of his setting out, to the time of his arrival in the city, he had taken care that both the world at large, and his enemies in particular, should have abundant opportunity of marking his movements, and of discovering, in his whole conduct and demeanour, the pregnant symptoms of some great and momentous event. It was the concourse and observation, which his presence was producing at the time, to which we must ascribe the words of the Pharisees, Luke xiii. 31 : and the proceedings, so minutely described, at the final entry into Jerusalem, are but indications of what had been going on, with more or less of the same pomp and celebrity, at every period of the progress previously. The passage through Jericho, in particular, is a case in point.

II. The women, who stood about our Saviour's cross, and were afterwards present at his interment, are described in general as women who had *followed him*, or, *come up* with him *from Galilee*—who had *followed him from Galilee*, ministering unto him—who, when he *was in Galilee, followed him*, ministering unto him—and had *come up* with him *unto Jerusalem* [a]—and, consequently, upon this occa-

---

[a] Luke xxiii. 49. 55.   Matt. xxvii. 55.   Mark xv. 41.

sion, and in attendance upon this feast, which had brought them all alike up to Jerusalem, but after some journey, beginning in Galilee, and ending in Jerusalem. And what is here asserted of the *female* disciples in our Saviour's train, St. Paul asserts in the synagogue of Pisidian Antioch also of the male disciples in general, and of the Apostles in particular [r]. The common progress, therefore, of both our Lord, and his disciples of either sex, had been commenced in Galilee, before it was brought to a close in Jerusalem— and if so, nobody, perhaps, will doubt that it was begun from Capernaum : to proceed therefore.

The final end of despatching the Seventy in thirty-five, or thirty-six, companies, (as their number was seventy, or seventy-two,) was evidently to facilitate the labours of each division, and so to expedite the common purpose of the ministry of all. By this means, each of these companies being engaged, in as many different places, at once, according to the specific directions which they had each received, they could not be long in accomplishing their commission, and so returning to their Master. In the charge, which was given to them before their departure [s], there is the same allusion to the shortness of the time, for which they might expect to be absent, and to the dependence, which they were to place on the providence of God, for their support·during their absence, which occurred in the former charge to the Twelve upon their mission also ; but there is no allusion now, as there was then, to the possibility of a continued stay in particular places ; there is no direction that, into whatever city, or whatever house, they might enter, *there* they should *abide*, and *thence* they should *depart*. The directions, which do occur, seem rather to intimate that they should stay long no where—that their appearance, and their preaching, in any quarter, should partake of the nature of a passing visit.

We may conclude, therefore, that the errand of the Seventy would not be of long duration ; and that Jesus might

[r] Acts xiii. 31.   [s] x. 2—16.

continue in Capernaum, or wherever else he was, without any memorable occurrence, until the time of their return. The mention, indeed, of this return [t], so instantly after the charge, is a presumptive proof to the same effect. Nor, when our Lord came to follow in their steps, is it necessary to suppose he visited every place, which they had visited before him, but simply that he visited himself no place, which they had not visited before him; and that every place, which they had visited before him, lay somewhere upon the route in which he followed after them; so that all, who had heard the preaching of the Seventy, (which was doubtless the effect consulted by their mission,) might be prepared to expect, and be ready to resort to, his own. It was not, in fact, possible that one man, however indefatigable his exertions, should singly have travelled over the same ground, or performed the same work, as thirty-five, or thirty-six, except in a proportionably longer time; or not by visiting in person every place, which they might have visited, but by visiting in person simply the principal places of that description, and passing in the vicinity of the rest.

The first event recorded after the return is the question of the Lawyer, Luke x. 25: which must have happened while our Lord was teaching; and, consequently, in some private house, or in the synagogue. It might have happened, therefore, in Capernaum itself—and so have preceded the commencement of the circuit. But the next—or Christ's reception into the house of Martha [u]—shews that he was actually on his journey, or that the circuit was now begun.

From this point, to the time when he was certainly arrived in Judæa, there are clear internal evidences, scattered up and down the narrative, the united effect of all which is to determine the nature and character of the period, to which they all alike belong, as one and the same—and that, the concluding period of our Lord's public ministry in general: and those parts of the whole, concerning whose chro-

[t] x. 17.　　[u] Ib. 38.

nological position there is commonly the greatest doubt, are the very parts, which upon examination supply these indications the most decidedly.

During all this period, too, there are, as we observed at the outset, similar intimations—beginning at Luke x. 38. when our Lord is first seen to be upon the road, and extending to xix. 1. when he is seen to have passed through Jericho—which all shew that he was journeying, and journeying in the direction of Jerusalem. There are others, not so direct, which nevertheless shew that he was journeying somewhither or other—and some of them, as plainly as the more direct, that he was journeying to Jerusalem.

For example, xi. 1. and xi. 14: at the former of which periods he was by himself—at the latter, in the company of the multitude—xiii. 10. and xiii. 32—35: from the last of which it is impossible to doubt that he was both journeying at the time, and journeying expressly to Jerusalem, and very probably not far off from it, when he delivered those words—xiv. 1: as a different occasion, and, consequently, a different time and place, from those of the similar incident mentioned xi. 37; xiv. 25. xvii. 6: from the last of which we may conclude he was in Lower Galilee at the time. If the distinction, laid down by the Rabbinical writers, is true, sycamine trees were to be found in Lower Galilee only; and, where they first began to grow, discriminated Lower Galilee, from Upper Galilee, itself [v].

And with regard to the intimations of time or place, which are furnished by particular passages, in addition to those which have been already pointed out, I shall shew hereafter that Luke x. 38—42. did not happen in Bethany, as it is commonly supposed, but in some village, most probably of Galilee, and certainly different from that. I shall shew, too, that Luke xi. 14—36. is not to be confounded with Matt. xii. 22—45. If the substance also of Luke xi. 37—54. be compared with Matt. xxiii. throughout, which belongs beyond a question either to the Tuesday, or to the

---

[v] Mishna. i. 189. 2. Relandi Palæst. i. 306.   1 Kings x. 27.   1 Chron. xxvii. 28.

Wednesday, in Passion-week, no person of moderate judgment will consider it probable that our Lord would have provoked the hostility of this proud, inveterate, and influential, sect, by so open and so sharp an attack, except at a time when he knew it was no longer necessary to be careful about giving them offence—that is, until the conclusion of his ministry was arrived, or not far distant.

What indications of the same fact are supplied by xii. throughout, and by xiii. 1—9. will also appear hereafter. The discourse, which ensues xiii. 23—30. in answer to the question, εἰ ὀλίγοι οἱ σωζόμενοι, becomes much more significant and impressive, if the period of our Lord's ministry was rapidly drawing to its close. But, with regard to the rest of the chapter, from verse 31. downwards, referring to an incident, which happened the same day, the mere perusal of the words must be sufficient to prove that Jesus was journeying at the time, and journeying to Jerusalem, on an occasion which would be followed by his death and passion. Go, and say to that fox, Behold, I am casting out devils, and I am performing healings, this day, and to-morrow ; and the third day I am perfected : only I must journey this day, and to-morrow, and the next day; because it is not possible for a prophet to perish out of Jerusalem. What can be the meaning of this declaration, unless our Lord, when he delivered it, was both going to Jerusalem, and, by that unhappy necessity which rendered Jerusalem the destined scene of the destruction of the prophets, was going thither to perish ? Every one, at least, will allow that it becomes, on this construction, wonderfully natural and apposite—a construction too, which has nothing to do with the further question in what sense the terms, *to-day*, *to-morrow*, and the *next day**, are to be understood. Whether these are literal notes of time, or not, the drift of the answer remains the same—that Jesus, however long he might be in travelling through the dominions of Herod,

---

* There may be an allusion in this number of days to the three years of his personal ministry.

would yet be safe; because, being a prophet, he could not perish except in Jerusalem.

It will be admitted, also, that the pathetic apostrophe which follows, as it must have been produced by some association of ideas with what goes before, so would be as naturally produced by no association, as by that of the idea of his approaching death. It must be evident, likewise, that the effort, which he was now making, and still should make, to gather her children together, was the *last* effort of the kind —upon the failure of which, their house should be left unto them desolate. Besides which, it is declared that they should not see him again, until the time should come, when they should say, Blessed is he, who is coming in the name of the Lord : a declaration, which a comparison with Matt. xxiii. 39. proves not to have been fulfilled merely when he entered Jerusalem in triumph [w]; but to belong to some period much later even than that. As *now* delivered, therefore, it was clearly *proleptically* delivered—and, if this present occasion of the journeying to Jerusalem was the last occasion of all, the *prolepsis* itself is naturally accounted for. For the whole journey, wheresoever it might have begun, and wheresoever it might end, and whatsoever course it might take between, was still one occasion from first to last—directed to a single purpose, that of producing, by a final effort, the conversion and repentance of the Jews : at the end of which, if it failed, and at any period of which, if it was foreseen that it would fail, (both which things are true of the last circuit,) it might be said with an equal propriety, Ye shall see me no more again, as ye have seen me heretofore, until ye shall be prepared to say, Blessed is he, who is coming in the name of the Lord ! Could it have been said, however, with the same consistency at any time before the feast of Dedication—after which the Jews were to see our Lord on *three* several occasions, at least, making *three* several efforts for their conversion—first, at the feast of Dedication—secondly, at the raising of Lazarus—and, thirdly, at the last Passover ?

[w] Matt. xxi. 9.

The address to the multitude, xiv. 26—35. argues the existence at the time of a more than usual expectation that his kingdom—such as they all anticipated—was at hand ; the same expectation, which produced the question of the Pharisees—the ambitious petition of the sons of Zebedee—and the parable of the minæ[x]—and gave occasion to that concourse of the people from all parts, and to that publicity of our Lord's motions and proceedings, alluded to before as characteristic of the last journey to Jerusalem in particular. Traces of the same peculiarity are perceptible also in the places noted below[y]; during all which time he was yet in Galilee, or, up to xviii. 30. (which Matt. xix. 29. 30. xx. 1. proves to have converged directly upon the parable of the labourers hired for the vineyard) was still in Peræa. Nor is the subject-matter of the prophecy, xvii. 20—xviii. 1—8. so readily accounted for on any principle, as on that of our Lord's speedy departure, and of its consequent speedy fulfilment by the event. A similar prophecy was afterwards delivered, but only on the last day of his appearance in public, and as a part of the discourse on Mount Olivet. Yet this also there are Harmonists who assign to a period earlier than the feast of Dedication itself.

With so many internal evidences as these, all pointing distinctly to one and the same conclusion—both that of the unity and regularity of all this portion of St. Luke, and that of the time and place in the course of the Christian ministry, which it ought to be supposed to occupy—to doubt whether it belongs to the last six months of the Gospel-history, and to the last portion of those six months, or no—appears to me the perfection of scepticism and incredulity[z]. I shall conclude, therefore, with the assumption of this point, as sufficiently proved—and confine the remainder of the present Dissertation to the consideration of the probable period when the three accounts, after having continued so long

---

[x] Luke xvii. 20. Matt. xx. 20. Mark x. 35. Luke xix. 11. [y] xi. 14. 29. 53. xii. 1. 13. 54. xiii. 1. 14. 24. 31. xiv. 25. xv. 1. xvi. 14.
[z] Vide also Vol. i. Diss. i. 20—22.

separated, may most justly be believed to coincide ; and to go on, in conjunction, afresh.

The omission of these last six months, in the Gospel of St. Mark, is a natural consequence of their omission, in the Gospel of St. Matthew ; and their omission in the Gospel of St. Matthew may be vindicated on various grounds. First, a great part of the time was spent in Judæa ; in residing at Capernaum, or at Ephraim ; which he either summarily supposes, or omits to notice only in common with St. Luke. Secondly, some portion more of it was occupied by the mission of the Seventy—an incident both in its cause, in its design, and in its effect, so similar to the previous mission of the Twelve, that one who had given so minute and particular an account of the latter might well be excused from taking any notice of the former. Thirdly, even after our Lord's circuit in person was begun, a great part of its events, and, consequently, of what must have entered into a regular historical account of it, as it may be seen from St. Luke, consisted of matters which had transpired before, and been related by St. Matthew in their proper place previously. I do not mean that these were identical, which is far from having been the case—but merely that they were similar ; and consequently that, whether actions or discourses, there was no necessity, *a priori*, why they should be repeated by St. Matthew. On this subject, however, I refer the reader to my first Dissertation in the preceding volume, page 45.

It is a singular coincidence, however, that the precise point of time, at which St. Matthew and St. Mark do each resume the proper thread of their accounts, is with the passage of Jesus from Galilee into Peræa, as such. The renewal of his ministerial duties, and consequently their implicit suspension since the last return to Capernaum, (which was prior to the feast of Tabernacles) are also specified at the same time ; Καὶ συμπορεύονται πάλιν ὄχλοι πρὸς αὐτόν, καὶ ὡς εἰώθει πάλιν ἐδίδασκεν αὐτούς[a]. This was, in fact, to resume the proper thread of the account as soon as the scene of our

[a] Mark x. 1.

Saviour's ministry was become strictly speaking *new*, or could be said to have got upon ground not absolutely familiar to their Gospels : and such was the case when it had once passed into Persæa.

The time of this passage is intimated by Matt. xix. 1—2. and by Mark x. 1; the most likely position of both which, as it appears to me, is between Luke xvii. 19. and xvii. 20 —xviii. 14. For, at the time of the performance of the miracle upon the lepers, the exordium of the account shews that our Lord was still in Galilee ; and at the time of the subsequent discourses, wheresoever he was, he was in some *one* place ; for all of them were consecutively delivered.

It is no difficulty that St. Matthew says, He came εἰς τὰ ὅρια τῆς Ἰουδαίας, πέραν τοῦ Ἰορδάνου : that is, he came, on the other side the Jordan, to the confines of Judæa : not, as some commentators, and writers on the geography of Palestine, have supposed—to the confines of Judæa beyond the Jordan—as if there were a Judæa, πέραν τοῦ Ἰορδάνου. The boundary of Judæa, and of Persæa, in the vicinity of Jericho, was the Jordan ; and one who had reached the Jordan in that direction on the eastern side might truly be said to have come to the confines of Judæa on the western. St. Mark, however, as if on purpose to explain St. Matthew, expresses himself without ambiguity as follows: Ἔρχεται ΕΙΣ τὰ ὅρια τῆς Ἰουδαίας, ΔΙΑ τοῦ πέραν τοῦ Ἰορδάνου—on which no other construction can possibly be put.

The plain of Jericho was seventy stades in length, and twenty in breadth : its chief productions being the palm, and the balsam, tree[b]—as alluded to by Horace in this line,

Præferat Herodis palmetis pinguibus.

Epistol. II. ii. 184.

Its distance from Jerusalem was 150 stades, and from the banks of the Jordan was 60[c]: and the way from thence to Jerusalem was rocky, steep, and desert or solitary. The first indication that our Lord had now crossed the Jordan

[b] B. Jud. i. vi. 6.   iv. viii. 3.   Strabo xvi. 1085.   Plin. H. N. xiii. 4. Justin. xxxvi. 3.   [c] B. Jud. iv. viii. 3.   Ant. Jud. v. 1. 4.

seems to be supplied at Matt. xx. 17—19. Mark x. 32—34. Luke xviii. 31—34: for both this prediction could no where have been so well timed, as when he was just entering Judæa, and the term ἀναβαίνομεν, found in each of the accounts, must be some presumptive proof that they were upon the high-road between the Jordan and Jerusalem; which was really an *ascent*, especially after it had arrived at Jericho. The same locality was, therefore, the scene of the petition of the sons of Zebedee, and of the first miracle on the blind man—each before the entrance into Jericho.

It is probable, consequently, that Jesus was arrived at the borders of Judæa, or within a day's journey of being so, when the Pharisees put their question concerning divorce[d] —especially as it may be made to appear, that this question was put just before he withdrew into some private house— and the next incident recorded, but one, the application of the rich young ruler, followed in its consequences by the parable of the labourers, took place as he was coming out εἰς ὁδόν—which means in resumption of his journey. The scene of this parable was probably Peræa; and the time, as probably, was morning. For Peræa, which was rich in vineyards[e]—not the plain of Jericho, where none were planted—was much the most likely to have suggested the parable on the spot: and the time of the parable itself is laid in the spring of the year, and on the morning of some day—both which things would also be true of our Saviour's journey, if he was now only one day's journey distant from Jerusalem, and preparing to renew his progress ἅμα πρωΐ, or with sunrise, in the day.

I infer, then, that the question of the Pharisees was put towards the close of *one* day—and that the proceedings of *another* are specified with the resumption of the journey, and the application of the Ruler, directly after. If our Saviour was at this very time at the ford of Bethabara, only 210 stades distant from Jerusalem, or even further off, I shall shew hereafter that by setting out in the morning, at

d Matt. xix. 3. Mark x. 7.   e B. Jud. iii. iii. 3.

the ordinary time of commencing a journey in the East, and travelling leisurely at the rate of only two or three miles to the hour, he might yet pass through Jericho, and stop with Zaccheus, before the ninth hour of the day, within three or four Roman miles of Jerusalem.   I shall shew also that this was the Friday before Passion-week—or one day before he actually arrived at Bethany, and seven days, or exactly one week, before he suffered.

DISSERTATION XVII.

On the village of Martha and Mary.

THAT the scene of the incident, which is recorded Luke x. 38—42. was some village of Galilee, the name of which, because it was altogether unnecessary to mention, the narrative has left indefinite, appears to me so certain a point, that I know not how it can reasonably be questioned; nor is there a stronger proof of the implicit submission, with which opinions are handed down from one commentator to another, as if prescriptively entitled to reception, than the very ancient, and very general, mistake, which has hitherto confounded it with Bethany.

Had the village been really Bethany, there is no conceivable reason why St. Luke should have suppressed its name —and those, who can be content with the reason which is commonly assigned, would be content with any thing. Nor is such an omission more improbable in itself, than contrary to the usage of the writer; especially in what, upon this principle, must have been the first instance of the occurrence of the name in his Gospel. With regard to the designations of places generally, throughout the Gospels, this rule may be observed to hold good—that, among a vast number of πόλεις and κῶμαι, little short of a thousand, which might have been mentioned, though the names of what are called *cities* are sometimes specified, the names of towns or villages (including every thing below the rank or population of a city) all bearing appellations of Jewish, or native, etymon—all extremely barbarous and uncouth in their structure—and all, consequently, proportionably difficult to express intelligibly in Greek—never are. To this rule, the villages of Bethany, and of Bethphage—both in the neighbourhood of Jerusalem, both upon the high road from Jericho, over the mount of Olives, and both memorable for some of the most interesting particulars in the Gospel-history—were as likely to be exceptions as any : and as they are, one or other of them, specified by name in all the Gospels—thrice by St. Matthew—five times by St. Mark—thrice by St. Luke—and thrice by St. John—it is manifest that they are exceptions.

The origin of the mistake may be traced up to these two assumptions : first, that Martha and Mary were the sisters of Lazarus ; secondly, that Lazarus, and consequently they also, were natives of Bethany. The former of these I am not disposed to question ; but of the latter, there is good reason to doubt ; and, even had it been true, still it would not have justified the inference grounded upon it. A native, and much more a mere inhabitant, of Bethany might yet have had possessions in Galilee.

But the antecedent probability is altogether in favour of the presumption that the family of Lazarus were natives of Galilee. All our Lord's followers, and especially the chief and the most devoted among them—the Twelve—the Seventy—the one hundred and twenty on the day of Pentecost—every female disciple in particular, Mary of Magdala—Mary, the mother of James and Joses—Salome—Susanna—Johanna, the wife of Chuzas—it may be concluded with an assurance, almost amounting to certainty, were natives of Galilee, and none of them of Judæa. And as to this one family, however doubtful it might be concerning the rest, I think it may be shewn even upon the testimony of St. John himself, that though all, or some, of them might be resident at Bethany, they were not born there; and, consequently, must have been natives of some other part ; which part we may reasonably suppose was Galilee.

St. John has a singular idiom, affecting the use of the prepositions ἀπὸ and ἐξ, of which this is an instance[a]—Ἦν δὲ ὁ Φίλιππος ἀπὸ Βηθσαϊδά, ἐκ τῆς πόλεως Ἀνδρέου καὶ Πέτρου. The sense of the preposition ἀπὸ is not the same with the sense of the preposition ἐξ—and, consequently, the phrase ἀπὸ Βηθσαϊδά, strictly rendered, cannot be identical with the

---

[a] i. 45.

phrase ἐκ τῆς πόλεως. Ἀνδρέου καὶ Πέτρου, strictly rendered also. The natural sense of ἀπὸ, as thus employed, is to designate an *inhabitant*, and the natural sense of ἐκ, similarly employed, is to designate a *native*, of a particular place. The former would answer to our vernacular use of *of*, *of*; the latter we have no corresponding preposition to express at once, nor any thing but a periphrasis. That the former is thus used in the present instance no one will dispute; or if they do, it may be proved by a reference to parallel places—τῷ ἀπὸ Βηθσαϊδά—Ἰωσήφ, ὁ ἀπὸ Ἀριμαθαίας—ὁ ἀπὸ Κανᾶ τῆς Γαλιλαίας[b]—in all which it stands for an *inhabitant* of one of those places. Philip, therefore, ὁ ἀπὸ Βηθσαϊδά, means Philip who was *of* Bethsaida—that is, Philip who was an inhabitant of Bethsaida; and how different this would be from Philip ὁ ἐκ Βηθσαϊδά may appear from the following considerations.

I. The phrase, Ἰησοῦς, ὁ ἀπὸ Ναζαρὲτ, to express the quarter which our Saviour was known to be *of*, is of standing occurrence in all the Gospels[c]—the phrase, Ἰησοῦς, ὁ ἐκ Ναζαρὲτ, is never once to be met with in any of them; and good reason why—it would have asserted a falsehood. A person, who had been both born and bred up at Nazareth, might well be said to be both ἀπὸ and ἐκ Ναζαρέτ—but one, who had not been born there, though he might have lived from his birth, and been brought up, there, never could be said to be ἐκ Ναζαρέτ—only ἀπὸ Ναζαρέτ. Nor can the distinct and proper force of these two modes of description respectively be better illustrated, than by the instance which follows upon John i. 45. itself. Philip, after conversing with Jesus, is said to have found Nathanael, and to have addressed him thus; We have found him, of whom Moses in the Law, and the Prophets, have written—Jesus, the son of Joseph, τὸν ἀπὸ Ναζαρέτ—which designates our Lord merely from the place of his residence as such. But Nathanael, concluding that the place of his residence must needs

---

[b] John xii. 21. xix. 38. xxi. 2. Compare also, Matt. xv. 1. xxvii. 57. Mark xv. 43. Luke xxiii. 51. John vii. 42. Acts vi. 9. x. 23. xxi. 10. 27. xxiv. 18. xxv. 7.   [c] Matt. xxi. 11. Mark i. 9. John i. 46. Acts x. 38.

have been the place of his birth, expresses his surprize accordingly; 'Εκ Ναζαρὲτ δύναταί τι ἀγαθὸν εἶναι[d];

II. Μὴ γὰρ ἐκ τῆς Γαλιλαίας ὁ Χριστὸς ἔρχεται; οὐχὶ ἡ γραφὴ εἶπεν ὅτι ἐκ τοῦ σπέρματος Δαβὶδ, καὶ ἀπὸ Βηθλεὲμ, τῆς κώμης ὅπου ἦν Δαβὶδ, ὁ Χριστὸς ἔρχεται[c]; The use of *ἐξ*, in the first of these questions, is to designate a native of Galilee; and in the second, to designate a lineal descendant of David: but the use of *ἀπὸ*, in the words ἀπὸ Βηθλεὲμ, is not to describe a *native*, but merely one *of*, that is, an *inhabitant*, of Bethlehem. This may be made to appear, first by a comparison with vii. 27. before—Τοῦτον οἴδαμεν πόθεν ἐστίν· ὁ δὲ Χριστὸς ὅταν ἔρχηται, οὐδεὶς γινώσκει πόθεν ἐστίν. If the words, πόθεν ἐστὶν, in this last assertion, are to be understood of the *family* of the Christ, they would be contradictory to what was asserted above—viz. that he should be of the seed of David. And if they are not to be understood of the *family* of the Christ, they must be understood of the *place* of his *birth*. It was known that the Christ should be *of* the seed of David—it was not known *where* he should be born. They cannot refer even to the place where he should appear; for then, they would contradict another part of the preceding assertion—which affirmed that he should be *of* Bethlehem. Here it is said, that when the Christ came, it should not be known *whence* he was—there it was said to be known already that he should be *of* Bethlehem—and these assertions would still be consistent, if the former refers to the place of his birth as such—the latter to the place of his residence—and both, prior to his appearance as the Christ.

Secondly, there are passages in Justin Martyr, which critically accord to this hypothesis; shewing that the Jews in his time, and by parity of consequence in our Saviour's time, so little before his, entertained such an idea about the Messias, as might naturally induce them to think he would be manifested at Bethlehem, but not necessarily that he

---

[d] Vide also, Matt. i. 20. ii. 6. Luke i. 5. 27. ii. 4. 36. v. 17. xxiii. 7. John iv. 7. 22. 39. vii. 52. viii. 23. Many more might be produced.   [c] John vii. 41. 42.

would be born there. Χριστὸς δὲ, εἰ καὶ γεγέννηται καὶ ἔστι που, ἄγνωστός ἐστι, καὶ οὐδὲ αὐτός πω ἑαυτὸν ἐπίσταται· οὐδὲ ἔχει δύναμίν τινα, μέχρις ἂν ἐλθὼν Ἠλίας χρίσῃ αὐτὸν, καὶ φανερὸν πᾶσι ποιήσῃ—Καὶ γὰρ πάντες ἡμεῖς τὸν Χριστὸν ἄνθρωπον ἐξ ἀνθρώπων προσδοκῶμεν γενήσεσθαι, καὶ τὸν Ἠλίαν χρίσαι αὐτὸν ἐλθόντα——And again, where Justin himself is speaking ; Καὶ αὐτὸν ὅτι οὐδέπω φασὶν ἐληλυθέναι, καὶ τοῦτο γινώσκω· εἰ δὲ καὶ ἐληλυθέναι λέγουσιν, οὐ γινώσκεται ὅς ἐστιν, ἀλλ᾽ ὅταν ἐμφανὴς καὶ ἔνδοξος γένηται, τότε γνωσθήσεται ὅς ἐστι, φασὶ[f].

They, who could believe these things, could not possibly expect the Christ to be born at any particular place, though they might perhaps expect him to be manifested at some such place. The phrase too, ὅπου Δαβὶδ ἦν, not ὅθεν Δαβὶδ ἦν, is more in accordance with this supposition, than with the other ; implying that the Christ should be *at*, or *of*, Bethlehem, when Elias should anoint him, as David was, when he was anointed by Samuel. Nor does Matt. ii. 4. 5. present any difficulty—since they, who returned that answer to Herod, could not have entertained this opinion, nor any opinion like this, concerning the Christ ; but must have had truer, and better, notions. Nor are we considering the rectitude of opinions, but the use of terms ; according to which, πόθεν ἐστὶν, in the one instance, and ἀπὸ Βηθλεὲμ, in the other, if they are not to assert a contradiction, must imply different things. To return, then, from this digression.

In our original proposition, Φίλιππος ἀπὸ Βηθσαϊδὰ, ἐκ τῆς πόλεως Ἀνδρέου καὶ Πέτρου, if the use of ἀπὸ, in the first member, is to describe an *inhabitant* of Bethsaida, the use of ἐξ, in the second, is not to do the same thing : for that would make Philip, and Andrew, and Peter, all of them, inhabitants of Bethsaida. But, though this might be the case with Philip, it would be false of Andrew and Peter ; whom Mark i. 21. 29. Luke iv. 31. 38. demonstrate to have been inhabitants of Capernaum. If, however, the use of ἐξ is not to describe an inhabitant, it must be to describe a

[f] Dialog. 153. 235. 371.

native, of the same city with Andrew and Peter; and the proposition will affirm either that Philip and Andrew and Peter had all been born at Bethsaida—where Philip had lived ever since—or that Philip and Andrew and Peter had all been born in Capernaum, where Andrew and Peter had lived ever since, though Philip had settled in Bethsaida. Now this is by far the most probable supposition; for ἐκ τῆς πόλεως Ἀνδρέου καὶ Πέτρου never can be merely synonymous with ἀπὸ Βηθσαϊδά—which it must be on the contrary supposition—and Peter and Andrew, both settled in Capernaum, and the former of them even married there, and both in partnership with two other inhabitants of the place, it is highly reasonable to conclude must have been both born and brought up there. In any case while the ἀπὸ is still to be distinguished from the ἐκ, neither of them can be dropped, as in the received translation, nor the latter rendered, except by a periphrasis, as follows: Now Philip was *of* Bethsaida—*but a native* of the city of Andrew and Peter—*this* circumstance being specified in contradistinction to *that*, in all probability, to account for some acquaintance between themselves, before any of them became acquainted with Jesus.

I have been the more particular in explanation of this idiom, because John xi. 1. the very outset of the history of Lazarus is exactly a case in point: Ἦν δέ τις ἀσθενῶν, Λάζαρος ἀπὸ Βηθανίας, ἐκ τῆς κώμης Μαρίας, καὶ Μάρθας τῆς ἀδελφῆς αὐτῆς—which we shall now understand accordingly—There was a certain person sick, Lazarus, who was of Bethany; a native of the village of Mary, and of Martha, her sister. The name of Lazarus, which occurs no where in the Gospels, except in St. John, and no where in St. John before this passage, is here introduced to the reader, as the name of a stranger naturally would be, first, indefinitely—there was one Lazarus—secondly, with such additional particulars, as would contribute to make him better known; one, his being of Bethany, another, his belonging to the village of Mary and her sister Martha.

Now, by this reference to the village of Mary and her

sister Martha, it is indisputably clear in my opinion that he refers to this present account of St. Luke—which speaks of a certain κώμη, or village—of two sisters, Martha and Mary, as belonging to it—and of something, affecting the personal history of them both, which transpired in it. Out of the Gospel of St. Luke, if we except what follows from the xi. to the xii. of St. John, no such persons, nor any such allusions to their history, are to be met with ; nor, in the Gospel of St. Luke itself, in any passage but the present.

And as St. John expected to make Lazarus better known, by referring his readers to the village of Martha and Mary, whose brother he was, so he expected to make Mary better known, by referring them to the performance of a memorable act, mentioned indeed by St. Matthew and St. Mark, but not ascribed to any one by name, the unction of our Lord at Bethany ; which unction he tells them was the act of Mary, the sister of this Lazarus, who was sick : in which statement, I think it must be admitted, he refers as plainly to St. Matthew or to St. Mark, as in the former instance he referred to St. Luke.

This part, then, of the Gospel of St. John, compared with St. Luke's, places it beyond a question that the Martha and the Mary of St. Luke were the two sisters of Lazarus —which otherwise could not have been inferred for certain. But it proves also that as Lazarus was not a native of Bethany, so neither was either of them ; and, therefore, that the village, to which they all belonged, might still be some village in Galilee—and certainly was none of Judæa, near to Jerusalem. The history of the unction, too, which he afterwards records, compared in like manner with the account of St. Matthew, or St. Mark, enables us to resolve the remaining problem—if the family of Lazarus were not natives of Bethany, how any part, or all, of it, came to be living there.

The supper, which was made for our Saviour, on the night of his arrival at Bethany, took place in the house of Martha—as may be inferred for the following reasons. I. Because it was manifestly intended out of gratitude for the recent miracle in behalf of Lazarus. II. Because Lazarus, her brother, was one of the guests. III. Because Martha herself ministered or waited—which she never could, or never would, have done, in any house but her own: and Theophylact reasons upon this fact accordingly. Διὰ δὲ τοῦ εἰπεῖν ὅτι ἡ Μάρθα διηκόνει, ἐσήμανεν ὅτι ἐν τῇ οἰκίᾳ αὐτῆς ἡ ἑστίασις ἦν [g]. IV. Because Mary, the sister of Martha, anointed our Lord, on the same occasion, as he sat at meat. This act being judged of in reference to the usages of the time could properly have been the act of no one, except either the owner of the house, or one, who stood in some near relation to the owner: for it was designed on purpose to do honour to their guest, and it was as striking (though by no means an unusual mode) as any which could have been employed. And this circumstance alone (if there were no other reason to the same effect) would be sufficient to discriminate the present unction of Mary's in St. John, from the former unction recorded by St. Luke [h]—that Mary's unction was entirely an expression of personal compliment, and for the sake of the patient—St. Luke's, an expression of penitence, and for the sake of the agent: Mary's had no object except to do honour to our Saviour, and to declare the two sisters' respect for their guest, or their gratitude to the preserver of their brother—St. Luke's was an earnest of the woman's contrition, a declaration that she believed our Saviour could forgive her sins, and only a more humble mode of entreating that he would.

The entertainment, then, according to St. John, was doubtless given in the house of Martha. But, according to St. Matthew and St. Mark [i], it was given in the house of Simon, surnamed the Leper. If both these representations are true, it was given in the house of both—and, consequently, either what Theophylact asserts was the tradition in his time—Τὸν δὲ Σίμωνα τοῦτον τὸν Λεπρὸν φασί τινες καὶ πατέρα εἶναι τοῦ Λαζάρου [k]—that Simon was the father of Lazarus, and, therefore, of Martha, becomes true of the relation

[g] Comm. in Joh. xii. 733. [h] vii. 37—end. [i] Matt. xxvi. 6. Mark xiv. 3. [k] In Matt. xxvi. 158.

between them, or, what is much more probable, Simon was the *husband* of Martha, and either of them might be called indifferently the owner of the house.

As he is called the Leper, we must needs suppose that he had once been such; though we cannot suppose he was so still. Hence it is probable that our Saviour had cured him of his leprosy; and if he was the husband of Martha, that would be a sufficient foundation for the faith of himself, and of his family, in Christ; a faith, prior to the time of the subsequent miracle, and, therefore, not produced, however much it might be strengthened, by it. Now Simon himself, it is possible, might be a native of Bethany, and yet, notwithstanding, married to a native of Galilee; and, consequently, to one who might have possessions in Galilee. And if Martha, who seems to have been the oldest of the family of Lazarus, was married to a native of Bethany, it is nothing extraordinary that her sister and brother, both of them younger than herself, and all three united together, by the closest and tenderest ties of attachment, should be permanently resident there also with her, yet so as occasionally to visit Galilee. It was a maxim of Jewish law, Maritus non habet ullam possessionem in bonis uxoris suæ, nec uxor in bonis mariti; it was another maxim, Filii, filiæque, jus idem est in hæreditate[1]. The first born received a double portion—the rest, of either sex, shared alike. This maxim, therefore, proves that Martha might have property of her own, though she had a brother, a sister, and a husband, all alive at the same time: the former proves in like manner that our Lord might as properly be said to be entertained in *her house* in Galilee, as in Simon's at Bethany.

When Jesus quitted Jerusalem, to retire to Ephraim, the family of Lazarus might have left its vicinity also; for, after his resurrection, the safety of Lazarus would have been as much endangered by a personal continuance in Bethany, as our Lord's. And this conjecture, I think, is so

[1] Mishn. iv. 169. 3. 191. 5.

far confirmed by the course of the subsequent history that, from John xii. 9—11. we may safely conclude Lazarus had not been in the neighbourhood, any more than Jesus, since the time of that miracle, until they both reappeared there, six days before the last Passover. It is possible that, when our Lord retired to Ephraim, the two sisters at least removed to Galilee; and knowing that Jesus was shortly to make his final circuit of that country, preparatory to visiting Jerusalem, might purposely have awaited his arrival in their native village; and, after entertaining him there, have accompanied him upon the rest of his journey. These, therefore, may be intended among others, as persons who had recently come up with him from Galilee [m]; and who, even in that country, had followed after, and ministered unto, him.

I cannot do better, then, than to conclude this Dissertation with some general observations.

I. Though Lazarus also had accompanied his sisters into Galilee, there would still be no reason to suppose his name would be mentioned by St. Luke, in the account of an incident which had nothing at all to do with him. What, therefore, Epiphanius [n] asserts, Ἀλλὰ καὶ ἐν παραδόσεσιν εὑρομεν ὅτι τριάκοντα ἐτῶν ἦν τότε ὁ Λάζαρος, ὅτε ἐγήγερται, μετὰ δὲ τὸ ἀναστῆναι αὐτὸν, ἄλλα τριάκοντα ἔτη ἔζησε—may be true or may be false, or partly the one and partly the other—but it cannot, in the slightest degree, apply to the case in point. The silence of St. Luke about Lazarus here would have been a natural consequence, even though he had related his resurrection elsewhere.

II. I have assumed that our Lord was now on his last progress; journeying from place to place, and, consequently, stopping only for the purpose of necessary refreshment, or of the discharge of the duties of his ministry, or of both. The circumstances of this little history prove all these things —his entering into a certain village, as he was on the road somewhither—his being entertained and his teaching both,

---

[m] Mark xv. 41. Luke xxiii. 49. 55.   [n] Adv. Hær. i. 652.

in a certain house—and, therefore, they are all in perfect consistency with the supposition of a circuit already begun, and still going on ; but not yet complete, much less concluded by its arrival at Jerusalem.

III. Among the circumstances of peculiarity, which characterize the unction at Bethany, two only would require any particular illustration—one, the supposed value of the unguent in proportion to its quantity, the other, the peculiarity of the denomination, which is given to it.

The quantity of the unguent was an alabaster box, or vase, full, estimated at a pound in weight ; the propriety of which estimation is explained by the following passage from Epiphanius [o]: Ἀλάβαστρον μύρου βικίον μέν ἐστιν ὑέλινον, χωροῦν λίτραν ἐλαίου· τὸ δὲ μέτρον ἐστὶ ξέστου τὸ ἥμισυ· ἀλάβαστρον δὲ κέκληται διὰ τὸ εὔθρυπτον. Boxes of this material were especially appropriated for the reception of unguents [*]. Unguenta optime servantur in alabastris, odores in oleo— Hunc aliqui lapidem alabastriten vocant, quem cavant ad vasa unguentaria ; quoniam optime servare incorrupta dicitur [p]. Ἀλάβαστρον, ἄγγος μύρου, μὴ ἔχον λαβὰς, λίθινον [q].

Ἔπειτ᾽ ἀλάβαστος εὐθέως ἥξει μύρου.
Athenæi Deipnos. vi. 94.

Οὐ γὰρ ἐμυρίζετ᾽ ἐξ ἀλαβάστου, πρᾶγμά τι γινόμενον ἀεὶ, Κρονικόν.
Ibid. xv. 44.

Tradite, nudantes rejecta veste papillas,
   Quam jucunda mihi munera libet onyx :
Vester onyx, casto colitis quæ jura cubili.
Catulli Coma Berenices. 81.

* In shape, the alabaster vase was round, and tapering from the bottom to the top : whence Pliny, (ix. 35.) Alabastrorum figura, in pleniorem orbem desinentes. Sometimes the receptacles of unguents were conchs, or shells, if they happened to be naturally strung with pearls. Cohærentes videmus (sc. margaritas) in conchis, hac dote unguenta circumferentibus. *Ibid.*

∘ ii. 182. De Mensuris et Ponderibus.   p Plin. H. N. xiii. 2. xxxvi. 8.
q Suidas. Ἀλάβαστρον. Vide also Pollucis Onomasticon vi. 19.

Quod quacunque venis Cosmum migrare putamus,
   Et fluere excusso cinnama fusa vitro,
Nolo peregrinis placeas tibi, Gellia, nugis.

> Martialis Epigramm. lib. v.

Unguentum fuerat, quod onyx modo parva gerebat :
   Olfecit postquam Papilus, ecce garum est.

> Ibid. vii.

Nunc furtiva lucri fieri bombycina possunt,
Profertur Cosmi nunc mihi siccus onyx.

> Ibid. xi. In Phyllidem.

The price of the unguent is computed, both in St. Mark and in St. John, at three hundred pence, denarii, or drachmæ, or more than that sum ; which would amount to between nine and ten pounds of English money : that is to say, the unguent was valued at almost one pound *per* ounce. There can be no question, however, that it was of a rich and costly description, in which case a pound's weight of it, as we shall see, might be worth even more than that price. The name of μύρον νάρδινον was given to a species of unguent composed of a variety of sweet spices, besides the nard : Syrian unguents (of which this would probably be one) were reckoned the most excellent in general [r], and the trade in unguents was so exclusively confined to Syrian or Phenician dealers [s], that, according to Juvenal, Syrophœnix is but another name for an *unguentarius*, or vender of unguents.

Obvius assiduo Syrophœnix * udus amomo
Currit, Idumææ Syrophœnix incola portæ.

> Sat. viii. 159.

........Συρίω δὲ μύρω χρύσει᾽ ἀλάβαστρα.

> Theocriti Idyll. xv. 114.

Among the Syrians themselves none was more esteemed than the nardine.

---

* This term illustrates the propriety of St. Mark's Συροφοίνισσα, as applied to the woman of Canaan, vii. 26.

[r] Athenæi Deipnos. xv. 38.   [s] Vide Arriani Exped. Alex. vi. 22.

'Ηδὺ τὸ μύρον, παῖ· (παιδίον) πῶς γὰρ οὐχί; (οὐ) νάρδινον*.

Athenæi xv. 42.

De folio nardi, observes Pliny, plura dici par est; ut principali in unguentis: and again, In nostro orbe proxime laudatur Syriacum; mox Gallicum; tertio loco Creticum[t].

Now even the spikenard, unprepared, was worth an hundred denarii a pound[u]; and the same substance after all the trouble and loss of preparation might easily fetch three times that sum. Athenæus asserts[v] that a cotyla of unguent, the content of which measure, like the alabaster vase full, must be reckoned, according to Arbuthnot, at half the ξέστης or pint, was sold at Athens for five minæ, or five hundred drachmæ; almost fifteen pounds English: and even at twice that sum. A sextarius, or pint, of balm of Gilead, opobalsamum, was commonly sold in the time of Pliny, by the retail dealers, for one thousand denarii, and, at the custom house itself, for three hundred[w]: to which unguent Juvenal alludes in these lines;

Sed tamen unde

Hæc emis, hirsuto spirant opobalsama collo
Quæ tibi? ne pudeat dominum monstrare tabernæ.

ii. 40.

One of the old comedians writes thus;

Στακτὴ δυοῖν μναῖν οὐκ ἀρέσκει μ' οὐδαμῶς.

Athenæi Deipnos. xv. 44.

and Pliny mentions an unguent, obtained from the *malobathrum*, a Syrian shrub, which he describes as a variety of the nard, the common price of which, when the best of its kind, was 300 denarii to the pound[x]. It is to this that Horace refers,

Coronatus nitentes
Malobathro Syrio capillos.　　　　Od. II. vii. 7.

* According to Schweighaeuser, this quotation from Menander stands thus:

'Ηδὺ τὸ μύρον γ' ὦ παιδίον, ἡδύ. πῶς γὰρ οὐ;
νάρδινον.

----

[t] H. N. xii. 12.　　[u] Plin. H. N. xii. 12.　　[v] xv. 44.　　[w] H. N. xii. 25.
[x] H. N. xii. 26.

We may collect also that from three to four hundred denarii was the common price of the best unguents at Rome. Excedunt, says Pliny[y], quadringenos denarios libræ : and there was so much variety among them that even of one sort, unguent of cinnamomum, the price might vary from thirty-five, to three hundred, denarii[z]; and there was a time when the raw material of this unguent was worth one thousand denarii a pound. With regard to this circumstance, then, its propriety is unquestionable; and the supposed value of the unguent might be strictly in accordance with the truth.

As to the name which is given it both by St. Mark and by St. John[a], νάρδος πιστικὴ, this is a denomination to be reckoned among the ἅπαξ λεγόμενα of the Gospels ; and as such it has occasioned some trouble to the critics. Nor do I mean to enumerate the various explanations which have been given of it: I shall notice only that one which derives πιστικὸς from πιστὸς, and πιστὸς from πιὼ, *potare facio* or *potandum do ;* because this at first sight may appear the most plausible, and yet, in my humble judgment, is far from being correct.

That there is such a verbal derivative as πιστὸς, used by good authors in the Greek language, and that πιστικὸς might be thence deducible, I should not think of denying. I would ask, however, assuming that it was so derived, what it must mean? nard *liquid,* as such, or nard *potable,* as such? nard the reverse of solid, or nard fit to be drunk ? With regard to the first of these, it would be a distinction without a difference ; for nard *liquid* could not be so designated, except in opposition to nard *solid ;* and who ever heard or read of nard *solid ?* It was peculiar to every species of μύρον, as such, to be made with oil, and ἀρώματα, of some kind or another ; and consequently to be liquid.

> Sic ut amaracini blandum, stactæque, liquorem,
> Et nardi florem, nectar qui naribus halat,
> Quom facere instituas, cum primis quærere par est

[y] xiii. 3.   [z] Ibid. i. xii. 19.   [a] Mark xiv. 3.   John xii. 3.

Quoad lĭcet, ac possis reperire, inolentis olivi
Naturam, nullam quæ mittat naribus auram.

> Lucretii ii. 846.

Nec casia liquidi corrumpitur usus olivi.

> Virgilii Georgic. ii. 466.

Quod nec Virgilius, nec carmine dixit Homerus,
Hoc ex unguento constat, et ex balano.

> Martialis Epigramm. Lib. xiv. De Myrobalano.

Pliny, indeed, observes, Sed quosdam crassitudo maxime delectat...linique jam, non solum perfundi, unguentis gaudent[b]: but this implies merely that some unguents were thicker or grosser than others; not that all were not, or should not be, more or less liquid : and he mentions it (xviii. 11.) as a common saying concerning Campania, Plus apud Campanos unguenti, quam apud cæteros olei, fieri. And as to unguent of nard in particular, its excellence was made to consist in its fineness or tenuity more than in any thing else.

With regard to the second, nard, considered as *potable*, or πιστικὴ in the literal sense, would be an absolute nonentity. I can cite but one instance only where any thing like μύρον seems to have been made to serve the purpose of oil ; and that is supplied by Suetonius and Plutarch, in their Lives of Julius Cæsar[c]. Pliny, it is true, speaks of the introduction of unguents into wine; but even of that, only to reprobate the practice, as both new and disgusting *.

My own exposition of the sense of πιστικὸς would be as follows. The precious unguent called nard was obtained either wholly, or in part, from a vegetable production

---

* A kind of spiced beverage, or sweet wine, called myrrhina (sc. potio) was, indeed, anciently known among the Romans : Plin. H. N. xiv. 13—but this is manifestly a different thing.

b H. N. xiii. 3.   c Suet. Vit. 53. Plutarchi Vit. 17. Vide also Hor. Sat. ii. 2. 68.

which bore the same name: and though it may be a contested point with the learned, whether the root, ῥίζα, or the spike, στάχυς, of this shrub was the most used for the purpose, still whatever uncertainty there may be about the former, there can be none about the latter. Cacumina, says Pliny in his description of the plant, in aristas se spargunt ; ideo gemina dote nardi spicas et folia celebrant [d].

> Tinge caput nardi *folio*, cervical olebit ;
>   Perdidit unguentum cum coma, pluma tenet.
> Martialis Epigramm. xiv.

Ovid, de Phœnice,

> Quo simul ac casias, et nardi lenis aristas,
> Quassaque cum fulva substravit cinnama myrrha,
> Se super imponit, finitque in odoribus ævum.
> Metamorphosewn xv. 398.

and to the like effect the author of the poem, on the same subject, ascribed to Claudian.

> His addit teneras nardi pubentis aristas,
>   Et sociat myrrhæ pascua grata nimis.

That the aromatic property at least was possessed in perfection by the *leaves*, the *stalks*, and the *spikes*, appears from the following passage of Arrian, where he is giving an account of Alexander's march over the desert of Gedrosia: Ἔχειν δὲ τὴν ἔρημον ταύτην καὶ νάρδου ῥίζαν, πολλήν τε καὶ εὔοσμον —πολὺ δὲ εἶναι αὐτῆς τὸ καταπατούμενον πρὸς τῆς στρατιᾶς, καὶ ἀπὸ τοῦ πατουμένου ὀδμὴν ἡδεῖαν κατέχειν ἐπιπολὺ τῆς χώρας [e]. The best nard is said to have been produced about Tarsus in Cilicia [f]; whence the epithet *Cilissa,* as applied to the spikenard.

> Cernis odoratis ut luceat ignibus æther,
>   Et sonet accensis spica Cilissa focis.
> Ovidii Fast. i. 75.

> Vinaque fundantur prelis elisa Falernis,
>   Terque lavet nostras spica Cilissa comas.
> Propertii iv. vi. 73.

---

[d] H. N. xii. 12.   [e] vi. 22.   [f] Athenæi Deipnos. xv. 38.

Now one of the modes, by which the unguentarii obtained their perfumes, whether from the roots, or from the leaves and stalks, or from any other part, of the aromatic shrub, was by pounding or braying in mortars; with a view to extract the essential oil. Hence, Horace,

Pressa tuis balanus capillis.

Carm. iii. xxix. 4.

Pliny, de Myrobalano, Unguentarii...tantum cortices *premuntᵍ:* again, Malobathron...ex quo *exprimitur* oleum ad unguenta ʰ: de Omphacio, Fit et alio modo cum in *mortariis* uva immatura *teriturⁱ:* de Caryopo, Hic est succus nuci *expressus:* De Metopio—Oleum hoc est, amygdalis amaris *expressumⁱ.*

Now, there are many themes in the Greek language, which, though obsolete or nearly so themselves, have yet given birth to derivatives, still in existence, and, consequently, proving that their themes or roots also once existed. That verb, which expresses in Greek at present the act of pounding, is πτίσσω: but πτίσσω, it will be readily admitted, is only another form for πίσσω. The existence of πίσσω some time or other is implied by the Latin *pinso,* (the original form whereof was *piso,* of which many instances are still to be met with,) *pistrinum,* and the like, in kindred senses, evidently deducible from that; but more especially from the Greek substantives πισμός and πιστήρ, both synonymous with ληνὸς or *torcular*ᵏ, which can be immediately derived only from πέπισμαι and πέπισται, the perfect passive of πίσσω: πίττω, too, which is *Attice* for πίσσω, is recognized by Pollux, in a sense equivalent to that of ἀλεῖν, *molere.* Πιστικὸς, in the corresponding signification of *apt,* or *fit, for pounding,* would be regularly obtained from πέπισται: and πτιστικὸς, in a similar sense, as derived from ἔπτισται is actually in use.

To admit, then, that such may be the real etymon of the term; it would be an obvious inference that the phrase

ᵍ xii. 21.   ʰ Ib. 26.   ⁱ Ib. 27. 28. xiii. 1.   ᵏ Phavorini Lexicon.

νάρδος πιστικὴ is intended to denote nard, which had undergone, or was proper to undergo, the process in question: that is, in one word, spikenard, or such part of the shrub as alone was qualified to yield the best ointment. If every part was not useful for this purpose alike, a term of distinction, expressing also the mode in which the ointment was to be obtained from any, would naturally be applied to that which was.

The word μύρον is said to have been unknown to the Greek language before the time of Archilochus[1]; and, probably, the use of unguents was unknown as long also. It was one of the luxuries which the West borrowed from the East, or the Greeks derived from the Persians[m] *: and its application, according to its first and most natural intention, was restricted to the upper part of the person. In the age of Pliny its application to the feet, among the Romans at least, was still a recent refinement: Vidinius etiam vestigia pedum tingi; quod M. Othonem monstrasse Neroni principi ferebant[n]. In the East such an abuse of it must have been ancient and very general: for Quintus Curtius speaks of it as an Indian custom in Alexander's time[o], and the practice had long been familiar among the Greeks.

Καὶ τοὺς πόδας
ἀλείψατ' αὐτοῦ τῷ Μεγαλλίῳ μύρῳ.
Athenæi xii. 78.

* Illi madent eo; says Pliny (*loco cit.*) and again, Primum, quod equidem inveniam, castris Darii regis expugnatis Alexander cepit scrinium unguentorum. Vide also vii. 29. where the same casquet is described as consisting of gold, richly enchased with precious stones; and as appropriated by Alexander to the preservation of the poems of Homer. The use of unguents, among the Greeks, and for a time at least, was considered a mark of effeminacy. Aristippus, says Seneca, aliquando delectatus unguento, Male, inquit, istis effeminatis eveniat, qui rem tam bellam infamaverunt. *De Beneficiis* vii. 25.

[1] Athenæi xv. 37.　　[m] Plin. H. N. xiii. 1.　　[n] Ibid. 3.　　[o] Lib. viii. 9.

'Εκ χρυσοκολλήτου γε κάλπιδος μύρῳ,
Αἰγυπτίῳ μὲν τοὺς πόδας, καὶ τὰς χέρας.

Ibid.

Yet even this will render it less extraordinary that on both occasions of our Lord's unctions, and especially on the first of them, this part of his person should have been anointed in particular.

The unguentarii were expelled from Lacedæmon by a public decree of the state, and there was a similar prohibition against the introduction of ointments at Rome, so late as A. U. 565. in the censorship of Crassus and Cæsar. (Seneca Nat. Quæst. iv. 13. Plin. H. N. xiii. 3.) Yet, before the death of Julius Cæsar, the use of unguents had become so common, that Lucius Plotius, a noble Roman, who had been included in the proscription which ensued, and was lying in concealment at the time, was betrayed by the scent of his perfumes; Quo dedecore, says Pliny, tota absoluta proscriptio est : quis enim non merito judicet periisse tales ? How passionately fond, indeed, of the sensuality in question the Romans were at this period of their history appears from the many references to it in the poets, and from the various modes in which we find it described as employed. It was lavished, in the shape of water of crocus, upon the stage.

Recte, necne, crocum floresque perambulet Attæ
Fabula, si dubitem, clament periisse pudorem.

Horatii Epistolarum lib. ii. i. 79.

Et quom scena croco Cilici perfusa recens est,
Araque Panchæos exhalat propter odores.

Lucretii ii. 416.

Tunc neque marmoreo pendebant vela theatro,
  Nec fuerant liquido pulpita rubra croco.

Ovidii De Arte Amandi i. 103.

Hoc rogo non melius, quam rubro pulpita nimbo
  Spargere, et effuso permaduisse croco?

Martialis Epigramm. v. De Chærestrato.

κ k 2

It was an expression of gallantry to apply it to the posts of
doors—nay even to anoint beds and couches with it.

> At lacrumans exclusus amator limina sæpe
> Floribus et sertis operit, posteisque superbos
> Unguit amaracino.
>
> *Lucretii iv.* 1170.

> Nam te non viduas jacere noctes
> Nequidquam tacitum cubile clamat,
> Sertis ac Syrio fragrans olivo.
>
> *Catulli vi. 6.*

As a personal luxury or indulgence, as part of the plea-
sures of the banquet, and as an inseparable ingredient in
every species of festivity, its use was universal : and to cite
passages in proof of it would be almost an endless task *.

> Unguentum dabo, quod meæ puellæ
> Donarunt Veneres, Cupidinesque :
> Quod tu cum olfacies, Deos rogabis
> Totum ut te faciant, Fabulle, nasum.
>
> *Catulli xiii.* 11.

> Cur non sub alta vel platano, vel hac
> Pinu, jacentes sic temerè, et rosa
>   Canos odorati capillos,
>   Dum licet, Assyriaque nardo
> Potamus uncti ?
>
> *Horatii Carm. ii. xi.* 13.

* Necnon aliquem ex privatis, says Pliny, audivimus jussisse
spargi parietes balinearum unguentis, atque Caium principem
solia temperari ... Maxime tamen mirum est hanc gratiam pene-
trasse et in castra : aquilæ certe ac signa, pulverulenta illa, et
custodiis horrida, inunguntur festis diebus. H: N. xiii. 3. We
read even of the anointing of a dolphin by a proconsul of Africa.
Ibid. ix. 8. Solini Polyhistor. cap. xii. Parum est, says Seneca,
sumere unguentum, ni bis die terque renovetur ; ne evanescat in
corpore. Epist. 86.

Sed pressum Calibus ducere Liberum
Si gestis, juvenum nobilium cliens,
    Nardo vina merebere ;
Nardi parvus onyx eliciet cadum.

Ibid. iv. xii. 14.

Illius e nitido stillent unguenta capillo,
    Et capite et collo mollia serta gerat.

Tibulli i. vii. 51.

Intonsi crines longa cervice fluebant,
    Spirabat Syrio myrtea rore coma.

iii. iv. 27.

Jamdudum Syria madefactus tempora nardo
    Debueram sertis implicuisse comas.

iii. vi. 63.

Sit mensæ ratio, noxque inter pocula currat,
    Et crocino nares myrrheus ungat onyx.

Propertii iii. x. 21.

Lævis odorato cervix manabit olivo,
    Et feries nudos veste fluente pedes.

iii. xvii. 31.

Veste tegor vili ; nullum est in crinibus aurum ;
    Non Arabo noster rore capillus olet.

Sappho Phaoni 75.

Sæpe coronatis stillant unguenta capillis,
    Et trahitur multo splendida palla croco.

Cydippe Acontio 161.

Projicit ipse suas deducta fronte coronas,
    Spissaque de nitidis tergit amoma comis.

Ibid. 165.

Nec coma vos fallat, liquida nitidissima nardo,
    Nec brevis in rugas cingula pressa suas.

Ovidii de Arte Amandi iii. 443.

Et matutino sudans Crispinus amomo,
Quantum vix redolent duo funera.

Juvenalis Sat. iv. 108.

The use of aromata, unguents, or perfumes, among the Jews, was as ancient as the institution of their temple ser-

K k 3

vice; but that use was purely religious.   In other respects
it seems to have been chiefly confined to funeral honours,
or the last offices about the persons of the dead[p].   At the
funeral of Herod, five hundred slaves or freedmen are said
to have been employed in carrying the spices merely[q].   Yet
this custom also was not more peculiar to the Jews than to
the rest of the East; and in Seneca's or Pliny's time it was
a regular part of the burial of the dead, to burn odours and
unguents along with them: Æque qui in *odoribus* jacet
mortuus est, quam qui rapitur unco, observes the one, and
Honosque is et ad defunctos pertinere cœpit, the other[r].
Poppæa, the wife of Nero, was so interred, Regum exter-
norum consuetudine[s]; concerning which fact Pliny informs
us, Periti rerum asseverant, non ferre (*leg.* ferri) tantum
annuo fetu, quantum Nero princeps novissimo Poppææ suæ
die concremaverit[t].   Nor were merely spices, but also μύρα,
employed for this purpose.

> Illuc quas mittit dives Panchaïa merces,
>   Eoïque Arabes, dives et Assyria,   ·
> Et nostri memores lacrymæ fundantur eodem;
>   Sic ego componi, versus in ossa, velim.
>
>   Tibulli iii. ii. 23.
>
> Desit odoriferis ordo mihi lancibus, adsint
>   Plebeii parvæ funeris exequiæ.
>
>   Propertii ii. xiii. 23.
>
> Osculaque in gelidis ponas suprema labellis,
>   Quum dabitur Syrio munere plenus onyx.
>
>   Ibid. 29.
>
> Cur ventos non ipse rogis, ingrate, petisti,
>   Cur nardo flammæ non oluere meæ?
>
>   iv. vii. 31.
>
> Ille tibi exequias, et magni funus honoris,
>   Fecit, et in gelidos versit amoma sinus.
> Diluit et lacrymis mœrens unguenta profusis,
>   Ossaque vicina condita texit humo.
>
>   Ovidii Epp. ex Ponto i. ix. 51.

---

[p] 2 Chron. xvi. 14.   Jeremiah xxxiv. 5.   Vide however Isaiah lvii. 9.
[q] Jos. B. Jud. i. xxxiii. 9.   [r] Seneca Epist. lxxxii. H. N. xiii. 1. Vide
also xii. 18.   [s] Tac. Ann. xvi. 6.   [t] xii. 18.

Unguenta, et casias, et olentem funera myrrham,
  Turaque de medio semicremata rogo,
Et quæ de Stygio rapuisti cinnama lecto,
  Improbe de turpi, Zoile, redde sinu.

                                  Martialis Epigramm. lib. xi.

Sparge mero cineres, bene olentis et unguine nardi,
  Hospes, et adde rosis balsama puniceis.

                                  Ausonii Epitaph.

Upon this usage was founded our Lord's prophetical,
and at the same time benevolent, interpretation of the act
of Mary[u], when the disciples in general, or Judas in particular, were complaining of the needless waste of a precious
article.   Let the woman alone—why are ye troubling her?
She hath done unto me a becoming deed—against the day
of my embalment hath she reserved it.   The office, which
she had just performed, was a good and a proper office,
insomuch as it was, or should be, the embalment of our
Lord's body against his burial.   For this was, strictly
speaking, the only embalment his body should receive;
and for that purpose, κατὰ συμβεβηκὸς, if not *per se*, it
might be said to be intended; and its effect should ultimately be reserved: which is the import of the prophetical
preterite, τετήρηκε, John xii. 7.

          [u] Mark xiv. 6. 8. John xii. 7.

DISSERTATION XVIII.

On the two dispossessions, and the blasphemy against the Holy Ghost: or the comparison of Matt. xii. 22—45. with Luke xi. 14—36.

I HAVE purposely reserved this comparison for the present period of the work, because, the more certain it might be that the occasions, to which these distinct portions of St. Matthew's and of St. Luke's Gospels, respectively, relate, were altogether different, the more necessary it would become to consider the question of their identity upon the last instance of their occurrence, rather than upon the first.

Against the supposition of this distinctness there is nothing to object on the score of antecedent improbability. Miracles of dispossession in general were among the most familiar of our Saviour's miraculous acts—and miracles of dispossession in particular were the only such effects, which either in their own nature admitted of the charge in question, or, by the matter of fact, can be proved to have had it advanced against them. St. Matthew's Gospel alone demonstrates the reality of two such instances—one, ix. 32—34. the other, xii. 22—the former of which was not merely distinct from, but actually in point of time posterior to, the latter. It is nothing extraordinary that St. Luke should have added a third.

The reality of these miracles was never disputed, even when the agency by which they were wrought was called in question—it could not be, and it was not, denied that dispossession had been produced, even when the cause of the dispossession was attributed to Satan. For if there were such beings as the devils or demons, and such a person as the ruler of the devils or demons, then it would be self-evident that the former must be subject to the latter—and at *his* command, any how expressed, might be supposed either to evacuate, or to take possession of, the bodies of men. The ruler of the demons, therefore, if he chose to cooperate with a man, might enable even a man to work such miracles as these—miracles of simple dispossession—attended at the utmost with the removal of those effects only, of which possession had been the cause. But more than this, there is no reason to suppose that the prince of the devils as such, though he cooperated with a man, could enable a man to perform : nor, as I have already observed, is the same charge of working by diabolical assistance found to be advanced against any class of miracles except this.

Now miracles of simple dispossession were among the earliest and the commonest of our Saviour's miracles in general—and as miracles of this description, *a priori*, were peculiarly liable to such an insinuation, it is not improbable that it might be frequently levelled against them ; and that our Lord might have repeated occasions, in the course of his ministry, to expose its absurdity. And if any one Evangelist had given a full and particular account both of the charge and of its refutation, upon a certain former instance of their occurrence, that alone would be a sufficient reason why he should pass them over, or only notice them in general, upon a second and a later. Accordingly, though St. Matthew himself specifies the fact of the insinuation *twice*, yet he particularizes the fact of the refutation only *once ;* and that, as we have seen, after the *first* occasion of their occurrence, in the order of succession, though the *second*, in the order of narration.

Still less improbable is the supposed repetition of the demand of a sign—of which there is one instance, John ii. 18. another, Matt. xii. 38. a third, Matt. xvi. 1. Mark viii. 11. besides this, xi. 16. in St. Luke. The testimony of St. Paul —Ἰουδαῖοι σημεῖον αἰτοῦσι, καὶ Ἕλληνες σοφίαν ζητοῦσι[a]—shews it, in fact, to have been a regular demand in his time still ; and from the emissaries of Christianity, as much as from our Saviour himself. It is further confirmed also by this characteristic circumstance in the appearance and demeanour

[a] 1 Cor. i. 22.

of the false Christs, or false Prophets, who rose up, from
time to time, among the Jews, subsequent to the Christian
era—that all such impostors came with *signs* of some kind
or other: which Josephus, indeed, describes in general as
signs of one sort, signs of liberty or deliverance.   But Bar-
chocheb, in the time of Hadrian, assumed that name in
reference to a sign from heaven; Ὡς δὴ ἐξ οὐρανοῦ φωστὴρ
αὐτοῖς κατεληλυθὼς, κακουμένοις τε ἐπιλάμψαι, τερατευόμενος[b].
The true name, indeed, of the sign, which the Jews demanded from our Saviour, was the sign from heaven—not
a sign of deliverance as such—and tradition might have
taught them to expect that something of the kind would
precede the advent or the appearance of the Messias.   For
the mission of Moses had been specially attested by signs:
and they might expect the same fact to hold good of the
Christ.   Moreover our Saviour has taught us that some
sign, which he calls the sign of the Son of man, shall precede the second appearance of the Christ, at least; and *that*
sign will appear in the heavens[c].   Nor can it be denied
that, howsoever the knowledge of them might have been
obtained, many mysterious truths relating to the second
coming of the Messias, and which may yet be fully verified
of that, were already not obscurely understood by the Jews;
and so implicitly referred to the first, that their not being
realized in respect to that was, probably, one of the chief
reasons of the rejection of our Lord himself.

Not to dwell, however, upon general arguments, but to
approach the discussion of the question on its proper grounds,
I observe first, that if these two accounts are to be considered identical, St. Luke is directly set at variance, on some
points, with St. Matthew, and, on others, with St. Matthew
and with St. Mark.

I. St. Matthew affirms that, when our Saviour went out
of the house, where the blasphemy against the Spirit had
been committed, he went to the shore of the lake, and he
went thither to teach—St. Luke that, when he had done

---

b Eus. Hist. Eccles. iv. 6.   c Matt. xxiv. 30.

refuting the charge, he went to the house of a Pharisee, and he went thither to dine.

II. St. Matthew and St. Mark both affirm that our Lord repaired to the lake not merely with a view to teach, but to teach in *parables;* and consequently that, for that day at least, he spake nothing, in the way of general instruction, distinct from parables—St. Luke affirms that he delivered both to his own disciples, and also to the people, a *moral discourse* of considerable length, which occupies the whole of his twelfth chapter; and immediately after that, another and a shorter, but not a less instructive, recorded xiii. 1—9. All this he must have done between the close of the previous discussion, and the beginning to teach in parables.

III. St. Matthew very plainly implies[d] that, until this day, neither the disciples, nor the multitude, had ever heard a *parable;* and, consequently, that the parables which were now delivered were the first instances of their kind, as yet known or remembered to have transpired. But St. Luke must shew that, on this very morning, and, perhaps, only a few minutes before, *four* separate parables[e], the first a moral parable, the three last all allegorical parables, had already been pronounced.

Now these are inconsistencies which lie upon the face of the respective accounts; and except on one supposition, viz. that the occasions themselves are perfectly distinct, they are as difficult to reconcile or to explain satisfactorily, as they are obvious and palpable.

Secondly—upon a more minute inspection of either narrative, there appears to be scarcely a single *individuating*, and at the same time *identical*, mark of agreement between them. The time—the place—the subjects of the miracle—the circumstances which preceded and drew forth the discourse—the parties addressed—the arrangement, substance, and particulars, of the discourse itself—the circumstances which followed upon it—all are more or less discriminated asunder in each: as may thus be shewn, by considering them in their order.

[d] xiii. 1. 10. 13.   [e] xii. 16—21. 35—40. 41—46. xiii. 6—9.

I. The times of the two events.   The time of the dispossession in St. Matthew, it appears from a comparison with
St. Mark, was the time of some meal in the day—which I
endeavoured to prove elsewhere was the morning's[f]—or not
much later than it.   The time of the morning's meal, among
the Jews, at every period of the year alike, was πρωὶ, or the
first hour of the day[g].   But the time of the dispossession in
St. Luke was manifestly either the time, or only just before
the time, of the ἄριστον, or midday's repast—which, on every
day, but the sabbath, when it was taken one hour later, was
taken at the *fifth* hour of the morning[h].   Nor was it much
otherwise among the Greeks or Romans[i].   Between this
time and the former, there would, consequently, be three or
four hours' difference.

II. The place.   The scene of the dispossession in St.
Matthew was doubtless Capernaum itself—but the scene
of the dispossession in St. Luke, though it might be some
other city of Galilee, could scarcely have been Capernaum.
For our Lord, so early as x. 38. had already begun his circuit—and at xi. 1. he is described as *alone* in a certain place
—which we may conclude infallibly was no town, nor village, and certainly not such an one as Capernaum.   Or,
though there should be any difficulty still raised on this
point, yet the place of the dispossession in St. Matthew
was unquestionably some *private* house, so completely beset by the multitude, that even our Lord's relations could
not procure an access to him—whereas the place of the dispossession in St. Luke was the *open* air, and while Jesus,
at first, was comparatively *alone;* but whither the people
could afterwards flock round about him.   For such is the
meaning of the expressions, Τῶν δὲ ὄχλων ἐπαθροιζομένων—
xi. 29.

III. The subjects of the miracle.   The subject of the
miracle in St. Matthew is a demoniac *blind* and *dumb*—the
subject of the miracle in St. Luke is a demoniac simply
dumb.

    [f] Vol. ii. Diss. viii. 305. 306.   [g] John xxi. 4. 12.   [h] Jos. B. Jud.
ii. viii. 5. Vita 54.   [i] Suidas ἄριστον.

There cannot be a clearer discrimination, between the personal identity of the two different subjects of a common miracle, than this. Had St. Luke's demoniac been really the same with St. Matthew's, then—not to insist on the improbability of his suppressing any part of his case at all—if he must suppress one, it would have been the *dumbness*, and not the *blindness ;* for the former was a very common, and a very obvious, characteristic of possession, but not the latter. Of a *blind* demoniac, if we except this in St. Matthew, there is not an example in all the Gospels—of *dumb*, and what is just as common, and very much akin to dumb, of *deaf*, demoniacs there are many instances; or, to speak more correctly, there are scarcely any other.

We may infer, therefore, that the blindness in this case was no consequence of mere possession ; nor, therefore, naturally or necessarily to be removed, upon the mere removal of possession. Hence, though St. Luke might not have specified the dumbness, as almost too common a feature of the case to require specification, he would never have omitted the blindness—a truly singular and characteristic circumstance—the removal of which was to change the nature of the miracle, or materially to exalt it. For to give sight to the blind, especially to one naturally, or born, blind, was always accounted one of the most illustrious of miracles ; and, considered in a moral or a typical point of view, was not more illustrious, than characteristic of a spiritual Messiah. Simple dispossession even the Jewish exorcists, and much more our Lord's disciples in his life time, might attempt, and be able, to effect—but not the restoration of sight : nor was simple dispossession, though accompanied by the removal of its ordinary effect, the loss of speech, or of hearing, on any principle so splendid an exertion of divine power, nor so likely to affect the spectators with admiration, as dispossession, accompanied not only by that, but by the removal of a much more uncommon, and otherwise an incurable, evil, the want of sight.

The case of the two demoniacs at Gadara is no instance of a similar omission—for *there* the same identical miracle was performed on two individually distinct subjects—but *here* a double specific miracle is performed on the same sub-ject; *there* it was not necessary for the sake of the miracle to describe its single operation on more than one of its dif-ferent subjects—*here* it was manifestly necessary to specify its double operation on the same subject. The miracle was the same in that instance, whether as wrought upon one person, or as wrought upon two persons—but it was not the same in this, if it did not open the eyes, as well as eject the spirit. St. Luke might have special reasons, at that time, for limiting the account of the cure to one of its cases—but he could have none here which would not have re-quired him to omit the miracle entirely, if he did not re-cord the whole. He must as soon have thought of divid-ing the person, or making one man into two, as of con-founding the miracle, or representing his double cure as a single.

IV. The cause which produced the discourse, and the parties concerned in the former, and addressed by the lat-ter. As the discourse, in each of the Evangelists, is alike divided into two general heads, and alike directed to two specific purposes, so have they each assigned to these heads a proper, but a different, origin. The cause of the first was the charge affecting the miracle—the cause of the second was the demand of the sign. But St. Matthew affirms that the charge was made at a separate time from the demand—St. Luke, that they were both made together: St. Matthew, that the demand was preferred *after* our Saviour had begun to refute, but *before* he had made an end of refuting, the charge—St. Luke, that both had taken place before he be-gan to refute, or to answer, either: St. Matthew, that the authors of the charge, and the demanders of the sign, were the *same*, viz. the Scribes and the Pharisees—St. Luke, that the authors of each respectively were *distinct*, and nei-ther of them Scribes or Pharisees; some of the multitude advanced the charge, and others of the multitude demand-ed the sign. Now this is not the way in which either he, or any other of the Evangelists, ever speaks of the Scribes and the Pharisees, as such—where those are expressly intended—but always by their proper name.

V. The order, substance, and particulars, of the discourse in each—and first, its order. As St. Matthew represents the demand to have been interposed while our Saviour was refuting the charge, so he represents the answer, which declines the demand, to be also interposed before the conclusion of the reply to the charge : as he makes the Scribes and the Pharisees interrupt Jesus to put the demand, so he makes him stop with his previous reply to the charge, in order to answer the demand. For it is evident that, from xii. 38—42. every thing in his account relates to the sign— and from xii. 43—45. every thing relates to the charge ; and still more evident it is that the whole of xii. 38—42. comes between xii. 22—37. and xii. 43. And this arrangement, if it follows the order of the event, would still be consistent and natural ; but not so, if it has purposely inverted it.

Again ; as St. Luke represents the charge, which produced one part of our Lord's discourse, and the demand, which produced the other, both to have been preferred at once, so he represents the answer to the one as made and concluded, before the answer to the other was begun. For, as distinct things in themselves, they would require to be answered distinctly—one answer could not have served for both. Hence, they must be answered one after the other— they could not both have been answered at once : and as the charge was first mentioned as made, so the answer to the charge is first specified as returned ; and then the reply to the demand. Besides which, the charge, as affecting the miracle, was a much more serious thing than the demand of the sign—and, therefore, though they both had been preferred together, the former would require to be answered before the other. This arrangement of St. Luke's, if he also is the faithful narrator of a real event, is just as consistent and natural as, on the same principle, was St. Matthew's. But, in this case, the two accounts cannot be the same. And should any one question whether the answer to the charge, as represented by St. Luke, was actually over when the reply to the demand was begun, there are two facts in his narrative, one at the end of the former, and the other at the end of the latter, either of which is sufficient to prove it.   The first is the exclamation of the woman[k], expressly directed to the wisdom and strength of the reply to the charge, and, consequently, implying that that was over—the second is the gathering of the people together[l] about the spot where our Lord was, which was either the moving cause, or at least the circumstance of situation, from which, or under which, he proceeded to answer the demand.

II. The substance.   The most cursory inspection of the two discourses shews that, while they agree in some things, they differ in others : a more particular examination proves that this agreement is far from entire, or absolute—and this disagreement is far from partial or unsignificant.   There is much in St. Matthew, not even hinted at in St. Luke— and much in St. Luke, altogether missing in St. Matthew. Upon the question of agreement I shall speak hereafter —but on the question of disagreement let me observe, at present, that the mere circumstance of one Evangelist's omitting some things, supplied by another, or supplying some things, omitted by another, even in a common account, would be nothing extraordinary ; for omission would not be contradiction, nor supplement, refutation, even where agreement might be most to be expected, in the record of words or discourses, as such, not merely of actions or proceedings.   But, here, there is reason to conclude, neither the omission, nor the supplement, in question were arbitrarily or undesignedly made ; but for a very sufficient motive, viz. that neither of them was part of the transaction to which the rest of the narrative belongs.

The omission in St. Matthew, as collected from what is present, over and above, in St. Luke, xi. 33—36. relates altogether to the demand of the sign ; the omission in St.

<hr />

[k] xi. 27. 28.   [l] Ib. 29.

Luke, as similarly ascertained from St. Matthew, xii. 31—37. relates altogether to the question of the charge. We shall find, moreover, that the general subject of St. Luke's omission is the particular denunciation of the heinousness of the charge, in one of its bearings, and the personal denunciation of the malignity of its authors, in reference to the same; but the subject of the omission in St. Matthew is a general statement of the means or evidences of conviction, in regard to their natural effect on the understanding—a general description of the proper faculty, whose business it is to judge of them—and a general denunciation or warning what is to be finally expected, if this proper faculty is not employed, in its proper department, and on its proper subject, with becoming simplicity of purpose, and its natural good effect. In the first of these omissions, consequently, there is nothing to encourage, but every thing to alarm; in the second there is much to alarm, but something withal to encourage: in the former there is not a hope expressed that the parties addressed could ever be reclaimed, or become better; in the latter, however uncertain that they will, it is yet implied that they may.

If, now, we compare St. Mark's account of this transaction with St. Matthew's, the agreement between which, as far as they go together, is unquestionable, we shall see that, though St. Matthew records only *one*, there were in reality *two* insinuations urged upon this occasion—the one, ὅτι Βεελζεβοὺλ ἔχει—explained and confirmed by what follows, ὅτι ἔλεγον πνεῦμα ἀκάθαρτον ἔχει—which clearly implies that, by saying Christ had Beelzebul, they meant to say Christ had an unclean spirit; the other, ὅτι ἐν τῷ ἄρχοντι τῶν δαιμονίων ἐκβάλλει τὰ δαιμόνια [m]. The reality of both these insinuations, therefore, is placed beyond a question: and their distinct tendency is not less indubitable. The former was a personal charge, levelled against the Spirit by whom our Saviour was inspired—the latter was a personal charge, levelled against himself, and affecting the

---

reality of his character as a prophet. The former would have made him a demoniac, or worse than a demoniac—because inspired by the Devil—but not an impostor, nor a deceiver; the latter would have made him an impostor or a deceiver, but not a demoniac—because only in league with, not possessed, nor actuated, by the Devil. The absurdity of each supposition was, also, evidently the same; and, consequently, as far as they required or deserved to be refuted at all, so far the propriety and pertinency of refuting them both by exactly the same arguments likewise must be apparent.

But with respect to the comparative heinousness, or veniality, of both, there was that in the nature of the object, in the specific direction, of each—in the party respectively affected by the charge—which made a very great difference between them. The one was levelled against God—the other, against man : the one personally affected the Holy Ghost—the other, only our Saviour, as a mere man. The one was blasphemy, that is, *slander*, of the Spirit—the other was blasphemy, or *slander*, of the Son of man. Our Saviour, therefore, might, if he pleased, not impute the latter—but he could not, on any principle, not impute the former. He could not, indeed, but denounce the *sinfulness* of both : yet he might, consistently with his character, and his demeanour in other respects, declare himself willing to *forgive* the one, which simply concerned himself; but he could not, on the same principle, undertake to forgive the other, which affected the Holy Ghost.

Hence, then, the substance of the whole omission in St. Luke, and of the whole supplement in St. Matthew—who, though he specifically records the second of these insinuations only, yet gives us conjointly the answer to both ; just as St. Mark, who specifically records them both, supplies in particular the answer only to one, or touches but very cursorily on that to the other. Hence, also, the denunciation of the greater atrocity of the blasphemy, levelled against the Spirit, and personally impugning the Spirit, than of the blasphemy, levelled against the Son of man, and personally affecting our Saviour: hence, the declaration that the forgiveness of the one was *possible*, but the forgiveness of the other was *impossible*—that the one should actually be forgiven, that is, *not imputed*, but the other should not be forgiven, and, therefore, necessarily must be *imputed :* hence too, the denunciation of the personal malignity of the authors of each—which, in respect to the offence pronounced unpardonable, is justly described as *incurable*, but in respect to that which was to be, or might be, forgiven, whether really *incurable* or not, still is not described as such. For these are the utmost purposes, to which Matthew xii. 31—37. containing the supplement in question, admits of being generally reduced; and they are clearly all of a *personal* nature, in resentment of a *personal* charge as concerns the party who is speaking, and *personally* denouncing its authors as concerns the parties addressed.

If we compare with this the account of the same things in St. Luke, we shall perceive that he recounts so much of the same charge as personally affected our Saviour, but not that part of it, which personally affected the Holy Ghost; and he omits, in his account of the reply, all the personal matter in respect to both. If the former charge was the only charge, made on the occasion in question, he has done no more than was to be expected : for, if the same personal charge against our Saviour was not now, as it had been before, accompanied by the same personal charge against the Holy Ghost, he would have no need now, as he had before, to mix up the charge against the Spirit with the reply to the charge against himself—and what he had said before of the personal offence against himself, he might wave in the answer, because not combined with the other in the provocation ; that is, he might consent to forgive or to overlook this totally, *now*, when it stood by itself, as he had said that he would forgive or overlook it comparatively, *then*, when it had been coupled with the other. But if this second charge was really preferred, and really answered, now, as well as the first, I know not upon what principle we could excuse St. Luke for the omission of a *part*, and that, the most important *part*, of the same continuous detail, which would not have required him to omit the *whole.*

If, however, the charge against our Saviour alone was now repeated, a charge, which so far as it was the subject of argument, concerned the question by *whose* power, God's or Satan's, our Lord was enabled to cast out devils—and so far as it bore a personal relation, concerned the question whether Christ was what he claimed to be, a Prophet sent from God, and empowered by God, or an Impostor in league with, and empowered by, the Devil—there is one observable distinction in the two accounts, which becomes on this supposition consistent and critical; but on any other singular and inexplicable. The *status quæstionis* in St. Matthew was virtually this—whether these miracles were wrought by the Spirit of God, or by Beelzebul, *dwelling in Christ :* the *status quæstionis* in St. Luke, whether the same miracles were wrought by the power of God, or by the power of Satan, *cooperating with Christ.* Now, when the answer, in each case, has occasion to revert to this question, how is it expressed in St. Matthew? Εἰ ἐγὼ ἐν πνεύματι Θεοῦ—and how in St. Luke? Εἰ (ἐγὼ) ἐν δακτύλῳ Θεοῦ—and this is a difference in the terms of the same proposition, which the Evangelist, except on the authority of our Lord himself, and out of deference to the matter of fact, would not have made ; because it would have been to change an appropriate and intelligible expression, for one much more ambiguous and difficult to be understood. The Gentile reader was likely to comprehend at once the meaning of ἐν πνεύματι Θεοῦ—but not the idiomatic Hebraïsm ἐν δακτύλῳ Θεοῦ, in general, nor the refined distinction of its meaning here, in particular.

There are three words in the Hebrew, all used to express not only the several energies, but also the several degrees of the energies, of the power of God, with respect to the comparative sensible magnitude of its effects—the finger (δάκτυλος) the hand (χείρ) the arm (βραχίων) of God. The expression ἐν δακτύλῳ Θεοῦ, then, would be a very proper description for the degree of the power of God, in opposition to the power of Satan, where the subject of discussion was the production of such miracles as these—miracles of simple dispossession—miracles of the simplest kind—so far from the hardest and most stupendous, as to rank among the easiest, of the works of God—miracles which, together with another class, almost as inferior, the healing diseases, even the Twelve, and the Seventy, had been already empowered to perform; and the ability of performing which continued with the Church, long after all its other miraculous graces either had totally ceased, or were still very rarely exerted. But the same term would not have been applied to express a like degree of power, with respect to the production of such a miracle as opening the eyes of the blind—had that also now taken place. No Prophet under the old dispensation, no Apostle, nor Evangelist, under the new, before the commencement of formal Christianity, none but our Saviour himself, had ever yet performed, or been enabled to perform, a miracle of this description; so that the assertion of the man in St. John, who had himself experienced such a miracle, might be more than the effusion of gratitude for his recent cure—might be even historically true—'Εκ τοῦ αἰῶνος οὐκ ἠκούσθη ὅτι ἤνοιξέ τις ὀφθαλμοὺς τυφλοῦ γεγεννημένου [n]. Philo Judæus was well aware of this distinction of terms, when he made the following observations on the plague of lice [o]. Τί γὰρ εὐτελέστερον σκνιπός; ἀλλ᾽ ὅμως τοσοῦτον ἴσχυσεν ὥστ᾽ ἀπαγορεῦσαι πᾶσαν Αἴγυπτον, καὶ ἐκβοᾶν ἀναγκασθῆναι ὅτι δάκτυλος Θεοῦ τοῦτ᾽ ἔστι· χεῖρα γὰρ Θεοῦ μηδὲ τὴν σύμπασαν οἰκουμένην ὑποστῆναι ἂν, ἀπὸ περάτων ἐπὶ πέρατα, μᾶλλον δὲ οὐδὲ τὸν σύμπαντα κόσμον.

Again, with regard to the omission in St. Matthew, or what is distinctly supplied by St. Luke, we may observe, it is expressly subjoined to the account of the answer to the demand of the sign: it is doubtless, therefore, subservient to the use and purpose of that answer in general. And as he has made the demand, which produced the answer, proceed from the people at large, so he has made the answer,

[n] ix. 32.   [o] Exod. viii. 19. Vit. Mosis. 619.

which replies to the demand, be returned to the people at large.

Now, though we knew no more of the nature of the sign in question, than is implied in the terms of the demand, yet thus much we might reasonably presume concerning it—it must have been something *extraordinary ;* totally different from what had yet occurred, or might still be expected to occur, in the way of proof: it must have been something decisive, something which would leave no doubt that he, by whom it had been given, was the Messias ; and such a Messias, as they, who required the sign expected. Thus much, I say, we might justly conclude concerning this particular sign, from *their* importunity who request it, and from our Saviour's refusal, who steadily and pointedly declines it.

It was some sign, therefore, which, as the true Messias, and consistently with his own character, he could not consent to give ; it was some sign which, to prove himself the true Messias, it was not necessary he should give. And whatever other reasons, for dispensing with this extraordinary medium of proof, there might be besides, this also, we may presume, would be one—that he had other proofs, both worthy of his character to produce, and adequate to the end, for which they might be produced ; among which proofs, however numerous or various they might be, his miracles at least could not fail to constitute an integral and an important class.

Reasoning, then, specifically in answer to the demand of an extraordinary proof, our Saviour, it might naturally be expected, would do *two* things—appeal to his miracles in general, and insist on their sufficiency in general. And, if there were any one among his miracles in general which approximated most nearly to the nature of an extraordinary sign, and consequently of an extraordinary proof, in particular, he might with equal consistency appeal especially to this, and insist especially on this. Such was the miracle of the Resurrection—a sign of the divine power of Christ, which is unquestionably the corner stone of the miraculous evidence in its behalf.   Accordingly, both in St. Matthew, and in St. Luke, so far as they agree together, he is represented as appealing to this, and as insisting on its sufficiency, in particular : but in St. Matthew, he is represented as doing only this—in St. Luke, as doing something more —appealing to his miracles in general, and insisting on the sufficiency of his miracles in general.

Now when a competent medium of conviction on any point is addressed to a competent medium of apprehension, the failure of conviction must needs be due to a moral incapacity, distinct from both, and not to a physical defect, peculiar to either.   On the question, whether our Saviour was, or was not, the Messias, his miracles supplied the one, and the common sense of mankind supplied the other.   If, then, the people came to a wrong conclusion upon the question at last, the fault would attach neither to the inadequacy of the means of conviction, nor to the incompetency of their natural faculties ; but solely to the perversity of their will ; producing a moral impossibility of being duly influenced by the strongest proofs—biassing the judgment in spite of instinct—and clouding the light of the clearest evidence.

It was natural, therefore, that speaking as before of the character and sufficiency of his proper media of proof, our Saviour should say something of the only cause, which prevented them from attaining their end, or justifying the efficiency of their nature itself : which, as a cause, in its origin, attributable to the hearers themselves, he might stigmatize in terms of becoming severity ; as a cause, in its effects, so fatally prejudicial to their good, he might as feelingly lament and deplore ; as a cause, considered in each of these bearings, he might both stigmatize and lament.   Accordingly, in each of the Evangelists, he is represented as doing both these things ; in St. Matthew, however, with respect to the miracle of the Resurrection in particular—in St. Luke, and that, in the part omitted by St. Matthew, with respect also to his miracles in general.   The analysis of the Epilogus itself will set this assertion in the clearest light.

ʟ l 4

For first, he reminds the hearers that they themselves do nothing, even in the commonest acts of life, without a proper end and purpose in view by it ; nor in such a manner as would defeat that end and purpose itself. He wishes them to infer from this that neither were his miracles wrought, without a specific design in view, nor in any manner, but what was necessary to give effect to that design—publicly, and in the face of the world, so that all might see them—demonstrably and sensibly, so that none might mistake them—exceeding the ability of man, and overstepping the course of nature, so that none might dispute them.

Secondly, he tells them that their common sense, and their understandings, were just as much intended, and just as effectual, for directing and assisting their judgments, as the faculty of sight for guiding the motions of the body. The eye, as they well knew, never failed to perform this service for the body, so long as it was sound and vigorous—nor continued competent to perform it, when it was distempered or decayed. He argues, therefore, that their understandings also, exerted upon a competent medium of proof, and if there was nothing besides within them, to interfere with their natural operation, would not fail to lead them to a right conclusion concerning himself. Under this image of a single and a double, that is, a good or an evil, eye, he describes a clear and unperverted, or a clouded and contaminated, faculty of judgment ; and, consequently, plainly implies that the obscuring and perverting cause is *moral*—the obliquity of the will—the force of prejudice—the corrupting influence of evil habits, or evil passions—and the like : for the same faculty of judgment, or power of reasoning in general, in conjunction with the will, and left free, or not free, to its natural effect, as that will is simple or disingenuous, honest or depraved, is always in Scripture denoted by the metaphor of the same eye, producing or not producing its natural effects, as the qualities, by which it is affected, are friendly or unfriendly to the natural energies of vision.

Hence, if they did not consider his miracles a sufficient proof that he was the Messiah, the blame must ultimately rest with the disinclination of their own minds, however produced, to attend to those proofs—to acquiesce in that conclusion—to receive and be satisfied with the natural decision of their judgments upon them. The true cause of their incredulity must, consequently, be sought within themselves —in the *evil* heart of unbelief. Consider, says he, whether the *light* within thee is not *dark*—whether that, which would otherwise be the natural medium of bringing thee to the truth, is not so corrupted and depraved by other principles, as to be now, of necessity, the medium of error. For it is in vain to deny that the understandings of men may be influenced by their passions—and the conclusions of the judgment may be as sensibly affected by its sympathy with the will and the feelings, as the impressions of sight by the medium through which the rays are transmitted to the eye. If the result of this scrutiny should be favourable, or the light of the mind be still clear and genuine, he bids them follow its spontaneous directions—it would not fail to exhibit things as they were, and to mark out the path before them : the simple drift of all which is to assure them that their own understandings, fairly and dispassionately applied to the means of conviction submitted to them, could not but conclude that Jesus was the Messias.

I have been the more diffuse in this exposition, with a view to demonstrate how great is the difference in our Saviour's manner of treating the enquirers, concerned in the demand of a sign in St. Luke, and the enquirers, concerned in the same demand in St. Matthew : and we have seen that there was a similar difference in his manner of dealing with the authors of the charge in each. With the one he deals in the language of just indignation, and of stern rebuke—with the other, in the tone of grave displeasure, and serious, but affectionate, admonition. What was personal in the one, becomes general in the other—and where he thundered, and threatened, before, he reasons, he expostulates, now. There is enough of severity, to shew he was

offended—there is so much of gentleness, as shews his anger
to have been mixed with pity. He represents the case of
his hearers as sufficiently dangerous to create alarm, yet not
so far gone as to justify despair. Before, however, in the
personal part of St. Matthew's account—the part omitted
by St. Luke—if any one spirit predominated in the whole,
and actuated the whole, it was a feeling of utter abhorrence
at the atrociousness of the crime—a feeling of utter repro-
bation of the malignity of its motive—a feeling of utter
despair of the reformation of its authors. We cannot conceive the most exalted and perfect of beings capable of expressing his feelings towards the most wicked and depraved,
consistently with his own dignity and purity, in terms more
severe than these[p]—Γεννήματα ἐχιδνῶν, πῶς δύνασθε ἀγαθὰ
λαλεῖν, πονηροὶ ὄντες; which are equalled, but not excelled,
in the same respects by these, delivered on another, and a
later, occasion to the same persons[q]—Ὄφεις, γεννήματα ἐχιδνῶν, πῶς φύγητε ἀπὸ τῆς κρίσεως τῆς γεέννης; What is there in
St. Luke, which approaches in severity to this?

The use, which I make of this fact in the difference of
our Lord's manner, upon two distinct occurrences, towards
an apparently similar offence, is to infer first, that the authors of the offence in either case are what they are—some
of the Pharisees in St. Matthew, and some of the people in
St. Luke: secondly, that in the commission of the offence
the Scribes and the Pharisees acted deliberately, and with
malice prepense; the people, only as they had been taught
by them. The former, then, had been instigated by their
own malignity; the latter had been misled by the former.
Neither, indeed, disputed the miracle; but both resolved
it into a cause, distinct from the true: neither denied that
miracles might furnish signs; but both would have it be
understood that these miracles were not *the* sign. The
Pharisees, however, did not believe in their own solution of
the miracle, on the one hand, nor expect compliance with
their demand of a sign, on the other: but they threw out
the solution, to discredit the authority of the real cause,

[p] xii. 34.   [q] xxiii. 33.

and to counteract the natural impression of the miracle—and they preferred the demand that they might reduce our Saviour to the necessity of publicly refusing it at least. The people took up the solution, as coming from them, and urged it again in a besotted deference to the judgment of their teachers; and so long as the demand was refused, it was easy to say *no* sign, independent of *that*, which our Saviour could exhibit, was sufficient to prove him the Messias. There was *one* sign which would prove this; and while that was withheld, none other should be considered satisfactory.

To make out each of these positions by itself would require a longer discussion than my present limits would admit of: I shall, therefore, barely observe that there is no proof of either the charge against these miracles, or the demand of a sign from heaven, until they were each advanced by the Pharisees first; nor any instance of the allegation of the charge, except in the case of a recent miracle, and a miracle which had produced a *lively* effect. We may perceive a reason, then, why our Lord might possibly compassionate the ignorant and deluded multitude, while he could only abhor and reprobate the artful malignity of their teachers; and, consequently, why he might *argue* with the one, while he denounces nothing but penal retribution against the other. Hence, too, in the ensuing discourse, Luke xii. 57. and in allusion to this very subject, he might address the people with the pointed question, there recorded; Τί δὲ καὶ ἀφ' ἑαυτῶν οὐ κρίνετε τὸ δίκαιον;

It may, however, be objected that the allegory of the unclean spirit, which the particle δὲ in St. Matthew[r] shews to be the resumption of a former topic, and a comparison with St. Luke, that this topic is the topic of the charge, is inconsistent with the supposition of a different spirit in the later address, as contrasted with the former. To refute this objection, we will consider the allegory somewhat at large.

This comparison or illustration, for it is nothing more,

[r] 43.

proceeds on two self-evident positions, one, that an unclean or wicked spirit delights in an unclean and impure abode; the other, that he who has not been made better, by what has been done to reclaim him, has necessarily been rendered worse. The result to which they would lead in conjunction is, consequently, this: an evil or impure spirit, once dispossest, if he gains possession of the same soul again, gains possession of what is fitter to receive him than before, and so is more firmly rooted than ever; that is, the case of the man's recovery is sevenfold more hopeless than before. Now let us see how the story developes these principles, or brings this result to pass.

First, the foundation of the argument, or the circumstance which suggested the analogy, was the recent dispossession which had taken place. Hence the first particular in each, which supposes the spirit ejected.

Secondly, according to the opinion of the times, the proper abode of evil spirits, banished from the society, or the souls, of men, were waste places, deserts, and rocks. Hence the next particular—the walking of the spirit δι' ἀνύδρων τόπων—and, in defect of his former habitation, seeking for a place of rest—but, from the superior fitness or attractions of that, finding none: all which supposes the fact of the dispossession complete, and the recovery of the party possest, for some time at least, to be certain.

Thirdly, according to the same belief, and, perhaps, the truth of the case, evil spirits, which had once taken possession of the souls of men, not only were hard to be dislodged, but, as finding nothing elsewhere so congenial to the impurity of their own nature, were ever after longing to take possession of them again. Hence the next particular—the spirit's determining to return, and to see if, haply, his former habitation might afford an opening for his entering into it again.

Fourthly, the next particular is the supposed result of this experiment. He finds it empty, or rather at *leisure*; unoccupied by any better tenant, and, therefore, at liberty for such as him; nor merely empty, and so open to the first comer, but σεσαρωμένον καὶ κεκοσμημένον—swept and furnished—better fitted in all respects for his inhabitation than before : that is, the man, for whom all this had been previously done, has not been rendered better, and, therefore, is necessarily become worse.

Fifthly, upon this discovery, which- was more than *he* could have expected who did not know whether he should again procure admission for himself, not content to enter in alone, and to dwell there singly, he goes and invites seven others, worse than himself—and they all enter in, and dwell there in conjunction ever after ; that is, he is more indissolubly united to his former habitation than before—the soul of the recipient, in league with *seven* spirits, more wicked than the first, is seven times as wicked as before.   Hence, on every principle, the last state, or the last things, of that man become worse than the first : all which St. Matthew has applied, in the words which conclude his account, οὕτως ἔσται καὶ τῇ γενεᾷ ταύτῃ τῇ πονηρᾷ, to the men of that generation, to the Jews of our Saviour's time in particular.

Now St. Peter[a], by quoting the same declaration, γέγονεν αὐτοῖς τὰ ἔσχατα χείρονα τῶν πρώτων—has shewn that it may refer to the case of those who, having once believed in Christianity, have subsequently apostatized from it ; and, by parity of consequence, to the case of those who, having been once convinced, or had the means of conviction in their power, have afterwards renounced their conviction, or have never used those means aright.   This was the case of the Jews in our Saviour's time.   The spirit of infidelity, which he had hitherto been combating, and still should continue to combat, by every means of proof to be expected from him, was so far ousted and dispossest.   But if the national incredulity should remain unsubdued to the last, when those means of proof would cease to be furnished, the spirit, which was kept in check only by their presence, would be free to return with sevenfold vigour—would take

* [a] 2 Ep. ii. 20.

sevenfold as firm possession of their minds—and, consequently, become entitled to sevenfold as great a punishment,
as before.

Throughout this representation, in every declaration except the last, So shall it be unto this evil generation also,
St. Luke goes along with St. Matthew ; and this one exception is a point of difference which makes a great change in
the character of all that precedes.   For with this declaration the whole is converted into a prophecy, and a fearful
prophecy too—levelled against that generation in particular ; without it, it becomes merely a continuance of the same
general argument, concerning the right use of means and
opportunities, with no more of a personal application than
the rest.   It is not, therefore, a part of a penal denunciation, like the whole of the matter in St. Matthew, but a
friendly warning, and a serious admonition, in character
with every thing else in St. Luke.

To proceed, then, to the remainder of the two discourses,
or what they contain in common, after the omissions in each
have been respectively taken into account.   The agreement
between them is not so complete, as ought to be exhibited
in two narratives confessedly the same—nor the disagreement greater than might be produced by the repetition of
the same sentiments, by the same speaker, on a later, which
he had already delivered on a former, occasion.   I have
instanced one example of this in the difference of the terms
πνεῦμα and δάκτυλος—and I might instance another in the
omission of σχολάζοντα by St. Luke, though expressed by
St. Matthew—which yet is so important to the order of
consequences, that, even though not present in St. Luke,
it must still be understood.   I might instance also in the
similar omission of μεθ' ἑαυτοῦ—which is even more important than that of σχολάζοντα, and, besides being implied in
the ἕτερα, would be just as necessarily to be understood.

But not to dwell on verbal discrepancies, which may be
pointed out in almost every verse of the two accounts, let
17. of St. Luke be compared with 25. of St. Matthew—and
21. 22. of St. Luke with 29. of St. Matthew—and 29. 30.

of St. Luke with 39. 40. of St. Matthew—and lastly, 31. 32. of St. Luke with 41. 42. of St. Matthew—and there will appear to be reasonable cause for doubting how both can possibly be the record of one and the same discourse.

In the last case referred to, the order of the examples in St. Matthew, it must be evident, would be the natural order, because the order suggested by the principle of association itself. The mention of Jonas, as a sign to the Ninevites, and a type of the resurrection, which was to be a sign κατ' ἐξοχὴν to the men of that generation, leads at once to the contrast between the known, historical, effect of the former sign upon the Ninevites, and the equally known, though future, effect of the latter, or of our Saviour's miracles in general, upon the men of that generation. If, however, St. Matthew's order was the *natural* order, St. Luke's, which differs from St. Matthew's, we may infer was the *actual* order, and the two accounts must have been distinct. Our Saviour, on one occasion, cited these examples in the order exhibited by St. Matthew—and, on another, in the order retained by St. Luke. For there is no more reason why St. Matthew should have altered the *actual* order, for the sake of the *natural,* than why St. Luke should; and still less reason is there, why St. Luke should have altered the *natural* and the *actual* both, for one which was neither.

VI. The circumstances which followed on the discourse in each. St. Luke relates one fact, the exclamation of the woman, which St. Matthew omits—and St. Matthew relates another, in which he is supported by St. Mark, the visit of our Lord's relations, which St. Luke omits. But St. Luke records *his* fact between the answer to the charge, and that to the demand—St. Matthew records *his* after both; and from the arrangement of these answers in St. Matthew, no fact, like that in St. Luke, could possibly have intervened in his account—nor, from their arrangement in St. Luke, and from the other circumstances specified by him, any such fact, as that in St. Matthew, have followed upon his account. That he was not ignorant of the fact appears from this—that he relates a similar fact [t], which happened on the same day with St. Matthew's; and yet was not the same with it, but a second attempt, as we have seen elsewhere, to accomplish in the evening, what our Lord's relations had not been able to effect in the morning.

There are other objections, which might still be urged in disproof of the hypothesis that any part of this transaction in St. Luke could have been the same with any part of the transaction in St. Matthew; which yet, for brevity's sake, I shall state only in general.

For instance, if the accounts are the same, then Matt. xii. 22. to the end of the chapter, was comprehended between some hour in the morning, and the time of noon, when, according to St. Luke, after the previous discourse, the Pharisee invited our Lord to dine. At the end of this dinner, which, as it was, took up more time than usual, Jesus must have delivered the whole of Luke xii. a very long chapter, abounding in interruptions, and a frequent change of topics. When this discourse, too, was over, there would still be some interval necessary for Luke xiii. 1—9. or the account relating to the Galileans, whose blood Pilate had mingled with their sacrifices; and for the reflections which it drew from our Lord.

All this must have been interposed between Matt. xii. 50. and xiii. 1. at which point of time he is first made to proceed to the lake—and, we may ask, from whence? not certainly from his own house, or that where he was at Matt. xii. 22. when the demoniac was dispossest—for, according to St. Luke, xi. 37. he must have quitted this house, when he went to the Pharisee's to dine—and yet this is the house, from which Matt. xiii. 1. evidently supposes him to proceed *to* the lake, and whither Matt. xiii. 36. makes him return *from* the lake. On the shore of the lake, he must have delivered a number of parables, sufficient to occupy a day's teaching; and then have returned to Capernaum, and shut himself up with his disciples, and interpreted his parables to them in private, as well as conversed with them on other

[t] viii. 19.

topics; all before the time of evening or sunset, when St. Mark shews he came out of the house again [u], and gave commandment to cross the lake. It is impossible that so many distinct events should have followed each other, and in this order, all during so disproportionate a time.

I shall conclude, therefore, with observing that the above discussion enables us to determine, by way of corollary, the answer to the celebrated question, what was the sin against the Holy Ghost? The offence, committed on the former of these occasions, was *that* sin against the Holy Ghost. The sin against the Holy Ghost was, consequently, committed *there* and *then*, and *by those persons*, *when* and *where*, and *by whom*, this charge was insinuated against our Saviour's miracles. But it is no where called the *sin* against the Holy Ghost; it is designated by no name except that of the *blasphemy* against the Holy Ghost: and this distinction is of manifold importance.

For, first, the strain of our Lord's denunciations against both the offence, and its authors, is a sufficient proof that, whatever it was, it was a sin of *words*—whatever was the guilt of its authors, they had contracted this guilt by an offence in words. Ὅς ἂν εἴπῃ λόγον κατὰ τοῦ υἱοῦ τοῦ ἀνθρώπου ... Ὅς δ' ἂν εἴπῃ (λόγον) κατὰ τοῦ Πνεύματος τοῦ ἁγίου .... Γεννήματα ἐχιδνῶν, πῶς δύνασθε ἀγαθὰ λαλεῖν, πονηροὶ ὄντες; ἐκ γὰρ τοῦ περισσεύματος τῆς καρδίας τὸ στόμα λαλεῖ—Ὁ ἀγαθὸς ἄνθρωπος ἐκ τοῦ ἀγαθοῦ θησαυροῦ τῆς καρδίας ἐκβάλλει τὰ ἀγαθὰ (ῥήματα·) καὶ ὁ πονηρὸς ἄνθρωπος ἐκ τοῦ πονηροῦ θησαυροῦ ἐκβάλλει πονηρά—Λέγω δὲ ὑμῖν ὅτι πᾶν ῥῆμα ἀργὸν, ὃ ἐὰν λαλήσωσιν οἱ ἄνθρωποι, ἀποδώσουσι περὶ αὐτοῦ λόγον ἐν ἡμέρᾳ κρίσεως· ἐκ γὰρ τῶν λόγων σου δικαιωθήσῃ, καὶ ἐκ τῶν λόγων σου καταδικασθήσῃ.

Secondly, the very essence of blasphemy is to be a sin in words. If any one will take the trouble to peruse the earlier, or what is more to the purpose the contemporary, Greek writers, he will soon be satisfied that the term, which expresses the sin of blasphemy, has but one original and proper meaning, and but one common and ordinary acceptation. In the sense of evil, or injurious, speaking—of

[u] iv. 35.

slander, traduction, calumny, or the like—it is precisely ἀντίστοιχον to εὐλογία, ἔπαινος, εὐφημία, or to any similar term[v].

It is, consequently, in a derivative or secondary sense,
that it comes to denote what divines, or moralists, understand by the offence of blasphemy, as such. It is not impossible for the Supreme Being himself to be made the object of injurious aspersion, or of obloquy ; and in that case,
what would be simply *evil-speaking,* as levelled against a
man, becomes *blasphemy,* as directed against God. Nor
can it be denied that they who, according to St. Mark, had
called the Spirit, by which our Saviour was inspired, ἀκάθαρτον πνεῦμα—and had confounded the pure and holy Spirit of God, with the impure and malignant spirit of Beelzebul, had spoken *evil* of that Spirit—had traduced and ma-
ligned that Spirit—in the strictest sense. Hence, if that
Spirit was really a person, and divine, such injurious speaking of that Spirit was strict and proper blasphemy—that is,
injurious speaking levelled against God. And who will contend that such blasphemy against the Holy Ghost would
not be sin against the Holy Ghost ? because sin, of which
the Holy Ghost himself was directly the object, and from
the effects of which, if there was any proper sufferer, that
sufferer was the Holy Ghost.

But is the proposition convertible that all sin, of which
the Holy Ghost may be any how the object, is such sin as
this? All unrighteousness, according to St. John [w], is sin ;
and all unrighteousness in Christians, who are supposed to
be regenerate, and under grace, of which the only source
and fountain is the Holy Ghost, must so far be sin against
the Holy Ghost ; because it must be sin against grace. But
even in this sense, according to the same authority, there
would be a sin *not unto death,* as well as a sin *unto death ;*
both, such as might be committed by a brother Christian.

---

[v] Compare Matt. xv. 19. xxvii. 39. Mark vii. 22. xv. 29. Luke xxii. 65.
xxiii. 39. Acts vi. 11. 13. xlii. 45. xviii. 6. xxvi. 11. Rom. ii. 24. iii. 8.
xiv. 16. 1 Cor. iv. 13. x. 30. 1 Tim. i. 13. vi. 1. 4. Tit. iii. 2. Ephes. iv.
31. Col. iii. 8. 1 Pet. iv. 14. 2 Pet. ii. 2. 11. Jude 9. &c.   [w] 1 Ep. v.
17. 16.

The sin unto death, which might be so committed, and for which the Apostle gives no encouragement even to pray, might be that sin against the Holy Ghost, which our Lord had pronounced unpardonable, both in this world and in the next. But the sin not unto death, which must include all other sins beside that, could not be the sin against the Holy Ghost in particular ; though, if committed, as the Apostle supposes, by a fellow Christian, sin against the Holy Ghost, in a general sense, it must still be.

In the application of human laws to human crimes, it is an acknowledged principle that the terms of every *penal* statute are to be rigidly and literally construed. The same rule is, surely, to be taken for our guide in interpreting this one, and the sole, instance of God's extreme, and severest, malediction against some offence, which may, indeed, be really committed—but, if really committed, becomes thenceforward unpardonable : for which neither the intercession of fellow-believers, nor the penitence of the offender—if penitence in such a case be possible—nor, what is more, the efficacy of the Christian atonement (which, for ought we know to the contrary, extends to every crime besides) can avail to procure forgiveness.

Now the denunciations ἡ τοῦ πνεύματος βλασφημία—and ὃς δ᾽ ἂν βλασφημήσῃ εἰς τὸ πνεῦμα τὸ ἅγιον—and, what is equivalent to them both, τῷ δὲ εἰς τὸ ἅγιον πνεῦμα βλασφημήσαντι—occur *ῥητῶς* [x]. But where do we meet with the expressions, ἡ δὲ τοῦ πνεύματος ἁμαρτία—or, if that is not sufficiently correct for the meaning, with ἡ δὲ κατὰ τοῦ πνεύματος ἁμαρτία, or, τῷ δὲ εἰς τὸ ἅγιον πνεῦμα ἁμαρτόντι ? And yet, on this distinction between sin against the Holy Ghost in general, and the blasphemy against the Holy Ghost, or one such sin in particular, the whole question what was the offence, now committed, and by whom, must be acknowledged to depend.

It always appeared to me so irrelevant to the present occasion—so irreconcileable with the context—so inconsistent

---

[x] Matt. xii. 31.   Mark iii. 29.   Luke xii. 10.

with the known laws of the association of ideas—so destructive of the necessary connection between desert and punishment, or cause and effect—to suppose the malediction pronounced *now*, and the crime on which it is pronounced committed *hereafter*—to see the Scribes and the Pharisees addressed in terms of the most indignant personal rebuke, and yet to have given no personal offence—to believe that our Saviour was resenting, as just committed, a crime which could not take place until almost two years afterwards— that I should dismiss, as unworthy of serious notice, the opinion which understands the blasphemy proleptically of the scoffers on the day of Pentecost, who ridiculed the Apostles as full of new wine.

It is more necessary to observe that even the phrase τοῖς ἀνθρώποις, which stands absolutely in this passage, must yet be construed with the ellipsis of τῆς γενεᾶς ταύτης—an ellipsis, which Matt. x. 17. 32. 33. and other instances, capable of being produced, would shew to be nothing extraordinary. In this case, the specific reference of both the crime, and its denunciation, to the persons then present, becomes so much the more demonstrable. We may conceive too, why upon this principle the blasphemy against our Lord in particular, considered as the Son of man—in which light only his enemies could have ventured to traduce him at all —might be pardonable; but not, on the same account, the blasphemy against the Holy Ghost. The former might be pardonable on the same score that every other injury, already inflicted, or still to be inflicted, on our Lord in his human capacity might be pardonable. For it was a part of his humiliation to hear himself reviled, and not to revile again—nor, consequently, to resent the reviling—to endure the gainsaying and obloquy of sinners patiently—and to be set, in short, as holy Symeon had long before predicted of him, εἰς σημεῖον ἀντιλεγόμενον y. But no such reason could apply to extenuate the blasphemy against the Holy Ghost; especially, if that blasphemy had been deliberately com-

y Luke ii. 34.

mitted. For such an outrage upon the majesty and the holiness of God, to serve the most malignant purposes, and not more repugnant to truth, and derogatory to the Deity, than at variance with the common sense of mankind, no excuse could be assigned at all ; and, therefore, as inexcusable, it might justly be pronounced unpardonable.

DISSERTATION XIX.

On the notices of time supplied by Luke xii.

I HAVE elsewhere[a] asserted that the twelfth chapter of St. Luke's Gospel contains numerous decisive indications of the period to which it belongs; and that, the concluding period of our Lord's ministry. If the proof of this position can be made out, the error committed by such schemes, as place it before even the beginning to teach in parables, which was the middle of our Saviour's ministry, must be apparent without further comment. They introduce an anachronism of nearly eighteen months in extent.

The foundation of this mistake, which is the supposed identity of Luke xi. 14. and what follows, with the parallel instance of dispossession, and its consequences, related by St. Matthew, has sufficiently, I think, been overthrown in the preceding Dissertation. Yet among the ill consequences of the mistake, so long as it remains uncorrected, this must necessarily be one—that we are thereby deprived of all means of appreciating rightly the force, the beauty, the propriety, of this one of the longest, and the most admirable, of our Lord's discourses in public. In order to the due perception of such qualities in a given instance, regard must needs be had to the time when the discourse was delivered—to the occasion, which called it forth—to the circumstances and situation of the speaker, and of his hearers, at the time, as well as to the topics or sentiments themselves. Much might be said with fitness and effect, at one time, which would not be apposite, nor in character, at another.

To instance only in the virtue of Christian watchfulness —and the part of the ensuing discourse, from verse 35. downwards, devoted to that—a virtue, which at no period, during the actual presence of Christ upon earth, could have

---

[a] Diss. xvi. supra.

any room for its exertion, or begin to be practically incumbent upon his followers.   For being altogether founded on the doctrine, and the expectation, of some second coming of Christ, it was dependent, conditionally, on the previous fact of his departure ; and until that had taken place, by his personal removal into heaven, no principle of duty, with a view exclusively to his return, could as yet be in force. Reasonably, then, might it be expected that the first mention of such a duty, and the proper arguments by which it would be substantiated, should both occur towards the close of our Lord's ministry only ; when the time of his departure was at hand.   If the place of the chapter is rightly assigned by me, this expectation would be verified in the present instance ; and it is still more indubitably true of the next, and the only remaining, instance, of a discourse upon the same topic, Matt. xxiv. 42. and the parallel places of St. Mark and of St. Luke, almost to the end of the prophecy upon Mount Olivet.

More examples of the same accommodation of the topics of the discourse to the time, when I suppose it to have been delivered, might be pointed out *now ;* were it not that this would be to anticipate that very examination of those topics in detail, which may be requisite to the confirmation of the assertion alluded to above.   To this examination, then, but no further than may suffice for that purpose, I shall accordingly proceed.

That the chapter contains the particulars of a series of discourses, all belonging to the same period of time, may be proved by various considerations.

First, the reference at the outset to the collection of a numerous multitude, during something else which had been going on meanwhile, is clearly to the circumstances related in the preceding chapter ; more especially, to the time taken up by the sitting at meat, and by the protracted conversation, consequent upon it, in the house of the Pharisee.   The same reference is implied in the nature of the topic, first insisted on, the ζύμη τῶν Φαρισαίων, or ὑπόκρισις—which is best explained upon the principles of association, by the recollec-

tion of what had just occurred; not merely their unfounded
pretensions to superior purity and virtue (which were instanced at xi. 38.) but also that series of captious interro-
gations, designed to make our Lord commit himself in some
manner or other, which is alluded to, xi. 53. 54.

Secondly, when he returned into public, and had begun
to address those about him, it was his disciples whom he
addressed *first;* which clearly implies that, some time in
the course of the same occasion, he must have addressed the
people also.   Accordingly, this is seen to have happened in
two different instances, one xii. 13—21. and the other xii.
54—the end; to one, or to both, of which the Evangelist
must consequently have referred.   Now there is this circumstance of distinction between them that, in the second,
our Lord spoke to the multitude of his own accord—in the
first, in consequence of an interruption; in the second, upon
a general subject, connected with his ministry as such—in
the first, upon a particular topic, suggested by the interruption itself.   The second, then, was the more likely of the
two to be thus referred to; and the second is the conclusion
of the chapter.   But if the end and the beginning of a certain discourse belong to the same point of time, the intermediate parts, whatever be the subject to which they relate,
cannot belong to a different.

Besides which, the topic of this last address to the people
is evidently connected with the demand of an extraordinary
sign; and verse tenth, in the course of the original address
to the disciples, with the fact of the blasphemy against the
Son of man, as contradistinguished from the blasphemy
against the Holy Ghost: both which were subjects suggested by recent events, and largely discussed a little before.   It follows, then, that the *whole* of this twelfth chapter
is strictly consecutive upon the course of proceedings from
xi. 14. forwards; and it is not less apparent that xiii. 1—9.
at least is strictly consecutive upon it: so that from xi. 14. to
xiii. 9. we possess a continuous account of events, belonging
to either the *whole,* or but the *same* part, of only one day.

This conclusion being established, the substance of 35—

48. which is in general the doctrine of Christian watchfulness, besides being parabolic in its nature, and, therefore, not a fit subject for the present work, as far as it was qualified to supply any argument respecting the time of the chapter, has been in fact anticipated.   The next division, which contains either clear, or presumptive, intimations to the same effect, is that which concludes the chapter, from verse 49—59; distributable into two parts; one from 49—53; the other from 54—59: the former, a continuation of the address to the disciples, and the latter, the substance of an address to the people.

In the first of these divisions itself, there is also a double reference—one, to the speaker, 49—50. the other, to the parties addressed, and, consequently, the disciples, 51—53. Upon each of these we may observe in common that it would be in vain to search for the connection of either, with the discourse which goes before, in any community of topics, or in the usual laws which regulate the transition of ideas; nor in any principle but that of the proximity of the close of our Lord's personal ministry, and of the natural effect, in reference both to himself and to his hearers, which the contemplation of that proximity was likely to produce upon his mind.

For to consider the latter division first.   The address to the disciples is obviously levelled against something in their present opinions or persuasions, concerning the speaker, and the final event of his coming, which the result would prove to be diametrically the reverse of the truth.   This same thing, it cannot admit of a question, is their persuasion of the nature of the kingdom of the Messiah, or what would be the effect of the appearance of Christ, both upon him and upon them.   Their minds at this present time were possessed with one idea, that his kingdom would be a temporal, and the immunity of his person perpetual; so that, before the event of the crucifixion itself, they could not comprehend the most simple and direct assurances of the fact, because they could not conceive the possibility, of his future sufferings.   Much less were they prepared to entertain the distinct apprehension of those personal dangers and inconveniences, which, under the general name of persecution, as emanating from the enmity of their unbelieving countrymen, were sometime to redound upon themselves, who believed in Christ.

· What, however, I would particularly observe is this—that the substance of these verses, in St. Luke, occurred before, and at a much earlier period, not less than a year from the present time, at Matt. x. 34—37. or 39: where, with the same specific allusion to the future fortunes of the disciples, in consequence of their master's coming, there was none to his own—with the same general prediction of the fact, there was no such express intimation of the instant proximity of the fact, of persecution and suffering, as concerned either him or them, which is here conveyed in the terms ἤδη ἀνήφθη, and still more in those of the ἀπὸ τοῦ νῦν. It is reasonable to infer that the *time* of the fulfilment of the prediction was much nearer now than then; for, if that was the case, it would account for the distinction at once. ·

With respect to the first of the same divisions—that apostrophe to our Lord's personal sufferings, so forcible, as to shew that he felt them in prospect deeply, so abrupt, as to seem the effect of a sudden emotion, is by nothing so easily to be accounted for, as by the contemplation of the near approach of his passion itself. Neither the kind, nor the degree, of those sufferings, was unknown to our Lord from the first; and if the prospect of their futurity, combined with this perfect understanding of their nature, could not but be, at all times, revolting to the ὁμοιοπάθεια of his common humanity, it is likely it would be most so, when the crisis was nearest at hand. The intensity of the agony in Gethsemane, whatever else might contribute towards it, must partly, if not mainly, be ascribed to this cause. What I have to observe here also is that, if the idea of his personal sufferings is seen to have ever, even momentarily, disturbed the equanimity of our Lord, it is only on the very eve of their arrival. At the beginning of his ministry, when they were yet comparatively distant, and even when two thirds of its duration were over[b], he alludes to their futurity with the same calmness and composure, which he displayed at last in their endurance.

And that the words do contain an allusion to these sufferings is proved by verse 50. in the use of the term βάπτισμα. The same term, along with another still more significant, in the use of a similar metaphorical expression for the same idea, occurs in the answer to the sons of Zebedee; Can *ye* drink of the *cup*, which *I* am to drink? and be baptized with the *baptism*, with which *I* am baptized[c]? The word βαπτίζεσθαι, in this figurative sense of persecution or suffering, endured for the sake of religion in general, or of any main article of religion in particular, seems to be so employed in that celebrated passage, Ἐπεὶ τί ποιήσουσιν οἱ βαπτιζόμενοι ὑπὲρ τῶν νεκρῶν, εἰ ὅλως νεκροὶ οὐκ ἐγείρονται; τί καὶ βαπτίζονται ὑπὲρ τῶν νεκρῶν; τί καὶ ἡμεῖς κινδυνεύομεν πᾶσαν ὥραν[d]; the context of which proves that βαπτίζεσθαι ὑπὲρ τῶν νεκρῶν is κινδυνεύειν ὑπὲρ τῶν νεκρῶν—the fire of which baptism, the brunt of which danger, in vindication of one of the main articles of the Christian faith, the resurrection of the dead, falling principally on the champions of all those articles κατ᾽ ἐξοχήν, the Apostles, St. Paul naturally specifies them in general, or himself in particular, directly afterwards, Τί καὶ ἡμεῖς κινδυνεύομεν πᾶσαν ὥραν; and, καθ᾽ ἡμέραν ἀποθνήσκω· κ. τ. λ.

The parallel passage of St. Matthew being compared with that of St. Luke[c],

Μὴ νομίσητε, ὅτι   ...   .
ἦλθον βαλεῖν εἰρήνην ἐπὶ τὴν γῆν.   Πῦρ ἦλθον βαλεῖν εἰς τὴν γῆν.

it follows that what our Lord did not come to cast upon the land, in the one, must be the ἀντίστοιχον of what he did come to cast upon the land, in the other: and if πῦρ be the latter, and εἰρήνη the former, then πῦρ in the one must be the ἀντίστοιχον of εἰρήνη in the other—and *vice versa*. Now nothing can be the proper ἀντίστοιχον of εἰρήνη, but πόλεμος;

[b] John ii. 19. vi. 51—58. 70.   [c] Matt. xx. 22. Mark x. 38.   [d] 1 Cor. xv. 29.   [c] Matt. x. 34. Luke xii. 49.

nor of πόλεμος but εἰρήνη : and, consequently, the signification of πῦρ, as so opposed, must be the signification of πόλεμος.   Nor, in fact, can any metaphor, or interchange of
ideas, be more natural than this, which personifies the idea
of war by the idea of a fire or conflagration.

But this is not all : for if by εἰρήνη here must be meant
the quiet and unmolested exercise of the Christian religion
—a kind of peace in which none could have a proper interest except the professors of the religion themselves—then
by the war, opposed to it, must be intended the turbulence
and contrariety by which that quiet and unmolested exercise should be forcibly obstructed ; a turbulence and contrariety, beginning from the enemies of the religion, but
spending their fury on its friends and advocates—a war,
which should originate in the bosom of private families,
and ripen the seeds of discord in the lap of natural chari-
ties—a war, which should spread from thence to the community at large, and operate to the dissolution of the social
order—a war, which the strong and violent should every
where wage against the weak and unresisting—which, from
the rapidity of its propagation, the universality of its operation, the searching nature of its effects, might well be
compared to a fire, kindled, perhaps, by a spark, but, finding materials at hand, soon blown up into a blaze, and
wrapping eventually an entire country in the same conflag-
gration.

Such a fire, and such a war, were the coming of Christ,
and the propagation of the Gospel, to produce in the Jewish
community.   What shall we say, then, to the time of its
beginning, and to the first subjects of its effects?   Were
this violence and this fire to be directed against the Master,
or against the disciples, first?   Doubtless against the Master
first, and against the disciples next.   For they were to drink
of *his* cup ; that is, not until *he* had drunk of it before
them : they were to be bathed in *his* fire ; that is, not
until *he* had been baptized therein himself.   In all things
it behoved him to be made like unto his brethren, both as
an example of patience, and as a pattern of virtue.   If so,

and Christ must of necessity have suffered, before, it is true, but still in the same way in kind as, his disciples, then the fiery ordeal, which hereafter awaited them, was first to be undergone by him.   Yet the period of his sufferings, strictly so called, was a determinate period; as may be collected from that peculiar, but regular, mode of designation by which St. John especially speaks of it—his hour, his hour κατ' ἐξοχὴν, and the power of darkness; which hour we, consequently, perceive to have been the time of his apprehension, trial, and passion; that is, the last act of his ministry upon earth.   As this period drew nigh, the fire, though not yet kindled, was nearer and nearer the time of its birth; and when it was close at hand, it might be said to be already lighted up: and this is the very manner in which it is referred to here.   Εἰ ἤδη ἀνήφθη, spoken of this fire, cannot imply less than that it was either then kindled, or shortly to be so.   The end of our Lord's ministry, therefore, was not far off.

· Let the whole passage, then, be rendered as, perhaps, it ought to be rendered, with a short paraphrase of each verse subjoined.   I came to cast a fire on the land—the very purpose of my mission was to excite such a fire, and to endure its first effects myself: and if even now it is kindled, what would I desire? if the purpose of my mission is so much nearer its attainment, why should I wish it otherwise?   But I have a baptism to be baptized withal, and how am I straitened until it be accomplished!   How anxious I am that it should soon be completed; how dearly do I wish it were over!

Compare with this the following from St. John[f], which refers to the same prospect of his sufferings, but only at a later period; Now is my soul troubled! and what would I say? (τί εἴπω;) Father, deliver me from this hour! yet, διὰ τοῦτο, for the sake of this hour, am I come unto it.   Why, then, should I pray to be delivered from it?   There is sufficient agreement not only in the general sentiment, but even in the particular phraseology, of these two passages, to shew that each is the same kind of apostrophe, produced by the common sensibility, and by the emotion arising from the common sensibility, on two distinct, but cognate, occasions, of the near prospect of the same painful and disastrous event.

The part addressed to the multitude, which concludes the chapter, admits also of distribution into the substance of 54—56. and the substance of 57—59. The first of these contains a distinct allusion to the demand of a sign, that is, an extraordinary proof of the truth of our Saviour's character, preferred and declined in the eleventh chapter. If there were any doubt upon this point, it would be removed by a comparison with Matt. xvi. 1—4. where the demand of such a sign, characterized by its proper name, as the sign from heaven, is found to have been put, and declined, in terms almost the same; the account of which was probably omitted, at the time, in the corresponding part of St. Luke's Gospel, because he knew that something of the same kind would come over again here. Ὀψίας γενομένης, λέγετε εὐδία (ἔσται·) πυῤῥάζει γὰρ ὁ οὐρανός· καὶ πρωῒ σήμερον χειμών πυῤῥάζει γὰρ στυγνάζων ὁ οὐρανός. Ὑποκριταὶ, τὸ μὲν πρόσωπον τοῦ οὐρανοῦ γινώσκετε διακρίνειν, τὰ δὲ σημεῖα τῶν καιρῶν οὐ δύνασθε;

In both these instances, the nature of the reasoning employed is to proceed upon the acknowledged observation of certain natural phenomena, as indicating certain natural effects, the connection between which was obvious to every one; and as a case in point, they constitute the principles of a *reductio ad absurdum*, that it was mere hypocrisy to be able thus to judge of the signs of the weather, or to draw the proper inference from the affections of the heavens, and yet to mistake the signs of the times—not to draw the proper inference from the events which were daily passing before their eyes.

That the demand, then, of an extraordinary means of conviction, distinct from the ordinary, or the evidence daily produced, may be equally referred to in both these instances must be apparent. There is some difference, however, in the later, compared with the former, which convinces me

that more is intended by that, than was by this. It is
not without reason that St. Matthew's general designation
of σημεῖα τῶν καιρῶν διακρίνειν is changed in St. Luke, for
the particular one of τὸν δὲ καιρὸν τοῦτον πῶς οὐ δοκιμάζετε;
The truth is our Lord in St. Matthew is reproaching his
hearers with not discerning, in the proofs of his divine commission daily vouchsafed before, the time or season of the
Messiah in general; in St. Luke, with not discovering, from
the same proofs, as now vouchsafed, the last time or season
of the Messias in particular. The illustrations, which he
employs, will lead to no other conclusion.

It is a well known fact, with respect to Judæa, that the
seasons of rain, and of fair weather, in that country, were
fixed and determinate: each had its proper commencement,
and each its proper termination; and there was a definite
interval between them. No allusion occurs in the sacred
writers, except to two such periods of rain, at opposite quarters of the year, and called respectively the former and the
latter rain. From the last passage, quoted below ^g, which
is to this effect, He will cause to come down for you the
rain, the former rain, and the *latter* rain, in the *first* month
—it appears that the latter rain was the rain which fell in
the spring, in or about the first month of the sacred year,
Abib or Nisan, answering partly to April and partly to
March with us. The same thing is implied by Jerome in his
commentary upon Amos ^h; Quæ locusta venit in principio
imbris serotini, quando cuncta virent, et parturit omnis
ager, et diversarum arborum flores in sui generis poma
erumpuntur: for this is a description of the month Adar
among the Jews. This, then, is the rain alluded to by
Solomon ⁱ; For lo! the winter is past; the rain is over and
gone; the flowers appear on the earth; the time of the
singing of birds is come; and the voice of the turtle is
heard in our land. The fig-tree putteth forth her green
figs, and the vines with the tender grapes give a good smell.
Amos iv. 7. it is said, And, also, I have withholden the

<hr>

^g Lev. xxvi. 4. Deut. xi. 14. xxviii. 12. Jerem. iii. 3. v. 24. Hos. vi. 3.
Zech. x. 1. Joel ii. 23.　　^h Oper. iii. 1432.　　ⁱ Canticles ii. 11—13.

rain from you, when there were yet *three* months to the harvest—which harvest being necessarily the wheat harvest, the season whereof was Pentecost, the period of the rain, three months prior to that, is at least the close of the last, or the beginning of the first, month in the sacred year. Jerome's commentary, *ut supra*, is to this effect, Significat vernum tempus extremi mensis Aprilis, a quo ad messem frumenti tres menses supersunt, Maius, Junius, Julius— which, however, is not altogether a correct statement; for wheat harvest in Judæa, no more than in Egypt, was ever later than the beginning of June. Δυομένης Πλειάδος, that is, about the end of the brumal quarter*, is specified by

* I am well aware that the notes of time, δυομένης Πλειάδος, περὶ Πλειάδων δύσιν, and the like, in their ordinary acceptation imply just the reverse of this ; the commencement of the autumnal, not the end of the brumal, quarter. But that Josephus intended to describe the period of the vernal rains, whether he has described it by its proper characteristics, or no, appears from the fact that this supply of water from heaven was early in the duration of the siege, and long prior to the feast of Tabernacles. Now the feast of Tabernacles could never be later than the period ordinarily meant by the Πλειάδων δύσις—which the ancient Calendaria[k] place about forty-three or forty-four days after the autumnal equinox, as they do their rising about the same time after the vernal. Forty-four days after the autumnal equinox would bring us to the seventh of November; almost a month later than the latest time when the feast of Tabernacles could fall. The necessity of the case, then, requires that Josephus should be understood of the Πλειάδων ἐπιτολὴ, not the δύσις—the time of which would be early in May, not much posterior to the ordinary termination of the vernal rains.

There is a passage in Æschylus which, as implying a similar inaccuracy, admits of comparison with this of Josephus. Speaking of the capture of Troy, he describes the ἵππου νεοσσός, *equus durateus*, as

Πήδημ' ὀρούσας ἀμφὶ Πλειάδων δύσιν. Agam. 799.

whereas the uniform historical tradition is that Troy was taken in the Attic month Thargelion, Scirrophorion, or the like,

Et Danaûm *decimo vere* redisse rates.

[k] Plin. H. N. xviii. 25. ii. 47. xi. 16. xvii. 18.

Josephus[1] as the beginning of one of the rainy seasons; consequently, of the vernal or latter rain as such. Now as the period of barley-harvest coincided with the anniversary of the Passover, and the effect of the latter rains, as indeed of the rainy season in general, when over, was necessarily to swell the Jordan, hence it is stated in the Book of Joshua[m], Jordan overfloweth all his banks, all the time of harvest, that is, of barley-harvest; for the river was crossed on the tenth of Nisan[n]. Before the time of barley-harvest, that is, before the middle of Nisan, which in a rectified year would answer to the middle of April, the vernal rains would almost always be long over: and in most years by the middle of March. There is a case in point, mentioned by Josephus, when the Jordan was impassable on account of the rain, on the fourth of Dystrus; which corresponded in that year to February 25[o].

After the cessation of the last or the spring rains, the continuance of fine weather until the periodic recurrence of the first or the autumnal, that is, all through the vernal and summer quarters, is equally well attested. Σπάνιον δὲ, εἴ ποτε, τὸ κλίμα τοῦτο θέρους ὕεται[p]: Nunquam in fine mensis Junii, sive in mense Julio, in his provinciis, maximeque in Judæa, pluvias vidimus[q]. Hence, at the inauguration of Saul, which 1 Sam. xii. 17. proves to have taken place about the feast of Pentecost, or in the ἀκμὴ of wheat-harvest, thunder and rain were so strange a phenomenon, as justly to be appealed to in token of the displeasure of God.

Nor is this all. The interval between the latter and the former rains seems to have been in general as near as possible the interval between the autumnal and the vernal equinox, or about six months. The one were over before the Passover, and the other set in shortly after the Scenopegia[r]. The duration of the dearth in the time of Elijah, though not specified in the Old Testament, further than as almost

[1] Ant. Jud. xiii. viii. 2.　　[m] iii. 15.　　[n] iv. 19. Vide also 1 Chron. xii. 15. Jerem. xii. 5. xlix. 19.　　[o] B. Jud. iv. vii. 3. 5. Vol. i. p. 580. Note.　　[p] B. Jud. iii. vii. 12. Vide also Ant. xviii. viii. 6.　　[q] Hieronymi Oper. iii. 1401.　　[r] Ezra x. 9—13.

three years, is twice specified in the New[s], and each time as a dearth of three years and six months in length ; which is to be accounted for in this manner.   The strictly preternatural period of the drought both began and terminated, as was to be expected, with the ordinary season of the first rain ; that is, the autumnal quarter of the year : and lasted just three years in all.   The six months, in addition to that, were, consequently, the ordinary interval between the latter and the former rain : which, though they did certainly aggravate the whole duration, and the consequent effects, of the drought, could not by themselves have been considered unnatural or extraordinary.

That this explanation is correct appears from Josephus[t], who cites Menander, the Tyrian historian, in testimony to a drought in the reign of Ithobal, the Ethbaal of Scripture, and father of Jezebel, which extended from Hyperberetæus, or Tisri, in one year, to the same month in the next. And hence we may better appreciate the maternal piety of Rizpah, the daughter of Aiah, and concubine of Saul, which is instanced in 2 Sam. xxi. 9. 10.   For these seven men were put to death in the first days of barley-harvest, that is, so early as the sixteenth of Nisan—and her watching over their bodies, which lasted until water dropped upon them out of heaven, must have continued past the same time in the month of Tisri.   The Mishna places the recurrence of the autumnal rains, one year with another, about the end of the first week in Marchesvan ; a fortnight after the close of the feast of Tabernacles [u] *.

* Josephus supplies a case in point when they appear to have so begun[v].   The remarkable storm of rain and wind, which is there described, being not many days later than the arrival of John of Gischala at Jerusalem, nor that arrival than the end of the month Tisri, must have coincided with about the middle of Marchesvan, and have been, consequently, the setting in of the autumnal rains.   See also a similar instance, in Diodorus Siculus[w],

[s] Luke iv. 25.   James v. 17.   [t] Ant. Jud. viii. xiii. 2.   [u] ii. 357.
[v] B. Jud. iv. iv. 5.   [w] xx. 74.

Now the natural phenomena, referred to by our Saviour, are referred to as indicating not merely certain natural consequences in general, but certain stated and regular consequences in particular. Γίνεται οὕτω, or καὶ γίνεται, is subjoined to each. The natural effects, supposed to be of this regular kind, are these two, *rain* and καύσων, which may well be understood of dry, and hot or sultry, weather. The appearance, which indicates the former, is the rising of the cloud from the west; the appearance, which prognosticates the latter, is the beginning of the south wind to blow.

Now the very terms, in which the first of these symptoms is alluded to—ὅταν ἴδητε τὴν νεφέλην ἀνατέλλουσαν ἀπὸ δυσμῶν—authorize the following conclusions respecting it. First, it was some well known and memorable cloud; secondly, it was never observed in any quarter but the west: and we have seen it was always the harbinger of rain. The west in Judæa is the region of the Mediterranean sea; this cloud from the west, therefore, was necessarily a cloud from that sea. The cloud itself, the quarter where it first appeared, the effect by which it was followed, are all satisfactorily explained by a case in point, at the end of the great drought before alluded to [x]. This cloud (ἡ νεφέλη) was that cloud, in the shape of a man's hand, which the servant of Elijah, at his seventh errand, saw and reported to be rising from the sea: after which, in a very short time, and almost before Ahab could prepare his chariot for departing, The heaven was black with clouds and wind, and there was a great rain. It is reasonable to presume that this was a familiar phenomenon in Judæa; the natural effect of a long continuance of dry and sultry weather; and the natural prognostic also of its speedy termination, by the setting in of the autumnal rain.

With regard to the other phenomenon, the south, in reference to Judæa, is the region of the sandy deserts of Idu-

---

of a storm encountered περὶ Πλειάδος δύσιν, when Demetrius Poliorcetes was sailing with a fleet to invade Egypt.

[x] 1 Kings xviii. 41—end.

mæa and of Arabia ; that is, the region of barrenness, heat, and thirst : a wind from that quarter, therefore, must needs be the forerunner of sultry weather.   Concerning the south winds in that quarter, Diodorus writes thus ; Θερμοὶ γίνονται καθ᾽ ὑπερβολὴν, ὥστε καὶ τὰς ὕλας ἐκπυροῦν, καὶ τῶν καταφευγόντων εἰς τὰς ἐν ταῖς καλύβαις σκιὰς ἐκλύειν τὰ σώματα [y] : Seneca ; Auster quoque, qui ex illo tractu venit, ventorum calidissimus est [z] : Pliny ; Austros ibi tam ardentes flare, ut æstatibus sylvas incendant, invenimus apud auctores [a] : Philo Judæus ; Ξηρός τε γάρ ἐστι, καὶ κεφαλαλγὴς, καὶ βαρυήκοος, ἄσας τε καὶ ἀδημονίας ἐμποιεῖν ἱκανὸς, καὶ μάλιστ᾽ ἐν Αἰγύπτῳ, κειμένῃ κατὰ τὰ νότια, ᾽δι᾽ ὧν αἱ περιπολήσεις τῶν φωσφόρων ἀστέρων, ὡς ἅμα τῷ διακινηθῆναι, τὸν ἀφ᾽ ἡλίου φλογμὸν συνεπωθεῖσθαι, καὶ πάντα καίειν [b].

But this is not all.   A variety of notices, relating to the south wind, may be specified from ancient authors, which, it appears to me, would be applicable to the case in point.

I. The year being taken throughout, the prevailing winds, almost every where, are described as the north, and the south.   Πλεῖστοι γὰρ βορέαι καὶ νότοι γίγνονται τῶν ἀνέμων [c]— Πλείστων δὲ ὄντων, ὥσπερ εἴρηται, βορείων καὶ νοτίων [d].

II. The south wind, in southern regions, was a fair wind ; and hence one of its names, and perhaps the most appropriate, was that of Λευκόνοτος.   Ἀργέστην δὲ νότον, τὸν Λευκόνοτον· οὗτος γὰρ ὀλίγα τὰ νέφη ποιεῖ [e]—Permutant et duo naturam cum situ : auster Africæ serenus ; aquilo nubilus [f]—Ὁ μὲν γὰρ νότος ἀεὶ τοῖς ἑαυτοῦ τόποις αἴθριος [g]—Ὁμοίως δὲ καὶ ὁ νότος αἴθριος τοῖς περὶ τὴν Λιβύην [h].

> ALBUS ut obscuro deterget nubila cœlo
>   Sæpe NOTUS, neque parturit imbres
> Perpetuos——
>
> Hor. Carm. I. vii. 15.

III. The south wind was etesian, or a monsoon, as well

---

[y] Diod. Sic. iii. 47. Vide also Herod. ii. 22.

[z] H. N. xii. 19.

[a] De Vit. Mos. 621.

ii. 3.

[c] Arist. Meteorol. ii. 4.

[e] Strabo i. 43.

[f] Plin. H. N. ii. 47.

[h] Arist. Meteorol. ii. 3.

[z] Nat. Quæst. iv. 2.

Vide also Arist. Meteorol. ii. 3.

[d] Theophrastus De Ventis.

[g] Theophrastus De Ventis.

as the northern.   Both Pliny and Diodorus[i] assert that
the etesian winds were not confined to the northern quarter of the heavens. Ὅθεν καὶ τὸ θαυμαζόμενον ὡς οὐκ ὄν, διατὶ
βορέαι μὲν ἐτησίαι γίνονται, νότοι δὲ οὐ γίνονται, φαίνεται πῶς
συμβαίνειν[k]——Etesiæ et prodromi...certo tempore anni, cum
Canis oritur, ex alia atque alia parte cœli spirant——P. Nigi-
dii in secundo librorum, quos de vento composuit, verba
hæc sunt; Etesiæ et austri anniversarii, secundo sole, flant[l].

   IV. The northern monsoons were in general the summer
wind; and the southern the winter.   Hence Lucretius, in
his beautiful chart of the seasons :

> It ver, et Venus; et Veris prænuncius ante
> Pennatus graditur Zephyrus, vestigia propter
> Flora quibus mater, præspargens ante viaï
> Cuncta, coloribus egregiis et odoribus obplet.
> Inde loci sequitur Calor aridus, et comes una
> Pulverulenta Ceres, et Etesia flabra Aquilonum.
> Inde Auctumnus adit, graditur simul Euius Euan:
> Inde aliæ Tempestates, Venteique, sequuntur,
> Altitonans Volturnus, et Auster fulmine pollens.
> Tandem Bruma niveis adfert, pigrumque rigorem
> Reddit; Hyems sequitur, crepitans ac dentibus Algu.
>
>   V. 736.

Hence also his description of the equinoctial points themselves :

> Nam medio cursu flatûs Aquilonis et Austri,
> Distinet æquato cœlum discrimine metas.   Ib. 688.

Γίνονται μὲν γὰρ καὶ οἱ καλούμενοι Λευκόνοτοι τὴν ἀντικειμένην
ὥραν (τοῖς βορείοις)[m]. Quia flatibus *etesiarum* implentur vada
(Caspii sc. maris); *hybernus* auster revolvit fluctus [n].

   V. The southern monsoon, among its other times, blew
most regularly at the close of the brumal quarter, and the
beginning of the vernal.   Columella De Re Rustica ; xvii.
kal. Febr. africus, interdum auster, cum pluvia. v. kal.
Febr. auster, aut africus, hiemat——Sex diebus ante idus

[i] Plin. H. N. ii. 47.   Diod. i. 39.   [k] Theophrastus De Ventis.   [l] Aulus
Gell. ii. 22.   [=] Arist. Meteorol. ii. 5.   [n] Tac. Ann. vi. 33.

                         N n 3

Maias; quod tempus austrinum est °. Ἑκατέρων οἶον τάξις, ἐν οἷς χρόνοις μάλιστα πνέουσι, κατὰ λόγον ἐστί· τοῖς μὲν βορείοις, χειμῶνός τε, καὶ θέρους, καὶ μετοπώρου ... τοῖς δὲ νοτίοις, κατὰ χειμῶνά τε, καὶ ἀρχομένου ἔαρος, καὶ μετοπώρου λήγοντος—Οἱ γὰρ ἠρινοὶ νότοι καθάπερ ἐτησίαι τινές εἰσιν· οὖς καλοῦσι Λευκονότους· αἴθριοι γὰρ, καὶ ἀσυννεφεῖς, ὡς ἐπίπαν—Τὸν βορέαν ἐπιπνεῖν τῷ νότῳ, τὸν δὲ νότον μὴ τῷ βορέᾳ ᴘ—Ζῶσι δ' ἀπὸ ἀκρίδων, ἃς οἱ ἐαρινοὶ λίβες καὶ ζέφυροι, πνέοντες μεγάλοι, συνελαύνουσιν εἰς τοὺς τόπους τούτους—Ὑπὸ .. τὴν ἐαρινὴν ἰσημερίαν, ὅτε λίβες παρ' αὐτοῖς καὶ ζέφυροι πνέουσι, παμμεγεθῶν ἀκρίδων πλῆθος ἀμύθητον .. μετὰ τῶν ἀνέμων παραγίνεται ٩. This wind from its bringing the birds of passage Aristotle and Pliny call ornithian, or chelidonian; Καὶ γὰρ οὗτοι ἐτησίαι εἰσὶν ἀσθενεῖς· ἐλάττους δὲ καὶ ὀψιαίτεροι τῶν ἐτησίων πνέουσιν· ἐβδομηκοστῇ γὰρ (which he dates from the τροπαὶ χειμεριναὶ, or winter solstice) ἄρχονται πνεῖν ʳ. Spirant autem et a bruma, cum vocantur ornithiæ; sed leniores, et paucis diebus—Favonium quidam ad ᴠɪɪ. kal. Martias chelidoniam vocant, ab hirundinis visu; nonnulli vero ornithian, uno et ʟxx. die post brumam, ab adventu avium, flantem per dies novem ˢ.

Accordingly Josephus speaks of the south wind as blowing in a given instance, the time of the recapture of Masada ᵗ, on the fifteenth of Xanthicus, Tuesday April 11. A. U. 826; and Solomon, Canticles iv. 16. alludes to both the north and the south as winds peculiar to the vernal quarter, and wont to succeed each other; Awake O north wind! and come thou south! blow upon my garden, that the spices thereof may flow out. Moreover, the Indian caravans, which set out upon their return between the end of December and the middle of January in every year, upon entering the Red sea, which they did after forty days' voyage, are said to have finished the rest of the journey, which took up thirty days more ᵘ, africo vel austro—each of them a monsoon, or trade wind. On this principle these

---

° Plin. H. N. ii. 47.   ᴘ Theophrastus De Ventis.   ٩ Strabo. xvi. 1098. Agatharchides, ap. Geographos Veteres i. 42.   ʳ Aristotle ut supra. ˢ Plin. H. N. ii. 47.   ᵗ B. Jud. vii. viii. 5.   Vol. i. Diss. xiii. 579.   ᵘ Plin. H. N. vi. 23.   Vide also Solin. Polyhist. liv.

winds must have begun, and continued, to blow, in the Red sea, contiguous to Judæa, seventy days after the beginning of January; that is, until as late as the first or second week in March: which would be the beginning of the dry season in that country.

Laying these testimonies together, we may fairly come to the conclusion that the south wind's commencing to blow was a natural indication of the approach of the dry, and therefore of the close of the rainy, season, in Judæa: as the appearance of the cloud was of the reverse. If so, our Lord intends to reproach his hearers with not being able, from the signs of the times, as a case in point, to discover that this was the last and concluding period of his ministry. For there was truly something, and had been, for some time past, in his manner and demeanour, which might have warranted this presumption. His diligence, activity, and earnestness, ever since the feast of Tabernacles, up to the present circuit, were sufficient to have raised the reflection that his time was at hand—the exigency of the occasion was pressing—the intermediate period was short, and no part of it to be idly or unprofitably spent. He delivered more discourses, he spake more parables, he wrought more miracles, and, perhaps, he visited more places, within the last three months of his ministry, than ever, within an equal time, before. St. Luke's Gospel, which in less than nine chapters comprized the account of two years and nine months previously, is taken up, for more than fourteen chapters, with the history of these two or three months alone subsequently. Within this period, too, the Seventy had been sent out; that is, the service, before rendered by the Twelve, had been increased sixfold by *their* mission: and our Lord himself was now following in their track, and visiting personally either all, or most, of the places which had been recently evangelized by them.

The same conclusion, respecting the nature of the present time, is obtruded also by the last member of the division, beginning, And why, even of yourselves, do ye not judge of that is just? The reasoning, immediately subjoined, supposes two parties—a creditor who is reclaiming, and a debtor who is withholding, the same *just* debt. It supposes the creditor, after trying every other expedient in vain, to be having recourse to the law, and bringing his debtor before the judge : it supposes the two parties to be actually on the way to the court of justice ; but not yet arrived there. It supposes, consequently, a remaining interval—but a short and finite interval—within which it is still possible for the refractory party to make up the matter, by satisfying the debt of his own accord ; and to stop all further proceedings. But it supposes that, if he persists in his obstinacy to the last, and the case comes before the judge, there will be no longer the means of retreat ; the law must take its usual course : the judge will deliver him to the exactor ; the exactor will consign him to prison ; and he will never come out from thence, until he have repaid the uttermost farthing.

Now, all this might be applicable to the case of our Lord, and of the Jewish people, the former of whom, upon the strength of sufficient evidence, had long been claiming to be received as their Messias, and the latter, notwithstanding this evidence, had long been refusing to receive him as such. But it would be applicable only on the further supposition that, at this present time, he was making a last and a final appeal to the same people, with a view to their conversion—that the period both of his own ministry, and of their probation, was fast drawing to its close—beyond which should the national impenitence be still protracted, they must expect to be given up to the penal consequences of an obstinate unbelief. This part, therefore, demonstrates the same conclusion, as clearly as any before it.

DISSERTATION XX.

On the incident relating to the Galileans, Luke xiii. 1—9.

THE connection of this section with the preceding chapter, which would otherwise be the first thing to require pointing out, has been demonstrated already. The phrase ἐν αὐτῷ τῷ καιρῷ, as equivalent to ἐν τῷ αὐτῷ καιρῷ, at the *self-same* season, instead of at *the same* season, is among the peculiar idioms of St. Luke[a]; and by its occurrence here ascertains the time of the following account, as directly consecutive upon the preceding. This allusion, then, to the fate of the Galileans took place soon after the previous discourse; and the matter of fact alluded to, if we proceed to examine into it, will, perhaps, be found to conspire with that discourse itself, in leading to the same conclusion, which the consideration of the discourse enabled us to deduce in the preceding Dissertation.

With a view to this examination I am not aware that it would make much difference whether we supposed the Galileans in question to be some of the sect, who are known in contemporary history by their relation to Judas, surnamed the Galilean—or certain of the people of Galilee. The same conclusions might follow in either case; yet the latter, and not the former, is indisputably the more correct opinion.

For first, when a word possesses both a *general* and *proper*, and also a *particular* and *improper*, signification, like this of the Galileans, it is impossible that it should be used ἁπλῶς, as it is here, except in the former. Those, for whom St. Luke was writing, might very well comprehend what was meant by the people of Galilee, as such; but could not, without some further explanation, what was meant by the followers of Judas of Galilee.

Secondly, the name of Galileans, as descriptive of any

[a] vii. 21. x. 21. xii. 12. xiii. 31. xx. 19. xxiii. 12. xxiv. 13. 33.

such sect, occurs no where in the Gospels: the principles of
the sect may often be alluded to, but the name is regularly
kept out of sight. St. Luke in particular suppresses even
the name of the Herodians, which neither St. Matthew, nor
St. Mark, does; though the principles of that sect, as the second of the passages cited below must serve to demonstrate[b],
if they were not the same with the principles of the Galileans, bordered very closely upon them.

The truth is, the denomination of Galileans was never the
peculiar name of this sect: it may be given, indeed, to their
founder, as at Acts v. 37. in reference either to his supposed
country, or to the persons of whom his followers, at the
time, might principally have consisted; but, as a specific
designation for his party, it is as little to be met with in Josephus, as in the Gospels. Judas himself was a Gaulanite,
ἐκ πόλεως ὄνομα Γάμαλα[c]: though he may also be called the
Galilean; and if his party had any distinctive appellation,
it was that of the Zealots or Sicarii. As such they are
enumerated by Josephus, in their proper place, among the
other sects of the Jews[d]. But even the Zealots were a
branch of the Pharisees: and their founder was Zadok the
Pharisee, as much as Judas the Galilean.

Thirdly, it may very well be questioned whether, after
the rise and dispersion of the party, A. U. 760. until near
the time of the Jewish war, when it again started into being,
the sect of the Zealots existed except in abeyance. The attempt of Judas had been speedily followed by his death;
and the reasoning of Gamaliel in the Acts necessarily supposes that both he, and his followers, had come to nothing.
Had not this been notoriously the fact, his very example,
as a case in point, would have made against him. At the
time of our Saviour's trial before Pilate[e], he was very
plainly charged with maintaining the principles of Judas—
but he was not himself called either a Zealot or a Galilean.
In Josephus too, though certain of the sons or descendants

[b] Luke vi. 11. xx. 20.   [c] Ant. xviii. i. 1. 6. xx. v. 2. B. ii. viii. 1.
xvii. 8.   [d] Ant. xviii. i. 1—6. B. ii. viii. 1—14. vii. viii. 1.   [e] Luke
xxiii. 2.

of Judas may be alluded to at intermediate periods, and on distinct occasions[f], yet no overt act similar to the first insurrection, A. U. 760. in which any of his party or his family were concerned, can be found on record, prior to A. U. 819. when Manahem, a descendant of his it is true, seized upon Masada[g], and usurped the tyranny of his countrymen, at the outset of the Jewish war.

It was not, in fact, possible that in peaceful and quiet times such a sect could be tolerated for a moment. Their principles led directly to anarchy and insubordination. It was a point of conscience with them to disclaim the authority of the Roman Emperor, or of his Procurators—to withhold the payment of tribute—to resist, in short, the imposition of any foreign yoke, and to acknowledge no master but God. From the time, therefore, of the census of Quirinius, and of the mission of Coponius, the civil constitution of Judæa and this sect could not both subsist together; their principles on the one hand allowed of no compromise between liberty or death—the stability of the existing government on the other, none between its own entire ascendancy and their utter annihilation. If the Galileans had survived the first contest, the Roman yoke must have been for ever shaken off: if the Roman government had triumphed, the Galileans must have perished in the struggle.

Fourthly, it is probable, from xiii. 31. that Jesus was at this very time in Galilee; and it is certain that he must have been somewhere in the dominions of Herod. This circumstance might account for the communication, xiii. 1. itself; but it supposes that the sufferers alluded to were inhabitants of Galilee. For where would a misfortune, which had happened to Galileans in particular, be so likely to excite an interest as in Galilee? and about whom were the people of Galilee so likely to feel an interest, as about their own countrymen?

Fifthly, the reasoning, which our Lord grounds upon the communication, must be decisive as to whom it refers to.

[f] Ant. xx. v. 2.　B. vii. viii. 1.　　　　　　　　[g] B. ii. xvii. 8.

He opposes these Galileans, who had perished, as a *part* to the Galileans, who still survived, as a *whole ;* and he urges the fact of what had befallen the *part,* as a warning of what might be expected by the *whole.* There can be no doubt that, in the latter instance, he means the people of Galilee, for he identifies them with his hearers at the time ; and, consequently, there can be as little that he meant them also in the former. In like manner, directly after[h], he opposes a certain number of the inhabitants of Jerusalem to the rest of the people of the same city ; and from the fact of what had befallen the former, he derives the same inference of what, unless they repented, might be expected by the latter. In each instance, a part is opposed to a whole ; a less number to a greater ; but each of the same kind, and both included within the same complex. We may take it for granted, therefore, that the persons alluded to here were no partisans of Judas of Galilee ; but strictly and properly Galileans.

Again, it seems equally reasonable to conclude that, whatever had befallen them in general, it was something which had befallen them *recently.* An event like this would naturally be talked about only as soon as it happened, and those who apprized our Saviour of it *now,* it is manifest, could not suppose he was aware of it already. His own language is in favour of this conclusion : Think ye, that these Galileans were sinners above all the Galileans, that they *have suffered* such things ? when he is referring to a fact, of unquestionably more ancient date, his language is perceptibly different ; Or they, the eighteen, on whom the tower in Siloam *fell,* and *slew* them, think ye that these were offenders, above all that were dwelling at Jerusalem ?

Again, whatever had befallen them in particular, it was something which had befallen them innocently ; that is, they had not brought it upon themselves. The very construction, put upon their misfortune, seems to be a proof of this. If they had been anywise instrumental to it, it would not have been accidental ; and if it had not been accidental, it

[h] xiii. 4.

could not have been construed into a judgment for sin. These men must have perished at a time, and in a manner, which, humanly speaking, would acquit them of all blame, as having drawn down their own death; and would resolve it solely into the controlling providence of God.

Again, there is no proof, in contemporary history, of any disturbance in Jerusalem, the scene of which is not principally, if not exclusively, the temple; and the time of which is not, still more invariably, about the time of some feast. Μάλιστα...ἐν ταῖς εὐωχίαις αὐτῶν στάσις ἅπτεται[i]. Such disturbances always took place when the Jews were assembled in greater numbers than usual : and they were never so assembled, except before and during the feasts[k]. Now the scene of the outrage upon these Galileans was manifestly the temple—for the outrage occurred in the midst of sacrifice—either of *their* sacrifices, or of the sacrifices *themselves,* according as we choose to render τῶν θυσιῶν αὐτῶν. And if Pilate also was present at Jerusalem, the time when it happened was the time of some feast. Cæsarea, and not Jerusalem, was the seat of the civil government[l]; so that he would never be ordinarily resident at Jerusalem, except during the periods of the feasts; when, for the same reason that a guard was always kept stationed in Antonia, (ἔνοπλοι δὲ ἀεὶ τὰς ἑορτὰς παραφυλάττουσιν, ὡς μή τι νεωτερίζοι τὸ πλῆθος συνηθροισμένον[m], that is, because the risk of extraordinary danger required extraordinary precaution to prevent it,) the supreme magistrate also took care to be on the spot.

Again, the case of Barabbas, as specified in each of the Gospels, is a proof that, before the last Passover, there had been a tumult in the city, accompanied by bloodshed[n]: for he was still in prison, on that account, at the time of our Saviour's condemnation: and the same case is equally a

[i] B. Jud. i. iv. 3.   [k] Ant. xvii. ix. 3. x. 2. B. ii. i. 3. iii. 1. Ant. xviii. ii. 2. xx. v. 3. B. ii. xii. 1.   [l] Tac. Hist. ii. 79. Acts xxiii. 23—end. xxv. 1—6. 13. Ant. Jud. xviii. iii. 1. iv. 3. B. ii. ix. 2. 4. Ant. xx. v. 4. viii. 7. B. ii. xii. 2. 5. xiii. 7. xiv. 4. 6.   [m] B. ii. xii. 1. Ant. xx. v. 3. Vide also B. v. v. 8.   [n] Luke xxiii. 19. Matt. xxvii. 16. Mark xv. 7. John xviii. 40.

proof that the tumult itself was a recent occurrence; for
though both he, and his accomplices, had been imprisoned,
none of them had yet been executed, on that account. The
bloodshed which had accompanied this disturbance, it is
reasonable to suppose, was the bloodshed of Roman soldiers,
not of native Jews; in which case, nothing was more likely
to have provoked the retaliatory vengeance of the Governor.
There is not the least ground for imagining that Barabbas,
who seems to have been so popular a character, notwithstanding the recent outrage, at the time of our Lord's crucifixion, had headed one party of Jews against another—or
that the contest, which terminated in death to some, had
lain between Jews, on both sides, as such, and not between
Jews, and the Roman military.

Again, at the time of our Lord's trial, not only Pilate,
but Herod, also, the Tetrarch of Galilee, was in Jerusalem[o].
There is no reason to suppose that, before this, the latter
had been a regular attendant at the feasts: on the contrary,
if Luke xxiii. 8. be true, it follows demonstratively that he
had not attended either the feast of Dedication, or the feast
of Tabernacles, last; at both of which times Jesus had been
in Jerusalem, teaching and performing miracles upon the
spot.   But, if he was now in attendance against his usage,
he must have had express reasons to bring him there—especially as he was accompanied by a train of soldiers[p]; which,
in a season of profound peace and tranquillity, like the present, except for some very urgent reasons, would be a still
more extraordinary circumstance.

Again, there was at this time a quarrel in existence between Herod and Pilate[q]; the cause of which, consequently,
must have been some ground of offence, on one side, or on
both sides.   But it would not be easy to conceive what offence Herod could have given to Pilate, at least in his offi-
cial capacity; for an offence to Pilate, in that capacity,
would also be an offence to the Emperor.   It is very possible, on the other hand, that Pilate might have given

o Luke xxiii. 7.   p Ib. 11.   q Ib. 12.

offence to Herod. The mere circumstance that the one was the petty Tetrarch of Galilee, and the other the representative of the majesty of Cæsar, without any reference to the personal character of the parties, might suffice to account for that.

Again, the quarrel in question was made up this day, and in consequence of something which passed this day— whence we may infer it was a quarrel of no long standing: the parties, between whom it existed, had probably never met since it had taken place, until they met on this occasion in Jerusalem. If it was so speedily made up now when they did meet, had they met before this period, we may suppose it would have been made up sooner.

Again, it is impossible to peruse the account of St. Luke, xxiii. 6—12. and not to come to the conclusion that the moving cause of the reconciliation was the mission of Jesus to Herod by Pilate. Now this mission is expressly attributed to the discovery that Jesus belonged to the jurisdiction of Herod. The mission, therefore, was a compliment paid to the jurisdiction of Herod; it was as much as to declare that, without the consent of Herod, Pilate would not interfere in the disposal of a person, whose proper master Herod might appear to be. And Herod understood it accordingly; for, by first sitting in judgment on our Lord himself, and then sending him back to Pilate, he both asserted his authority over him, and resigned it voluntarily up to Pilate. But if the cause of the final reconciliation was this deference to the rights of Herod, it becomes an argument that the cause of the misunderstanding previously had been some injury done to those rights; which could not be repaired except by a public acknowledgment like this. The reputation of Jesus would necessarily render it an important question to whose jurisdiction in particular he ought to be considered amenable—and in sending him upon this occasion to Herod, Pilate was not only flattering the pride of that prince, but ministering also to the gratification of a wish to see Jesus, which he had long since formed.

Again, it may be inferred from Luke xiii. 31—35. that

our Lord could not have been far from Jerusalem, that is, his circuit was fast drawing to its close, when he heard of this misfortune of the Galileans: and before his arrival at Bethany, six days anterior to the Passover, numbers of the Jews were already assembled at Jerusalem[r]. These are described as Jews from the country; and the purpose for which they went up, so much before the time, was to purify themselves against the feast. There can be no question that considerations of this kind—such as the close of the vow of separation—the purification of women after childbirth, whom their husbands would naturally accompany—besides various accidental pollutions, dependent upon circumstances—would bring up numbers to Jerusalem, some a greater, others a less, time, before the feast, in every year[s]. Οὔτε γὰρ λεπροῖς, says Josephus, οὔτε γονορροίοις, οὔτε γυναιξὶν ἐπεμμήνοις, οὔτε τοῖς ἄλλως μεμιασμένοις, ἐξῆν τῆσδε τῆς θυσίας μεταλαμβάνειν[t]. It is not to be supposed that any one, however previously clean, would delay his arrival later than the tenth of Nisan—and there is a case in point, mentioned accidentally by Josephus, which proves that the resort of visitants, against the Passover, was going forward on, and before, the eighth[u]: Ἀθροιζομένου τοῦ λαοῦ πρὸς τὴν τῶν Ἀζύμων ἑορτήν· ὀγδόη δ᾽ ἦν Ξανθικοῦ μηνός.

Laying these several particulars together, I think we may come to the inference, partly with an absolute certainty, and partly with a high degree of probability, first, that a contest had taken place in Jerusalem, arising out of a disturbance of the public peace, between the Jews and the Roman soldiers, attended by bloodshed on both sides, the scene of which was partially the temple—secondly, that this was the sedition of Barabbas, for which he was in prison, when Jesus was brought before Pilate—thirdly, that some of the Galileans, the native subjects of Herod, while engaged in the act of sacrificing, had been innocently sufferers by it—fourthly, that this violence done to them was the

---

[r] John xi. 55.   [s] Vide 2 Chron. xxix. xxx.   [t] B. Jud. vi. ix. 3.
[u] B. vi. v. 3.

cause of the enmity existing between Herod and Pilate, and the reason why the former was present in Jerusalem, at the time of the last Passover, with an armed force, for his own protection, or for that of his subjects—fifthly, that, all this was of recent occurrence, between the time denoted by John xi. 53. and xii. 1: after the commencement of our Lord's final circuit, and not long before its close.

It is some confirmation of the connection between this incident, thus alluded to Luke xiii. 1. and what subsequently passed at our Lord's examination, xxiii. 6—12. that the former does serve to clear up the latter, and that both are related by St. Luke, and by him alone.   There is no proof, it is true, in Josephus of any disturbance in Jerusalem, about this time: but neither is there any account, given by him, of the administration of Pilate generally, except after the close of our Lord's personal history, and so far as regards one or two particulars—his introduction of the ensigns into the city—his sequestration of the corban—and his violence towards the Samaritans—the last of which led to his removal from office, and the two former, as I apprehend, had not yet taken place.   Nor could any greater objection be deducible from the silence of Josephus as to this fact in particular, than from his silence with respect to Christianity in general.   If this fact was connected with the sedition of Barabbas, then the history of Barabbas was too intimately connected also with the personal history of Christ, to be noticed distinctly by an author, who has preserved so deep, and undoubtedly so deliberate, a secrecy with respect to that.

It seems to have been ordained by Providence, and with an evident fitness and expediency, that the whole period of our Lord's public ministry, until this time, should have passed over with no such events as these: nor can I help thinking that the occurrence of something of the kind, at last, was more permissive, than accidental; and as providential as any thing else.   For had not this been the case, no such notorious criminal as Barabbas could have been in confinement at the time of the trial of our Lord; and if Barabbas had not then been in prison, whom could the infidel Jews have demanded instead of the Christ? and without this preference of Barabbas to the Christ, what room could there have been for that last and most convincing testimony to the national impenitence and guilt, the deliberate predilection of a robber and an outlaw, a ringleader of sedition, with hands embrued in blood, instead not merely of a person whose innocence was undoubted, and whose purity of character was unimpeachable, but of their own Messias, the Prince of peace, and Saviour of mankind?

DISSERTATION XXI.

On the question concerning divorce, Matt. xix. 3—12.
Mark x. 2—12.

THE reason why St. Luke has omitted all mention of this question, and of its answer, appears to be, because a similar, and very probably a recent, decision on the same subject was recorded by him[a], not long before the point of time[b] where his narrative again joins St. Matthew and St. Mark. In the accounts of the two latter Evangelists themselves, compared together, there is the same evidence of omissions on the one hand, and of supplements on the other, as repeatedly occurs elsewhere; and this fact being once established, it will naturally go some way in reconciling the differences between them.

For example, when Jesus had replied to the question of the Pharisees—which was put in public, and answered in public—he retired into some private house[c]. There is no notice, either express or implicit, of this fact in St. Matthew. While he was in this house, the disciples, according to the same authority, renewed the enquiry concerning the question: neither is this fact noticed by St. Matthew. Yet what he attributes to the disciples[d] must have made a part of this conversation in private: it has all the appearance of a remark, produced by the repetition to them in particular of what had lately been pronounced to all in common. If so, it becomes implicitly a proof that our Lord, at this period in St. Matthew's account, was actually in private; and the conclusion is confirmed by the incident next subjoined, the bringing of little children to Christ[e]; for that transaction took place *after* he came into the house, and *before* he left it again; that is, while he was still within[f].

[a] xvi. 18. [b] xviii. 15. [c] Mark x. 10. [d] xix. 10. [e] xix.
13—15. [f] Mark x. 10. 17.

We may conclude, therefore, that the final end, which St. Mark has here in view, is to supply certain particulars in a common account, omitted by St. Matthew. Hence he is in some respects fuller, and in some respects more concise, than he: fuller, where St. Matthew had been most defective, and more concise, where he had been most minute. On this principle they may easily be accommodated to each other.

For first, the question, according to St. Matthew, stood thus—Εἰ ἔξεστιν ἀνθρώπῳ ἀπολῦσαι τὴν γυναῖκα αὐτοῦ κατὰ πᾶσαν αἰτίαν; according to St. Mark—Εἰ ἔξεστιν ἀνδρὶ γυναῖκα ἀπολῦσαι; in which, consequently, there is an omission of κατὰ πᾶσαν αἰτίαν: and this is an omission which must have been intentional. For the decision of our Lord himself [g] shews that, on *one* account, the account of fornication, which in a married woman amounts to adultery, it *was lawful* to put away a wife. The question, then, Is it lawful for a husband to put away his wife? so expressed, might be answered in the affirmative; the question, Is it lawful for a man to put away his wife, on *any account?* must be answered in the negative. The true drift of the question, therefore, as stated by St. Mark, supposes its statement by St. Matthew also to be carried along with his.

Secondly, in reply to the question, our Lord, according to St. Mark, began with referring to the decision of Moses —according to St. Matthew, he proceeded to decide it himself [h]. If he did both these things, there is no inconsistency between the statements; and in favour of that supposition we may argue as follows.

When, in other instances, a question was put to our Saviour, which either had been actually decided by the Law, or was easily to be collected from it, we observe him refer in the first place to the Law [i]; and, as this was a case in point, it might naturally be expected he would do the same now. But, had he never done so, on any other occasion, there were yet special reasons why he should do so on this.

[g] Matt. xix. 9. [h] Mark x. 3. Matt. xix. 4. [i] Matt. xix. 16. 17. 18. Luke x. 25. 26.

It was notorious that liberty of divorce had been conceded by the Law of Moses [k] : it was certain also that, at the first institution of marriage, marriage had been pronounced inseparable. It follows, therefore, that the concession of the Law had been contrary to the original statute ; and, consequently, a special indulgence, vouchsafed to the Jews. Hence, as there was once a time, when no such indulgence yet existed, so there might be a time, when it should be again repealed.

If, then, the original law was to be revived by the Gospel, and made binding on Christians, the temporary indulgence, granted subsequently to the Jews, was necessarily to cease. The design, therefore, of referring in the first place to the decision of the Law was to give greater solemnity to the decision of Christ. It would intimate so much the more clearly both the abrogation of the existing commandment, and the grounds on which it would be made. What did Moses command you? was, consequently, a natural, and even a necessary, question before any declaration of our Lord himself. The judgment, which he meant to pronounce, would commit his authority apparently with the authority of Moses ; and he proposes to shew beforehand that this committal was only apparent, not real. The Mosaic injunction itself was an extraordinary and a temporary concession——not more opposed to his own decision, than to an original and prior law, recorded by Moses himself ; which, as it had once prevailed before the dispensation, so, notwithstanding that, might well recover its ascendancy again.

The interrogation recorded even by St. Matthew [l], Τί οὖν Μωσῆς ἐνετείλατο, κ.τ.λ. contains an implicit allusion to some such reference concerning the dictum of the Law. The parties, who put that question, are the same as before ; and it is manifest, that they put it by way of objection to the decision just pronounced. Our Saviour, it is true, had anticipated the objection in the decision itself ; but that the

[k] Deut. xxiv. 1. 2.   [l] xix. 7.

Pharisees should not have been satisfied with *his* reasons would be nothing extraordinary : and, if they thought proper to start the same difficulty afresh, it would be just as natural that he should reply to it as before. They had not originally put their question, out of a genuine deference to his authority, or with a candid disposition to receive instruction on an important rule of duty—but from some insidious motive; either to elicit a declaration, which they knew would be repugnant to the mandate of the Law, or to render Jesus obnoxious to the people. They could not be ignorant that, twice at least in the course of his ministry, once in the sermon on the mount, and again, still more recently in their own hearing [m], he had peremptorily laid down a new principle of conduct upon this very point.

Nor was there any thing more palatable to the people at large, nor yet more grossly abused, than this liberty of divorce. The license of polygamy allowed by the doctors of the Law, and practised by the Jews every where, was almost unrestrained. Justin Martyr tells us that the former openly permitted any man to have four or five wives individually; and that the latter freely availed themselves of this permission, marrying as many as they pleased [n]. Besides this, however, the right of divorce was carried to an excess, which rendered the marriage union, whatever it might be in profession, little better in practice than the liberty of promiscuous concubinage. There was no conceivable reason, however slight, for which a man might not put away one woman, and marry another. Γυναικὸς τῆς συνοικούσης βουλόμενος διαζευχθῆναι, καθ᾽ ἃς δηποτοῦν αἰτίας· πολλαὶ δ᾽ ἂν τοῖς ἀνθρώποις τοιαῦται γίνοιντο [o]. Josephus himself is a case in point [p], and proves the universality of the practice, as well as the slightness of the reasons for which it might be resorted to, as much as any thing. With respect, however, to the grounds of separation, considered justifiable by the Rabbins, *pudet, pigetque!* If a wife had spoiled her husband's dinner—nay more, if she was no longer to his liking,

---

[m] Matt. v. 31. 32. Luke xvi. 14. 18. [n] Dialog. 423. 436. [o] Ant. Jud. iv. viii. 23. [p] Vit. 76.

if he had found one that would suit him better—he was at liberty to put her away [q].   Schola Schamai dicit, nemo repudiabit uxorem, nisi in ea repertum fuerit quid inhonesti ... Schola Hellelis dicit, etiamsi combusserit decoctum ejus ... R. Akiba dicit, etiamsi illa pulchriorem inveniat aliam.   And yet while the husbands were thus freely allowed to divorce their wives, the wives were not allowed to divorce their husbands.

On a subject like this, where the temporary indulgence, permitted by the Law, had come to be so flagrantly abused, it is not credible that our Saviour would shrink from the discharge of his duty, or hesitate to repeat a decision, so worthy of himself.   On the contrary he repeats it now, as it might be expected an ultimate and solemn declaration would be repeated, with more emphasis and distinctness of expression, with more weight of authority, and force of reasoning, than ever before.   Yet for all this might not the Pharisees in particular be convinced by it ; and if *his* decision was any ways opposed to the decision of Moses, it was easy to see which *they* would affect to defer to.   There was no means, however, of answering our Saviour, except by appealing to Moses ; and though he had met that appeal already, yet an argument, which supposed any part of their law to be designed for a temporary purpose, was not likely to satisfy them.   Nor is it more extraordinary that *they* should have continued, or pretended to continue, unconvinced, than that the disciples of our Lord himself, from the strangeness, and probably the disagreeableness, of his doctrine should have enquired about it again.

The arrangement, then, of the two narratives will stand as follows.

I. Matt. xix. 3. Mark x. 2: the question, as reported by St. Matthew.

II. Mark x. 3. 4. 5: the demand of our Lord—the reply to that demand—and the declaration subjoined to the reply, shewing the grounds of the legal injunction.

[q] Mishna. iii. 358. 10

o o 4

III. Matt. xix. 4. 5. 6. Mark x. 6. 7. 8. 9 : which proceed in conjunction, down to the close of St. Mark's account of what passed in public ; and may be harmonized thus.

First, if we retain the interrogatory form of St. Matthew, and supply the particle δὲ from St. Mark, Οὐκ ἀνέγνωτε (δὲ) ὅτι ὁ ποιήσας ἀπ' ἀρχῆς κτίσεως, ἄρσεν καὶ θῆλυ ἐποίησεν αὐτοὺς, ὁ Θεός ;

Secondly, as supplied by St. Matthew, and as part of the quotation from Genesis, Καὶ εἶπεν (sc. ὁ Θεός)· ἕνεκεν τούτου .. down to χωριζέτω—which is all *verbatim* the same in both.

IV. Matt. xix. 7 : the objection from the Law, as repeated by the Pharisees—xix. 8 : our Lord's reply to it, as before, but more concisely than before—xix. 9 : a renewed declaration concerning the unlawfulness of promiscuous divorce, similar to what had been pronounced Matt. v. 31. 32. Luke xvi. 18. upon former occasions, but not as yet on this occasion : which concludes St. Matthew's account of what passed in public.

V. Mark x. 10. 11. 12 : the renewal of the conversation with the disciples in private ; where at verses 11. 12. there is a clear reference to Matt. xix. 9. the concluding declaration in public : which yet, without that, would not have been intelligible.

VI. And, lastly, Matt. xix. 10. 11. 12 : which will close not only St. Matthew's, but also the *whole*, account. The remark of the disciples that it was better not to marry at all, than to marry on such terms as these, is manifestly such as might have been produced by Mark x. 11. 12 ; and the reason why St. Matthew has mentioned it after xix. 9. in particular is that it followed upon the repetition of the same declaration *within*, which had recently been pronounced *without*, and it was due to the same cause, the dislike of the doctrine, or at least the surprize entertained at the doctrine, whether as prescribed *without* to the people, or as prescribed *within* to the disciples.

DISSERTATION XXII.

On the miracles performed at Jericho.

IN the account of these miracles St. Luke is apparently at variance with St. Mark, and St. Matthew apparently at variance with both[a]; the former, on the question of place, or where the miracle was performed in each—the latter, on the question of persons, or on whom the miracle was performed in each.

St. Luke's language is so clear as to the performance of *his* miracle, before the procession of Jesus arrived at Jericho, and St. Mark's, as to the performance of *his*, when the procession had passed through it, that it would be a vain attempt to prove the locality of the two events the same; or that either miracle was performed as Jesus drew nigh to Jericho, or as Jesus was leaving Jericho. It would be equally preposterous to suppose that he made any stay at Jericho; and so might perform one miracle as he first came thither, and another, as he finally left it again. The first verse of the nineteenth chapter of St. Luke is decisive that Jesus passed through Jericho without stopping; or, if there is any doubt on this subject, the next Dissertation, I trust, will place it beyond a question. The two accounts, then, are still as much at variance as before—relating to the course of one and the same procession from the banks of the Jordan, through Jericho, without interruption, until it stopped for a time with Zaccheus. Or, if the miracle in St. Luke is to be considered the same with the miracle in St. Mark, they are even more at variance than before.

I know no means, therefore, of reconciling either of them with the other, or both with St. Matthew, except one—a mode of reconciliation, handed down from the earliest times, and not more recommended by its antiquity, than by its

---

[a] Luke xviii. 35—43. Mark x. 46—52. Matt. xx. 29—34.

simplicity—which is to suppose two miracles, each at distinct times, and on a different individual; the one, as our Lord was approaching to Jericho, the other, as he was leaving it again; the former, related by St. Luke, the latter, by St. Mark, and both, by St. Matthew; each, as distinctly related, related in its proper place; and the two, as related conjointly, not absolutely related out of their's: for one or the other of the two, even in St. Matthew, must be regularly related, though the other may not.

The general conciseness of this Evangelist, in the account of miracles as such, has been often pointed out already; and on the principle of this conciseness, his blending together the history of two miracles, the same in kind—very similar in their circumstances—and almost contiguous in point of time—if any such events really occurred, was *a priori* to be expected from-him: in which case, it is infinitely most probable that he would connect the history of the first performed, with the history of the last, or would relate the last performed in its place, and the first performed out of it, rather than do the contrary. The approach of Jesus to Jericho he does not even mention; but the departure from it again he does: unless, therefore, he had purposely travelled out of his way, in order to record the first miracle for its own sake (to do which would not have been consistent with his practice) he had not even an opportunity of recounting *that*, until the time arrived for the history of the other. Nor, when he is proceeding to recount them both, or to give the history of one *out* of its order, along with the history of the other *in* it, does he employ any formula of transition, which establishes an immediate succession. He ushers in the account by merely his idiomatic expression, καὶ ἰδού [b]—a phrase which, in numberless instances, is simply a note of admonition to the reader, preparing him for something remarkable about to be related, but is no note of time or sequence, as referred to the order and connection of events.

The Gospel of St. Mark coming after St. Matthew's, and

[b] xx. 30.

every where closely treading in the steps of St. Matthew's, it was quite sufficient that St. Matthew had recorded both the miracles in conjunction, to induce St. Mark to record only one of them in particular. St. Luke's Gospel coming after both their's, and written with a perfect knowledge of the accounts of both, it was equally sufficient to make him record only one that St. Mark had recorded the other; and to make him record this one in its proper place that St. Matthew had recorded it, but with the other, out of it. The time of the *double* miracle in St. Matthew is clearly the time of the *single* miracle in St. Mark; that is, the miracle on Bartimæus, recorded by the latter, is the second of the miracles, recorded by the former. By restricting, therefore, *his* account to this one miracle, St. Mark still went along with St. Matthew; and by specifying this, as a single miracle, he not only went along with him, but so far rectified his order; for this was to detach the one miracle from another of like kind but upon a different occasion, which St. Matthew had combined with it. The approach to Jericho is not mentioned by him, no more than by St. Matthew; so that, unless he had purposely chosen to relate the other miracle also, he could have no opportunity of recording *that*, except in conjunction with the second. But this his scrupulous regard for historical precision would not allow him to do—nor in fact was it likely he should have done it; for it would have been merely to repeat what St. Matthew had done previously, and to perpetuate the very anachronism, which, as it was, he desired to remove. There was something, also, in the case of the second blind man, different from that of the first; as the very description given of him—Υἱὸς Τιμαίου, Βαρ-τίμαιος, ὁ τυφλός[c]—is alone sufficient to prove: and this would be an additional reason for confining the account of the miracle to him.

It remains, then, that the details of the first miracle, as a part of the general narrative, could be given by St. Luke alone. St. Matthew's account, as to the number of the miracles, was complete—as to their order, was irregular: St.

[c] x. 46.

Mark's account, as to the order, was regular—as to the number, was incomplete. St. Luke's serves an equal purpose with respect to both; filling up the deficiency in St. Mark, and reducing to order the irregularity in St. Matthew. The *two single* miracles, therefore, of the later Evangelists are exactly equivalent to the *one double* miracle of the earlier, and the accounts of the two former, laid together, will be just coextensive with the account of the latter by itself. Nor is there any thing in them separately to militate against such a construction of their relation in common. Had St. Matthew affirmed that both his miracles were wrought *after* Jesus left Jericho, then indeed St. Luke's miracle could not have been one of *those*, though it might still have been matter of fact. Had St. Luke asserted that the name and description of *his* blind man were Timæus, the son of Timæus, *his* authority would have been committed *recta fronte* with St. Mark's. But, as it is, each account in particular may be true—and all in common may be consistent.

The nature of the case itself is enough to prove that it is by no means an improbable supposition, which merely assumes that *two* blind men, neither of whom had any means of subsistence, except from the benevolence of private charity, should have been found sitting and begging, in the vicinity of a city like Jericho, in point of size, only one third, or not much more, less than Jerusalem[d], and containing, probably, more than one hundred thousand inhabitants; and upon two such thoroughfares, as the road from the Jordan to Jericho, and from Jericho to Jerusalem. But, even in this case, it is much more likely they would be found apart, than in conjunction. The procession of our Saviour would, consequently, pass by them at separate times; and there is no circumstance in the situation, behaviour, or treatment, of the one, which was not *a priori* to be just as much expected of the other. The similarity, then, of the different accounts is no proof of the identity of these occasions; for they could not have been otherwise than similar. It was

d Epiphanius Oper. i. 702.

this very similarity which brought them readily within the scope of St. Matthew's plan of conciseness in such details as these, and induced him to blend them both into one narrative. The particulars of the story, which he has thus given in reference to both, must have been individually applicable to either. Both must have been sitting by the road side, and both must have been begging, when Jesus passed by—both must have enquired who was passing, and both must have been told it was Jesus of Nazareth—both must have implored his mercy—both must have been rebuked by the people—both must have cried out the more—both must have been conducted to Christ—both must have been questioned alike—both must have returned the same answer—both must have been restored to sight by a word and a touch—and both must have followed him in the way. Each I say must have done all these things, if either of them did: and St. Luke, or St. Mark, will merely have related of one, what St. Matthew, with equal truth, had recorded of two.

END OF VOL. II.

Check Out More Titles From HardPress Classics Series In this collection we are offering thousands of classic and hard to find books. This series spans a vast array of subjects — so you are bound to find something of interest to enjoy reading and learning about.

Subjects:
Architecture
Art
Biography & Autobiography
Body, Mind &Spirit
Children & Young Adult
Dramas
Education
Fiction
History
Language Arts & Disciplines
Law
Literary Collections
Music
Poetry
Psychology
Science
…and many more.

Visit us at www.hardpress.net

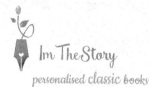

Im TheStory

personalised classic books

"Beautiful gift., lovely finish.
My Niece loves it, so precious!"

Helen R Brumfieldon

⭐⭐⭐⭐⭐

UNIQUE
GIFT

FOR KIDS, PARTNERS
AND FRIENDS

Timeless books such as:

Kids

Alice in Wonderland · The Jungle Book · The Wonderful Wizard of Oz
Peter and Wendy · Robin Hood · The Prince and The Pauper
The Railway Children · Treasure Island · A Christmas Carol

Adults

Romeo and Juliet · Dracula

Highly
Customizable

Change
Books Title

Replace
Characters Name
with yours

Upload
Photo into
inside page!

Add
Inscriptions

Visit
Im TheStory .com
and order yours today!